C# 11 and .NET 7 – Cross-Platform Development Fundamentals

Seventh Edition

Start building websites and services with ASP.NET Core 7, Blazor, and EF Core 7

Mark J. Price

BIRMINGHAM—MUMBAI

C# 11 and .NET 7 — Modern Cross-Platform Development Fundamentals

Seventh Edition

Senior Publishing Product Manager: Suman Sen

Acquisition Editor – Peer Reviews: Saby Dsilva

Project Editor: Janice Gonsalves

Content Development Editor: Lucy Wan

Copy Editor: Safis Editing

Technical Editor: Tejas Mhasvekar

Proofreader: Safis Editing

Indexer: Tejal Daruwale Soni

Presentation Designer: Pranit Padwal

First published: March 2016

Second edition: March 2017

Third edition: November 2017

Fourth edition: October 2019

Fifth edition: November 2020

Sixth edition: November 2021

Seventh edition: November 2022

Production reference: 2161122

Published by Packt Publishing Ltd.

Livery Place

35 Livery Street

Birmingham

B3 2PB, UK.

ISBN 978-1-80323-780-0

www.packt.com

Contributors

About the author

Mark J. Price is a Microsoft Specialist: Programming in C# and Architecting Microsoft Azure Solutions, with over 20 years of experience. Since 1993, he has passed more than 80 Microsoft programming exams and specializes in preparing others to pass them. Between 2001 and 2003, Mark was employed to write official courseware for Microsoft in Redmond, USA. His team wrote the first training courses for C# while it was still an early alpha version. While with Microsoft, he taught "train-the-trainer" classes to get Microsoft Certified Trainers up-to-speed on C# and .NET. Mark has spent most of his career training a wide variety of students from 16-year-old apprentices to 70-year-old retirees, with the majority being professional developers. Mark holds a Computer Science BSc. Hons. degree.

About the reviewer

Dave Brock is a development lead with experience in the architecture, design, and development of distributed, cloud-native applications. He was awarded a master's degree in software engineering from DePaul University. With a focus on Microsoft technologies such as .NET and Azure, Dave writes at daveabrock.com and has been awarded the Microsoft MVP award twice for his community contributions. He resides in Madison, Wisconsin, and, when not reviewing books, enjoys running, hiking, and playing music, and, of course, is a proud dad to his two wonderful children, Emma and Colin.

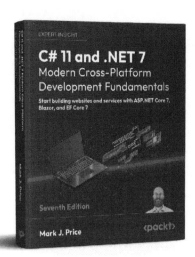

Target audience:
Beginner-to-intermediate in the C# language, .NET libraries, and ASP.NET Core web development

Topics include:
C# language, .NET libraries, ASP.NET Core, object-oriented programming, testing, EF Core, and more

Learn the fundamentals

Take your apps to the next level

Target audience:
Beginner-to-intermediate in building apps and services

Topics include:
Common .NET-adjacent technologies like Cosmos DB, GraphQL, .NET MAUI, Blazor, gRPC, and more

Join our book's Discord space

Join the book's Discord workspace for *Ask me Anything* sessions with the author.

https://packt.link/csharp11dotnet7

Quick Chapter Reference

Table of Contents

Chapter 8: Working with Common .NET Types   355

Chapter 15: Building and Consuming Web Services 657

Chapter 16: Building User Interfaces Using Blazor   703

Preface

There are programming books that are thousands of pages long that aim to be comprehensive references to the C# language, the .NET libraries, and app models like websites, services, and desktop and mobile apps.

This book is different. It is concise and aims to be a brisk, fun read packed with practical hands-on walk-throughs of each subject. The breadth of the overarching narrative comes at the cost of some depth, but you will find many signposts to explore further if you wish.

This book is simultaneously a step-by-step guide to learning modern C# proven practices using cross-platform .NET and a brief introduction to the fundamentals of web development and the websites and services that can be built with them. This book is best for beginners to C# and .NET or programmers who have worked with C# in the past but feel left behind by the changes in the past few years.

If you already have experience with older versions of the C# language, then in the first topic of *Chapter 2, Speaking C#*, you can review tables of the new language features and jump straight to them.

If you already have experience with older versions of the .NET libraries, then in the first topic of *Chapter 7, Packaging and Distributing .NET Types*, you can review tables of the new library features and jump straight to them.

I will point out the cool corners and gotchas of C# and .NET, so you can impress colleagues and get productive fast. Rather than slowing down and boring some readers by explaining every little thing, I will assume that you are smart enough to Google an explanation for topics that are related but not necessary to include in a beginner-to-intermediate guide that has limited space in the printed book.

Where to find the code solutions

You can download solutions for the step-by-step guided tasks and exercises from the GitHub repository at the following link: https://github.com/markjprice/cs11dotnet7.

If you don't know how, then I provide instructions on how to do this at the end of *Chapter 1, Hello, C#! Welcome, .NET!*.

What this book covers

Chapter 1, Hello, C#! Welcome, .NET!, is about setting up your development environment and using either Visual Studio 2022 or Visual Studio Code to create the simplest application possible with C# and .NET. For simplified console apps, you will see the use of the top-level program feature introduced in C# 9 and then used by the default project templates in C# 10 onwards. To learn how to write simple language constructs and library features, you will see the use of .NET Interactive Notebooks in an online section. You will also learn about some good places to look for help and ways to contact me to get help with an issue or give me feedback to improve the book today through its GitHub repository and in future print editions.

Chapter 2, Speaking C#, introduces the versions of C# and has tables showing which version introduced new features. I explain the grammar and vocabulary that you will use every day to write the source code for your applications. In particular, you will learn how to declare and work with variables of different types, and you will see how useful the C# 11 raw string literal feature is.

Chapter 3, Controlling Flow, Converting Types, and Handling Exceptions, covers using operators to perform simple actions on variables including comparisons, writing code that makes decisions, pattern matching in C# 7 to C# 11, repeating a block of statements, and converting between types. It also covers writing code defensively to handle exceptions when they inevitably occur.

Chapter 4, Writing, Debugging, and Testing Functions, is about following the **Don't Repeat Yourself** (**DRY**) principle by writing reusable functions using both imperative and functional implementation styles. You will also learn how to use debugging tools to track down and remove bugs, Hot Reload to make changes while your app is running, monitor your code while it executes to diagnose problems, and rigorously test your code to remove bugs and ensure stability and reliability before it gets deployed into production.

Chapter 5, Building Your Own Types with Object-Oriented Programming, discusses all the different categories of members that a type can have, including fields to store data and methods to perform actions. You will use **object-oriented programming** (**OOP**) concepts, such as aggregation and encapsulation. You will learn about language features such as tuple syntax support and out variables, operators and local functions, and default literals and inferred tuple names, as well as how to define and work with immutable types using the `record` keyword, `init`-only properties, and `with` expressions introduced in C# 9. We will also look at how C# 11 introduces the `required` keyword to help avoid the overuse of constructors to control initialization.

Chapter 6, Implementing Interfaces and Inheriting Classes, explains deriving new types from existing ones using OOP. You will learn how to define delegates and events, how to implement interfaces about base and derived classes, how to override a member of a type, how to use polymorphism, how to create extension methods, how to cast between classes in an inheritance hierarchy, and about the big changes in C# 8 with the introduction of nullable reference types and the switch to make this the default in C# 10 and later. You will also learn how analyzers can help you write better code.

Chapter 7, Packaging and Distributing .NET Types, introduces the versions of .NET and has tables showing which version introduced new library features. I then present the .NET types that are compliant with .NET Standard, and how they relate to C#.

You will learn how to write and compile code on any of the supported operating systems: Windows, macOS, and Linux variants. You will learn how to package, deploy, and distribute your own apps and libraries.

Chapter 8, Working with Common .NET Types, discusses the types that allow your code to perform common practical tasks, such as manipulating numbers and text, storing items in collections, and working with the network in an online section. You will also learn about regular expressions and the improvements that make them easier to write and how to improve their performance in .NET 7 by using source generators.

Chapter 9, Working with Files, Streams, and Serialization, covers interacting with the filesystem, reading and writing to files and streams, text encoding, and serialization formats like JSON and XML, including the improved functionality and performance of the System.Text.Json classes.

Chapter 10, Working with Data Using Entity Framework Core, explains reading and writing to relational databases, such as Microsoft SQL Server and SQLite, using the **object-relational mapping** (ORM) technology named **Entity Framework Core** (**EF Core**). You will learn how to define entity models that map to existing tables in a database using Database First models, as well as how to define Code First models that can create the tables and database at runtime in an online section.

Chapter 11, Querying and Manipulating Data Using LINQ, teaches you **Language INtegrated Queries** (**LINQ**)—language extensions that add the ability to work with sequences of items and filter, sort, and project them into different outputs. This chapter includes the new LINQ methods introduced in .NET 6 like TryGetNonEnumeratedCount and DistinctBy and in .NET 7 like Order and OrderDescending. You will learn about the special capabilities of LINQ to XML. In an online section, you will learn how to improve efficiency with **Parallel LINQ** (**PLINQ**).

Chapter 12, Introducing Web Development Using ASP.NET Core, introduces you to the types of web applications that can be built using C# and .NET. You will also build an EF Core model to represent the database for a fictional organization named Northwind that will be used throughout the rest of the chapters in the book. Finally, you will be introduced to common web technologies.

Chapter 13, Building Websites Using ASP.NET Core Razor Pages, is about learning the basics of building websites with a modern HTTP architecture on the server side using ASP.NET Core. You will learn how to implement the ASP.NET Core feature known as Razor Pages, which simplifies creating dynamic web pages for small websites, about building the HTTP request and response pipeline, and how to enable HTTP/3 in your website project.

Chapter 14, Building Websites Using the Model-View-Controller Pattern, is about learning how to build large, complex websites in a way that is easy to unit test and manage with teams of programmers using ASP.NET Core MVC. You will learn about startup configuration, authentication, routes, models, views, and controllers. You will learn about a feature eagerly anticipated by the .NET community called output caching that was finally implemented in ASP.NET Core 7.

Chapter 15, Building and Consuming Web Services, explains building backend REST architecture web services using the ASP.NET Core Web API. We cover how to document and test them using OpenAPI. Then we see how to properly consume them using factory-instantiated HTTP clients.

We explore Minimal APIs, introduced in ASP.NET Core 6, which reduce the number of code statements needed to implement simple web services.

Chapter 16, Building User Interfaces Using Blazor, introduces how to build web user interface components using Blazor that can be executed either on the server side or inside the web browser. You will see the differences between Blazor Server and Blazor WebAssembly and how to build components that are easier to switch between the two hosting models.

Epilogue describes your options for further study of C# and .NET.

Appendix, Answers to the Test Your Knowledge Questions, has the answers to the test questions at the end of each chapter.

You can read the appendix at the following link: `https://packt.link/9RuLP`.

What you need for this book

You can develop and deploy C# and .NET apps using Visual Studio Code and the command-line tools on most operating systems, including Windows, macOS, and many varieties of Linux. An operating system that supports Visual Studio Code and an internet connection are all you need to complete this book.

If you prefer to use Visual Studio 2022 for Windows or macOS, or a third-party tool like JetBrains Rider, then you can.

Download the example code files

The code bundle for the book is hosted on GitHub at `https://github.com/markjprice/cs11dotnet7`. We also have other code bundles from our rich catalog of books and videos available at `https://github.com/PacktPublishing/`. Check them out!

Download the color images

We also provide a PDF file that has color images of the screenshots/diagrams used in this book. You can download it here: `https://packt.link/hmdd1`.

Conventions used

In this book, you will find a number of text styles that distinguish between different kinds of information. Here are some examples of these styles and an explanation of their meaning.

Bold: Indicates a new **term**, an important **word**, or words that you see on the screen, for example, in menus or dialog boxes. For example: ".NET versions are either **Long Term Support (LTS)**, **Standard Term Support (STS)**, formerly known as **Current**, or **Preview**."

`CodeInText`: Indicates code words in text, database table names, folder names, filenames, file extensions, pathnames, dummy URLs, user input, and Twitter handles. For example: "The `Controllers`, `Models`, and `Views` folders contain ASP.NET Core classes and the `.cshtml` files for execution on the server."

A block of code is set as follows:

```
// storing items at index positions
names[0] = "Kate";
names[1] = "Jack";
names[2] = "Rebecca";
names[3] = "Tom";
```

When we wish to draw your attention to a particular part of a code block, the relevant lines or items are highlighted:

```
// storing items at index positions
names[0] = "Kate";
names[1] = "Jack";
names[2] = "Rebecca";
names[3] = "Tom";
```

Any command-line input or output is written as follows:

```
dotnet new console
```

 Warnings or important notes appear like this.

 Tips and tricks appear like this.

Get in touch

Feedback from our readers is always welcome.

General feedback: Email feedback@packtpub.com and mention the book's title in the subject of your message. If you have questions about any aspect of this book, please email us at questions@packtpub.com.

Errata: Although we have taken every care to ensure the accuracy of our content, mistakes do happen. If you have found a mistake in this book, we would be grateful if you reported this to us. Please visit http://www.packtpub.com/submit-errata, click **Submit Errata**, and fill in the form.

Piracy: If you come across any illegal copies of our works in any form on the internet, we would be grateful if you would provide us with the location address or website name. Please contact us at copyright@packtpub.com with a link to the material.

If you are interested in becoming an author: If there is a topic that you have expertise in and you are interested in either writing or contributing to a book, please visit http://authors.packtpub.com.

Share your thoughts

Once you've read *C# 11 and .NET 7 - Modern Cross-Platform Development Fundamentals, Seventh Edition*, we'd love to hear your thoughts! Scan the QR code below to go straight to the Amazon review page for this book and share your feedback.

https://packt.link/r/1803237805

Your review is important to us and the tech community and will help us make sure we're delivering excellent quality content.

Download a free PDF copy of this book

Thanks for purchasing this book!

Do you like to read on the go but are unable to carry your print books everywhere? Is your eBook purchase not compatible with the device of your choice?

Don't worry, now with every Packt book you get a DRM-free PDF version of that book at no cost.

Read anywhere, any place, on any device. Search, copy, and paste code from your favorite technical books directly into your application.

The perks don't stop there, you can get exclusive access to discounts, newsletters, and great free content in your inbox daily

Follow these simple steps to get the benefits:

1. Scan the QR code or visit the link below

https://packt.link/free-ebook/9781803237800

2. Submit your proof of purchase
3. That's it! We'll send your free PDF and other benefits to your email directly

1

Hello, C#! Welcome, .NET!

In this first chapter, the goals are setting up your development environment; understanding the similarities and differences between modern .NET, .NET Core, .NET Framework, Mono, Xamarin, and .NET Standard; creating the simplest application possible with C# 11 and .NET 7 using various code editors; and then discovering good places to look for help.

The GitHub repository for this book has solutions using full application projects for all code tasks and notebooks when possible:

https://github.com/markjprice/cs11dotnet7

Simply press the `.` (dot) key or manually change `.com` to `.dev` in the link to convert the GitHub repository into a live code editor based on Visual Studio Code using GitHub Codespaces, as shown in *Figure 1.1*:

Figure 1.1: GitHub Codespaces live editing the book's GitHub repository

We provide you with a PDF file that has color images of the screenshots and diagrams used in this book. You can download this file from `https://packt.link/hmdd1`.

Visual Studio Code in a web browser is great to run alongside your chosen local code editor as you work through the book's coding tasks. You can compare your code to the solution code and easily copy and paste parts if needed.

You do not need to use or know anything about Git to get the solution code of this book. You can download a ZIP file containing all the code solutions by using the following direct link, and then extract the ZIP file into your local filesystem: `https://github.com/markjprice/cs11dotnet7/archive/refs/heads/main.zip`.

Throughout this book, I use the term **modern .NET** to refer to .NET 7 and its predecessors like .NET 5 and .NET 6 that come from .NET Core. I use the term **legacy .NET** to refer to .NET Framework, Mono, Xamarin, and .NET Standard. Modern .NET is a unification of those legacy platforms and standards.

After this first chapter, the book can be divided into three parts: first, the grammar and vocabulary of the C# language; second, the types available in .NET for building app features; and third, the fundamentals of cross-platform websites, services, and browser apps that you can build using C# and .NET.

Most people learn complex topics best by imitation and repetition rather than reading a detailed explanation of the theory; therefore, I will not overload you with detailed explanations of every step throughout this book. The idea is to get you to write some code and see it run.

You don't need to know all the nitty-gritty details immediately. That will be something that comes with time as you build your own apps and go beyond what any book can teach you.

In the words of Samuel Johnson, author of the English dictionary in 1755, I have committed "a few wild blunders, and risible absurdities, from which no work of such multiplicity is free." I take sole responsibility for these and hope you appreciate the challenge of my attempt to lash the wind by writing this book about rapidly evolving technologies like C# and .NET, and the apps that you can build with them.

If you have a complaint about this book, then please contact me before writing a negative review on Amazon. Authors cannot respond to Amazon reviews so I cannot contact you to resolve the problem and help you, or at least listen to your feedback and try to do better in the next edition. Please ask a question on the Discord channel for this book at `https://packt.link/csharp11dotnet7`, email me (my address is on the GitHub repository for the book), or raise an issue in the GitHub repository for the book at the following link: `https://github.com/markjprice/cs11dotnet7/issues`.

This chapter covers the following topics:

- Setting up your development environment

- Understanding .NET
- Building console apps using Visual Studio 2022
- Building console apps using Visual Studio Code
- Exploring code using .NET Interactive Notebooks (online section)
- Reviewing the folders and files for projects
- Making good use of the GitHub repository for this book
- Looking for help

Setting up your development environment

Before you start programming, you'll need a code editor for C#. Microsoft has a family of code editors and **Integrated Development Environments (IDEs)**, which include:

- Visual Studio 2022 for Windows
- Visual Studio 2022 for Mac
- Visual Studio Code for Windows, Mac, or Linux
- Visual Studio Code for the Web
- GitHub Codespaces

Third parties have created their own C# code editors, for example, JetBrains Rider.

Choosing the appropriate tool and application type for learning

What is the best tool and application type for learning C# and .NET?

When learning, the best tool is one that helps you write code and configuration but does not hide what is really happening. IDEs provide graphical user interfaces that are friendly to use, but what are they doing for you underneath? A more basic code editor that is closer to the action while providing help to write your code is better while you are learning.

Having said that, you can make the argument that the best tool is the one you are already familiar with or that you or your team will use as your daily development tool. For that reason, I want you to be free to choose any C# code editor or IDE to complete the coding tasks in this book, including Visual Studio Code, Visual Studio for Windows, Visual Studio for Mac, or even JetBrains Rider.

In this book, I give detailed step-by-step instructions for how to create multiple projects in both Visual Studio 2022 for Windows and Visual Studio Code, in *Chapter 1*. After that, I give names of projects and general instructions that work with all tools so you can use whichever tool you prefer.

The best application type for learning the C# language constructs and many of the .NET libraries is one that does not distract with unnecessary application code. For example, there is no need to create an entire Windows desktop application or a website just to learn how to write a `switch` statement.

For that reason, I believe the best method for learning the C# and .NET topics in *Chapters 1* to *11* is to build console apps. Then, in *Chapters 12* to *16*, you will build websites, services, and web browser apps.

Pros and cons of the .NET Interactive Notebooks extension

Another benefit of Visual Studio Code is the .NET Interactive Notebooks extension. This extension provides an easy and safe place to write simple code snippets for experimenting and learning. For example, data scientists use notebooks to analyze and visualize data. Students use them to learn how to write small pieces of code for language constructs and to explore APIs.

.NET Interactive Notebooks enables you to create a single notebook file that mixes "cells" of Markdown (richly formatted text) and code using C# and other related languages, such as PowerShell, F#, and SQL (for databases).

However, .NET Interactive Notebooks do have some limitations:

- They cannot be used to create websites, services, and apps.
- They cannot read input from the user, for example, you cannot use `ReadLine` or `ReadKey`.
- They cannot have arguments passed to them.
- They do not allow you to define your own namespaces.
- They do not have any debugging tools (but these will come).

Using Visual Studio Code for cross-platform development

The most modern and lightweight code editor to choose from, and the only one from Microsoft that is cross-platform, is Visual Studio Code. It can run on all common operating systems, including Windows, macOS, and many varieties of Linux, including **Red Hat Enterprise Linux (RHEL)** and Ubuntu.

Visual Studio Code is a good choice for modern cross-platform development because it has an extensive and growing set of extensions to support many languages beyond C#.

Being cross-platform and lightweight, it can be installed on all platforms that your apps will be deployed to for quick bug fixes and so on. Choosing Visual Studio Code means a developer can use a cross-platform code editor to develop cross-platform apps.

Visual Studio Code has strong support for web development, although it currently has weak support for mobile and desktop development.

Visual Studio Code is supported on ARM processors so that you can develop on Apple Silicon computers and Raspberry Pi.

Visual Studio Code is by far the most popular integrated development environment, with over 70% of professional developers selecting it in the Stack Overflow 2021 survey.

Using GitHub Codespaces for development in the cloud

GitHub Codespaces is a fully configured development environment based on Visual Studio Code that can be spun up in an environment hosted in the cloud and accessed through any web browser. It supports Git repos, extensions, and a built-in command-line interface so you can edit, run, and test from any device.

Using Visual Studio for Mac for general development

Microsoft Visual Studio 2022 for Mac can create most types of applications, including console apps, websites, web services, desktop, and mobile apps.

To compile apps for Apple operating systems like iOS to run on devices like the iPhone and iPad, you must have Xcode, which only runs on macOS.

Using Visual Studio for Windows for general development

Microsoft Visual Studio 2022 for Windows can create most types of applications, including console apps, websites, web services, desktop, and mobile apps. Although you can use Visual Studio 2022 for Windows with its Xamarin extensions to write a cross-platform mobile app, you still need macOS and Xcode to compile it.

It only runs on Windows, version 7 SP1 or later. You must run it on Windows 10 or Windows 11 to create **Universal Windows Platform** (**UWP**) apps that are installed from the Microsoft Store and run in a sandbox to protect your computer.

What I used

To write and test the code for this book, I used the following hardware:

- HP Spectre (Intel) laptop
- Apple Silicon Mac mini (M1) desktop
- Raspberry Pi 400 (ARM v8) desktop

And I used the following software:

- Visual Studio Code on:

    - macOS on an Apple Silicon Mac mini (M1) desktop
    - Windows 11 on an HP Spectre (Intel) laptop
    - Ubuntu 64 on a Raspberry Pi 400

- Visual Studio 2022 for Windows on:

    - Windows 11 on an HP Spectre (Intel) laptop

- Visual Studio 2022 for Mac on:

    - macOS on an Apple Silicon Mac mini (M1) desktop

I hope that you have access to a variety of hardware and software too, because seeing the differences in platforms deepens your understanding of development challenges, although any one of the above combinations is enough to learn the fundamentals of C# and .NET and how to build practical apps and websites.

You can learn how to write code with C# and .NET using a Raspberry Pi 400 with Ubuntu Desktop 64-bit by reading an extra article that I wrote at the following link: `https://github.com/markjprice/cs11dotnet7/tree/main/docs/raspberry-pi-ubuntu64`.

Deploying cross-platform

Your choice of code editor and operating system for development does not limit where your code gets deployed.

.NET 7 supports the following platforms for deployment:

- **Windows:** Windows 7 SP1 or later. Windows 8.1 or later. Windows 10 version 1607 or later. Windows 11 version 22000 or later. Windows Server 2012 R2 SP1 or later. Nano Server version 1809 or later.
- **Mac:** macOS Catalina version 10.15 or later.
- **Linux:** Alpine Linux 3.15 or later. CentOS 7 or later. Debian 10 or later. Fedora 33 or later. openSUSE 15 or later. RHEL 7 or later. SUSE Enterprise Linux 12 SP2 or later. Ubuntu 18.04 or later. Note that .NET 6 is now included with Ubuntu 22.04, as you can read about at the following link: `https://devblogs.microsoft.com/dotnet/dotnet-6-is-now-in-ubuntu-2204/`.
- **Android:** API 21 or later.
- **iOS:** 10.0 or later.

Although .NET supports Windows 7 and 8.1 at the time of publishing, .NET support for Windows 7 and 8.1 will end in January 2023: `https://github.com/dotnet/core/issues/7556`.

Windows Arm64 support in .NET 5 and later means you can develop on, and deploy to, Windows Arm devices like Microsoft Surface Pro X. Developing on an Apple M1 Mac using Parallels and a Windows 11 Arm virtual machine is twice as fast.

You can review the latest supported operating systems and versions at the following link: `https://github.com/dotnet/core/blob/main/release-notes/7.0/supported-os.md`.

Downloading and installing Visual Studio 2022 for Windows

Many professional Microsoft developers use Visual Studio 2022 for Windows in their day-to-day development work. Even if you choose to use Visual Studio Code to complete the coding tasks in this book, you might want to familiarize yourself with Visual Studio 2022 for Windows too. It is not until you have written a decent amount of code with a tool that you can really judge if it fits your needs.

If you do not have a Windows computer, then you can skip this section and continue to the next section where you will download and install Visual Studio Code on macOS or Linux.

Since October 2014, Microsoft has made a professional-quality edition of Visual Studio for Windows available to students, open-source contributors, and individuals for free. It is called Community Edition. Any of the editions are suitable for this book. If you have not already installed it, let's do so now:

1. Download Microsoft Visual Studio 2022 version 17.4 or later for Windows from the following link: `https://visualstudio.microsoft.com/downloads/`.

2. Start the installer.

3. On the **Workloads** tab, select the following:

   - **ASP.NET** and **web development**
   - **.NET desktop development** (because this includes Console Apps)

4. On the **Individual components** tab, in the **Code tools** section, select the following:

   - **Git for Windows**

5. Click **Install** and wait for the installer to acquire the selected software and install it.

6. When the installation is complete, click **Launch**.

7. The first time that you run Visual Studio, you will be prompted to sign in. If you have a Microsoft account, you can use that account. If you don't, then register for a new one at the following link: `https://signup.live.com/`.

8. The first time that you run Visual Studio, you will be prompted to configure your environment. For **Development Settings**, choose **Visual C#**. For the color theme, I chose **Blue**, but you can choose whatever tickles your fancy.

9. If you want to customize your keyboard shortcuts, navigate to **Tools | Options...**, and then select the **Keyboard** section.

Microsoft Visual Studio for Windows keyboard shortcuts

In this book, I will avoid showing keyboard shortcuts since they are often customized. Where they are consistent across code editors and commonly used, I will try to show them. If you want to identify and customize your keyboard shortcuts, then you can, as shown at the following link: `https://docs.microsoft.com/en-us/visualstudio/ide/identifying-and-customizing-keyboard-shortcuts-in-visual-studio`.

Downloading and installing Visual Studio Code

Visual Studio Code has rapidly improved over the past couple of years and has pleasantly surprised Microsoft with its popularity. If you are brave and like to live on the bleeding edge, then there is an **Insiders** edition, which is a daily build of the next version.

Even if you plan to only use Visual Studio 2022 for Windows for development, I recommend that you download and install Visual Studio Code and try the coding tasks in this chapter using it, and then decide if you want to stick with just using Visual Studio 2022 for the rest of the book.

Let's now download and install Visual Studio Code, the .NET SDK, and the C# and .NET Interactive Notebooks extensions:

1. Download and install either the Stable build or the Insiders edition of Visual Studio Code from the following link: `https://code.visualstudio.com/`.

 More Information: If you need more help installing Visual Studio Code, you can read the official setup guide at the following link: `https://code.visualstudio.com/docs/setup/setup-overview`.

2. Download and install the .NET SDKs for versions 6.0 and 7.0 from the following link: `https://www.microsoft.com/net/download`.

 To fully learn how to control .NET SDKs, we need multiple versions installed. .NET 6.0 and .NET 7.0 are two currently supported versions. You can safely install multiple SDKs side by side. Although .NET 6.0 is not the most recent, it is the most recent **Long-Term Support (LTS)** version, so that is another good reason to install it.

3. To install the C# extension, you must first launch the Visual Studio Code application.

4. In Visual Studio Code, click the **Extensions** icon or navigate to **View | Extensions**.

5. C# is one of the most popular extensions available, so you should see it at the top of the list, or you can enter `C#` in the search box.

6. Click **Install** and wait for supporting packages to download and install.

7. Enter `.NET Interactive` in the search box to find the **.NET Interactive Notebooks** extension.

8. Click **Install** and wait for it to install.

Installing other extensions

In later chapters of this book, you will use more Visual Studio Code extensions. If you want to install them now, all the extensions that we will use are shown in the following table:

Extension name and identifier	Description
C# for Visual Studio Code (powered by OmniSharp) `ms-dotnettools.csharp`	C# editing support, including syntax highlighting, IntelliSense, Go To Definition, Find All References, debugging support for .NET, and support for `csproj` projects on Windows, macOS, and Linux.
.NET Interactive Notebooks `ms-dotnettools.dotnet-interactive-vscode`	This extension adds support for using .NET Interactive in a Visual Studio Code notebook. It has a dependency on the Jupyter extension (`ms-toolsai.jupyter`) that itself has dependencies.
MSBuild project tools `tintoy.msbuild-project-tools`	Provides IntelliSense for MSBuild project files, including autocomplete for `<PackageReference>` elements.

REST Client `humao.rest-client`	Send an HTTP request and view the response directly in Visual Studio Code.
ilspy-vscode `icsharpcode.ilspy-vscode`	Decompile MSIL assemblies – support for modern .NET, .NET Framework, .NET Core, and .NET Standard.

Managing Visual Studio Code extensions at the command line

You can install a Visual Studio Code extension at the command line or terminal, as shown in the following table:

Command	Description
`code --list-extensions`	List installed extensions
`code --install-extension <extension-id>`	Install the specified extension
`code --uninstall-extension <extension-id>`	Uninstall the specified extension

For example, to install the C# extension, enter the following at the command line or terminal:

```
code --install-extension ms-dotnettools.csharp
```

 I have created a PowerShell script to install all the Visual Studio Code extensions in the preceding table. You can find it at the following link: https://github.com/markjprice/cs11dotnet7/blob/main/vscode/Scripts/install-vs-code-extensions.ps1.

Understanding Microsoft Visual Studio Code versions

Microsoft releases a new feature version of Visual Studio Code (almost) every month and bug fix versions more frequently. For example:

- Version 1.64.0, February 2022 feature release
- Version 1.64.1, February 2022 bug fix release

The version used in this book is 1.71.0, September 2022 feature release, but the version of Microsoft Visual Studio Code is less important than the version of the C# for Visual Studio Code extension that you installed.

While the C# extension is not required, it provides IntelliSense as you type, code navigation, and debugging features, so it's something that's very handy to install and keep updated to support the latest C# language features.

Microsoft Visual Studio Code keyboard shortcuts

In this book, I will avoid showing keyboard shortcuts used for tasks like creating a new file since they are often different on different operating systems. The situations where I will show keyboard shortcuts are when you need to repeatedly press the key, for example, while debugging. These are also more likely to be consistent across operating systems.

If you want to customize your keyboard shortcuts for Visual Studio Code, then you can, as shown at the following link: https://code.visualstudio.com/docs/getstarted/keybindings.

I recommend that you download a PDF of keyboard shortcuts for your operating system from the following list:

- Windows: https://code.visualstudio.com/shortcuts/keyboard-shortcuts-windows.pdf
- macOS: https://code.visualstudio.com/shortcuts/keyboard-shortcuts-macos.pdf
- Linux: https://code.visualstudio.com/shortcuts/keyboard-shortcuts-linux.pdf

Understanding .NET

.NET 7, .NET Core, .NET Framework, and Xamarin are related and overlapping platforms for developers used to build applications and services. In this section, I'm going to introduce you to each of these .NET concepts.

Understanding .NET Framework

.NET Framework is a development platform that includes a **Common Language Runtime (CLR)**, which manages the execution of code, and a **Base Class Library (BCL)**, which provides a rich library of classes to build applications from.

Microsoft originally designed .NET Framework to have the possibility of being cross-platform, but Microsoft put their implementation efforts into making it work best with Windows.

Since .NET Framework 4.5.2, it has been an official component of the Windows operating system. Components have the same support as their parent products, so 4.5.2 and later follow the life cycle policy of the Windows OS on which they are installed. .NET Framework is installed on over one billion computers, so it must change as little as possible. Even bug fixes can cause problems, so it is updated infrequently.

For .NET Framework 4.0 or later, all the apps on a computer written for .NET Framework share the same version of the CLR and libraries stored in the **Global Assembly Cache (GAC)**, which can lead to issues if some of them need a specific version for compatibility.

 Good Practice: Practically speaking, .NET Framework is Windows-only and a legacy platform. Do not create new apps using it.

Understanding the Mono, Xamarin, and Unity projects

Third parties developed a .NET Framework implementation named the **Mono** project. Mono is cross-platform, but it fell behind the official implementation of .NET Framework.

Mono has found a niche as the foundation of the **Xamarin** mobile platform as well as cross-platform game development platforms like **Unity**.

Microsoft purchased Xamarin in 2016 and now gives away what used to be an expensive Xamarin extension for free with Visual Studio. Microsoft renamed the Xamarin Studio development tool, which could only create mobile apps, to Visual Studio for Mac, and gave it the ability to create other types of projects like console apps and web services.

With Visual Studio 2022 for Mac, Microsoft has replaced parts of the Xamarin Studio editor with parts from Visual Studio 2022 for Windows to provide closer parity of experience and performance. Visual Studio 2022 for Mac was also rewritten to be a truly native macOS UI app to improve reliability and work with macOS's built-in assistive technologies.

Understanding .NET Core

Today, we live in a truly cross-platform world where modern mobile and cloud development have made Windows, as an operating system, much less important. Because of that, Microsoft has been working since 2015 on an effort to decouple .NET from its close ties with Windows. While rewriting .NET Framework to be truly cross-platform, they've taken the opportunity to refactor and remove major parts that are no longer considered core.

This new modernized product was initially branded **.NET Core** and includes a cross-platform implementation of the CLR known as **CoreCLR** and a streamlined BCL known as **CoreFX**.

Scott Hunter, Microsoft Partner Director Program Manager for .NET, has said that "Forty percent of our .NET Core customers are brand-new developers to the platform, which is what we want with .NET Core. We want to bring new people in."

.NET Core is fast-moving, and because it can be deployed side by side with an app, it can change frequently, knowing those changes will not affect other .NET Core apps on the same machine. Most improvements that Microsoft makes to .NET Core and modern .NET cannot be easily added to .NET Framework.

Understanding the journey to one .NET

At the Microsoft Build developer conference in May 2020, the .NET team announced that their plans for the unification of .NET had been delayed. They said that .NET 5 would be released on November 10, 2020, and it would unify all the various .NET platforms except mobile. It would not be until .NET 6 in November 2021 that mobile would also be supported by the unified .NET platform. Unfortunately, in September 2021 they had to announce a six-month delay to .NET MAUI, their new cross-platform platform for mobile and desktop app development. .NET MAUI finally released to **General Availability (GA)** in May 2022. You can read the announcement at the following link:

```
https://devblogs.microsoft.com/dotnet/introducing-dotnet-maui-one-codebase-many-
platforms/
```

.NET Core has been renamed .NET and the major version number has skipped 4 to avoid confusion with .NET Framework 4.x. Microsoft plans on annual major version releases every November, rather like Apple does major version number releases of iOS every September.

The following table shows when the key versions of modern .NET were released, when future releases are planned, and which version is used by the published editions of this book:

Version	Released	Edition	Published
.NET Core RC1	November 2015	First	March 2016
.NET Core 1.0	June 2016		
.NET Core 1.1	November 2016		
.NET Core 1.0.4 and .NET Core 1.1.1	March 2017	Second	March 2017
.NET Core 2.0	August 2017		
.NET Core for UWP in Windows 10 Fall Creators Update	October 2017	Third	November 2017
.NET Core 2.1 (LTS)	May 2018		
.NET Core 2.2 (Current)	December 2018		
.NET Core 3.0 (Current)	September 2019	Fourth	October 2019
.NET Core 3.1 (LTS)	December 2019		
Blazor WebAssembly 3.2 (Current)	May 2020		
.NET 5.0 (Current)	November 2020	Fifth	November 2020
.NET 6.0 (LTS)	November 2021	Sixth	November 2021
.NET 7.0 (Standard)	November 2022	Seventh	November 2022
.NET 8.0 (LTS)	November 2023	Eighth	November 2023
.NET 9.0 (Standard)	November 2024	Ninth	November 2024
.NET 10.0 (LTS)	November 2025	Tenth	November 2025

Understanding Blazor WebAssembly versioning

.NET Core 3.1 included Blazor Server for building web components. Microsoft had also planned to include Blazor WebAssembly in that release, but it was delayed. Blazor WebAssembly was later released as an optional add-on for .NET Core 3.1. I include it in the table above because it was versioned as 3.2 to exclude it from the LTS of .NET Core 3.1.

Understanding .NET support

.NET releases are either **Long Term Support (LTS)**, **Standard Support** formerly known as **Current**, or **Preview**, as described in the following list:

- **LTS** releases are stable and require fewer updates over their lifetime. These are a good choice for applications that you do not intend to update frequently. LTS releases are supported by Microsoft for 3 years after general availability, or 1 year after the next LTS release ships, whichever is longer.

- **Standard** or **Current** releases include features that may change based on feedback. These are a good choice for applications that you are actively developing because they provide access to the latest improvements. Standard releases are supported by Microsoft for 18 months after general availability, or 6 months after the next Standard or LTS release ships, whichever is longer.

- **Preview** releases are for public testing. These are a good choice for adventurous programmers who want to live on the bleeding edge, or programming book writers who need to have early access to new language features, libraries, and app platforms. Preview releases are not supported by Microsoft but Preview or **Release Candidate** (**RC**) releases may be declared **Go Live**, meaning they are supported by Microsoft in production.

Standard and LTS releases receive critical fixes throughout their lifetime for security and reliability. You must stay up to date with the latest patches to get support. For example, if a system is running 1.0.0 and 1.0.1 has been released, 1.0.1 will need to be installed to get support.

 End of support or **end of life** means the date after which bug fixes, security updates, and technical assistance are no longer available from Microsoft.

To better understand your choice between Standard (aka Current) and LTS releases, it is helpful to see it visually, with 3-year-long black bars for LTS releases, and variable-length gray bars for Standard/Current releases that end with cross-hatching for the 6 months after a new major or minor release that they retain support for, as shown in *Figure 1.2*:

Figure 1.2: Support durations for Standard and LTS releases

For example, if you had created a project using .NET 5.0, then when Microsoft released .NET 6.0 on November 8, 2021, you had to upgrade your project to .NET 6.0 by May 8, 2022, if you wanted to get fixes and updates and be supported by Microsoft.

If you need long-term support from Microsoft, then choose .NET 6.0 today and stick with it until .NET 8.0, even though Microsoft has released .NET 7.0. This is because .NET 7.0 is a Standard release, and it will therefore lose support before .NET 6.0 does. Just remember that even with LTS releases, you must upgrade to bug fix releases like .NET 6.0.9 and .NET SDK 6.0.401, which were released on September 13, 2022, because updates are released every month.

At the time of publishing in November 2022, all versions of .NET Core and modern .NET have reached their end of life except those shown in the following list that are ordered by their end-of-life dates:

- .NET Core 3.1 will reach end of life on December 13, 2022.
- .NET 7.0 will reach end of life on May 14, 2024.
- .NET 6.0 will reach end of life on November 12, 2024.

 You can check which .NET versions are currently supported and when they will reach end of life at the following link: `https://github.com/dotnet/core/blob/main/releases.md`.

Understanding .NET Runtime and .NET SDK versions

.NET Runtime versioning follows semantic versioning, that is, a major increment indicates breaking changes, minor increments indicate new features, and patch increments indicate bug fixes.

.NET SDK versioning does not follow semantic versioning. The major and minor version numbers are tied to the runtime version it is matched with. The patch number follows a convention that indicates the major and minor versions of the SDK.

You can see an example of this in the following table:

Change	Runtime	SDK
Initial release	7.0.0	7.0.100
SDK bug fix	7.0.0	7.0.101
Runtime and SDK bug fix	7.0.1	7.0.102
SDK new feature	7.0.1	7.0.200

Listing and removing versions of .NET

.NET Runtime updates are compatible with a major version such as 7.x, and updated releases of the .NET SDK maintain the ability to build applications that target previous versions of the runtime, which enables the safe removal of older versions.

You can see which SDKs and runtimes are currently installed using the following commands:

```
dotnet --list-sdks
dotnet --list-runtimes
dotnet --info
```

On Windows, use the **Apps & features** section to remove .NET SDKs.

On macOS or Windows, use the `dotnet-core-uninstall` tool. This tool is not installed by default.

For example, while writing the fourth edition, I used the following command every month:

```
dotnet-core-uninstall remove --all-previews-but-latest --sdk
```

What is different about modern .NET?

Modern .NET is modularized compared to the legacy .NET Framework, which is monolithic. It is open source and Microsoft makes decisions about improvements and changes in the open. Microsoft has put particular effort into improving the performance of modern .NET.

It can be smaller than the last version of .NET Framework due to the removal of legacy and non-cross-platform technologies. For example, workloads such as **Windows Forms** and **Windows Presentation Foundation (WPF)** can be used to build **graphical user interface (GUI)** applications, but they are tightly bound to the Windows ecosystem, so they are not included with .NET on macOS and Linux.

Windows desktop development

One of the features of modern .NET is support for running old Windows Forms and WPF desktop applications using the Windows Desktop Pack that is included with the Windows version of .NET Core 3.1 or later. This is why it is bigger than the SDKs for macOS and Linux. You can make changes to your legacy Windows desktop app, and then rebuild it for modern .NET to take advantage of new features and performance improvements. I do not cover Windows desktop development in this book.

Web development

ASP.NET Web Forms and **Windows Communication Foundation (WCF)** are old web application and service technologies that fewer developers are choosing to use for new development projects today, so they have also been removed from modern .NET. Instead, developers prefer to use ASP.NET MVC, ASP.NET Web API, SignalR, and gRPC. These technologies have been refactored and combined into a platform that runs on modern .NET, named **ASP.NET Core**.

You'll learn about the web development technologies in *Chapter 12, Introducing Web Development Using ASP.NET Core, Chapter 13, Building Websites Using ASP.NET Core Razor Pages, Chapter 14, Building Websites Using the Model-View-Controller Pattern, Chapter 15, Building and Consuming Web Services*, and *Chapter 16, Building User Interfaces Using Blazor*.

> **More Information:** Some .NET Framework developers are upset that ASP.NET Web Forms, WCF, and **Windows Workflow (WF)** are missing from modern .NET and would like Microsoft to change their minds. There are open-source projects to enable WCF and WF to migrate to modern .NET. You can read more at the following link: `https://devblogs.microsoft.com/dotnet/supporting-the-community-with-wf-and-wcf-oss-projects/`. CoreWCF 1.0 was released in April 2022: `https://devblogs.microsoft.com/dotnet/corewcf-v1-released/`. There is an open-source project for Blazor Web Forms components at the following link: `https://github.com/FritzAndFriends/BlazorWebFormsComponents`.

Database development

Entity Framework (EF) 6 is an object-relational mapping technology that is designed to work with data that is stored in relational databases such as Oracle and SQL Server. It has gained baggage over the years, so the cross-platform API has been slimmed down, has been given support for non-relational databases like Azure Cosmos DB, and has been renamed **Entity Framework Core**.

You will learn about it in *Chapter 10, Working with Data Using Entity Framework Core*.

If you have existing apps that use the old EF, then version 6.3 is supported on .NET Core 3.0 or later.

Understanding .NET Standard

The situation with .NET in 2019 was that there were three forked .NET platforms controlled by Microsoft, as shown in the following list:

- **.NET Core**: For cross-platform and new apps.
- **.NET Framework**: For legacy apps.
- **Xamarin**: For mobile apps.

Each had strengths and weaknesses because they were all designed for different scenarios. This led to the problem that a developer had to learn three platforms, each with annoying quirks and limitations.

Because of that, Microsoft defined .NET Standard – a specification for a set of APIs that all .NET platforms could implement to indicate what level of compatibility they have. For example, basic support is indicated by a platform being compliant with .NET Standard 1.4.

With .NET Standard 2.0 and later, Microsoft made all three platforms converge on a modern minimum standard, which made it much easier for developers to share code between any flavor of .NET.

For .NET Core 2.0 and later, this added most of the missing APIs that developers need to port old code written for .NET Framework to the cross-platform .NET Core. However, some APIs are implemented but throw an exception to indicate to a developer that they should not actually be used! This is usually due to differences in the operating system on which you run .NET. You'll learn how to handle these platform-specific exceptions in *Chapter 2, Speaking C#*.

It is important to understand that .NET Standard is just a standard. You are not able to install .NET Standard in the same way that you cannot install HTML5. To use HTML5, you must install a web browser that implements the HTML5 standard.

To use .NET Standard, you must install a .NET platform that implements the .NET Standard specification. The last .NET Standard, version 2.1, is implemented by .NET Core 3.0, Mono, and Xamarin. Some features of C# 8.0 require .NET Standard 2.1. .NET Standard 2.1 is not implemented by .NET Framework 4.8.

With the release of .NET 5 and later, the need for .NET Standard has reduced significantly because there is now a single .NET for all platforms, including mobile. Modern .NET has a single BCL and two CLRs: CoreCLR is optimized for server or desktop scenarios like websites and Windows desktop apps, and the Mono runtime is optimized for mobile and web browser apps that have limited resources.

In August 2021, Stephen Toub (Partner Software Engineer, .NET) wrote the article "Performance Improvements in .NET 6." It has a section about Blazor and Mono where he wrote:

> *The runtime is itself compiled to WASM, downloaded to the browser, and used to execute the application and library code on which the app depends. I say "the runtime" here, but in reality, there are actually multiple incarnations of a runtime for .NET. In .NET 6, all of the .NET core libraries for all of the .NET app models, whether it be console apps or ASP.NET Core or Blazor WASM or mobile apps, come from the same source in dotnet/runtime, but there are actually two runtime implementations in dotnet/runtime: "coreclr" and "mono."*

 Read more about the two runtimes at the following link: `https://devblogs.microsoft.com/dotnet/performance-improvements-in-net-6/#blazor-and-mono`.

Even now, apps and websites created for .NET Framework will need to be supported, so it is important to understand that you can create .NET Standard 2.0 class libraries that are backward compatible with legacy .NET platforms.

 .NET Standard is now officially legacy. There will be no new versions of .NET Standard so its GitHub repository is archived, as you can read about in the following tweet: `https://twitter.com/dotnet/status/1569725004690128898`.

.NET platforms and tools used by the C# and .NET book editions

For the first edition of this book, which was published in March 2016, I focused on .NET Core functionality but used .NET Framework when important or useful features had not yet been implemented in .NET Core. That was necessary because it was before the final release of .NET Core 1.0. Visual Studio 2015 was used for most examples, with Visual Studio Code shown only briefly.

The second edition was (almost) completely purged of all .NET Framework code examples so that readers were able to focus on .NET Core 1.1 examples that truly run cross-platform and it was an LTS release.

The third edition completed the switch. It was rewritten so that all the code was pure .NET Core 2.0. But giving step-by-step instructions for both Visual Studio Code and Visual Studio 2017 for all tasks added complexity.

The fourth edition continued the trend by only showing coding examples using Visual Studio Code for all but the last two chapters. In *Chapter 20, Building Windows Desktop Apps*, it used Visual Studio running on Windows 10, and in *Chapter 21, Building Cross-Platform Mobile Apps*, it used Visual Studio for Mac.

In the fifth edition, *Chapter 20, Building Windows Desktop Apps*, was moved to an online-only *Appendix B* to make space for a new *Chapter 20, Building Web User Interfaces Using Blazor*. Blazor projects can be created using Visual Studio Code.

In the sixth edition, *Chapter 19, Building Mobile and Desktop Apps Using .NET MAUI*, was updated to show how mobile and desktop cross-platform apps can be created using Visual Studio 2022 and **.NET MAUI (Multi-platform App UI)**.

In this seventh edition, I refocused the book on three areas: language, libraries, and web development fundamentals. Readers can use Visual Studio Code for all examples in the book, or any other code editor of their choice.

Topics covered by Apps and Services with .NET 7

The following topics are available in a new book, *Apps and Services with .NET 7*:

- **Data:** SQL Server, Azure Cosmos DB.
- **Libraries:** Dates, times, time zones, and internationalization; reflection and source code generators; third-party libraries for image handling, logging, mapping, generating PDFs; benchmarking performance and multitasking; and so on.
- **Services:** gRPC, OData, GraphQL, Azure Functions, SignalR, Minimal Web APIs.
- **User Interfaces:** ASP.NET Core, Blazor WebAssembly, .NET MAUI.

Understanding intermediate language

The C# compiler (named **Roslyn**) used by the dotnet CLI tool converts your C# source code into **intermediate language (IL)** code and stores the IL in an **assembly** (a DLL or EXE file). IL code statements are like assembly language instructions, which are executed by .NET's virtual machine, known as CoreCLR.

At runtime, CoreCLR loads the IL code from the assembly, the **just-in-time (JIT)** compiler compiles it into native CPU instructions, and then it is executed by the CPU on your machine.

The benefit of this two-step compilation process is that Microsoft can create CLRs for Linux and macOS, as well as for Windows. The same IL code runs everywhere because of the second compilation step, which generates code for the native operating system and CPU instruction set.

Regardless of which language the source code is written in, for example, C#, Visual Basic, or F#, all .NET applications use IL code for their instructions stored in an assembly. Microsoft and others provide disassembler tools that can open an assembly and reveal this IL code, such as the ILSpy .NET Decompiler extension.

Comparing .NET technologies

We can summarize and compare .NET technologies today, as shown in the following table:

Technology	Description	Host operating systems
Modern .NET	A modern feature set, full C# 8 to 11 support, used to port existing apps or create new desktop, mobile, and web apps and services. Can target older .NET platforms.	Windows, macOS, Linux, Android, iOS, Tizen
.NET Framework	A legacy feature set, limited C# 8 support, no C# 9 to 11 support, used to maintain existing applications only.	Windows only
Xamarin	Mobile and desktop apps only.	Android, iOS, macOS

Building console apps using Visual Studio 2022

The goal of this section is to showcase how to build a console app using Visual Studio 2022 for Windows.

If you do not have a Windows computer or want to use Visual Studio Code, then you can skip this section since the code will be the same; just the tooling experience is different.

Managing multiple projects using Visual Studio 2022

Visual Studio 2022 has a concept named a **solution** that allows you to open and manage multiple projects simultaneously. We will use a solution to manage the two projects that you will create in this chapter.

Writing code using Visual Studio 2022

Let's get started writing code!

1. Start Visual Studio 2022.
2. In the Start window, click **Create a new project**.
3. In the **Create a new project** dialog, enter console in the **Search for templates** box, and select **Console App**, making sure that you have chosen the C# project template rather than another language, such as Visual Basic or C++, and that it is cross-platform, not for .NET Framework, which is Windows-only, as shown in *Figure 1.3*:

Figure 1.3: Selecting the Console App project template for modern cross-platform .NET

4. Click **Next**.
5. In the **Configure your new project** dialog, enter HelloCS for the project name, enter C:\cs11dotnet7 for the location, and enter Chapter01 for the solution name.

6. Click **Next**.

7. In the **Additional information** dialog, in the **Target Framework** drop-down list, note the choices of short-term support and long-term support versions of .NET, and then select either **.NET 6.0** or **.NET 7.0**. For the projects in this chapter, we will not need any .NET 7-specific functionality.

 If you are missing .NET SDK versions, then you can install them from the following link: https://dotnet.microsoft.com/en-us/download/dotnet.

8. Leave the check box labeled **Do not use top-level statements** cleared, and then click **Create**.

9. If code is not shown, then in **Solution Explorer**, double-click to open the file named `Program.cs` and note that **Solution Explorer** shows the **HelloCS** project, as shown in *Figure 1.4*:

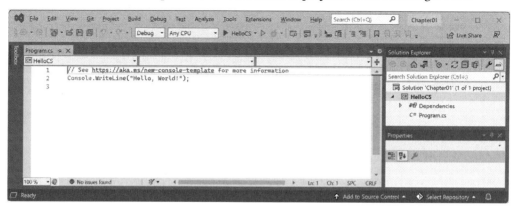

Figure 1.4: Editing Program.cs in Visual Studio 2022

10. In `Program.cs`, note the code consists of only a comment and a single statement because it uses the top-level program feature introduced in C# 9, as shown in the following code:

```
// See https://aka.ms/new-console-template for more information
Console.WriteLine("Hello, World!");
```

 As the comment in the code says, you can read more about this template at the following link: https://aka.ms/new-console-template.

11. In `Program.cs`, modify line 2 so that the text that is being written to the console says `Hello, C#!`.

All code examples and commands that the reader must review or type are shown in plain text as in *Step 10*. You will never have to read code or commands from a screenshot like in *Figure 1.4* that might be too faint in print.

Compiling and running code using Visual Studio

The next task is to compile and run the code:

1. In Visual Studio, navigate to **Debug | Start Without Debugging**.

Good Practice: When you start a project in Visual Studio 2022, you can choose to attach a debugger or not. If you do not need to debug, then it is better not to attach one because attaching a debugger requires more resources and slows everything down. Attaching a debugger also limits you to only starting one project. If you want to run more than one project, each with a debugger attached, then you must start multiple instances of Visual Studio. In the toolbar, click the green outline triangle button to start without debugging instead of the green solid triangle button unless you need to debug.

2. The output in the console window will show the result of running your application, as shown in *Figure 1.5*:

Figure 1.5: Running the console app on Windows

3. Press any key to close the console app window and return to Visual Studio.
4. Optionally, close the **Properties** pane to make more vertical space for **Solution Explorer**.
5. Double-click the **HelloCS** project and note the `HelloCS.csproj` project file shows that this console app targets either `net6.0` or `net7.0`, depending on what you selected when you created the project, as shown in *Figure 1.6*.

6. In the **Solution Explorer** toolbar, toggle on the **Show All Files** button, and note that the compiler-generated bin and obj folders are visible, as shown in *Figure 1.6*:

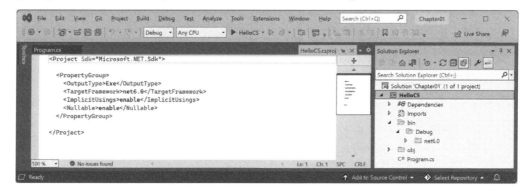

Figure 1.6: Showing the compiler-generated folders and files

Understanding the compiler-generated folders and files

Two compiler-generated folders were created, named obj and bin. You do not need to look inside these folders or understand their files yet (but feel free to browse around if you are curious).

Just be aware that the compiler needs to create temporary folders and files to do its work. You could delete these folders and their files, and they will be automatically recreated the next time you "build" or run the project. Developers often delete these temporary folders and files to "clean" a project. Visual Studio even has a command on the **Build** menu named **Clean Solution** that deletes some of these temporary files for you. The equivalent command with Visual Studio Code is dotnet clean. Brief descriptions of what the two folders contain are in the following list:

*   The obj folder contains one compiled *object* file for each source code file. These objects haven't been linked together into a final executable yet.
*   The bin folder contains the *binary* executable for the application or class library. We will look at this in more detail in *Chapter 7, Packaging and Distributing .NET Types*.

Understanding top-level programs

If you have seen older .NET projects before then you might have expected more code, even just to output a simple message. This is because some code is written for you by the compiler when you target .NET 6 or later.

If you had created the project with .NET SDK 5.0 or earlier, or if you had selected the check box labeled **Do not use top-level statements**, then the Program.cs file would have more statements, as shown in the following code:

```
using System; // Not needed in .NET 6 or later.


namespace HelloCS
{
  class Program
  {
```

```
      static void Main(string[] args)
      {
        Console.WriteLine("Hello, World!");
      }
    }
  }
```

During compilation with .NET SDK 6.0 or later, all the boilerplate code to define a namespace, the Program class, and its Main method, is generated and wrapped around the statements you write. This uses a feature introduced in .NET 5 called **top-level programs**, but it was not until .NET 6 that Microsoft updated the project template for console apps to use it by default.

Key points to remember about top-level programs include the following:

- There can be only one file like this in a project.
- Any using statements must go at the top of the file.
- If you declare any classes or other types, they must go at the bottom of the file.
- Although you should name the method Main if you explicitly define it, the method is named <Main>$ when created by the compiler.

The using System; statement at the top of the file imports the System namespace. This enables the Console.WriteLine statement to work. Why do we not have to import it in our project?

Implicitly imported namespaces

The trick is that we do still need to import the System namespace, but it is now done for us using a combination of features introduced in C# 10 and .NET 6. Let's see how:

1. In **Solution Explorer**, expand the obj folder, expand the Debug folder, expand the net6.0 or net7.0 folder, and open the file named HelloCS.GlobalUsings.g.cs.
2. Note that this file is automatically created by the compiler for projects that target .NET 6 or later, and that it uses a feature introduced in C# 10 called **global namespace imports** that imports some commonly used namespaces like System for use in all code files, as shown in the following code:

```
// <autogenerated />
global using global::System;
global using global::System.Collections.Generic;
global using global::System.IO;
global using global::System.Linq;
global using global::System.Net.Http;
global using global::System.Threading;
global using global::System.Threading.Tasks;
```

3. In **Solution Explorer**, click the **Show All Files** button to hide the bin and obj folders.

I will explain more about the implicit imports feature in the next chapter. For now, just note that a significant change that happened between .NET 5 and .NET 6 is that many of the project templates, like the one for console apps, use new SDK and language features to hide what is really happening.

Revealing the hidden code by throwing an exception

Now let's discover how the hidden code has been written:

1. In `Program.cs`, after the statement that outputs the message, add a statement to throw a new exception, as shown in the following code:

    ```
    throw new Exception();
    ```

2. In Visual Studio, navigate to **Debug | Start Without Debugging**. (Do not start the project with debugging or the exception will be caught by the debugger!)

3. The output in the console window will show the result of running your application, including that a hidden `Program` class was defined by the compiler with a method named `<Main>$` that has a parameter named args for passing in arguments, as shown in *Figure 1.7*:

Figure 1.7: Throwing an exception to reveal the hidden Program.<Main>$ method

4. Press any key to close the console app window and return to Visual Studio.

Adding a second project using Visual Studio 2022

Let's add a second project to our solution to explore how to work with multiple projects:

1. In Visual Studio, navigate to **File | Add | New Project**.

2. In the **Add a new project** dialog, in **Recent project templates**, select **Console App [C#]** and then click **Next**.

3. In the **Configure your new project** dialog, for **Project name**, enter `AboutMyEnvironment`, leave the location as `C:\cs11dotnet7\Chapter01`, and then click **Next**.

4. In the **Additional information** dialog, select **.NET 6.0** or **.NET 7.0**, and then click **Create**.

5. In the `AboutMyEnvironment` project, in `Program.cs`, modify the statement to output the current directory and the version of the operating system, as shown highlighted in the following code:

    ```
    // See https://aka.ms/new-console-template for more information
    Console.WriteLine(Environment.CurrentDirectory);
    Console.WriteLine(Environment.OSVersion.VersionString);
    ```

6. In **Solution Explorer**, right-click the **Chapter01** solution, select **Set Startup Projects...**, set **Current** selection, and then click **OK**.

7. In **Solution Explorer**, click the AboutMyEnvironment project (or any file or folder within it), and note that Visual Studio indicates that AboutMyEnvironment is now the startup project by making the project name bold.

8. Navigate to **Debug | Start Without Debugging** to run the AboutMyEnvironment project, and note the result, as shown in *Figure 1.8*:

Figure 1.8: Running a top-level program in a Visual Studio solution with two projects on Windows 11

 Windows 11 is just branding. Its official major version number is still 10! But its patch version is 22000 or higher.

9. Press any key to close the console app window and return to Visual Studio.

 When using Visual Studio 2022 for Windows to run a console app, it executes the app from the `<projectname>\bin\Debug\net7.0` or `net6.0` folder. It will be important to remember this when we work with the filesystem in later chapters. When using Visual Studio Code, or more accurately, the dotnet CLI, it has different behavior, as you are about to see.

Building console apps using Visual Studio Code

The goal of this section is to showcase how to build a console app using Visual Studio Code and the dotnet **command-line interface (CLI)**.

If you never want to try Visual Studio Code or .NET Interactive Notebooks, then please feel free to skip this section and the next, and then continue with the *Reviewing the folders and files for projects* section.

Both the instructions and screenshots in this section are for Windows, but the same actions will work with Visual Studio Code on the macOS and Linux variants.

The main differences will be native command-line actions such as deleting a file: both the command and the path are likely to be different on Windows or macOS and Linux. Luckily, the dotnet CLI tool is identical on all platforms.

Managing multiple projects using Visual Studio Code

Visual Studio Code has a concept named a **workspace** that allows you to open and manage multiple projects simultaneously. We will use a workspace to manage the two projects that you will create in this chapter.

Writing code using Visual Studio Code

Let's get started writing code!

1. Start Visual Studio Code.
2. Make sure that you do not have any open files, folders, or workspaces.
3. Navigate to **File** | **Save Workspace As...**.
4. In the dialog box, navigate to your C: drive on Windows, your user folder on macOS (mine is named markjprice), or any directory or drive in which you want to save your projects.
5. Click the **New Folder** button and name the folder cs11dotnet7. (If you completed the section for Visual Studio 2022, then this folder will already exist.)
6. In the cs11dotnet7 folder, create a new folder named Chapter01-vscode.
7. In the Chapter01-vscode folder, save the workspace as Chapter01.code-workspace.
8. Navigate to **File** | **Add Folder to Workspace...** or click the **Add Folder** button.
9. In the Chapter01-vscode folder, create a new folder named HelloCS.
10. Select the HelloCS folder and click the **Add** button.
11. When you see the dialog asking if you trust the authors of the files in this folder, click **Yes**, as shown in *Figure 1.9*:

Figure 1.9: Trusting a folder in Visual Studio Code

12. Under the menu bar, note the blue bar that explains **Restricted Mode**, and click **Manage**.
13. In the **Workspace Trust** tab, click the **Trust** button, as shown in *Figure 1.10*:

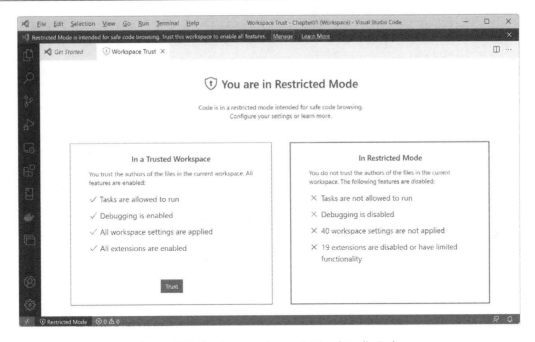

Figure 1.10: Trusting a workspace in Visual Studio Code

 When working with Visual Studio Code in the future, if some features seem to be broken, it might be because your workspace or folder is in restricted mode. You can scroll down the **Workspace Trust** window and manually manage which folders and workspaces you currently trust.

14. Close the **Workspace Trust** tab.

15. Navigate to **View | Terminal**.

16. In **TERMINAL**, make sure that you are in the HelloCS folder, and then use the dotnet CLI to create a new console app, as shown in the following command:

```
dotnet new console
```

 The dotnet new console command targets your latest .NET SDK version by default. To target a different version, use the -f switch to specify a target framework like .NET 6.0, as shown in the following command:

```
dotnet new console -f net6.0
```

17. You will see that the dotnet command-line tool creates a new **Console App** project for you in the current folder, and the **EXPLORER** window shows the two files created, HelloCS.csproj and Program.cs, and the obj folder, as shown in *Figure 1.11*:

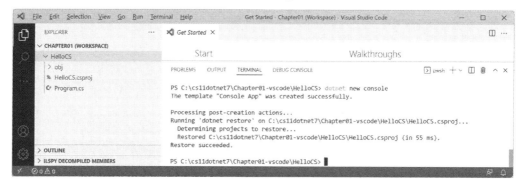

Figure 1.11: The EXPLORER window will show that two files and a folder have been created

 By default, the name of the project will match the folder name. The dotnet new console command created a project file named HelloCS.csproj in the HelloCS folder. If you want to create a folder and project simultaneously, then you can use the -o switch. For example, if you are in the Chapter01-vscode folder and you want to create a subfolder and project named HelloCS, then you enter the following command:

```
dotnet new console -o HelloCS
```

18. In **EXPLORER**, click on the file named Program.cs to open it in the editor window. The first time that you do this, Visual Studio Code may have to download and install C# dependencies like OmniSharp, .NET Core Debugger, and Razor Language Server, if it did not do this when you installed the C# extension or if they need updating. Visual Studio Code will show progress in the **Output** window and eventually the message Finished, as shown in the following output:

```
Installing C# dependencies...
Platform: win32, x86_64
Downloading package 'OmniSharp for Windows (.NET 4.6 / x64)' (36150
KB).................. Done!
Validating download...
Integrity Check succeeded.
Installing package 'OmniSharp for Windows (.NET 4.6 / x64)'
Downloading package '.NET Core Debugger (Windows / x64)' (45048
KB).................. Done!
Validating download...
Integrity Check succeeded.
Installing package '.NET Core Debugger (Windows / x64)'
Downloading package 'Razor Language Server (Windows / x64)' (52344
KB).................. Done!
```

```
Installing package 'Razor Language Server (Windows / x64)'
Finished
```

The preceding output is from Visual Studio Code on Windows. When run on macOS or Linux, the output will look slightly different, but the equivalent components for your operating system will be downloaded and installed.

19. Folders named `obj` and `bin` will have been created and when you see a notification saying that required assets are missing, click **Yes**, as shown in *Figure 1.12*:

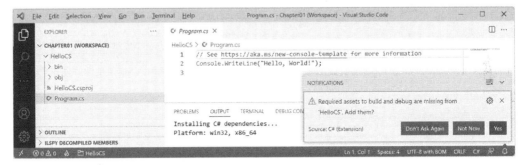

Figure 1.12: Warning message to add required build and debug assets

 If the notification disappears before you can interact with it, then you can click the bell icon in the far-right corner of the status bar to show it again.

20. After a few seconds, another folder named `.vscode` will be created with some files that are used by Visual Studio Code to provide features like IntelliSense during debugging, which you will learn more about in *Chapter 4, Writing, Debugging, and Testing Functions*.

21. In `Program.cs`, modify line 2 so that the text that is being written to the console says `Hello, C#!`.

 Good Practice: Navigate to **File | Auto Save**. This toggle will save the annoyance of remembering to save before rebuilding your application each time.

Compiling and running code using the dotnet CLI

The next task is to compile and run the code:

1. Navigate to **View | Terminal** and enter the following command:

```
dotnet run
```

2. The output in the **TERMINAL** window will show the result of running your application, as shown in *Figure 1.13*:

Figure 1.13: The output of running your first console app

3. In `Program.cs`, after the statement that outputs the message, add a statement to throw a new exception, as shown in the following code:

```
throw new Exception();
```

4. Navigate to **View** | **Terminal** and enter the following command:

```
dotnet run
```

In **TERMINAL**, you can press the up and down arrows to loop through previous commands and then press the left and right arrows to edit the command before pressing *Enter* to run them.

5. The output in the **TERMINAL** window will show the result of running your application, including that a hidden `Program` class was defined by the compiler with a method named `<Main>$` that has a parameter named `args` for passing in arguments, as shown in the following output:

```
Hello, C#!
   at Program.<Main>$(String[] args) in C:\cs11dotnet7\Chapter01-vscode\
HelloCS\Program.cs:line 3
```

Adding a second project using Visual Studio Code

Let's add a second project to our workspace to explore how to work with multiple projects:

1. In Visual Studio Code, navigate to **File** | **Add Folder to Workspace....**

2. In the `Chapter01-vscode` folder, use the **New Folder** button to create a new folder named `AboutMyEnvironment`, select it, and click **Add**.

3. When asked if you trust the folder, click **Yes**.

4. Navigate to **Terminal** | **New Terminal**, and in the drop-down list that appears, select **About-MyEnvironment**. Alternatively, in **EXPLORER**, right-click the `AboutMyEnvironment` folder and then select **Open in Integrated Terminal**.

5. In **TERMINAL**, confirm that you are in the `AboutMyEnvironment` folder, and then enter the command to create a new console app, as shown in the following command:

```
dotnet new console
```

 Good Practice: Be careful when entering commands in **TERMINAL**. Be sure that you are in the correct folder before entering potentially destructive commands! That is why I got you to create a new terminal for `AboutMyEnvironment` before issuing the command to create a new console app.

6. Navigate to **View | Command Palette**.

7. Enter omni, and then, in the drop-down list that appears, select **OmniSharp: Select Project**.

8. In the drop-down list of two projects, select the **AboutMyEnvironment** project, and when prompted, click **Yes** to add required assets to debug.

 Good Practice: To enable debugging and other useful features, like code formatting and Go To Definition, you must tell OmniSharp which project you are actively working on in Visual Studio Code. You can quickly toggle active projects by clicking the project/folder to the right of the flame icon on the left side of the status bar.

9. In **EXPLORER**, in the `AboutMyEnvironment` folder, select `Program.cs` and then change the existing statement to output the current directory and the operating system version string, as shown in the following code:

```
Console.WriteLine(Environment.CurrentDirectory);
Console.WriteLine(Environment.OSVersion.VersionString);
```

10. In **TERMINAL**, enter the command to run a program, as shown in the following command:

```
dotnet run
```

11. Note the output in the **TERMINAL** window, as shown in *Figure 1.14*:

Figure 1.14: Running a top-level program in a Visual Studio Code workspace with two projects on Windows

When using Visual Studio Code, or more accurately, the dotnet CLI, to run a console app, it executes the app from the `<projectname>` folder. When using Visual Studio 2022 for Windows, it executes the app from the `<projectname>\bin\Debug\net7.0` or net6.0 folder. It will be important to remember this when we work with the filesystem in later chapters.

If you were to run the program on macOS Big Sur, the environment operating system would be different, as shown in the following output:

```
Unix 11.2.3
```

Exploring code using .NET Interactive Notebooks

This is a bonus section for the chapter that is available online at `https://github.com/markjprice/cs11dotnet7/blob/main/docs/bonus/notebooks.md`

Using .NET Interactive Notebooks for the code in this book

Throughout the rest of the chapters, I will not give explicit instructions to use notebooks, but the GitHub repository for the book has solution notebooks when appropriate. I expect many readers will want to run my pre-created notebooks for language and library features covered in *Chapters 1* to *11* that they want to see in action and learn about without having to write a complete application:

`https://github.com/markjprice/cs11dotnet7/tree/main/notebooks`

Reviewing the folders and files for projects

In this chapter, you created two projects named `HelloCS` and `AboutMyEnvironment`.

Visual Studio Code uses a workspace file to manage multiple projects. Visual Studio 2022 uses a solution file to manage multiple projects. You might have also created a .NET Interactive notebook.

The result is a folder structure and files that will be repeated in subsequent chapters, although with more than just two projects, as shown in *Figure 1.20*:

Figure 1.20: Folder structure and files for the two projects in this chapter

Understanding the common folders and files

Although `.code-workspace` and `.sln` files are different, the project folders and files such as `HelloCS` and `AboutMyEnvironment` are identical for Visual Studio 2022 and Visual Studio Code. This means that you can mix and match between both code editors if you like:

- In Visual Studio 2022, with a solution open, navigate to **File | Add Existing Project...** to add a project file created by another tool.
- In Visual Studio Code, with a workspace open, navigate to **File | Add Folder to Workspace...** to add a project folder created by another tool.

Good Practice: Although the source code, like the `.csproj` and `.cs` files, is identical, the `bin` and `obj` folders that are automatically generated by the compiler could have mismatched file versions that show you errors. If you want to open the same project in both Visual Studio 2022 and Visual Studio Code, delete the temporary `bin` and `obj` folders before opening the project in the other code editor. This explains why I asked you to create a different folder for the Visual Studio Code projects in this chapter.

Understanding the solution code on GitHub

The solution code in the GitHub repository for this book includes separate folders for Visual Studio Code, Visual Studio 2022, and .NET Interactive notebook files, as shown in the following list:

- Visual Studio 2022 solutions: `https://github.com/markjprice/cs11dotnet7/tree/main/vs4win`
- Visual Studio Code solutions: `https://github.com/markjprice/cs11dotnet7/tree/main/vscode`
- .NET Interactive Notebook solutions: `https://github.com/markjprice/cs11dotnet7/tree/main/notebooks`

Good Practice: If you need to, return to this chapter to remind yourself how to create and manage multiple projects in the code editor of your choice. The GitHub repository has step-by-step instructions for four code editors (Visual Studio 2022 for Windows, Visual Studio Code, Visual Studio 2022 for Mac, and JetBrains Rider), along with additional screenshots: `https://github.com/markjprice/cs11dotnet7/blob/main/docs/code-editors/`.

Making good use of the GitHub repository for this book

Git is a commonly used source code management system. GitHub is a company, website, and desktop application that makes it easier to manage Git. Microsoft purchased GitHub in 2018, so it will continue to become more closely integrated with Microsoft tools.

I created a GitHub repository for this book, and I use it for the following:

- To store the solution code for the book that can be maintained after the print publication date.
- To provide extra materials that extend the book, like errata fixes, small improvements, lists of useful links, and longer articles that cannot fit in the printed book.
- To provide a place for readers to get in touch with me if they have issues with the book.

Raising issues with the book

If you get stuck following any of the instructions in this book, or if you spot a mistake in the text or the code in the solutions, please raise an issue in the GitHub repository:

1. Use your favorite browser to navigate to the following link: `https://github.com/markjprice/cs11dotnet7/issues`.
2. Click **New Issue**.
3. Enter as much detail as possible that will help me to diagnose the issue. For example:

   - For a mistake in the book, the page number and section title.
   - Your operating system, for example, Windows 11 64-bit, or macOS Big Sur version 11.2.3.
   - Your hardware, for example, Intel, Apple Silicon, or ARM CPU.
   - Your code editor, for example, Visual Studio 2022, Visual Studio Code, or something else, including the version number.
   - As much of your code and configuration that you feel is relevant and necessary.
   - Description of expected behavior and the behavior experienced.
   - Screenshots (you can drag and drop image files into the issue box).

I cannot always respond immediately to issues. But I want all my readers to be successful with my book, so if I can help you (and others) without too much trouble, then I will gladly do so.

Giving me feedback

If you'd like to give me more general feedback about the book, then either email me, ask me a question on Discord, or the GitHub repository `README.md` page will have links to some surveys. You can provide the feedback anonymously, or if you would like a response from me, then you can supply an email address. I will only use this email address to answer your feedback.

Please join me and your fellow readers on Discord using this invite: `https://packt.link/csharp11dotnet7`.

I love to hear from my readers about what they like about my book, as well as suggestions for improvements and how they are working with C# and .NET, so don't be shy. Please get in touch!

Thank you in advance for your thoughtful and constructive feedback.

Downloading solution code from the GitHub repository

I use GitHub to store solutions to all the hands-on, step-by-step coding examples throughout chapters and the practical exercises that are featured at the end of each chapter. You will find the repository at the following link: `https://github.com/markjprice/cs11dotnet7`.

I recommend that you add the preceding link to your favorite bookmarks.

If you just want to download all the solution files without using Git, click the green **Code** button and then select **Download ZIP**, as shown in *Figure 1.21*:

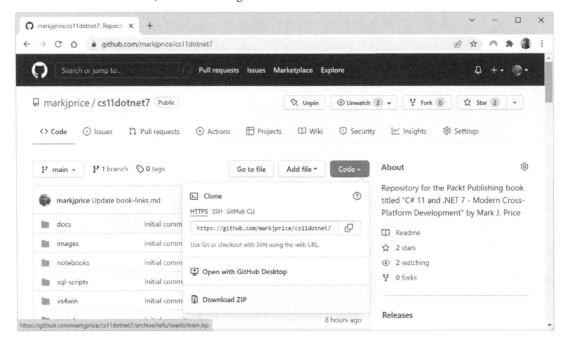

Figure 1.21: Downloading the repository as a ZIP file

 Good Practice: It is best to clone or download the code solutions to a short folder path, like `C:\cs11dotnet7\` or `C:\book\`, to avoid build-generated files exceeding the maximum path length. You should also avoid special characters like #, for example, do not use a folder name like `C:\C# projects\`. That folder name might work for a simple console app project, but once you start adding features that automatically generate code you are likely to have strange issues. Keep your folder names short and simple.

Using Git with Visual Studio Code and the command line

Visual Studio Code has support for Git, but it will use your operating system's Git installation, so you must install Git 2.0 or later first before you get these features.

You can install Git from the following link: `https://git-scm.com/download`.

If you like to use a GUI, you can download GitHub Desktop from the following link: `https://desktop.` `github.com`.

> You do not need to use or know anything about Git to get the solution code of this book. You can directly download a ZIP by using the following link and then extract it in your local filesystem: `https://github.com/markjprice/cs11dotnet7/archive/refs/heads/` `main.zip`.

Cloning the book solution code repository

Let's clone the book solution code repository. In the steps that follow, you will use the Visual Studio Code terminal, but you could enter the commands at any command prompt or terminal window:

1. Create a folder named `Repos-vscode` in your user or `Documents` folder, or wherever you want to store your Git repositories.
2. In Visual Studio Code, open the `Repos-vscode` folder.
3. Navigate to **View | Terminal**, and enter the following command:

```
git clone https://github.com/markjprice/cs11dotnet7.git
```

> Note that cloning all the solutions for all the chapters will take a minute or so, so please be patient.

Looking for help

This section is all about how to find quality information about programming on the web.

Reading Microsoft documentation

The definitive resource for getting help with Microsoft developer tools and platforms is Microsoft Docs, and you can find it at the following link: `https://docs.microsoft.com/`.

Getting help for the dotnet tool

At the command line, you can ask the `dotnet` tool for help with its commands:

1. To open the official documentation in a browser window for the `dotnet new` command, enter the following at the command line or in the Visual Studio Code terminal:

```
dotnet help new
```

2. To get help output at the command line, use the `-h` or `--help` flag, as shown in the following command:

```
dotnet new console -h
```

3. You will see the following partial output:

```
Console App (C#)
Author: Microsoft
Description: A project for creating a command-line application that can
run on .NET Core on Windows, Linux and macOS
Options:
  -f|--framework. The target framework for the project.
                      net7.0              - Target net7.0
                      net6.0              - Target net6.0
                      net5.0              - Target net5.0
                      netcoreapp3.1.    - Target netcoreapp3.1
                  Default: net7.0


  --langVersion    Sets langVersion in the created project file
                   text - Optional


  --no-restore    If specified, skips the automatic restore of the
project on create.
                   bool - Optional
                   Default: false


To see help for other template languages (F#, VB), use --language option:
   dotnet new console -h --language F#
```

Getting definitions of types and their members

One of the most useful features of a code editor is **Go To Definition**. It is available in Visual Studio Code and Visual Studio 2022. It will show what the public definition of the type or member looks like by reading the metadata in the compiled assembly or by loading from a source link.

Some tools, such as ILSpy .NET Decompiler, will even reverse-engineer from the metadata and IL code back into C# or another language for you.

Let's see how to use the **Go To Definition** feature:

1. In Visual Studio 2022 or Visual Studio Code, open the solution/workspace named Chapter01.
2. In the HelloCS project, at the bottom of Program.cs, enter the following statement to declare an integer variable named z:

   ```
   int z;
   ```

3. Click inside int and then right-click and choose **Go To Definition**.

4. In the code window that appears, you can see how the `int` data type is defined, as shown in *Figure 1.22*:

Figure 1.22: The int data type metadata

You can see that `int`:

- Is defined using the `struct` keyword
- Is in the `System.Runtime` assembly
- Is in the `System` namespace
- Is named `Int32`
- Is therefore an alias for the `System.Int32` type
- Implements interfaces such as `IComparable`
- Has constant values for its maximum and minimum values
- Has methods such as `Parse`

> **Good Practice:** When you try to use **Go To Definition** in Visual Studio Code, you will sometimes see an error saying **No definition found**. This is because the C# extension does not know about the current project. To fix this issue, navigate to **View | Command Palette**, enter omni, select **OmniSharp: Select Project**, and then select the project that you want to work with.

Right now, the **Go To Definition** feature is not that useful to you because you do not yet know what all of this information means.

By the end of the first part of this book, which consists of *Chapters 2* to *6*, and which teaches you about the C# language, you will know enough for this feature to become very handy.

5. In the code editor window, scroll down to find the `Parse` method with a single `string` parameter, as shown in the following code:

```
public static int Parse(string s)
```

6. Expand the code and review the comments that document this method, as shown in *Figure 1.23*:

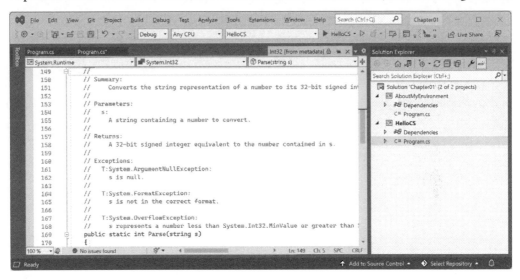

Figure 1.23: The comments for the Parse method with a single string parameter

 Figure 1.23 shows the code generated from metadata which includes the comments. Visual Studio 2022 might alternatively show code from a source link that does not include the comments.

In the comments, you will see that Microsoft has documented the following:

- A summary that describes the method.
- Parameters like the `string` value that can be passed to the method.
- The return value of the method, including its data type.
- Three exceptions that might occur if you call this method, including `ArgumentNullException`, `FormatException`, and `OverflowException`. Now, we know that we could choose to wrap a call to this method in a `try` statement and which exceptions to catch.

Hopefully, you are getting impatient to learn what all this means!

Be patient for a little longer. You are almost at the end of this chapter, and in the next chapter, you will dive into the details of the C# language. But first, let's see where else you can look for help.

Looking for answers on Stack Overflow

Stack Overflow is the most popular third-party website for getting answers to difficult programming questions. It's so popular that search engines such as DuckDuckGo have a special way to write a query to search the site:

1. Start your favorite web browser.

2. Navigate to `DuckDuckGo.com`, enter the following query, and note the search results, which are also shown in *Figure 1.24*:

```
!so securestring
```

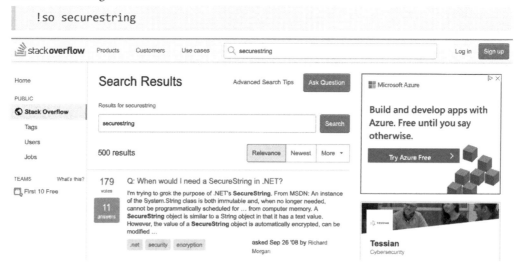

Figure 1.24: Stack Overflow search results for securestring

Searching for answers using Google

You can search Google with advanced search options to increase the likelihood of finding what you need:

1. Navigate to Google.

2. Search for information about `garbage collection` using a simple Google query and note that you will probably see a lot of ads for garbage collection services in your local area before you see the Wikipedia definition of garbage collection in computer science.

3. Improve the search by restricting it to a useful site such as Stack Overflow, and by removing languages that we might not care about, such as C++, Rust, and Python, or by adding C# and .NET explicitly, as shown in the following search query:

```
garbage collection site:stackoverflow.com +C# -Java
```

Subscribing to the official .NET blog

To keep up to date with .NET, an excellent blog to subscribe to is the official .NET Blog, written by the .NET engineering teams, and you can find it at the following link: `https://devblogs.microsoft.com/dotnet/`.

Watching Scott Hanselman's videos

Scott Hanselman from Microsoft has an excellent YouTube channel about computer stuff they didn't teach you: http://computerstufftheydidntteachyou.com/.

I recommend it to everyone working with computers.

A companion book to continue your learning journey

I have created a second book that continues your learning journey, so it acts as a companion to this book.

This first book covers the fundamentals of C#, .NET, and ASP.NET Core for web development. The second book covers more specialized topics like managing data in relational and cloud databases, and building services with Minimal APIs, OData, GraphQL, gRPC, SignalR, and Azure Functions. You will learn how to build graphical user interfaces for websites, desktop, and mobile apps with ASP.NET Core, Blazor, and .NET MAUI, as shown in *Figure 1.25*:

1. **C# language,** including new C# 11 features, object-oriented programming, and debugging and unit testing.

2. **.NET libraries,** including numbers, text, and collections, file I/O, and data with EF Core 7.

3. **Websites and web services** with ASP.NET Core 7 and Blazor.

1. **More .NET libraries** like internationalization, multitasking, and security.

2. **More data** with SQL Server and Azure Cosmos DB.

3. **More services** with Minimal Web API, OData, GraphQL, gRPC, SignalR, and Azure Functions.

4. **More graphical user interfaces** with ASP.NET Core MVC, Razor, Blazor, and .NET MAUI.

Fundamentals   *Practical Applications*

Figure 1.25: A companion book for learning C# and .NET

The first book is best read linearly, chapter by chapter, because it builds up fundamental skills and knowledge.

The second book can be read more like a cookbook, so if you are especially interested in building gRPC services, then you could read that chapter first. The main exception is *Chapter 2*, which covers SQL Server, because one of the coding tasks in that chapter walks you through creating an EF Core model in class libraries that are then used in many other chapters.

To see a list of all the books that I have published with Packt, you can use the following link:

https://subscription.packtpub.com/search?query=mark+j.+price

A similar list is available on Amazon, and, of course, you can search other book-selling sites for my books too:

https://www.amazon.com/Mark-J-Price/e/B071DW3QGN/

Practicing and exploring

Let's now test your knowledge and understanding by trying to answer some questions, getting some hands-on practice, and going into the topics covered throughout this chapter in greater detail.

Exercise 1.1 – Test your knowledge

Try to answer the following questions, remembering that although most answers can be found in this chapter, you should do some online research or code writing to answer others:

1. Is Visual Studio 2022 better than Visual Studio Code?

2. Is .NET 5 and later better than .NET Framework?

3. What is .NET Standard and why is it still important?

4. Why can a programmer use different languages, for example, C# and F#, to write applications that run on .NET?

5. What is a top-level program and how do you access any command-line arguments?

6. What is the name of the entry point method of a .NET console app and how should it be explicitly declared if you are not using the top-level program feature?

7. What do you type at the command line to build and execute C# source code?

8. What are some benefits of using .NET Interactive Notebooks to write C# code?

9. Where would you look for help for a C# keyword?

10. Where would you look first for solutions to common programming problems?

 Appendix, Answers to the Test Your Knowledge Questions, is available to download from a link in the README on the GitHub repository: `https://github.com/markjprice/cs11dotnet7`.

Exercise 1.2 – Practice C# anywhere with a browser

You don't need to download and install Visual Studio Code or even Visual Studio 2022 for Windows or Mac to write C#. You can start coding online at any of the following links:

*   Visual Studio Code for Web: `https://vscode.dev/`
*   SharpLab: `https://sharplab.io/`
*   C# Online Compiler | .NET Fiddle: `https://dotnetfiddle.net/`
*   W3Schools C# Online Compiler: `https://www.w3schools.com/cs/cs_compiler.php`

Exercise 1.3 – Explore topics

A book is a curated experience. I have tried to find the right balance of topics to include in the printed book. Other content that I have written can be found in the GitHub repository for this book.

I believe that this book covers all the fundamental knowledge and skills a C# and .NET developer should have or be aware of. Some longer examples are best included as links to Microsoft documentation or third-party article authors.

Use the links on the following page to learn more details about the topics covered in this chapter:

```
https://github.com/markjprice/cs11dotnet7/blob/main/book-links.md#chapter-1---hello-
c-welcome-net
```

Exercise 1.4 — Explore themes of modern .NET

Microsoft has created a website using Blazor that shows the major themes of modern .NET:

```
https://themesof.net/
```

Summary

In this chapter, we:

- Set up your development environment.
- Discussed the similarities and differences between modern .NET, .NET Core, .NET Framework, Xamarin, and .NET Standard.
- Used Visual Studio 2022 for Windows and Visual Studio Code with the .NET SDK to create some simple console apps managed with a solution or workspace.
- Used .NET Interactive Notebooks to execute snippets of code.
- Learned how to download the solution code for this book from its GitHub repository.
- And, most importantly, learned how to find help.

In the next chapter, you will learn how to "speak" C#.

Join our book's Discord space

Join the book's Discord workspace for *Ask me Anything* sessions with the author.

```
https://packt.link/csharp11dotnet7
```

2

Speaking C#

This chapter is all about the basics of the C# programming language. Over the course of this chapter, you'll learn how to write statements using the grammar of C#, as well as being introduced to some of the common vocabulary that you will use every day. In addition to this, by the end of the chapter, you'll feel confident in knowing how to temporarily store and work with information in your computer's memory.

This chapter covers the following topics:

- Introducing the C# language
- Understanding C# grammar and vocabulary
- Working with variables
- Exploring more about console apps
- Understanding async and await

Introducing the C# language

This part of the book is about the C# language—the grammar and vocabulary that you will use every day to write the source code for your applications.

Programming languages have many similarities to human languages, except that in programming languages, you can make up your own words, just like Dr. Seuss!

In a book written by Dr. Seuss in 1950, *If I Ran the Zoo*, he states this:

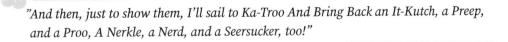

> "And then, just to show them, I'll sail to Ka-Troo And Bring Back an It-Kutch, a Preep, and a Proo, A Nerkle, a Nerd, and a Seersucker, too!"

Understanding language versions and features

This part of the book covers the C# programming language and is written primarily for beginners, so it covers the fundamental topics that all developers need to know, from declaring variables to storing data to how to define your own custom data types.

This book covers features of the C# language from version 1 up to the latest version, 11.

If you already have some familiarity with older versions of C# and are excited to find out about the new features in the most recent versions of C#, I have made it easier for you to jump around by listing language versions and their important new features below, along with the chapter number and topic title where you can learn about them.

Project COOL

Before the first release of C#, it had the codename COOL (C-like Object-Oriented Language).

C# 1

C# 1 was released in February 2002 and included all the important features of a statically typed object-oriented modern language, as you will see throughout *Chapters 2 to 6*.

C# 1.2

C# 1.2, with a few minor improvements like automatic disposal at the end of foreach statements, was released with Visual Studio .NET 2003.

C# 2

C# 2 was released in 2005 and focused on enabling strong data typing using generics, to improve code performance and reduce type errors, including the topics listed in the following table:

Feature	Chapter	Topic
Nullable value types	6	Making a value type nullable
Generics	6	Making types more reusable with generics

C# 3

C# 3 was released in 2007 and focused on enabling declarative coding with **Language INtegrated Queries (LINQ)** and related features like anonymous types and lambda expressions, including the topics listed in the following table:

Feature	Chapter	Topic
Implicitly typed local variables	2	Inferring the type of a local variable
LINQ	11	All topics in *Chapter 11, Querying and Manipulating Data Using LINQ*

C# 4

C# 4 was released in 2010 and focused on improving interoperability with dynamic languages like F# and Python, including the topics listed in the following table:

Feature	Chapter	Topic
Dynamic types	2	Storing dynamic types
Named/optional arguments	5	Optional parameters and named arguments

C# 5

C# 5 was released in 2012 and focused on simplifying asynchronous operation support by automatically implementing complex state machines while writing what looks like synchronous statements, including the topics listed in the following table:

Feature	Chapter	Topic
Simplified asynchronous tasks	2	Understanding async and await

C# 6

C# 6 was released in 2015 and focused on minor refinements to the language, including the topics listed in the following table:

Feature	Chapter	Topic
static imports	2	Simplifying the usage of the console
Interpolated strings	2	Displaying output to the user
Expression-bodied members	5	Defining read-only properties

C# 7.0

C# 7.0 was released in March 2017 and focused on adding functional language features like tuples and pattern matching, as well as minor refinements to the language, including the topics listed in the following table:

Feature	Chapter	Topic
Binary literals and digit separators	2	Storing whole numbers
Pattern matching	3	Pattern matching with the if statement
out variables	5	Controlling how parameters are passed
Tuples	5	Combining multiple values with tuples
Local functions	6	Defining local functions

C# 7.1

C# 7.1 was released in August 2017 and focused on minor refinements to the language, including the topics listed in the following table:

Feature	Chapter	Topic
`async` Main	2	Improving responsiveness for console apps
Default literal expressions	5	Setting fields with default literal
Inferred tuple element names	5	Inferring tuple names

C# 7.2

C# 7.2 was released in November 2017 and focused on minor refinements to the language, including the topics listed in the following table:

Feature	Chapter	Topic
Leading underscores in numeric literals	2	Storing whole numbers
Non-trailing named arguments	5	Optional parameters and named arguments
`private protected` access modifier	5	Understanding access modifiers
You can test `==` and `!=` with tuple types	5	Comparing tuples

C# 7.3

C# 7.3 was released in May 2018 and focused on performance-oriented safe code that improves `ref` variables, pointers, and `stackalloc`. These are advanced and rarely needed for most developers, so they are not covered in this book.

C# 8

C# 8 was released in September 2019 and focused on a major change to the language related to null handling, including the topics listed in the following table:

Feature	Chapter	Topic
Switch expressions	3	Simplifying `switch` statements with switch expressions
Nullable reference types	6	Making a reference type nullable
Default interface methods	6	Understanding default interface methods

C# 9

C# 9 was released in November 2020 and focused on record types, refinements to pattern matching, and minimal-code projects, including the topics listed in the following table:

Feature	Chapter	Topic
Minimal-code console apps	1	Top-level programs
Target-typed new	2	Using target-typed new to instantiate objects
Enhanced pattern matching	5	Pattern matching with objects
Records	5	Working with records

C# 10

C# 10 was released in November 2021 and focused on features that minimize the amount of code needed in common scenarios, including the topics listed in the following table:

Feature	Chapter	Topic
Global namespace imports	2	Importing namespaces
Constant string literals	2	Formatting using interpolated strings
File-scoped namespaces	5	Simplifying namespace declarations
Record structs	6	Working with record struct types
`ArgumentNullException.ThrowIfNull`	6	Checking for null in method parameters

C# 11

C# 11 was released in November 2022 and focused on features that simplify your code, including the topics listed in the following table:

Feature	Chapter	Topic
Raw string literals	2	Understanding raw string literals
Line breaks in interpolated string expressions	2	Formatting using interpolated strings
Required properties	5	Requiring properties to be set during instantiation

Understanding C# standards

Over the years, Microsoft has submitted a few versions of C# to standards bodies, as shown in the following table:

C# version	ECMA standard	ISO/IEC standard
1.0	ECMA-334:2003	ISO/IEC 23270:2003
2.0	ECMA-334:2006	ISO/IEC 23270:2006
5.0	ECMA-334:2017	ISO/IEC 23270:2018

The ECMA standard for C# 6 is still a draft, and work on adding C# 7 features is progressing. Microsoft made C# open source in 2014. You can read the C# ECMA standard document at the following link: `https://www.ecma-international.org/publications-and-standards/standards/ecma-334/`.

More practically useful than the ECMA standards are the public GitHub repositories for making the work on C# and related technologies as open as possible, as shown in the following table:

Description	Link
C# language design	`https://github.com/dotnet/csharplang`
Compiler implementation	`https://github.com/dotnet/roslyn`
Standard to describe the language	`https://github.com/dotnet/csharpstandard`

Discovering your C# compiler versions

The .NET language compiler for C# and Visual Basic, also known as **Roslyn**, along with a separate compiler for F#, is distributed as part of the .NET SDK. To use a specific version of C#, you must have at least that version of the .NET SDK installed, as shown in the following table:

.NET SDK	Roslyn compiler	Default C# language
1.0.4	2.0 - 2.2	7.0
1.1.4	2.3 - 2.4	7.1
2.1.2	2.6 - 2.7	7.2
2.1.200	2.8 - 2.10	7.3
3.0	3.0 - 3.4	8.0
5.0	3.8	9.0
6.0	4.0	10.0
7.0	4.4	11.0

When you create class libraries, you can choose to target .NET Standard as well as versions of modern .NET. They have default C# language versions, as shown in the following table:

.NET Standard	C#
2.0	7.3
2.1	8.0

 Although you must have a minimum version of the .NET SDK installed to have access to a specific compiler version, the projects that you create can target older versions of .NET and still use a modern compiler version. For example, if you have the .NET 7 SDK or later installed, then you could use C# 11 language features in a console app that targets .NET Core 3.0.

How to output the SDK version

Let's see what .NET SDK and C# language compiler versions you have available:

1. On Windows, start **Windows Terminal** or **Command Prompt**. On macOS, start **Terminal**.
2. To determine which version of the .NET SDK you have available, enter the following command:

```
dotnet --version
```

3. Note that the version at the time of publishing is 7.0.100, indicating that it is the initial version of the SDK without any bug fixes or new features yet, as shown in the following output:

```
7.0.100
```

Enabling a specific language version compiler

Developer tools like Visual Studio and the dotnet command-line interface assume that you want to use the latest major version of a C# language compiler by default. Before C# 8.0 was released, C# 7.0 was the latest major version and was used by default. To use the improvements in a C# point release like 7.1, 7.2, or 7.3, you had to add a <LangVersion> configuration element to the project file, as shown in the following markup:

```
<LangVersion>7.3</LangVersion>
```

After the release of C# 11 with .NET 7, if Microsoft releases a C# 11.1 compiler and you want to use its new language features, then you will have to add a configuration element to your project file, as shown in the following markup:

```
<LangVersion>11.1</LangVersion>
```

Potential values for the <LangVersion> are shown in the following table:

LangVersion	Description
7, 7.1, 7.2, 7.3, 8, 9, 10, 11	Entering a specific version number will use that compiler if it has been installed.
latestmajor	Uses the highest major number, for example, 7.0 in August 2019, 8 in October 2019, 9 in November 2020, 10 in November 2021, and 11 in November 2022.
latest	Uses the highest major and highest minor number, for example, 7.2 in 2017, 7.3 in 2018, 8 in 2019, and perhaps 11.1 in H1 2023.
preview	Uses the highest available preview version, for example, 11.0 in July 2022 with .NET 7.0 Preview 6 installed.

After creating a new project, you can edit the .csproj file and add the <LangVersion> element, as shown highlighted in the following markup:

```
<Project Sdk="Microsoft.NET.Sdk">
  <PropertyGroup>
    <OutputType>Exe</OutputType>
```

```
    <TargetFramework>net7.0</TargetFramework>
    <LangVersion>preview</LangVersion>
  </PropertyGroup>
</Project>
```

Switching the C# compiler for .NET 6

.NET 6 is an LTS release, so Microsoft must support developers who continue to use .NET 6 for six months longer than .NET 7. With .NET SDK 6.0.200 and later, which was released in February 2022, you can set the language version to preview to start exploring C# 11 language features. I expect that whatever version is released alongside .NET SDK 7.0.100 on November 8, 2022 (probably .NET SDK 6.0.500), it will default to using the C# 10 compiler unless you explicitly set the language version to 11, as shown highlighted in the following markup:

```
<Project Sdk="Microsoft.NET.Sdk">

  <PropertyGroup>
    <OutputType>Exe</OutputType>
    <TargetFramework>net6.0</TargetFramework>
    <ImplicitUsings>enable</ImplicitUsings>
    <Nullable>enable</Nullable>
    <LangVersion>11</LangVersion>
  </PropertyGroup>

</Project>
```

If you target net7.0, which your projects will do by default if you have installed the .NET 7 SDK, then the default language will be C# 11 so it does not need to be explicitly set.

 Good Practice: If you are using Visual Studio Code and you have not done so already, install the Visual Studio Code extension named **MSBuild project tools**. This will give you IntelliSense while editing .csproj files, including making it easy to add the <LangVersion> element with appropriate values.

Understanding C# grammar and vocabulary

To learn simple C# language features, you can use .NET Interactive Notebooks, which remove the need to create an application of any kind.

To learn some other C# language features, you will need to create an application. The simplest type of application is a console app.

Let's start by looking at the basics of the grammar and vocabulary of C#. Throughout this chapter, you will create multiple console apps, with each one showing related features of the C# language.

Showing the compiler version

We will start by writing code that shows the compiler version:

1. If you've completed *Chapter 1, Hello, C#! Welcome, .NET!*, then you will already have a `cs11dotnet7` folder. If not, then you'll need to create it.

2. Use your preferred code editor to create a new project, as defined in the following list:

    *   Project template: **Console App [C#]**/`console`
    *   Project file and folder: `Vocabulary`
    *   Workspace/solution file and folder: `Chapter02`

     Good Practice: If you have forgotten how, or did not complete the previous chapter, then step-by-step instructions for creating a workspace/solution with multiple projects are given in *Chapter 1, Hello, C#! Welcome, .NET!*.

3. Open the `Program.cs` file, and under the comment, add a statement to show the C# version as an error, as shown in the following code:

    ```
    #error version
    ```

4. Run the console app:

    *   If you are using Visual Studio Code, then in a terminal, enter the command `dotnet run`.
    *   If you are using Visual Studio 2022, then navigate to **Debug** | **Start Without Debugging**. When prompted to continue and run the last successful build, click **No**.

5. Note that the compiler version and the language version appear as a compiler error message number `CS8304`, as shown in *Figure 2.1*:

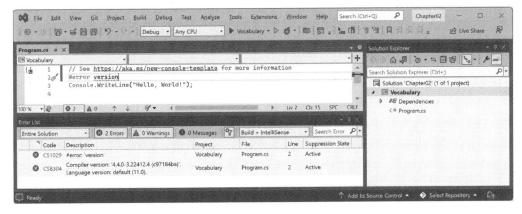

Figure 2.1: A compiler error that shows the C# language version

6. The error message in the Visual Studio Code **PROBLEMS** window or Visual Studio **Error List** window says **Compiler version: '4.4.0...'** with language version **default (11.0)**.

7. Comment out the statement that causes the error, as shown in the following code:

    ```
    // #error version
    ```

8. Note that the compiler error messages disappear.

Understanding C# grammar

The grammar of C# includes statements and blocks. To document your code, you can use comments.

 Good Practice: Comments should not be the only way that you document your code. Choosing sensible names for variables and functions, writing unit tests, and creating actual documents are other ways to document your code.

Statements

In English, we indicate the end of a sentence with a full stop. A sentence can be composed of multiple words and phrases, with the order of words being part of the grammar. For example, in English, we say "the black cat."

The adjective, *black*, comes before the noun, *cat*. Whereas French grammar has a different order; the adjective comes after the noun: "le chat noir." What's important to take away from this is that the order matters.

C# indicates the end of a **statement** with a semicolon. A statement can be composed of multiple **variables** and **expressions**. For example, in the following statement, `totalPrice` is a variable and `subtotal + salesTax` is an expression:

```
var totalPrice = subtotal + salesTax;
```

The expression is made up of an operand named `subtotal`, an operator +, and another operand named `salesTax`. The order of operands and operators matters.

Comments

Comments are the primary method of documenting your code to increase understanding of how it works, for other developers to read, or even yourself when you come back to it months later.

 In *Chapter 4, Writing, Debugging, and Testing Functions*, you will learn about XML comments that work with a tool to generate web pages to document your code.

You can add comments to explain your code using a double slash, //. The compiler will ignore everything after the // until the end of the line, as shown in the following code:

```
// sales tax must be added to the subtotal
var totalPrice = subtotal + salesTax;
```

To write a multiline comment, use /* at the beginning and */ at the end of the comment, as shown in the following code:

```
/*
This is a
multi-line comment.
*/
```

Although /* */ is most commonly used for multiline comments, it is also useful for commenting in the middle of a statement, as shown in the following code:

```
var totalPrice = subtotal /* for this item */ + salesTax;
```

 Good Practice: Well-designed code, including function signatures with well-named parameters and class encapsulation, can be somewhat self-documenting. When you find yourself putting too many comments and explanations in your code, ask yourself: can I rewrite, aka refactor, this code to make it more understandable without long comments?

Your code editor has commands to make it easier to add and remove comment characters, as shown in the following list:

- Visual Studio 2022 for Windows: Navigate to **Edit | Advanced | Comment Selection** or **Uncomment Selection**.
- Visual Studio Code: Navigate to **Edit | Toggle Line Comment** or **Toggle Block Comment**.

 Good Practice: You **comment** code by adding descriptive text above or after code statements. You **comment out** code by adding comment characters before or around statements to make them inactive. **Uncommenting** means removing the comment characters.

Blocks

In English, we indicate a new paragraph by starting a new line. C# indicates a **block** of code with the use of curly brackets, { }.

Blocks start with a declaration to indicate what is being defined. For example, a block can define the start and end of many language constructs including namespaces, classes, methods, or statements like foreach.

You will learn more about namespaces, classes, and methods later in this chapter and subsequent chapters, but to briefly introduce some of those concepts now:

- A **namespace** contains types like classes to group them together.
- A **class** contains the members of an object, including methods.
- A **method** contains statements that implement an action that an object can take.

Examples of statements and blocks

In a simple console app that does not use the top-level program feature, I've added some comments to the statements and blocks, as shown in the following code:

```
using System; // a semicolon indicates the end of a statement

namespace Basics
{ // an open brace indicates the start of a block
  class Program
  {
    static void Main(string[] args)
    {
      Console.WriteLine("Hello World!"); // a statement
    }
  }
} // a close brace indicates the end of a block
```

Understanding C# vocabulary

The C# vocabulary is made up of **keywords**, **symbol characters**, and **types**.

Some of the predefined, reserved keywords that you will see in this book include using, namespace, class, static, int, string, double, bool, if, switch, break, while, do, for, foreach, and, or, not, record, and init.

Some of the symbol characters that you will see include ", ', +, -, *, /, %, @, and $.

There are other contextual keywords that only have a special meaning in a specific context.

However, that still means that there are only about 100 actual C# keywords in the language.

> **Good Practice:** C# keywords use all lowercase. Although you can use all lowercase for your own names in your type names, you should not. With C# 11 and later, the compiler will give a warning if you do, as shown in the following output:
>
> ```
> Warning CS8981 The type name 'person' only contains lower-
> cased ascii characters. Such names may become reserved for the
> language.
> ```

Comparing programming languages to human languages

The English language has more than 250,000 distinct words, so how does C# get away with only having about 100 keywords? Moreover, why is C# so difficult to learn if it has only 0.0416% of the number of words in the English language?

One of the key differences between a human language and a programming language is that developers need to be able to define the new "words" with new meanings. Apart from the (about) 100 keywords in the C# language, this book will teach you about some of the hundreds of thousands of "words" that other developers have defined, but you will also learn how to define your own "words."

Programmers all over the world must learn English because most programming languages use English words such as "namespace" and "class." There are programming languages that use other human languages, such as Arabic, but they are rare. If you are interested in learning more, this YouTube video shows a demonstration of an Arabic programming language: `https://youtu.be/dkO8cdwf6v8`.

Changing the color scheme for C# syntax

By default, Visual Studio 2022 and Visual Studio Code show C# keywords in blue to make them easier to differentiate from other code. Both tools allow you to customize the color scheme.

In Visual Studio 2022:

1. Navigate to **Tools | Options**.
2. In the **Options** dialog box, in the **Environment** section, select **Fonts and Colors**, and then select the display items that you would like to customize. You can also search for the section instead of browsing for it.

In Visual Studio Code:

1. Navigate to **File | Preferences | Color Theme**. It is in the **Code** menu on macOS.
2. Select a color theme. For reference, I'll use the **Light+ (default light)** color theme so that the screenshots look better in a printed book.

Help for writing correct code

Plain text editors such as Notepad don't help you write correct English. Likewise, Notepad won't help you write correct C# either.

Microsoft Word can help you write English by highlighting spelling mistakes with red squiggles, with Word saying that "icecream" should be ice-cream or ice cream, and grammatical errors with blue squiggles, such as a sentence should have an uppercase first letter.

Similarly, Visual Studio 2022 and Visual Studio Code's C# extension help you write C# code by highlighting spelling mistakes, such as the method name should be `WriteLine` with an uppercase `L`, and grammatical errors, such as statements that must end with a semicolon.

The C# extension constantly watches what you type and gives you feedback by highlighting problems with colored squiggly lines, like that of Microsoft Word.

Let's see it in action:

1. In `Program.cs`, change the `L` in the `WriteLine` method to lowercase.
2. Delete the semicolon at the end of the statement.

3. In Visual Studio Code, navigate to **View** | **Problems**, or in Visual Studio, navigate to **View** | **Error List**, and note that a red squiggle appears under the code mistakes and details are shown, as you can see in *Figure 2.2*:

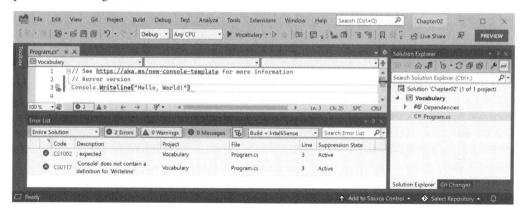

Figure 2.2: The Error List window showing two compile errors

4. Fix the two coding errors.

Importing namespaces

System is a namespace, which is like an address for a type. To refer to someone's location exactly, you might use Oxford.HighStreet.BobSmith, which tells us to look for a person named Bob Smith on the High Street in the city of Oxford.

System.Console.WriteLine tells the compiler to look for a method named WriteLine in a type named Console in a namespace named System.

To simplify our code, the **Console App** project template for every version of .NET before 6.0 added a statement at the top of the code file to tell the compiler to always look in the System namespace for types that haven't been prefixed with their namespace, as shown in the following code:

```
using System; // import the System namespace
```

We call this *importing the namespace*. The effect of importing a namespace is that all available types in that namespace will be available to your program without needing to enter the namespace prefix, and will be seen in IntelliSense while you write code.

.NET Interactive Notebooks have most namespaces imported automatically.

Implicitly and globally importing namespaces

Traditionally, every .cs file that needs to import namespaces would have to start with using statements to import those namespaces. Namespaces like System and System.Linq are needed in almost all .cs files, so the first few lines of every .cs file often had at least a few using statements, as shown in the following code:

```
using System;
using System.Linq;
using System.Collections.Generic;
```

When creating websites and services using ASP.NET Core, there are often dozens of namespaces that each file would have to import.

C# 10 introduced a new keyword combination and .NET SDK 6 introduced a new project setting that work together to simplify importing common namespaces.

The global using keyword combination means you only need to import a namespace in one .cs file and it will be available throughout all .cs files. You could put global using statements in the Program.cs file, but I recommend creating a separate file for those statements named something like GlobalUsings.cs with the contents being all your global using statements, as shown in the following code:

```
global using System;
global using System.Linq;
global using System.Collections.Generic;
```

 Good Practice: As developers get used to this new C# feature, I expect one naming convention for this file to become the standard. As you are about to see, the related .NET SDK feature uses a similar naming convention.

Any projects that target .NET 6.0 or later, and therefore use the C# 10 or later compiler, generate a <ProjectName>.GlobalUsings.g.cs file in the obj\Debug\net7.0 folder to implicitly globally import some common namespaces like System. The specific list of implicitly imported namespaces depends on which SDK you target, as shown in the following table:

SDK	Implicitly imported namespaces
Microsoft.NET.Sdk	System System.Collections.Generic System.IO System.Linq System.Net.Http System.Threading System.Threading.Tasks

Microsoft.NET.Sdk.Web	Same as `Microsoft.NET.Sdk` and:
	`System.Net.Http.Json`
	`Microsoft.AspNetCore.Builder`
	`Microsoft.AspNetCore.Hosting`
	`Microsoft.AspNetCore.Http`
	`Microsoft.AspNetCore.Routing`
	`Microsoft.Extensions.Configuration`
	`Microsoft.Extensions.DependencyInjection`
	`Microsoft.Extensions.Hosting`
	`Microsoft.Extensions.Logging`

Microsoft.NET.Sdk.Worker	Same as `Microsoft.NET.Sdk` and:
	`Microsoft.Extensions.Configuration`
	`Microsoft.Extensions.DependencyInjection`
	`Microsoft.Extensions.Hosting`
	`Microsoft.Extensions.Logging`

Let's see the current autogenerated implicit imports file:

1. If you are using Visual Studio 2022, then in **Solution Explorer**, select the `Vocabulary` project, toggle on the **Show All Files** button, and note the compiler-generated `bin` and `obj` folders are now visible.

2. Expand the `obj` folder, expand the `Debug` folder, expand the `net7.0` folder, and open the file named `Vocabulary.GlobalUsings.g.cs`.

 The naming convention for this file is `<ProjectName>.GlobalUsings.g.cs`. Note the g for **generated** to differentiate from developer-written code files.

3. Remember that this file is automatically created by the compiler for projects that target .NET 6.0, and that it imports some commonly used namespaces, including `System.Threading`, as shown in the following code:

```
// <autogenerated />
global using global::System;
global using global::System.Collections.Generic;
global using global::System.IO;
global using global::System.Linq;
global using global::System.Net.Http;
global using global::System.Threading;
global using global::System.Threading.Tasks;
```

4. Close the `Vocabulary.GlobalUsings.g.cs` file.

5. In **Solution Explorer**, select the project, and then add additional entries to the project file to control which namespaces are implicitly imported, as shown highlighted in the following markup:

```
<Project Sdk="Microsoft.NET.Sdk">

  <PropertyGroup>
    <OutputType>Exe</OutputType>
    <TargetFramework>net7.0</TargetFramework>
    <Nullable>enable</Nullable>
    <ImplicitUsings>enable</ImplicitUsings>
  </PropertyGroup>

  <ItemGroup>
    <Using Remove="System.Threading" />
    <Using Include="System.Numerics" />
  </ItemGroup>

</Project>
```

 Note that `<ItemGroup>` is different from `<ImportGroup>`. Be sure to use the correct one! Also note that the order of elements in a project group or item group does not matter. For example, `<Nullable>` can be before or after `<ImplicitUsings>`.

6. Save the changes to the project file.

7. Expand the `obj` folder, expand the `Debug` folder, expand the `net7.0` folder, and open the file named `Vocabulary.GlobalUsings.g.cs`.

8. Note this file now imports `System.Numerics` instead of `System.Threading`, as shown highlighted in the following code:

```
// <autogenerated />
global using global::System;
global using global::System.Collections.Generic;
global using global::System.IO;
global using global::System.Linq;
global using global::System.Net.Http;
global using global::System.Numerics;
global using global::System.Threading.Tasks;
```

9. Close the `Vocabulary.GlobalUsings.g.cs` file.

You can disable the implicitly imported namespaces feature for all SDKs by removing the `<ImplicitUsings>` element completely from the project file, or changing its value to `disable`, as shown in the following markup:

```
<ImplicitUsings>disable</ImplicitUsings>
```

If you are using Visual Studio 2022, then you can control project settings in the user interface:

1. In **Solution Explorer**, right-click the Vocabulary project and select **Properties**.
2. Click **Build** and note it has a **General** section opened by default.
3. Scroll down and note the sections to control nullability and implicit imports, as shown in *Figure 2.3*:

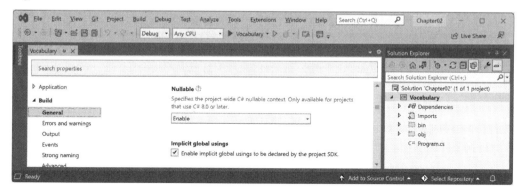

Figure 2.3: Controlling project settings in the Visual Studio 2022 user interface

4. Close the project properties.

Verbs are methods

In English, verbs are doing or action words, like "run" and "jump." In C#, doing or action words are called **methods**. There are hundreds of thousands of methods available to C#. In English, verbs change how they are written based on when in time the action happens. For example, Amir *was jumping* in the past, Beth *jumps* in the present, they *jumped* in the past, and Charlie *will jump* in the future.

In C#, methods such as WriteLine change how they are called or executed based on the specifics of the action. This is called overloading, which we'll cover in more detail in *Chapter 5, Building Your Own Types with Object-Oriented Programming*. But for now, consider the following example:

```
// Outputs the current line terminator string.
// By default, this is a carriage-return and line feed.
Console.WriteLine();

// Outputs the greeting and the current line terminator string.
Console.WriteLine("Hello Ahmed");

// Outputs a formatted number and date and the current line terminator string.
Console.WriteLine("Temperature on {0:D} is {1}°C.", DateTime.Today, 23.4);
```

When I show code snippets without numbered step-by-step instructions for you to enter the code, I do not expect you to enter the code, so it might not execute out-of-context.

A different analogy is that some words are spelled the same but have different meanings depending on the context.

Nouns are types, variables, fields, and properties

In English, nouns are names that refer to things. For example, Fido is the name of a dog. The word "dog" tells us the type of thing that Fido is, and so to order Fido to fetch a ball, we would use his name.

In C#, their equivalents are **types**, **variables**, **fields**, and **properties**. For example:

- `Animal` and `Car` are types; they are nouns for categorizing things.
- `Head` and `Engine` might be fields or properties; they are nouns that belong to `Animal` and `Car`.
- `Fido` and `Bob` are variables; they are nouns for referring to a specific object.

There are tens of thousands of types available to C#, though have you noticed how I didn't say, "There are tens of thousands of types *in* C#?" The difference is subtle but important. The language of C# only has a few keywords for types, such as `string` and `int`, and strictly speaking, C# doesn't define any types. Keywords such as `string` that look like types are **aliases**, which represent types provided by the platform on which C# runs.

It's important to know that C# cannot exist alone; after all, it's a language that runs on variants of .NET. In theory, someone could write a compiler for C# that uses a different platform, with different underlying types. In practice, the platform for C# is .NET, which provides tens of thousands of types to C#, including `System.Int32`, which is the C# keyword alias `int` maps to, as well as many more complex types, such as `System.Xml.Linq.XDocument`.

It's worth taking note that the term **type** is often confused with **class**. Have you ever played the parlor game *Twenty Questions*, also known as *Animal, Vegetable, or Mineral?* In the game, everything can be categorized as an animal, vegetable, or mineral. In C#, every **type** can be categorized as a `class`, `struct`, `enum`, `interface`, or `delegate`. You will learn what these mean in *Chapter 6, Implementing Interfaces and Inheriting Classes*. As examples, the C# keyword `string` is a `class`, but `int` is a `struct`. So, it is best to use the term **type** to refer to both.

Revealing the extent of the C# vocabulary

We know that there are more than 100 keywords in C#, but how many types are there? Let's write some code to find out how many types (and their methods) are available to C# in our simple console app.

Don't worry about exactly how this code works for now, but know that it uses a technique called **reflection**:

1. Delete all the existing statements in `Program.cs`.
2. We'll start by importing the `System.Reflection` namespace at the top of the `Program.cs` file, as shown in the following code:

```
using System.Reflection;
```

Good Practice: We could use the implicit imports and `global using` features to import this namespace for all `.cs` files in this project, but since there is only one file, it is better to import the namespace in the one file in which it is needed.

3. Write statements to get the compiled console app and loop through all of the types that it has access to, outputting the names and number of methods each has, as shown in the following code:

```
Assembly? myApp = Assembly.GetEntryAssembly();

if (myApp == null) return; // quit the app

// loop through the assemblies that my app references
foreach (AssemblyName name in myApp.GetReferencedAssemblies())
{
  // load the assembly so we can read its details
  Assembly a = Assembly.Load(name);

  // declare a variable to count the number of methods
  int methodCount = 0;

  // loop through all the types in the assembly
  foreach (TypeInfo t in a.DefinedTypes)
  {
    // add up the counts of methods
    methodCount += t.GetMethods().Count();
  }

  // output the count of types and their methods
  Console.WriteLine(
    "{0:N0} types with {1:N0} methods in {2} assembly.",
    arg0: a.DefinedTypes.Count(),
    arg1: methodCount,
    arg2: name.Name);
}
```

N0 is uppercase N followed by the digit zero. It is not uppercase N followed by uppercase O. It means "format a number (N) with zero (0) decimal places."

4. Run the code. You will see the actual number of types and methods that are available to you in the simplest application when running on your OS. The number of types and methods displayed will be different depending on the operating system that you are using, as shown in the following outputs:

```
// Output on Windows
0 types with 0 methods in System.Runtime assembly.
44 types with 645 methods in System.Console assembly.
106 types with 1,126 methods in System.Linq assembly.
```

```
// Output on macOS
0 types with 0 methods in System.Runtime assembly.
57 types with 701 methods in System.Console assembly.
103 types with 1,094 methods in System.Linq assembly.
```

 Why does the `System.Runtime` assembly contain zero types? This assembly is special because it contains only **type-forwarders** rather than actual types. A type-forwarder represents a type that has been implemented outside of .NET or for some other advanced reason.

5. Add statements to the top of the file (after importing the namespace) to declare some variables, as shown in the following code:

```
using System.Reflection;

// declare some unused variables using types
// in additional assemblies
System.Data.DataSet ds;
HttpClient client;
```

By declaring variables that use types in other assemblies, those assemblies are loaded with our application, which allows our code to see all the types and methods in them. The compiler will warn you that you have unused variables, but that won't stop your code from running.

6. Run the console app again and view the results, which should look like the following outputs:

```
// Output on Windows
0 types with 0 methods in System.Runtime assembly.
383 types with 6,854 methods in System.Data.Common assembly.
456 types with 4,590 methods in System.Net.Http assembly.
44 types with 645 methods in System.Console assembly.
106 types with 1,126 methods in System.Linq assembly.
```

```
// Output on macOS
0 types with 0 methods in System.Runtime assembly.
376 types with 6,763 methods in System.Data.Common assembly.
522 types with 5,141 methods in System.Net.Http assembly.
57 types with 701 methods in System.Console assembly.
103 types with 1,094 methods in System.Linq assembly.
```

Now, you have a better sense of why learning C# is a challenge – because there are so many types and methods to learn. Methods are only one category of a member that a type can have, and you and other programmers are constantly defining new types and members!

Working with variables

All applications process data. Data comes in, data is processed, and then data goes out.

Data usually comes into our program from files, databases, or user input, and it can be put temporarily into variables that will be stored in the memory of the running program. When the program ends, the data in memory is lost. Data is usually output to files and databases, or to the screen or a printer. When using variables, you should think about, firstly, how much space the variable takes in the memory, and, secondly, how fast it can be processed.

We control this by picking an appropriate type. You can think of simple common types such as int and double as being different-sized storage boxes, where a smaller box would take less memory but may not be as fast at being processed; for example, adding 16-bit numbers might not be processed as quickly as adding 64-bit numbers on a 64-bit operating system. Some of these boxes may be stacked close by, and some may be thrown into a big heap further away.

Naming things and assigning values

There are naming conventions for things, and it is good practice to follow them, as shown in the following table:

Naming convention	Examples	Used for
Camel case	cost, orderDetail, dateOfBirth	Local variables, private fields.
Title case aka Pascal case	String, Int32, Cost, DateOfBirth, Run	Types, non-private fields, and other members like methods.

 Some C# programmers like to prefix the names of private fields with an underscore, for example, _dateOfBirth instead of dateOfBirth. The naming of private members of all kinds is not formally defined because they will not be visible outside the class, so both are valid. My preference is without an underscore.

Good Practice: Following a consistent set of naming conventions will enable your code to be easily understood by other developers (and yourself in the future!).

The following code block shows an example of declaring a named local variable and assigning a value to it with the = symbol. You should note that you can output the name of a variable using a keyword introduced in C# 6.0, nameof:

```
// Let the heightInMetres variable become equal to the value 1.88
double heightInMetres = 1.88;
Console.WriteLine($"The variable {nameof(heightInMetres)} has the value
{heightInMetres}.");
```

Warning! The message in double quotes in the preceding code wraps onto a second line because the width of a printed page is too narrow. When entering a statement like this in your code editor, type it all in a single line.

Literal values

When you assign to a variable, you often, but not always, assign a **literal** value. But what is a literal value? A literal is a notation that represents a fixed value. Data types have different notations for their literal values, and over the next few sections, you will see examples of using literal notation to assign values to variables.

Storing text

For text, a single letter, such as an A, is stored as a char type.

Good Practice: Actually, it can be more complicated than that. Egyptian Hieroglyph A002 (U+13001) needs two System.Char values (known as surrogate pairs) to represent it: \uD80C and \uDC01. Do not always assume one char equals one letter or you could introduce hard-to-notice bugs into your code.

A char is assigned using single quotes around the literal value, or assigning the return value of a function call, as shown in the following code:

```
char letter = 'A'; // assigning literal characters
char digit = '1';
char symbol = '$';
char userChoice = GetSomeKeystroke(); // assigning from a fictitious function
```

For text, multiple letters, such as Bob, are stored as a string type and are assigned using double quotes around the literal value, or by assigning the return value of a function call or constructor, as shown in the following code:

```
string firstName = "Bob"; // assigning literal strings
string lastName = "Smith";
string phoneNumber = "(215) 555-4256";

// assigning a string returned from the string class constructor
string horizontalLine = new('-', count: 74); // 74 hyphens

// assigning a string returned from a fictitious function
string address = GetAddressFromDatabase(id: 563);

// assigning an emoji by converting from Unicode
string grinningEmoji = char.ConvertFromUtf32(0x1F600);
```

To output emoji at the command line on Windows, you must use Windows Terminal because Command Prompt does not support emoji, and set the output encoding to use UTF-8, as shown in the following code:

```
Console.OutputEncoding = System.Text.Encoding.UTF8;
string grinningEmoji = char.ConvertFromUtf32(0x1F600);
Console.WriteLine(grinningEmoji);
```

Verbatim strings

When storing text in a string variable, you can include escape sequences, which represent special characters like tabs and new lines using a backslash, as shown in the following code:

```
string fullNameWithTabSeparator = "Bob\tSmith";
```

But what if you are storing the path to a file on Windows, and one of the folder names starts with a T, as shown in the following code?

```
string filePath = "C:\televisions\sony\bravia.txt";
```

The compiler will convert the \t into a tab character and you will get errors!

You must prefix with the @ symbol to use a verbatim literal string, as shown in the following code:

```
string filePath = @"C:\televisions\sony\bravia.txt";
```

Raw string literals

Introduced in C# 11, raw string literals are convenient for entering any arbitrary text without needing to escape the contents. They make it easy to define literals containing other languages like XML, HTML, or JSON.

Raw string literals start and end with three or more double-quote characters, as shown in the following code:

```
string xml = """
              <person age="50">
                <first_name>Mark</first_name>
              </person>
              """;
```

Why three *or more* double-quote characters? That is for scenarios where the content itself needs to have three double-quote characters; you can then use four double-quote characters to indicate the beginning and end of the contents. Where the content needs to have four double-quote characters, you can then use five double-quote characters to indicate the beginning and end of the contents. And so on.

In the previous code, the XML is indented by 13 spaces. The compiler looks at the indentation of the last three or more double-quote characters, and then automatically removes that level of indentation from all the content inside the raw string literal. The results of the previous code would therefore not be indented as in the defining code, but instead be aligned with the left margin, as shown in the following markup:

```
<person age="50">
  <first_name>Mark</first_name>
</person>
```

Raw interpolated string literals

You can mix interpolated strings that use curly braces { } with raw string literals. You specify the number of braces that indicate a replaced expression by adding that number of dollar signs to the start of the literal. Any fewer braces than that are treated as raw content.

For example, if we want to define some JSON, single braces will be treated as normal braces, but the two dollar symbols tell the compiler that any two curly braces indicate a replaced expression value, as shown in the following code:

```
var person = new { FirstName = "Alice", Age = 56 };

string json = $$"""
                {
                  "first_name": "{{person.FirstName}}",
                  "age": {{person.Age}},
                  "calculation", "{{{ 1 + 2 }}}"
                }
                """;

Console.WriteLine(json);
```

The previous code would generate the following JSON document:

```json
{
  "first_name": "Alice",
  "age": 56,
  "calculation", "{3}"
}
```

The number of dollars tells the compiler how many curly braces are needed for something to become recognized as an interpolated expression.

Summarizing options for storing text

To summarize:

- **Literal string:** Characters enclosed in double-quote characters. They can use escape characters like \t for tab. To represent a backslash, use two: \\.
- **Raw string literal:** Characters enclosed in three or more double-quote characters.
- **Verbatim string:** A literal string prefixed with @ to disable escape characters so that a backslash is a backslash. It also allows the string value to span multiple lines because the whitespace characters are treated as themselves instead of instructions to the compiler.
- **Interpolated string:** A literal string prefixed with $ to enable embedded formatted variables. You will learn more about this later in this chapter.

Storing numbers

Numbers are data that we want to perform an arithmetic calculation on, for example, multiplying. A telephone number is not a number. To decide whether a variable should be stored as a number or not, ask yourself whether you need to perform arithmetic operations on the number or whether the number includes non-digit characters such as parentheses or hyphens to format the number, such as (414) 555-1234. In this case, the "number" is a sequence of characters, so it should be stored as a string.

Numbers can be natural numbers, such as 42, used for counting (also called whole numbers); they can also include negative numbers, such as -42 (called integers); or they can be real numbers, such as 3.9 (with a fractional part), which are called single- or double-precision floating-point numbers in computing.

Let's explore numbers:

1. Use your preferred code editor to add a new **Console App**/console project named Numbers to the Chapter02 workspace/solution.

   - If you are using Visual Studio Code, then select Numbers as the active OmniSharp project. When you see the pop-up warning message saying that required assets are missing, click **Yes** to add them.
   - If you are using Visual Studio 2022, then set the startup project to the current selection.

2. In `Program.cs`, delete the existing code and then type statements to declare some number variables using various data types, as shown in the following code:

```
// unsigned integer means positive whole number or 0
uint naturalNumber = 23;

// integer means negative or positive whole number or 0
int integerNumber = -23;

// float means single-precision floating point
// F suffix makes it a float literal
float realNumber = 2.3F;

// double means double-precision floating point
// double is the default type for a number value with a decimal point .
double anotherRealNumber = 2.3; // double literal
```

Storing whole numbers

You might know that computers store everything as bits. The value of a bit is either 0 or 1. This is called a **binary number system**. Humans use a **decimal number system**.

The decimal number system, also known as Base 10, has 10 as its **base**, meaning there are 10 digits, from 0 to 9. Although it is the number base most used by human civilizations, other number base systems are popular in science, engineering, and computing. The binary number system, also known as Base 2, has two as its base, meaning there are two digits, 0 and 1.

The following table shows how computers store the decimal number 10. Take note of the bits with the value 1 in the 8 and 2 columns; 8 + 2 = 10:

128	64	32	16	8	4	2	1
0	0	0	0	1	0	1	0

So, 10 in decimal is 00001010 in binary.

Improving legibility by using digit separators

Two of the improvements seen in C# 7.0 and later are the use of the underscore character _ as a digit separator, and support for binary literals.

You can insert underscores anywhere into the digits of a number literal, including decimal, binary, or hexadecimal notation, to improve legibility.

For example, you could write the value for 1 million in decimal notation, that is, Base 10, as 1_000_000.

You can even use the 2/3 grouping common in India: 10_00_000.

Using binary or hexadecimal notation

To use binary notation, that is, Base 2, using only 1s and 0s, start the number literal with `0b`. To use hexadecimal notation, that is, Base 16, using 0 to 9 and A to F, start the number literal with `0x`.

Exploring whole numbers

Let's enter some code to see some examples:

1. In `Program.cs`, type statements to declare some number variables using underscore separators, as shown in the following code:

    ```
    // three variables that store the number 2 million
    int decimalNotation = 2_000_000;
    int binaryNotation = 0b_0001_1110_1000_0100_1000_0000;
    int hexadecimalNotation = 0x_001E_8480;


    // check the three variables have the same value
    // both statements output true
    Console.WriteLine($"{decimalNotation == binaryNotation}");
    Console.WriteLine($"{decimalNotation == hexadecimalNotation}");
    ```

2. Run the code and note the result is that all three numbers are the same, as shown in the following output:

    ```
    True
    True
    ```

Computers can always exactly represent integers using the `int` type or one of its sibling types, such as `long` and `short`.

Storing real numbers

Computers cannot always represent real, aka decimal or non-integer, numbers precisely. The `float` and `double` types store real numbers using single- and double-precision floating points.

Most programming languages implement the IEEE Standard for Floating-Point Arithmetic. IEEE 754 is a technical standard for floating-point arithmetic established in 1985 by the **Institute of Electrical and Electronics Engineers (IEEE)**.

The following table shows a simplification of how a computer represents the number 12.75 in binary notation. Note the bits with the value 1 in the 8, 4, ½, and ¼ columns.

$$8 + 4 + ½ + ¼ = 12¾ = 12.75.$$

128	64	32	16	8	4	2	1	.	½	¼	1/8	1/16
0	0	0	0	1	1	0	0	.	1	1	0	0

So, 12.75 in decimal is 00001100.1100 in binary. As you can see, the number 12.75 can be exactly represented using bits. However, some numbers can't, which is something that we'll be exploring shortly.

Writing code to explore number sizes

C# has an operator named sizeof() that returns the number of bytes that a type uses in memory. Some types have members named MinValue and MaxValue, which return the minimum and maximum values that can be stored in a variable of that type. We are now going to use these features to create a console app to explore number types:

1. In Program.cs, type statements to show the size of three number data types, as shown in the following code:

```
Console.WriteLine($"int uses {sizeof(int)} bytes and can store numbers in
the range {int.MinValue:N0} to {int.MaxValue:N0}.");
Console.WriteLine($"double uses {sizeof(double)} bytes and can store
numbers in the range {double.MinValue:N0} to {double.MaxValue:N0}.");
Console.WriteLine($"decimal uses {sizeof(decimal)} bytes and can store
numbers in the range {decimal.MinValue:N0} to {decimal.MaxValue:N0}.");
```

 Warning! The width of the printed pages in this book makes the string values (in double quotes) wrap over multiple lines. You must type them on a single line, or you will get compile errors.

2. Run the code and view the output, as shown in *Figure 2.4*:

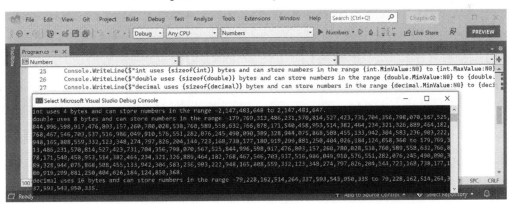

Figure 2.4: Size and range information for common number data types

An int variable uses four bytes of memory and can store positive or negative numbers up to about 2 billion. A double variable uses 8 bytes of memory and can store much bigger values! A decimal variable uses 16 bytes of memory and can store big numbers, but not as big as a double type.

But you may be asking yourself, why might a double variable be able to store bigger numbers than a decimal variable, yet it's only using half the space in memory? Well, let's now find out!

Comparing double and decimal types

You will now write some code to compare `double` and `decimal` values. Although it isn't hard to follow, don't worry about understanding the syntax right now:

1. Type statements to declare two `double` variables, add them together, and compare them to the expected result. Then, write the result to the console, as shown in the following code:

```
Console.WriteLine("Using doubles:");
double a = 0.1;
double b = 0.2;
if (a + b == 0.3)
{
  Console.WriteLine($"{a} + {b} equals {0.3}");
}
else
{
  Console.WriteLine($"{a} + {b} does NOT equal {0.3}");
}
```

2. Run the code and view the result, as shown in the following output:

```
Using doubles:
0.1 + 0.2 does NOT equal 0.3
```

In locales that use a comma for the decimal separator the result will look slightly different, as shown in the following output:

```
0,1 + 0,2 does NOT equal 0,3
```

The `double` type is not guaranteed to be accurate because some numbers like `0.1` literally cannot be represented as floating-point values.

As a rule of thumb, you should only use `double` when accuracy, especially when comparing the equality of two numbers, is not important. An example of this might be when you're measuring a person's height; you will only compare values using greater than or less than, but never equals.

The problem with the preceding code is illustrated by how the computer stores the number `0.1`, or multiples of it. To represent `0.1` in binary, the computer stores 1 in the 1/16 column, 1 in the 1/32 column, 1 in the 1/256 column, 1 in the 1/512 column, and so on.

The number `0.1` in decimal is `0.00011001100110011...` in binary, repeating forever:

4	2	1	.	½	¼	1/8	1/16	1/32	1/64	1/128	1/256	1/512	1/1024	1/2048
0	0	0	.	0	0	0	1	1	0	0	1	1	0	0

Good Practice: Never compare `double` values using `==`. During the First Gulf War, an American Patriot missile battery used `double` values in its calculations. The inaccuracy caused it to fail to track and intercept an incoming Iraqi Scud missile, and 28 soldiers were killed. You can read about this at `https://www.ima.umn.edu/~arnold/disasters/patriot.html`.

1. Copy and paste the statements that you wrote before (which used the `double` variables).

2. Modify the statements to use `decimal` and rename the variables to c and d, as shown in the following code:

```
Console.WriteLine("Using decimals:");
decimal c = 0.1M; // M suffix means a decimal literal value
decimal d = 0.2M;

if (c + d == 0.3M)
{
  Console.WriteLine($"{c} + {d} equals {0.3M}");
}
else
{
  Console.WriteLine($"{c} + {d} does NOT equal {0.3M}");
}
```

3. Run the code and view the result, as shown in the following output:

```
Using decimals:
0.1 + 0.2 equals 0.3
```

The `decimal` type is accurate because it stores the number as a large integer and shifts the decimal point. For example, `0.1` is stored as 1, with a note to shift the decimal point one place to the left. `12.75` is stored as 1275, with a note to shift the decimal point two places to the left.

Good Practice: Use `int` for whole numbers. Use `double` for real numbers that will not be compared for equality to other values; it is okay to compare `double` values being less than or greater than, and so on. Use `decimal` for money, CAD drawings, general engineering, and wherever the accuracy of a real number is important.

The `float` and `double` types have some useful special values: `NaN` represents not-a-number (for example, the result of dividing by zero), `Epsilon` represents the smallest positive number that can be stored in a `float` or `double`, and `PositiveInfinity` and `NegativeInfinity` represent infinitely large positive and negative values. They also have methods for checking for these special values like `IsInfinity` and `IsNan`.

Storing Booleans

Booleans can only contain one of the two literal values `true` or `false`, as shown in the following code:

```
bool happy = true;
bool sad = false;
```

They are most used to branch and loop. You don't need to fully understand them yet, as they are covered more in *Chapter 3, Controlling Flow, Converting Types, and Handling Exceptions*.

Storing any type of object

There is a special type named `object` that can store any type of data, but its flexibility comes at the cost of messier code and possibly poor performance. Because of those two reasons, you should avoid it whenever possible. The following steps show you how to use object types if you need to use them:

1. Use your preferred code editor to add a new **Console App**/console project named `Variables` to the `Chapter02` workspace/solution.

    •   If you are using Visual Studio Code, then select `Variables` as the active OmniSharp project. When you see the pop-up warning message saying that required assets are missing, click **Yes** to add them.

2. In `Program.cs`, delete the existing statements and then type statements to declare and use some variables using the `object` type, as shown in the following code:

```
object height = 1.88; // storing a double in an object
object name = "Amir"; // storing a string in an object
Console.WriteLine($"{name} is {height} metres tall.");


int length1 = name.Length; // gives compile error!
int length2 = ((string)name).Length; // tell compiler it is a string
Console.WriteLine($"{name} has {length2} characters.");
```

3. Run the code and note that the fourth statement cannot compile because the data type of the `name` variable is not known by the compiler, as shown in *Figure 2.5*:

Figure 2.5: The object type does not have a Length property

4. Add double slashes to the beginning of the statement that cannot compile to comment out the statement, making it inactive.

5. Run the code again and note that the compiler can access the length of a string if the programmer explicitly tells the compiler that the object variable contains a string by prefixing with a cast expression like (string), as shown in the following output:

```
Amir is 1.88 metres tall.
Amir has 4 characters.
```

The object type has been available since the first version of C#, but C# 2.0 and later have a better alternative called **generics**, which we will cover in *Chapter 6, Implementing Interfaces and Inheriting Classes*. This will provide us with the flexibility we want, but without the performance overhead.

Storing dynamic types

There is another special type named dynamic that can also store any type of data, but even more than object, its flexibility comes at the cost of performance. The dynamic keyword was introduced in C# 4.0. However, unlike object, the value stored in the variable can have its members invoked without an explicit cast. Let's make use of a dynamic type:

1. Add statements to declare a dynamic variable. Assign a string literal value, and then an integer value, and then an array of integer values, as shown in the following code:

```
// storing a string in a dynamic object
// string has a Length property
dynamic something = "Ahmed";

// int does not have a Length property
// something = 12;
// an array of any type has a Length property
// something = new[] { 3, 5, 7 };
```

2. Add a statement to output the length of the dynamic variable, as shown in the following code:

```
// this compiles but would throw an exception at run-time
// if you later stored a data type that does not have a
// property named Length
Console.WriteLine($"Length is {something.Length}");
```

3. Run the code and note it works because a string value does have a Length property, as shown in the following output:

```
Length is 5
```

4. Uncomment the statement that assigns an int value of 12 to the something variable.

5. Run the code and note the runtime error because int does not have a Length property, as shown in the following output:

```
Unhandled exception. Microsoft.CSharp.RuntimeBinder.
RuntimeBinderException: 'int' does not contain a definition for 'Length'
```

6. Uncomment the statement that assigns the array of three integers 3, 5, and 7 to the something variable.

7. Run the code and note the output because an array of three int values does have a Length property, as shown in the following output:

```
Length is 3
```

One limitation of dynamic is that code editors cannot show IntelliSense to help you write the code. This is because the compiler cannot check what the type is during build time. Instead, the CLR checks for the member at runtime and throws an exception if it is missing.

Exceptions are a way to indicate that something has gone wrong at runtime. You will learn more about them and how to handle them in *Chapter 3, Controlling Flow, Converting Types, and Handling Exceptions*.

Declaring local variables

Local variables are declared inside methods, and they only exist during the execution of that method. Once the method returns, the memory allocated to any local variables is released.

Strictly speaking, value types are released while reference types must wait for a garbage collection. You will learn about the difference between value types and reference types in *Chapter 6, Implementing Interfaces and Inheriting Classes*.

Specifying the type of a local variable

Let's explore local variables declared with specific types and using type inference:

- Type statements to declare and assign values to some local variables using specific types, as shown in the following code:

```
int population = 67_000_000; // 67 million in UK
double weight = 1.88; // in kilograms
decimal price = 4.99M; // in pounds sterling
string fruit = "Apples"; // strings use double-quotes
char letter = 'Z'; // chars use single-quotes
bool happy = true; // Booleans have value of true or false
```

Depending on your code editor and color scheme, it will show green squiggles under each of the variable names and lighten their text color to warn you that the variable is assigned but its value is never used.

Inferring the type of a local variable

You can use the var keyword to declare local variables with C# 3 and later. The compiler will infer the type from the value that you assign after the assignment operator, =.

A literal number without a decimal point is inferred as an int variable, that is, unless you add a suffix, as described in the following list:

- L: Compiler infers long
- UL: Compiler infers ulong
- M: Compiler infers decimal
- D: Compiler infers double
- F: Compiler infers float

A literal number with a decimal point is inferred as double unless you add the M suffix, in which case the compiler infers a decimal variable, or the F suffix, in which case it infers a float variable.

Double quotes indicate a string variable, single quotes indicate a char variable, and the true and false values infer a bool type:

1. Modify the previous statements to use var, as shown in the following code:

    ```
    var population = 67_000_000; // 67 million in UK
    var weight = 1.88; // in kilograms
    var price = 4.99M; // in pounds sterling
    var fruit = "Apples"; // strings use double-quotes
    var letter = 'Z'; // chars use single-quotes
    var happy = true; // Booleans have value of true or false
    ```

2. Hover your mouse over each of the var keywords and note that your code editor shows a tooltip with information about the type that has been inferred.

3. At the top of Program.cs, import the namespace for working with XML to enable us to declare some variables using types in that namespace, as shown in the following code:

    ```
    using System.Xml;
    ```

    Good Practice: If you are using .NET Interactive Notebooks, then add using statements in a separate code cell above the code cell where you write the main code. Then, click **Execute Cell** to ensure the namespaces are imported. They will then be available in subsequent code cells.

4. Under the previous statements, add statements to create some new objects, as shown in the following code:

    ```
    // good use of var because it avoids the repeated type
    // as shown in the more verbose second statement
    ```

```
var xml1 = new XmlDocument(); // C# 3 and later
XmlDocument xml2 = new XmlDocument(); // all C# versions

// bad use of var because we cannot tell the type, so we
// should use a specific type declaration as shown in
// the second statement
var file1 = File.CreateText("something1.txt");
StreamWriter file2 = File.CreateText("something2.txt");
```

Good Practice: Although using **var** is convenient, some developers avoid using it to make it easier for a code reader to understand the types in use. Personally, I use it only when the type is obvious. For example, in the preceding code statements, the first statement is just as clear as the second in stating what the types of the **xml** variables are, but it is shorter. However, the third statement isn't clear in showing the type of the **file** variable, so the fourth is better because it shows that the type is **StreamWriter**. If in doubt, spell it out!

Using target-typed new to instantiate objects

With C# 9, Microsoft introduced another syntax for instantiating objects known as **target-typed new**. When instantiating an object, you can specify the type first and then use new without repeating the type, as shown in the following code:

```
XmlDocument xml3 = new(); // target-typed new in C# 9 or later
```

If you have a type with a field or property that needs to be set, then the type can be inferred, as shown in the following code:

```
// In Program.cs
Person kim = new();
kim.BirthDate = new(1967, 12, 26); // instead of: new DateTime(1967, 12, 26)

// In a separate Person.cs file or at the bottom of Program.cs
class Person
{
    public DateTime BirthDate;
}
```

This way of instantiating objects is especially useful with arrays and collections because they have multiple objects often of the same type, as shown in the following code:

```
List<Person> people = new()
{
    new() { FirstName = "Alice" },
    new() { FirstName = "Bob" },
```

```
  new() { FirstName = "Charlie" }
};
```

You will learn about arrays in *Chapter 3, Controlling Flow, Converting Types, and Handling Exceptions,* and collections in *Chapter 8, Working with Common .NET Types.*

 Good Practice: Use target-typed new to instantiate objects unless you must use a pre-version 9 C# compiler. I have used target-typed new throughout the remainder of this book. Please let me know if you spot any cases that I missed!

Getting and setting the default values for types

Most of the primitive types except string are **value types**, which means that they must have a value. You can determine the default value of a type by using the default() operator and passing the type as a parameter. You can assign the default value of a type by using the default keyword.

The string type is a **reference type**. This means that string variables contain the memory address of a value, not the value itself. A reference type variable can have a null value, which is a literal that indicates that the variable does not reference anything (yet). null is the default for all reference types.

You'll learn more about value types and reference types in *Chapter 6, Implementing Interfaces and Inheriting Classes.*

Let's explore default values:

1. Add statements to show the default values of an int, bool, DateTime, and string, as shown in the following code:

    ```
    Console.WriteLine($"default(int) = {default(int)}");
    Console.WriteLine($"default(bool) = {default(bool)}");
    Console.WriteLine($"default(DateTime) = {default(DateTime)}");
    Console.WriteLine($"default(string) = {default(string)}");
    ```

2. Run the code and view the result. Note that your output for the date and time might be formatted differently if you are not running it in the UK and that null values output as an empty string, as shown in the following output:

    ```
    default(int) = 0
    default(bool) = False
    default(DateTime) = 01/01/0001 00:00:00
    default(string) =
    ```

3. Add statements to declare a number, assign a value, and then reset it to its default value, as shown in the following code:

    ```
    int number = 13;
    Console.WriteLine($"number has been set to: {number}");
    ```

```
number = default;
Console.WriteLine($"number has been reset to its default: {number}");
```

4. Run the code and view the result, as shown in the following output:

```
number has been set to: 13
number has been reset to its default: 0
```

Exploring more about console apps

We have already created and used basic console apps, but we're now at a stage where we should delve into them more deeply.

Console apps are text-based and are run at the command line. They typically perform simple tasks that need to be scripted, such as compiling a file or encrypting a section of a configuration file.

Equally, they can also have arguments passed to them to control their behavior.

An example of this would be to create a new console app using the F# language with a specified name instead of using the name of the current folder, as shown in the following command line:

```
dotnet new console -lang "F#" --name "ExploringConsole"
```

Displaying output to the user

The two most common tasks that a console app performs are writing and reading data. We have already been using the `WriteLine` method to output, but if we didn't want a carriage return at the end of a line, for example, if we later wanted to continue to write more text to the end of that line, we could have used the `Write` method.

Formatting using numbered positional arguments

One way of generating formatted strings is to use numbered positional arguments.

This feature is supported by methods like `Write` and `WriteLine`, and for methods that do not support the feature, the `string` parameter can be formatted using the `Format` method of `string`.

Let's begin formatting:

1. Use your preferred code editor to add a new **Console App**/console project named `Formatting` to the `Chapter02` workspace/solution.

    •   If you are using Visual Studio Code, then select `Formatting` as the active OmniSharp project.

2. In `Program.cs`, delete the existing statements and then type statements to declare some number variables and write them to the console, as shown in the following code:

```
int numberOfApples = 12;
decimal pricePerApple = 0.35M;
```

```
Console.WriteLine(
  format: "{0} apples cost {1:C}",
  arg0: numberOfApples,
  arg1: pricePerApple * numberOfApples);

string formatted = string.Format(
  format: "{0} apples cost {1:C}",
  arg0: numberOfApples,
  arg1: pricePerApple * numberOfApples);

//WriteToFile(formatted); // writes the string into a file
```

The `WriteToFile` method is a nonexistent method used to illustrate the idea.

The `Write`, `WriteLine`, and `Format` methods can have up to four numbered arguments, named `arg0`, `arg1`, `arg2`, and `arg3`. If you need to pass more than four values, then you cannot name them, as shown in the following code:

```
// Four parameter values can use named arguments.
Console.WriteLine(
  format: "{0} {1} lived in {2}, {3}.",
  arg0: "Roger", arg1: "Cevung",
  arg2: "Stockholm", arg3: "Sweden");

// Five or more parameter values cannot use named arguments.
Console.WriteLine(
  format: "{0} {1} lived in {2}, {3} and worked in the {4} team at {5}.",
  "Roger", "Cevung", "Stockholm", "Sweden", "Education", "Optimizely");
```

Good Practice: Once you become more comfortable with formatting strings, you should stop naming the parameters, for example, stop using `format:`, `arg0:`, and `arg1:`. The preceding code uses a non-canonical style to show where the 0 and 1 came from while you are learning.

Formatting using interpolated strings

C# 6.0 and later have a handy feature named **interpolated strings**. A `string` prefixed with `$` can use curly braces around the name of a variable or expression to output the current value of that variable or expression at that position in the `string`, as the following shows:

1. Enter a statement at the bottom of the `Program.cs` file, as shown in the following code:

    ```
    // The following statement must be all on one line.
    Console.WriteLine($"{numberOfApples} apples cost {pricePerApple *
    numberOfApples:C}");
    ```

2. Run the code and view the result, as shown in the following partial output:

```
12 apples cost £4.20
```

For short formatted `string` values, an interpolated `string` can be easier for people to read. But for code examples in a book, where lines need to wrap over multiple lines, this can be tricky. For many of the code examples in this book, I will use numbered positional arguments, although an improvement introduced in C# 11 is support for line breaks within the "hole" made by an interpolated expression, as shown in the following code:

```
Console.WriteLine($"{numberOfApples} apples cost {pricePerApple
                                     *
                                     numberOfApples:C}");
```

Another reason to avoid interpolated strings is that they can't be read from resource files to be localized.

Before C# 10, `string` constants could only be combined by using concatenation with the + operator, as shown in the following code:

```
private const string firstname = "Omar";
private const string lastname = "Rudberg";
private const string fullname = firstname + " " + lastname;
```

With C# 10, interpolated strings (prefixed with $) can now be used, as shown in the following code:

```
private const string fullname = $"{firstname} {lastname}";
```

This only works for combining `string` constant values. It cannot work with other types like numbers that would require runtime data type conversions.

Understanding format strings

A variable or expression can be formatted using a format string after a comma or colon.

An `N0` format string means a number with thousands separators and no decimal places, while a `C` format string means currency. The currency format will be determined by the current thread.

For instance, if you run code that uses the number or currency format on a PC in the UK, you'll get pounds sterling with commas as the thousands separators, but if you run it on a PC in Germany, you will get euros with dots as the thousands separators.

The full syntax of a format item is:

```
{ index [, alignment ] [ : formatString ] }
```

Each format item can have an alignment, which is useful when outputting tables of values, some of which might need to be left- or right-aligned within a width of characters. Alignment values are integers. Positive integers mean right-aligned and negative integers mean left-aligned.

For example, to output a table of fruit and how many of each there are, we might want to left-align the names within a column of 10 characters and right-align the counts formatted as numbers with zero decimal places within a column of six characters:

1. At the bottom of Program.cs, enter the following statements:

```
string applesText = "Apples";
int applesCount = 1234;
string bananasText = "Bananas";
int bananasCount = 56789;

Console.WriteLine(
  format: "{0,-10} {1,6}",
  arg0: "Name",
  arg1: "Count");
Console.WriteLine(
  format: "{0,-10} {1,6:N0}",
  arg0: applesText,
  arg1: applesCount);
Console.WriteLine(
  format: "{0,-10} {1,6:N0}",
  arg0: bananasText,
  arg1: bananasCount);
```

2. Run the code and note the effect of the alignment and number format, as shown in the following output:

```
Name          Count
Apples        1,234
Bananas      56,789
```

Getting text input from the user

We can get text input from the user using the ReadLine method. This method waits for the user to type some text. Then, as soon as the user presses *Enter*, whatever the user has typed is returned as a string value.

> **Good Practice:** If you are using a .NET Interactive Notebook for this section, then note that it does not support reading input from the console using Console.ReadLine(). Instead, you must set literal values, as shown in the following code: string? firstName = "Gary";. This is often quicker to experiment with because you can simply change the literal string value and click the **Execute Cell** button instead of having to restart a console app each time you want to enter a different string value.

Let's get input from the user:

1. Type statements to ask the user for their name and age and then output what they entered, as shown in the following code:

```
Console.Write("Type your first name and press ENTER: ");
string firstName = Console.ReadLine();

Console.Write("Type your age and press ENTER: ");
string age = Console.ReadLine();

Console.WriteLine($"Hello {firstName}, you look good for {age}.");
```

By default, with .NET 6 and later, nullability checks are enabled, so the C# compiler gives two warnings because the ReadLine method could return a null value instead of a string value.

2. For the firstName variable, append a ? after string. This tells the compiler that we are expecting a possible null value so it does not need to warn us. If the variable is null then when it is later output with WriteLine, it will just be blank, so that works fine in this case. If we were going to access any of the members of the firstName variable, then we would need to handle the case where it is null.

3. For the firstName variable, append a ! before the semi-colon at the end of the statement. This is called the **null-forgiving operator** because it tells the compiler that, in this case, ReadLine will not return null, so it can stop showing the warning. It is now our responsibility to ensure this is the case. Luckily, the Console type's implementation of ReadLine always returns a string even if it is just an empty string value.

 You have now seen two common ways to handle nullability warnings from the compiler. We will cover nullability and how to handle it in more detail in *Chapter 6, Implementing Interfaces and Inheriting Classes*.

4. Run the code, and then enter a name and age, as shown in the following output:

```
Type your name and press ENTER: Gary
Type your age and press ENTER: 34
Hello Gary, you look good for 34.
```

Simplifying the usage of the console

In C# 6.0 and later, the using statement can be used not only to import a namespace but also to further simplify our code by importing a static class. Then, we won't need to enter the Console type name throughout our code.

Importing a static type for a single file

You can use your code editor's Find and Replace feature to remove the times we have previously written Console:

1. At the top of the Program.cs file, add a statement to **statically import** the System.Console class, as shown in the following code:

    ```
    using static System.Console;
    ```

2. Select the first Console. in your code, ensuring that you select the dot after the word Console too.

3. In Visual Studio, navigate to **Edit | Find and Replace | Quick Replace**, or in Visual Studio Code, navigate to **Edit | Replace**, and note that an overlay dialog appears ready for you to enter what you would like to replace Console. with, as shown in *Figure 2.6*:

Figure 2.6: Using the Replace feature in Visual Studio to simplify your code

4. Leave the replace box empty, click on the **Replace all** button (the second of the two buttons to the right of the replace box), and then close the replace box by clicking on the cross in its top-right corner.

5. Run the console app and note the behavior is the same as before.

Importing a static type for all code files in a project

Instead of statically importing the Console class just for one code file, it would probably be better to import it for all code files in the project:

1. Delete the statement to statically import System.Console.

2. Open Formatting.csproj, and after the <PropertyGroup> section, add a new <ItemGroup> section to statically import System.Console using the implicit usings .NET SDK feature, as shown in the following markup:

    ```
    <ItemGroup>
      <Using Include="System.Console" Static="true" />
    </ItemGroup>
    ```

3. Run the console app and note the behavior is the same as before.

Good Practice: In future, for all console app projects you create for this book, add the section above to simplify the code you need to write in all C# files to work with the `Console` class.

Getting key input from the user

We can get key input from the user using the `ReadKey` method. This method waits for the user to press a key or key combination that is then returned as a `ConsoleKeyInfo` value.

You will not be able to execute the call to the `ReadKey` method using a .NET Interactive Notebook, but if you have created a console app, then let's explore reading key presses:

1. Type statements to ask the user to press any key combination and then output information about it, as shown in the following code:

    ```
    Write("Press any key combination: ");
    ConsoleKeyInfo key = ReadKey();
    WriteLine();
    WriteLine("Key: {0}, Char: {1}, Modifiers: {2}",
      arg0: key.Key,
      arg1: key.KeyChar,
      arg2: key.Modifiers);
    ```

2. Run the code, press the *K* key, and note the result, as shown in the following output:

    ```
    Press any key combination: k
    Key: K, Char: k, Modifiers: 0
    ```

3. Run the code, hold down *Shift* and press the *K* key, and note the result, as shown in the following output:

    ```
    Press any key combination: K
    Key: K, Char: K, Modifiers: Shift
    ```

4. Run the code, press the *F12* key, and note the result, as shown in the following output:

    ```
    Press any key combination:
    Key: F12, Char: , Modifiers: 0
    ```

When running a console app in a terminal within Visual Studio Code, some keyboard combinations will be captured by the code editor before they can be processed by your console app. For example, *Ctrl + Shift + X* in Visual Studio Code activates the **Extensions** view in the side bar. To fully test this console app, open a command prompt or terminal in the project folder and run the console app from there.

Passing arguments to a console app

When you run a console app, you often want to change its behavior by passing arguments. For example, with the dotnet command-line tool, you can pass the name of a new project template, as shown in the following commands:

```
dotnet new console
dotnet new mvc
```

You might have been wondering how to get any arguments that might be passed to a console app.

In every version of .NET prior to version 6.0, the console app project template made it obvious, as shown in the following code:

```
using System;

namespace Arguments
{
  class Program
  {
    static void Main(string[] args)
    {
      Console.WriteLine("Hello World!");
    }
  }
}
```

The `string[] args` arguments are declared and passed in the `Main` method of the `Program` class. They're an array used to pass arguments into a console app. But in top-level programs, as used by the console app project template in .NET 6.0 and later, the `Program` class and its `Main` method are hidden, along with the declaration of the `args` array. The trick is that you must know it still exists.

Command-line arguments are separated by spaces. Other characters like hyphens and colons are treated as part of an argument value.

To include spaces in an argument value, enclose the argument value in single or double quotes.

Imagine that we want to be able to enter the names of some colors for the foreground and background and the dimensions of the terminal window at the command line. We would be able to read the colors and numbers by reading them from the `args` array, which is always passed into the `Main` method, aka the entry point of a console app:

1. Use your preferred code editor to add a new **Console App**/console project named `Arguments` to the `Chapter02` workspace/solution. You will not be able to use a .NET Interactive Notebook because you cannot pass arguments to a notebook.

    *   If you are using Visual Studio Code, then select `Arguments` as the active OmniSharp project.

2. Open `Arguments.csproj`, and after the `<PropertyGroup>` section, add a new `<ItemGroup>` section to statically import `System.Console` for all C# files using the implicit usings .NET SDK feature, as shown in the following markup:

```
<ItemGroup>
  <Using Include="System.Console" Static="true" />
</ItemGroup>
```

 Good Practice: Remember to use the implicit usings .NET SDK feature to statically import the `System.Console` type in all future console app projects to simplify your code, as these instructions will not be repeated every time.

3. In `Program.cs`, delete the existing statements and then add a statement to output the number of arguments passed to the application, as shown in the following code:

```
WriteLine($"There are {args.Length} arguments.");
```

4. Run the console app and view the result, as shown in the following output:

```
There are 0 arguments.
```

If you are using Visual Studio 2022:

1. Navigate to **Project | Arguments Properties**.
2. Select the **Debug** tab, click **Open debug launch profiles UI**, and in the **Command line arguments** box, enter the following arguments: `firstarg second-arg third:arg "fourth arg"`, as shown in *Figure 2.7*:

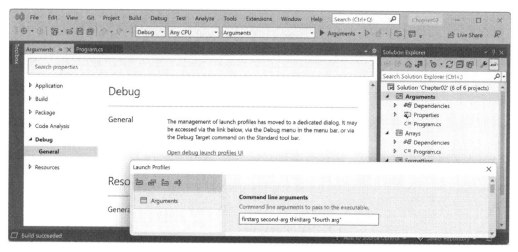

Figure 2.7: Entering command-line arguments in the Visual Studio project properties

3. Close the **Launch Profiles** window.

4. Run the console app.

If you are using Visual Studio Code:

- In **Terminal**, enter some arguments after the dotnet run command, as shown in the following command:

```
dotnet run firstarg second-arg third:arg "fourth arg"
```

For both coding tools:

1. Note the result indicates four arguments, as shown in the following output:

```
There are 4 arguments.
```

2. In Program.cs, to enumerate or iterate (that is, loop through) the values of those four arguments, add the following statements after outputting the length of the array:

```
foreach (string arg in args)
{
  WriteLine(arg);
}
```

3. Run the code again and note the result shows the details of the four arguments, as shown in the following output:

```
There are 4 arguments.
firstarg
second-arg
third:arg
fourth arg
```

Setting options with arguments

We will now use these arguments to allow the user to pick a color for the background, foreground, and cursor size of the output window. The cursor size can be an integer value from 1, meaning a line at the bottom of the cursor cell, up to 100, meaning a percentage of the height of the cursor cell.

We have statically imported the System.Console class. It has properties like ForegroundColor, BackgroundColor, and CursorSize that we can now set just by using their names without needing to prefix with Console.

The System namespace is already imported so that the compiler knows about the ConsoleColor and Enum types:

1. Add statements to warn the user if they do not enter three arguments, and then parse those arguments and use them to set the color and dimensions of the console window, as shown in the following code:

```
if (args.Length < 3)
{
  WriteLine("You must specify two colors and cursor size, e.g.");
  WriteLine("dotnet run red yellow 50");
  return; // stop running
}

ForegroundColor = (ConsoleColor)Enum.Parse(
  enumType: typeof(ConsoleColor),
  value: args[0],
  ignoreCase: true);

BackgroundColor = (ConsoleColor)Enum.Parse(
  enumType: typeof(ConsoleColor),
  value: args[1],
  ignoreCase: true);

CursorSize = int.Parse(args[2]);
```

 Note the compiler warning that setting the `CursorSize` is only supported on Windows.

- If you are using Visual Studio 2022, navigate to **Project | Arguments Properties**, and change the arguments to red yellow 50. Run the console app and note the cursor is half the size and the colors have changed in the window, as shown in *Figure 2.8*:

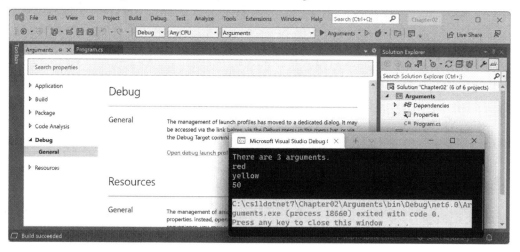

Figure 2.8: Setting colors and cursor size on Windows

- If you are using Visual Studio Code, then run the code with arguments to set the foreground color to red, the background color to yellow, and the cursor size to 50%, as shown in the following command:

```
dotnet run red yellow 50
```

On macOS, you'll see an unhandled exception, as shown in *Figure 2.9*:

Figure 2.9: An unhandled exception on unsupported macOS

Although the compiler did not give an error or warning, at runtime some API calls may fail on some platforms. Although a console app running on Windows can change its cursor size, on macOS, it cannot, and complains if you try.

Handling platforms that do not support an API

So how do we solve this problem? We can solve this by using an exception handler. You will learn more details about the try-catch statement in *Chapter 3, Controlling Flow, Converting Types, and Handling Exceptions*, so for now, just enter the code:

1. Modify the code to wrap the lines that change the cursor size in a try statement, as shown in the following code:

```
try
{
  CursorSize = int.Parse(args[2]);
}
catch (PlatformNotSupportedException)
{
  WriteLine("The current platform does not support changing the size of
the cursor.");
}
```

2. If you were to run the code on macOS, then you would see the exception is caught, and a friendlier message is shown to the user.

Another way to handle differences in operating systems is to use the `OperatingSystem` class in the `System` namespace, as shown in the following code:

```
if (OperatingSystem.IsWindows())
{
  // execute code that only works on Windows
}
else if (OperatingSystem.IsWindowsVersionAtLeast(major: 10))
{
  // execute code that only works on Windows 10 or later
}
else if (OperatingSystem.IsIOSVersionAtLeast(major: 14, minor: 5))
{
  // execute code that only works on iOS 14.5 or later
}
else if (OperatingSystem.IsBrowser())
{
  // execute code that only works in the browser with Blazor
}
```

The `OperatingSystem` class has equivalent methods for other common operating systems like Android, iOS, Linux, macOS, and even the browser, which is useful for Blazor web components.

A third way to handle different platforms is to use conditional compilation statements.

There are four preprocessor directives that control conditional compilation: `#if`, `#elif`, `#else`, and `#endif`.

You define symbols using `#define`, as shown in the following code:

```
#define MYSYMBOL
```

Many symbols are automatically defined for you, as shown in the following table:

Target Framework	Symbols
.NET Standard	`NETSTANDARD2_0`, `NETSTANDARD2_1`, and so on
Modern .NET	`NET7_0`, `NET7_0_ANDROID`, `NET7_0_IOS`, `NET7_0_WINDOWS`, and so on

You can then write statements that will compile only for the specified platforms, as shown in the following code:

```
#if NET7_0_ANDROID
// compile statements that only works on Android
#elif NET7_0_IOS
// compile statements that only works on iOS
#else
```

```
// compile statements that work everywhere else
#endif
```

Understanding async and await

C# 5 introduced two C# keywords when working with the `Task` type that enables easy multithreading. The pair of keywords are especially useful for the following:

- Implementing multitasking for a **graphical user interface** (GUI).
- Improving the scalability of web applications and web services.
- Preventing blocking calls when interacting with the filesystem, databases, and remote services, all of which tend to take a long time to complete their work.

In *Chapter 14, Building Websites Using the Model-View-Controller Pattern*, we will see how the `async` and `await` keywords can improve scalability for websites. But for now, let's see an example of how they can be used in a console app, and then later you will see them used in a more practical example within web projects.

Improving responsiveness for console apps

One of the limitations with console apps is that you can only use the `await` keyword inside methods that are marked as `async`, but C# 7 and earlier do not allow the `Main` method to be marked as async! Luckily, a new feature introduced in C# 7.1 was support for `async` in `Main`.

Let's see it in action:

1. Use your preferred code editor to add a new **Console App**/console project named `AsyncConsole` to the `Chapter02` solution/workspace.

    - If you are using Visual Studio Code, then select `AsyncConsole` as the active OmniSharp project.

2. Open `AsyncConsole.csproj`, and after the `<PropertyGroup>` section, add a new `<ItemGroup>` section to statically import `System.Console` for all C# files using the implicit usings .NET SDK feature, as shown in the following markup:

    ```
    <ItemGroup>
      <Using Include="System.Console" Static="true" />
    </ItemGroup>
    ```

3. In `Program.cs`, delete the existing statements and then add statements to create an `HttpClient` instance, make a request for Apple's home page, and output how many bytes it has, as shown in the following code:

    ```
    HttpClient client = new();

    HttpResponseMessage response =
      await client.GetAsync("http://www.apple.com/");
    ```

```
WriteLine("Apple's home page has {0:N0} bytes.",
    response.Content.Headers.ContentLength);
```

4. Navigate to **Build | Build AsyncConsole** and note that the project builds successfully.

In .NET 5 and earlier, you would have seen an error message, as shown in the following output:

```
Program.cs(14,9): error CS4033: The 'await' operator can
only be used within an async method. Consider marking
this method with the 'async' modifier and changing its
return type to 'Task'. [/Users/markjprice/Code/ Chapter02/
AsyncConsole/AsyncConsole.csproj]
```

You would have had to add the `async` keyword to your `Main` method and change its return type from `void` to `Task`. With .NET 6 and later, the console app project template uses the top-level program feature to automatically define the `Program` class with an asynchronous `<Main>$` method for you.

5. Run the code and view the result, which is likely to have a different number of bytes since Apple changes its home page frequently, as shown in the following output:

```
Apple's home page has 40,252 bytes.
```

Practicing and exploring

Test your knowledge and understanding by answering some questions, getting some hands-on practice, and exploring the topics covered in this chapter with deeper research.

Exercise 2.1 – Test your knowledge

To get the best answer to some of these questions, you will need to do your own research. I want you to "think outside the book," so I have deliberately not provided all the answers in the book.

I want to encourage you to get into the good habit of looking for help elsewhere, following the principle of "teach a person to fish."

1. What statement can you type in a C# file to discover the compiler and language version?
2. What are the two types of comments in C#?
3. What is the difference between a verbatim string and an interpolated string?
4. Why should you be careful when using `float` and `double` values?
5. How can you determine how many bytes a type like `double` uses in memory?
6. When should you use the `var` keyword?
7. What is the newest syntax to create an instance of a class like `XmlDocument`?
8. Why should you be careful when using the `dynamic` type?
9. How do you right-align a format string?

10. What character separates arguments for a console app?

 Appendix, Answers to the Test Your Knowledge Questions, is available to download from a link in the README in the GitHub repository: `https://github.com/markjprice/cs11dotnet7`.

Exercise 2.2 — Test your knowledge of number types

What type would you choose for the following "numbers"?

1. A person's telephone number
2. A person's height
3. A person's age
4. A person's salary
5. A book's ISBN
6. A book's price
7. A book's shipping weight
8. A country's population
9. The number of stars in the universe
10. The number of employees in each of the small or medium businesses in the United Kingdom (up to about 50,000 employees per business)

Exercise 2.3 — Practice number sizes and ranges

In the `Chapter02` solution/workspace, create a console app project named `Ch02Ex03Numbers` that outputs the number of bytes in memory that each of the following number types uses and the minimum and maximum values they can have: `sbyte`, `byte`, `short`, `ushort`, `int`, `uint`, `long`, `ulong`, `float`, `double`, and `decimal`.

The result of running your console app should look something like *Figure 2.10*:

Type	Byte(s) of memory	Min	Max
sbyte	1	-128	127
byte	1	0	255
short	2	-32768	32767
ushort	2	0	65535
int	4	-2147483648	2147483647
uint	4	0	4294967295
long	8	-9223372036854775808	9223372036854775807
ulong	8	0	18446744073709551615
float	4	-3.4028235E+38	3.4028235E+38
double	8	-1.7976931348623157E+308	1.7976931348623157E+308
decimal	16	-79228162514264337593543950335	79228162514264337593543950335

Figure 2.10: The result of outputting number type sizes

As a bonus exercise, output a row for the System.Half type that was introduced in .NET 5.

Code solutions for all exercises are available to download or clone from the GitHub repository at the following link: https://github.com/markjprice/cs11dotnet7.

Exercise 2.4 – Explore topics

Use the links on the following page to learn more details about the topics covered in this chapter:

https://github.com/markjprice/cs11dotnet7/blob/main/book-links.md#chapter-2---speaking-c

Summary

In this chapter, you learned how to:

- Declare variables with a specified or an inferred type.
- Use some of the built-in types for numbers, text, and Booleans.
- Choose between number types.
- Control output formatting in console apps.

In the next chapter, you will learn about operators, branching, looping, converting between types, and how to handle exceptions.

3

Controlling Flow, Converting Types, and Handling Exceptions

This chapter is all about writing code that performs simple operations on variables, makes decisions, performs pattern matching, repeats statements or blocks, works with arrays to store multiple values, converts variable or expression values from one type to another, handles exceptions, and checks for overflows in number variables.

This chapter covers the following topics:

- Operating on variables
- Understanding selection statements
- Understanding iteration statements
- Storing multiple values in an array
- Casting and converting between types
- Handling exceptions
- Checking for overflow

Operating on variables

Operators apply simple operations such as addition and multiplication to **operands** such as variables and literal values. They usually return a new value that is the result of the operation and that can be assigned to a variable.

Most operators are binary, meaning that they work on two operands, as shown in the following pseudo-code:

```
var resultOfOperation = firstOperand operator secondOperand;
```

Examples of binary operators include adding and multiplying, as shown in the following code:

```
int x = 5;
int y = 3;
int resultOfAdding = x + y;
int resultOfMultiplying = x * y;
```

Some operators are unary, meaning they work on a single operand, and can apply before or after the operand, as shown in the following pseudocode:

```
var resultOfOperationAfter = onlyOperand operator;
var resultOfOperationBefore = operator onlyOperand;
```

Examples of unary operators include incrementors and retrieving a type or its size in bytes, as shown in the following code:

```
int x = 5;
int postfixIncrement = x++;
int prefixIncrement = ++x;
Type theTypeOfAnInteger = typeof(int);
string nameOfVariable = nameof(x);
int howManyBytesInAnInteger = sizeof(int);
```

A ternary operator works on three operands, as shown in the following pseudocode:

```
var resultOfOperation = firstOperand firstOperator
  secondOperand secondOperator thirdOperand;
```

Exploring unary operators

Two common unary operators are used to increment, ++, and decrement, --, a number. Let us write some example code to show how they work:

1. If you've completed the previous chapters, then you will already have a `cs11dotnet7` folder. If not, then you'll need to create it.

2. Use your preferred coding tool to create a new project, as defined in the following list:

    *   Project template: **Console App**/console
    *   Project file and folder: Operators
    *   Workspace/solution file and folder: Chapter03

3. Open `Operators.csproj`, and after the `<PropertyGroup>` section, add a new `<ItemGroup>` section to statically import `System.Console` for all C# files using the `implicit usings` .NET SDK feature, as shown in the following markup:

    ```
    <ItemGroup>
      <Using Include="System.Console" Static="true" />
    </ItemGroup>
    ```

4. In `Program.cs`, delete the existing statements and then declare two integer variables named a and b, set a to 3, increment a while assigning the result to b, and then output their values, as shown in the following code:

```
int a = 3;
int b = a++;
WriteLine($"a is {a}, b is {b}");
```

5. Before running the console app, ask yourself a question: what do you think the value of b will be when output? Once you've thought about that, run the code, and compare your prediction against the actual result, as shown in the following output:

```
a is 4, b is 3
```

The variable b has the value 3 because the ++ operator executes *after* the assignment; this is known as a **postfix operator**. If you need to increment *before* the assignment, then use the **prefix operator**.

6. Copy and paste the statements, and then modify them to rename the variables and use the prefix operator, as shown in the following code:

```
int c = 3;
int d = ++c; // increment c before assigning it
WriteLine($"c is {c}, d is {d}");
```

7. Rerun the code and note the result, as shown in the following output:

```
a is 4, b is 3
c is 4, d is 4
```

Good Practice: Due to the confusion between prefix and postfix for the increment and decrement operators when combined with an assignment, the Swift programming language designers decided to drop support for this operator in version 3. My recommendation for usage in C# is to never combine the use of ++ and -- operators with an assignment operator, =. Perform the operations as separate statements.

Exploring binary arithmetic operators

Increment and decrement are unary arithmetic operators. Other arithmetic operators are usually binary and allow you to perform arithmetic operations on two numbers, as the following shows:

1. Add statements to declare and assign values to two integer variables named e and f, and then apply the five common binary arithmetic operators to the two numbers, as shown in the following code:

```
int e = 11;
int f = 3;
```

```
WriteLine($"e is {e}, f is {f}");
WriteLine($"e + f = {e + f}");
WriteLine($"e - f = {e - f}");
WriteLine($"e * f = {e * f}");
WriteLine($"e / f = {e / f}");
WriteLine($"e % f = {e % f}");
```

2. Run the code and note the result, as shown in the following output:

```
e is 11, f is 3
e + f = 14
e - f = 8
e * f = 33
e / f = 3
e % f = 2
```

To understand the divide / and modulo % operators when applied to integers, you need to think back to primary school. Imagine you have eleven sweets and three friends.

How can you divide the sweets between your friends? You can give three sweets to each of your friends, and there will be two left over. Those two sweets are the **modulus**, also known as the **remainder** after dividing. If you had twelve sweets, then each friend would get four of them, and there would be none left over, so the remainder would be 0.

3. Add statements to declare and assign a value to a double variable named g to show the difference between whole number and real number divisions, as shown in the following code:

```
double g = 11.0;
WriteLine($"g is {g:N1}, f is {f}");
WriteLine($"g / f = {g / f}");
```

4. Run the code and note the result, as shown in the following output:

```
g is 11.0, f is 3
g / f = 3.6666666666666665
```

If the first operand is a floating-point number, such as g with the value 11.0, then the divide operator returns a floating-point value, such as 3.6666666666665, rather than a whole number.

Assignment operators

You have already been using the most common assignment operator, =.

To make your code more concise, you can combine the assignment operator with other operators like arithmetic operators, as shown in the following code:

```
int p = 6;
p += 3; // equivalent to p = p + 3;
p -= 3; // equivalent to p = p - 3;
p *= 3; // equivalent to p = p * 3;
p /= 3; // equivalent to p = p / 3;
```

Exploring logical operators

Logical operators operate on Boolean values, so they return either true or false. Let's explore binary logical operators that operate on two Boolean values:

1. Use your preferred coding tool to add a new **Console App**/console project named BooleanOperators to the Chapter03 workspace/solution.

   - In Visual Studio Code, select BooleanOperators as the active OmniSharp project. When you see the pop-up warning message saying that required assets are missing, click **Yes** to add them.

   - In Visual Studio 2022, set the startup project for the solution to the current selection.

 Good Practice: Remember to statically import System.Console for all C# files using the implicit usings .NET SDK feature.

2. In Program.cs, delete the existing statements and then add statements to declare two Boolean variables with values of true and false, and then output truth tables showing the results of applying AND, OR, and XOR (exclusive OR) logical operators, as shown in the following code:

```
bool a = true;
bool b = false;
WriteLine($"AND    | a      | b      ");
WriteLine($"a      | {a & a,-5} | {a & b,-5} ");
WriteLine($"b      | {b & a,-5} | {b & b,-5} ");
WriteLine();
WriteLine($"OR     | a      | b      ");
WriteLine($"a      | {a | a,-5} | {a | b,-5} ");
WriteLine($"b      | {b | a,-5} | {b | b,-5} ");
WriteLine();
WriteLine($"XOR    | a      | b      ");
WriteLine($"a      | {a ^ a,-5} | {a ^ b,-5} ");
WriteLine($"b      | {b ^ a,-5} | {b ^ b,-5} ");
```

3. Run the code and note the results, as shown in the following output:

```
AND   | a      | b
a     | True   | False
b     | False  | False

OR    | a      | b
a     | True   | True
b     | True   | False

XOR   | a      | b
```

```
a     | False | True
b     | True  | False
```

For the AND & logical operator, both operands must be `true` for the result to be `true`. For the OR | logical operator, either operand can be `true` for the result to be `true`. For the XOR ^ logical operator, either operand can be `true` (but not both!) for the result to be `true`.

Exploring conditional logical operators

Conditional logical operators are like logical operators, but you use two symbols instead of one, for example, && instead of &, or || instead of |.

In *Chapter 4, Writing, Debugging, and Testing Functions*, you will learn about functions in more detail, but I need to introduce functions now to explain conditional logical operators, also known as short-circuiting Boolean operators.

A function executes statements and then returns a value. That value could be a Boolean value like `true` that is used in a Boolean operation. Let's make use of conditional logical operators:

1. At the bottom of `Program.cs`, write statements to declare a function that writes a message to the console and returns `true`, as shown in the following code:

```
static bool DoStuff()
{
  WriteLine("I am doing some stuff.");
  return true;
}
```

 Good Practice: If you are using a .NET Interactive Notebook, write the `DoStuff` function in a separate code cell and then execute it to make its context available to other code cells.

2. After the previous `WriteLine` statements, perform an AND & operation on the a and b variables, which you defined in *step 2* of the previous section, and the result of calling the function, as shown in the following code:

```
WriteLine();
WriteLine($"a & DoStuff() = {a & DoStuff()}");
WriteLine($"b & DoStuff() = {b & DoStuff()}");
```

3. Run the code, view the result, and note that the function was called twice, once for a and once for b, as shown in the following output:

```
I am doing some stuff.
a & DoStuff() = True
I am doing some stuff.
b & DoStuff() = False
```

4. Copy and paste the three statements and then change the & operators into && operators, as shown in the following code:

```
WriteLine();
WriteLine($"a && DoStuff() = {a && DoStuff()}");
WriteLine($"b && DoStuff() = {b && DoStuff()}");
```

5. Run the code, view the result, and note that the function does run when combined with the a variable. It does not run when combined with the b variable because the b variable is `false` so the result will be `false` anyway, so it does not need to execute the function, as shown in the following output:

```
I am doing some stuff.
a && DoStuff() = True
b && DoStuff() = False // DoStuff function was not executed!
```

Good Practice: Now you can see why the conditional logical operators are described as being short-circuiting. They can make your apps more efficient, but they can also introduce subtle bugs in cases where you assume that the function will always be called. It is safest to avoid them when used in combination with functions that cause side effects.

Exploring bitwise and binary shift operators

Bitwise operators affect the bits in a number. Binary shift operators can perform some common arithmetic calculations much faster than traditional operators, for example, any multiplication by a factor of 2.

Let's explore bitwise and binary shift operators:

1. Use your preferred coding tool to add a new **Console App**/console project named BitwiseAndShiftOperators to the Chapter03 workspace/solution.

   • In Visual Studio Code, select BitwiseAndShiftOperators as the active OmniSharp project. When you see the pop-up warning message saying that required assets are missing, click **Yes** to add them.

2. In Program.cs, delete the existing statements, then type statements to declare two integer variables with values 10 and 6, and then output the results of applying AND, OR, and XOR bitwise operators, as shown in the following code:

```
int a = 10; // 00001010
int b = 6;  // 00000110

WriteLine($"a = {a}");
WriteLine($"b = {b}");
WriteLine($"a & b = {a & b}"); // 2-bit column only e.g. 00000010
WriteLine($"a | b = {a | b}"); // 8, 4, and 2-bit columns e.g. 00001110
WriteLine($"a ^ b = {a ^ b}"); // 8 and 4-bit columns e.g. 00001100
```

3. Run the code and note the results, as shown in the following output:

```
a = 10
b = 6
a & b = 2
a | b = 14
a ^ b = 12
```

4. In `Program.cs`, add statements to output the results of applying the left-shift operator to move the bits of the variable a by three columns, multiplying a by 8, and right-shifting the bits of the variable b by one column, as shown in the following code:

```
// 01010000 left-shift a by three bit columns
WriteLine($"a << 3 = {a << 3}");

// multiply a by 8
WriteLine($"a * 8 = {a * 8}");

// 00000011 right-shift b by one bit column
WriteLine($"b >> 1 = {b >> 1}");
```

5. Run the code and note the results, as shown in the following output:

```
a << 3 = 80
a * 8 = 80
b >> 1 = 3
```

The 80 result is because the bits in it were shifted three columns to the left, so the 1-bits moved into the 64- and 16-bit columns and 64 + 16 = 80. This is the equivalent of multiplying by 8, but CPUs can perform a bit-shift faster. The 3 result is because the 1-bits in b were shifted one column into the 2- and 1-bit columns.

 Good Practice: Remember that when operating on integer values, the & and | symbols are bitwise operators, and when operating on Boolean values like true and false, the & and | symbols are logical operators.

We can illustrate the operations by converting the integer values into binary strings of zeros and ones:

1. At the bottom of `Program.cs`, add a function to convert an integer value into a binary (Base2) string of up to eight zeros and ones, as shown in the following code:

```
static string ToBinaryString(int value)
{
  return Convert.ToString(value, toBase: 2).PadLeft(8, '0');
}
```

2. Above the function, add statements to output a, b, and the results of the various bitwise operators, as shown in the following code:

```
WriteLine();
WriteLine("Outputting integers as binary:");
WriteLine($"a =      {ToBinaryString(a)}");
WriteLine($"b =      {ToBinaryString(b)}");
WriteLine($"a & b = {ToBinaryString(a & b)}");
WriteLine($"a | b = {ToBinaryString(a | b)}");
WriteLine($"a ^ b = {ToBinaryString(a ^ b)}");
```

3. Run the code and note the results, as shown in the following output:

```
Outputting integers as binary:
a =      00001010
b =      00000110
a & b = 00000010
a | b = 00001110
a ^ b = 00001100
```

Miscellaneous operators

nameof and sizeof are convenient operators when working with types:

*   nameof returns the short name (without the namespace) of a variable, type, or member as a string value, which is useful when outputting exception messages.

*   sizeof returns the size in bytes of simple types, which is useful for determining the efficiency of data storage.

For example:

```
int age = 50;
WriteLine($"The {nameof(age)} variable uses {sizeof(int)} bytes of memory.");
```

There are many other operators; for example, the dot between a variable and its members is called the **member access operator** and the round brackets at the end of a function or method name are called the **invocation operator**, as shown in the following code:

```
int age = 50;

// How many operators in the following statement?
char firstDigit = age.ToString()[0];

// There are four operators:
// = is the assignment operator
// . is the member access operator
// () is the invocation operator
// [] is the indexer access operator
```

Understanding selection statements

Every application needs to be able to select from choices and branch along different code paths. The two selection statements in C# are if and switch. You can use if for all your code, but switch can simplify your code in some common scenarios, such as when there is a single variable that can have multiple values that each requires different processing.

Branching with the if statement

The if statement determines which branch to follow by evaluating a Boolean expression. If the expression is true, then the block executes. The else block is optional, and it executes if the if expression is false. The if statement can be nested.

The if statement can be combined with other if statements as else if branches, as shown in the following code:

```
if (expression1)
{
  // runs if expression1 is true
}
else if (expression2)
{
  // runs if expression1 is false and expression2 if true
}
else if (expression3)
{
  // runs if expression1 and expression2 are false
  // and expression3 is true
}
else
{
  // runs if all expressions are false
}
```

Each if statement's Boolean expression is independent of the others and, unlike switch statements, does not need to reference a single value.

Let's write some code to explore selection statements like if:

1. Use your preferred coding tool to add a new **Console App**/console project named SelectionStatements to the Chapter03 workspace/solution.

    *   In Visual Studio Code, select SelectionStatements as the active OmniSharp project.

2. In Program.cs, delete the existing statements and then add statements to check if a password is at least eight characters, as shown in the following code:

    ```
    string password = "ninja";

    if (password.Length < 8)
    ```

```
  {
    WriteLine("Your password is too short. Use at least 8 characters.");
  }
  else
  {
    WriteLine("Your password is strong.");
  }
```

3. Run the code and note the result, as shown in the following output:

```
Your password is too short. Use at least 8 characters.
```

Why you should always use braces with if statements

As there is only a single statement inside each block, the preceding code could be written without the curly braces, as shown in the following code:

```
if (password.Length < 8)
  WriteLine("Your password is too short. Use at least 8 characters.");
else
  WriteLine("Your password is strong.");
```

This style of if statement should be avoided because it can introduce serious bugs, for example, the infamous #gotofail bug in Apple's iPhone iOS operating system.

For 18 months after Apple's iOS 6 was released, in September 2012, it had a bug in its **Secure Sockets Layer (SSL)** encryption code, which meant that any user running Safari, the device's web browser, who tried to connect to secure websites, such as their bank, was not properly secure because an important check was being accidentally skipped.

Just because you can leave out the curly braces doesn't mean you should. Your code is not "more efficient" without them; instead, it is less maintainable and potentially more dangerous.

Pattern matching with the if statement

A feature introduced with C# 7.0 and later is pattern matching. The if statement can use the is keyword in combination with declaring a local variable to make your code safer:

1. Add statements so that if the value stored in the variable named o is an int, then the value is assigned to the local variable named i, which can then be used inside the if statement. This is safer than using the variable named o because we know for sure that i is an int variable and not something else, as shown in the following code:

```
// add and remove the "" to change the behavior
object o = "3";
int j = 4;

if (o is int i)
{
  WriteLine($"{i} x {j} = {i * j}");
```

```
    }
    else
    {
      WriteLine("o is not an int so it cannot multiply!");
    }
```

2. Run the code and view the results, as shown in the following output:

```
o is not an int so it cannot multiply!
```

3. Delete the double-quote characters around the "3" value so that the value stored in the variable named o is an int type instead of a string type.

4. Rerun the code to view the results, as shown in the following output:

```
3 x 4 = 12
```

Branching with the switch statement

The switch statement is different from the if statement because switch compares a single expression against a list of multiple possible case statements. Every case statement is related to the single expression. Every case section must end with:

- The break keyword (like case 1 in the following code)
- Or the goto case keywords (like case 2 in the following code)
- Or they should have no statements (like case 3 in the following code)
- Or the goto keyword that references a named label (like case 5 in the following code)
- Or the return keyword to leave the current function (not shown in the code)

Let's write some code to explore the switch statements:

1. Type code for a switch statement. You should note that the penultimate statement is a label that can be jumped to, and the first statement generates a random number between 1 and 6 (the number 7 in the code is an exclusive upper bound). The switch statement branches are based on the value of this random number, as shown in the following code:

```
int number = Random.Shared.Next(1, 7);
WriteLine($"My random number is {number}");

switch (number)
{
  case 1:
    WriteLine("One");
    break; // jumps to end of switch statement
  case 2:
    WriteLine("Two");
    goto case 1;
  case 3: // multiple case section
  case 4:
```

```
      WriteLine("Three or four");
      goto case 1;
    case 5:
      goto A_label;
    default:
      WriteLine("Default");
      break;
} // end of switch statement
WriteLine("After end of switch");
A_label:
WriteLine($"After A_label");
```

Good Practice: You can use the goto keyword to jump to another case or a label. The goto keyword is frowned upon by most programmers but can be a good solution to code logic in some scenarios. However, you should use it sparingly.

2. Run the code multiple times to see what happens in various cases of random numbers, as shown in the following example output:

```
// first random run
My random number is 4
Three or four
One
After end of switch
After A_label

// second random run
My random number is 2
Two
One
After end of switch
After A_label

// third random run
My random number is 6
Default
After end of switch
After A_label

// fourth random run
My random number is 1
One
After end of switch
After A_label
```

```
// fifth random run
My random number is 5
After A_label
```

 Good Practice: The Random class that we used to generate a random number has a Next method that allows you to specify an inclusive lower bound and an exclusive upper bound and will generate a pseudo-random number. Instead of creating a new instance of Random that is not thread-safe, since .NET 6 you can use a Shared instance that is thread-safe so it can be used concurrently from any thread.

Pattern matching with the switch statement

Like the if statement, the switch statement supports pattern matching in C# 7.0 and later. The case values no longer need to be literal values; they can be patterns.

In C# 7.0 and later, your code can more concisely branch, based on the subtype of a class, and declare and assign a local variable to safely use it. Additionally, case statements can include a when keyword to perform more specific pattern matching.

Let's see an example of pattern matching with the switch statement using a custom class hierarchy of animals with different properties:

 You will learn more details about defining classes in *Chapter 5, Building Your Own Types with Object-Oriented Programming*. For now, you should be able to get the idea from reading the code.

1. In the SelectionStatements project, navigate to **Project | Add Class...**, enter a filename of Animals.cs, and then click **Add**.

2. In Animals.cs, define three classes, a base class and two inherited classes, as shown in the following code:

```
class Animal // This is the base type for all animals.
{
  public string? Name;
  public DateTime Born;
  public byte Legs;
}

class Cat : Animal // This is a subtype of animal.
{
  public bool IsDomestic;
}

class Spider : Animal // This is another subtype of animal.
```

```
{
  public bool IsPoisonous;
}
```

3. In `Program.cs`, add statements to declare an array of nullable animals, and then show a message based on what type and attributes each animal has, as shown in the following code:

```
Animal?[] animals = new Animal?[]
{
  new Cat { Name = "Karen", Born = new(year: 2022, month: 8, day: 23),
    Legs = 4, IsDomestic = true },
  null,
  new Cat { Name = "Mufasa", Born = new(year: 1994, month: 6, day: 12) },
  new Spider { Name = "Sid Vicious", Born = DateTime.Today,
    IsPoisonous = true},
  new Spider { Name = "Captain Furry", Born = DateTime.Today }
};

foreach (Animal? animal in animals)
{
  string message;

  switch (animal)
  {
    case Cat fourLeggedCat when fourLeggedCat.Legs == 4:
      message = $"The cat named {fourLeggedCat.Name} has four legs.";
      break;
    case Cat wildCat when wildCat.IsDomestic == false:
      message = $"The non-domestic cat is named {wildCat.Name}.";
      break;
    case Cat cat:
      message = $"The cat is named {cat.Name}.";
      break;
    default: // default is always evaluated last
      message = $"The animal named {animal.Name} is a {animal.GetType().
      Name}.";
      break;
    case Spider spider when spider.IsPoisonous:
      message = $"The {spider.Name} spider is poisonous. Run!";
      break;
    case null:
      message = "The animal is null.";
      break;
  }
  WriteLine($"switch statement: {message}");
}
```

4. Run the code and note that the array named `animals` is declared to contain the `Animal?` type so it could be any subtype of `Animal`, such as a `Cat` or a `Spider`, or a `null` value. In this code, we create four instances of `Animal` of different types with different properties, and one `null` one, so the result will be five messages that describe each of the animals, as shown in the following output:

```
switch statement: The cat named Karen has four legs.
switch statement: The animal is null.
switch statement: The non-domestic cat is named Mufasa.
switch statement: The Sid Vicious spider is poisonous. Run!
switch statement: The animal named Captain Furry is a Spider.
```

Simplifying switch statements with switch expressions

In C# 8.0 or later, you can simplify `switch` statements using **switch expressions**.

Most `switch` statements are very simple, yet they require a lot of typing. `switch` expressions are designed to simplify the code you need to type while still expressing the same intent in scenarios where all cases return a value to set a single variable. `switch` expressions use a lambda, `=>`, to indicate a return value.

Let's implement the previous code that used a `switch` statement using a `switch` expression so that you can compare the two styles:

1. In `Program.cs`, at the bottom and inside of the `foreach` loop, add statements to set the message based on what type and attributes the animal has, using a `switch` expression, as shown in the following code:

```
message = animal switch
{
  Cat fourLeggedCat when fourLeggedCat.Legs == 4
    => $"The cat {fourLeggedCat.Name} has four legs.",
  Cat wildCat when wildCat.IsDomestic == false
    => $"The non-domestic cat is named {wildCat.Name}.",
  Cat cat
    => $"The cat is named {cat.Name}.",
  Spider spider when spider.IsPoisonous
    => $"The {spider.Name} spider is poisonous. Run!",
  null
    => "The animal is null.",
  _
    => $"The animal named {animal.Name} is a {animal.GetType().Name}."
};
WriteLine($"switch expression: {message}");
```

The main differences are the removal of the case and break keywords. The underscore character _ is used to represent the default return value. It is known as a **discard** and you can read more about it at the following link: https://docs. microsoft.com/en-us/dotnet/csharp/fundamentals/functional/discards.

2. Run the code, and note that the result is the same as before, as shown in the following output:

```
switch statement: The cat named Karen has four legs.
switch expression: The cat named Karen has four legs.
switch statement: The animal is null.
switch expression: The animal is null.
switch statement: The non-domestic cat is named Mufasa.
switch expression: The non-domestic cat is named Mufasa.
switch statement: The Sid Vicious spider is poisonous. Run!
switch expression: The Sid Vicious spider is poisonous. Run!
switch statement: The animal named Captain Furry is a Spider.
switch expression: The animal named Captain Furry is a Spider.
```

Understanding iteration statements

Iteration statements repeat a block of statements either while a condition is true (while and for statements) or for each item in a collection (foreach statement). The choice of which statement to use is based on a combination of ease of understanding to solve the logic problem and personal preference.

Looping with the while statement

The while statement evaluates a Boolean expression and continues to loop while it is true. Let's explore iteration statements:

1. Use your preferred coding tool to add a new **Console App**/console project named IterationStatements to the Chapter03 workspace/solution.

    • In Visual Studio Code, select IterationStatements as the active OmniSharp project.

2. In Program.cs, delete the existing statements and then add statements to define a while statement that loops while an integer variable has a value less than 10, as shown in the following code:

```
int x = 0;
while (x < 10)
{
  WriteLine(x);
  x++;
}
```

3. Run the code and view the results, which should be the numbers 0 to 9, as shown in the following output:

```
0
1
2
3
4
5
6
7
8
9
```

Looping with the do statement

The do statement is like while, except the Boolean expression is checked at the bottom of the block instead of the top, which means that the block always executes at least once, as the following shows:

1. Type statements to define a do loop, as shown in the following code:

```
string? password;
do
{
  Write("Enter your password: ");
  password = ReadLine();
}
while (password != "Pa$$w0rd");
WriteLine("Correct!");
```

2. Run the code, and note that you are prompted to enter your password repeatedly until you enter it correctly, as shown in the following output:

```
Enter your password: password
Enter your password: 12345678
Enter your password: ninja
Enter your password: correct horse battery staple
Enter your password: Pa$$w0rd
Correct!
```

3. As an optional challenge, add statements so that the user can only make ten attempts before an error message is displayed.

Looping with the for statement

The for statement is like while, except that it is more succinct. It combines:

- An optional **initializer expression**, which executes once at the start of the loop.

- An optional **conditional expression**, which executes on every iteration at the start of the loop to check whether the looping should continue. If the expression returns `true` or it is missing, the loop will execute again.
- An optional **iterator expression**, which executes on every loop at the bottom of the statement. This is often used to increment a counter variable.

The `for` statement is commonly used with an integer counter. Let's explore some code:

1. Type a `for` statement to output the numbers 1 to 10, as shown in the following code:

```
for (int y = 1; y <= 10; y++)
{
  WriteLine(y);
}
```

2. Run the code to view the result, which should be the numbers 1 to 10.

Looping with the foreach statement

The `foreach` statement is a bit different from the previous three iteration statements.

It is used to perform a block of statements on each item in a sequence, for example, an array or collection. Each item is usually read-only, and if the sequence structure is modified during iteration, for example, by adding or removing an item, then an exception will be thrown.

Try the following example:

1. Type statements to create an array of string variables and then output the length of each one, as shown in the following code:

```
string[] names = { "Adam", "Barry", "Charlie" };

foreach (string name in names)
{
  WriteLine($"{name} has {name.Length} characters.");
}
```

2. Run the code and view the results, as shown in the following output:

```
Adam has 4 characters.
Barry has 5 characters.
Charlie has 7 characters.
```

Understanding how foreach works internally

A creator of any type that represents multiple items, like an array or collection, should make sure that a programmer can use the `foreach` statement to enumerate through the type's items.

Technically, the `foreach` statement will work on any type that follows these rules:

- The type must have a method named `GetEnumerator` that returns an object.

- The returned object must have a property named `Current` and a method named `MoveNext`.

- The `MoveNext` method must change the value of `Current` and return `true` if there are more items to enumerate through or return `false` if there are no more items.

There are interfaces named `IEnumerable` and `IEnumerable<T>` that formally define these rules, but technically the compiler does not require the type to implement these interfaces.

The compiler turns the `foreach` statement in the preceding example into something like the following pseudocode:

```
IEnumerator e = names.GetEnumerator();

while (e.MoveNext())
{
  string name = (string)e.Current; // Current is read-only!
  WriteLine($"{name} has {name.Length} characters.");
}
```

Due to the use of an iterator and its read-only `Current` property, the variable declared in a `foreach` statement cannot be used to modify the value of the current item.

Storing multiple values in an array

When you need to store multiple values of the same type, you can declare an **array**. For example, you may do this when you need to store four names in a `string` array.

Working with single-dimensional arrays

The code that you will write next will allocate memory for an array for storing four `string` values. It will then store `string` values at index positions 0 to 3 (arrays usually have a lower bound of zero, so the index of the last item is one less than the length of the array).

We could visualize the array like this:

0	1	2	3
Kate	Jack	Rebecca	Tom

 Good Practice: Do not assume that all arrays count from zero. The most common type of array in .NET is an **szArray**, a single-dimension zero-indexed array, and these use the normal [ ] syntax. But .NET also has **mdArray**, a multi-dimensional array, and they do not have to have a lower bound of zero. These are rarely used, but you should know they exist.

Finally, it will loop through each item in the array using a `for` statement.

Let's look at how to use an array:

1. Use your preferred code editor to add a new **Console App**/console project named `Arrays` to the `Chapter03` workspace/solution.

- In Visual Studio Code, select Arrays as the active OmniSharp project. When you see the pop-up warning message saying that required assets are missing, click **Yes** to add them.

2. In Program.cs, delete the existing statements and then type statements to declare and use an array of string values, as shown in the following code:

```
string[] names; // can reference any size array of strings

// allocating memory for four strings in an array
names = new string[4];

// storing items at index positions
names[0] = "Kate";
names[1] = "Jack";
names[2] = "Rebecca";
names[3] = "Tom";

// looping through the names
for (int i = 0; i < names.Length; i++)
{
  // output the item at index position i
  WriteLine(names[i]);
}
```

3. Run the code and note the result, as shown in the following output:

```
Kate
Jack
Rebecca
Tom
```

Arrays are always of a fixed size at the time of memory allocation, so you need to decide how many items you want to store before instantiating them.

An alternative to defining the array in three steps as above is to use array initializer syntax:

1. Before the for loop, add a statement to declare, allocate memory, and instantiate the values of a similar array, as shown in the following code:

```
string[] names2 = new[] { "Kate", "Jack", "Rebecca", "Tom" };
```

2. Change the for loop to use names2, run the console app, and note that the results are the same.

When you use the new[] syntax to allocate memory for the array, you must have at least one item in the curly braces so that the compiler can infer the data type.

Working with multi-dimensional arrays

Instead of a single-dimension array for storing a row of string values (or any other data type), what if we want to store a grid of values? Or a cube? Or even higher dimensions?

We could visualize a two-dimensional array, aka grid, of `string` values like this:

	0	1	2	3
0	Alpha	Beta	Gamma	Delta
1	Anne	Ben	Charlie	Doug
2	Aardvark	Bear	Cat	Dog

Let's look at how to use multi-dimensional arrays:

1. At the bottom of `Program.cs`, add statements to declare and instantiate a two-dimensional array of `string` values, as shown in the following code:

    ```
    string[,] grid1 = new[,] // two dimensions
    {
      { "Alpha", "Beta", "Gamma", "Delta" },
      { "Anne", "Ben", "Charlie", "Doug" },
      { "Aardvark", "Bear", "Cat", "Dog" }
    };
    ```

2. We can discover the lower and upper bounds of this array using helpful methods, as shown in the following code:

    ```
    WriteLine($"Lower bound of the first dimension is: {grid1.
    GetLowerBound(0)}");
    WriteLine($"Upper bound of the first dimension is: {grid1.
    GetUpperBound(0)}");
    WriteLine($"Lower bound of the second dimension is: {grid1.
    GetLowerBound(1)}");
    WriteLine($"Upper bound of the second dimension is: {grid1.
    GetUpperBound(1)}");
    ```

3. Run the code and note the result, as shown in the following output:

    ```
    Lower bound of the first dimension is: 0
    Upper bound of the first dimension is: 2
    Lower bound of the second dimension is: 0
    Upper bound of the second dimension is: 3
    ```

4. We can then use these values in nested `for` statements to loop through the `string` values, as shown in the following code:

    ```
    for (int row = 0; row <= grid1.GetUpperBound(0); row++)
    {
      for (int col = 0; col <= grid1.GetUpperBound(1); col++)
      {
        WriteLine($"Row {row}, Column {col}: {grid1[row, col]}");
      }
    }
    ```

5. Run the code and note the result, as shown in the following output:

```
Row 0, Column 0: Alpha
Row 0, Column 1: Beta
Row 0, Column 2: Gamma
Row 0, Column 3: Delta
Row 1, Column 0: Anne
Row 1, Column 1: Ben
Row 1, Column 2: Charlie
Row 1, Column 3: Doug
Row 2, Column 0: Aardvark
Row 2, Column 1: Bear
Row 2, Column 2: Cat
Row 2, Column 3: Dog
```

You must supply a value for every row and every column when it is instantiated, or you will get compile errors. If you need to indicate a missing `string` value, then use `string.Empty`. Or if you declare the array to be nullable `string` values by using `string?[]`, then you can also use `null` for a missing value.

If you cannot use the array initialization syntax, perhaps because you are loading values from a file or database, then you can separate the declaration of the array dimension and the allocation of memory from the assigning of values, as shown in the following code:

```
// alternative syntax
string[,] grid2 = new string[3,4]; // allocate memory

grid2[0, 0] = "Alpha"; // assign values
grid2[0, 1] = "Beta";
// and so on
grid2[2, 3] = "Dog";
```

When declaring the size of the dimensions, you specify the length, not the upper bound. The expression `new string[3,4]` means the array can have 3 items in its first dimension (0) with an upper bound of 2, and the array can have 4 items in its second dimension (1) with an upper bound of 3.

Working with jagged arrays

If you need a multi-dimensional array but the number of items stored in each dimension is different, then you can define an array of arrays, aka a jagged array.

We could visualize a jagged array like this:

0	0	1	2	
	Alpha	Beta	Gamma	
1	0	1	2	3
	Anne	Ben	Charlie	Doug
2	0	1		
	Aardvark	Bear		

Let's look at how to use a jagged array:

1. At the bottom of `Program.cs`, add statements to declare and instantiate an array of arrays of `string` values, as shown in the following code:

    ```
    string[][] jagged = new[] // array of string arrays
    {
      new[] { "Alpha", "Beta", "Gamma" },
      new[] { "Anne", "Ben", "Charlie", "Doug" },
      new[] { "Aardvark", "Bear" }
    };
    ```

2. We can discover the lower and upper bounds of the array of arrays, and then each array with it, as shown in the following code:

    ```
    WriteLine("Upper bound of array of arrays is: {0}",
      jagged.GetUpperBound(0));

    for (int array = 0; array <= jagged.GetUpperBound(0); array++)
    {
      WriteLine("Upper bound of array {0} is: {1}",
        arg0: array,
        arg1: jagged[array].GetUpperBound(0));
    }
    ```

3. Run the code and note the result, as shown in the following output:

    ```
    Upper bound of array of arrays is: 2
    Upper bound of array 0 is: 2
    Upper bound of array 1 is: 3
    Upper bound of array 2 is: 1
    ```

4. We can then use these values in nested `for` statements to loop through the `string` values, as shown in the following code:

    ```
    for (int row = 0; row <= jagged.GetUpperBound(0); row++)
    {
    ```

```
    for (int col = 0; col <= jagged[row].GetUpperBound(0); col++)
    {
      WriteLine($"Row {row}, Column {col}: {jagged[row][col]}");
    }
  }
```

5. Run the code and note the result, as shown in the following output:

```
Row 0, Column 0: Alpha
Row 0, Column 1: Beta
Row 0, Column 2: Gamma
Row 1, Column 0: Anne
Row 1, Column 1: Ben
Row 1, Column 2: Charlie
Row 1, Column 3: Doug
Row 2, Column 0: Aardvark
Row 2, Column 1: Bear
```

List pattern matching with arrays

Earlier in this chapter, you saw how an individual object supports pattern matching against their type and their properties. Pattern matching also works with arrays and collections.

List pattern matching works with any type that has a public Length or Count property and has an indexer using an int or System.Index parameter. You will learn about indexers in *Chapter 5, Building Your Own Types with Object-Oriented Programming*.

When you define multiple list patterns in the same switch expression, you must order them so that the more specific one comes first, or the compiler will complain because a more general pattern will match all the more specific patterns too and make the more specific one unreachable.

The following table shows examples of list pattern matching, assuming a list of int values:

Example	Description
[]	Matches an empty array or collection.
[..]	Matches an array or collection with any number of items including zero, so [..] must come after [] if you need to switch on both.
[1, 2]	Matches exactly a list of two items with those values in that order.
[_]	Matches a list with any single item.
[int item1] or [var item1]	Matches a list with any single item and can use the value in the return expression by referring to item1.
[_, _]	Matches a list with any two items.
[var item1, var item2]	Matches a list with any two items and can use the values in the return expression by referring to item1 and item2.
[_, _, _]	Matches a list with any three items.

`[var item1, ..]`	Matches a list with one or more items. Can refer to the value of the first item in its return expression by referring to `item1`.
`[var firstItem, ..,` `var lastItem]`	Matches a list with two or more items. Can refer to the value of the first and last item in its return expression by referring to `firstItem` and `lastItem`.
`[.., var lastItem]`	Matches a list with one or more items. Can refer to the value of the last item in its return expression by referring to `lastItem`.

Let's see some examples in code:

1. At the bottom of `Program.cs`, add statements to define some arrays of `int` values, and then pass them to a method that returns descriptive text depending on the pattern that matches best, as shown in the following code:

```
int[] sequentialNumbers = new int[] { 1, 2, 3, 4, 5, 6, 7, 8, 9, 10 };
int[] oneTwoNumbers = new int[] { 1, 2 };
int[] oneTwoTenNumbers = new int[] { 1, 2, 10 };
int[] oneTwoThreeTenNumbers = new int[] { 1, 2, 3, 10 };
int[] primeNumbers = new int[] { 2, 3, 5, 7, 11, 13, 17, 19, 23, 29 };
int[] fibonacciNumbers = new int[] { 0, 1, 1, 2, 3, 5, 8, 13, 21, 34, 55,
89 };
int[] emptyNumbers = new int[] { };
int[] threeNumbers = new int[] { 9, 7, 5 };
int[] sixNumbers = new int[] { 9, 7, 5, 4, 2, 10 };

WriteLine($"{nameof(sequentialNumbers)}:
{CheckSwitch(sequentialNumbers)}");
WriteLine($"{nameof(oneTwoNumbers)}: {CheckSwitch(oneTwoNumbers)}");
WriteLine($"{nameof(oneTwoTenNumbers)}:
{CheckSwitch(oneTwoTenNumbers)}");
WriteLine($"{nameof(oneTwoThreeTenNumbers)}:
{CheckSwitch(oneTwoThreeTenNumbers)}");
WriteLine($"{nameof(primeNumbers)}: {CheckSwitch(primeNumbers)}");
WriteLine($"{nameof(fibonacciNumbers)}:
{CheckSwitch(fibonacciNumbers)}");
WriteLine($"{nameof(emptyNumbers)}: {CheckSwitch(emptyNumbers)}");
WriteLine($"{nameof(threeNumbers)}: {CheckSwitch(threeNumbers)}");
WriteLine($"{nameof(sixNumbers)}: {CheckSwitch(sixNumbers)}");

static string CheckSwitch(int[] values) => values switch
{
  [] => "Empty array",
  [1, 2, _, 10] => "Contains 1, 2, any single number, 10.",
  [1, 2, .., 10] => "Contains 1, 2, any range including empty, 10.",
  [1, 2] => "Contains 1 then 2.",
  [int item1, int item2, int item3] =>
    $"Contains {item1} then {item2} then {item3}.",
```

```
    [0, _] => "Starts with 0, then one other number.",
    [0, ..] => "Starts with 0, then any range of numbers.",
    [2, .. int[] others] => $"Starts with 2, then {others.Length} more
    numbers.",
    [..] => "Any items in any order.",
};
```

2. Run the code and note the result, as shown in the following output:

```
sequentialNumbers: Contains 1, 2, any range including empty, 10.
oneTwoNumbers: Contains 1 then 2.
oneTwoTenNumbers: Contains 1, 2, any range including empty, 10.
oneTwoThreeTenNumbers: Contains 1, 2, any single number, 10.
primeNumbers: Starts with 2, then 9 more numbers.
fibonacciNumbers: Starts with 0, then any range of numbers.
emptyNumbers: Empty array
threeNumbers: Contains 9 then 7 then 5.
sixNumbers: Any items in any order.
```

> You can learn more about list pattern matching at the following link: https://
> learn.microsoft.com/en-us/dotnet/csharp/language-reference/operators/
> patterns#list-patterns.

Summarizing arrays

We use slightly different syntax to declare different types of arrays, as shown in the following table:

Type of array	Declaration syntax
Single dimension	datatype[], for example, string[]
Two dimensions	string[,]
Three dimensions	string[,,]
Ten dimensions	string[,,,,,,,,,]
Array of arrays aka jagged array	string[][]
Array of arrays of arrays	string[][][]

Arrays are useful for temporarily storing multiple items, but collections are a more flexible option when adding and removing items dynamically. You don't need to worry about collections right now, as we will cover them in *Chapter 8, Working with Common .NET Types*.

> **Good Practice:** If you will not dynamically add and remove items, then you should use an array instead of a collection like List<T>.

Casting and converting between types

You will often need to convert values of variables between different types. For example, data input is often entered as text at the console, so it is initially stored in a variable of the string type, but it then needs to be converted into a date/time, number, or some other data type, depending on how it should be stored and processed.

Sometimes you will need to convert between number types, like between an integer and a floating point, before performing calculations.

Converting is also known as **casting**, and it has two varieties: **implicit** and **explicit**. Implicit casting happens automatically, and it is safe, meaning that you will not lose any information.

Explicit casting must be performed manually because it may lose information, for example, the precision of a number. By explicitly casting, you are telling the C# compiler that you understand and accept the risk.

Casting numbers implicitly and explicitly

Implicitly casting an int variable into a double variable is safe because no information can be lost, as the following shows:

1. Use your preferred coding tool to add a new **Console App**/console project named CastingConverting to the Chapter03 workspace/solution.

    *   In Visual Studio Code, select CastingConverting as the active OmniSharp project.

2. In Program.cs, delete the existing statements and then type statements to declare and assign an int variable and a double variable, and then implicitly cast the integer's value when assigning it to the double variable, as shown in the following code:

    ```
    int a = 10;
    double b = a; // an int can be safely cast into a double
    WriteLine(b);
    ```

3. Type statements to declare and assign a double variable and an int variable, and then implicitly cast the double value when assigning it to the int variable, as shown in the following code:

    ```
    double c = 9.8;
    int d = c; // compiler gives an error for this line
    WriteLine(d);
    ```

4. Run the code and note the error message, as shown in the following output:

    ```
    Error: (6,9): error CS0266: Cannot implicitly convert type 'double' to
    'int'. An explicit conversion exists (are you missing a cast?)
    ```

    This error message will also appear in the Visual Studio **Error List** or Visual Studio Code **PROBLEMS** window.

You cannot implicitly cast a double variable into an int variable because it is potentially unsafe and could lose data, like the value after the decimal point. You must explicitly cast a double variable into an int variable using a pair of round brackets around the type you want to cast the double type into. The pair of round brackets is the **cast operator**. Even then, you must beware that the part after the decimal point will be trimmed off without warning because you have chosen to perform an explicit cast and therefore understand the consequences.

5. Modify the assignment statement for the d variable, as shown in the following code:

```
int d = (int)c;
WriteLine(d); // d is 9 Losing the .8 part
```

6. Run the code to view the results, as shown in the following output:

```
10
9
```

We must perform a similar operation when converting values between larger integers and smaller integers. Again, beware that you might lose information because any value too big will have its bits copied and then be interpreted in ways that you might not expect!

7. Enter statements to declare and assign a long 64-bit variable to an int 32-bit variable, both using a small value that will work and a too-large value that will not, as shown in the following code:

```
long e = 10;
int f = (int)e;
WriteLine($"e is {e:N0} and f is {f:N0}");

e = long.MaxValue;
f = (int)e;
WriteLine($"e is {e:N0} and f is {f:N0}");
```

8. Run the code to view the results, as shown in the following output:

```
e is 10 and f is 10
e is 9,223,372,036,854,775,807 and f is -1
```

9. Modify the value of e to 5 billion, as shown in the following code:

```
e = 5_000_000_000;
```

10. Run the code to view the results, as shown in the following output:

```
e is 5,000,000,000 and f is 705,032,704
```

Converting with the System.Convert type

You can only cast between similar types, for example, between whole numbers like byte, int, and long, or between a class and its subclasses. You cannot cast a long to a string or a byte to a DateTime.

An alternative to using the cast operator is to use the System.Convert type. The System.Convert type can convert to and from all the C# number types, as well as Booleans, strings, and date and time values.

Let's write some code to see this in action:

1. At the top of Program.cs, statically import the System.Convert class, as shown in the following code:

    ```
    using static System.Convert;
    ```

2. At the bottom of Program.cs, type statements to declare and assign a value to a double variable, convert it to an integer, and then write both values to the console, as shown in the following code:

    ```
    double g = 9.8;
    int h = ToInt32(g); // a method of System.Convert
    WriteLine($"g is {g} and h is {h}");
    ```

3. Run the code and view the result, as shown in the following output:

    ```
    g is 9.8 and h is 10
    ```

 An important difference between casting and converting is that converting rounds the double value 9.8 up to 10 instead of trimming the part after the decimal point.

Rounding numbers

You have now seen that the cast operator trims the decimal part of a real number and that the System.Convert methods round up or down. However, what is the rule for rounding?

Understanding the default rounding rules

In British primary schools for children aged 5 to 11, pupils are taught to round *up* if the decimal part is .5 or higher and round *down* if the decimal part is less.

Let's explore if C# follows the same primary school rule:

1. Type statements to declare and assign an array of double values, convert each of them to an integer, and then write the result to the console, as shown in the following code:

    ```
    double[] doubles = new[]
      { 9.49, 9.5, 9.51, 10.49, 10.5, 10.51 };

    foreach (double n in doubles)
    {
      WriteLine($"ToInt32({n}) is {ToInt32(n)}");
    }
    ```

2. Run the code and view the result, as shown in the following output:

```
ToInt32(9.49) is 9
ToInt32(9.5) is 10
ToInt32(9.51) is 10
ToInt32(10.49) is 10
ToInt32(10.5) is 10
ToInt32(10.51) is 11
```

We have shown that the rule for rounding in C# is subtly different from the primary school rule:

- It always rounds *down* if the decimal part is less than the midpoint .5.
- It always rounds *up* if the decimal part is more than the midpoint .5.
- It will round *up* if the decimal part is the midpoint .5 and the non-decimal part is *odd*, but it will round *down* if the non-decimal part is *even*.

This rule is known as **banker's rounding**, and it is preferred because it reduces bias by alternating when it rounds up or down. Sadly, other languages such as JavaScript use the primary school rule.

Taking control of rounding rules

You can take control of the rounding rules by using the Round method of the Math class:

1. Type statements to round each of the double values using the "away from zero" rounding rule, also known as rounding "up," and then write the result to the console, as shown in the following code:

```
foreach (double n in doubles)
{
  WriteLine(format:
    "Math.Round({0}, 0, MidpointRounding.AwayFromZero) is {1}",
    arg0: n,
    arg1: Math.Round(value: n, digits: 0,
          mode: MidpointRounding.AwayFromZero));
}
```

2. Run the code and view the result, as shown in the following output:

```
Math.Round(9.49, 0, MidpointRounding.AwayFromZero) is 9
Math.Round(9.5, 0, MidpointRounding.AwayFromZero) is 10
Math.Round(9.51, 0, MidpointRounding.AwayFromZero) is 10
Math.Round(10.49, 0, MidpointRounding.AwayFromZero) is 10
Math.Round(10.5, 0, MidpointRounding.AwayFromZero) is 11
Math.Round(10.51, 0, MidpointRounding.AwayFromZero) is 11
```

 Good Practice: For every programming language that you use, check its rounding rules. They may not work the way you expect!

Converting from any type to a string

The most common conversion is from any type into a string variable for outputting as human-readable text, so all types have a method named ToString that they inherit from the System.Object class.

The ToString method converts the current value of any variable into a textual representation. Some types can't be sensibly represented as text, so they return their namespace and type name instead.

Let's convert some types into a string:

1. Type statements to declare some variables, convert them to their string representation, and write them to the console, as shown in the following code:

```
int number = 12;
WriteLine(number.ToString());
bool boolean = true;
WriteLine(boolean.ToString());
DateTime now = DateTime.Now;
WriteLine(now.ToString());
object me = new();
WriteLine(me.ToString());
```

2. Run the code and view the result, as shown in the following output:

```
12
True
08/28/2022 17:33:54
System.Object
```

Converting from a binary object to a string

When you have a binary object like an image or video that you want to either store or transmit, you sometimes do not want to send the raw bits because you do not know how those bits could be misinterpreted, for example, by the network protocol transmitting them or another operating system that is reading the stored binary object.

The safest thing to do is to convert the binary object into a string of safe characters. Programmers call this **Base64** encoding.

The Convert type has a pair of methods, ToBase64String and FromBase64String, that perform this conversion for you. Let's see them in action:

1. Type statements to create an array of bytes randomly populated with byte values, write each byte nicely formatted to the console, and then write the same bytes converted to Base64 to the console, as shown in the following code:

```
// allocate array of 128 bytes
byte[] binaryObject = new byte[128];

// populate array with random bytes
```

```
Random.Shared.NextBytes(binaryObject);

WriteLine("Binary Object as bytes:");
for(int index = 0; index < binaryObject.Length; index++)
{
  Write($"{binaryObject[index]:X} ");
}
WriteLine();

// convert to Base64 string and output as text
string encoded = ToBase64String(binaryObject);
WriteLine($"Binary Object as Base64: {encoded}");
```

By default, an int value would output assuming decimal notation, that is, Base10. You can use format codes such as :X to format the value using hexadecimal notation.

2. Run the code and view the result, as shown in the following output:

```
Binary Object as bytes:
B3 4D 55 DE 2D E BB CF BE 4D E6 53 C3 C2 9B 67 3 45 F9 E5 20 61 7E 4F 7A
81
EC 49 F0 49 1D 8E D4 F7 DB 54 AF A0 81 5 B8 BE CE F8 36 90 7A D4 36 42
4 75 81 1B AB 51 CE 5 63 AC 22 72 DE 74 2F 57 7F CB E7 47 B7 62 C3 F4 2D
61 93 85 18 EA 6 17 12 AE 44 A8 D B8 4C 89 85 A9 3C D5 E2 46 E0 59 C9 DF
10 AF ED EF 8AA1 B1 8D EE 4A BE 48 EC 79 A5 A 5F 2F 30 87 4A C7 7F 5D C1
D
26 EE
Binary Object as Base64: s01V3i0Ou8++TeZTw8KbZwNF
+eUgYX5PeoHsSfBJHY7U99tU
r6CBBbi+zvg2kHrUNkIEdYEbq1HOBWOsInLedC9Xf8vnR7diw/
QtYZOFGOoGFxKuRKgNuEyJha k81eJG4FnJ3xCv7e+KobGN7kq+SO x5pQpfLzCHSsd/
XcENJu4=
```

Parsing from strings to numbers or dates and times

The second most common conversion is from strings to numbers or date and time values.

The opposite of ToString is Parse. Only a few types have a Parse method, including all the number types and DateTime.

Let's see Parse in action:

1. Type statements to parse an integer and a date and time value from strings and then write the result to the console, as shown in the following code:

```
int age = int.Parse("27");
DateTime birthday = DateTime.Parse("4 July 1980");
WriteLine($"I was born {age} years ago.");
WriteLine($"My birthday is {birthday}.");
WriteLine($"My birthday is {birthday:D}.");
```

2. Run the code and view the result, as shown in the following output:

```
I was born 27 years ago.
My birthday is 04/07/1980 00:00:00.
My birthday is 04 July 1980.
```

By default, a date and time value outputs with the short date and time format. You can use format codes such as D to output only the date part using the long date format.

 Good Practice: Use the standard date and time format specifiers, as shown at the following link: https://docs.microsoft.com/en-us/dotnet/standard/base-types/standard-date-and-time-format-strings#table-of-format-specifiers.

Errors using Parse

One problem with the Parse method is that it gives errors if the string cannot be converted:

1. Type a statement to attempt to parse a string containing letters into an integer variable, as shown in the following code:

```
int count = int.Parse("abc");
```

2. Run the code and view the result, as shown in the following output:

```
Unhandled Exception: System.FormatException: Input string was not in a
correct format.
```

As well as the preceding exception message, you will see a stack trace. I have not included stack traces in this book because they take up too much space.

Avoiding exceptions using the TryParse method

To avoid errors, you can use the TryParse method instead. TryParse attempts to convert the input string and returns true if it can convert it and false if it cannot. Exceptions are a relatively expensive operation so they should be avoided when you can.

The out keyword is required to allow the TryParse method to set the count variable when the conversion works.

Let's see TryParse in action:

1. Replace the int count declaration with statements to use the TryParse method and ask the user to input a count for a number of eggs, as shown in the following code:

```
Write("How many eggs are there? ");
string? input = ReadLine(); // or use "12" in notebook

if (int.TryParse(input, out int count))
{
  WriteLine($"There are {count} eggs.");
```

```
    }
    else
    {
        WriteLine("I could not parse the input.");
    }
```

2. Run the code, enter 12, and view the result, as shown in the following output:

```
How many eggs are there? 12
There are 12 eggs.
```

3. Run the code, enter `twelve` (or change the `string` value to `"twelve"` in a notebook), and view the result, as shown in the following output:

```
How many eggs are there? twelve
I could not parse the input.
```

You can also use methods of the `System.Convert` type to convert `string` values into other types; however, like the `Parse` method, it gives an error if it cannot convert.

Handling exceptions

You've seen several scenarios where errors have occurred when converting types. Some languages return error codes when something goes wrong. .NET uses exceptions that are richer and designed only for failure reporting. When this happens, we say *a runtime exception has been thrown*.

Other systems might use return values that could have multiple uses. For example, if the return value is a positive number, it might represent the count of rows in a table, or if the return value is a negative number it might represent some error code.

When an exception is thrown, the thread is suspended and if the calling code has defined a `try-catch` statement, then it is given a chance to handle the exception. If the current method does not handle it, then its calling method is given a chance, and so on up the call stack.

As you have seen, the default behavior of a console app or a .NET Interactive notebook is to output a message about the exception, including a stack trace, and then stop running the code. The application is terminated. This is better than allowing the code to continue executing in a potentially corrupt state. Your code should only catch and handle exceptions that it understands and can properly fix.

 Good Practice: Avoid writing code that will throw an exception whenever possible, perhaps by performing `if` statement checks. Sometimes you can't, and sometimes it is best to allow the exception to be caught by a higher-level component that is calling your code. You will learn how to do this in *Chapter 4, Writing, Debugging, and Testing Functions*.

Wrapping error-prone code in a try block

When you know that a statement can cause an error, you should wrap that statement in a `try` block. For example, parsing from text to a number can cause an error. Any statements in the `catch` block will be executed only if an exception is thrown by a statement in the `try` block.

We don't have to do anything inside the `catch` block. Let's see this in action:

1. Use your preferred coding tool to add a new **Console App**/`console` project named `HandlingExceptions` to the `Chapter03` workspace/solution.

   • In Visual Studio Code, select `HandlingExceptions` as the active OmniSharp project.

2. Type statements to prompt the user to enter their age and then write their age to the console, as shown in the following code:

```
WriteLine("Before parsing");
Write("What is your age? ");
string? input = ReadLine(); // or use "49" in a notebook
try
{
  int age = int.Parse(input);
  WriteLine($"You are {age} years old.");
}
catch
{
}
WriteLine("After parsing");
```

You will see the following compiler message: `Warning CS8604 Possible null reference argument for parameter 's' in 'int int.Parse(string s)'`.

By default, in new .NET 6 projects, Microsoft has enabled nullable reference types so you will see many more compiler warnings like this. In production code, you should add code to check for `null` and handle that possibility appropriately. In this book, I will not include these `null` checks because the code samples are not designed to be production-quality and having `null` checks everywhere will clutter the code and use up valuable pages.

You will see hundreds more examples of potentially `null` variables throughout the code samples in this book. Those warnings are safe to ignore for the book code examples. You only need similar warnings when you write your own production code. You will see more about null handling in *Chapter 6, Implementing Interfaces and Inheriting Classes.*

In this case, it is impossible for `input` to be `null` because the user must press *Enter* for `ReadLine` to return and that will return an empty `string`:

1. To disable the compiler warning, change `input` to `input!`. An exclamation mark `!` after an expression is called the **null-forgiving operator** and it disables the compiler warning. The **null-forgiving operator** has no effect at runtime. If the expression could evaluate to `null` at runtime, perhaps because we assigned it in another way, then an exception would be thrown.

   This code includes two messages to indicate *before* parsing and *after* parsing to make clearer the flow through the code. These will be especially useful as the example code grows more complex.

2. Run the code, enter 49, and view the result, as shown in the following output:

```
Before parsing
What is your age? 49
You are 49 years old.
After parsing
```

3. Run the code, enter Kermit, and view the result, as shown in the following output:

```
Before parsing
What is your age? Kermit
After parsing
```

When the code was executed, the error exception was caught and the default message and stack trace were not output, and the console app continued running. This is better than the default behavior, but it might be useful to see the type of error that occurred.

> **Good Practice:** You should never use an empty catch statement like this in production code because it "swallows" exceptions and hides potential problems. You should at least log the exception if you cannot or do not want to handle it properly, or rethrow it so that higher-level code can decide instead. You will learn about logging in *Chapter 4, Writing, Debugging, and Testing Functions*.

Catching all exceptions

To get information about any type of exception that might occur, you can declare a variable of type System.Exception to the catch block:

1. Add an exception variable declaration to the catch block and use it to write information about the exception to the console, as shown in the following code:

```
catch (Exception ex)
{
  WriteLine($"{ex.GetType()} says {ex.Message}");
}
```

2. Run the code, enter Kermit again, and view the result, as shown in the following output:

```
Before parsing
What is your age? Kermit
System.FormatException says Input string was not in a correct format.
After parsing
```

Catching specific exceptions

Now that we know which specific type of exception occurred, we can improve our code by catching just that type of exception and customizing the message that we display to the user:

1. Leave the existing `catch` block, and above it, add a new `catch` block for the format exception type, as shown in the following highlighted code:

```
catch (FormatException)
{
  WriteLine("The age you entered is not a valid number format.");
}
catch (Exception ex)
{
  WriteLine($"{ex.GetType()} says {ex.Message}");
}
```

2. Run the code, enter `Kermit` again, and view the result, as shown in the following output:

```
Before parsing
What is your age? Kermit
The age you entered is not a valid number format.
After parsing
```

The reason we want to leave the more general catch below is that there might be other types of exceptions that can occur.

3. Run the code, enter `9876543210`, and view the result, as shown in the following output:

```
Before parsing
What is your age? 9876543210
System.OverflowException says Value was either too large or too small for
an Int32.
After parsing
```

Let's add another `catch` block for this type of exception.

4. Leave the existing `catch` blocks, and add a new `catch` block for the overflow exception type, as shown in the following highlighted code:

```
catch (OverflowException)
{
  WriteLine("Your age is a valid number format but it is either too big
or small.");
}
catch (FormatException)
{
  WriteLine("The age you entered is not a valid number format.");
}
```

5. Run the code, enter 9876543210, and view the result, as shown in the following output:

```
Before parsing
What is your age? 9876543210
Your age is a valid number format but it is either too big or small.
After parsing
```

The order in which you catch exceptions is important. The correct order is related to the inheritance hierarchy of the exception types. You will learn about inheritance in *Chapter 5, Building Your Own Types with Object-Oriented Programming*. However, don't worry too much about this—the compiler will give you build errors if you get exceptions in the wrong order anyway.

 Good Practice: Avoid over-catching exceptions. They should often be allowed to propagate up the call stack to be handled at a level where more information is known about the circumstances that could change the logic of how they should be handled. You will learn about this in *Chapter 4, Writing, Debugging, and Testing Functions*.

Catching with filters

You can also add filters to a catch statement using the when keyword, as shown in the following code:

```
Write("Enter an amount: ");
string amount = ReadLine()!;
if (string.IsNullOrEmpty(amount)) return;

try
{
  decimal amountValue = decimal.Parse(amount);
  WriteLine($"Amount formatted as currency: {amountValue:C}");
}
catch (FormatException) when (amount.Contains("$"))
{
  WriteLine("Amounts cannot use the dollar sign!");
}
catch (FormatException)
{
  WriteLine("Amounts must only contain digits!");
}
```

Checking for overflow

Earlier, we saw that when casting between number types, it was possible to lose information, for example, when casting from a long variable to an int variable. If the value stored in a type is too big, it will overflow.

Throwing overflow exceptions with the checked statement

The checked statement tells .NET to throw an exception when an overflow happens instead of allowing it to happen silently, which is done by default for performance reasons.

We will set the initial value of an int variable to its maximum value minus one. Then, we will increment it several times, outputting its value each time. Once it gets above its maximum value, it overflows to its minimum value and continues incrementing from there. Let's see this in action:

1. Use your preferred coding tool to add a new **Console App**/console named CheckingForOverflow to the Chapter03 workspace/solution.

   - In Visual Studio Code, select CheckingForOverflow as the active OmniSharp project.

2. In Program.cs, delete the existing statements and then type statements to declare and assign an integer to one less than its maximum possible value, and then increment it and write its value to the console three times, as shown in the following code:

```
int x = int.MaxValue - 1;
WriteLine($"Initial value: {x}");
x++;
WriteLine($"After incrementing: {x}");
x++;
WriteLine($"After incrementing: {x}");
x++;
WriteLine($"After incrementing: {x}");
```

3. Run the code and view the result that shows the value overflowing silently and wrapping around to large negative values, as shown in the following output:

```
Initial value: 2147483646
After incrementing: 2147483647
After incrementing: -2147483648
After incrementing: -2147483647
```

4. Now, let's get the compiler to warn us about the overflow by wrapping the statements using a checked statement block, as shown highlighted in the following code:

```
checked
{
    int x = int.MaxValue - 1;
    WriteLine($"Initial value: {x}");
    x++;
    WriteLine($"After incrementing: {x}");
    x++;
    WriteLine($"After incrementing: {x}");
```

```
    x++;
    WriteLine($"After incrementing: {x}");
}
```

5. Run the code and view the result that shows the overflow being checked and causing an exception to be thrown, as shown in the following output:

```
Initial value: 2147483646
After incrementing: 2147483647
Unhandled Exception: System.OverflowException: Arithmetic operation
resulted in an overflow.
```

6. Just like any other exception, we should wrap these statements in a try statement block and display a nicer error message for the user, as shown in the following code:

```
try
{
    // previous code goes here
}
catch (OverflowException)
{
    WriteLine("The code overflowed but I caught the exception.");
}
```

7. Run the code and view the result, as shown in the following output:

```
Initial value: 2147483646
After incrementing: 2147483647
The code overflowed but I caught the exception.
```

Disabling compiler overflow checks with the unchecked statement

The previous section was about the default overflow behavior at *runtime* and how to use the checked statement to change that behavior. This section is about *compile-time* overflow behavior and how to use the unchecked statement to change that behavior.

A related keyword is unchecked. This keyword switches off overflow checks performed by the compiler within a block of code. Let's see how to do this:

1. Type the following statement at the end of the previous statements. The compiler will not compile this statement because it knows it would overflow:

```
int y = int.MaxValue + 1;
```

2. Hover your mouse pointer over the error, and note that a compile-time check is shown as an error message, as shown in *Figure 3.1*:

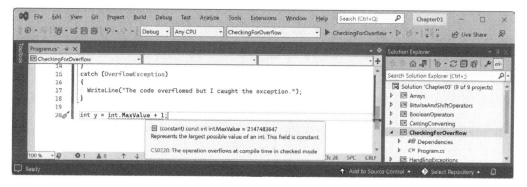

Figure 3.1: A compile-time check in the PROBLEMS window

3. To disable compile-time checks, wrap the statement in an unchecked block, write the value of y to the console, decrement it, and repeat, as shown in the following code:

```
unchecked
{
    int y = int.MaxValue + 1;
    WriteLine($"Initial value: {y}");
    y--;
    WriteLine($"After decrementing: {y}");
    y--;
    WriteLine($"After decrementing: {y}");
}
```

4. Run the code and view the results, as shown in the following output:

```
Initial value: -2147483648
After decrementing: 2147483647
After decrementing: 2147483646
```

Of course, it would be rare that you would want to explicitly switch off a check like this because it allows an overflow to occur. But perhaps you can think of a scenario where you might want that behavior.

Practicing and exploring

Test your knowledge and understanding by answering some questions, getting some hands-on practice, and exploring with deeper research this chapter's topics.

Exercise 3.1 – Test your knowledge

Answer the following questions:

1. What happens when you divide an int variable by 0?
2. What happens when you divide a double variable by 0?
3. What happens when you overflow an int variable, that is, set it to a value beyond its range?

4. What is the difference between x = y++; and x = ++y;?

5. What is the difference between break, continue, and return when used inside a loop statement?

6. What are the three parts of a for statement and which of them are required?

7. What is the difference between the = and == operators?

8. Does the following statement compile?

```
for ( ; ; ) ;
```

9. What does the underscore _ represent in a switch expression?

10. What interface must an object "implement" to be enumerated over using the foreach statement?

Exercise 3.2 – Explore loops and overflow

What will happen if this code executes?

```
int max = 500;
for (byte i = 0; i < max; i++)
{
  WriteLine(i);
}
```

Create a console app in Chapter03 named Ch03Ex02LoopsAndOverflow and enter the preceding code. Run the console app and view the output. What happens?

What code could you add (don't change any of the preceding code) to warn us about the problem?

Exercise 3.3 – Practice loops and operators

FizzBuzz is a group game for children to teach them about division. Players take turns to count incrementally, replacing any number divisible by three with the word *fizz*, any number divisible by five with the word *buzz*, and any number divisible by both with *fizzbuzz*.

Create a console app in Chapter03 named Ch03Ex03FizzBuzz that outputs a simulated FizzBuzz game that counts up to 100. The output should look something like *Figure 3.2*:

Figure 3.2: A simulated FizzBuzz game output

Exercise 3.4 – Practice exception handling

Create a console app in `Chapter03` named `Ch03Ex04Exceptions` that asks the user for two numbers in the range 0-255 and then divides the first number by the second:

```
Enter a number between 0 and 255: 100
Enter another number between 0 and 255: 8
100 divided by 8 is 12
```

Write exception handlers to catch any thrown errors, as shown in the following output:

```
Enter a number between 0 and 255: apples
Enter another number between 0 and 255: bananas
FormatException: Input string was not in a correct format.
```

Exercise 3.5 – Test your knowledge of operators

What are the values of x and y after the following statements execute? Create a console app in `Chapter03` named `Ch03Ex05Operators` to test your assumptions:

1. Increment and addition operators:

   ```
   x = 3;
   y = 2 + ++x;
   ```

2. Binary shift operators:

   ```
   x = 3 << 2;
   y = 10 >> 1;
   ```

3. Bitwise operators:

   ```
   x = 10 & 8;
   y = 10 | 7;
   ```

Exercise 3.6 – Explore topics

Use the links on the following page to learn about the topics covered in this chapter in more detail:

```
https://github.com/markjprice/cs11dotnet7/blob/main/book-links.md#chapter-3---
controlling-flow-converting-types-and-handling-exceptions
```

Summary

In this chapter, you learned how to:

- Use operators to perform simple tasks.
- Use branch and loop statements to implement logic.
- Work with single- and multi-dimensional arrays.
- Convert between types.
- Catch exceptions.

You are now ready to learn how to reuse blocks of code by defining functions, how to pass values into them and get values back, and how to track down bugs in your code and squash them using debugging and testing tools!

4

Writing, Debugging, and Testing Functions

This chapter is about writing functions to reuse code, debugging logic errors during development, logging exceptions during runtime, unit testing your code to remove bugs, and ensuring stability and reliability.

This chapter covers the following topics:

- Writing functions
- Debugging during development
- Hot reloading during development
- Logging during development and runtime
- Unit testing
- Throwing and catching exceptions in functions

Writing functions

A fundamental principle of programming is **Don't Repeat Yourself (DRY)**.

While programming, if you find yourself writing the same statements over and over again, then turn those statements into a function. Functions are like tiny programs that complete one small task. For example, you might write a function to calculate sales tax and then reuse that function in many places in a financial application.

Like programs, functions usually have inputs and outputs. They are sometimes described as black boxes, where you feed some raw materials in one end, and a manufactured item emerges at the other. Once created and thoroughly debugged and tested, you don't need to think about how they work.

Understanding top-level programs and functions

In *Chapter 1, Hello, C#! Welcome, .NET!*, we learned that since .NET 6, the default project template for console apps uses the top-level program feature introduced with C# 9.

Once you start writing functions, it is important to understand how they work with the automatically generated `Program` class and its `<Main>$` method.

In `Program.cs`, you might write statements to import a class, call one of its methods, and define and call a function, as shown in the following code:

```csharp
using static System.Console;

WriteLine("Hello, World!");

DoSomething(); // call the function

void DoSomething() // define a function
{
  WriteLine("Doing something!");
}
```

The compiler automatically generates a `Program` class with a `<Main>$` function, then moves your statements and function inside the `<Main>$` method, and renames the function, as shown highlighted in the following code:

```csharp
using static System.Console;

partial class Program
{
  static void <Main>$(String[] args)
  {
    WriteLine("Hello, World!");

    <<Main>$>g__DoSomething|0_0(); // call the function

    void <<Main>$>g__DoSomething|0_0() // define a local function
    {
      WriteLine("Doing something!");
    }
  }
}
```

For the compiler to know what statements need to go where, you must follow some rules:

- Import statements (`using`) must go at the top of the `Program.cs` file.
- Statements that will go in the `<Main>$` function must go in the middle of the `Program.cs` file.
- Functions must go at the bottom of the `Program.cs` file. They will become **local functions**.

The last point is important because local functions have limitations, as you will see later in this chapter.

 You are about to see some C# keywords like `static` and `partial` that will be formally introduced in *Chapter 5, Building Your Own Types with Object-Oriented Programming*.

A better approach is to define the function in a separate file and to add it as a `static` member of the `Program` class, as shown in the following code:

```csharp
// in a file named Program.Functions.cs
partial class Program
{
  static void DoSomething() // define a non-local static function
  {
    WriteLine("Doing something!");
  }
}

// in the Program.cs file
using static System.Console;

WriteLine("Hello, World!");

DoSomething(); // call the function
```

The compiler defines a `Program` class with a `<Main>$` function and moves your statements inside the `<Main>$` method, and then merges your function as a member of the `Program` class, as shown in the following highlighted code:

```csharp
using static System.Console;

partial class Program
{
  static void <Main>$(String[] args)
  {
    WriteLine("Hello, World!");
    DoSomething(); // call the function
  }

  static void DoSomething() // define a function
  {
    WriteLine("Doing something!");
  }
}
```

Good Practice: Create any functions that you will call in `Program.cs` in a separate file and manually define them inside a `partial Program` class. This will merge them into the automatically generated `Program` class *at the same level* as the `<Main>$` method, instead of as local functions *inside* the `<Main>$` method.

Times table example

Let's say that you want to help your child learn their times tables, so you want to make it easy to generate a times table for a number, such as the 7 times table:

```
1 x 7 = 7
2 x 7 = 14
3 x 7 = 21
...
10 x 7 = 70
11 x 7 = 77
12 x 7 = 84
```

Most times tables have either 10, 12, or 20 rows, depending on how advanced the child is.

You learned about the `for` statement earlier in this book, so you know that it can be used to generate repeated lines of output when there is a regular pattern, such as a 7 times table with 12 rows, as shown in the following code:

```
for (int row = 1; row <= 12; row++)
{
  Console.WriteLine($"{row} x 7 = {row * 7}");
}
```

However, instead of always outputting the 7 times table with 12 rows, we want to make this more flexible so it can output any size times table for any number. We can do this by creating a function.

Writing a times table function

Let's explore functions by creating one to output any times table for numbers 0 to 255 of any size up to 255 rows (but it defaults to 12 rows):

1. Use your preferred coding tool to create a new project, as defined in the following list:

    • Project template: **Console App**/`console`
    • Project file and folder: `WritingFunctions`
    • Workspace/solution file and folder: `Chapter04`

2. Open WritingFunctions.csproj, and after the <PropertyGroup> section, add a new <ItemGroup>
    section to statically import System.Console for all C# files using the implicit usings .NET
    SDK feature, as shown in the following markup:

```
<ItemGroup>
  <Using Include="System.Console" Static="true" />
</ItemGroup>
```

3. Add a new class file to the project named Program.Functions.cs.

    •   In Visual Studio 2022, navigate to **Project** | **Add Class...**, type the name, and then click
        Add.
    •   In Visual Studio Code, click the **New File...** button.

4. In Program.Functions.cs, write statements to define a function named TimesTable in the
    partial Program class, as shown in the following code:

```
partial class Program
{
  static void TimesTable(byte number, byte size = 12)
  {
    WriteLine($"This is the {number} times table with {size} rows:");
    for (int row = 1; row <= size; row++)
    {
      WriteLine($"{row} x {number} = {row * number}");
    }
    WriteLine();
  }
}
```

In the preceding code, note the following:

   •   TimesTable must have a byte value passed to it as a parameter named number.
   •   TimesTable can optionally have a byte value passed to it as a parameter named size.
       If a value is not passed, it defaults to 12.
   •   TimesTable is a static method because it will be called by the static method <Main>$.
   •   TimesTable does not return a value to the caller, so it is declared with the void keyword
       before its name.
   •   TimesTable uses a for statement to output the times table for the number passed to it
       with a number of rows equal to size.

5. In Program.cs, delete the existing statements and then call the function. Pass in a byte value
    for the number parameter, for example, 7, as shown in the following code:

```
TimesTable(7);
```

6.   Run the code and then view the result, as shown in the following output:

```
This is the 7 times table with 12 rows:
1 x 7 = 7
2 x 7 = 14
3 x 7 = 21
4 x 7 = 28
5 x 7 = 35
6 x 7 = 42
7 x 7 = 49
8 x 7 = 56
9 x 7 = 63
10 x 7 = 70
11 x 7 = 77
12 x 7 = 84
```

7.   Set the `size` parameter to 20, as shown in the following code:

```
TimesTable(7, 20);
```

8.   Run the console app and confirm that the times table now has twenty rows.

 Good Practice: If a function has one or more parameters where just passing the values may not provide enough meaning, then you can optionally specify the name of the parameter as well as its value, as shown in the following code: `TimesTable(number: 7, size: 10)`.

9.   Change the number passed into the `TimesTable` function to other byte values between 0 and 255 and confirm that the output times tables are correct.

10. Note that if you try to pass a non-byte number, for example, an `int`, `double`, or `string`, an error is returned, as shown in the following output:

```
Error: (1,12): error CS1503: Argument 1: cannot convert from 'int' to
'byte'
```

A brief aside about arguments and parameters

In daily usage, most developers will use the terms **argument** and **parameter** interchangeably. Strictly speaking, the two terms have specific and subtly different meanings. But just like a person can be both a parent and a doctor, the two terms often apply to the same thing.

A *parameter* is a variable in a function definition. For example, `startDate` is a parameter of the `Hire` function, as shown in the following code:

```
void Hire(DateTime startDate)
{
    // implementation
}
```

When a method is called, an *argument* is the data you pass into the method's parameters. For example, when is a variable passed as an argument to the `Hire` function, as shown in the following code:

```
DateTime when = new(year: 2022, month: 11, day: 8);
Hire(when);
```

You might prefer to specify the parameter name when passing the argument, as shown in the following code:

```
DateTime when = new(year: 2022, month: 11, day: 8);
Hire(startDate: when);
```

When talking about the call to the `Hire` function, `startDate` is the parameter, and when is the argument.

> If you read the official Microsoft documentation, they use the phrase "named and option-al arguments" and "named and optional parameters" interchangeably, as shown at the following link: `https://learn.microsoft.com/en-us/dotnet/csharp/programming-guide/classes-and-structs/named-and-optional-arguments`.

It gets complicated because a single object can act as both a parameter and an argument depending on context. For example, within the `Hire` function implementation, the `startDate` parameter could be passed as an argument to another function like `SaveToDatabase`, as shown in the following code:

```
void Hire(DateTime startDate)
{
    ...
    SaveToDatabase(startDate, employeeRecord);
    ...
}
```

Naming things is one of the hardest parts of computing. A classic example is the parameter to the most important function in C#, `Main`. It defines a parameter named args, short for "arguments", as shown in the following code:

```
static void Main(String[] args)
{
    ...
}
```

To summarize, parameters define inputs to a function, and arguments are passed to a function when calling the function.

> **Good Practice:** Try to use the correct term depending on the context, but do not get pedan-tic with other developers if they "misuse" a term. I must have used the terms "parameter" and "argument" thousands of times in this book. I'm sure some of those times I've been imprecise. Please do not @ me about it. ☺

Writing a function that returns a value

The previous function performed actions (looping and writing to the console), but it did not return a value. Let's say that you need to calculate sales or **value-added tax** (**VAT**). In Europe, VAT rates can range from 8% in Switzerland to 27% in Hungary. In the United States, state sales taxes can range from 0% in Oregon to 8.25% in California.

 Tax rates change all the time, and they vary based on many factors. The values used in this example do not need to be accurate.

Let's implement a function to calculate taxes in various regions around the world:

1. In `Program.Functions.cs`, write a function named `CalculateTax`, as shown in the following code:

```
partial class Program
{
  ...

  static decimal CalculateTax(
    decimal amount, string twoLetterRegionCode)
  {
    decimal rate = 0.0M;

    switch (twoLetterRegionCode)
    {
      case "CH": // Switzerland
        rate = 0.08M;
        break;
      case "DK": // Denmark
      case "NO": // Norway
        rate = 0.25M;
        break;
      case "GB": // United Kingdom
      case "FR": // France
        rate = 0.2M;
        break;
      case "HU": // Hungary
        rate = 0.27M;
        break;
      case "OR": // Oregon
      case "AK": // Alaska
      case "MT": // Montana
        rate = 0.0M;
```

```
          break;
        case "ND": // North Dakota
        case "WI": // Wisconsin
        case "ME": // Maine
        case "VA": // Virginia
          rate = 0.05M;
          break;
        case "CA": // California
          rate = 0.0825M;
          break;
        default: // most US states
          rate = 0.06M;
          break;
    }
    return amount * rate;
  }
}
```

In the preceding code, note the following:

- CalculateTax has two inputs: a parameter named amount that will be the amount of money spent, and a parameter named twoLetterRegionCode that will be the region the amount is spent in.

- CalculateTax will perform a calculation using a switch statement and then return the sales tax or VAT owed on the amount as a decimal value; so, before the name of the function, we have declared the data type of the return value to be decimal.

2. Comment out any TimesTable method calls and then call the CalculateTax method, passing values for the amount such as 149 and a valid region code such as FR, as shown in the following code:

```
decimal taxToPay = CalculateTax(amount: 149, twoLetterRegionCode: "FR");
WriteLine($"You must pay {taxToPay} in tax.");
```

3. Run the code and view the result, as shown in the following output:

```
You must pay 29.8 in tax.
```

We could format the taxToPay output as currency by using {taxToPay:C}, but it will use your local culture to decide how to format the currency symbol and decimals. For example, for me in the UK, I would see £29.80.

Can you think of any problems with the CalculateTax function as written? What would happen if the user enters a code such as fr or UK? How could you rewrite the function to improve it? Would using a switch *expression* instead of a switch *statement* be clearer?

Converting numbers from cardinal to ordinal

Numbers that are used to count are called **cardinal** numbers, for example, 1, 2, and 3, whereas numbers used to order are **ordinal** numbers, for example, 1st, 2nd, and 3rd. Let's create a function to convert cardinals to ordinals:

1. In `Program.Functions.cs`, write a function named `CardinalToOrdinal` that converts a cardinal `int` value into an ordinal `string` value; for example, it converts 1 into 1st, 2 into 2nd, and so on, as shown in the following code:

```csharp
static string CardinalToOrdinal(int number)
{
    int lastTwoDigits = number % 100;

    switch (lastTwoDigits)
    {
        case 11: // special cases for 11th to 13th
        case 12:
        case 13:
            return $"{number:N0}th";
        default:
            int lastDigit = number % 10;

            string suffix = lastDigit switch
            {
                1 => "st",
                2 => "nd",
                3 => "rd",
                _ => "th"
            };

            return $"{number:N0}{suffix}";
    }
}
```

From the preceding code, note the following:

- `CardinalToOrdinal` has one input, a parameter of the `int` type named `number`, and one output: a return value of the `string` type.
- A `switch` *statement* is used to handle the special cases of 11, 12, and 13.
- A `switch` *expression* then handles all other cases: if the last digit is 1, then use `st` as the suffix; if the last digit is 2, then use `nd` as the suffix; if the last digit is 3, then use `rd` as the suffix; and if the last digit is anything else, then use `th` as the suffix.

2. In `Program.Functions.cs`, write a function named `RunCardinalToOrdinal` that uses a `for` statement to loop from 1 to 150, calling the `CardinalToOrdinal` function for each number and writing the returned `string` to the console, separated by a space character, as shown in the following code:

```
static void RunCardinalToOrdinal()
{
  for (int number = 1; number <= 150; number++)
  {
    Write($"{CardinalToOrdinal(number)} ");
  }
  WriteLine();
}
```

3. In `Program.cs`, comment out the `CalculateTax` statements, and call the `RunCardinalToOrdinal` method, as shown in the following code:

```
RunCardinalToOrdinal();
```

4. Run the console app and view the results, as shown in the following output:

```
1st 2nd 3rd 4th 5th 6th 7th 8th 9th 10th 11th 12th 13th 14th 15th 16th
17th 18th 19th 20th 21st 22nd 23rd 24th 25th 26th 27th 28th 29th 30th
31st 32nd 33rd 34th 35th 36th 37th 38th 39th 40th 41st 42nd 43rd 44th
45th 46th 47th 48th 49th 50th 51st 52nd 53rd 54th 55th 56th 57th 58th
59th 60th 61st 62nd 63rd 64th 65th 66th 67th 68th 69th 70th 71st 72nd
73rd 74th 75th 76th 77th 78th 79th 80th 81st 82nd 83rd 84th 85th 86th
87th 88th 89th 90th 91st 92nd 93rd 94th 95th 96th 97th 98th 99th 100th
101st 102nd 103rd 104th 105th 106th 107th 108th 109th 110th 111th 112th
113th 114th 115th 116th 117th 118th 119th 120th 121st 122nd 123rd 124th
125th 126th 127th 128th 129th 130th 131st 132nd 133rd 134th 135th 136th
137th 138th 139th 140th 141st 142nd 143rd 144th 145th 146th 147th 148th
149th 150th
```

5. In the `RunCardinalToOrdinal` function, change the maximum number to `1500`.

6. Run the console app and view the results, as shown partially in the following output:

```
1,480th 1,481st 1,482nd 1,483rd 1,484th 1,485th 1,486th 1,487th 1,488th
1,489th 1,490th 1,491st 1,492nd 1,493rd 1,494th 1,495th 1,496th 1,497th
1,498th 1,499th 1,500th
```

Calculating factorials with recursion

The factorial of 5 is 120, because factorials are calculated by multiplying the starting number by one less than itself, and then by one less again, and so on, until the number is reduced to 1. An example can be seen here: 5 x 4 x 3 x 2 x 1 = 120.

The factorial function is defined for non-negative integers only, i.e. for 0, 1, 2, 3, and so on, and it is defined as:

```
0! = 1
n! = n × (n - 1)!, for n ∈ { 1, 2, 3, ... }
```

Factorials are written like this: 5!, where the exclamation mark is read as "bang," so 5! = 120, that is, *five bang equals one hundred and twenty*. Bang is a good term to use in the context of factorials because they increase in size very rapidly, just like an explosion.

We will write a function named `Factorial`; this will calculate the factorial for an `int` passed to it as a parameter. We will use a clever technique called **recursion**, which means a function that calls itself within its implementation, either directly or indirectly:

1. In `Program.Functions.cs`, write a function named `Factorial`, as shown in the following code:

    ```
    static int Factorial(int number)
    {
      if (number < 0)
      {
          throw new ArgumentException(message:
            $"The factorial function is defined for non-negative integers
            only. Input: {number}",
            paramName: nameof(number));
      }
      else if (number == 0)
      {
        return 1;
      }
      else
      {
        return number * Factorial(number - 1);
      }
    }
    ```

As before, there are several noteworthy elements of the preceding code, including the following:

*   If the input parameter `number` is negative, `Factorial` throws an exception.
*   If the input parameter `number` is zero, `Factorial` returns 1.
*   If the input parameter `number` is more than 1, which it will be in all other cases, `Factorial` multiplies the number by the result of calling itself and passing one less than `number`. This makes the function recursive.

More Information: Recursion is clever, but it can lead to problems, such as a stack overflow due to too many function calls because memory is used to store data on every function call, and it eventually uses too much. Iteration is a more practical, if less succinct, solution in languages such as C#. You can read more about this at the following link: `https://en.wikipedia.org/wiki/Recursion_(computer_science)#Recursion_versus_iteration`.

2. In `Program.Functions.cs`, write a function named `RunFactorial` that uses a `for` statement to output the factorials of numbers from 1 to 15, calls the `Factorial` function inside its loop, and then outputs the result, formatted using the code `N0`, which means number format using thousand separators with zero decimal places, as shown in the following code:

```
static void RunFactorial()
{
  for (int i = 1; i <= 15; i++)
  {
    WriteLine($"{i}! = {Factorial(i):N0}");
  }
}
```

3. Comment out the `RunCardinalToOrdinal` method call and call the `RunFactorial` method.

4. Run the code and view the results, as shown in the following output:

```
1! = 1
2! = 2
3! = 6
4! = 24
5! = 120
6! = 720
7! = 5,040
8! = 40,320
9! = 362,880
10! = 3,628,800
11! = 39,916,800
12! = 479,001,600
13! = 1,932,053,504
14! = 1,278,945,280
15! = 2,004,310,016
```

It is not immediately obvious in the previous output, but factorials of 13 and higher overflow the `int` type because they are so big. 12! is 479,001,600, which is about half a billion. The maximum positive value that can be stored in an `int` variable is about two billion. 13! is 6,227,020,800, which is about six billion, and when stored in a 32-bit integer it overflows silently without showing any problems.

What should you do to get notified when an overflow happens? Of course, we could solve the problem for 13! and 14! by using a `long` (64-bit integer) instead of an `int` (32-bit integer), but we will quickly hit the overflow limit again.

The point of this section is to understand and show you that numbers can overflow, and not specifically how to calculate factorials higher than 12! Let's take a look:

1. Modify the `Factorial` function to check for overflows, as shown highlighted in the following code:

    ```
    checked // for overflow
    {
        return number * Factorial(number - 1);
    }
    ```

2. Modify the `RunFactorial` function to change the starting number to be -2 and to handle overflow and other exceptions when calling the `Factorial` function, as shown highlighted in the following code:

    ```
    static void RunFactorial()
    {
        for (int i = -2; i <= 15; i++)
        {
            try
            {
                WriteLine($"{i}! = {Factorial(i):N0}");
            }
            catch (OverflowException)
            {
                WriteLine($"{i}! is too big for a 32-bit integer.");
            }
            catch (Exception ex)
            {
                WriteLine($"{i}! throws {ex.GetType()}: {ex.Message}");
            }
        }
    }
    ```

3. Run the code and view the results, as shown in the following output:

    ```
    -2! throws System.ArgumentException: The factorial function is defined
    for non-negative integers only. Input: -2 (Parameter 'number')
    -1! throws System.ArgumentException: The factorial function is defined
    for non-negative integers only. Input: -1 (Parameter 'number')
    0! = 1
    1! = 1
    2! = 2
    3! = 6
    ```

```
 4! = 24
 5! = 120
 6! = 720
 7! = 5,040
 8! = 40,320
 9! = 362,880
10! = 3,628,800
11! = 39,916,800
12! = 479,001,600
13! is too big for a 32-bit integer.
14! is too big for a 32-bit integer.
15! is too big for a 32-bit integer.
```

Documenting functions with XML comments

By default, when calling a function such as CardinalToOrdinal, code editors will show a tooltip with basic information, as shown in *Figure 4.1*:

Figure 4.1: A tooltip showing the default simple method signature

Let's improve the tooltip by adding extra information:

1. If you are using Visual Studio Code with the **C#** extension, you should navigate to **View | Command Palette | Preferences: Open Settings (UI)**, and then search for formatOnType and make sure that it is enabled. C# XML documentation comments are a built-in feature of Visual Studio 2022.

2. On the line above the CardinalToOrdinal function, type three forward slashes ///, and note that they are expanded into an XML comment that recognizes that the function has a single parameter named number, as shown in the following code:

```
/// <summary>
///
/// </summary>
/// <param name="number"></param>
/// <returns></returns>
```

3. Enter suitable information for the XML documentation comment for the `CardinalToOrdinal` function. Add a summary, and describe the input parameter and the return value, as shown highlighted in the following code:

```
/// <summary>
/// Pass a 32-bit integer and it will be converted into its ordinal
equivalent.
/// </summary>
/// <param name="number">Number as a cardinal value e.g. 1, 2, 3, and so
on.</param>
/// <returns>Number as an ordinal value e.g. 1st, 2nd, 3rd, and so on.</
returns>
```

4. Now, when calling the function, you will see more details, as shown in *Figure 4.2*:

Figure 4.2: A tooltip showing the more detailed method signature

It is worth emphasizing that this feature is primarily designed to be used with a tool that converts the comments into documentation, like Sandcastle, which you can read more about at the following link: `https://github.com/EWSoftware/SHFB`. The tooltips that appear while entering code or hovering over the function name are a secondary feature.

Local functions do not support XML comments because local functions cannot be used outside the member in which they are declared, so it makes no sense to generate documentation from them. Sadly, this also means no tooltip, which would still be useful, but neither Visual Studio 2022 nor Visual Studio Code recognize that.

 Good Practice: Add XML documentation comments to all your functions except local functions.

Using lambdas in function implementations

F# is Microsoft's strongly typed functional-first programming language that, like C#, compiles to IL to be executed by .NET. Functional languages evolved from lambda calculus, a computational system based only on functions. The code looks more like mathematical functions than steps in a recipe.

Some of the important attributes of functional languages are defined in the following list:

- **Modularity**: The same benefit of defining functions in C# applies to functional languages. Break up a large complex code base into smaller pieces.
- **Immutability**: Variables in the C# sense do not exist. Any data value inside a function cannot change. Instead, a new data value can be created from an existing one. This reduces bugs.
- **Maintainability**: Code is cleaner and clearer (for mathematically inclined programmers!).

Since C# 6, Microsoft has worked to add features to the language to support a more functional approach, for example, adding **tuples** and **pattern matching** in C# 7, **non-null reference types** in C# 8, and improving pattern matching and adding records, that is, **immutable objects**, in C# 9.

In C# 6, Microsoft added support for **expression-bodied function members.** We will look at an example of this now. In C#, lambdas are the use of the => character to indicate a return value from a function.

The **Fibonacci sequence** of numbers always starts with 0 and 1. Then the rest of the sequence is generated using the rule of adding together the previous two numbers, as shown in the following sequence of numbers:

$$0\ 1\ 1\ 2\ 3\ 5\ 8\ 13\ 21\ 34\ 55\ ...$$

The next term in the sequence would be 34 + 55, which is 89.

We will use the Fibonacci sequence to illustrate the difference between an imperative and declarative function implementation:

1. In `Program.Functions.cs`, write a function named `FibImperative` that will be written in an imperative style, as shown in the following code:

```csharp
static int FibImperative(int term)
{
  if (term == 1)
  {
    return 0;
  }
  else if (term == 2)
  {
    return 1;
  }
  else
  {
    return FibImperative(term - 1) + FibImperative(term - 2);
  }
}
```

2. In `Program.Functions.cs`, write a function named `RunFibImperative` that calls `FibImperative` inside a for statement that loops from 1 to 30, as shown in the following code:

```csharp
static void RunFibImperative()
```

```
{
  for (int i = 1; i <= 30; i++)
  {
    WriteLine("The {0} term of the Fibonacci sequence is {1:N0}.",
      arg0: CardinalToOrdinal(i),
      arg1: FibImperative(term: i));
  }
}
```

3. In `Program.cs`, comment out the other method calls and call the `RunFibImperative` method.

4. Run the console app and view the results, as shown in the following partial output:

```
The 1st term of the Fibonacci sequence is 0.
The 2nd term of the Fibonacci sequence is 1.
The 3rd term of the Fibonacci sequence is 1.
The 4th term of the Fibonacci sequence is 2.
The 5th term of the Fibonacci sequence is 3.
The 6th term of the Fibonacci sequence is 5.
The 7th term of the Fibonacci sequence is 8.
...
The 28th term of the Fibonacci sequence is 196,418.
The 29th term of the Fibonacci sequence is 317,811.
The 30th term of the Fibonacci sequence is 514,229.
```

5. In `Program.Functions.cs`, write a function named `FibFunctional` written in a declarative style, as shown in the following code:

```
static int FibFunctional(int term) =>
  term switch
  {
    1 => 0,
    2 => 1,
    _ => FibFunctional(term - 1) + FibFunctional(term - 2)
  };
```

6. In `Program.Functions.cs`, write a function to call it inside a `for` statement that loops from 1 to 30, as shown in the following code:

```
static void RunFibFunctional()
{
  for (int i = 1; i <= 30; i++)
  {
    WriteLine("The {0} term of the Fibonacci sequence is {1:N0}.",
      arg0: CardinalToOrdinal(i),
      arg1: FibFunctional(term: i));
  }
}
```

7. In `Program.cs`, comment out the `RunFibImperative` method call, and call the `RunFibFunctional` method.

8. Run the code and view the results (which will be the same as before).

Debugging during development

In this section, you will learn how to debug problems at development time. You must use a code editor that has debugging tools, such as Visual Studio 2022 or Visual Studio Code. At the time of writing, you cannot use .NET Interactive Notebooks to debug code, but this is expected to be added in the future.

 More Information: Some people find it tricky setting up the OmniSharp debugger for Visual Studio Code. I have included instructions for the most common issues, but if you still have trouble, try reading the information at the following link: `https://github.com/OmniSharp/omnisharp-vscode/blob/master/debugger.md`.

Using the Visual Studio Code integrated terminal during debugging

By default, OmniSharp sets the console to use the internal console during debugging, which does not allow interactions like entering text from the `ReadLine` method.

To improve the experience, we can change a setting to use the integrated terminal instead:

1. In any project where you want to set breakpoints and step through code, in the `.vscode` folder, open the `launch.json` file.

2. Change the `console` setting from `internalConsole` to `integratedTerminal`, as shown highlighted in the following partial configuration:

```
{
    "version": "0.2.0",
    "configurations": [
        {
            ...
            "console": "integratedTerminal",
            ...
        }
    ]
}
```

Creating code with a deliberate bug

Let's explore debugging by creating a console app with a deliberate bug that we will then use the debugger tools in your code editor to track down and fix:

1. Use your preferred coding tool to add a new **Console App**/console project named Debugging to the Chapter04 workspace/solution.

    *   In Visual Studio Code, select Debugging as the active OmniSharp project. When you see the pop-up warning message saying that required assets are missing, click **Yes** to add them.

    *   In Visual Studio 2022, set the startup project for the solution to the current selection.

2. Modify Debugging.csproj to statically import System.Console for all code files.

3. In Program.cs, at the bottom of the file, add a function with a deliberate bug, as shown in the following code:

```
double Add(double a, double b)
{
  return a * b; // deliberate bug!
}
```

4. Above the Add function, write statements to declare and set some variables and then add them together using the buggy function, as shown in the following code:

```
double a = 4.5;
double b = 2.5;
double answer = Add(a, b);

WriteLine($"{a} + {b} = {answer}");
WriteLine("Press ENTER to end the app.");
ReadLine(); // wait for user to press ENTER
```

5. Run the console application and view the result, as shown in the following output:

```
4.5 + 2.5 = 11.25
Press ENTER to end the app.
```

    But wait, there's a bug! 4.5 added to 2.5 should be 7, not 11.25!

We will use the debugging tools to hunt for and squish the bug.

Setting a breakpoint and starting debugging

Breakpoints allow us to mark a line of code that we want to pause at to inspect the program state and find bugs.

Using Visual Studio 2022

Let's set a breakpoint and then start debugging using Visual Studio 2022:

1. Click in line 1, which is the statement that declares the variable named a.

2. Navigate to **Debug | Toggle Breakpoint** or press *F9*. A red circle will appear in the margin bar on the left-hand side and the statement will be highlighted in red to indicate that a breakpoint has been set, as shown in *Figure 4.3*:

Figure 4.3: Toggling breakpoints using Visual Studio 2022

Breakpoints can be toggled off with the same action. You can also left-click in the margin to toggle a breakpoint on and off, or right-click a breakpoint to see more options, such as delete, disable, or edit conditions or actions for an existing breakpoint.

3. Navigate to **Debug | Start Debugging** or press *F5*. Visual Studio starts the console application and then pauses when it hits the breakpoint. This is known as break mode. Extra windows titled **Locals** (showing current values of local variables), **Watch 1** (showing any watch expressions you have defined), **Call Stack**, **Exception Settings**, and **Immediate Window** appear. The **Debugging** toolbar appears. The line that will be executed next is highlighted in yellow, and a yellow arrow points at the line from the margin bar, as shown in *Figure 4.4*:

Figure 4.4: Break mode in Visual Studio 2022

If you do not want to see how to use Visual Studio Code to start debugging, then you can skip the next section and continue to the section titled *Navigating with the debugging toolbar*.

Navigating with the debugging toolbar

Visual Studio Code shows a floating toolbar with buttons to make it easy to access debugging features. Visual Studio 2022 has two debug-related buttons in its **Standard** toolbar to start or continue debugging and to hot reload changes to the running code, and a separate **Debug** toolbar for the rest of the tools.

Both are shown in *Figure 4.5* and as described in the following list:

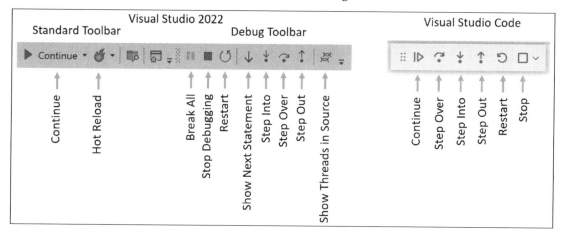

Figure 4.5: Debugging toolbars in Visual Studio 2022 and Visual Studio Code

- **Start/Continue/***F5*: This button is context-sensitive. It will either start a project running or continue running the project from the current position until it ends or hits a breakpoint.
- **Hot Reload:** This button will reload compiled code changes without needing to restart the app.
- **Break All:** This button will break into the next available line of code in a running app.
- **Stop Debugging/Stop/***Shift + F5* (red square): This button will stop the debugging session.
- **Restart/***Ctrl* or *Cmd + Shift + F5* (circular arrow): This button will stop and then immediately restart the program with the debugger attached again.
- **Show Next Statement:** This button will move the current cursor to the next statement that will execute.
- **Step Into/***F11*, **Step Over/***F10*, and **Step Out/***Shift + F11* (blue arrows over dots): These buttons step through the code statements in various ways, as you will see in a moment.
- **Show Threads in Source:** This button allows you to examine and work with threads in the application that you're debugging.

Using Visual Studio Code

Let's set a breakpoint and then start debugging using Visual Studio Code:

1. Click in line 1, which is the statement that declares the variable named a.

2. Navigate to **Run** | **Toggle Breakpoint** or press *F9*. A red circle will appear in the margin bar on the left-hand side to indicate that a breakpoint has been set.

    Breakpoints can be toggled off with the same action. You can also left-click in the margin to toggle a breakpoint on and off, or right-click to see more options, such as remove, edit, or disable an existing breakpoint; or add a breakpoint, conditional breakpoint, or logpoint when a breakpoint does not yet exist.

    Logpoints, also known as **tracepoints,** indicate that you want to record some information without having to stop executing the code at that point.

3. Navigate to **View** | **Run**, or in the left navigation bar you can click the **Run and Debug** icon (the triangle "play" button and "bug").

4. At the top of the **RUN AND DEBUG** window, click on the dropdown to the right of the **Start Debugging** button (green triangular "play" button) and select **.NET Core Launch (console) (Debugging)**, as shown in *Figure 4.6*:

Figure 4.6: Selecting the project to debug using Visual Studio Code

Good Practice: If you do not see a choice in the drop-down list for the **Debugging** project, it is because that project does not have the assets needed to debug. Those assets are stored in the .vscode folder. To create the .vscode folder for a project, navigate to **View** | **Command Palette**, select **OmniSharp: Select Project**, and then select the **Debugging** project. After a few seconds, when prompted with **Required assets to build and debug are missing from 'Debugging'. Add them?**, click **Yes** to add the missing assets.

5. At the top of the **RUN AND DEBUG** window, either click the **Start Debugging** button (green triangular "play" button), navigate to **Run | Start Debugging**, or press *F5*. Visual Studio Code starts the console app and then pauses when it hits the breakpoint. This is known as **break mode**. The line that will be executed next is highlighted in yellow, and a yellow block points at the line from the margin bar, as shown in *Figure 4.7*:

Figure 4.7: Break mode in Visual Studio Code

Debugging windows

While debugging, both Visual Studio Code and Visual Studio 2022 show extra windows that allow you to monitor useful information, such as variables, while you step through your code.

The most useful windows are described in the following list:

- **VARIABLES**, including **Locals**, which shows the name, value, and type for any local variables automatically. Keep an eye on this window while you step through your code.
- **WATCH**, or **Watch 1**, which shows the value of variables and expressions that you manually enter.
- **CALL STACK**, which shows the stack of function calls.
- **BREAKPOINTS**, which shows all your breakpoints and allows finer control over them.

When in break mode, there is also a useful window at the bottom of the edit area:

- **DEBUG CONSOLE** or **Immediate Window** enables live interaction with your code. You can interrogate the program state, for example, by entering the name of a variable. For example, you can ask a question such as "What is 1+2?" by typing 1+2 and pressing *Enter*.

Stepping through code

Let's explore some ways to step through the code using either Visual Studio or Visual Studio Code:

1. Navigate to **Run** or **Debug | Step Into**, click on the **Step Into** button in the toolbar, or press *F11*. The yellow highlight steps forward one line.
2. Navigate to **Run** or **Debug | Step Over**, click on the **Step Over** button in the toolbar, or press *F10*. The yellow highlight steps forward one line. At the moment, you can see that there is no difference between using **Step Into** or **Step Over**.

3. You should now be on the line that calls the Add method.

    The difference between **Step Into** and **Step Over** can be seen when you are about to execute a method call:

    • If you click on **Step Into**, the debugger steps *into* the method so that you can step through every line in that method.

    • If you click on **Step Over**, the whole method is executed in one go; it does not skip over the method without executing it.

4. Click on **Step Into** to step inside the method.

5. Hover your mouse pointer over the a or b parameters in the code editing window and note that a tooltip appears showing their current value.

6. Select the expression a * b, right-click the expression, and select **Add to Watch** or **Add Watch**. The expression is added to the **WATCH** or **Watch 1** window, showing that this operator is multiplying a by b to give the result 11.25.

7. In the **WATCH** or **Watch 1** window, right-click the expression and choose **Remove Expression** or **Delete Watch**.

8. Fix the bug by changing * to + in the Add function.

9. Stop debugging, recompile, and restart debugging by clicking the circular arrow **Restart** button or pressing *Ctrl* or *Cmd + Shift + F5*.

10. Step over the function, take a minute to note how it now calculates correctly, and click the **Continue** button or press *F5*.

11. With Visual Studio Code, note that when writing to the console during debugging, the output appears in the **DEBUG CONSOLE** window instead of the **TERMINAL** window, as shown in *Figure 4.8*:

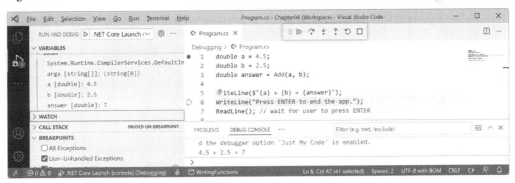

Figure 4.8: Writing to the DEBUG CONSOLE during debugging

Customizing breakpoints

It is easy to make more complex breakpoints:

1. If you are still debugging, click the **Stop** button in the debugging toolbar, navigate to **Run** or **Debug | Stop Debugging**, or press *Shift + F5*.

2. Navigate to **Run | Remove All Breakpoints** or **Debug | Delete All Breakpoints**.

3. Click on the `WriteLine` statement that outputs the answer.

4. Set a breakpoint by pressing *F9* or navigating to **Run** or **Debug | Toggle Breakpoint**.

5. Right-click the breakpoint and choose the appropriate menu for your code editor:

    • In Visual Studio Code, choose **Edit Breakpoint...**

    • In Visual Studio 2022, choose **Conditions...**

6. Type an expression, such as the `answer` variable must be greater than 9, and then press *Enter* to accept it, and note the expression must evaluate to *true* for the breakpoint to activate, as shown in *Figure 4.9*:

Figure 4.9: Customizing a breakpoint with an expression using Visual Studio Code

7. Start debugging and note the breakpoint is not hit.

8. Stop debugging.

9. Edit the breakpoint or its conditions and change its expression to less than 9.

10. Start debugging and note the breakpoint is hit.

11. Stop debugging.

12. Edit the breakpoint or its conditions (in Visual Studio 2022 click **Add condition**), select **Hit Count**, then enter a number such as 3, meaning that you would have to hit the breakpoint three times before it activates, as shown in *Figure 4.10*:

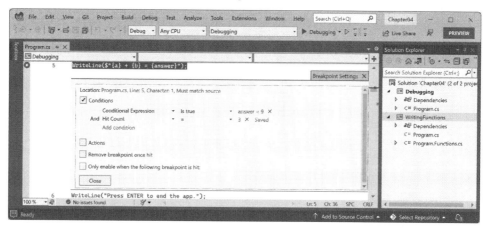

Figure 4.10: Customizing a breakpoint with an expression and hit count using Visual Studio 2022

13. Hover your mouse over the breakpoint's red circle to see a summary, as shown in *Figure 4.11*:

Figure 4.11: A summary of a customized breakpoint in Visual Studio Code

You have now fixed a bug using some debugging tools and seen some advanced possibilities for setting breakpoints.

Hot reloading during development

Hot Reload is a feature that allows a developer to apply changes to code while the app is running and immediately see the effect. This is great for fixing bugs quickly. Hot Reload is also known as **Edit and Continue**. A list of the types of changes that you can make that support Hot Reload is found at the following link: `https://aka.ms/dotnet/hot-reload`.

Just before the release of .NET 6, a high-level Microsoft employee caused controversy by attempting to make the feature Visual Studio-only. Luckily the open-source contingent within Microsoft successfully had the decision overturned. Hot Reload remains available using the command-line tool as well.

Let's see it in action:

1. Use your preferred coding tool to add a new **Console App** / `console` project named `HotReloading` to the `Chapter04` workspace/solution.

   - In Visual Studio Code, select `HotReloading` as the active OmniSharp project. When you see the pop-up warning message saying that required assets are missing, click **Yes** to add them.

2. Modify `HotReloading.csproj` to statically import `System.Console` for all code files.

3. In `Program.cs`, delete the existing statements and then write a message to the console output every two seconds, as shown in the following code:

```
/* Visual Studio: run the app, change the message, click Hot Reload
button.
 * Visual Studio Code: run the app using dotnet watch, change the
message. */

while (true)
{
  WriteLine("Hello, Hot Reload!");
  await Task.Delay(2000);
}
```

Hot reloading using Visual Studio 2022

If you are using Visual Studio, Hot Reload is built into the user interface:

1. In Visual Studio, start the console app and note that the message is output every two seconds.

2. Change Hello to Goodbye, navigate to **Debug | Apply Code Changes** or click the **Hot Reload** button in the toolbar, and note the change is applied without needing to restart the console app.

3. Drop down the **Hot Reload** button menu and select **Hot Reload on File Save**, as shown in *Figure 4.12*:

Figure 4.12: Changing Hot Reload options

4. Change the message again, save the file, and note the console app updates automatically.

Hot reloading using Visual Studio Code and the command line

If you are using Visual Studio Code, you must issue a special command when starting the console app to activate Hot Reload:

1. In Visual Studio Code, in **TERMINAL**, start the console app using dotnet watch, and note the output that shows that hot reload is active, as shown in the following output:

```
dotnet watch 🔥 Hot reload enabled. For a list of supported edits, see
https://aka.ms/dotnet/hot-reload.
  💡 Press "Ctrl + R" to restart.
dotnet watch 🖊 Building...
  Determining projects to restore...
  All projects are up-to-date for restore.
  HotReloading -> C:\cs11dotnet7\Chapter04\HotReloading\bin\Debug\net7.0\
HotReloading.dll
dotnet watch 🚀 Started
Hello, Hot Reload!
Hello, Hot Reload!
Hello, Hot Reload!
```

2. In Visual Studio Code, change Hello to Goodbye, and note that after a couple of seconds the change is applied without needing to restart the console app, as shown in the following output:

```
Hello, Hot Reload!
```

```
dotnet watch ⊘ File changed: .\Program.cs.
Hello, Hot Reload!
Hello, Hot Reload!
dotnet watch ◊ Hot reload of changes succeeded.
Goodbye, Hot Reload!
Goodbye, Hot Reload!
```

3. Press *Ctrl + C* to stop it running, as shown in the following output:

```
Goodbye, Hot Reload!
dotnet watch ● Shutdown requested. Press Ctrl+C again to force exit.
```

Logging during development and runtime

Once you believe that all the bugs have been removed from your code, you will then compile a release version and deploy the application, so that people can use it. But no code is ever bug-free, and during runtime, unexpected errors can occur.

End users are notoriously bad at remembering, admitting to, and then accurately describing what they were doing when an error occurred. You should not rely on them accurately providing useful information to reproduce the problem so that you can understand what caused the problem and then fix it. Instead, you can **instrument your code**, which means logging events of interest.

> **Good Practice:** Add code throughout your application to log what is happening, and especially when exceptions occur, so that you can review the logs and use them to trace the issue and fix the problem. Although we will see logging again in *Chapter 10, Working with Data Using Entity Framework Core*, and in *Chapter 14, Building Websites Using the Model-View-Controller Pattern*, logging is a huge topic, so we can only cover the basics in this book.

Understanding logging options

.NET includes some built-in ways to instrument your code by adding logging capabilities. We will cover the basics in this book. But logging is an area where third parties have created a rich ecosystem of powerful solutions that extend what Microsoft provides. I cannot make specific recommendations because the best logging framework depends on your needs. But I include some common ones in the following list:

*   Apache log4net
*   NLog
*   Serilog

Instrumenting with Debug and Trace

There are two types that can be used to add simple logging to your code: Debug and Trace.

Before we delve into them in more detail, let's look at a quick overview of each one:

*   The Debug class is used to add logging that gets written only during development.

- The Trace class is used to add logging that gets written during both development and runtime.

You have seen the use of the Console type and its WriteLine method writing out to the console window. There is also a pair of types named Debug and Trace that have more flexibility in where they write out to.

The Debug and Trace classes write to any trace listener. A trace listener is a type that can be configured to write output anywhere you like when the WriteLine method is called. There are several trace listeners provided by .NET, including one that outputs to the console, and you can even make your own by inheriting from the TraceListener type.

Writing to the default trace listener

One trace listener, the DefaultTraceListener class, is configured automatically and writes to Visual Studio Code's **DEBUG CONSOLE** window or Visual Studio's **Debug** window. You can configure other trace listeners using code.

Let's see trace listeners in action:

1. Use your preferred coding tool to add a new **Console App**/console project named Instrumenting to the Chapter04 workspace/solution.

   - In Visual Studio Code, select Instrumenting as the active OmniSharp project. When you see the pop-up warning message saying that required assets are missing, click **Yes** to add them.

2. In Program.cs, delete the existing statements and then import the System.Diagnostics namespace, as shown in the following code:

   ```
   using System.Diagnostics;
   ```

3. In Program.cs, write a message from the Debug and Trace classes, as shown in the following code:

   ```
   Debug.WriteLine("Debug says, I am watching!");
   Trace.WriteLine("Trace says, I am watching!");
   ```

4. In Visual Studio, navigate to **View** | **Output** and make sure **Show output from: Debug** is selected.

5. Start debugging the Instrumenting console app, and note that **DEBUG CONSOLE** in Visual Studio Code or the **Output** window in Visual Studio 2022 shows the two messages, mixed with other debugging information, such as loaded assembly DLLs, as shown in *Figures 4.13* and *4.14*:

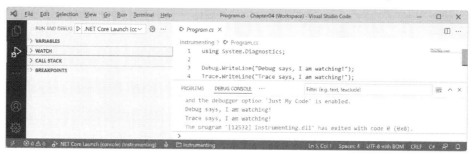

Figure 4.13: Visual Studio Code DEBUG CONSOLE shows the two messages in blue

Figure 4.14: Visual Studio 2022 Output window shows Debug output including the two messages

Configuring trace listeners

Now, we will configure another trace listener that will write to a text file:

1. Before the Debug and Trace calls to WriteLine, add statements to create a new text file on the desktop and pass it into a new trace listener that knows how to write to a text file, and enable automatic flushing for its buffer, as shown in the following code:

```
string logPath = Path.Combine(Environment.GetFolderPath(
    Environment.SpecialFolder.DesktopDirectory), "log.txt");

Console.WriteLine($"Writing to: {logPath}");

TextWriterTraceListener logFile = new(File.CreateText(logPath));

Trace.Listeners.Add(logFile);

// text writer is buffered, so this option calls
// Flush() on all listeners after writing
Trace.AutoFlush = true;
```

Good Practice: Any type that represents a file usually implements a buffer to improve performance. Instead of writing immediately to the file, data is written to an in-memory buffer and only once the buffer is full will it be written in one chunk to the file. This behavior can be confusing while debugging because we do not immediately see the results! Enabling AutoFlush means the Flush method is called automatically after every write.

2. Run the release configuration of the console app:

    •   In Visual Studio Code, enter the following command in the **TERMINAL** window for the
        Instrumenting project and note that nothing will appear to have happened:

    ```
    dotnet run --configuration Release
    ```

    •   In Visual Studio 2022, in the standard toolbar, select **Release** in the **Solution
        Configurations** drop-down list and then navigate to **Debug | Start Without Debugging**,
        as shown in *Figure 4.15*:

Figure 4.15: Selecting the Release configuration in Visual Studio

3. On your desktop, open the file named log.txt and note that it contains the message Trace
    says, I am watching!.

4. Run the debug configuration of the console app:

    •   In Visual Studio Code, enter the following command in the **TERMINAL** window for
        the Instrumenting project:

    ```
    dotnet run --configuration Debug
    ```

    •   In Visual Studio, in the standard toolbar, select **Debug** in the **Solution Configurations**
        drop-down list and then navigate to **Debug | Start Debugging**.

5. On your desktop, open the file named log.txt and note that it contains both the message
    Debug says, I am watching! and also Trace says, I am watching!, as shown in *Figure 4.16*:

Figure 4.16: Opening the log.txt file in Visual Studio Code

 Good Practice: When running with the Debug configuration, both Debug and Trace
are active and will write to any trace listeners. When running with the Release
configuration, only Trace will write to any trace listeners. You can therefore use
Debug.WriteLine calls liberally throughout your code, knowing they will be
stripped out automatically when you build the release version of your application
and will therefore not affect performance.

Switching trace levels

The `Trace.WriteLine` calls are left in your code even after release. So, it would be great to have fine control over when they are output. This is something we can do with a **trace switch**.

The value of a trace switch can be set using a number or a word. For example, the number 3 can be replaced with the word `Info`, as shown in the following table:

Number	Word	Description
0	Off	This will output nothing.
1	Error	This will output only errors.
2	Warning	This will output errors and warnings.
3	Info	This will output errors, warnings, and information.
4	Verbose	This will output all levels.

Let's explore using trace switches. First, we will add some NuGet packages to our project to enable loading configuration settings from a JSON `appsettings` file.

Adding packages to a project in Visual Studio 2022

Visual Studio has a graphical user interface for adding packages:

1. In **Solution Explorer**, right-click the `Instrumenting` project and select **Manage NuGet Packages**.
2. Select the **Browse** tab.
3. In the search box, enter `Microsoft.Extensions.Configuration`.
4. Select each of these NuGet packages and click the **Install** button, as shown in *Figure 4.17*:

    - **Microsoft.Extensions.Configuration**
    - **Microsoft.Extensions.Configuration.Binder**
    - **Microsoft.Extensions.Configuration.FileExtensions**
    - **Microsoft.Extensions.Configuration.Json**

Figure 4.17: Installing NuGet packages using Visual Studio 2022

Good Practice: There are also packages for loading configuration from XML files, INI files, environment variables, and the command line. Use the most appropriate technique for setting configuration in your projects.

Adding packages to a project in Visual Studio Code

Visual Studio Code does not have a mechanism to add NuGet packages to a project, so we will use the command-line tool:

1. Navigate to the **TERMINAL** window for the `Instrumenting` project.
2. Enter the following command:

```
dotnet add package Microsoft.Extensions.Configuration
```

3. Enter the following command:

```
dotnet add package Microsoft.Extensions.Configuration.Binder
```

4. Enter the following command:

```
dotnet add package Microsoft.Extensions.Configuration.FileExtensions
```

5. Enter the following command:

```
dotnet add package Microsoft.Extensions.Configuration.Json
```

`dotnet add package` adds a reference to a NuGet package to your project file. It will be downloaded during the build process. `dotnet add reference` adds a project-to-project reference to your project file. The referenced project will be compiled if needed during the build process.

Reviewing project packages

After adding the NuGet packages, we can see the references in the project file:

1. Open `Instrumenting.csproj` and note the `<ItemGroup>` section with the added NuGet packages, as shown highlighted in the following markup:

```xml
<Project Sdk="Microsoft.NET.Sdk">

  <PropertyGroup>
    <OutputType>Exe</OutputType>
    <TargetFramework>net7.0</TargetFramework>
    <Nullable>enable</Nullable>
    <ImplicitUsings>enable</ImplicitUsings>
  </PropertyGroup>

  <ItemGroup>
```

```xml
        <PackageReference
          Include="Microsoft.Extensions.Configuration"
          Version="7.0.0" />
        <PackageReference
          Include="Microsoft.Extensions.Configuration.Binder"
          Version="7.0.0" />
        <PackageReference
          Include="Microsoft.Extensions.Configuration.FileExtensions"
          Version="7.0.0" />
        <PackageReference
          Include="Microsoft.Extensions.Configuration.Json"
          Version="7.0.0" />
    </ItemGroup>

</Project>
```

2. Add a file named appsettings.json to the Instrumenting project folder.

3. In appsettings.json, define a setting named PacktSwitch with a Level value, as shown in the following code:

```json
{
  "PacktSwitch": {
    "Level": "Info"
  }
}
```

4. In Visual Studio 2022, in **Solution Explorer**, right-click appsettings.json, select **Properties**, and then in the **Properties** window, change **Copy to Output Directory** to **Copy if newer**. This is necessary because unlike Visual Studio Code, which runs the console app in the project folder, Visual Studio runs the console app in Instrumenting\bin\Debug\net7.0 or Instrumenting\bin\Release\net7.0.

5. In Program.cs, import the Microsoft.Extensions.Configuration namespace, as shown in the following code:

```csharp
using Microsoft.Extensions.Configuration;
```

6. Add some statements to the end of Program.cs to create a configuration builder that looks in the current folder for a file named appsettings.json, build the configuration, create a trace switch, set its level by binding to the configuration, and then output the four trace switch levels, as shown in the following code:

```csharp
Console.WriteLine("Reading from appsettings.json in {0}",
  arg0: Directory.GetCurrentDirectory());

ConfigurationBuilder builder = new();

builder.SetBasePath(Directory.GetCurrentDirectory());
```

```csharp
builder.AddJsonFile("appsettings.json",
    optional: true, reloadOnChange: true);

IConfigurationRoot configuration = builder.Build();

TraceSwitch ts = new(
  displayName: "PacktSwitch",
  description: "This switch is set via a JSON config.");

configuration.GetSection("PacktSwitch").Bind(ts);

Trace.WriteLineIf(ts.TraceError, "Trace error");
Trace.WriteLineIf(ts.TraceWarning, "Trace warning");
Trace.WriteLineIf(ts.TraceInfo, "Trace information");
Trace.WriteLineIf(ts.TraceVerbose, "Trace verbose");

Console.ReadLine();
```

7. Set a breakpoint on the `Bind` statement.

8. Start debugging the `Instrumenting` console app.

9. In the **VARIABLES** or **Locals** window, expand the `ts` variable expression, and note that its `Level` is `Off` and its `TraceError`, `TraceWarning`, and so on are all `false`, as shown in *Figure 4.18*:

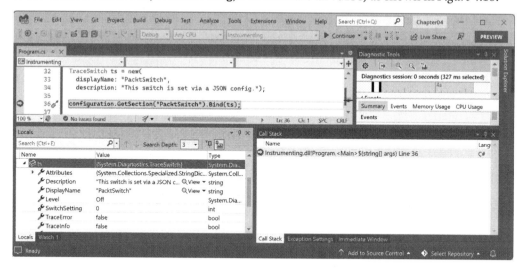

Figure 4.18: Watching the trace switch variable properties in Visual Studio 2022

10. Step into the call to the `Bind` method by clicking the **Step Into** or **Step Over** buttons or pressing *F11* or *F10*, and note the `ts` variable watch expression updates to the `Info` level.

11. Step into or over the four calls to `Trace.WriteLineIf` and note that all levels up to `Info` are written to the **DEBUG CONSOLE** or **Output - Debug** window, but not `Verbose`, as shown in *Figure 4.19*:

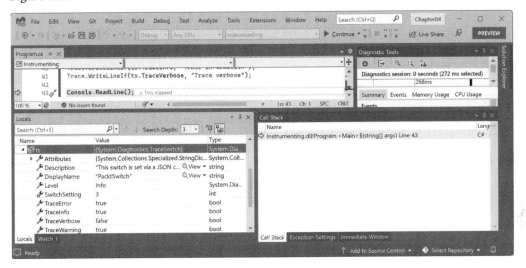

Figure 4.19: Different trace levels shown in the DEBUG CONSOLE in Visual Studio Code

12. Stop debugging.

13. Modify `appsettings.json` to set a level of 2, which means warning, as shown in the following JSON file:

```json
{
    "PacktSwitch": {
      "Level": "2"
    }
}
```

14. Save the changes.

15. In Visual Studio Code, run the console application by entering the following command in the **TERMINAL** window for the `Instrumenting` project:

```
dotnet run --configuration Release
```

16. In Visual Studio, in the standard toolbar, select **Release** in the **Solution Configurations** drop-down list and then run the console app by navigating to **Debug | Start Without Debugging**.

17. Open the file named `log.txt` and note that this time, only trace error and warning levels are the output of the four potential trace levels, as shown in the following text file:

```
Trace says, I am watching!
Trace error
Trace warning
```

If no argument is passed, the default trace switch level is `Off` (0), so none of the switch levels are output.

Logging information about your source code

When you write to a log, you will often want to include the name of the source code file, the name of the method, and the line number. In C# 10 and later, you can even get any expressions passed as an argument to a function as a string value so you can log them.

You can get all this information from the compiler by decorating function parameters with special attributes, as shown in the following table:

Parameter example	Description
`[CallerMemberName] string member = ""`	Sets the `string` parameter named `member` to the name of the method or property that is executing the method that defines this parameter.
`[CallerFilePath] string filepath = ""`	Sets the `string` parameter named `filepath` to the name of the source code file that contains the statement that is executing the method that defines this parameter.
`[CallerLineNumber] int line = 0`	Sets the `int` parameter named `line` to the line number in the source code file of the statement that is executing the method that defines this parameter.

`[CallerArgumentExpression(`
`nameof(argumentExpression))]`
`string expression = ""`
	Sets the `string` parameter named `expression` to the expression that has been passed to the parameter named `argumentExpression`.

You must make these parameters optional by assigning default values to them.

Let's see some code in action:

1. In the `Instrumenting` project, add a class file named `Program.Methods.cs`, and modify its content to define a function named `LogSourceDetails` that uses the four special attributes to log information about the calling code, as shown in the following code:

```
using System.Diagnostics; // Trace
using System.Runtime.CompilerServices; // [Caller...] attributes

partial class Program
{
  static void LogSourceDetails(
    bool condition,
    [CallerMemberName] string member = "",
    [CallerFilePath] string filepath = "",
    [CallerLineNumber] int line = 0,
    [CallerArgumentExpression(nameof(condition))] string expression = "")
```

```
  {
    Trace.WriteLine(string.Format(
      "[{0}]\n   {1} on line {2}. Expression: {3}",
      filepath, member, line, expression));
  }
}
```

2. In `Program.cs`, before the call to `Console.ReadLine()` at the bottom of the file, add statements to declare and set a variable that will be used in an expression that is passed to the function named `LogSourceDetails`, as shown highlighted in the following code:

```
Trace.WriteLineIf(ts.TraceVerbose, "Trace verbose");

int unitsInStock = 12;
LogSourceDetails(unitsInStock > 10);

Console.ReadLine();
```

 We are just making up an expression in this scenario. In a real project, this might be an expression that is dynamically generated by the user making user interface selections to query a database.

3. Run the console app without debugging, press *Enter* and close the console app, and then open the `log.txt` file and note the result, as shown in the following output:

```
[C:\cs11dotnet7\Chapter04\Instrumenting\Program.cs]
   <Main>$ on line 44. Expression: unitsInStock > 10
```

Unit testing

Fixing bugs in code is expensive. The earlier that a bug is discovered in the development process, the less expensive it will be to fix.

Unit testing is a good way to find bugs early in the development process. Some developers even follow the principle that programmers should create unit tests before they write code, and this is called **Test-Driven Development (TDD)**.

Microsoft has a proprietary unit testing framework known as **MSTest**. There is also a framework named **NUnit**. However, we will use the free and open-source third-party framework **xUnit.net**. xUnit was created by the same team that built NUnit, but they fixed the mistakes they felt they made previously. xUnit is more extensible and has better community support.

Understanding types of testing

Unit testing is just one of many types of testing, as described in the following table:

Type of testing	Description
Unit	Tests the smallest unit of code, typically a method or function. Unit testing is performed on a unit of code isolated from its dependencies by mocking them if needed. Each unit should have multiple tests: some with typical inputs and expected outputs, some with extreme input values to test boundaries, and some with deliberately wrong inputs to test exception handling.
Integration	Tests if the smaller units and larger components work together as a single piece of software. Sometimes involves integrating with external components that you do not have source code for.
System	Tests the whole system environment in which your software will run.
Performance	Tests the performance of your software; for example, your code must return a web page full of data to a visitor in under 20 milliseconds.
Load	Tests how many requests your software can handle simultaneously while maintaining required performance, for example, 10,000 concurrent visitors to a website.
User Acceptance	Tests if users can happily complete their work using your software.

Creating a class library that needs testing

First, we will create a function that needs testing. We will create it in a class library project separate from a console app project. A class library is a package of code that can be distributed and referenced by other .NET applications:

1. Use your preferred coding tool to add a new **Class Library**/classlib project named CalculatorLib to the Chapter04 workspace/solution. At this point, you will have created about a dozen new console app projects and added them to a Visual Studio 2022 solution or a Visual Studio Code workspace. The only difference when adding a **Class Library**/classlib is to select a different project template. The rest of the steps are the same as adding a **Console App**/console project. For your convenience, I repeat them below for both Visual Studio 2022 and Visual Studio Code.

    • If you are using Visual Studio 2022:

        1. Navigate to **File** | **Add** | **New Project**.
        2. In the **Add a new project** dialog, in **Recent project templates**, select **Class Library [C#]** and then click **Next**.
        3. In the **Configure your new project** dialog, for the **Project name**, enter CalculatorLib, leave the location as C:\cs11dotnet7\Chapter04, and then click **Next**.

    4.   In the **Additional information** dialog, select **.NET 7.0**, and then click **Create**.

- If you are using Visual Studio Code:

    1.   Navigate to File | **Add Folder to Workspace....**

    2.   In the Chapter04 folder, use the **New Folder** button to create a new folder named CalculatorLib, select it, and click **Add**.

    3.   When prompted if you trust the folder, click **Yes**.

    4.   Navigate to **Terminal** | **New Terminal**, and in the drop-down list that appears, select **CalculatorLib**.

    5.   In **TERMINAL**, confirm that you are in the CalculatorLib folder, and then enter the command to create a new class library, as shown in the following command: dotnet new console.

    6.   Navigate to **View** | **Command Palette**, and then select **OmniSharp: Select Project**.

    7.   In the drop-down list, select the **CalculatorLib** project, and when prompted, click **Yes** to add required assets to debug.

2. In the CalculatorLib project, rename the file named Class1.cs to Calculator.cs.

3. Modify the file to define a Calculator class (with a deliberate bug!), as shown in the following code:

```
namespace CalculatorLib
{
  public class Calculator
  {
    public double Add(double a, double b)
    {
      return a * b;
    }
  }
}
```

4. Compile your class library project:

- In Visual Studio 2022, navigate to **Build** | **Build CalculatorLib**.
- In Visual Studio Code, in **TERMINAL**, enter the command dotnet build.

5. Use your preferred coding tool to add a new **xUnit Test Project [C#]** / xunit project named CalculatorLibUnitTests to the Chapter04 workspace/solution.

6. Add a project reference to the CalculatorLib project:

- If you are using Visual Studio 2022, in **Solution Explorer**, select the CalculatorLibUnitTests project, navigate to **Project** | **Add Project Reference...**, check the box to select the CalculatorLib project, and then click **OK**.

- If you are using Visual Studio Code, use the `dotnet add reference` command or click on the file named `CalculatorLibUnitTests.csproj`, and modify the configuration to add an item group with a project reference to the `CalculatorLib` project, as shown highlighted in the following markup:

```xml
<Project Sdk="Microsoft.NET.Sdk">

  <PropertyGroup>
    <TargetFramework>net7.0</TargetFramework>
    <ImplicitUsings>enable</ImplicitUsings>
    <Nullable>enable</Nullable>
    <IsPackable>false</IsPackable>
  </PropertyGroup>

  <ItemGroup>
    <PackageReference Include="Microsoft.NET.Test.Sdk"
    Version="17.0.0" />
    <PackageReference Include="xunit" Version="2.4.1" />
    <PackageReference Include="xunit.runner.visualstudio"
    Version="2.4.3">
      <IncludeAssets>runtime; build; native; contentfiles;
        analyzers; buildtransitive</IncludeAssets>
      <PrivateAssets>all</PrivateAssets>
    </PackageReference>
    <PackageReference Include="coverlet.collector" Version="3.1.0">
      <IncludeAssets>runtime; build; native; contentfiles;
        analyzers; buildtransitive</IncludeAssets>
      <PrivateAssets>all</PrivateAssets>
    </PackageReference>
  </ItemGroup>

  <ItemGroup>
    <ProjectReference
      Include="..\CalculatorLib\CalculatorLib.csproj" />
  </ItemGroup>

</Project>
```

7. Build the `CalculatorLibUnitTests` project.

Writing unit tests

A well-written unit test will have three parts:

- **Arrange:** This part will declare and instantiate variables for input and output.

- **Act**: This part will execute the unit that you are testing. In our case, that means calling the method that we want to test.
- **Assert**: This part will make one or more assertions about the output. An assertion is a belief that, if not true, indicates a failed test. For example, when adding 2 and 2, we would expect the result to be 4.

Now, we will write some unit tests for the `Calculator` class:

1. Rename the file `UnitTest1.cs` to `CalculatorUnitTests.cs` and then open it.
2. In Visual Studio Code, rename the class to `CalculatorUnitTests`. (Visual Studio prompts you to rename the class when you rename the file.)
3. Import the `CalculatorLib` namespace.
4. Modify the `CalculatorUnitTests` class to have two test methods; one for adding 2 and 2, and another for adding 2 and 3, as shown in the following code:

```csharp
using CalculatorLib;

namespace CalculatorLibUnitTests
{
  public class CalculatorUnitTests
  {
    [Fact]
    public void TestAdding2And2()
    {
      // arrange
      double a = 2;
      double b = 2;
      double expected = 4;
      Calculator calc = new();
      // act
      double actual = calc.Add(a, b);
      // assert
      Assert.Equal(expected, actual);
    }
    [Fact]
    public void TestAdding2And3()
    {
      // arrange
      double a = 2;
      double b = 3;
      double expected = 5;
      Calculator calc = new();
      // act
      double actual = calc.Add(a, b);
      // assert
```

```
        Assert.Equal(expected, actual);
    }
  }
}
```

Running unit tests using Visual Studio 2022

Now we are ready to run the unit tests and see the results:

1. In Visual Studio, navigate to **Test | Run All Tests**.

2. In **Test Explorer**, note that the results indicate that two tests ran, one test passed, and one test failed, as shown in *Figure 4.20*:

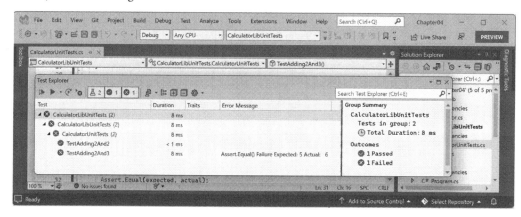

Figure 4.20: The unit test results in Visual Studio 2022's Test Explorer

Running unit tests using Visual Studio Code

Now we are ready to run the unit tests and see the results:

1. In Visual Studio Code, in the `CalculatorLibUnitTest` project's **TERMINAL** window, run the tests, as shown in the following command:

```
dotnet test
```

2.   Note that the results indicate that two tests ran, one test passed, and one test failed, as shown in *Figure 4.21*:

Figure 4.21: The unit test results in Visual Studio Code's TERMINAL

Fixing the bug

Now you can fix the bug:

1.   Fix the bug in the Add method.
2.   Run the unit tests again to see that the bug has now been fixed and both tests pass.

Throwing and catching exceptions in functions

In *Chapter 3, Controlling Flow, Converting Types, and Handling Exceptions*, you were introduced to exceptions and how to use a try-catch statement to handle them. But you should only catch and handle an exception if you have enough information to mitigate the issue. If you do not, then you should allow the exception to pass up through the call stack to a higher level.

Understanding usage errors and execution errors

Usage errors are when a programmer misuses a function, typically by passing invalid values as parameters. They could be avoided by that programmer changing their code to pass valid values. When some programmers first learn C# and .NET, they sometimes think exceptions can always be avoided because they assume all errors are usage errors. Usage errors should all be fixed before production runtime.

Execution errors are when something happens at runtime that cannot be fixed by writing "better" code. Execution errors can be split into **program errors** and **system errors**. If you attempt to access a network resource but the network is down, you need to be able to handle that system error by logging an exception, and possibly backing off for a time and trying again. But some system errors, such as running out of memory, simply cannot be handled. If you attempt to open a file that does not exist, you might be able to catch that error and handle it programmatically by creating a new file. Program errors can be programmatically fixed by writing smart code. System errors often cannot be fixed programmatically.

Commonly thrown exceptions in functions

Very rarely should you define new types of exceptions to indicate usage errors. .NET already defines many that you should use.

When defining your own functions with parameters, your code should check the parameter values and throw exceptions if they have values that will prevent your function from properly functioning.

For example, if an argument to a function should not be `null`, throw `ArgumentNullException`. For other problems, you might throw `ArgumentException`, `NotSupportedException`, or `InvalidOperationException`. For any exception, include a message that describes the problem for whoever will have to read it (typically a developer audience for class libraries and functions, or end users if it is at the highest level of a GUI app), as shown in the following code:

```
static void Withdraw(string accountName, decimal amount)
{
  if (accountName is null)
  {
    throw new ArgumentNullException(paramName: nameof(accountName));
  }

  if (amount < 0)
  {
    throw new ArgumentException(
      message: $"{nameof(amount)} cannot be less than zero.");
  }

  // process parameters
}
```

 Good Practice: If a function cannot successfully perform its operation, you should consider that a function failure and report it by throwing an exception.

Instead of writing an `if` statement and then throwing a new exception, .NET 6 introduced a convenience method to throw an exception if an argument is `null`, as shown in the following code:

```
static void Withdraw(string accountName, decimal amount)
{
    ArgumentNullException.ThrowIfNull(accountName);
```

C# 11 previews introduced a null check operator `!!` to do the same thing but it was removed in later previews after complaints from critics, as shown in the following code:

```
static void Withdraw(string accountName!!, decimal amount)
```

You should never need to write a `try-catch` statement to catch these usage-type errors. You want the application to terminate. These exceptions should cause the programmer who is calling the function to fix their code to prevent the problem. They should be fixed before production deployment. That does not mean that your code does not need to throw usage error type exceptions. It should—to force other programmers to call your functions correctly!

Understanding the call stack

The entry point for a .NET console application is the method named `Main` (if you have explicitly defined this class) or `<Main>$` (if it was created for you by the top-level program feature) of the `Program` class.

The Main method will call other methods, which call other methods, and so on, and these methods could be in the current project or referenced projects and NuGet packages, as shown in *Figure 4.22*:

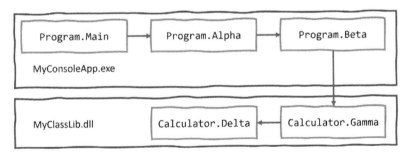

Figure 4.22: A chain of method calls that create a call stack

Let's create a similar chain of methods to explore where we could catch and handle exceptions:

1. Use your preferred coding tool to add a new **Class Library**/`classlib` project named `CallStackExceptionHandlingLib` to the `Chapter04` workspace/solution.

2. Rename the `Class1.cs` file to `Calculator.cs`.

3. In `Calculator.cs`, modify its contents, as shown in the following code:

```
using static System.Console;

namespace CallStackExceptionHandlingLib
{
```

```
public class Calculator
{
  public static void Gamma() // public so it can be called from outside
  {
    WriteLine("In Gamma");
    Delta();
  }

  private static void Delta()
  // private so it can only be called internally
  {
    WriteLine("In Delta");
    File.OpenText("bad file path");
  }
}
}
```

4. Use your preferred coding tool to add a new **Console App**/console project named
    CallStackExceptionHandling to the Chapter04 workspace/solution.

    - In Visual Studio Code, select CallStackExceptionHandling as the active OmniSharp
      project. When you see the pop-up warning message saying that required assets are
      missing, click **Yes** to add them.

5. In the CallStackExceptionHandling project, add a reference to the
    CallStackExceptionHandlingLib project.

6. In Program.cs, delete the existing statements and then add statements to define two methods
    and chain calls to them, and the methods in the class library, as shown in the following code:

```
using CallStackExceptionHandlingLib;
using static System.Console;

WriteLine("In Main");
Alpha();

void Alpha()
{
  WriteLine("In Alpha");
  Beta();
}

void Beta()
{
  WriteLine("In Beta");
  Calculator.Gamma();
}
```

7. Run the console app *without* the debugger attached, and note the results, as shown in the following partial output:

```
In Main
In Alpha
In Beta
In Gamma
In Delta
Unhandled exception. System.IO.FileNotFoundException: Could not find file
'C:\cs11dotnet7\Chapter04\CallStackExceptionHandling\bin\Debug\net7.0\bad
file path'.
File name: 'C:\cs11dotnet7\Chapter04\CallStackExceptionHandling\bin\
Debug\net7.0\bad file path'
   at Microsoft.Win32.SafeHandles.SafeFileHandle.CreateFile(String
fullPath, FileMode mode, FileAccess access, FileShare share, FileOptions
options)
   at Microsoft.Win32.SafeHandles.SafeFileHandle.Open(String fullPath,
FileMode mode, FileAccess access, FileShare share, FileOptions options,
Int64 preallocationSize)
   at System.IO.Strategies.OSFileStreamStrategy..ctor(String path,
FileMode mode, FileAccess access, FileShare share, FileOptions options,
Int64 preallocationSize)
   at System.IO.Strategies.FileStreamHelpers.ChooseStrategyCore(String
path, FileMode mode, FileAccess access, FileShare share, FileOptions
options, Int64 preallocationSize)
   at System.IO.StreamReader.ValidateArgsAndOpenPath(String path,
Encoding encoding, Int32 bufferSize)
   at System.IO.File.OpenText(String path)
   at CallStackExceptionHandlingLib.Calculator.Delta() in C:\cs11dotnet7\
Chapter04\CallStackExceptionHandlingLib\Calculator.cs:line 16
   at CallStackExceptionHandlingLib.Calculator.Gamma() in C:\cs11dotnet7\
Chapter04\CallStackExceptionHandlingLib\Calculator.cs:line 10
   at Program.<<Main>$>g__Beta|0_1() in C:\cs11dotnet7\Chapter04\
CallStackExceptionHandling\Program.cs:line 16
   at Program.<<Main>$>g__Alpha|0_0() in C:\cs11dotnet7\Chapter04\
CallStackExceptionHandling\Program.cs:line 10
   at Program.<Main>$(String[] args) in C:\cs11dotnet7\Chapter04\
CallStackExceptionHandling\Program.cs:line 5
```

Note that the call stack is upside-down. Starting from the bottom, you see:

- The first call is to the `<Main>$` entry point function in the auto-generated `Program` class. This is where arguments are passed in as a `String` array.
- The second call is to the `<<Main>$>g__Alpha|0_0` function. (The C# compiler renames it from `Alpha` when it adds it as a local function.)
- The third call is to the `Beta` function.
- The fourth call is to the `Gamma` function.

- The fifth call is to the Delta function. This function attempts to open a file by passing a bad file path. This causes an exception to be thrown. Any function with a try-catch statement could catch this exception. If it does not, the exception is automatically passed up the call stack until it reaches the top, where .NET outputs the exception (and the details of this call stack).

 Good Practice: Unless you need to step through your code to debug it, you should always run your code without the debugger attached. In this case, it is especially important not to attach the debugger because if you do, then it will catch the exception and show it in a GUI dialog box instead of outputting it as shown in the book.

Where to catch exceptions

Programmers can decide if they want to catch an exception near the failure point, or centralized higher up the call stack. This allows your code to be simplified and standardized. You might know that calling an exception could throw one or more types of exception, but you do not need to handle any of them at the current point in the call stack.

Rethrowing exceptions

Sometimes you want to catch an exception, log it, and then rethrow it. For example, if you are writing a low-level class library that will be called from an application, your code may not have enough information to programmatically fix the error in a smart way, but the calling application might have more information and could. Your code should log the error in case the calling application does not, and then rethrow it up the call stack in case the calling application chooses to handle it better.

There are three ways to rethrow an exception inside a catch block, as shown in the following list:

- To throw the caught exception with its original call stack, call throw.
- To throw the caught exception as if it was thrown at the current level in the call stack, call throw with the caught exception, for example, throw ex. This is usually poor practice because you have lost some potentially useful information for debugging but can be useful when you want to deliberately remove that information when it contains sensitive data.
- To wrap the caught exception in another exception that can include more information in a message that might help the caller understand the problem, throw a new exception, and pass the caught exception as the innerException parameter.

If an error could occur when we called the Gamma function, then we could catch the exception and then perform one of the three techniques of rethrowing an exception, as shown in the following code:

```
try
{
  Gamma();
}
catch (IOException ex)
{
  LogException(ex);
```

```
// throw the caught exception as if it happened here
// this will lose the original call stack
throw ex;

// rethrow the caught exception and retain its original call stack
throw;

// throw a new exception with the caught exception nested within it
throw new InvalidOperationException(
  message: "Calculation had invalid values. See inner exception for why.",
  innerException: ex);
}
```

Let's see this in action with our call stack example:

1. In the `CallStackExceptionHandling` project, in `Program.cs`, in the `Beta` function, add a `try-catch` statement around the call to the `Gamma` function, as shown highlighted in the following code:

```
void Beta()
{
  WriteLine("In Beta");
  try
  {
    Calculator.Gamma();
  }
  catch (Exception ex)
  {
    WriteLine($"Caught this: {ex.Message}");
    throw ex;
  }
}
```

 Note the green squiggle under the `throw ex` to warn you that you will lose call stack information.

2. Run the console app and note that the output excludes some details of the call stack, as shown in the following output:

```
Caught this: Could not find file 'C:\cs11dotnet7\Chapter04\
CallStackExceptionHandling\bin\Debug\net7.0\bad file path'.
Unhandled exception. System.IO.FileNotFoundException: Could not find file
'C:\cs11dotnet7\Chapter04\CallStackExceptionHandling\bin\Debug\net7.0\bad
file path'.
```

```
File name: 'C:\cs11dotnet7\Chapter04\CallStackExceptionHandling\bin\
Debug\net7.0\bad file path'
   at Program.<<Main>$>g__Beta|0_1() in C:\cs11dotnet7\Chapter04\
CallStackExceptionHandling\Program.cs:line 23
   at Program.<<Main>$>g__Alpha|0_0() in C:\cs11dotnet7\Chapter04\
CallStackExceptionHandling\Program.cs:line 10
   at Program.<Main>$(String[] args) in C:\cs11dotnet7\Chapter04\
CallStackExceptionHandling\Program.cs:line 5
```

3. Remove the ex by replacing the statement `throw ex;` with `throw;`.

4. Run the console app and note that the output includes all the details of the call stack.

Implementing the tester-doer pattern

The **tester-doer pattern** can avoid some thrown exceptions (but not eliminate them completely). This pattern uses pairs of functions: one to perform a test and the other to perform an action that would fail if the test is not passed.

.NET implements this pattern itself. For example, before adding an item to a collection by calling the `Add` method, you can test to see if it is read-only, which would cause `Add` to fail and therefore throw an exception.

For example, before withdrawing money from a bank account, you might test that the account is not overdrawn, as shown in the following code:

```
if (!bankAccount.IsOverdrawn())
{
  bankAccount.Withdraw(amount);
}
```

Problems with the tester-doer pattern

The tester-doer pattern can add performance overhead, so you can also implement the **try pattern**, which in effect combines the `test` and do parts into a single function, as we saw with `TryParse`.

Another problem with the tester-doer pattern occurs when you are using multiple threads. In this scenario, one thread could call the test function and it returns okay. But then another thread executes that changes the state. Then the original thread continues executing assuming everything is fine, but it is not fine. This is called a race condition. This topic is too advanced to cover how to handle it in this book.

If you implement your own `try` pattern function and it fails, remember to set the out parameter to the default value of its type and then return `false`, as shown in the following code:

```
static bool TryParse(string? input, out Person value)
{
  if (someFailure)
  {
    value = default(Person);
    return false;
  }
}
```

```
    // successfully parsed the string into a Person
    value = new Person() { ... };
    return true;
}
```

Practicing and exploring

Test your knowledge and understanding by answering some questions, getting some hands-on practice, and exploring with deeper research the topics covered in this chapter.

Exercise 4.1 – Test your knowledge

Answer the following questions. If you get stuck, try googling the answers if necessary, while remembering that if you get totally stuck, the answers are in the *Appendix*:

1. What does the C# keyword void mean?
2. What are some differences between imperative and functional programming styles?
3. In Visual Studio Code or Visual Studio, what is the difference between pressing *F5*, *Ctrl* or *Cmd* + *F5*, *Shift* + *F5*, and *Ctrl* or *Cmd* + *Shift* + *F5*?
4. Where does the Trace.WriteLine method write its output to?
5. What are the five trace levels?
6. What is the difference between the Debug and Trace classes?
7. When writing a unit test, what are the three "A"s?
8. When writing a unit test using xUnit, which attribute must you decorate the test methods with?
9. What dotnet command executes xUnit tests?
10. What statement should you use to rethrow a caught exception named ex without losing the stack trace?

Exercise 4.2 – Practice writing functions with debugging and unit testing

Prime factors are the combination of the smallest prime numbers that, when multiplied together, will produce the original number. Consider the following examples:

- Prime factors of 4 are: 2 x 2
- Prime factors of 7 are: 7
- Prime factors of 30 are: 5 x 3 x 2
- Prime factors of 40 are: 5 x 2 x 2 x 2
- Prime factors of 50 are: 5 x 5 x 2

Create three projects:

- A class library named Ch04Ex02PrimeFactorsLib with a static class and static method named PrimeFactors that, when passed an int variable as a parameter, returns a string showing its prime factors

- A unit test project named Ch04Ex02PrimeFactorsTests with a few suitable unit tests
- A console application to use it named Ch04Ex02PrimeFactorsApp

To keep it simple, you can assume that the largest number entered will be 1,000.

Use the debugging tools and write unit tests to ensure that your function works correctly with multiple inputs and returns the correct output.

Exercise 4.3 – Explore topics

Use the links on the following page to learn more about the topics covered in this chapter:

https://github.com/markjprice/cs11dotnet7/blob/main/book-links.md#chapter-4---writing-debugging-and-testing-functions

Summary

In this chapter, you learned:

- How to write reusable functions with input parameters and return values, in both an imperative and functional style.
- How to use the Visual Studio and Visual Studio Code debugging and diagnostic features like logging and unit tests to identify and fix any bugs in them.
- How to throw and catch exceptions in functions and understand the call stack.

In the next chapter, you will learn how to build your own types using object-oriented programming techniques.

5

Building Your Own Types with Object-Oriented Programming

This chapter is about making your own types using **object-oriented programming** (OOP). You will learn about all the different categories of members that a type can have, including fields to store data and methods to perform actions. You will use OOP concepts such as aggregation and encapsulation. You will also learn about language features such as tuple syntax support, out variables, inferred tuple names, and default literals. You will learn about defining operators and local functions for performing simple actions.

This chapter will cover the following topics:

- Talking about OOP
- Building class libraries
- Storing data within fields
- Writing and calling methods
- Splitting classes using partial
- Controlling access with properties and indexers
- More about methods
- Pattern matching with objects
- Working with records

Talking about OOP

An object in the real world is a thing, such as a car or a person, whereas an object in programming often represents something in the real world, such as a product or bank account, but it can also be something more abstract.

In C#, we use the `class` and `record` (mostly) or `struct` (sometimes) C# keywords to define a type of object. You will learn about the difference between classes and structs in *Chapter 6, Implementing Interfaces and Inheriting Classes*. You can think of a type as being a blueprint or template for an object.

The concepts of OOP are briefly described here:

- **Encapsulation** is the combination of the data and actions that are related to an object. For example, a `BankAccount` type might have data, such as `Balance` and `AccountName`, as well as actions, such as `Deposit` and `Withdraw`. When encapsulating, you often want to control what can access those actions and the data; for example, restricting how the internal state of an object can be accessed or modified from the outside.

- **Composition** is about what an object is made of. For example, a `Car` is composed of different parts, such as four `Wheel` objects, several `Seat` objects, and an `Engine`.

- **Aggregation** is about what can be combined with an object. For example, a `Person` is not part of a `Car` object, but they could sit in the driver's `Seat` and then become the car's `Driver`—two separate objects that are aggregated together to form a new component.

- **Inheritance** is about reusing code by having a **subclass** derive from a **base** or **superclass**. All functionality in the base class is inherited by, and becomes available in, the **derived** class. For example, the base or super `Exception` class has some members that have the same implementation across all exceptions, and the sub or derived `SqlException` class inherits those members and has extra members only relevant to when a SQL database exception occurs, like a property for the database connection.

- **Abstraction** is about capturing the core idea of an object and ignoring the details or specifics. C# has the `abstract` keyword that formalizes this concept. If a class is not explicitly **abstract**, then it can be described as being **concrete**. Base or superclasses are often abstract; for example, the superclass `Stream` is abstract, and its subclasses, like `FileStream` and `MemoryStream`, are concrete. Only concrete classes can be used to create objects; abstract classes can only be used as the base for other classes because they are missing some implementation. Abstraction is a tricky balance. If you make a class more abstract, more classes will be able to inherit from it, but at the same time, there will be less functionality to share.

- **Polymorphism** is about allowing a derived class to override an inherited action to provide custom behavior.

Building class libraries

Class library assemblies group types together into easily deployable units (DLL files). Apart from when you learned about unit testing, you have only created console applications or .NET Interactive notebooks to contain your code. To make the code that you write reusable across multiple projects, you should put it in class library assemblies, just like Microsoft does.

Creating a class library

The first task is to create a reusable .NET class library:

1. Use your preferred coding tool to create a new project, as defined in the following list:

   - Project template: **Class Library**/classlib
   - Project file and folder: PacktLibraryNetStandard2
   - Workspace/solution file and folder: Chapter05

2. Open the PacktLibraryNetStandard2.csproj file, and note that, by default, class libraries created by the .NET SDK 7 target .NET 7 and, therefore, can only be referenced by other .NET 7-compatible assemblies, as shown in the following markup:

```
<Project Sdk="Microsoft.NET.Sdk">

  <PropertyGroup>
    <TargetFramework>net7.0</TargetFramework>
    <Nullable>enable</Nullable>
    <ImplicitUsings>enable</ImplicitUsings>
  </PropertyGroup>

</Project>
```

3. Modify the framework to target .NET Standard 2.0, add an entry to explicitly use the C# 11 compiler, and statically import the System.Console class to all C# files, as shown highlighted in the following markup:

```
<Project Sdk="Microsoft.NET.Sdk">

  <PropertyGroup>
    <TargetFramework>netstandard2.0</TargetFramework>
    <LangVersion>11</LangVersion>
    <Nullable>enable</Nullable>
    <ImplicitUsings>enable</ImplicitUsings>
  </PropertyGroup>

  <ItemGroup>
    <Using Include="System.Console" Static="true" />
  </ItemGroup>

</Project>
```

4. Save and close the file.

5. Delete the file named `Class1.cs`.

6. Compile the project so that other projects can reference it later.

   - In Visual Studio 2022, navigate to **Build | Build PacktLibraryNetStandard2**.
   - In Visual Studio Code, enter the following command: `dotnet build`.

> **Good Practice:** To use the latest C# language and .NET platform features, put types in a .NET 7 class library. To support legacy .NET platforms like .NET Core, .NET Framework, and Xamarin, put types that you might reuse in a .NET Standard 2.0 class library. By default, targeting .NET Standard 2.0 uses the C# 7.0 compiler, but this can be overridden so you get the benefits of the newer SDK and compiler even though you are limited to .NET Standard 2.0 APIs.

Defining a class in a namespace

The next task is to define a class that will represent a person:

1. In the `PacktLibraryNetStandard2` project, add a new class file named `Person.cs`.

2. Set the namespace to `Packt.Shared`, end the namespace definition with a semi-colon, and remove the curly braces associated with the namespace (Visual Studio 2022 does this automatically for you), to specify that the types defined in this file are part of this namespace, as shown in the following code:

```
namespace Packt.Shared; // file-scoped namespace
```

> **Good Practice:** We're doing this because it is important to put your classes in a logically named namespace. A better namespace name would be domain-specific, for example, `System.Numerics` for types related to advanced numbers. In this case, the types we will create are `Person`, `BankAccount`, and `WondersOfTheWorld`, and they do not have a typical domain so we will use the more generic `Packt.Shared`.

3. For the `Person` class, change the keyword `internal` to `public`.

Your class file should now look like the following code:

```
namespace Packt.Shared; // file-scoped namespace

public class Person
{
}
```

Note that the C# keyword `public` is applied before `class`. This keyword is an **access modifier**, and it allows for any other code to access this class even outside this class library.

If you do not explicitly apply the public keyword, then it will only be accessible within the assembly that defined it. This is because the implicit access modifier for a class is internal. We need this class to be accessible outside the assembly, so we must make sure it is public.

To simplify your code if you are targeting .NET 6.0 or later, and therefore using C# 10 or later, you can end a namespace declaration with a semicolon and remove the curly braces, so the type definitions do not need to be indented. This is known as a **file-scoped namespace** declaration. You can only have one file-scoped namespace per file. This feature is especially useful for book writers who have limited horizontal space.

 Good Practice: Put each type that you create in its own file so that you can use file-scoped namespace declarations.

Understanding members

This type does not yet have any members encapsulated within it. We will create some over the following pages. Members can be fields, methods, or specialized versions of both. You'll find a description of them here:

- **Fields** are used to store data. There are also three specialized categories of field, as shown in the following bullets:

    - **Constant:** The data never changes. The compiler literally copies the data into any code that reads it.

    - **Read-only:** The data cannot change after the class is instantiated, but the data can be calculated or loaded from an external source at the time of instantiation.

    - **Event:** The data references one or more methods that you want to execute when something happens, such as clicking on a button or responding to a request from some other code. Events will be covered in *Chapter 6, Implementing Interfaces and Inheriting Classes*.

- **Methods** are used to execute statements. You saw some examples when you learned about functions in *Chapter 4, Writing, Debugging, and Testing Functions*. There are also four specialized categories of method:

    - **Constructor:** The statements execute when you use the new keyword to allocate memory to instantiate a class.

    - **Property:** The statements execute when you get or set data. The data is commonly stored in a field, but could be stored externally or calculated at runtime. Properties are the preferred way to encapsulate fields unless the memory address of the field needs to be exposed.

    - **Indexer:** The statements execute when you get or set data using "array" syntax [ ].

    - **Operator:** The statements execute when you use an operator like + and / on operands of your type.

Instantiating a class

In this section, we will make an instance of the Person class.

Before we can instantiate a class, we need to reference the assembly that contains it from another project. We will use the class in a console app:

1. Use your preferred coding tool to add a new **Console App**/console named PeopleApp to the Chapter05 workspace/solution.

2. If you are using Visual Studio 2022:

    1. Set the startup project for the solution to the current selection.

    2. In **Solution Explorer,** select the PeopleApp project, navigate to **Project | Add Project Reference...,** check the box to select the PacktLibraryNetStandard2 project, and then click **OK.**

    3. In PeopleApp.csproj, add an entry to statically import the System.Console class, as shown in the following markup:

        ```xml
        <ItemGroup>
          <Using Include="System.Console" Static="true" />
        </ItemGroup>
        ```

    4. Navigate to **Build | Build PeopleApp.**

3. If you are using Visual Studio Code:

    1. Select PeopleApp as the active OmniSharp project. When you see the pop-up warning message saying that required assets are missing, click **Yes** to add them.

    2. Edit PeopleApp.csproj to add a project reference to PacktLibraryNetStandard2, and add an entry to statically import the System.Console class, as shown highlighted in the following markup:

        ```xml
        <Project Sdk="Microsoft.NET.Sdk">

          <PropertyGroup>
            <OutputType>Exe</OutputType>
            <TargetFramework>net7.0</TargetFramework>
            <Nullable>enable</Nullable>
            <ImplicitUsings>enable</ImplicitUsings>
          </PropertyGroup>

          <ItemGroup>
            <ProjectReference Include=
              "../PacktLibraryNetStandard2/PacktLibraryNetStandard2.
              csproj" />
          </ItemGroup>
        ```

```
<ItemGroup>
  <Using Include="System.Console" Static="true" />
</ItemGroup>

</Project>
```

3. In a terminal, compile the `PeopleApp` project and its dependency `PacktLibraryNetStandard2` project, as shown in the following command:

```
dotnet build
```

Importing a namespace to use a type

Now, we are ready to write statements to work with the `Person` class:

1. In the `PeopleApp` project/folder, in `Program.cs` file, delete the existing statements, and then add statements to import the namespace for our `Person` class, as shown in the following code:

```
using Packt.Shared;
```

 Although we could import this namespace globally, it will be clearer to anyone reading this code where we are importing the types we use from if the import statement is at the top of the file, and the `PeopleApp` project will only have this one `Program.cs` file that needs the namespace imported.

2. In `Program.cs`, add statements to:

    -   Create an instance of the `Person` type.
    -   Output the instance using a textual description of itself.

    The new keyword allocates memory for the object and initializes any internal data, as shown in the following code:

```
// Person bob = new Person(); // C# 1.0 or later
// var bob = new Person(); // C# 3.0 or later

Person bob = new(); // C# 9.0 or later
WriteLine(bob.ToString());
```

You might be wondering, "Why does the bob variable have a method named `ToString`? The Person class is empty!" Don't worry, we're about to find out!

3. Run the code and view the result, as shown in the following output:

```
Packt.Shared.Person
```

Avoiding a namespace conflict with a using alias

It is possible that there are two namespaces that contain the same type name, and importing both namespaces causes ambiguity. For example:

```
// France.Paris.cs
namespace France
{
  public class Paris
  {
  }
}

// Texas.Paris.cs
namespace Texas
{
  public class Paris
  {
  }
}

// Program.cs
using France;
using Texas;

Paris p = new();
```

The compiler would give `Error CS0104`:

```
'Paris' is an ambiguous reference between 'France.Paris' and 'Texas.Paris'
```

We can define an alias for one of the namespaces to differentiate it, as shown in the following code:

```
using France;
using us = Texas; // us becomes alias for the namespace and it is not imported

Paris p1 = new(); // France.Paris
us.Paris p2 = new(); // Texas.Paris
```

Renaming a type with a using alias

Another situation where you might want to use an alias is if you would like to rename a type. For example, if you use the `Environment` class a lot, you could rename it, as shown in the following code:

```
using Env = System.Environment;

WriteLine(Env.OSVersion);
WriteLine(Env.MachineName);
WriteLine(Env.CurrentDirectory);
```

Understanding objects

Although our Person class did not explicitly choose to inherit from a type, all types ultimately inherit directly or indirectly from a special type named System.Object.

The implementation of the ToString method in the System.Object type outputs the full namespace and type name.

Back in the original Person class, we could have explicitly told the compiler that Person inherits from the System.Object type, as shown in the following code:

```
public class Person : System.Object
```

When class B inherits from class A, we say that A is the base or superclass and B is the derived or subclass. In this case, System.Object is the base or superclass and Person is the derived or subclass.

You can also use the C# alias keyword object, as shown in the following code:

```
public class Person : object
```

Inheriting from System.Object

Let's make our class explicitly inherit from object and then review what members all objects have:

1. Modify your Person class to explicitly inherit from object.
2. Click inside the object keyword and press *F12*, or right-click on the object keyword and choose **Go to Definition**.

You will see the Microsoft-defined System.Object type and its members. This is something you don't need to understand the details of yet, but notice that it has a method named ToString, as shown in *Figure 5.1*:

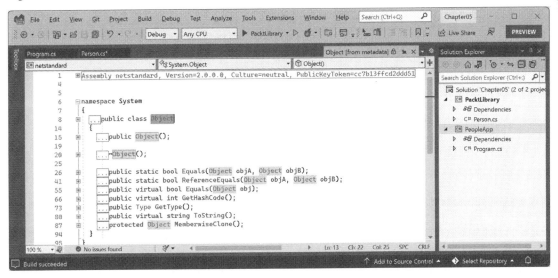

Figure 5.1: System.Object class definition in .NET Standard 2.0

Good Practice: Assume other programmers know that if inheritance is not specified, the class will inherit from `System.Object`.

Storing data within fields

In this section, we will be defining a selection of fields in the class to store information about a person.

Defining fields

Let's say that we have decided that a person is composed of a name and a date of birth. We will encapsulate these two values inside a person, and the values will be visible outside it:

- Inside the `Person` class, write statements to declare two public fields for storing a person's name and date of birth, as shown highlighted in the following code:

```
public class Person : object
{
    // fields
    public string? Name;
    public DateTime DateOfBirth;
}
```

 We have multiple choices for the data type of the `DateOfBirth` field. .NET 6 introduced the `DateOnly` type. This would store only the date without a time value. `DateTime` stores the date and time of when the person was born. An even better choice might be `DateTimeOffset`, which stores the date, time, and time zone. The choice depends on how much detail you need to store.

Since C# 8, the compiler has had the ability to warn you if a reference type like a `string` could have a `null` value and therefore potentially throw a `NullReferenceException`. Since .NET 6, the SDK enables those warnings by default. You can suffix the `string` type with a question mark ? to indicate that you accept this, and the warning disappears. You will learn more about nullability and how to handle it in *Chapter 6, Implementing Interfaces and Inheriting Classes*.

You can use any type for a field, including arrays and collections such as lists and dictionaries. These would be used if you needed to store multiple values in one named field. In this example, a person only has one name and one date of birth.

Understanding access modifiers

Part of encapsulation is choosing how visible the members are.

Note that, as we did with the class, we explicitly applied the `public` keyword to these fields. If we hadn't, then they would be implicitly `private` to the class, which means they are accessible only inside the class.

There are four access modifier keywords, and two combinations of access modifier keywords that you can apply to a class member, like a field or method, as shown in the following table:

Access Modifier	Description
private	Member is accessible inside the type only. This is the default.
internal	Member is accessible inside the type and any type in the same assembly.
protected	Member is accessible inside the type and any type that inherits from the type.
public	Member is accessible everywhere.
internal protected	Member is accessible inside the type, any type in the same assembly, and any type that inherits from the type. Equivalent to a fictional access modifier named internal_or_protected.
private protected	Member is accessible inside the type and any type that inherits from the type and is in the same assembly. Equivalent to a fictional access modifier named internal_and_protected. This combination is only available with C# 7.2 or later.

Good Practice: Explicitly apply one of the access modifiers to all type members, even if you want to use the implicit access modifier for members, which is private. Additionally, fields should usually be private or protected, and you should then create public properties to get or set the field values. This is because the property then controls access. You will do this later in the chapter.

Setting and outputting field values

Now we will use those fields in your code:

1. In Program.cs, after instantiating bob, add statements to set his name and date of birth, and then output those fields formatted nicely, as shown in the following code:

```
bob.Name = "Bob Smith";
bob.DateOfBirth = new DateTime(1965, 12, 22); // C# 1.0 or later

WriteLine(format: "{0} was born on {1:dddd, d MMMM yyyy}",
  arg0: bob.Name,
  arg1: bob.DateOfBirth);
```

We could have used string interpolation too, but for long strings it will wrap over multiple lines, which can be harder to read in a printed book. In the code examples in this book, remember that {0} is a placeholder for arg0, and so on.

2. Run the code and view the result, as shown in the following output:

```
Bob Smith was born on Wednesday, 22 December 1965
```

Your output may look different based on your locale, that is, language and culture.

The format code for arg1 is made of several parts. dddd means the name of the day of the week. d means the number of the day of the month. MMMM means the name of the month. Lowercase m is used for minutes in time values. yyyy means the full number of the year. yy would mean the two-digit year.

You can also initialize fields using a shorthand **object initializer** syntax using curly braces, which was introduced with C# 3.0. Let's see how:

1. Add statements underneath the existing code to create another new person named Alice. Note the different format code for the date of birth when writing her to the console, as shown in the following code:

    ```
    Person alice = new()
    {
      Name = "Alice Jones",
      DateOfBirth = new(1998, 3, 7) // C# 9.0 or later
    };
    WriteLine(format: "{0} was born on {1:dd MMM yy}",
      arg0: alice.Name,
      arg1: alice.DateOfBirth);
    ```

2. Run the code and view the result, as shown in the following output:

    ```
    Alice Jones was born on 07 Mar 98
    ```

Storing a value using an enum type

Sometimes, a value needs to be one of a limited set of options. For example, there are seven ancient wonders of the world, and a person may have one favorite. At other times, a value needs to be a combination of a limited set of options. For example, a person may have a bucket list of ancient world wonders they want to visit. We are able to store this data by defining an enum type.

An enum type is a very efficient way of storing one or more choices because, internally, it uses integer values in combination with a lookup table of string descriptions:

1. Add a new file to the PacktLibraryNetStandard2 project named WondersOfTheAncientWorld. cs.

2. Modify the WondersOfTheAncientWorld.cs file, as shown in the following code:

    ```
    namespace Packt.Shared;

    public enum WondersOfTheAncientWorld
    {
      GreatPyramidOfGiza,
      HangingGardensOfBabylon,
      StatueOfZeusAtOlympia,
      TempleOfArtemisAtEphesus,
      MausoleumAtHalicarnassus,
      ColossusOfRhodes,
    ```

```
        LighthouseOfAlexandria
    }
```

 Good Practice: If you are writing code in a .NET Interactive notebook, then the code cell containing the enum must be above the code cell defining the Person class.

3. In `Person.cs`, add the following statement to your list of fields:

```
public WondersOfTheAncientWorld FavoriteAncientWonder;
```

4. In `Program.cs`, add the following statements:

```
bob.FavoriteAncientWonder =
    WondersOfTheAncientWorld.StatueOfZeusAtOlympia;

WriteLine(
    format: "{0}'s favorite wonder is {1}. Its integer is {2}.",
    arg0: bob.Name,
    arg1: bob.FavoriteAncientWonder,
    arg2: (int)bob.FavoriteAncientWonder);
```

5. Run the code and view the result, as shown in the following output:

```
Bob Smith's favorite wonder is StatueOfZeusAtOlympia. Its integer is 2.
```

The enum value is internally stored as an `int` for efficiency. The `int` values are automatically assigned starting at 0, so the third world wonder in our enum has a value of 2. You can assign `int` values that are not listed in the enum. They will output as the `int` value instead of a name, since a match will not be found.

Storing multiple values using an enum type

For the bucket list, we could create an array or collection of instances of the enum, and collections will be explained later in this chapter, but there is a better way. We can combine multiple choices into a single value using enum flags:

1. Modify the enum by decorating it with the `[Flags]` attribute, and explicitly set a byte value for each wonder that represents different bit columns, as shown in the following code:

```
namespace Packt.Shared;

[Flags]
public enum WondersOfTheAncientWorld : byte
{
    None                      = 0b_0000_0000, // i.e. 0
    GreatPyramidOfGiza        = 0b_0000_0001, // i.e. 1
    HangingGardensOfBabylon   = 0b_0000_0010, // i.e. 2
```

```
    StatueOfZeusAtOlympia     = 0b_0000_0100, // i.e. 4
    TempleOfArtemisAtEphesus  = 0b_0000_1000, // i.e. 8
    MausoleumAtHalicarnassus  = 0b_0001_0000, // i.e. 16
    ColossusOfRhodes          = 0b_0010_0000, // i.e. 32
    LighthouseOfAlexandria    = 0b_0100_0000  // i.e. 64
}
```

We are assigning explicit values for each choice that will not overlap when looking at the bits stored in memory. We should also decorate the enum type with the System.Flags attribute so that when the value is returned, it can automatically match with multiple values as a comma-separated string instead of returning an int value.

Normally, an enum type uses an int variable internally, but since we don't need values that big, we can reduce memory requirements by 75%, that is, 1 byte per value instead of 4 bytes, by telling it to use a byte variable. As another example, if you wanted to define an enum for days of the week, there will only ever be seven of them.

If we want to indicate that our bucket list includes the *Hanging Gardens of Babylon* and the *Mausoleum at Halicarnassus* ancient world wonders, then we would want the 16 and 2 bits set to 1. In other words, we would store the value 18:

64	32	16	8	4	2	1
0	0	1	0	0	1	0

2. In Person.cs, add the following statement to your list of fields, as shown in the following code:

    ```
    public WondersOfTheAncientWorld BucketList;
    ```

3. In Program.cs, add statements to set the bucket list using the | operator (bitwise logical OR) to combine the enum values. We could also set the value using the number 18 cast into the enum type, as shown in the comment, but we shouldn't because that would make the code harder to understand, as shown in the following code:

    ```
    bob.BucketList =
      WondersOfTheAncientWorld.HangingGardensOfBabylon
      | WondersOfTheAncientWorld.MausoleumAtHalicarnassus;

    // bob.BucketList = (WondersOfTheAncientWorld)18;

    WriteLine($"{bob.Name}'s bucket list is {bob.BucketList}");
    ```

4. Run the code and view the result, as shown in the following output:

    ```
    Bob Smith's bucket list is HangingGardensOfBabylon,
    MausoleumAtHalicarnassus
    ```

Good Practice: Use the enum values to store combinations of discrete options. Derive an enum type from byte if there are up to eight options, from ushort if there are up to 16 options, from uint if there are up to 32 options, and from ulong if there are up to 64 options.

Storing multiple values using collections

Let's now add a field to store a person's children. This is an example of aggregation because children are instances of a class that is related to the current person, but are not part of the person itself. We will use a generic List<T> collection type that can store an ordered collection of any type. You will learn more about collections in *Chapter 8, Working with Common .NET Types*. For now, just follow along:

- In Person.cs, declare a new field to store multiple Person instances that represent the children of this person, as shown in the following code:

```
public List<Person> Children = new();
```

List<Person> is read aloud as "list of Person," for example, "the type of the property named Children is a list of Person instances."

We must ensure the collection is initialized to a new instance before we can add items to it, otherwise the field will be null and it will throw runtime exceptions when we try to use any of its members, like Add.

Understanding generic collections

The angle brackets in the List<T> type is a feature of C# called **generics** that was introduced in 2005 with C# 2.0. It's a fancy term for making a collection **strongly typed**, that is, the compiler knows specifically what type of object can be stored in the collection. Generics improve the performance and correctness of your code.

Strongly typed has a different meaning than **statically typed**. The old System.Collection types are statically typed to contain weakly typed System.Object items. The newer System.Collection.Generic types are statically typed to contain strongly typed <T> instances.

Ironically, the term *generics* means we can use a more specific static type!

1. In Program.cs, add statements to add two children for Bob and then show how many children he has and what their names are, as shown in the following code:

```
bob.Children.Add(new Person { Name = "Alfred" }); // C# 3.0 and later
bob.Children.Add(new() { Name = "Zoe" }); // C# 9.0 and later

WriteLine($"{bob.Name} has {bob.Children.Count} children:");

for (int childIndex = 0; childIndex < bob.Children.Count; childIndex++)
{
  WriteLine($"> {bob.Children[childIndex].Name}");
}
```

We could also use a `foreach` statement to enumerate over the collection. As an extra challenge, change the `for` statement to output the same information using `foreach`.

2. Run the code and view the result, as shown in the following output:

```
Bob Smith has 2 children:
> Alfred
> Zoe
```

Making a field static

The fields that we have created so far have all been **instance** members, meaning that a different value of each field exists for each instance of the class that is created. The `alice` and `bob` variables have different `Name` values.

Sometimes, you want to define a field that only has one value that is shared across all instances.

These are called **static members** because fields are not the only members that can be static. Let's see what can be achieved using `static` fields:

1. In the `PacktLibraryNetStandard2` project, add a new class file named `BankAccount.cs`.

2. Modify the class to give it three fields – two instance fields and one static field – as shown in the following code:

```
namespace Packt.Shared;

public class BankAccount
{
  public string AccountName; // instance member
  public decimal Balance; // instance member
  public static decimal InterestRate; // shared member
}
```

Each instance of `BankAccount` will have its own `AccountName` and `Balance` values, but all instances will share a single `InterestRate` value.

3. In `Program.cs`, add statements to set the shared interest rate and then create two instances of the `BankAccount` type, as shown in the following code:

```
BankAccount.InterestRate = 0.012M; // store a shared value

BankAccount jonesAccount = new();
jonesAccount.AccountName = "Mrs. Jones";
jonesAccount.Balance = 2400;
WriteLine(format: "{0} earned {1:C} interest.",
  arg0: jonesAccount.AccountName,
  arg1: jonesAccount.Balance * BankAccount.InterestRate);
```

```
BankAccount gerrierAccount = new();
gerrierAccount.AccountName = "Ms. Gerrier";
gerrierAccount.Balance = 98;
WriteLine(format: "{0} earned {1:C} interest.",
  arg0: gerrierAccount.AccountName,
  arg1: gerrierAccount.Balance * BankAccount.InterestRate);
```

4. Run the code and view the additional output:

```
Mrs. Jones earned £28.80 interest.
Ms. Gerrier earned £1.18 interest.
```

:C is a format code that tells .NET to use the currency format for the numbers. It will use the default for your operating system installation. I live in Great Britain, hence my output shows British Pounds (£).

You can control the culture that determines the currency symbol and other data formatting by setting a property on the current thread. For example, you could set the culture to British English near the top of Program.cs, as shown in the following code:

```
Thread.CurrentThread.CurrentCulture =
  System.Globalization.CultureInfo.GetCultureInfo("en-GB");
```

 If you would like to learn more about working with languages and cultures, as well as dates, times, and time zones, then there is a chapter about globalization and localization in my companion book, *Apps and Services with .NET 7*.

Fields are not the only members that can be static. Constructors, methods, properties, and other members can also be static.

Making a field constant

If the value of a field will never ever change, you can use the const keyword and assign a literal value at compile time:

1. In Person.cs, add a string constant for the species of a person, as shown in the following code:

    ```
    // constants
    public const string Species = "Homo Sapiens";
    ```

2. To get the value of a constant field, you must write the name of the class, not the name of an instance of the class. In Program.cs, add a statement to write Bob's name and species to the console, as shown in the following code:

    ```
    WriteLine($"{bob.Name} is a {Person.Species}");
    ```

3. Run the code and view the result, as shown in the following output:

    ```
    Bob Smith is a Homo Sapiens
    ```

Examples of `const` fields in Microsoft types include `System.Int32.MaxValue` and `System.Math.PI` because neither value will ever change, as you can see in *Figure 5.2*:

Figure 5.2: Examples of constants in the Math class

Good Practice: Constants are not always the best choice for two important reasons: the value must be known at compile time, and it must be expressible as a literal `string`, `Boolean`, or number value. Every reference to the `const` field is replaced with the literal value at compile time, which will, therefore, not be reflected if the value changes in a future version and you do not recompile any assemblies that reference it to get the new value.

Making a field read-only

Often, a better choice for fields that should not change is to mark them as read-only:

1. In `Person.cs`, add a statement to declare an instance read-only field to store a person's home planet, as shown in the following code:

    ```
    // read-only fields
    public readonly string HomePlanet = "Earth";
    ```

2. In `Program.cs`, add a statement to write Bob's name and home planet to the console, as shown in the following code:

    ```
    WriteLine($"{bob.Name} was born on {bob.HomePlanet}");
    ```

3. Run the code and view the result, as shown in the following output:

    ```
    Bob Smith was born on Earth
    ```

Good Practice: Use read-only fields over constant fields for two important reasons: the value can be calculated or loaded at runtime and can be expressed using any executable statement. So, a read-only field can be set using a constructor or a field assignment. Every reference to the read-only field is a live reference, so any future changes will be correctly reflected by the calling code.

You can also declare `static readonly` fields whose values will be shared across all instances of the type.

Initializing fields with constructors

Fields often need to be initialized at runtime. You do this in a constructor that will be called when you make an instance of the class using the `new` keyword. Constructors execute before any fields are set by the code that is using the type:

1. In `Person.cs`, add statements after the existing read-only `HomePlanet` field to define a second read-only field and then set the `Name` and `Instantiated` fields in a constructor, as shown in the following code:

    ```
    // read-only fields
    public readonly string HomePlanet = "Earth";
    public readonly DateTime Instantiated;

    // constructors
    public Person()
    {
      // set default values for fields
      // including read-only fields
      Name = "Unknown";
      Instantiated = DateTime.Now;
    }
    ```

2. In `Program.cs`, add statements to instantiate a new person and then output its initial field values, as shown in the following code:

    ```
    Person blankPerson = new();

    WriteLine(format:
      "{0} of {1} was created at {2:hh:mm:ss} on a {2:dddd}.",
      arg0: blankPerson.Name,
      arg1: blankPerson.HomePlanet,
      arg2: blankPerson.Instantiated);
    ```

3. Run the code and view the result, as shown in the following output:

    ```
    Unknown of Earth was created at 11:58:12 on a Sunday
    ```

Defining multiple constructors

You can have multiple constructors in a type. This is especially useful to encourage developers to set initial values for fields:

1. In `Person.cs`, add statements to define a second constructor that allows a developer to set initial values for the person's name and home planet, as shown in the following code:

    ```
    public Person(string initialName, string homePlanet)
    {
    ```

```
    Name = initialName;
    HomePlanet = homePlanet;
    Instantiated = DateTime.Now;
  }
```

2. In `Program.cs`, add statements to create another person using the constructor with two pa-
    rameters, as shown in the following code:

    ```
    Person gunny = new(initialName: "Gunny", homePlanet: "Mars");

    WriteLine(format:
      "{0} of {1} was created at {2:hh:mm:ss} on a {2:dddd}.",
      arg0: gunny.Name,
      arg1: gunny.HomePlanet,
      arg2: gunny.Instantiated);
    ```

3. Run the code and view the result:

    ```
    Gunny of Mars was created at 11:59:25 on a Sunday
    ```

Constructors are a special category of method. Let's look at methods in more detail.

Writing and calling methods

Methods are members of a type that execute a block of statements. They are functions that belong
to a type.

Returning values from methods

Methods can return a single value or return nothing:

*   A method that performs some actions but does not return a value indicates this with the void
    type before the name of the method.
*   A method that performs some actions and returns a value indicates this with the type of the
    return value before the name of the method.

For example, in the next task, you will create two methods:

*   `WriteToConsole`: This will perform an action (writing some text to the console), but it will
    return nothing from the method, indicated by the void keyword.
*   `GetOrigin`: This will return a text value, indicated by the string keyword.

Let's write the code:

1. In `Person.cs`, add statements to define the two methods that I described earlier, as shown in
    the following code:

    ```
    // methods
    public void WriteToConsole()
    {
      WriteLine($"{Name} was born on a {DateOfBirth:dddd}.");
    ```

```
}

public string GetOrigin()
{
    return $"{Name} was born on {HomePlanet}.";
}
```

2. In `Program.cs`, add statements to call the two methods, as shown in the following code:

```
bob.WriteToConsole();
WriteLine(bob.GetOrigin());
```

3. Run the code and view the result, as shown in the following output:

```
Bob Smith was born on a Wednesday.
Bob Smith was born on Earth.
```

Combining multiple returned values using tuples

Each method can only return a single value that has a single type. That type could be a simple type, such as `string` in the previous example; a complex type, such as `Person`; or a collection type, such as `List<Person>`.

Imagine that we want to define a method named `GetTheData` that needs to return both a `string` value and an `int` value. We could define a new class named `TextAndNumber` with a `string` field and an `int` field, and return an instance of that complex type, as shown in the following code:

```
public class TextAndNumber
{
    public string Text;
    public int Number;
}

public class LifeTheUniverseAndEverything
{
    public TextAndNumber GetTheData()
    {
        return new TextAndNumber
        {
            Text = "What's the meaning of life?",
            Number = 42
        };
    }
}
```

But defining a class just to combine two values together is unnecessary because, in modern versions of C#, we can use **tuples**. Tuples are an efficient way to combine two or more values into a single unit. I pronounce them as *tuh-ples* but I have heard other developers pronounce them as *too-ples*. To-may-toe, to-mah-toe, po-tay-toe, po-tah-toe, I guess.

Tuples have been a part of some languages, such as F#, since their first version, but .NET only added support for them with .NET 4.0 in 2010 using the `System.Tuple` type.

C# language support for tuples

It was only with C# 7.0 in 2017 that C# added language syntax support for tuples using the parentheses characters ( ) and, at the same time, .NET added a new `System.ValueTuple` type that is more efficient in some common scenarios than the old .NET 4.0 `System.Tuple` type. The C# tuple syntax uses the more efficient one.

Let's explore tuples:

1. In `Person.cs`, add statements to define a method that returns a tuple that combines a `string` and `int`, as shown in the following code:

```
public (string, int) GetFruit()
{
  return ("Apples", 5);
}
```

2. In `Program.cs`, add statements to call the `GetFruit` method and then output the tuple's fields, which are automatically named `Item1` and `Item2`, as shown in the following code:

```
(string, int) fruit = bob.GetFruit();
WriteLine($"{fruit.Item1}, {fruit.Item2} there are.");
```

3. Run the code and view the result, as shown in the following output:

```
Apples, 5 there are.
```

Naming the fields of a tuple

To access the fields of a tuple, the default names are `Item1`, `Item2`, and so on.

You can explicitly specify the field names:

1. In `Person.cs`, add statements to define a method that returns a tuple with named fields, as shown in the following code:

```
public (string Name, int Number) GetNamedFruit()
{
  return (Name: "Apples", Number: 5);
}
```

2. In `Program.cs`, add statements to call the method and output the tuple's named fields, as shown in the following code:

```
var fruitNamed = bob.GetNamedFruit();
WriteLine($"There are {fruitNamed.Number} {fruitNamed.Name}.");
```

3. Run the code and view the result, as shown in the following output:

```
There are 5 Apples.
```

If you are constructing a tuple from another object, you can use a feature introduced in C# 7.1 called **tuple name inference**.

4. In `Program.cs`, create two tuples, made of a `string` and `int` value each, as shown in the following code:

```
var thing1 = ("Neville", 4);
WriteLine($"{thing1.Item1} has {thing1.Item2} children.");


var thing2 = (bob.Name, bob.Children.Count);
WriteLine($"{thing2.Name} has {thing2.Count} children.");
```

In C# 7.0, both things would use the `Item1` and `Item2` naming schemes. In C# 7.1 and later, `thing2` can infer the names `Name` and `Count`.

Deconstructing tuples

You can also deconstruct tuples into separate variables. The deconstructing declaration has the same syntax as named field tuples, but without a named variable for the tuple, as shown in the following code:

```
// store return value in a tuple variable with two fields
(string TheName, int TheNumber) tupleWithNamedFields = bob.GetNamedFruit();
// tupleWithNamedFields.TheName
// tupleWithNamedFields.TheNumber
// deconstruct return value into two separate variables
(string name, int number) = bob.GetNamedFruit();
// name
// number
```

This has the effect of splitting the tuple into its parts and assigning those parts to new variables:

1. In `Program.cs`, add statements to deconstruct the tuple returned from the `GetFruit` method, as shown in the following code:

```
(string fruitName, int fruitNumber) = bob.GetFruit();
WriteLine($"Deconstructed: {fruitName}, {fruitNumber}");
```

2. Run the code and view the result, as shown in the following output:

```
Deconstructed: Apples, 5
```

Deconstructing types

Tuples are not the only type that can be deconstructed. Any type can have special methods, named `Deconstruct`, that break down the object into parts. Let's implement some for the `Person` class:

1. In `Person.cs`, add two `Deconstruct` methods with out parameters defined for the parts we want to deconstruct into, as shown in the following code:

```
// deconstructors
public void Deconstruct(out string? name, out DateTime dob)
{
```

```
    name = Name;
    dob = DateOfBirth;
  }

  public void Deconstruct(out string? name,
    out DateTime dob, out WondersOfTheAncientWorld fav)
  {
    name = Name;
    dob = DateOfBirth;
    fav = FavoriteAncientWonder;
  }
```

 Although I introduce the out keyword in the preceding code, you will learn about it properly in a few pages' time.

2.   In `Program.cs`, add statements to deconstruct `bob`, as shown in the following code:

```
// Deconstructing a Person
var (name1, dob1) = bob; // implicitly calls the Deconstruct method
WriteLine($"Deconstructed: {name1}, {dob1}");


var (name2, dob2, fav2) = bob;
WriteLine($"Deconstructed: {name2}, {dob2}, {fav2}");
```

 You do not explicitly call the **Deconstruct** method. It is called implicitly when you assign an object to a tuple variable.

3.   Run the code and view the result, as shown in the following output:

```
Deconstructed: Bob Smith, 22/12/1965 00:00:00
Deconstructed: Bob Smith, 22/12/1965 00:00:00, StatueOfZeusAtOlympia
```

Defining and passing parameters to methods

Methods can have parameters passed to them to change their behavior. Parameters are defined a bit like variable declarations but inside the parentheses of the method, as you saw earlier in this chapter with constructors. Let's see more examples:

1.   In `Person.cs`, add statements to define two methods, the first without parameters and the second with one parameter, as shown in the following code:

```
public string SayHello()
{
```

```
    return $"{Name} says 'Hello!'";
}

public string SayHelloTo(string name)
{
    return $"{Name} says 'Hello, {name}!'";
}
```

2. In `Program.cs`, add statements to call the two methods and write the return value to the console, as shown in the following code:

```
WriteLine(bob.SayHello());
WriteLine(bob.SayHelloTo("Emily"));
```

3. Run the code and view the result:

```
Bob Smith says 'Hello!'
Bob Smith says 'Hello, Emily!'
```

When typing a statement that calls a method, IntelliSense shows a tooltip with the name, the type of any parameters, and the return type of the method.

Overloading methods

Instead of having two different method names, we could give both methods the same name. This is allowed because the methods each have a different signature. You saw an example of this with the two `Deconstruct` methods.

A **method signature** is a list of parameter types that can be passed when calling the method. Overloaded methods cannot differ only in the return type:

1. In `Person.cs`, change the name of the `SayHelloTo` method to `SayHello`.

2. In `Program.cs`, change the method call to use the `SayHello` method, and note that the quick info for the method tells you that it has an additional overload, **1 of 2**, as well as **2 of 2**, as shown in *Figure 5.3*:

Figure 5.3: An IntelliSense tooltip for an overloaded method

> **Good Practice:** Use overloaded methods to simplify your class by making it appear to have fewer methods.

Passing optional and named parameters

Another way to simplify methods is to make parameters optional. You make a parameter optional by assigning a default value inside the method parameter list. Optional parameters must always come last in the list of parameters.

We will now create a method with three optional parameters:

1. In `Person.cs`, add statements to define the method, as shown in the following code:

```
public string OptionalParameters(string command  = "Run!",
  double number = 0.0, bool active = true)
{
  return string.Format(
    format: "command is {0}, number is {1}, active is {2}",
    arg0: command,
    arg1: number,
    arg2: active);
}
```

2. In `Program.cs`, add a statement to call the method and write its return value to the console, as shown in the following code:

```
WriteLine(bob.OptionalParameters());
```

3. Watch IntelliSense appear as you type the code. You will see a tooltip showing the three optional parameters with their default values, as shown in *Figure 5.4*:

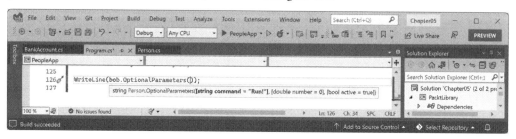

Figure 5.4: IntelliSense showing optional parameters as you type code

4. Run the code and view the result, as shown in the following output:

```
command is Run!, number is 0, active is True
```

5. In `Program.cs`, add a statement to pass a `string` value for the `command` parameter and a `double` value for the `number` parameter, as shown in the following code:

```
WriteLine(bob.OptionalParameters("Jump!", 98.5));
```

6. Run the code and see the result, as shown in the following output:

```
command is Jump!, number is 98.5, active is True
```

The default values for the `command` and `number` parameters have been replaced, but the default for `active` is still `true`.

Naming parameter values when calling methods

Optional parameters are often combined with naming parameters when you call the method, because naming a parameter allows the values to be passed in a different order than how they were declared:

1. In `Program.cs`, add a statement to pass a `string` value for the `command` parameter and a `double` value for the `number` parameter but using named parameters, so that the order they are passed through can be swapped around, as shown in the following code:

   ```
   WriteLine(bob.OptionalParameters(number: 52.7, command: "Hide!"));
   ```

2. Run the code and view the result, as shown in the following output:

   ```
   command is Hide!, number is 52.7, active is True
   ```

   You can even use named parameters to skip over optional parameters.

3. In `Program.cs`, add a statement to pass a `string` value for the `command` parameter using positional order, skip the `number` parameter, and use the named `active` parameter, as shown in the following code:

   ```
   WriteLine(bob.OptionalParameters("Poke!", active: false));
   ```

4. Run the code and view the result, as shown in the following output:

   ```
   command is Poke!, number is 0, active is False
   ```

Controlling how parameters are passed

When a parameter is passed into a method, it can be passed in one of three ways:

- By **value** (this is the default): Think of these as being *in-only*.
- As an out parameter: Think of these as being *out-only*. out parameters cannot have a default value assigned in the parameter declaration and they cannot be left uninitialized. They must be set inside the method or the compiler will give an error.
- By **reference** as a `ref` parameter: Think of these as being *in-and-out*. Like out parameters, `ref` parameters also cannot have default values, but since they can already be set outside the method, they do not need to be set inside the method.

Let's see some examples of passing parameters in and out:

1. In `Person.cs`, add statements to define a method with three parameters, one in parameter, one `ref` parameter, and one out parameter, as shown in the following method:

   ```
   public void PassingParameters(int x, ref int y, out int z)
   {
     // out parameters cannot have a default
     // AND must be initialized inside the method
     z = 99;
   ```

```
    // increment each parameter
    x++;
    y++;
    z++;
}
```

2. In `Program.cs`, add statements to declare some `int` variables and pass them into the method, as shown in the following code:

```
int a = 10;
int b = 20;
int c = 30;
WriteLine($"Before: a = {a}, b = {b}, c = {c}");
bob.PassingParameters(a, ref b, out c);
WriteLine($"After: a = {a}, b = {b}, c = {c}");
```

3. Run the code and view the result, as shown in the following output:

```
Before: a = 10, b = 20, c = 30
After: a = 10, b = 21, c = 100
```

-   When passing a variable as a parameter by default, its current value gets passed, not the variable itself. Therefore, x has a copy of the value of the a variable. The a variable retains its original value of 10.

-   When passing a variable as a `ref` parameter, a reference to the variable gets passed into the method. Therefore, y is a reference to b. The b variable gets incremented when the y parameter gets incremented.

-   When passing a variable as an out parameter, a reference to the variable gets passed into the method. Therefore, z is a reference to c. The value of the c variable gets replaced by whatever code executes inside the method. We could simplify the code in the Main method by not assigning the value 30 to the c variable, since it will always be replaced anyway.

Simplified out parameters

In C# 7.0 and later, we can simplify code that uses the out parameter:

1. In `Program.cs`, add statements to declare some more variables, including an out parameter named f declared inline, as shown in the following code:

```
int d = 10;
int e = 20;
WriteLine($"Before: d = {d}, e = {e}, f doesn't exist yet!");

// simplified C# 7.0 or later syntax for the out parameter
bob.PassingParameters(d, ref e, out int f);
WriteLine($"After: d = {d}, e = {e}, f = {f}");
```

2. Run the code and view the result, as shown in the following output:

```
Before: d = 10, e = 20, f doesn't exist yet!
After: d = 10, e = 21, f = 100
```

Understanding ref returns

In C# 7.0 or later, the ref keyword is not just for passing parameters into a method; it can also be applied to the return value. This allows an external variable to reference an internal variable and modify its value after the method call. This might be useful in advanced scenarios, for example, passing around placeholders into big data structures, but it's beyond the scope of this book.

Splitting classes using partial

When working on large projects with multiple team members, or when working with especially large and complex class implementations, it is useful to be able to split the definition of a class across multiple files. You do this using the partial keyword.

Imagine we want to add statements to the Person class that are automatically generated by a tool like an object-relational mapper that reads schema information from a database. If the class is defined as partial, then we can split the class into an autogenerated code file and a manually edited code file.

Let's write some code that simulates this example:

1. In Person.cs, add the partial keyword, as shown highlighted in the following code:

```
public partial class Person
```

2. In the PacktLibraryNetStandard2 project/folder, add a new class file named PersonAutoGen.cs.
3. Add statements to the new file, as shown in the following code:

```
namespace Packt.Shared;

// this file simulates an autogenerated class

public partial class Person
{
}
```

The rest of the code we write for this chapter will be written in the PersonAutoGen.cs file.

Controlling access with properties and indexers

Earlier, you created a method named GetOrigin that returned a string containing the name and origin of the person. Languages such as Java do this a lot. C# has a better way: properties.

A **property** is simply a method (or a pair of methods) that acts and looks like a field when you want to get or set a value, thereby simplifying the syntax.

Defining read-only properties

A readonly property only has a get implementation:

1. In `PersonAutoGen.cs`, in the `Person` class, add statements to define three properties:

    *   The first property will perform the same role as the `GetOrigin` method using the property syntax that works with all versions of C#.

    *   The second property will return a greeting message using the lambda expression body `=>` syntax from C# 6 and later.

    *   The third property will calculate the person's age.

2. Here's the code:

    ```csharp
    // a readonly property defined using C# 1 - 5 syntax
    public string Origin
    {
      get
      {
        return string.Format("{0} was born on {1}",
          arg0: Name, arg1: HomePlanet);
      }
    }

    // two readonly properties defined using C# 6+ lambda expression body
    syntax
    public string Greeting => $"{Name} says 'Hello!'";
    public int Age => DateTime.Today.Year - DateOfBirth.Year;
    ```

     Good Practice: This isn't the best way to calculate someone's age, but we aren't learning how to calculate an age from a date of birth. If you need to do that properly, read the discussion at the following link: https://stackoverflow.com/questions/9/how-do-i-calculate-someones-age-in-c.

3. In `Program.cs`, add the statements to get the properties, as shown in the following code:

    ```csharp
    Person sam = new()
    {
      Name = "Sam",
      DateOfBirth = new(1969, 6, 25)
    };
    WriteLine(sam.Origin);
    WriteLine(sam.Greeting);
    WriteLine(sam.Age);
    ```

4. Run the code and view the result, as shown in the following output:

    ```
    Sam was born on Earth
    ```

```
Sam says 'Hello!'
53
```

The output shows 53 because I ran the console app on February 20, 2022, when Sam was 53 years old.

Defining settable properties

To create a settable property, you must use the older syntax and provide a pair of methods—not just a get part, but also a set part:

1. In PersonAutoGen.cs, add statements to define a string property that has both a get and set method (also known as a **getter** and **setter**), as shown in the following code:

    ```
    // a read-write property defined using C# 3.0 syntax
    public string? FavoriteIceCream { get; set; } // auto-syntax
    ```

    Although you have not manually created a field to store the person's favorite ice cream, it is there, automatically created by the compiler for you.

    Sometimes, you need more control over what happens when a property is set. In this scenario, you must use a more detailed syntax and manually create a private field to store the value for the property.

2. In PersonAutoGen.cs, add statements to define a string field and string property that has both a get and set, as shown in the following code:

    ```
    // a private field to store the property value
    private string? favoritePrimaryColor;

    // a public property to read and write to the field
    public string? FavoritePrimaryColor
    {
      get
      {
        return favoritePrimaryColor;
      }
      set
      {
        switch (value?.ToLower())
        {
          case "red":
          case "green":
          case "blue":
            favoritePrimaryColor = value;
            break;
          default:
            throw new ArgumentException(
              $"{value} is not a primary color. " +
              "Choose from: red, green, blue.");
    ```

```
        }
    }
}
```

Good Practice: Avoid adding too much code to your getters and setters. This could indicate a problem with your design. Consider adding private methods that you then call in setters and getters to simplify your implementations.

3. In `Program.cs`, add statements to set Sam's favorite ice cream and color, and then write them out, as shown in the following code:

```
sam.FavoriteIceCream = "Chocolate Fudge";
WriteLine($"Sam's favorite ice-cream flavor is {sam.FavoriteIceCream}.");

string color = "Red";
try
{
  sam.FavoritePrimaryColor = color;
  WriteLine($"Sam's favorite primary color is {sam.
FavoritePrimaryColor}.");
}
catch (Exception ex)
{
  WriteLine("Tried to set {0} to '{1}': {2}",
    nameof(sam.FavoritePrimaryColor), color, ex.Message);
}
```

The print book is limited to about 820 pages. If I added exception handling code to all code examples as we have done here, then I would have to remove at least one chapter from the book to make enough space. In future, I will not explicitly tell you to add exception handling code, but get into the habit of adding it yourself when needed.

4. Run the code and view the result, as shown in the following output:

```
Sam's favorite ice-cream flavor is Chocolate Fudge.
Sam's favorite primary color is Red.
```

5. Try to set the color to any value other than red, green, or blue, like black.

6. Run the code and view the result, as shown in the following output:

```
Tried to set FavoritePrimaryColor to 'Black': Black is not a primary
color. Choose from: red, green, blue.
```

Good Practice: Use properties instead of fields when you want to read and write to a field without using a method pair like `GetAge` and `SetAge`.

Requiring properties to be set during instantiation

C# 11 introduces the `required` modifier. If you use it on a property or field, the compiler will ensure that you set the property or field to a value when you instantiate it. It requires targeting .NET 7 or later, so we need to create a new class library first:

1. In the `Chapter05` solution or workspace, add a new class library project named `PacktLibraryModern` that targets .NET 7.0.

2. In the `PacktLibraryModern` project, add a new class file named `Book.cs`.

3. Modify the class to give it four properties, with two set as `required`, as shown in the following code:

```
namespace Packt.Shared;

public class Book
{
    // Needs .NET 7 or later as well as C# 11 or later.
    public required string? Isbn { get; set; }
    public required string? Title { get; set; }
    public string? Author { get; set; }
    public int PageCount { get; set; }
}
```

Note that all **three** string properties are nullable. Setting a property or field to be `required` does not mean that it cannot be `null`. It just means that it must be explicitly set to `null`.

4. In `Program.cs`, attempt to instantiate a `Book` without setting the `Isbn` and `Title` properties, as shown in the following code:

```
Book book = new();
```

5. Note that you will see a compiler error, as shown in the following output:

```
C:\cs11dotnet7-old\Chapter05\PeopleApp\Program.cs(164,13): error CS9035:
Required member 'Book.Isbn' must be set in the object initializer or
attribute constructor. [C:\cs11dotnet7-old\Chapter05\PeopleApp\PeopleApp.
csproj]
C:\cs11dotnet7-old\Chapter05\PeopleApp\Program.cs(164,13): error CS9035:
Required member 'Book.Title' must be set in the object initializer or
attribute constructor. [C:\cs11dotnet7-old\Chapter05\PeopleApp\PeopleApp.
csproj]
```

```
 0 Warning(s)
 2 Error(s)
```

6. In `Program.cs`, modify the statement to set the two required properties using object initialization syntax, as shown in the following code:

```
Book book = new()
{
  Isbn = "978-1803237800",
  Title = "C# 11 and .NET 7 - Modern Cross-Platform Development
Fundamentals"
};


WriteLine("{0}: {1} written by {2} has {3:N0} pages.",
  book.Isbn, book.Title, book.Author, book.PageCount);
```

7. Note that the statement now compiles without errors.

8. In the `PacktLibraryModern` project, in `Book.cs`, add statements to define a pair of constructors, one that supports initialization syntax and one to set the two required properties, as shown highlighted in the following code:

```
public class Book
{
  public Book() { } // For use with initialization syntax.

  public Book(string? isbn, string? title)
  {
    Isbn = isbn;
    Title = title;
  }
  ...
```

9. In `Program.cs`, comment out the statement that instantiates a book using initialization syntax, add a statement to instantiate a book using the constructor, and then set the non-required properties for the book, as shown in the following code:

```
/*
Book book = new()
{
  Isbn = "978-1803237800",
  Title = "C# 11 and .NET 7 - Modern Cross-Platform Development
  Fundamentals"
};
*/
Book book = new(isbn: "978-1803237800",
```

```
      title: "C# 11 and .NET 7 - Modern Cross-Platform Development
      Fundamentals")
  {
    Author = "Mark J. Price",
    PageCount = 821
  };
```

10. Note that you will see a compiler error as before, because the compiler cannot automatically tell that calling the constructor will have set the two required properties.

11. In the `PacktLibraryModern` project, in `Book.cs`, import the namespace for performing code analysis and then decorate the constructor with the attribute for telling the compiler that it sets all required properties and fields, as shown highlighted in the following code:

```
using System.Diagnostics.CodeAnalysis; // [SetsRequiredMembers]

namespace Packt.Shared;

public class Book
{
  public Book() { } // For use with initialization syntax.

  [SetsRequiredMembers]
  public Book(string isbn, string title)
```

12. In `Program.cs`, note that the statement that calls the constructor now compiles without errors.

13. Optionally, run the console app to confirm it behaves as expected, as shown in the following output:

```
978-1803237800: C# 11 and .NET 7 - Modern Cross-Platform Development
Fundamentals written by Mark J. Price has 821 pages.
```

Defining indexers

Indexers allow the calling code to use the array syntax to access a property. For example, the `string` type defines an indexer so that the calling code can access individual characters in the `string`, as shown in the following code:

```
string alphabet = "abcdefghijklmnopqrstuvwxyz";
char letterF = alphabet[5]; // 0 is a, 1 is b, and so on
```

We will define an indexer to simplify access to the children of a person:

1. In `PersonAutoGen.cs`, add statements to define an indexer to get and set a child using the index of the child, as shown in the following code:

```
// indexers
public Person this[int index]
{
  get
```

```
    {
      return Children[index]; // pass on to the List<T> indexer
    }
    set
    {
      Children[index] = value;
    }
  }
```

You can overload indexers so that different types can be used for their parameters. For example, as well as passing an int value, you could also pass a string value.

2. In `PersonAutoGen.cs`, add statements to define an indexer to get and set a child using the name of the child, as shown in the following code:

```
public Person this[string name]
{
  get
  {
    return Children.Find(p => p.Name == name);
  }
  set
  {
    Person found = Children.Find(p => p.Name == name);
    if (found is not null) found = value;
  }
}
```

 You will learn more about collections like List<T> in *Chapter 8, Working with Common .NET Types*, and how to write lambda expressions using => in *Chapter 11, Querying and Manipulating Data Using LINQ*.

3. In `Program.cs`, add statements to add two children to Sam, and then access the first and second child using the longer Children field and the shorter indexer syntax, as shown in the following code:

```
sam.Children.Add(new() { Name = "Charlie", DateOfBirth = new(2010, 3, 18)
});
sam.Children.Add(new() { Name = "Ella", DateOfBirth = new(2020, 12, 24)
});

// get using Children List
WriteLine($"Sam's first child is {sam.Children[0].Name}.");
WriteLine($"Sam's second child is {sam.Children[1].Name}.");

// get using integer position indexer
```

```
WriteLine($"Sam's first child is {sam[0].Name}.");
WriteLine($"Sam's second child is {sam[1].Name}.");

// get using name indexer
WriteLine($"Sam's child named Ella is {sam["Ella"].Age} years old.");
```

4. Run the code and view the result, as shown in the following output:

```
Sam's first child is Charlie.
Sam's second child is Ella.
Sam's first child is Charlie.
Sam's second child is Ella.
Sam's child named Ella is 2 years old.
```

More about methods

I wanted to think of some methods that would apply to a Person instance that could also become operators like + and *. What would adding two people together represent? What would multiplying two people represent? The obvious answers are getting married and making babies.

We might want two instances of Person to be able to marry and procreate. We can implement this by writing methods and overriding operators. Instance methods are actions that an object does to itself; static methods are actions the type does.

Which you choose depends on what makes the most sense for the action.

 Good Practice: Having both static and instance methods to perform similar actions often makes sense. For example, string has both a Compare static method and a CompareTo instance method. This puts the choice of how to use the functionality in the hands of the programmers using your type, giving them more flexibility.

Implementing functionality using methods

Let's start by implementing some functionality by using both static and instance methods:

1. In PersonAutoGen.cs, in the Person class, add read-only properties with private backing storage fields to indicate if that person is married and to whom, as shown in the following code:

```
private bool married = false;
public bool Married => married;

private Person? spouse = null;
public Person? Spouse => spouse;
```

2. In PersonAutoGen.cs, add one instance method and one static method to the Person class that will allow two Person objects to marry, as shown in the following code:

```
// static method to marry
public static void Marry(Person p1, Person p2)
```

```
{
  p1.Marry(p2);
}

// instance method to marry
public void Marry(Person partner)
{
  if (married) return;
  spouse = partner;
  married = true;
  partner.Marry(this); // this is the current object
}
```

Note the following:

- In the `static` method named `Marry`, the `Person` objects are passed as parameters named p1 and p2 to the instance method `Marry`.

- In the instance method named `Marry`, the spouse is set to the `partner` passed as a parameter, and the married Boolean is set to `true`.

3. In `PersonAutoGen.cs`, add one instance method and one static method to the `Person` class that will allow two `Person` objects to procreate, as shown in the following code:

```
// static method to "multiply"
public static Person Procreate(Person p1, Person p2)
{
  if (p1.Spouse != p2)
  {
    throw new ArgumentException("You must be married to procreate.");
  }

  Person baby = new()
  {
    Name = $"Baby of {p1.Name} and {p2.Name}",
    DateOfBirth = DateTime.Now
  };

  p1.Children.Add(baby);
  p2.Children.Add(baby);

  return baby;
}

// instance method to "multiply"
public Person ProcreateWith(Person partner)
{
  return Procreate(this, partner);
}
```

Note the following:

- In the `static` method named `Procreate`, the `Person` objects that will procreate are passed as parameters named p1 and p2.
- A new `Person` class named baby is created with a name composed of a combination of the two people who have procreated. This could be changed later by setting the returned baby variable's `Name` property.
- The baby object is added to the `Children` collection of both parents and then returned. Classes are reference types, meaning a reference to the baby object stored in memory is added, not a clone of the baby object. You will learn the difference between reference types and value types later in *Chapter 6, Implementing Interfaces and Inheriting Classes.*
- In the instance method named `ProcreateWith`, the `Person` object to procreate with is passed as a parameter named `partner`, and it, along with `this`, is passed to the static `Procreate` method to reuse the method implementation. `this` is a keyword that references the current instance of the class.

Good Practice: A method that creates a new object, or modifies an existing object, should return a reference to that object so that the caller can access the results.

We will tell the story of Lamech and his two wives and their children, as described at the following link: `https://www.kingjamesbibleonline.org/Genesis-4-19/`.

4. In `Program.cs`, create three people and have them marry and then procreate with each other, noting that to add a double-quote character into a `string`, you must prefix it with a backslash character like this, \", as shown in the following code:

```
Person lamech = new() { Name = "Lamech" };
Person adah = new() { Name = "Adah" };
Person zillah = new() { Name = "Zillah" };

lamech.Marry(adah);
Person.Marry(zillah, lamech);

WriteLine($"{lamech.Name} is married to {lamech.Spouse?.Name ??
"nobody"}");
WriteLine($"{adah.Name} is married to {adah.Spouse?.Name ?? "nobody"}");
WriteLine($"{zillah.Name} is married to {zillah.Spouse?.Name ??
"nobody"}");

// call instance method
Person baby1 = lamech.ProcreateWith(adah);
```

```
baby1.Name = "Jabal";
WriteLine($"{baby1.Name} was born on {baby1.DateOfBirth}");

// call static method
Person baby2 = Person.Procreate(zillah, lamech);
baby2.Name = "Tubalcain";

WriteLine($"{lamech.Name} has {lamech.Children.Count} children.");
WriteLine($"{adah.Name} has {adah.Children.Count} children.");
WriteLine($"{zillah.Name} has {zillah.Children.Count} children.");

for (int i = 0; i < lamech.Children.Count; i++)
{
  WriteLine(format: "{0}'s child #{1} is named \"{2}\".",
    arg0: lamech.Name, arg1: i, arg2: lamech[i].Name);
}
```

5. Run the code and view the result, as shown in the following output:

```
Lamech is married to Adah
Adah is married to Lamech
Zillah is married to Lamech
Jabal was born on 20/02/2022 16:26:35
Lamech has 2 children.
Adah has 1 children.
Zillah has 1 children.
Lamech's child #0 is named "Jabal".
Lamech's child #1 is named "Tubalcain".
```

Implementing functionality using operators

The System.String class has a static method named Concat that concatenates two string values and returns the result, as shown in the following code:

```
string s1 = "Hello ";
string s2 = "World!";
string s3 = string.Concat(s1, s2);
WriteLine(s3); // Hello World!
```

Calling a method like Concat works, but it might be more natural for a programmer to use the + symbol operator to "add" two string values together, as shown in the following code:

```
string s3 = s1 + s2;
```

A well-known biblical phrase is *Go forth and multiply*, meaning to procreate. Let's write code so that the * (multiply) symbol will allow two Person objects to procreate. And we will use the + operator to marry two people.

We do this by defining a `static` operator for the * symbol. The syntax is rather like a method, because in effect, an operator *is* a method, but uses a symbol instead of a method name, which makes the syntax more concise:

1. In `PersonAutoGen.cs`, create a `static` operator for the + symbol, as shown in the following code:

```
// operator to "marry"
public static bool operator +(Person p1, Person p2)
{
  Marry(p1, p2);
  return p1.Married && p2.Married; // confirm they are both now married
}
```

The return type for an operator does not need to match the types passed as parameters to the operator, but the return type cannot be void.

2. In `PersonAutoGen.cs`, create a `static` operator for the * symbol, as shown in the following code:

```
// operator to "multiply"
public static Person operator *(Person p1, Person p2)
{
  return Procreate(p1, p2);
}
```

Good Practice: Unlike methods, operators do not appear in IntelliSense lists for a type. For every operator that you define, make a method as well, because it may not be obvious to a programmer that the operator is available. The implementation of the operator can then call the method, reusing the code you have written. A second reason for providing a method is that operators are not supported by every language compiler; for example, although arithmetic operators like * are supported by Visual Basic and F#, there is no requirement that other languages support all operators supported by C#.

3. In `Program.cs`, comment out the statement that calls that static `Marry` method to marry Zillah and Lamech, and replace it with an `if` statement that uses the + operator to marry them, as shown in the following code:

```
// Person.Marry(zillah, lamech);
if (zillah + lamech)
{
  WriteLine($"{zillah.Name} and {lamech.Name} successfully got
married.");
}
```

4. In `Program.cs`, after calling the `Procreate` method and before the statements that write the children to the console, use the * operator for Lamech to make two more babies with his wives Adah and Zillah, as shown highlighted in the following code:

```
// use operator to "multiply"
Person baby3 = lamech * adah;
baby3.Name = "Jubal";


Person baby4 = zillah * lamech;
baby4.Name = "Naamah";
```

5. Run the code and view the result, as shown in the following output:

```
Zillah and Lamech successfully got married.
Lamech is married to Adah
Adah is married to Lamech
Zillah is married to Lamech
Jabal was born on 20/02/2022 16:49:43
Lamech has 4 children.
Adah has 2 children.
Zillah has 2 children.
Lamech's child #0 is named "Jabal".
Lamech's child #1 is named "Tubalcain".
Lamech's child #2 is named "Jubal".
Lamech's child #3 is named "Naamah".
```

Implementing functionality using local functions

A language feature introduced in C# 7.0 is the ability to define a **local function**.

Local functions are the method equivalent of local variables. In other words, they are methods that are only accessible from within the containing method in which they have been defined. In other languages, they are sometimes called **nested** or **inner functions**.

Local functions can be defined anywhere inside a method: the top, the bottom, or even somewhere in the middle!

We will use a local function to implement a factorial calculation:

1. In `PersonAutoGen.cs`, add statements to define a `Factorial` function that uses a local function inside itself to calculate the result, as shown in the following code:

```
// method with a local function
public static int Factorial(int number)
{
  if (number < 0)
  {
    throw new ArgumentException(
      $"{nameof(number)} cannot be less than zero.");
  }
```

```
    return localFactorial(number);

    int localFactorial(int localNumber) // Local function
    {
      if (localNumber == 0) return 1;
      return localNumber * localFactorial(localNumber - 1);
    }
}
```

2. In `Program.cs`, add statements to call the `Factorial` function and write the return value to the console, with exception handling, as shown in the following code:

```
int number = 5; // change to -1 to make the exception handling code
execute

try
{
  WriteLine($"{number}! is {Person.Factorial(number)}");
}
catch (Exception ex)
{
  WriteLine($"{ex.GetType()} says: {ex.Message} number was {number}.");
}
```

3. Run the code and view the result, as shown in the following output:

```
5! is 120
```

4. Change the number to -1 so we can check the exception handling.

5. Run the code and view the result, as shown in the following output:

```
System.ArgumentException says: number cannot be less than zero. number
was -1.
```

Pattern matching with objects

In *Chapter 3, Controlling Flow, Converting Types, and Handling Exceptions*, you were introduced to basic pattern matching. In this section, we will explore pattern matching in more detail.

Defining flight passengers

In this example, we will define some classes that represent various types of passengers on a flight and then we will use a switch expression with pattern matching to determine the cost of their flight:

1. In the `PacktLibraryNetStandard2` project/folder, add a new file named `FlightPatterns.cs`.

2. In `FlightPatterns.cs`, add statements to define three types of passenger with different properties, as shown in the following code:

```
namespace Packt.Shared;
```

```csharp
public class Passenger
{
  public string? Name { get; set; }
}

public class BusinessClassPassenger : Passenger
{
  public override string ToString()
  {
    return $"Business Class: {Name}";
  }
}

public class FirstClassPassenger : Passenger
{
  public int AirMiles { get; set; }

  public override string ToString()
  {
    return $"First Class with {AirMiles:N0} air miles: {Name}";
  }
}

public class CoachClassPassenger : Passenger
{
  public double CarryOnKG { get; set; }

  public override string ToString()
  {
    return $"Coach Class with {CarryOnKG:N2} KG carry on: {Name}";
  }
}
```

 You will learn about overriding the ToString method in *Chapter 6, Implementing Interfaces and Inheriting Classes.*

3. In `Program.cs`, add statements to define an object array containing five passengers of various types and property values, and then enumerate them, outputting the cost of their flight, as shown in the following code:

```csharp
Passenger[] passengers = {
  new FirstClassPassenger { AirMiles = 1_419, Name = "Suman" },
  new FirstClassPassenger { AirMiles = 16_562, Name = "Lucy" },
  new BusinessClassPassenger { Name = "Janice" },
  new CoachClassPassenger { CarryOnKG = 25.7, Name = "Dave" },
```

```
    new CoachClassPassenger { CarryOnKG = 0, Name = "Amit" },
};

foreach (Passenger passenger in passengers)
{
  decimal flightCost = passenger switch
  {
    FirstClassPassenger p when p.AirMiles > 35000 => 1500M,
    FirstClassPassenger p when p.AirMiles > 15000 => 1750M,
    FirstClassPassenger _                          => 2000M,
    BusinessClassPassenger _                       => 1000M,
    CoachClassPassenger p when p.CarryOnKG < 10.0 => 500M,
    CoachClassPassenger _                          => 650M,
    _                                              => 800M
  };
  WriteLine($"Flight costs {flightCost:C} for {passenger}");
}
```

While reviewing the preceding code, note the following:

- To pattern match on the properties of an object, you must name a local variable, like p, that can then be used in an expression.
- To pattern match on a type only, you can use _ to discard the local variable.
- The switch expression also uses _ to represent its default branch.

4. Run the code and view the result, as shown in the following output:

```
Flight costs £2,000.00 for First Class with 1,419 air miles: Suman
Flight costs £1,750.00 for First Class with 16,562 air miles: Lucy
Flight costs £1,000.00 for Business Class: Janice
Flight costs £650.00 for Coach Class with 25.70 KG carry on: Dave
Flight costs £500.00 for Coach Class with 0.00 KG carry on: Amit
```

Enhancements to pattern matching in C# 9 or later

The previous examples worked with C# 8. Now we will look at some enhancements in C# 9 and later. First, you no longer need to use the underscore to discard when doing type matching:

1. In Program.cs, comment out the C# 8 syntax and add C# 9 and later syntax to modify the branches for first-class passengers to use a nested switch expression and the new support for conditionals like >, as shown in the following code:

```
decimal flightCost = passenger switch
{
  /* C# 8 syntax
  FirstClassPassenger p when p.AirMiles > 35000 => 1500M,
  FirstClassPassenger p when p.AirMiles > 15000 => 1750M,
  FirstClassPassenger                           => 2000M, */
```

```
// C# 9 or later syntax
FirstClassPassenger p => p.AirMiles switch
{
   > 35000 => 1500M,
   > 15000 => 1750M,
          _ => 2000M
},
BusinessClassPassenger                        => 1000M,
CoachClassPassenger p when p.CarryOnKG < 10.0 => 500M,
CoachClassPassenger                           => 650M,
_                                             => 800M
};
```

2.   Run the code to view the results, and note they are the same as before.

You could also use the relational pattern in combination with the property pattern to avoid the nested switch expression, as shown in the following code:

```
FirstClassPassenger { AirMiles: > 35000 } => 1500,
FirstClassPassenger { AirMiles: > 15000 } => 1750M,
FirstClassPassenger                       => 2000M,
```

Working with records

Before we dive into the new records language feature, let us see some other related new features of C# 9 and later.

Init-only properties

You have used object initialization syntax to instantiate objects and set initial properties throughout this chapter. Those properties can also be changed after instantiation.

Sometimes, you want to treat properties like `readonly` fields so they can be set during instantiation but not after. The new `init` keyword enables this. It can be used in place of the `set` keyword:

1.   In the `PacktLibraryNetStandard2` project/folder, add a new file named `Records.cs`.

2.   In `Records.cs`, define a person class with two immutable properties, as shown in the following code:

```
namespace Packt.Shared;

public class ImmutablePerson
{
  public string? FirstName { get; init; }
  public string? LastName { get; init; }
}
```

3. In `Program.cs`, add statements to instantiate a new immutable person and then try to change one of its properties, as shown in the following code:

```
ImmutablePerson jeff = new()
{
  FirstName = "Jeff",
  LastName = "Winger"
};
jeff.FirstName = "Geoff";
```

4. Compile the console app and note the compile error, as shown in the following output:

```
Program.cs(254,7): error CS8852: Init-only property or indexer
'ImmutablePerson.FirstName' can only be assigned in an object
initializer, or on 'this' or 'base' in an instance constructor or an
'init' accessor. [/Users/markjprice/Code/Chapter05/PeopleApp/PeopleApp.
csproj]
```

5. Comment out the attempt to set the `FirstName` property after instantiation.

Understanding records

Init-only properties provide some immutability to C#. You can take the concept further by using **records**. These are defined by using the `record` keyword instead of the `class` keyword. That can make the whole object immutable, and it acts like a value when compared. We will discuss equality and comparisons of classes, records, and value types in more detail in *Chapter 6, Implementing Interfaces and Inheriting Classes.*

Records should not have any state (properties and fields) that changes after instantiation. Instead, the idea is that you create new records from existing ones. The new record has the changed state. This is called non-destructive mutation. To do this, C# 9 introduced the `with` keyword:

1. In `Records.cs`, add a record named `ImmutableVehicle`, as shown in the following code:

```
public record ImmutableVehicle
{
  public int Wheels { get; init; }
  public string? Color { get; init; }
  public string? Brand { get; init; }
}
```

2. In `Program.cs`, add statements to create a car and then a mutated copy of it, as shown in the following code:

```
ImmutableVehicle car = new()
{
  Brand = "Mazda MX-5 RF",
  Color = "Soul Red Crystal Metallic",
  Wheels = 4
};
```

```
ImmutableVehicle repaintedCar = car
  with { Color = "Polymetal Grey Metallic" };
WriteLine($"Original car color was {car.Color}.");
WriteLine($"New car color is {repaintedCar.Color}.");
```

3. Run the code to view the results, and note the change to the car color in the mutated copy, as shown in the following output:

```
Original car color was Soul Red Crystal Metallic.
New car color is Polymetal Grey Metallic.
```

Positional data members in records

The syntax for defining a record can be greatly simplified using positional data members.

Simplifying data members in records

Instead of using object initialization syntax with curly braces, sometimes you might prefer to provide a constructor with positional parameters, as you saw earlier in this chapter. You can also combine this with a deconstructor for splitting the object into individual parts, as shown in the following code:

```
public record ImmutableAnimal
{
  public string Name { get; init; }
  public string Species { get; init; }
  public ImmutableAnimal(string name, string species)
  {
    Name = name;
    Species = species;
  }
  public void Deconstruct(out string name, out string species)
  {
    name = Name;
    species = Species;
  }
}
```

The properties, constructor, and deconstructor can be generated for you:

1. In `Records.cs`, add statements to define another record using simplified syntax known as positional records, as shown in the following code:

```
// simpler way to define a record
// auto-generates the properties, constructor, and deconstructor
public record ImmutableAnimal(string Name, string Species);
```

2. In `Program.cs`, add statements to construct and deconstruct immutable animals, as shown in the following code:

```
ImmutableAnimal oscar = new("Oscar", "Labrador");
```

```
var (who, what) = oscar; // calls Deconstruct method
WriteLine($"{who} is a {what}.");
```

3. Run the application and view the results, as shown in the following output:

```
Oscar is a Labrador.
```

You will see records again when we look at C# 10 support for creating `struct` records in *Chapter 6, Implementing Interfaces and Inheriting Classes*.

Practicing and exploring

Test your knowledge and understanding by answering some questions, getting some hands-on practice, and exploring this chapter's topics with deeper research.

Exercise 5.1 – Test your knowledge

Answer the following questions:

1. What are the six combinations of access modifier keywords and what do they do?
2. What is the difference between the `static`, `const`, and `readonly` keywords when applied to a type member?
3. What does a constructor do?
4. Why should you apply the `[Flags]` attribute to an enum type when you want to store combined values?
5. Why is the `partial` keyword useful?
6. What is a tuple?
7. What does the `record` keyword do?
8. What does overloading mean?
9. What is the difference between a field and a property?
10. How do you make a method parameter optional?

Exercise 5.2 – Explore topics

Use the links on the following page to learn more detail about the topics covered in this chapter:

https://github.com/markjprice/cs11dotnet7/blob/main/book-links.md#chapter-5---building-your-own-types-with-object-oriented-programming

Summary

In this chapter, you learned about:

- Making your own types using OOP.
- Some of the different categories of members that a type can have, including fields to store data and methods to perform actions.
- OOP concepts, such as aggregation and encapsulation.

- How to use operators as an alternative to methods to implement simple functionality.
- How to use modern C# features like relational and property pattern matching enhancements, `init`-only properties, and records.

In the next chapter, you will take these concepts further by defining delegates and events, implementing interfaces, and inheriting from existing classes.

6

Implementing Interfaces and Inheriting Classes

This chapter is about deriving new types from existing ones using **object-oriented programming (OOP)**. You will learn about generics and how they make your code safer and more performant. You will learn about delegates and events for exchanging messages between types. You will see the differences between reference and value types. You will implement interfaces for common functionality. You will create a derived class to inherit from a base class to reuse functionality, override an inherited type member, and use polymorphism. You will learn how to create extension methods and how to cast between classes in an inheritance hierarchy. Finally, you will learn how to write better code with the help of static code analyzers.

This chapter covers the following topics:

- Setting up a class library and console application
- Making types safely reusable with generics
- Raising and handling events
- Implementing interfaces
- Managing memory with reference and value types
- Working with null values
- Inheriting from classes
- Casting within inheritance hierarchies
- Inheriting and extending .NET types
- Writing better code

Setting up a class library and console application

We will start by defining a workspace/solution with two projects like the one created in *Chapter 5, Building Your Own Types with Object-Oriented Programming*. Even if you completed all the exercises in that chapter, follow the instructions below so that you start this chapter with fresh working projects:

1. Use your preferred coding tool to create a new project, as defined in the following list:

    *   Project template: **Class Library**/classlib
    *   Project file and folder: PacktLibrary
    *   Workspace/solution file and folder: Chapter06

2. Add a new project, as defined in the following list:

    *   Project template: **Console App**/console
    *   Project file and folder: PeopleApp
    *   Workspace/solution file and folder: Chapter06

3. In the PacktLibrary project, rename the file named Class1.cs to Person.cs.

4. In both projects, add <ItemGroup> to globally and statically import the System.Console class, as shown in the following markup:

```
<ItemGroup>
    <Using Include="System.Console" Static="true" />
</ItemGroup>
```

5. Modify the Person.cs file contents, as shown in the following code:

```
namespace Packt.Shared;

public class Person : object
{
  // properties
  public string? Name { get; set; }
  public DateTime DateOfBirth { get; set; }

  // methods
  public void WriteToConsole()
  {
    WriteLine($"{Name} was born on a {DateOfBirth:dddd}.");
  }
}
```

6. In the PeopleApp project, add a project reference to PacktLibrary, as shown in the following markup:

```
<ItemGroup>
  <ProjectReference
```

```
      Include="..\PacktLibrary\PacktLibrary.csproj" />
  </ItemGroup>
```

7. In `Program.cs`, delete the existing statements and then write statements to create an instance of `Person` and write information about it to the console, as shown in the following code:

```
using Packt.Shared;

Person harry = new()
{
  Name = "Harry",
  DateOfBirth = new(year: 2001, month: 3, day: 25)
};

harry.WriteToConsole();
```

8. Run the `PeopleApp` project and note the result, as shown in the following output:

```
Harry was born on a Sunday.
```

Making types safely reusable with generics

In 2005, with C# 2.0 and .NET Framework 2.0, Microsoft introduced a feature named **generics**, which enables your types to be more safely reusable and more efficient. It does this by allowing a programmer to pass types as parameters, like how you can pass objects as parameters.

Working with non-generic types

First, let's look at an example of working with a non-generic type so that you can understand the problem that generics are designed to solve, such as weakly typed parameters and values, and performance problems caused by using `System.Object`.

`System.Collections.Hashtable` can be used to store multiple values each with a unique key that can later be used to quickly look up its value. Both the key and value can be any object because they are declared as `System.Object`. Although this provides flexibility when storing value types like integers, it is slow, and bugs are easier to introduce because no type checks are made when adding items.

Let's write some code:

1. In `Program.cs`, create an instance of the non-generic collection, `System.Collections.Hashtable`, and then add four items to it, as shown in the following code:

```
// non-generic lookup collection
System.Collections.Hashtable lookupObject = new();
lookupObject.Add(key: 1, value: "Alpha");
lookupObject.Add(key: 2, value: "Beta");
lookupObject.Add(key: 3, value: "Gamma");
lookupObject.Add(key: harry, value: "Delta");
```

2. Add statements to define a key with the value of 2 and use it to look up its value in the *hash table*, as shown in the following code:

```
int key = 2; // Look up the value that has 2 as its key

WriteLine(format: "Key {0} has value: {1}",
  arg0: key,
  arg1: lookupObject[key]);
```

3. Add statements to use the `harry` object to look up its value, as shown in the following code:

```
// Look up the value that has harry as its key
WriteLine(format: "Key {0} has value: {1}",
  arg0: harry,
  arg1: lookupObject[harry]);
```

4. Run the code and note that it works, as shown in the following output:

```
Key 2 has value: Beta
Key Packt.Shared.Person has value: Delta
```

Although the code works, there is potential for mistakes because literally any type can be used for the key or value. If another developer used your *lookup object* and expected all the items to be a certain type, they might cast them to that type and get exceptions because some values might be a different type. A lookup object with lots of items would also give poor performance.

 Good Practice: Avoid types imported into the `System.Collections` namespace. Use types imported in `System.Collections.Generics` and other namespaces instead.

Working with generic types

`System.Collections.Generic.Dictionary<TKey, TValue>` can be used to store multiple values, each with a unique key that can later be used to quickly look up its value. Both the key and value can be any object, but you must tell the compiler what the types of the key and value will be when you first instantiate the collection. You do this by specifying types for the **generic parameters** in angle brackets <>, TKey, and TValue.

 Good Practice: When a generic type has one definable type, it should be named T, for example, `List<T>`, where T is the type stored in the list. When a generic type has multiple definable types, they should use T as a name prefix and have a sensible name, for example, `Dictionary<TKey, TValue>`.

This provides flexibility, it is faster, and bugs are easier to avoid because type checks are made when adding items. We will not need to explicitly specify the `System.Collections.Generic` namespace that contains `Dictionary<TKey, TValue>` because it is implicitly and globally imported by default.

Let's write some code to solve the problem by using generics:

1. In `Program.cs`, create an instance of the generic lookup collection `Dictionary<TKey, TValue>` and then add four items to it, as shown in the following code:

    ```
    // generic lookup collection
    Dictionary<int, string> lookupIntString = new();
    lookupIntString.Add(key: 1, value: "Alpha");
    lookupIntString.Add(key: 2, value: "Beta");
    lookupIntString.Add(key: 3, value: "Gamma");
    lookupIntString.Add(key: harry, value: "Delta");
    ```

2. Note the compile error when using `harry` as a key, as shown in the following output:

    ```
    /Users/markjprice/Code/Chapter06/PeopleApp/Program.cs(98,32): error
    CS1503: Argument 1: cannot convert from 'Packt.Shared.Person' to 'int' [/
    Users/markjprice/Code/Chapter06/PeopleApp/PeopleApp.csproj]
    ```

3. Replace `harry` with **4**.

4. Add statements to set the key to 3 and use it to look up its value in the dictionary, as shown in the following code:

    ```
    key = 3;

    WriteLine(format: "Key {0} has value: {1}",
      arg0: key,
      arg1: lookupIntString[key]);
    ```

5. Run the code and note that it works, as shown in the following output:

    ```
    Key 3 has value: Gamma
    ```

Raising and handling events

Methods are often described as *actions that an object can perform, either on itself or on related objects*. For example, `List<T>` can add an item to itself or clear itself, and `File` can create or delete a file in the filesystem.

Events are often described as *actions that happen to an object*. For example, in a user interface, `Button` has a `Click` event, a click being something that happens to a button, and `FileSystemWatcher` listens to the filesystem for change notifications and raises events like `Created` and `Deleted` that are triggered when a directory or file changes.

Another way of thinking of events is that they provide a way of exchanging messages between two objects.

Events are built on **delegates**, so let's start by having a look at what delegates are and how they work.

Calling methods using delegates

You have already seen the most common way to call or execute a method: using the `.` operator to access the method using its name. For example, `Console.WriteLine` tells the `Console` type to call its `WriteLine` method.

The other way to call or execute a method is to use a delegate. If you have used languages that support **function pointers**, then think of a delegate as being a **type-safe method pointer**.

In other words, a delegate contains the memory address of a method that matches the same signature as the delegate so that it can be called safely with the correct parameter types.

For example, imagine there is a method in the `Person` class that must have a `string` type passed as its only parameter, and it returns an `int` type, as shown in the following code:

```
public int MethodIWantToCall(string input)
{
  return input.Length; // it doesn't matter what the method does
}
```

I can call this method on an instance of `Person` named p1 like this:

```
Person p1 = new();
int answer = p1.MethodIWantToCall("Frog");
```

Alternatively, I can define a delegate with a matching signature to call the method indirectly. Note that the names of the parameters do not have to match. Only the types of parameters and return values must match, as shown in the following code:

```
delegate int DelegateWithMatchingSignature(string s);
```

Now, I can create an instance of the delegate, point it at the method, and finally, call the delegate (which calls the method), as shown in the following code:

```
// create a delegate instance that points to the method
DelegateWithMatchingSignature d = new(p1.MethodIWantToCall);

// call the delegate, who then calls the method
int answer2 = d("Frog");
```

You are probably thinking, "What's the point of that?" Well, it provides flexibility.

For example, we could use delegates to create a queue of methods that need to be called in order. Queuing actions that need to be performed is common in services to provide improved scalability.

Another example is to allow multiple actions to perform in parallel. Delegates have built-in support for asynchronous operations that run on a different thread, and that can provide improved responsiveness.

The most important example is that delegates allow us to implement events for sending messages between different objects that do not need to know about each other. Events are an example of loose coupling between components because the components do not need to know about each other; they just need to know the event signature.

Delegates and events are two of the most confusing features of C# and can take a few attempts to understand, so don't worry if you feel lost as we walk through how they work!

Defining and handling delegates

Microsoft has two predefined delegates for use as events. They both have two parameters:

- `object? sender`: This parameter is a reference to the object raising the event or sending the message. The reference could be `null`.
- `EventArgs e` or `TEventArgs e`: This parameter contains additional relevant information about the event that is occurring. For example, in a GUI app, you might define `MouseMoveEventArgs` that has properties for the X and Y coordinates for the mouse pointer. A bank account might have a `WithdrawEventArgs` with a property for the `amount` to withdraw.

Their signatures are simple, yet flexible, as shown in the following code:

```
// for methods that do not need additional argument values passed in
public delegate void EventHandler(object? sender, EventArgs e);


// for methods that need additional argument values passed in as
// defined by the generic type TEventArgs
public delegate void EventHandler<TEventArgs>(object? sender, TEventArgs e);
```

 Good Practice: When you want to define an event in your own type, you should use one of these two predefined delegates.

Let's explore delegates and events:

1. Add statements to the `Person` class and note the following points, as shown in the following code:
   - It defines an `EventHandler` delegate field named `Shout`.
   - It defines an `int` field to store `AngerLevel`.
   - It defines a method named `Poke`.
   - Each time a person is poked, their `AngerLevel` increments. Once their `AngerLevel` reaches three, they raise the `Shout` event, but only if there is at least one event delegate pointing at a method defined somewhere else in the code; that is, it is not `null`:

     ```
     // delegate field
     public EventHandler? Shout;
     ```

```
// data field
public int AngerLevel;

// method
public void Poke()
{
  AngerLevel++;
  if (AngerLevel >= 3)
  {
    // if something is listening...
    if (Shout != null)
    {
      // ...then call the delegate
      Shout(this, EventArgs.Empty);
    }
  }
}
```

 Checking whether an object is not null before calling one of its methods is very common. C# 6.0 and later allows null checks to be simplified inline using a ? symbol before the . operator, as shown in the following code:

```
Shout?.Invoke(this, EventArgs.Empty);
```

2. In the `PeopleApp` project, add a new class file named `Program.EventHandlers.cs`.

3. In `Program.EventHandlers.cs`, add a method with a matching signature that gets a reference to the `Person` object from the `sender` parameter and outputs some information about them, as shown in the following code:

```
using Packt.Shared;

partial class Program
{
  // a method to handle the Shout event received by the harry object
  static void Harry_Shout(object? sender, EventArgs e)
  {
    if (sender is null) return;
    Person? p = sender as Person;
    if (p is null) return;

    WriteLine($"{p.Name} is this angry: {p.AngerLevel}.");
  }
}
```

Microsoft's convention for method names that handle events is `ObjectName_EventName`.

4. In `Program.cs`, add a statement to assign the method to the delegate field, and then add statements to call the `Poke` method four times, as shown in the following code:

```
// assign a method to the Shout delegate
harry.Shout = Harry_Shout;

// call the Poke method that raises the Shout event
harry.Poke();
harry.Poke();
harry.Poke();
harry.Poke();
```

5. Run the code and view the result, and note that Harry says nothing the first two times he is poked, and only gets angry enough to shout once he's been poked at least three times, as shown in the following output:

```
Harry is this angry: 3.
Harry is this angry: 4.
```

Defining and handling events

You've now seen how delegates implement the most important functionality of events: the ability to define a signature for a method that can be implemented by a completely different piece of code, and then call that method and any others that are hooked up to the delegate field.

But what about events? There is less to them than you might think.

When assigning a method to a delegate field, you should not use the simple assignment operator as we did in the preceding example.

Delegates are multicast, meaning that you can assign multiple delegates to a single delegate field. Instead of the = assignment, we could have used the += operator so that we could add more methods to the same delegate field. When the delegate is called, all the assigned methods are called, although you have no control over the order in which they are called.

If the `Shout` delegate field was already referencing one or more methods, by assigning a method, it would replace all the others. With delegates that are used for events, we usually want to make sure that a programmer only ever uses either the += operator or the -= operator to assign and remove methods:

1. To enforce this, in `Person.cs`, add the `event` keyword to the delegate field declaration, as shown highlighted in the following code:

```
public event EventHandler? Shout;
```

2. Build the `PeopleApp` project and note the compiler error message, as shown in the following output:

```
Program.cs(41,13): error CS0079: The event 'Person.Shout' can only appear
on the left hand side of += or -=
```

This is (almost) all that the event keyword does! If you will never have more than one method assigned to a delegate field, then technically you do not need "events," but it is still good practice to indicate your meaning and that you expect a delegate field to be used as an event.

3. In `Program.cs`, modify the comment and the method assignment to use +=, as shown in the following code:

```
// assign event handler methods to Shout event
harry.Shout += Harry_Shout;
```

4. Run the code and note that it has the same behavior as before.

5. In `Program.EventHandlers.cs`, copy and paste the method, and then change its comment, name, and output, as shown highlighted in the following code:

```
// another method to handle the Shout event received by the harry object
static void Harry_Shout2(object? sender, EventArgs e)
{
  if (sender is null) return;
  Person? p = sender as Person;
  if (p is null) return;

  WriteLine($"Stop it!");
}
```

6. In `Program.cs`, after the statement that assigns the `Harry_Shout` method to the `Shout` event, add a statement to attach the new event handler to the `Shout` event too, as shown highlighted in the following code:

```
harry.Shout += Harry_Shout;
harry.Shout += Harry_Shout2;
```

7. Run the code and view the result, and note that both event handlers execute whenever the event is raised, as shown in the following output:

```
Harry is this angry: 3.
Stop it!
Harry is this angry: 4.
Stop it!
```

Implementing interfaces

Interfaces are a way to implement standard functionality and connect different types to make new things. Think of them like the studs on top of LEGO™ bricks, which allow them to "stick" together, or electrical standards for plugs and sockets.

If a type implements an interface, then it is making a promise to the rest of .NET that it supports specific functionality. Therefore, they are sometimes described as contracts.

Common interfaces

Here are some common interfaces that your types might implement:

Interface	Method(s)	Description
IComparable	CompareTo(other)	This defines a comparison method that a type implements to order or sort its instances.
IComparer	Compare(first, second)	This defines a comparison method that a secondary type implements to order or sort instances of a primary type.
IDisposable	Dispose()	This defines a disposal method to release unmanaged resources more efficiently than waiting for a finalizer. See the *Releasing unmanaged resources* section later in this chapter for more details.
IFormattable	ToString(format, culture)	This defines a culture-aware method to format the value of an object into a string representation.
IFormatter	Serialize(stream, object) Deserialize(stream)	This defines methods to convert an object to and from a stream of bytes for storage or transfer.
IFormatProvider	GetFormat(type)	This defines a method to format inputs based on a language and region.

Comparing objects when sorting

One of the most common interfaces that you will want to implement is IComparable. It has one method named CompareTo. It has two variations, one that works with a nullable object type and one that works with a nullable generic type T, as shown in the following code:

```
namespace System
{
  public interface IComparable
  {
    int CompareTo(object? obj);
  }

  public interface IComparable<in T>
  {
    int CompareTo(T? other);
  }
}
```

For example, the `string` type implements `IComparable` by returning `-1` if the `string` should be sorted before the `string` being compared to, `1` if it should be sorted after, and `0` if they are equal. The `int` type implements `IComparable` by returning `-1` if the `int` is less than the `int` being compared to, `1` if it is greater, and `0` if they are equal.

If a type implements one of the `IComparable` interfaces, then arrays and collections containing instances of that type can be sorted.

Before we implement the `IComparable` interface and its `CompareTo` method for the `Person` class, let's see what happens when we try to sort an array of `Person` instances, including some that are `null` or have a `null` value for their `Name` property:

1. In the `PeopleApp` project, add a new class file named `Program.Helpers.cs`.

2. In `Program.Helpers.cs`, add a method to the `Program` class that will output all the names of a collection of people passed as a parameter with a title beforehand, as shown in the following code:

```csharp
using Packt.Shared;

partial class Program
{
  static void OutputPeopleNames(IEnumerable<Person?> people, string
title)
  {
    WriteLine(title);
    foreach (Person? p in people)
    {
      WriteLine("  {0}",
        p is null ? "<null> Person" : p.Name ?? "<null> Name");

      /* if p is null then output: <null> Person
         else output: p.Name
         unless p.Name is null in which case output: <null> Name */
    }
  }
}
```

3. In `Program.cs`, add statements that create an array of `Person` instances and call the `OutputPeopleNames` method to write the items to the console, and then attempt to sort the array and write the items to the console again, as shown in the following code:

```csharp
Person?[] people =
{
  null,
  new() { Name = "Simon" },
  new() { Name = "Jenny" },
  new() { Name = "Adam" },
  new() { Name = null },
```

```
    new() { Name = "Richard" }
};

OutputPeopleNames(people, "Initial list of people:");

Array.Sort(people);

OutputPeopleNames(people,
    "After sorting using Person's IComparable implementation:");
```

4. Run the code and an exception will be thrown. As the message explains, to fix the problem, our type must implement `IComparable`, as shown in the following output:

```
Unhandled Exception: System.InvalidOperationException: Failed to compare
two elements in the array. ---> System.ArgumentException: At least one
object must implement IComparable.
```

5. In `Person.cs`, after inheriting from `object`, add a comma and enter `IComparable<Person?>`, as shown highlighted in the following code:

```
public class Person : object, IComparable<Person?>
```

 Your code editor will draw a red squiggle under the new code to warn you that you have not yet implemented the method you promised to. Your code editor can write the skeleton implementation for you.

6. Click on the light bulb and then click **Implement interface**.

7. Scroll down to the bottom of the `Person` class to find the method that was written for you, as shown in the following code:

```
public int CompareTo(Person? other)
{
    throw new NotImplementedException();
}
```

8. Delete the statement that throws the `NotImplementedException` error.

9. Add statements to handle variations of input values, including `null`, and call the `CompareTo` method of the `Name` field, which uses the `string` type's implementation of `CompareTo`, and return the result, as shown in the following code:

```
int position;
if ((this is not null) && (other is not null))
{
    if ((Name is not null) && (other.Name is not null))
    {
        // if both Name values are not null,
        // use the string implementation of CompareTo
```

```
      position = Name.CompareTo(other.Name);
    }
    else if ((Name is not null) && (other.Name is null))
    {
      position = -1; // else this Person precedes other Person
    }
    else if ((Name is null) && (other.Name is not null))
    {
      position = 1; // else this Person follows other Person
    }
    else
    {
      position = 0; // this Person and other Person are at same position
    }
}
else if ((this is not null) && (other is null))
{
  position = -1; // this Person precedes other Person
}
else if ((this is null) && (other is not null))
{
  position = 1; // this Person follows other Person
}
else
{
  position = 0; // this Person and other Person are at same position
}
return position;
```

 We have chosen to compare two `Person` instances by comparing their `Name` fields. `Person` instances will, therefore, be sorted alphabetically by their name. `null` values will be sorted to the bottom of the collection. Storing the calculated `position` before returning it is useful when debugging.

10. Run the `PeopleApp` console app and note that this time it works as it should, sorted alphabetically by name, as shown in the following output:

```
Initial list of people:
  <null> Person
  Simon
  Jenny
  Adam
  <null> Name
  Richard
After sorting using Person's IComparable implementation:
```

```
    Adam
    Jenny
    Richard
    Simon
    <null> Name
    <null> Person
```

 Good Practice: If anyone wants to sort an array or collection of instances of your type, then implement the `IComparable` interface.

Comparing objects using a separate class

Sometimes, you won't have access to the source code for a type, and it might not implement the `IComparable` interface. Luckily, there is another way to sort instances of a type. You can create a separate type that implements a slightly different interface, named `IComparer`:

1. In the `PacktLibrary` project, add a new class file named `PersonComparer.cs` containing a class implementing the `IComparer` interface that will compare two people, that is, two `Person` instances. Implement it by comparing the length of their `Name` field, or if the names are the same length, then compare the names alphabetically, as shown in the following code:

```csharp
namespace Packt.Shared;

public class PersonComparer : IComparer<Person?>
{
  public int Compare(Person? x, Person? y)
  {
    int position;
    if ((x is not null) && (y is not null))
    {
      if ((x.Name is not null) && (y.Name is not null))
      {
        // if both Name values are not null...

        // ...compare the Name lengths...
        int result = x.Name.Length.CompareTo(y.Name.Length);

        /// ...if they are equal...
        if (result == 0)
        {
          // ...then compare by the Names...
          return x.Name.CompareTo(y.Name);
        }
        else
```

```
        {
          // ...otherwise compare by the lengths.
          position = result;
        }
      }
      else if ((x.Name is not null) && (y.Name is null))
      {
        position = -1; // else x Person precedes y Person
      }
      else if ((x.Name is null) && (y.Name is not null))
      {
        position = 1; // else x Person follows y Person
      }
      else
      {
        position = 0; // x Person and y Person are at same position
      }
    }
    else if ((x is not null) && (y is null))
    {
      position = -1; // x Person precedes y Person
    }
    else if ((x is null) && (y is not null))
    {
      position = 1; // x Person follows y Person
    }
    else
    {
      position = 0; // x Person and y Person are at same position
    }
    return position;
  }
}
```

2. In `Program.cs`, add statements to sort the array using this alternative implementation, as shown in the following code:

```
Array.Sort(people, new PersonComparer());

OutputPeopleNames(people,
  "After sorting using PersonComparer's IComparer implementation:");
```

3. Run the `PeopleApp` console app and view the result of sorting the people by the length of names and then alphabetically, as shown in the following output:

```
After sorting using PersonComparer's IComparer implementation:
  Adam
  Jenny
```

```
    Simon
    Richard
    <null> Name
    <null> Person
```

This time, when we sort the people array, we explicitly ask the sorting algorithm to use the PersonComparer type instead, so that the people are sorted with the shortest names first, like Adam, and the longest names last, like Richard; and when the lengths of two or more names are equal, to sort them alphabetically, like Jenny and Simon.

Implicit and explicit interface implementations

Interfaces can be implemented implicitly and explicitly. Implicit implementations are simpler and more common. Explicit implementations are only necessary if a type must have multiple methods with the same name and signature.

For example, both IGamePlayer and IKeyHolder might have a method called Lose with the same parameters because both a game and a key can be lost. In a type that must implement both interfaces, only one implementation of Lose can be the implicit method. If both interfaces can share the same implementation, that works, but if not, then the other Lose method will have to be implemented differently and called explicitly, as shown in the following code:

```
public interface IGamePlayer
{
  void Lose();
}

public interface IKeyHolder
{
  void Lose();
}

public class Person : IGamePlayer, IKeyHolder
{
  public void Lose() // implicit implementation
  {
    // implement losing a key
  }

  void IGamePlayer.Lose() // explicit implementation
  {
    // implement losing a game
  }
}
```

```
// calling implicit and explicit implementations of Lose
Person p = new();
p.Lose(); // calls implicit implementation of losing a key

((IGamePlayer)p).Lose(); // calls explicit implementation of losing a game

IGamePlayer player = p as IGamePlayer;
player.Lose(); // calls explicit implementation of losing a game
```

Defining interfaces with default implementations

A language feature introduced in C# 8.0 is **default implementations** for an interface. Let's see it in action:

1. In the PacktLibrary project, add a new file named IPlayable.cs.

2. Modify the statements to define a public IPlayable interface with two methods to Play and Pause, as shown in the following code:

    ```
    namespace Packt.Shared;

    public interface IPlayable
    {
      void Play();
      void Pause();
    }
    ```

3. In the PacktLibrary project, add a new class file named DvdPlayer.cs.

4. Modify the statements in the file to implement the IPlayable interface, as shown in the following code:

    ```
    namespace Packt.Shared;

    public class DvdPlayer : IPlayable
    {
      public void Pause()
      {
        WriteLine("DVD player is pausing.");
      }

      public void Play()
      {
        WriteLine("DVD player is playing.");
      }
    }
    ```

This is useful, but what if we decide to add a third method named Stop? Before C# 8.0, this would be impossible once at least one type is implemented in the original interface. One of the main points of an interface is that it is a fixed contract.

C# 8.0 allows an interface to add new members after release as long as they have a default implementation. C# purists do not like the idea, but for practical reasons, such as avoiding breaking changes or having to define a whole new interface, it is useful, and other languages such as Java and Swift enable similar techniques.

Support for default interface implementations requires some fundamental changes to the underlying platform, so they are only supported with C# if the target framework is .NET 5.0 or later, .NET Core 3.0 or later, or .NET Standard 2.1. They are therefore not supported by .NET Framework. Let's add a Stop method:

5. Modify the IPlayable interface to add a Stop method with a default implementation, as shown highlighted in the following code:

```
namespace Packt.Shared;

public interface IPlayable
{
  void Play();
  void Pause();
  void Stop() // default interface implementation
  {
    WriteLine("Default implementation of Stop.");
  }
}
```

6. Build the PeopleApp project and note that the projects compile successfully despite the DvdPlayer class not implementing Stop. In the future, we could override the default implementation of Stop by implementing it in the DvdPlayer class.

Managing memory with reference and value types

I have mentioned **reference types** a couple of times. Let's look at them in more detail.

There are two categories of memory: **stack** memory and **heap** memory. With modern operating systems, the stack and heap can be anywhere in physical or virtual memory.

Stack memory is faster to work with (because it is managed directly by the CPU and because it uses a last-in, first-out mechanism, it is more likely to have data in its L1 or L2 cache) but limited in size, while heap memory is slower but much more plentiful.

On Windows, for ARM64, x86, and x64 machines, the default stack size is 1 MB. It is 8 MB on a typical modern Linux-based operating system. For example, in a macOS terminal, I can enter the command ulimit -a to discover that the stack size is limited to 8,192 KB and that other memory is "unlimited." This limited amount of stack memory is why it is so easy to fill it up and get a "stack overflow."

Defining reference and value types

There are three C# keywords that you can use to define object types: class, record, and struct. All can have the same members, such as fields and methods. One difference between them is how memory is allocated:

- When you define a type using record or class, you are defining a **reference type**. This means that the memory for the object itself is allocated on the heap, and only the memory address of the object (and a little overhead) is stored on the stack.

- When you define a type using record struct or struct, you are defining a **value type**. This means that the memory for the object itself is allocated to the stack.

If a struct uses field types that are not of the struct type, then those fields will be stored on the heap, meaning the data for that object is stored in both the stack and the heap!

These are the most common struct types:

- Number System types: byte, sbyte, short, ushort, int, uint, long, ulong, float, double, and decimal
- Other System types: char, DateTime, DateOnly, TimeOnly, and bool
- System.Drawing types: Color, Point, PointF, Size, SizeF, Rectangle, and RectangleF

Almost all the other types are class types, including string aka System.String and object aka System.Object.

 Apart from the difference in terms of where in memory the data for a type is stored, the other major difference is that you cannot inherit from a struct.

How reference and value types are stored in memory

Imagine that you have a console app that declares some variables, as shown in the following code:

```
int number1 = 49;
long number2 = 12;
System.Drawing.Point location = new(x: 4, y: 5);
Person kevin = new() { Name = "Kevin",
  DateOfBirth = new(year: 1988, month: 9, day: 23) };
Person sally;
```

Let's review what memory is allocated on the stack and heap when these statements execute, as shown in *Figure 6.1* and as described in the following list:

- The number1 variable is a value type (also known as struct), so it is allocated on the stack, and it uses 4 bytes of memory since it is a 32-bit integer. Its value, 49, is stored directly in the variable

- The number2 variable is also a value type, so it is also allocated on the stack, and it uses 8 bytes since it is a 64-bit integer.
- The location variable is also a value type, so it is allocated on the stack, and it uses 8 bytes since it is made up of two 32-bit integers, x and y.
- The kevin variable is a reference type (also known as class), so 8 bytes for a 64-bit memory address (assuming a 64-bit operating system) are allocated on the stack and enough bytes on the heap to store an instance of a Person.
- The sally variable is a reference type, so 8 bytes for a 64-bit memory address are allocated on the stack. It is currently null, meaning no memory has yet been allocated for it on the heap. If we were to later assign kevin to sally, then the memory address of the Person on the heap would be copied into sally, as shown in the following code:

```
sally = kevin; // both variables point at the same Person on heap
```

Figure 6.1: How value and reference types are allocated in the stack and heap

All the allocated memory for a reference type is stored on the heap. If a value type such as DateTime is used for a field of a reference type like Person, then the DateTime value is stored on the heap, as shown in *Figure 6.1*.

If a value type has a field that is a reference type, then that part of the value type is stored on the heap. Point is a value type that consists of two fields, both of which are themselves value types, so the entire object can be allocated on the stack. If the Point value type had a field that was a reference type, like string, then the string bytes would be stored on the heap.

Equality of types

It is common to compare two variables using the == and != operators. The behavior of these two operators is different for reference types and value types.

When you check the equality of two value type variables, .NET literally compares the *values* of those two variables on the stack and returns `true` if they are equal.

1. In `Program.cs`, add statements to declare two integers with equal values and then compare them, as shown in the following code:

```
int a = 3;
int b = 3;
WriteLine($"a: {a}, b: {b}");
WriteLine($"a == b: {(a == b)}");
```

2. Run the console app and view the result, as shown in the following output:

```
a: 3, b: 3
a == b: True
```

When you check the equality of two reference type variables, .NET compares the memory addresses of those two variables and returns `true` if they are equal.

3. In `Program.cs`, add statements to declare two `Person` instances with equal names and then compare the variables and their names, as shown in the following code:

```
Person p1 = new() { Name = "Kevin" };
Person p2 = new() { Name = "Kevin" };
WriteLine($"p1: {p1}, p2: {p2}");
WriteLine($"p1 == p2: {(p1 == p2)}");
```

4. Run the console app and view the result, as shown in the following output:

```
p1: Packt.Shared.Person, p2: Packt.Shared.Person
p1 == p2: False
```

This is because they are not the same object. If both variables literally pointed to the same object on the heap, then they would be equal.

5. Add statements to declare a third `Person` object and assign p1 to it, as shown in the following code:

```
Person p3 = p1;
WriteLine($"p3: {p3}");
WriteLine($"p1 == p3: {(p1 == p3)}");
```

6. Run the console app and view the result, as shown in the following output:

```
p3: Packt.Shared.Person
p1 == p3: True
```

The one exception to this behavior of reference types is the `string` type. It is a reference type, but the equality operators have been overridden to make them behave as if they were value types.

7. Add statements to compare the `Name` properties of two `Person` instances, as shown in the following code:

```
WriteLine($"p1.Name: {p1.Name}, p2.Name: {p2.Name}");
WriteLine($"p1.Name == p2.Name: {(p1.Name == p2.Name)}");
```

8. Run the console app and view the result, as shown in the following output:

```
p1.Name: Kevin, p2.Name: Kevin
p1.Name == p2.Name: True
```

You can do something similar with your classes to make the equality operators return `true` even if they are not the same object (the same memory address on the heap) but instead their fields have the same values; that is beyond the scope of this book. Alternatively, use a `record class`, because one of its benefits is that it implements this behavior for you.

Defining struct types

Let's explore defining your own value types:

1. In the `PacktLibrary` project, add a file named `DisplacementVector.cs`.

2. Modify the file, as shown in the following code, and note the following:

   - The type is declared using `struct` instead of `class`.
   - It has two int properties, named X and Y, that will auto-generate two private fields with the same data type that will be allocated on the stack.
   - It has a constructor for setting initial values for X and Y.
   - It has an operator for adding two instances together that returns a new instance of the type with X added to X, and Y added to Y:

```
namespace Packt.Shared;

public struct DisplacementVector
{
  public int X { get; set; }
  public int Y { get; set; }

  public DisplacementVector(int initialX, int initialY)
  {
    X = initialX;
    Y = initialY;
  }

  public static DisplacementVector operator +(
    DisplacementVector vector1,
```

```
                     DisplacementVector vector2)
           {
             return new(
               vector1.X + vector2.X,
               vector1.Y + vector2.Y);
           }
         }
```

3. In `Program.cs`, add statements to create two new instances of `DisplacementVector`, add them together, and output the result, as shown in the following code:

```
DisplacementVector dv1 = new(3, 5);
DisplacementVector dv2 = new(-2, 7);
DisplacementVector dv3 = dv1 + dv2;
WriteLine($"({dv1.X}, {dv1.Y}) + ({dv2.X}, {dv2.Y}) = ({dv3.X},
{dv3.Y})");
```

4. Run the code and view the result, as shown in the following output:

```
(3, 5) + (-2, 7) = (1, 12)
```

    Value types always have a default constructor even if an explicit one is not defined because the values on the stack must be initialized, even if to default values. For the two integer fields in `DisplacementVector`, they will be initialized to 0.

5. In `Program.cs`, add statements to create a new instance of `DisplacementVector`, and output the object's properties, as shown in the following code:

```
DisplacementVector dv4 = new();
WriteLine($"({dv4.X}, {dv4.Y})");
```

6. Run the code and view the result, as shown in the following output:

```
(0, 0)
```

 Good Practice: If the total memory used by all the fields in your type is 16 bytes or less, your type only uses value types for its fields, and you will never want to derive from your type, then Microsoft recommends that you use `struct`. If your type uses more than 16 bytes of stack memory, if it uses reference types for its fields, or if you might want to inherit from it, then use `class`.

Defining record struct types

C# 10 introduced the ability to use the `record` keyword with `struct` types as well as with `class` types.

We could define the `DisplacementVector` type, as shown in the following code:

```
public record struct DisplacementVector(int X, int Y);
```

A record struct has all the same benefits over a record class that a struct has over a class. One difference between record struct and record class is that record struct is not immutable unless you also apply the readonly keyword to the record struct declaration. A struct does not implement the == and != operators, but they are automatically implemented with a record struct.

With this change, Microsoft recommends explicitly specifying class if you want to define a record class even though the class keyword is optional, as shown in the following code:

```
public record class ImmutableAnimal(string Name);
```

Releasing unmanaged resources

In the previous chapter, we saw that constructors can be used to initialize fields and that a type may have multiple constructors. Imagine that a constructor allocates an **unmanaged resource**, that is, anything that is not controlled by .NET, such as a file or mutex under the control of the operating system. The unmanaged resource must be manually released because .NET cannot do it for us using its automatic garbage collection feature.

Garbage collection is an advanced topic, so for this topic, I will show some code examples, but you do not need to write the code yourself.

Each type can have a single **finalizer** that will be called by the .NET runtime when the resources need to be released. A finalizer has the same name as a constructor, that is, the name of the type, but it is prefixed with a tilde, ~, as shown in the following code:

```
public class ObjectWithUnmanagedResources
{
  public ObjectWithUnmanagedResources() // constructor
  {
    // allocate any unmanaged resources
  }

  ~ObjectWithUnmanagedResources() // Finalizer aka destructor
  {
    // deallocate any unmanaged resources
  }
}
```

Do not confuse a finalizer (also known as a **destructor**) with a Deconstruct method. A destructor releases resources; that is, it destroys an object in memory. A Deconstruct method returns an object split up into its constituent parts and uses the C# deconstruction syntax, for example, when working with tuples. See *Chapter 5, Building Your Own Types with Object-Oriented Programming*, for details of Deconstruct methods.

The preceding code example is the minimum you should do when working with unmanaged resources. But the problem with only providing a finalizer is that the .NET garbage collector requires two garbage collections to completely release the allocated resources for this type.

Though optional, it is recommended to also provide a method to allow a developer who uses your type to explicitly release resources. This would allow the garbage collector to release managed parts of an unmanaged resource, such as a file, immediately and deterministically.

This would mean it releases the managed memory part of the object in a single garbage collection instead of two rounds of garbage collection.

There is a standard mechanism for doing this by implementing the IDisposable interface, as shown in the following example:

```csharp
public class ObjectWithUnmanagedResources : IDisposable
{
  public ObjectWithUnmanagedResources()
  {
    // allocate unmanaged resource
  }


  ~ObjectWithUnmanagedResources() // Finalizer
  {
    Dispose(false);
  }

  bool disposed = false; // have resources been released?

  public void Dispose()
  {
    Dispose(true);

    // tell garbage collector it does not need to call the finalizer
    GC.SuppressFinalize(this);
  }

  protected virtual void Dispose(bool disposing)
  {
    if (disposed) return;

    // deallocate the *unmanaged* resource
    // ...
    if (disposing)
    {
      // deallocate any other *managed* resources
      // ...
    }
```

```
      disposed = true;
    }
  }
}
```

There are two `Dispose` methods, one `public` and one `protected`:

- The `public void Dispose` method will be called by a developer using your type. When called, both unmanaged and managed resources need to be deallocated.

- The `protected virtual void Dispose` method with a `bool` parameter is used internally to implement the deallocation of resources. It needs to check the `disposing` parameter and `disposed` field because if the finalizer thread has already run and it called the `~ObjectWithUnmanagedResources` method, then only unmanaged resources need to be deallocated.

The call to `GC.SuppressFinalize(this)` is what notifies the garbage collector that it no longer needs to run the finalizer and removes the need for a second garbage collection.

Ensuring that Dispose is called

When someone uses a type that implements `IDisposable`, they can ensure that the public `Dispose` method is called with the `using` statement, as shown in the following code:

```
using (ObjectWithUnmanagedResources thing = new())
{
  // code that uses thing
}
```

The compiler converts your code into something like the following, which guarantees that even if an exception occurs, the `Dispose` method will still be called:

```
ObjectWithUnmanagedResources thing = new();
try
{
  // code that uses thing
}
finally
{
  if (thing != null) thing.Dispose();
}
```

When someone uses a type that implements `IAsyncDisposable`, they can ensure that the public `Dispose` method is called with the `using` statement, as shown in the following code:

```
await using (ObjectWithUnmanagedResources thing = new())
{
  // code that uses thing
}
```

You will see practical examples of releasing unmanaged resources with IDisposable, using statements, and try...finally blocks in *Chapter 9, Working with Files, Streams, and Serialization.*

Working with null values

You have seen how reference types are different from value types in how they are stored in memory, and how to store primitive values like numbers in struct variables. But what if a variable does not yet have a value? How can we indicate that? C# has the concept of a null value, which can be used to indicate that a variable has not been set.

Making a value type nullable

By default, **value types** like int and DateTime must always have a *value*, hence their name. Sometimes, for example, when reading values stored in a database that allows empty, missing, or null values, it is convenient to allow a value type to be null. We call this a **nullable value type**.

You can enable this by adding a question mark as a suffix to the type when declaring a variable.

Let's see an example:

1. Use your preferred coding tool to add a new **Console App**/console project named NullHandling to the Chapter06 workspace/solution.

    *   In Visual Studio Code, select NullHandling as the active OmniSharp project.
    *   In Visual Studio 2022, set NullHandling as the startup project.

2. In NullHandling.csproj, add an <ItemGroup> to globally and statically import the System. Console class.

3. In Program.cs, delete the existing statements and then add statements to declare and assign values, including null, to int variables, one suffixed with ? and one not, as shown in the following code:

```
int thisCannotBeNull  = 4;
thisCannotBeNull = null; // compile error!
WriteLine(thisCannotBeNull);

int? thisCouldBeNull = null;

WriteLine(thisCouldBeNull);
WriteLine(thisCouldBeNull.GetValueOrDefault());

thisCouldBeNull = 7;

WriteLine(thisCouldBeNull);
WriteLine(thisCouldBeNull.GetValueOrDefault());
```

4. Build the project and note the compile error, as shown in the following output:

```
Cannot convert null to 'int' because it is a non-nullable value type
```

5. Comment out the statement that gives the compile error.

6. Run the code and view the result, as shown in the following output:

```
0
7
7
```

7. The first line is blank because it is outputting the null value!

8. Add statements to use alternative syntax, as shown in the following code:

```
// the actual type of int? is Nullable<int>
Nullable<int> thisCouldAlsoBeNull = null;
thisCouldAlsoBeNull = 9;
WriteLine(thisCouldAlsoBeNull);
```

9. Click in Nullable<int> and press *F12*, or right-click and choose **Go To Definition**.

10. Note that the generic value type, Nullable<T>, must have a type T that is a struct aka a value type, and it has useful members like HasValue, Value, and GetValueOrDefault, as shown in *Figure 6.2*:

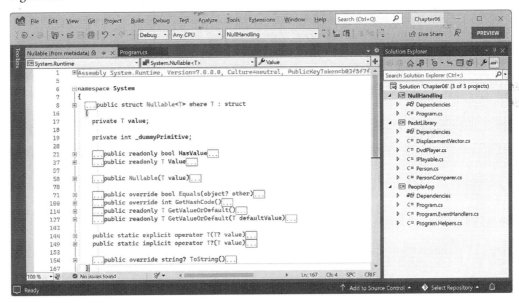

Figure 6.2: Revealing Nullable<T> members

 Good Practice: When you append a ? after a struct aka value type, you are changing it to a different struct aka value type.

Understanding null-related initialisms

Before we see some code, let's review some commonly used initialisms, as shown in the following table:

Initialism	Meaning	Description
NRT	Nullable reference types	A compiler feature introduced with C# 8 and enabled by default in new projects with C# 10 that performs static analysis of your code at design time and shows warnings of potential misuse of `null` values for reference types.
NRE	`NullReferenceException`	An exception thrown at runtime when **dereferencing** a `null` value, aka accessing a variable or member that has a `null` value.
ANE	`ArgumentNullException`	An exception thrown at runtime by a method invocation when an argument has a `null` value when that is not valid.

Understanding nullable reference types

The use of the `null` value is so common, in so many languages, that many experienced programmers never question the need for its existence. But there are many scenarios where we could write better, simpler code if a variable is not allowed to have a `null` value.

The most significant change to the C# 8 language compiler was the introduction of checks and warnings for nullable and non-nullable reference types. "But wait!", you are probably thinking, "Reference types are already nullable!"

And you would be right, but in C# 8 and later, reference types can be configured to no longer allow the `null` value by setting a file- or project-level option to enable this useful new feature. Since this is a big change for C#, Microsoft decided to make the feature opt in.

It will take multiple years for this new C# language compiler feature to make an impact since thousands of existing library packages and apps will expect the old behavior. Even Microsoft did not have time to fully implement this new feature in all the main .NET packages until .NET 6. Important libraries like `Microsoft.Extensions` for logging, dependency injections, and configuration were not annotated until .NET 7.

During the transition, you can choose between several approaches for your own projects:

- **Default:** For projects created using .NET 5 or earlier, no changes are needed. Non-nullable reference types are not checked. For projects created using .NET 6 or later, nullability checks are enabled by default, but this can be disabled by either deleting the `<Nullable>` entry in the project file or setting it to `disable`.
- **Opt-in project, opt-out files:** Enable the feature at the project level and, for any files that need to remain compatible with old behavior, opt out. This was the approach Microsoft was using internally while it updated its own packages to use this new feature.
- **Opt-in files:** Only enable the feature for individual files.

Controlling the nullability warning check feature

To enable the nullability warning check feature at the project level, add the following to your project file:

```
<PropertyGroup>
  ...
  <Nullable>enable</Nullable>
</PropertyGroup>
```

To disable the nullability warning check feature at the project level, add the following to your project file:

```
<PropertyGroup>
  ...
  <Nullable>disable</Nullable>
</PropertyGroup>
```

To disable the feature at the file level, add the following to the top of a code file:

```
#nullable disable
```

To enable the feature at the file level, add the following to the top of a code file:

```
#nullable enable
```

Declaring non-nullable variables and parameters

If you enable nullable reference types and you want a reference type to be assigned the null value, then you will have to use the same syntax as making a value type nullable, that is, adding a ? symbol after the type declaration.

So, how do nullable reference types work? Let's look at an example. When storing information about an address, you might want to force a value for the street, city, and region, but the building can be left blank, that is, null:

1. In NullHandling.csproj, add a class file named Address.cs.

2. In Address.cs, add statements to declare an Address class with four fields, as shown in the following code:

```
public class Address
{
  public string? Building;
  public string Street;
  public string City;
  public string Region;
}
```

3. After a few seconds, note the warnings about non-nullable fields, like `Street` not being initialized, as shown in *Figure 6.3*:

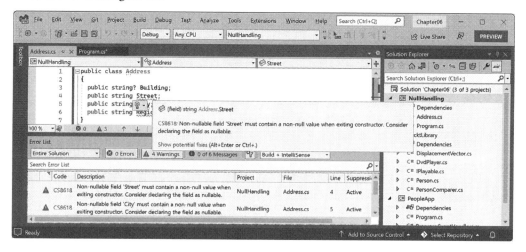

Figure 6.3: Warning messages about non-nullable fields in the Error List window

4. Assign the empty `string` value to each of the three fields that are non-nullable, as shown in the following code:

```
public string Street = string.Empty;
public string City = string.Empty;
public string Region = string.Empty;
```

5. In `Program.cs`, add statements to instantiate an `Address` and set its properties, as shown in the following code:

```
Address address = new()
{
  Building = null,
  Street = null,
  City = "London",
  Region = "UK"
};
```

6. Note the `Warning CS8625` on setting the `Street` but not the `Building`, as shown in the following output:

```
Cannot convert null literal to non-nullable reference type.
```

7. Append an exclamation mark after `null` when setting `Street`, as shown highlighted in the following code:

```
Street = null!, // null-forgiving operator
```

8. Note that the warning disappears.

9. Add statements that would dereference the `Building` and `Street` properties, as shown in the following code:

```
WriteLine(address.Building.Length);
WriteLine(address.Street.Length);
```

10. Note the `Warning CS8602` on setting the `Building` but not the `Street`, as shown in the following output:

```
Dereference of a possibly null reference.
```

At runtime it is still possible for an exception to be thrown when working with `Street`, but the compiler should continue to warn you of potential exceptions when working with `Building` so you can change your code to avoid them.

11. Use the null-conditional operator to return `null` instead of accessing the `Length`, as shown in the following code:

```
WriteLine(address.Building?.Length);
```

12. Run the console app and note that the statement that accesses the `Length` of the `Building` outputs a `null` value (blank line), but a runtime exception occurs when we access the `Length` of the `Street`, as shown in the following output:

```
Unhandled exception. System.NullReferenceException: Object reference not
set to an instance of an object.
```

It is worth reminding yourself that an NRT is only about asking the compiler to provide warnings about potential `null` values that might cause problems. It does not actually change the behavior of your code. It performs a static analysis of your code at compile time.

So, this explains why the new language feature is named nullable reference types. Starting with C# 8.0, unadorned reference types can become non-nullable, and the same syntax is used to make a reference type nullable as it is used for value types.

 Suffixing a reference type with ? does not change the type. This is different from suffixing a value type with ? that changes its type to `Nullable<T>`. Reference types can already have `null` values. All you are doing with **nullable reference types** (**NRTs**) is telling the compiler that you expect it could be `null`, so the compiler does not need to warn you. But this does not remove the need to perform `null` checks throughout your code.

Now let's see language features to work with `null` values that do change the behavior of your code and work well as a complement to NRTs.

Checking for null

Checking whether a nullable reference type or nullable value type variable currently contains `null` is important because if you do not, a `NullReferenceException` can be thrown, which results in an error. You should check for a `null` value before using a nullable variable, as shown in the following code:

```
// check that the variable is not null before using it
if (thisCouldBeNull != null)
{
  // access a member of thisCouldBeNull
  int length = thisCouldBeNull.Length; // could throw exception
  ...
}
```

C# 7 introduced `is` combined with the `!` (not) operator as an alternative to `!=`, as shown in the following code:

```
if (!(thisCouldBeNull is null))
{
}
```

C# 9 introduced `is not` as an even clearer alternative, as shown in the following code:

```
if (thisCouldBeNull is not null)
{
```

If you are trying to use a member of a variable that might be `null`, use the **null-conditional operator**, `?.`, as shown in the following code:

```
string authorName = null;

// the following throws a NullReferenceException
int x = authorName.Length;

// instead of throwing an exception, null is assigned to y
int? y = authorName?.Length;
```

Sometimes, you want to either assign a variable to a result or use an alternative value, such as 3, if the variable is `null`. You do this using the **null-coalescing operator**, `??`, as shown in the following code:

```
// result will be 3 if authorName?.Length is null
int result = authorName?.Length ?? 3;
Console.WriteLine(result);
```

Good Practice: Even if you enable nullable reference types, you should still check non-nullable parameters for `null` and throw an `ArgumentNullException`.

Checking for null in method parameters

When defining methods with parameters, it is good practice to check for `null` values.

In earlier versions of C#, you would have to write `if` statements to check for `null` parameter values and then throw an `ArgumentNullException` for any parameter that is `null`, as shown in the following code:

```
public void Hire(Person manager, Person employee)
{
  if (manager == null)
  {
    throw new ArgumentNullException(nameof(manager));
  }

  if (employee == null)
  {
    throw new ArgumentNullException(nameof(employee));
  }
  ...
}
```

C# 10 introduced a convenience method to throw an exception if an argument is `null`, as shown in the following code:

```
public void Hire(Person manager, Person employee)
{
  ArgumentNullException.ThrowIfNull(manager);
  ArgumentNullException.ThrowIfNull(employee);

  ...
}
```

C# 11 previews introduced a new `!!` operator that does this for you, as shown in the following code:

```
public void Hire(Person manager!!, Person employee!!)
{
  ...
}
```

The `if` statement and throwing of the exception are done for you. The code is injected and executes before any statements that you write.

This syntax is controversial within the C# developer community. Some would prefer the use of attributes to decorate parameters instead of a pair of characters. The .NET product team said they saved more than 10,000 lines of code throughout the .NET libraries by using this feature. That sounds like a good reason to use it to me! And no one must use it if they choose not to. Unfortunately, the team eventually decided to remove the feature, so now we all have to write the null checks manually, as described in the following link:

https://devblogs.microsoft.com/dotnet/csharp-11-preview-updates/#remove-parameter-null-checking-from-c-11

I include this story in this book because I think it's an interesting example of Microsoft being transparent by developing .NET in the open and listening to and responding to feedback from the community.

Good Practice: Always remember that nullable is a warning check, not an enforcement. You can read more about the compiler warnings relating to null at the following link: https://docs.microsoft.com/en-us/dotnet/csharp/language-reference/compiler-messages/nullable-warnings.

Inheriting from classes

The Person type we created earlier derived (inherited) from object, the alias for System.Object. Now, we will create a subclass that inherits from Person:

1. In the PacktLibrary project, add a new class file named Employee.cs.

2. Modify its contents to define a class named Employee that derives from Person, as shown in the following code:

```
namespace Packt.Shared;

public class Employee : Person
{
}
```

3. In the PeopleApp project, in Program.cs, add statements to create an instance of the Employee class, as shown in the following code:

```
Employee john = new()
{
  Name = "John Jones",
  DateOfBirth = new(year: 1990, month: 7, day: 28)
};
john.WriteToConsole();
```

4. Run the code and view the result, as shown in the following output:

```
John Jones was born on a Saturday.
```

Note that the Employee class has inherited all the members of Person.

Extending classes to add functionality

Now, we will add some employee-specific members to extend the class.

1. In `Employee.cs`, add statements to define two properties, for an employee code and the date they were hired, as shown in the following code:

```
public string? EmployeeCode { get; set; }
public DateTime HireDate { get; set; }
```

2. In `Program.cs`, add statements to set John's employee code and hire date, as shown in the following code:

```
john.EmployeeCode = "JJ001";
john.HireDate = new(year: 2014, month: 11, day: 23);
WriteLine($"{john.Name} was hired on {john.HireDate:dd/MM/yy}");
```

3. Run the code and view the result, as shown in the following output:

```
John Jones was hired on 23/11/14
```

Hiding members

So far, the `WriteToConsole` method is inherited from `Person`, and it only outputs the employee's name and date of birth. We might want to change what this method does for an employee:

1. In `Employee.cs`, add statements to redefine the `WriteToConsole` method, as shown highlighted in the following code:

```
namespace Packt.Shared;

public class Employee : Person
{
  public string? EmployeeCode { get; set; }
  public DateTime HireDate { get; set; }

  public void WriteToConsole()
  {
    WriteLine(format:
      "{0} was born on {1:dd/MM/yy} and hired on {2:dd/MM/yy}",
      arg0: Name,
      arg1: DateOfBirth,
      arg2: HireDate);
  }
}
```

2. Run the code and view the result, as shown in the following output:

```
John Jones was born on 28/07/90 and hired on 01/01/01
John Jones was hired on 23/11/14
```

Your coding tool warns you that your method now hides the method from `Person` by drawing a squiggle under the method name; the **PROBLEMS/Error List** window includes more details; and the compiler will output the warning when you build and run the console application, as shown in *Figure 6.4*:

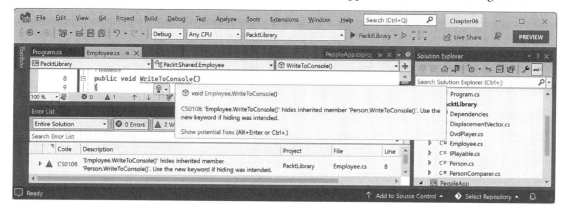

Figure 6.4: Hidden method warning

As the warning describes, you can hide this message by applying the `new` keyword to the method, to indicate that you are deliberately replacing the old method, as shown highlighted in the following code:

```
public new void WriteToConsole()
```

Overriding members

Rather than hiding a method, it is usually better to **override** it. You can only override if the base class chooses to allow overriding, by applying the `virtual` keyword to any methods that should allow overriding.

Let's see an example:

1. In `Program.cs`, add a statement to write the value of the `john` variable to the console using its `string` representation, as shown in the following code:

    ```
    WriteLine(john.ToString());
    ```

2. Run the code and note that the `ToString` method is inherited from `System.Object`, so the implementation returns the namespace and type name, as shown in the following output:

    ```
    Packt.Shared.Employee
    ```

3. In `Person.cs` (not in the `Employee` class!), override this behavior by adding a `ToString` method to output the name of the person as well as the type name, as shown in the following code:

    ```
    // overridden methods
    public override string ToString()
    {
      return $"{Name} is a {base.ToString()}";
    }
    ```

The base keyword allows a subclass to access members of its superclass, that is, the **base class** that it inherits or derives from.

4. Run the code and view the result. Now, when the ToString method is called, it outputs the person's name, as well as returning the base class's implementation of ToString, as shown in the following output:

```
John Jones is a Packt.Shared.Employee
```

 Good Practice: Many real-world APIs, for example, Microsoft's Entity Framework Core, Castle's DynamicProxy, and Optimizely CMS's content models, require the properties that you define in your classes to be marked as virtual so that they can be overridden. Carefully decide which of your method and property members should be marked as virtual.

Inheriting from abstract classes

Earlier in this chapter, you learned about interfaces that can define a set of members that a type must have to meet a basic level of functionality. These are very useful, but their main limitation is that until C# 8 they could not provide any implementation of their own.

This is a particular problem if you still need to create class libraries that will work with .NET Framework and other platforms that do not support .NET Standard 2.1.

In those earlier platforms, you could use abstract classes as a sort of halfway house between a pure interface and a fully implemented class.

When a class is marked as abstract, this means that it cannot be instantiated because you are indicating that the class is not complete. It needs more implementation before it can be instantiated. For example, the System.IO.Stream class is abstract because it implements common functionality that all streams would need but is not complete, so you cannot instantiate it using new Stream().

Let's compare the two types of interface and two types of class, as shown in the following code:

```
public interface INoImplementation // C# 1.0 and later
{
  void Alpha(); // must be implemented by derived type
}

public interface ISomeImplementation // C# 8.0 and later
{
  void Alpha(); // must be implemented by derived type

  void Beta()
  {
    // default implementation; can be overridden
  }
}
```

```
public abstract class PartiallyImplemented // C# 1.0 and later
{
  public abstract void Gamma(); // must be implemented by derived type

  public virtual void Delta() // can be overridden
  {
    // implementation
  }
}

public class FullyImplemented : PartiallyImplemented, ISomeImplementation
{
  public void Alpha()
  {
    // implementation
  }

  public override void Gamma()
  {
    // implementation
  }
}

// you can only instantiate the fully implemented class
FullyImplemented a = new();

// all the other types give compile errors
PartiallyImplemented b = new(); // compile error!
ISomeImplementation c = new(); // compile error!
INoImplementation d = new(); // compile error!
```

Preventing inheritance and overriding

You can prevent another developer from inheriting from your class by applying the sealed keyword to its definition. No one can inherit from Scrooge McDuck, as shown in the following code:

```
public sealed class ScroogeMcDuck
{
}
```

An example of `sealed` in .NET is the `string` class. Microsoft has implemented some extreme optimizations inside the `string` class that could be negatively affected by your inheritance, so Microsoft prevents that.

You can prevent someone from further overriding a `virtual` method in your class by applying the `sealed` keyword to the method. No one can change the way Lady Gaga sings, as shown in the following code:

```
namespace Packt.Shared;

public class Singer
{
  // virtual allows this method to be overridden
  public virtual void Sing()
  {
    WriteLine("Singing...");
  }
}

public class LadyGaga : Singer
{
  // sealed prevents overriding the method in subclasses
  public sealed override void Sing()
  {
    WriteLine("Singing with style...");
  }
}
```

You can only seal an overridden method.

Understanding polymorphism

You have now seen two ways to change the behavior of an inherited method. We can *hide* it using the new keyword (known as **non-polymorphic inheritance**), or we can *override* it (known as **polymorphic inheritance**).

Both ways can access members of the base or superclass by using the base keyword, so what is the difference?

It all depends on the type of variable holding a reference to the object. For example, a variable of the `Person` type can hold a reference to a `Person` class, or any type that derives from `Person`.

Let's see how this could affect your code:

1. In `Employee.cs`, add statements to override the `ToString` method so that it writes the employee's name and code to the console, as shown in the following code:

    ```
    public override string ToString()
    {
      return $"{Name}'s code is {EmployeeCode}";
    }
    ```

2. In `Program.cs`, write statements to create a new employee named Alice, store it in a variable of type `Person`, and call both variables' `WriteToConsole` and `ToString` methods, as shown in the following code:

    ```
    Employee aliceInEmployee = new()
      { Name = "Alice", EmployeeCode = "AA123" };

    Person aliceInPerson = aliceInEmployee;
    aliceInEmployee.WriteToConsole();
    aliceInPerson.WriteToConsole();
    WriteLine(aliceInEmployee.ToString());
    WriteLine(aliceInPerson.ToString());
    ```

3. Run the code and view the result, as shown in the following output:

    ```
    Alice was born on 01/01/01 and hired on 01/01/01
    Alice was born on a Monday
    Alice's code is AA123
    Alice's code is AA123
    ```

When a method is hidden with `new`, the compiler is not smart enough to know that the object is an `Employee`, so it calls the `WriteToConsole` method in `Person`.

When a method is overridden with `virtual` and `override`, the compiler is smart enough to know that although the variable is declared as a `Person` class, the object itself is an `Employee` class and, therefore, the `Employee` implementation of `ToString` is called.

The member modifiers and the effect they have are summarized in the following table:

Variable type	Member modifier	Method executed	In class
Person		WriteToConsole	Person
Employee	new	WriteToConsole	Employee
Person	virtual	ToString	Employee
Employee	override	ToString	Employee

In my opinion, polymorphism is academic to most programmers. If you get the concept, that's cool; but, if not, I suggest that you don't worry about it. Some people like to make others feel inferior by saying understanding polymorphism is important for all C# programmers, but IMHO it's not.

You can have a successful career with C# and never need to be able to explain polymorphism, just as a racing car driver doesn't need to be able to explain the engineering behind fuel injection.

 Good Practice: You should use `virtual` and `override` rather than `new` to change the implementation of an inherited method whenever possible.

Casting within inheritance hierarchies

Casting between types is subtly different from converting between types. Casting is between similar types, like between a 16-bit integer and a 32-bit integer, or between a superclass and one of its subclasses. **Converting** is between dissimilar types, such as between text and a number.

For example, if you need to work with multiple types of stream, then instead of declaring specific types of stream like `MemoryStream` or `FileStream`, you could declare an array of `Stream`, the supertype of `MemoryStream` and `FileStream`.

Implicit casting

In the previous example, you saw how an instance of a derived type can be stored in a variable of its base type (or its base's base type, and so on). When we do this, it is called **implicit casting**.

Explicit casting

Going the other way is an explicit cast, and you must use parentheses around the type you want to cast into as a prefix to do it:

1. In `Program.cs`, add a statement to assign the `aliceInPerson` variable to a new `Employee` variable, as shown in the following code:

    ```
    Employee explicitAlice = aliceInPerson;
    ```

2. Your coding tool displays a red squiggle and a compile error, as shown in *Figure 6.5*:

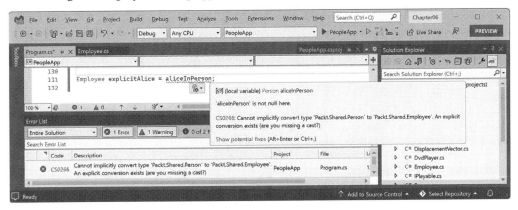

Figure 6.5: A missing explicit cast compile error

3. Change the statement to prefix the assigned variable named with a cast to the `Employee` type, as shown in the following code:

```
Employee explicitAlice = (Employee)aliceInPerson;
```

Avoiding casting exceptions

The compiler is now happy; but, because `aliceInPerson` might be a different derived type, like `Student` instead of `Employee`, we need to be careful. In a real application with more complex code, the current value of this variable could have been set to a `Student` instance, and then this statement would throw an `InvalidCastException` error.

Using is to check a type

We can handle this by writing a `try` statement, but there is a better way. We can check the type of an object using the `is` keyword:

1. Wrap the explicit cast statement in an `if` statement, as shown highlighted in the following code:

```
if (aliceInPerson is Employee)
{
    WriteLine($"{nameof(aliceInPerson)} IS an Employee");

    Employee explicitAlice = (Employee)aliceInPerson;

    // safely do something with explicitAlice
}
```

2. Run the code and view the result, as shown in the following output:

```
aliceInPerson IS an Employee
```

You could simplify the code further using a declaration pattern and this will avoid needing to perform an explicit cast, as shown in the following code:

```
if (aliceInPerson is Employee explicitAlice)
{
    WriteLine($"{nameof(aliceInPerson)} IS an Employee");
    // safely do something with explicitAlice
}
```

What if you want to execute a block of statements when Alice is *not* an employee?

In the past, you would have had to use the ! (not) operator, as shown in the following code:

```
if (!(aliceInPerson is Employee))
```

With C# 9 and later, you can use the not keyword, as shown in the following code:

```
if (aliceInPerson is not Employee)
```

Using as to cast a type

Alternatively, you can use the as keyword to cast. Instead of throwing an exception, the as keyword returns null if the type cannot be cast.

1. In Program.cs, add statements to cast Alice using the as keyword and then check whether the return value is not null, as shown in the following code:

```
Employee? aliceAsEmployee = aliceInPerson as Employee; // could be null

if (aliceAsEmployee is not null)
{
  WriteLine($"{nameof(aliceInPerson)} AS an Employee");

  // safely do something with aliceAsEmployee
}
```

Since accessing a member of a null variable will throw a NullReferenceException error, you should always check for null before using the result.

2. Run the code and view the result, as shown in the following output:

```
aliceInPerson AS an Employee
```

 Good Practice: Use the is and as keywords to avoid throwing exceptions when casting between derived types. If you don't do this, you must write **try-catch** statements for InvalidCastException.

Inheriting and extending .NET types

.NET has pre-built class libraries containing hundreds of thousands of types. Rather than creating your own completely new types, you can often get a head start by deriving from one of Microsoft's types to inherit some or all of its behavior and then overriding or extending it.

Inheriting exceptions

As an example of inheritance, we will derive a new type of exception:

1. In the PacktLibrary project, add a new class file named PersonException.cs.
2. Modify the contents of the file to define a class named PersonException with three constructors, as shown in the following code:

```
namespace Packt.Shared;

public class PersonException : Exception
{
  public PersonException() : base() { }
```

```
    public PersonException(string message) : base(message) { }

    public PersonException(string message, Exception innerException)
      : base(message, innerException) { }
}
```

Unlike ordinary methods, constructors are not inherited, so we must explicitly declare and explicitly call the base constructor implementations in System.Exception (or whichever exception class you derived from) to make them available to programmers who might want to use those constructors with our custom exception.

3. In Person.cs, add statements to define a method that throws an exception if a date/time parameter is earlier than a person's date of birth, as shown in the following code:

```
public void TimeTravel(DateTime when)
{
  if (when <= DateOfBirth)
  {
    throw new PersonException("If you travel back in time to a date
earlier than your own birth, then the universe will explode!");
  }
  else
  {
    WriteLine($"Welcome to {when:yyyy}!");
  }
}
```

4. In Program.cs, add statements to test what happens when employee John Jones tries to time-travel too far back, as shown in the following code:

```
try
{
  john.TimeTravel(when: new(1999, 12, 31));
  john.TimeTravel(when: new(1950, 12, 25));
}
catch (PersonException ex)
{
  WriteLine(ex.Message);
}
```

5. Run the code and view the result, as shown in the following output:

```
Welcome to 1999!
If you travel back in time to a date earlier than your own birth, then
the universe will explode!
```

Good Practice: When defining your own exceptions, give them the same three constructors that explicitly call the built-in ones in `System.Exception`. Other exceptions that you might inherit from may have more.

Extending types when you can't inherit

Earlier, we saw how the `sealed` modifier can be used to prevent inheritance.

Microsoft has applied the `sealed` keyword to the `System.String` class so that no one can inherit and potentially break the behavior of strings.

Can we still add new methods to strings? Yes, if we use a language feature named **extension methods**, which was introduced with C# 3.0. To properly understand extension methods, we need to review static methods first.

Using static methods to reuse functionality

Since the first version of C#, we've been able to create `static` methods to reuse functionality, such as the ability to validate that a `string` contains an email address. The implementation will use a regular expression that you will learn more about in *Chapter 8, Working with Common .NET Types*.

Let's write some code:

1. In the `PacktLibrary` project, add a new class file named `StringExtensions.cs`.
2. Modify `StringExtensions.cs`, as shown in the following code, and note the following:

   - The class imports a namespace for handling regular expressions.
   - The `IsValidEmail` method is `static` and it uses the `Regex` type to check for matches against a simple email pattern that looks for valid characters before and after the @ symbol:

```csharp
using System.Text.RegularExpressions; // to get Regex

namespace Packt.Shared;

public class StringExtensions
{
  public static bool IsValidEmail(string input)
  {
    // use a simple regular expression to check
    // that the input string is a valid email

    return Regex.IsMatch(input,
```

```
         @"[a-zA-Z0-9\.-_]+@[a-zA-Z0-9\.-_]+");
    }
}
```

3. In `Program.cs`, add statements to validate two examples of email addresses, as shown in the following code:

```
string email1 = "pamela@test.com";
string email2 = "ian&test.com";

WriteLine("{0} is a valid e-mail address: {1}",
  arg0: email1,
  arg1: StringExtensions.IsValidEmail(email1));

WriteLine("{0} is a valid e-mail address: {1}",
  arg0: email2,
  arg1: StringExtensions.IsValidEmail(email2));
```

4. Run the code and view the result, as shown in the following output:

```
pamela@test.com is a valid e-mail address: True
ian&test.com is a valid e-mail address: False
```

This works, but extension methods can reduce the amount of code we must type and simplify the usage of this function.

Using extension methods to reuse functionality

It is easy to make `static` methods into extension methods:

1. In `StringExtensions.cs`, add the `static` modifier before the class, and add the `this` modifier before the `string` type, as highlighted in the following code:

```
public static class StringExtensions
{
  public static bool IsValidEmail(this string input)
  {
```

These two changes tell the compiler that it should treat the method as one that extends the string type.

2. In `Program.cs`, add statements to use the extension method for `string` values that need to be checked for valid email addresses, as shown in the following code:

```
WriteLine("{0} is a valid e-mail address: {1}",
  arg0: email1,
  arg1: email1.IsValidEmail());

WriteLine("{0} is a valid e-mail address: {1}",
```

```
    arg0: email2,
    arg1: email2.IsValidEmail());
```

Note the subtle simplification in the syntax for calling the `IsValidEmail` method. The older, longer syntax still works too.

3. The `IsValidEmail` extension method now appears to be a method just like all the actual instance methods of the `string` type, such as `IsNormalized`, except with a small down arrow on the method icon to indicate an extension method, as shown in *Figure 6.6*:

Figure 6.6: Extension methods appear in IntelliSense alongside instance methods

4. Run the code and view the result, which will be the same as before.

 Good Practice: Extension methods cannot replace or override existing instance methods. You cannot, for example, redefine the `Insert` method. The extension method will appear as an overload in IntelliSense, but an instance method will be called in preference to an extension method with the same name and signature.

Although extension methods might not seem to give a big benefit, in *Chapter 11, Querying and Manipulating Data Using LINQ,* you will see some extremely powerful uses of extension methods.

Writing better code

Now that you have learned the fundamentals of the C# language, let's see some ways that you can write better code.

Treating warnings as errors

A simple yet effective way to write better code is to force yourself to fix compiler warnings. By default, warnings can be ignored. You can ask the compiler to prevent you from ignoring them.

Let's review the default experience and then see how we can improve it:

1. Use your preferred code editor to add a **Console App**/`console` project named `WarningsAsErrors` to the `Chapter06` solution/workspace.

2. In `Program.cs`, modify the existing statements to prompt the user to enter a name and then say hello to them, as shown highlighted in the following code:

```
// See https://aka.ms/new-console-template for more information
Console.Write("Enter a name: ");
string name = Console.ReadLine();
Console.WriteLine($"Hello, {name} has {name.Length} characters!");
```

3. Build the `WarningsAsErrors` project using `dotnet build` at the command line or terminal and note that the build succeeds but there are two warnings, as shown in the following output:

```
Build succeeded.

C:\cs11dotnet7\Chapter06\WarningsAsErrors\Program.cs(3,15): warning
CS8600: Converting null literal or possible null value to non-nullable
type. [C:\cs11dotnet7\Chapter06\WarningsAsErrors\WarningsAsErrors.csproj]
C:\cs11dotnet7-old\Chapter06\WarningsAsErrors\Program.cs(9,40): warning
CS8602: Dereference of a possibly null reference. [C:\cs11dotnet7\
Chapter06\WarningsAsErrors\WarningsAsErrors.csproj]
    2 Warning(s)
    0 Error(s)
```

4. Build the `WarningsAsErrors` project a second time using `dotnet build` at the command line or the terminal and note that the build succeeds but the warnings have gone, as shown in the following output:

```
Build succeeded.
    0 Warning(s)
    0 Error(s)
```

If you use the Visual Studio **Build** menu and look in the **Error List** then you will continue to see the two warnings because Visual Studio is not showing the true output from the compiler. Visual Studio runs its own checks on your code.

Good Practice: You can "clean" a project either using the Visual Studio **Build** menu or using the command `dotnet clean` so that the warnings reappear the next time you build.

5. In the project file, add an entry to ask the compiler to treat warnings as errors, as shown highlighted in the following markup:

```
<Project Sdk="Microsoft.NET.Sdk">

  <PropertyGroup>
    <OutputType>Exe</OutputType>
    <TargetFramework>net7.0</TargetFramework>
```

```
  <ImplicitUsings>enable</ImplicitUsings>
  <Nullable>enable</Nullable>
  <TreatWarningsAsErrors>true</TreatWarningsAsErrors>
</PropertyGroup>

</Project>
```

6. Build the `WarningsAsErrors` project and note that the build fails and there are two errors, as shown in the following output:

```
Build FAILED.
C:\cs11dotnet7\Chapter06\WarningsAsErrors\Program.cs(3,15): error CS8600:
Converting null literal or possible null value to non-nullable type. [C:\
cs11dotnet7\Chapter06\WarningsAsErrors\WarningsAsErrors.csproj]
C:\cs11dotnet7-old\Chapter06\WarningsAsErrors\Program.cs(9,40): error
CS8602: Dereference of a possibly null reference. [C:\cs11dotnet7\
Chapter06\WarningsAsErrors\WarningsAsErrors.csproj]
    0 Warning(s)
    2 Error(s)
```

7. Build the `WarningsAsErrors` project again and note that the build fails again, so we cannot run the console app until we fix the issues.

8. Fix the two errors by adding a nullable operator `?` after the string variable declaration and by checking for a `null` value and exiting the app if the variable is `null`, as shown highlighted in the following code:

```
Console.Write("Enter a name: ");
string? name = Console.ReadLine();
if (name == null)
{
  Console.WriteLine("You did not enter a name.");
  return;
}
Console.WriteLine($"Hello, {name} has {name.Length} characters!");
```

9. Build the `WarningsAsErrors` project and note that the build succeeds without errors.

In the scenario above, the `ReadLine` method always returns a non-`null` value, so we could have fixed the warning simply by suffixing the call to `ReadLine` with the null-forgiving operator, as shown in the following code:

```
string name = Console.ReadLine()!;
```

Good Practice: Do not ignore warnings. The compiler is warning you for a reason. At the project level, treat warnings as errors to force yourself to fix the issue. For an individual issue, like the compiler not knowing that the `ReadLine` method will not in practice return null, you can disable that individual warning.

Understanding warning waves

New warnings and errors may be introduced in each release of the C# compiler.

When new warnings could be reported on existing code, those warnings are introduced under an opt-in system referred to as a **warning wave**. The opt-in system means that you shouldn't see new warnings on existing code without taking action to enable them.

Warning waves are enabled using the `AnalysisLevel` element in your project file. For example, if you want to disable the warning wave warnings introduced with .NET 7, you set the analysis level to `6.0`, as shown highlighted in the following markup:

```xml
<Project Sdk="Microsoft.NET.Sdk">

  <PropertyGroup>
    <OutputType>Exe</OutputType>
    <TargetFramework>net7.0</TargetFramework>
    <ImplicitUsings>enable</ImplicitUsings>
    <Nullable>enable</Nullable>
    <AnalysisLevel>6.0</AnalysisLevel>
  </PropertyGroup>

</Project>
```

There are many potential values for the analysis level setting, as shown in the following table:

Level	Description
`5.0`	Enables only up to warning wave 5 warnings.
`6.0`	Enables only up to warning wave 6 warnings.
`7.0`	Enables only up to warning wave 7 warnings.
`latest` (default)	Enables all warning wave warnings.
`preview`	Enables all warning wave warnings, including preview waves.
`none`	Disables all warnings.

If you tell the compiler treat warnings as errors, enabled warning wave warnings generate errors.

Warning wave 5 diagnostics were added in C# 9. Some examples include:

- CS8073 - The result of the expression is always 'false' (or 'true'). The `==` and `!=` operators always return `false` (or `true`) when comparing an instance of a struct type `s` to `null`, as shown in the following code:

```csharp
if (s == null) { } // CS8073: The result of the expression is always
'false'
if (s != null) { } // CS8073: The result of the expression is always
'true'.
```

- CS8892 - Method will not be used as an entry point because a synchronous entry point 'method' was found. If you have both a normal Main method and an async one, then the normal one takes precedence and so the compiler warns that the async one will never be used.

Warning wave 6 diagnostics were added in C# 10:

- CS8826 - Partial method declarations have signature differences.

Warning wave 7 diagnostics were added in C# 11:

- CS8981 - The type name only contains lower-cased ascii characters. C# keywords are all lowercase ASCII characters. This warning makes sure that none of your types conflict with future C# keywords. Some source code generated by tools triggers this warning, for example, Google's design tools that generate .NET proxies for gRPC services.

 You can learn what warnings were added during warning waves at the following link: https://docs.microsoft.com/en-us/dotnet/csharp/language-reference/ compiler-messages/warning-waves.

Using an analyzer to write better code

We have now spent many chapters learning how to write C# code. Before we move on to learning about the .NET libraries, let's see how we can get help to write better code.

.NET analyzers find potential issues and suggest fixes for them. **StyleCop** is a commonly used analyzer for helping you write better C# code.

Let's see it in action:

1. Use your preferred code editor to add a **Console App**/console project named CodeAnalyzing to the Chapter06 solution/workspace.

   - If you are using Visual Studio 2022, then select the check box named **Do not use top-level statements**.
   - If you are using Visual Studio Code, then use the switch --use-program-main.

2. In the CodeAnalyzing project, add a package reference for StyleCop.Analyzers, as shown highlighted in the following configuration:

```
<Project Sdk="Microsoft.NET.Sdk">

  <PropertyGroup>
    <OutputType>Exe</OutputType>
    <TargetFramework>net7.0</TargetFramework>
    <ImplicitUsings>enable</ImplicitUsings>
    <Nullable>enable</Nullable>
  </PropertyGroup>
```

```xml
<ItemGroup>
    <PackageReference Include="StyleCop.Analyzers" Version="1.2.0-
beta.435">
        <PrivateAssets>all</PrivateAssets>
        <IncludeAssets>runtime; build; native; contentfiles; analyzers;
buildtransitive</IncludeAssets>
    </PackageReference>
</ItemGroup>

</Project>
```

The current version at the time of writing is `1.2.0-beta.435`. I recommend changing it to `1.2.0-*` so that you automatically get updates while it is still in preview. Once it has a GA release, you can remove the wildcard to fix it to that version, for example, `1.2.0`.

3. Add a JSON file to your project named `stylecop.json` for controlling StyleCop settings.

4. Modify its contents, as shown in the following markup:

```json
{
  "$schema": "https://raw.githubusercontent.com/DotNetAnalyzers/
StyleCopAnalyzers/master/StyleCop.Analyzers/StyleCop.Analyzers/Settings/
stylecop.schema.json",
  "settings": {

  }
}
```

The `$schema` entry enables IntelliSense while editing the `stylecop.json` file in your code editor.

5. Move the insertion point inside the `settings` section and press *Ctrl + Space*, and note the IntelliSense showing valid subsections of settings, as shown in *Figure 6.7*:

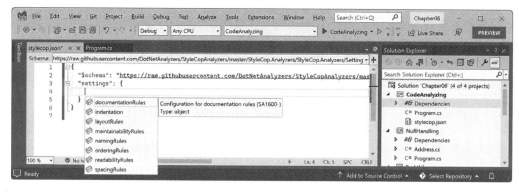

Figure 6.7: stylecop.json IntelliSense showing valid subsections of settings

6. In the `CodeAnalyzing` project file, add entries to configure the file named `stylecop.json` to not be included in published deployments, and to enable it as an additional file for processing during development, as highlighted in the following markup:

```xml
<Project Sdk="Microsoft.NET.Sdk">

  <PropertyGroup>
    <OutputType>Exe</OutputType>
    <TargetFramework>net7.0</TargetFramework>
    <ImplicitUsings>enable</ImplicitUsings>
    <Nullable>enable</Nullable>
  </PropertyGroup>

  <ItemGroup>
    <PackageReference Include="StyleCop.Analyzers" Version="1.2.0-*">
      <PrivateAssets>all</PrivateAssets>
      <IncludeAssets>runtime; build; native; contentfiles; analyzers</IncludeAssets>
    </PackageReference>
  </ItemGroup>

  <ItemGroup>
    <None Remove="stylecop.json" />
  </ItemGroup>

  <ItemGroup>
    <AdditionalFiles Include="stylecop.json" />
  </ItemGroup>

</Project>
```

7. In `Program.cs`, add some statements to import the namespace that will allow us to output a message to the debug output window instead of the console, as shown highlighted in the following code:

```csharp
using System.Diagnostics;

namespace CodeAnalyzing
{
  internal class Program
  {
    static void Main(string[] args)
    {
      Debug.WriteLine("Hello, Debugger!");
    }
  }
}
```

8. Build the `CodeAnalyzing` project.

9. You will see warnings for everything it thinks is wrong, as shown in *Figure 6.8*:

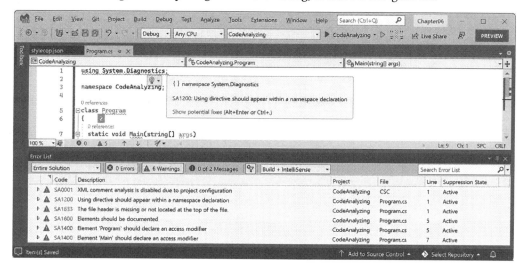

Figure 6.8: StyleCop code analyzer warnings

10. For example, it wants `using` directives to be put within the namespace declaration, as shown in the following output:

```
C:\cs11dotnet7\Chapter06\CodeAnalyzing\Program.cs(1,1): warning SA1200:
Using directive should appear within a namespace declaration [C:\
cs11dotnet7\Chapter06\CodeAnalyzing\CodeAnalyzing.csproj]
```

Suppressing warnings

To suppress a warning, you have several options, including adding code and setting configuration.

To suppress a warning using an attribute, add an assembly-level attribute, as shown in the following code:

```
[assembly:SuppressMessage("StyleCop.CSharp.OrderingRules",
"SA1200:UsingDirectivesMustBePlacedWithinNamespace", Justification =
"Reviewed.")]
```

To suppress a warning using a directive, add `#pragma` statements around the statement that is causing the warning, as shown in the following code:

```
#pragma warning disable SA1200 // UsingDirectivesMustBePlacedWithinNamespace
using System.Diagnostics;
#pragma warning restore SA1200 // UsingDirectivesMustBePlacedWithinNamespace
```

Let's suppress the warning by modifying the `stylecop.json` file:

1. In `stylecop.json`, add a configuration option to set `using` statements to be allowable outside a namespace, as shown highlighted in the following markup:

    ```json
    {
      "$schema": "https://raw.githubusercontent.com/DotNetAnalyzers/
    StyleCopAnalyzers/master/StyleCop.Analyzers/StyleCop.Analyzers/Settings/
    stylecop.schema.json",
        "settings": {
          "orderingRules": {
            "usingDirectivesPlacement": "outsideNamespace"
          }
        }
    }
    ```

2. Build the project and note that warning SA1200 has disappeared.

3. In `stylecop.json`, set the using directives placement to `preserve`, which allows `using` statements both inside and outside a namespace, as shown highlighted in the following markup:

    ```json
    "orderingRules": {
      "usingDirectivesPlacement": "preserve"
    }
    ```

Fixing the code

Now, let's fix all the other warnings:

1. In `CodeAnalyzing.csproj`, add an element to automatically generate an XML file for documentation, as shown highlighted in the following markup:

    ```xml
    <Project Sdk="Microsoft.NET.Sdk">

      <PropertyGroup>
        <OutputType>Exe</OutputType>
        <TargetFramework>net7.0</TargetFramework>
        <ImplicitUsings>enable</ImplicitUsings>
        <Nullable>enable</Nullable>
        <GenerateDocumentationFile>true</GenerateDocumentationFile>
      </PropertyGroup>
    ```

2. In `stylecop.json`, add a configuration option to provide values for documentation for the company name and copyright text, as shown highlighted in the following markup:

    ```json
    {
      "$schema": "https://raw.githubusercontent.com/DotNetAnalyzers/
    StyleCopAnalyzers/master/StyleCop.Analyzers/StyleCop.Analyzers/Settings/
    stylecop.schema.json",
        "settings": {
    ```

```
      "orderingRules": {
        "usingDirectivesPlacement": "preserve"
      },
      "documentationRules": {
        "companyName": "Packt",
        "copyrightText": "Copyright (c) Packt. All rights reserved."
      }
    }
  }
```

3. In `Program.cs`, add comments for a file header with the company and copyright text, move the `using System;` declaration inside the namespace, and set explicit access modifiers and XML comments for the class and method, as shown in the following code:

```csharp
// <copyright file="Program.cs" company="Packt">
// Copyright (c) Packt. All rights reserved.
// </copyright>
namespace CodeAnalyzing;

using System.Diagnostics;

/// <summary>
/// The main class for this console app.
/// </summary>
public class Program
{
  /// <summary>
  /// The main entry point for this console app.
  /// </summary>
  /// <param name="args">
  /// A string array of arguments passed to the console app.
  /// </param>
  public static void Main(string[] args)
  {
    Debug.WriteLine("Hello, Debugger!");
  }
}
```

4. Build the project.

5. Expand the `bin/Debug/net7.0` folder (remember to **Show All Files** if you are using Visual Studio 2022) and note the autogenerated file named `CodeAnalyzing.xml`, as shown in the following markup:

```xml
<?xml version="1.0"?>
<doc>
    <assembly>
        <name>CodeAnalyzing</name>
```

```
        </assembly>
        <members>
            <member name="T:CodeAnalyzing.Program">
                <summary>
                The main class for this console app.
                </summary>
            </member>
            <member name="M:CodeAnalyzing.Program.Main(System.String[])">
                <summary>
                The main entry point for this console app.
                </summary>
                <param name="args">
                A string array of arguments passed to the console app.
                </param>
            </member>
        </members>
    </doc>
```

The `CodeAnalyzing.xml` file can then be processed by a tool like DocFX to convert it into documentation files, as shown at the following link: `https://www.jamescroft.co.uk/building-net-project-docs-with-docfx-on-github-pages/`.

Understanding common StyleCop recommendations

Inside a code file, you should order the contents as shown in the following list:

1. External alias directives
2. Using directives
3. Namespaces
4. Delegates
5. Enums
6. Interfaces
7. Structs
8. Classes

Within a class, record, struct, or interface, you should order the contents as shown in the following list:

1. Fields
2. Constructors
3. Destructors (finalizers)
4. Delegates
5. Events
6. Enums
7. Interfaces

8. Properties

9. Indexers

10. Methods

11. Structs

12. Nested classes and records

 Good Practice: You can learn about all the StyleCop rules at the following link: `https://github.com/DotNetAnalyzers/StyleCopAnalyzers/blob/master/DOCUMENTATION.md`.

Practicing and exploring

Test your knowledge and understanding by answering some questions, getting some hands-on practice, and exploring this chapter's topics with more in-depth research.

Exercise 6.1 – Test your knowledge

Answer the following questions:

1. What is a delegate?

2. What is an event?

3. How are a base class and a derived class related, and how can the derived class access the base class?

4. What is the difference between `is` and `as` operators?

5. Which keyword is used to prevent a class from being derived from or a method from being further overridden?

6. Which keyword is used to prevent a class from being instantiated with the new keyword?

7. Which keyword is used to allow a member to be overridden?

8. What's the difference between a destructor and a deconstruct method?

9. What are the signatures of the constructors that all exceptions should have?

10. What is an extension method, and how do you define one?

Exercise 6.2 – Practice creating an inheritance hierarchy

Explore inheritance hierarchies by following these steps:

1. Add a new console app named `Ch06Ex02Inheritance` to your `Chapter06` solution/workspace.

2. Create a class named `Shape` with properties named `Height`, `Width`, and `Area`.

3. Add three classes that derive from it—`Rectangle`, `Square`, and `Circle`—with any additional members you feel are appropriate and that override and implement the `Area` property correctly.

4. In `Program.cs`, add statements to create one instance of each shape, as shown in the following code:

```
Rectangle r = new(height: 3, width: 4.5);
WriteLine($"Rectangle H: {r.Height}, W: {r.Width}, Area: {r.Area}");


Square s = new(5);
WriteLine($"Square H: {s.Height}, W: {s.Width}, Area: {s.Area}");


Circle c = new(radius: 2.5);
WriteLine($"Circle H: {c.Height}, W: {c.Width}, Area: {c.Area}");
```

5. Run the console app and ensure that the result looks like the following output:

```
Rectangle H: 3, W: 4.5, Area: 13.5
Square H: 5, W: 5, Area: 25
Circle H: 5, W: 5, Area: 19.6349540849362
```

Exercise 6.3 – Explore topics

Use the links on the following page to learn more about the topics covered in this chapter:

`https://github.com/markjprice/cs11dotnet7/blob/main/book-links.md#chapter-6---implementing-interfaces-and-inheriting-classes`

Summary

In this chapter, you learned about:

*   Generic types
*   Delegates and events
*   Implementing interfaces
*   Memory usage differences between reference and value types
*   Working with null values
*   Deriving types using inheritance
*   Base and derived classes, how to override a type member, and using polymorphism
*   Casting between types

In the next chapter, you will learn how .NET is packaged and deployed, and, in subsequent chapters, the types that it provides you with to implement common functionality such as file handling and database access.

Join our book's Discord space

Join the book's Discord workspace for *Ask me Anything* sessions with the author.

https://packt.link/csharp11dotnet7

7

Packaging and Distributing .NET Types

This chapter is about how C# keywords are related to .NET types, and about the relationship between namespaces and assemblies. You'll also become familiar with how to package and publish your .NET apps and libraries for cross-platform use, how to use legacy .NET Framework libraries in .NET libraries, and the possibility of porting legacy .NET Framework code bases to modern .NET.

This chapter covers the following topics:

- The road to .NET 7
- Understanding .NET components
- Publishing your applications for deployment
- Decompiling .NET assemblies
- Packaging your libraries for NuGet distribution
- Porting from .NET Framework to modern .NET
- Working with preview features

The road to .NET 7

This part of the book is about the functionality in the **Base Class Library** (BCL) APIs provided by .NET and how to reuse functionality across all the different .NET platforms using .NET Standard.

First, we will review the route to this point and why it is important to understand the past.

.NET Core 2.0 and later's support for a minimum of .NET Standard 2.0 is important because it provides many of the APIs that were missing from the first version of .NET Core. The 15 years' worth of libraries and applications that .NET Framework developers had available to them that are relevant for modern development have now been migrated to .NET and can run cross-platform on macOS and Linux variants, as well as on Windows.

.NET Standard 2.1 added about 3,000 new APIs. Some of those APIs need runtime changes that would break backward compatibility, so .NET Framework 4.8 only implements .NET Standard 2.0. .NET Core 3.0, Xamarin, Mono, and Unity implement .NET Standard 2.1.

.NET 5 removed the need for .NET Standard if all your projects could use .NET 5. The same applies to .NET 6 and .NET 7. Since you might still need to create class libraries for legacy .NET Framework projects or legacy Xamarin mobile apps, there is still a need to create .NET Standard 2.0 and 2.1 class libraries. In March 2021, I surveyed professional developers, and half still needed to create .NET Standard 2.0 compliant class libraries.

Now that .NET 6 and .NET 7 have full support for mobile and desktop apps built using .NET MAUI, the need for .NET Standard has been further reduced.

To summarize the progress that .NET has made over the past five years, I have compared the major .NET Core and modern .NET versions with the equivalent .NET Framework versions in the following list:

- **.NET Core 1.x:** Much smaller API compared to .NET Framework 4.6.1, which was the current version in March 2016.

- **.NET Core 2.x:** Reached API parity with .NET Framework 4.7.1 for modern APIs because they both implement .NET Standard 2.0.

- **.NET Core 3.x:** Larger API compared to .NET Framework for modern APIs because .NET Framework 4.8 does not implement .NET Standard 2.1.

- **.NET 5:** Even larger API compared to .NET Framework 4.8 for modern APIs, with much-improved performance.

- **.NET 6:** Continued improvements to performance and expanded APIs. Optional support for mobile apps in .NET MAUI added in May 2022.

- **.NET 7:** Final unification with the support for mobile apps in .NET MAUI.

.NET Core 1.0

.NET Core 1.0 was released in June 2016 and focused on implementing an API suitable for building modern cross-platform apps, including web and cloud applications and services for Linux using ASP. NET Core.

.NET Core 1.1

.NET Core 1.1 was released in November 2016 and focused on fixing bugs, increasing the number of Linux distributions supported, supporting .NET Standard 1.6, and improving performance, especially with ASP.NET Core for web apps and services.

.NET Core 2.0

.NET Core 2.0 was released in August 2017 and focused on implementing .NET Standard 2.0, the ability to reference .NET Framework libraries, and more performance improvements.

The third edition of this book was published in November 2017, so it covered up to .NET Core 2.0 and .NET Core for **Universal Windows Platform (UWP)** apps.

.NET Core 2.1

.NET Core 2.1 was released in May 2018 and focused on an extendable tooling system, adding new types like Span<T>, new APIs for cryptography and compression, a Windows Compatibility Pack with an additional 20,000 APIs to help port old Windows applications, Entity Framework Core value conversions, LINQ GroupBy conversions, data seeding, query types, and even more performance improvements, including the topics listed in the following table:

Feature	Chapter	Topic
Spans	8	Working with spans, indexes, and ranges
Brotli compression	9	Compressing with the Brotli algorithm
EF Core Lazy loading	10	Enabling lazy loading
EF Core Data seeding	10	Understanding data seeding

.NET Core 2.2

.NET Core 2.2 was released in December 2018 and focused on diagnostic improvements for the runtime, optional tiered compilation, and adding new features to ASP.NET Core and Entity Framework Core like spatial data support using types from the **NetTopologySuite** (**NTS**) library, query tags, and collections of owned entities.

.NET Core 3.0

.NET Core 3.0 was released in September 2019 and focused on adding support for building Windows desktop applications using Windows Forms (2001), **Windows Presentation Foundation** (**WPF**; 2006), and Entity Framework 6.3, side-by-side and app-local deployments, a fast JSON reader, serial port access and other pinout access for **Internet of Things** (**IoT**) solutions, and tiered compilation by default, including the topics listed in the following table:

Feature	Chapter	Topic
Embedding .NET in-app	7	Publishing your applications for deployment
Index and Range	8	Working with spans, indexes, and ranges
System.Text.Json	9	High-performance JSON processing

The fourth edition of this book was published in October 2019, so it covered some of the new APIs added in later versions up to .NET Core 3.0.

.NET Core 3.1

.NET Core 3.1 was released in December 2019 and focused on bug fixes and refinements so that it could be a **Long Term Support** (**LTS**) release, not losing support until December 2022.

.NET 5.0

.NET 5.0 was released in November 2020 and focused on unifying the various .NET platforms except mobile, refining the platform, and improving performance, including the topics listed in the following table:

Feature	Chapter	Topic
`Half` type	8	Working with numbers
Regular expression performance improvements	8	Regular expression performance improvements
`System.Text.Json` improvements	9	High-performance JSON processing
EF Core generated SQL	10	Getting the generated SQL
EF Core Filtered Include	10	Filtering included entities
EF Core Scaffold-DbContext now singularizes using Humanizer	10	Scaffolding models using an existing database

.NET 6.0

.NET 6.0 was released in November 2021 and focused on adding more features to EF Core for data management, new types for working with dates and times, and improving performance, including the topics listed in the following table:

Feature	Chapter	Topic
Check .NET SDK status	7	Checking your .NET SDKs for updates
Support for Apple Silicon	7	Creating a console application to publish
Link trim mode as default	7	Reducing the size of apps using app trimming
`EnsureCapacity` for `List<T>`	8	Improving performance by ensuring the capacity of a collection
Low-level file API using `RandomAccess`	9	Reading and writing with random access handles
EF Core configure conventions	10	Configuring preconvention models
New LINQ methods	11	Building LINQ expressions with the `Enumerable` class
`TryGetNonEnumeratedCount`	11	Aggregating sequences

.NET 7.0

.NET 7.0 was released in November 2022 and focused on unifying with the mobile platform, adding more features like string syntax coloring and IntelliSense, support for creating and extracting tar archives, and improving performance of inserts and updates with EF Core, including the topics listed in the following table:

Feature	Chapter	Topic
[StringSyntax] attribute	8	Activating regular expression syntax coloring
[GeneratedRegex] attribute	8	Improving regular expression performance with source generators
Tar archive support	9	Working with tar archives
ExecuteUpdate and ExecuteDelete	10	More efficient updates and deletes
Order and OrderDescending	11	Sorting by the item itself

Improving performance with .NET 5 and later

Microsoft has made significant improvements to performance in the past few years. You can read detailed blog posts at the following links:

https://devblogs.microsoft.com/dotnet/performance-improvements-in-net-5/

https://devblogs.microsoft.com/dotnet/performance-improvements-in-net-6/

https://devblogs.microsoft.com/dotnet/performance_improvements_in_net_7/

Checking your .NET SDKs for updates

With .NET 6, Microsoft added a command to check the versions of .NET SDKs and runtimes that you have installed and warn you if any need updating. For example, enter the following command:

```
dotnet sdk check
```

You will see results, including the status of available updates, as shown in the following partial output:

```
.NET SDKs:
Version                         Status
----------------------------------------------------------------------
3.1.421                         .NET Core 3.1 is going out of support soon.
5.0.406                         .NET 5.0 is out of support.
6.0.300                         Patch 6.0.301 is available.
7.0.100                         Up to date.
```

Understanding .NET components

.NET is made up of several pieces, which are shown in the following list:

- **Language compilers:** These turn your source code written with languages such as C#, F#, and Visual Basic into **intermediate language (IL)** code stored in assemblies. With C# 6.0 and later, Microsoft switched to an open-source rewritten compiler known as Roslyn that is also used by Visual Basic.

- **Common Language Runtime (CoreCLR):** This runtime loads assemblies, compiles the IL code stored in them into native code instructions for your computer's CPU, and executes the code within an environment that manages resources such as threads and memory.

- **Base Class Libraries (BCL or CoreFX):** These are prebuilt assemblies of types packaged and distributed using NuGet for performing common tasks when building applications. You can use them to quickly build anything you want, rather like combining LEGO™ pieces.

Assemblies, NuGet packages, and namespaces

An **assembly** is where a type is stored in the filesystem. Assemblies are a mechanism for deploying code. For example, the `System.Data.dll` assembly contains types for managing data. To use types in other assemblies, they must be referenced. Assemblies can be static (pre-created) or dynamic (generated at runtime). Dynamic assemblies are an advanced feature that we will not cover in this book. Assemblies can be compiled into a single file as a DLL (class library) or an EXE (console app).

Assemblies are distributed as **NuGet packages**, which are files downloadable from public online feeds and can contain multiple assemblies and other resources. You will also hear about **project SDKs**, **workloads**, and **platforms**, which are combinations of NuGet packages.

Microsoft's NuGet feed is found here: `https://www.nuget.org/`.

What is a namespace?

A namespace is the address of a type. Namespaces are a mechanism to uniquely identify a type by requiring a full address rather than just a short name. In the real world, *Bob of 34 Sycamore Street* is different from *Bob of 12 Willow Drive*.

In .NET, the `IActionFilter` interface of the `System.Web.Mvc` namespace is different from the `IActionFilter` interface of the `System.Web.Http.Filters` namespace.

Dependent assemblies

If an assembly is compiled as a class library and provides types for other assemblies to use, then it has the file extension `.dll` (**dynamic link library**), and it cannot be executed standalone.

Likewise, if an assembly is compiled as an application, then it has the file extension `.exe` (**executable**) and can be executed standalone. Before .NET Core 3.0, console apps were compiled to `.dll` files and had to be executed by the `dotnet run` command or a host executable.

Any assembly can reference one or more class library assemblies as dependencies, but you cannot have circular references. So, assembly *B* cannot reference assembly *A* if assembly *A* already references assembly *B*. The compiler will warn you if you attempt to add a dependency reference that would cause a circular reference. Circular references are often a warning sign of poor code design. If you are sure that you need a circular reference, then use an interface to solve it.

Microsoft .NET project SDKs

By default, console applications have a dependency reference on the Microsoft .NET project SDK. This platform contains thousands of types in NuGet packages that almost all applications would need, such as the System.Int32 and System.String types.

When using .NET, you reference the dependency assemblies, NuGet packages, and platforms that your application needs in a project file.

Let's explore the relationship between assemblies and namespaces:

1. Use your preferred code editor to create a new project, as defined in the following list:

    -   Project template: **Console App**/console
    -   Project file and folder: AssembliesAndNamespaces
    -   Workspace/solution file and folder: Chapter07

2. Open AssembliesAndNamespaces.csproj and note that it is a typical project file for a .NET application, as shown in the following markup:

    ```
    <Project Sdk="Microsoft.NET.Sdk">

      <PropertyGroup>
        <OutputType>Exe</OutputType>
        <TargetFramework>net7.0</TargetFramework>
        <Nullable>enable</Nullable>
        <ImplicitUsings>enable</ImplicitUsings>
      </PropertyGroup>

    </Project>
    ```

3. After the <PropertyGroup> section, add a new <ItemGroup> section to statically import System.Console for all C# files using the implicit usings .NET SDK feature, as shown in the following markup:

    ```
    <ItemGroup>
      <Using Include="System.Console" Static="true" />
    </ItemGroup>
    ```

Namespaces and types in assemblies

Many common .NET types are in the System.Runtime.dll assembly. There is not always a one-to-one mapping between assemblies and namespaces. A single assembly can contain many namespaces and a namespace can be defined in many assemblies. You can see the relationship between some assemblies and the namespaces that they supply types for, as shown in the following table:

Assembly	Example namespaces	Example types
System.Runtime.dll	System, System.Collections, System.Collections.Generic	Int32, String, IEnumerable\<T\>
System.Console.dll	System	Console
System.Threading.dll	System.Threading	Interlocked, Monitor, Mutex
System.Xml.XDocument.dll	System.Xml.Linq	XDocument, XElement, XNode

NuGet packages

.NET is split into a set of packages, distributed using a Microsoft-supported package management technology named NuGet. Each of these packages represents a single assembly of the same name. For example, the System.Collections package contains the System.Collections.dll assembly.

The following are the benefits of packages:

- Packages can be easily distributed on public feeds.
- Packages can be reused.
- Packages can ship on their own schedule.
- Packages can be tested independently of other packages.
- Packages can support different OSes and CPUs by including multiple versions of the same assembly built for different OSes and CPUs.
- Packages can have dependencies specific to only one library.
- Apps are smaller because unreferenced packages aren't part of the distribution. The following table lists some of the more important packages and their important types:

Package	Important types
System.Runtime	Object, String, Int32, Array
System.Collections	List\<T\>, Dictionary\<TKey, TValue\>
System.Net.Http	HttpClient, HttpResponseMessage
System.IO.FileSystem	File, Directory
System.Reflection	Assembly, TypeInfo, MethodInfo

Understanding frameworks

There is a two-way relationship between frameworks and packages. Packages define the APIs, while frameworks group packages. A framework without any packages would not define any APIs.

.NET packages each support a set of frameworks. For example, the `System.IO.FileSystem` package version 4.3.0 supports the following frameworks:

- .NET Standard, version 1.3 or later
- .NET Framework, version 4.6 or later
- Six Mono and Xamarin platforms (for example, Xamarin.iOS 1.0)

 More Information: You can read the details at the following link: `https://www.nuget.org/packages/System.IO.FileSystem/`.

Importing a namespace to use a type

Let's explore how namespaces are related to assemblies and types:

1. In the `AssembliesAndNamespaces` project, in `Program.cs`, delete the existing statements and then enter the following code:

   ```
   XDocument doc = new();
   ```

2. Build the project and note the compiler error message, as shown in the following output:

   ```
   The type or namespace name 'XDocument' could not be found (are you
   missing a using directive or an assembly reference?)
   ```

   The `XDocument` type is not recognized because we have not told the compiler what the namespace of the type is. Although this project already has a reference to the assembly that contains the type, we also need to either prefix the type name with its namespace or import the namespace.

3. Click inside the `XDocument` class name. Your code editor displays a light bulb, showing that it recognizes the type and can automatically fix the problem for you.

4. Click the light bulb, and select `using System.Xml.Linq;` from the menu.

This will *import the namespace* by adding a `using` statement to the top of the file. Once a namespace is imported at the top of a code file, then all the types within the namespace are available for use in that code file by just typing their name without the type name needing to be fully qualified by prefixing it with its namespace.

Sometimes I like to add a comment with a type name after importing a namespace to remind me which types require me to import that namespace, as shown in the following code:

```
using System.Xml.Linq; // XDocument
```

Relating C# keywords to .NET types

One of the common questions I get from new C# programmers is, "What is the difference between string with a lowercase s and String with an uppercase S?"

The short answer is easy: none. The long answer is that all C# type keywords like string or int are aliases for a .NET type in a class library assembly.

When you use the string keyword, the compiler recognizes it as a System.String type. When you use the int type, the compiler recognizes it as a System.Int32 type.

Let's see this in action with some code:

1. In Program.cs, declare two variables to hold string values, one using lowercase string and one using uppercase String, as shown in the following code:

```
string s1 = "Hello";
String s2 = "World";
WriteLine($"{s1} {s2}");
```

2. Run the code, and note that at the moment, they both work equally well, and literally mean the same thing.

3. In AssembliesAndNamespaces.csproj, add entries to prevent the System namespace from being globally imported, as shown in the following markup:

```
<ItemGroup>
  <Using Remove="System" />
</ItemGroup>
```

4. In Program.cs, note the compiler error message, as shown in the following output:

```
The type or namespace name 'String' could not be found (are you missing a
using directive or an assembly reference?)
```

5. At the top of Program.cs, import the System namespace with a using statement that will fix the error, as shown in the following code:

```
using System; // String
```

 Good Practice: When you have a choice, use the C# keyword instead of the actual type because the keywords do not need the namespace to be imported.

Mapping C# aliases to .NET types

The following table shows the 18 C# type keywords along with their actual .NET types:

Keyword	.NET type	Keyword	.NET type
string	System.String	char	System.Char
sbyte	System.SByte	byte	System.Byte
short	System.Int16	ushort	System.UInt16
int	System.Int32	uint	System.UInt32
long	System.Int64	ulong	System.UInt64
nint	System.IntPtr	nuint	System.UIntPtr
float	System.Single	double	System.Double
decimal	System.Decimal	bool	System.Boolean
object	System.Object	dynamic	System.Dynamic.DynamicObject

Other .NET programming language compilers can do the same thing. For example, the Visual Basic .NET language has a type named Integer that is its alias for System.Int32.

Understanding native-sized integers

C# 9 introduced the nint and nuint keyword aliases for **native-sized integers**, meaning that the storage size for the integer value is platform-specific. They store a 32-bit integer in a 32-bit process and sizeof() returns 4 bytes; they store a 64-bit integer in a 64-bit process and sizeof() returns 8 bytes. The aliases represent pointers to the integer value in memory, which is why their .NET names are IntPtr and UIntPtr. The actual storage type will be either System.Int32 or System.Int64 depending on the process.

In a 64-bit process, the following code:

```
WriteLine($"int.MaxValue = {int.MaxValue:N0}");
WriteLine($"nint.MaxValue = {nint.MaxValue:N0}");
```

produces this output:

```
int.MaxValue = 2,147,483,647
nint.MaxValue = 9,223,372,036,854,775,807
```

Revealing the location of a type

Code editors provide built-in documentation for .NET types. Let's explore:

1. Right-click inside XDocument and choose **Go to Definition**.

2. Navigate to the top of the code file and note the assembly filename is `System.Xml.XDocument. dll`, but the class is in the `System.Xml.Linq` namespace, as shown in *Figure 7.1*:

Figure 7.1: Assembly and namespace that contains the XDocument type

3. Close the **XDocument [from metadata]** tab.

4. Right-click inside `string` or `String` and choose **Go to Definition**.

5. Navigate to the top of the code file and note the assembly filename is `System.Runtime.dll` but the class is in the `System` namespace.

Your code editor is technically lying to you. If you remember when we wrote code in *Chapter 2, Speaking C#*, when we revealed the extent of the C# vocabulary, we discovered that the `System.Runtime.dll` assembly contains zero types.

What the `System.Runtime.dll` assembly does contain are type-forwarders. These are special types that appear to exist in an assembly but are implemented elsewhere. In this case, they are implemented deep inside the .NET runtime using highly optimized code.

Sharing code with legacy platforms using .NET Standard

Before .NET Standard, there were **Portable Class Libraries** (**PCLs**). With PCLs, you could create a library of code and explicitly specify which platforms you want the library to support, such as Xamarin, Silverlight, and Windows 8. Your library could then use the intersection of APIs that are supported by the specified platforms.

Microsoft realized that this is unsustainable, so they created .NET Standard—a single API that all future .NET platforms would support. There are older versions of .NET Standard, but .NET Standard 2.0 was an attempt to unify all important recent .NET platforms. .NET Standard 2.1 was released in late 2019 but only .NET Core 3.0 and that year's version of Xamarin support its new features. For the rest of this book, I will use the term .NET Standard to mean .NET Standard 2.0.

.NET Standard is like HTML5 in that they are both standards that a platform should support. Just as Google's Chrome browser and Microsoft's Edge browser implement the HTML5 standard, .NET Core, .NET Framework, and Xamarin all implement .NET Standard. If you want to create a library of types that will work across variants of legacy .NET, you can do so most easily with .NET Standard.

Good Practice: Since many of the API additions in .NET Standard 2.1 required runtime changes, and .NET Framework is Microsoft's legacy platform that needs to remain as unchanging as possible, .NET Framework 4.8 remained on .NET Standard 2.0 rather than implementing .NET Standard 2.1. If you need to support .NET Framework customers, then you should create class libraries on .NET Standard 2.0 even though it is not the latest and does not support all the recent language and BCL new features.

Your choice of which .NET Standard version to target comes down to a balance between maximizing platform support and available functionality. A lower version supports more platforms but has a smaller set of APIs. A higher version supports fewer platforms but has a larger set of APIs. Generally, you should choose the lowest version that supports all the APIs that you need.

Understanding defaults for class libraries with different SDKs

When using the dotnet SDK tool to create a class library, it might be useful to know which target framework will be used by default, as shown in the following table:

SDK	Default target framework for new class libraries
.NET Core 3.1	`netstandard2.0`
.NET 6	`net6.0`
.NET 7	`net7.0`

Of course, just because a class library targets a specific version of .NET by default does not mean you cannot change it after creating a class library project using the default template.

You can manually set the target framework to a value that supports the projects that need to reference that library, as shown in the following table:

Class library target framework	Can be used by projects that target
`netstandard2.0`	.NET Framework 4.6.1 or later, .NET Core 2.0 or later, .NET 5.0 or later, Mono 5.4 or later, Xamarin.Android 8.0 or later, Xamarin.iOS 10.14 or later
`netstandard2.1`	.NET Core 3.0 or later, .NET 5.0 or later, Mono 6.4 or later, Xamarin.Android 10.0 or later, Xamarin.iOS 12.16 or later
`net6.0`	.NET 6.0 or later
`net7.0`	.NET 7.0 or later

Good Practice: Always check the target framework of a class library and then manually change it to something more appropriate if necessary. Make a conscious decision about what it should be rather than accepting the default.

Creating a .NET Standard 2.0 class library

We will create a class library using .NET Standard 2.0 so that it can be used across all important .NET legacy platforms and cross-platform on Windows, macOS, and Linux operating systems, while also having access to a wide set of .NET APIs:

1. Use your preferred code editor to add a new **Class Library**/classlib project named SharedLibrary that targets .NET Standard 2.0 to the Chapter07 solution/workspace:

    *   If you use Visual Studio 2022, when prompted for the **Target Framework**, select **.NET Standard 2.0**, and then set the startup project for the solution to the current selection.
    *   If you use Visual Studio Code, include a switch to target .NET Standard 2.0, as shown in the following command, and then select SharedLibrary as the active OmniSharp project:

    ```
    dotnet new classlib -f netstandard2.0
    ```

 Good Practice: If you need to create types that use new features in .NET 7.0, as well as types that only use .NET Standard 2.0 features, then you can create two separate class libraries: one targeting .NET Standard 2.0 and one targeting .NET 7.0.

An alternative to manually creating two class libraries is to create one that supports **multi-targeting**. If you would like me to add a section about multi-targeting to the next edition, please let me know. You can read about multi-targeting here: https://docs.microsoft.com/en-us/dotnet/standard/library-guidance/cross-platform-targeting#multi-targeting.

Controlling the .NET SDK

By default, executing dotnet commands uses the most recent installed .NET SDK. There may be times when you want to control which SDK is used.

For example, one reader of the fourth edition wanted their experience to match the book steps that use the .NET Core 3.1 SDK. But they had installed the .NET 5.0 SDK as well and that was being used by default. As described in the previous section, the behavior when creating new class libraries changed to target .NET 5.0 instead of .NET Standard 2.0, and that confused the reader.

You can control the .NET SDK used by default by using a global.json file. The dotnet command searches the current folder and ancestor folders for a global.json file.

You do not need to complete the following steps, but if you want to try and do not already have .NET 6.0 SDK installed then you can install it from the following link:

https://dotnet.microsoft.com/download/dotnet/6.0

1. Create a subdirectory/folder in the Chapter07 folder named ControlSDK.
2. On Windows, start **Command Prompt** or **Windows Terminal**. On macOS, start **Terminal**. If you are using Visual Studio Code, then you can use the integrated terminal.

3. In the `ControlSDK` folder, at the command prompt or terminal, enter a command to list the installed .NET SDKs, as shown in the following command:

```
dotnet --list-sdks
```

4. Note the results and the version number of the latest .NET 6 SDK installed, as shown in the following output:

```
3.1.416 [C:\Program Files\dotnet\sdk]
6.0.200 [C:\Program Files\dotnet\sdk]
7.0.100 [C:\Program Files\dotnet\sdk]
```

5. Create a `global.json` file that forces the use of the latest .NET Core 6.0 SDK that you have installed (which might be later than mine), as shown in the following command:

```
dotnet new globaljson --sdk-version 6.0.200
```

6. Open the `global.json` file and review its contents, as shown in the following markup:

```
{
  "sdk": {
    "version": "6.0.200"
  }
}
```

7. In the `ControlSDK` folder, at the command prompt or terminal, enter a command to create a class library project, as shown in the following command:

```
dotnet new classlib
```

8. If you do not have the .NET 6.0 SDK installed then you will see an error, as shown in the following output:

```
Could not execute because the application was not found or a compatible
.NET SDK is not installed.
```

9. If you do have the .NET 6.0 SDK installed, then a class library project will be created that targets .NET 6.0 by default.

Publishing your code for deployment

If you write a novel and you want other people to read it, you must publish it.

Most developers write code for other developers to use in their own projects, or for users to run as an app. To do so, you must publish your code as packaged class libraries or executable applications.

There are three ways to publish and deploy a .NET application. They are:

*   **Framework-dependent deployment (FDD)**
*   **Framework-dependent executable (FDE)**
*   **Self-contained**

If you choose to deploy your application and its package dependencies, but not .NET itself, then you rely on .NET already being on the target computer. This works well for web applications deployed to a server because .NET and lots of other web applications are likely already on the server.

Framework-dependent deployment (FDD) means you deploy a DLL that must be executed by the dotnet command-line tool. **Framework-dependent executables** (FDE) means you deploy an EXE that can be run directly from the command line. Both require the appropriate version of the .NET runtime to be already installed on the system.

Sometimes, you want to be able to give someone a USB stick containing your application and know that it can execute on their computer. You want to perform a self-contained deployment. While the size of the deployment files will be larger, you'll know that it will work.

Creating a console app to publish

Let's explore how to publish a console app:

1. Use your preferred code editor to add a new **Console App**/console project named DotNetEverywhere to the Chapter07 solution/workspace:

    *   In Visual Studio Code, select DotNetEverywhere as the active OmniSharp project. When you see the pop-up warning message saying that required assets are missing, click **Yes** to add them.

2. Modify the project file to statically import the System.Console class in all C# files.

3. In Program.cs, delete the existing statements and then add a statement to output a message saying the console app can run everywhere and some information about the operating system, as shown in the following code:

```
WriteLine("I can run everywhere!");
WriteLine($"OS Version is {Environment.OSVersion}.");

if (OperatingSystem.IsMacOS())
{
  WriteLine("I am macOS.");
}
else if (OperatingSystem.IsWindowsVersionAtLeast(major: 10, build:
22000))
{
  WriteLine("I am Windows 11.");
}
else if (OperatingSystem.IsWindowsVersionAtLeast(major: 10))
{
  WriteLine("I am Windows 10.");
}
else
{
  WriteLine("I am some other mysterious OS.");
```

```
    }
    WriteLine("Press ENTER to stop me.");
    ReadLine();
```

4. Run the console app and note the results when run on Windows 11, as shown in the following output:

```
I can run everywhere!
OS Version is Microsoft Windows NT 10.0.22000.0.
I am Windows 11.
Press ENTER to stop me.
```

5. Open `DotNetEverywhere.csproj` and add the runtime identifiers to target three operating systems inside the `<PropertyGroup>` element, as shown highlighted in the following markup:

```
<Project Sdk="Microsoft.NET.Sdk">

  <PropertyGroup>
    <OutputType>Exe</OutputType>
    <TargetFramework>net7.0</TargetFramework>
    <Nullable>enable</Nullable>
    <ImplicitUsings>enable</ImplicitUsings>
    <RuntimeIdentifiers>
      win10-x64;osx-x64;osx.11.0-arm64;linux-x64;linux-arm64
    </RuntimeIdentifiers>
  </PropertyGroup>

</Project>
```

The highlighted items are as follows:

- The `win10-x64` RID value means Windows 10 or Windows Server 2016 64-bit. You could also use the `win10-arm64` RID value to deploy to a Microsoft Surface Pro X, Surface Pro 9 (SQ 3), or Windows Dev Kit 2023.
- The `osx-x64` RID value means macOS Sierra 10.12 or later. You can also specify version-specific RID values like `osx.10.15-x64` (Catalina), `osx.13.0-x64` (Ventura on Intel), or `osx.13.0-arm64` (Ventura on Apple Silicon).
- The `linux-x64` RID value means most desktop distributions of Linux, like Ubuntu, CentOS, Debian, or Fedora. Use `linux-arm` for Raspbian or Raspberry Pi OS 32-bit. Use `linux-arm64` for a Raspberry Pi running Ubuntu 64-bit.

There are two elements that you can use to specify runtime identifiers. Use `<RuntimeIdentifier>` if you only need to specify one. Use `<RuntimeIdentifiers>` if you need to specify multiple, as we did in the preceding example. If you use the wrong one, then the compiler will give an error and it can be difficult to understand why with only one character difference!

Understanding dotnet commands

When you install the .NET SDK, it includes a **command-line interface (CLI)** named dotnet.

Creating new projects

The .NET CLI has commands that work on the current folder to create a new project using templates:

1. On Windows, start **Command Prompt** or **Windows Terminal**. On macOS, start **Terminal**. If you are using Visual Studio Code, then you can use the integrated terminal.

2. Enter the dotnet new list (.NET 7), or dotnet new --list or dotnet new -l (.NET 6) command to list your currently installed templates, as shown in *Figure 7.2*:

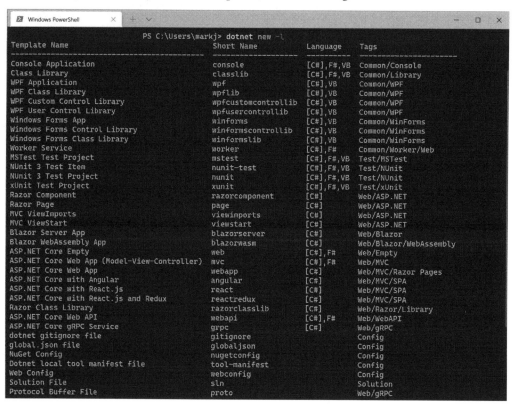

Figure 7.2: A list of installed dotnet new project templates

Most dotnet command-line switches have a long and a short version, for example, --list or -l. The short ones are quicker to type but more likely to be misinterpreted by you or other humans. Sometimes more typing is clearer.

Getting information about .NET and its environment

It is useful to see what .NET SDKs and runtimes are currently installed, alongside information about the operating system, as shown in the following command:

```
dotnet --info
```

Note the results, as shown in the following partial output:

```
.NET SDK (reflecting any global.json):
 Version:   7.0.100
 Commit:    129d2465c8

Runtime Environment:
 OS Name:     Windows
 OS Version:  10.0.22000
 OS Platform: Windows
 RID:         win10-x64
 Base Path:   C:\Program Files\dotnet\sdk\7.0.100\

Host (useful for support):
  Version: 7.0.0
  Commit:  405337939c

.NET SDKs installed:
  3.1.416 [C:\Program Files\dotnet\sdk]
  5.0.405 [C:\Program Files\dotnet\sdk]
  6.0.200 [C:\Program Files\dotnet\sdk]
  7.0.100 [C:\Program Files\dotnet\sdk]

.NET runtimes installed:
  Microsoft.AspNetCore.App 3.1.22 [...\dotnet\shared\Microsoft.AspNetCore.All]
...
```

Managing projects

The .NET CLI has the following commands that work on the project in the current folder, to manage the project:

- `dotnet help`: Shows the command line help.
- `dotnet new`: Create a new .NET project or file.
- `dotnet tool`: Install or manage tools that extend the .NET experience.
- `dotnet workload`: Manage optional workloads like .NET MAUI.
- `dotnet restore`: This downloads dependencies for the project.
- `dotnet build`: This builds, aka compiles, a .NET project.
- `dotnet build-server`: Interact with servers started by a build.
- `dotnet msbuild`: This runs MS Build Engine commands.
- `dotnet clean`: This removes the temporary outputs from a build.
- `dotnet test`: This builds and then runs unit tests for the project.
- `dotnet run`: This builds and then runs the project.
- `dotnet pack`: This creates a NuGet package for the project.

- `dotnet publish`: This builds and then publishes the project, either with dependencies or as a self-contained application.
- `dotnet add`: This adds a reference to a package or class library to the project.
- `dotnet remove`: This removes a reference to a package or class library from the project.
- `dotnet list`: This lists the package or class library references for the project.

Publishing a self-contained app

Now that you have seen some example `dotnet` tool commands, we can publish our cross-platform console app:

1. At the command line, make sure that you are in the `DotNetEverywhere` folder.

2. Enter a command to build and publish the self-contained release version of the console application for Windows 10, as shown in the following command:

```
dotnet publish -c Release -r win10-x64 --self-contained
```

3. Note the build engine restores any needed packages, compiles the project source code into an assembly DLL, and creates a `publish` folder, as shown in the following output:

```
MSBuild version 17.4.0+14c24b2d3 for .NET
  Determining projects to restore...
  All projects are up-to-date for restore.
  DotNetEverywhere -> C:\cs11dotnet7\Chapter07\DotNetEverywhere\bin\
Release\net7.0\win10-x64\DotNetEverywhere.dll
  DotNetEverywhere -> C:\cs11dotnet7\Chapter07\DotNetEverywhere\bin\
Release\net7.0\win10-x64\publish\
```

4. Enter the following commands to build and publish the release versions for macOS and Linux variants:

```
dotnet publish -c Release -r osx-x64 --self-contained
dotnet publish -c Release -r osx.11.0-arm64 --self-contained
dotnet publish -c Release -r linux-x64 --self-contained
dotnet publish -c Release -r linux-arm64 --self-contained
```

> **Good Practice:** You could automate these commands by using a scripting language like PowerShell and execute the script file on any operating system using the cross-platform PowerShell Core. Just create a file with the extension `.ps1` with the five commands in it. Then execute the file. Learn more about PowerShell at the following link: `https://github.com/markjprice/cs11dotnet7/tree/main/docs/powershell`.

5. Open Windows **File Explorer** or a macOS **Finder** window, navigate to `DotNetEverywhere\bin\Release\net7.0`, and note the output folders for the five operating systems.

6. In the `win10-x64` folder, select the `publish` folder, and note all the supporting assemblies like `Microsoft.CSharp.dll`.

7. Select the `DotNetEverywhere` executable file, and note it is 149 KB, as shown in *Figure 7.3*:

Figure 7.3: The DotNetEverywhere executable file for Windows 10 64-bit

8. If you are on Windows, then double-click to execute the program and note the result, as shown in the following output:

```
I can run everywhere!
OS Version is Microsoft Windows NT 10.0.22000.0.
I am Windows 11.
Press ENTER to stop me.
```

9. Press *Enter* to close the console app and its window.

10. Note that the total size of the `publish` folder and all its files is about 70 MB.

11. In the `osx.11.0-arm64` folder, select the `publish` folder, note all the supporting assemblies, and then select the `DotNetEverywhere` executable file. Note that the executable is 126 KB, and the `publish` folder is about 76 MB.

If you copy any of those `publish` folders to the appropriate operating system, the console app will run; this is because it is a self-contained deployable .NET application. For example, here it is on macOS Big Sur with Intel:

```
I can run everywhere!
OS Version is Unix 11.2.3
I am macOS.
Press ENTER to stop me.
```

This example used a console app, but you could just as easily create an ASP.NET Core website or web service, or a Windows Forms or WPF app. Of course, you can only deploy Windows desktop apps to Windows computers, not Linux or macOS.

Publishing a single-file app

To publish as a "single" file, you can specify flags when publishing. With .NET 5, single-file apps were primarily focused on Linux because there are limitations in both Windows and macOS that mean true single-file publishing is not technically possible. With .NET 6 or later, you can now create proper single-file apps on Windows.

If you can assume that .NET is already installed on the computer on which you want to run your app, then you can use the extra flags when you publish your app for release to say that it does not need to be self-contained and that you want to publish it as a single file (if possible), as shown in the following command (which must be entered on a single line):

```
dotnet publish -r win10-x64 -c Release --no-self-contained
/p:PublishSingleFile=true
```

This will generate two files: DotNetEverywhere.exe and DotNetEverywhere.pdb. The .exe file is the executable. The .pdb file is a **program debug database** file that stores debugging information.

There is no .exe file extension for published applications on macOS, so if you use osx-x64 in the command above, the filename will not have an extension.

If you prefer the .pdb file to be embedded in the .exe file, for example, to ensure it is deployed with its assembly, then add a <DebugType> element to the <PropertyGroup> element in your .csproj file and set it to embedded, as shown highlighted in the following markup:

```
<PropertyGroup>

  <OutputType>Exe</OutputType>
  <TargetFramework>net7.0</TargetFramework>
  <Nullable>enable</Nullable>
  <ImplicitUsings>enable</ImplicitUsings>

  <RuntimeIdentifiers>
    win10-x64;osx-x64;osx.11.0-arm64;linux-x64;linux-arm64
  </RuntimeIdentifiers>

  <DebugType>embedded</DebugType>

</PropertyGroup>
```

If you cannot assume that .NET is already installed on a computer, then although Linux also only generates the two files, expect the following additional files for Windows: coreclr.dll, clrjit.dll, clrcompression.dll, and mscordaccore.dll.

Let's see an example for Windows:

1. At the command line, enter the command to build the self-contained release version of the console app for Windows 10, as shown in the following command:

    ```
    dotnet publish -c Release -r win10-x64 --self-contained
    /p:PublishSingleFile=true
    ```

2. Navigate to the DotNetEverywhere\bin\Release\net7.0\win10-x64\publish folder and select the DotNetEverywhere executable file. Note that the executable is now about 64 MB, and there is also a .pdb file that is 11 KB. The sizes on your system will vary.

Reducing the size of apps using app trimming

One of the problems with deploying a .NET app as a self-contained app is that the .NET libraries take up a lot of space. One of the biggest needs is to reduce the size of Blazor WebAssembly components because all the .NET libraries need to be downloaded to the browser.

Luckily, you can reduce this size by not packaging unused assemblies with your deployments. Introduced with .NET Core 3.0, the app trimming system can identify the assemblies needed by your code and remove those that are not needed.

With .NET 5, the trimming went further by removing individual types, and even members like methods from within an assembly if they are not used. For example, with a Hello World console app, the System.Console.dll assembly is trimmed from 61.5 KB to 31.5 KB. For .NET 5, this is an experimental feature, so it is disabled by default.

With .NET 6, Microsoft added annotations to their libraries to indicate how they can be safely trimmed so the trimming of types and members was made the default. This is known as **link trim mode**.

The catch is how well the trimming identifies unused assemblies, types, and members. If your code is dynamic, perhaps using reflection, then it might not work correctly, so Microsoft also allows manual control.

Enabling assembly-level trimming

There are two ways to enable assembly-level trimming.

The first way is to add an element in the project file, as shown in the following markup:

```
<PublishTrimmed>true</PublishTrimmed>
```

The second way is to add a flag when publishing, as shown highlighted in the following command:

```
dotnet publish ... -p:PublishTrimmed=True
```

Enabling type-level and member-level trimming

There are two ways to enable type-level and member-level trimming.

The first way is to add two elements in the project file, as shown in the following markup:

```
<PublishTrimmed>true</PublishTrimmed>
<TrimMode>Link</TrimMode>
```

The second way is to add two flags when publishing, as shown highlighted in the following command:

```
dotnet publish ... -p:PublishTrimmed=True -p:TrimMode=Link
```

For .NET 6, link trim mode is the default, so you only need to specify the switch if you want to set an alternative trim mode, like copyused, which means assembly-level trimming.

Decompiling .NET assemblies

One of the best ways to learn how to code for .NET is to see how professionals do it.

 Good Practice: You could decompile someone else's assemblies for non-learning purposes like copying their code for use in your own production library or application, but remember that you are viewing their intellectual property, so please respect that.

Decompiling using the ILSpy extension for Visual Studio 2022

For learning purposes, you can decompile any .NET assembly with a tool like ILSpy:

1. In Visual Studio 2022 for Windows, navigate to **Extensions | Manage Extensions**.
2. In the search box, enter `ilspy`.
3. For the **ILSpy 2022** extension, click **Download**.
4. Click **Close**.
5. Close Visual Studio to allow the extension to install.
6. Restart Visual Studio and reopen the `Chapter07` solution.
7. In **Solution Explorer**, right-click the **DotNetEverywhere** project and select **Open output in ILSpy**.
8. In ILSpy, in the toolbar, make sure that **C#** is selected in the drop-down list of languages to decompile into.
9. In ILSpy, in the **Assemblies** navigation tree on the left, expand **DotNetEverywhere (1.0.0.0, .NETCoreApp, v7.0)**.
10. In ILSpy, in the **Assemblies** navigation tree on the left, expand **{ }**.
11. In ILSpy, in the **Assemblies** navigation tree on the left, expand **Program**.
12. In ILSpy, in the **Assemblies** navigation tree on the left, click **<Main>$(string[]) : void** to show the statements in the compiler-generated `Program` class and `<Main>$` method to reveal how interpolated strings work, as shown in *Figure 7.4*:

Figure 7.4: Revealing the <Main>$ method and how interpolated strings work using ILSpy

13. In ILSpy, navigate to **File | Open...**.

14. Navigate to the following folder:

```
cs11dotnet7/Chapter07/DotNetEverywhere/bin/Release/net7.0/linux-x64
```

15. Select the `System.Linq.dll` assembly and click **Open**.

16. In the **Assemblies** tree, expand the **System.Linq (7.0.0.0, .NETCoreApp, v7.0)** assembly, expand the **System.Linq** namespace, expand the **Enumerable** class, and then click the **Count<TSource>(this IEnumerable<TSource>) : int** method.

17. In the `Count` method, note the good practice of:

   - Checking the `source` parameter and throwing an `ArgumentNullException` if it is null.

   - Checking for interfaces that the source might implement with their own `Count` properties that would be more efficient to read.

   - The last resort of enumerating through all the items in the source and incrementing a counter, which would be the least efficient implementation.

This is shown in *Figure 7.5*:

Figure 7.5: Decompiled Count method of the Enumerable class on Linux

18. Review the C# source code for the `Count` method, as shown in the following code, in preparation for reviewing the same code in **Intermediate Language (IL)**:

```csharp
public static int Count<TSource>(this IEnumerable<TSource> source)
{
  if (source == null)
  {
    ThrowHelper.ThrowArgumentNullException(ExceptionArgument.source);
```

```
    }
    if (source is ICollection<TSource> collection)
    {
      return collection.Count;
    }
    if (source is IIListProvider<TSource> iIListProvider)
    {
      return iIListProvider.GetCount(onlyIfCheap: false);
    }
    if (source is ICollection collection2)
    {
      return collection2.Count;
    }
    int num = 0;
    using IEnumerator<TSource> enumerator = source.GetEnumerator();
    while (enumerator.MoveNext())
    {
      num = checked(num + 1);
    }
    return num;
}
```

19. In the ILSpy toolbar, click the **Select language to decompile** dropdown and select **IL**, and then review the IL source code of the Count method, as shown in the following code:

```
.method public hidebysig static
  int32 Count<TSource> (
    class [System.Runtime]System.Collections.Generic.
IEnumerable'1<!!TSource> source
  ) cil managed
{
  .custom instance void [System.Runtime]System.Runtime.CompilerServices.
ExtensionAttribute::.ctor() = (
    01 00 00 00
  )
  .param type TSource
    .custom instance void System.Runtime.CompilerServices.
NullableAttribute::.ctor(uint8) = (
      01 00 02 00 00
    )
  // Method begins at RVA 0x42050
  // Header size: 12
  // Code size: 103 (0x67)
  .maxstack 2
  .locals (
    [0] class [System.Runtime]System.Collections.Generic.
ICollection'1<!!TSource>,
```

```
    [1] class System.Linq.IIListProvider'1<!!TSource>,
    [2] class [System.Runtime]System.Collections.ICollection,
    [3] int32,
    [4] class [System.Runtime]System.Collections.Generic.
IEnumerator'1<!!TSource>
  )

  IL_0000: ldarg.0
  IL_0001: brtrue.s IL_000a

  IL_0003: ldc.i4.s 16
  IL_0005: call void System.Linq.
ThrowHelper::ThrowArgumentNullException(valuetype System.Linq.
ExceptionArgument)

  IL_000a: ldarg.0
  IL_000b: isinst class [System.Runtime]System.Collections.Generic.
ICollection'1<!!TSource>
  IL_0010: stloc.0
  IL_0011: ldloc.0
  IL_0012: brfalse.s IL_001b

  IL_0014: ldloc.0
  IL_0015: callvirt instance int32 class [System.Runtime]System.
Collections.Generic.ICollection'1<!!TSource>::get_Count()
  IL_001a: ret
...
  IL_003e: ldc.i4.0
  IL_003f: stloc.3
  IL_0040: ldarg.0
  IL_0041: callvirt instance class [System.Runtime]System.Collections.
Generic.IEnumerator'1<!0> class [System.Runtime]System.Collections.
Generic.IEnumerable'1<!!TSource>::GetEnumerator()
  IL_0046: stloc.s 4
  .try
  {
    IL_0048: br.s IL_004e
    // loop start (head: IL_004e)
      IL_004a: ldloc.3
      IL_004b: ldc.i4.1
      IL_004c: add.ovf
      IL_004d: stloc.3

      IL_004e: ldloc.s 4
      IL_0050: callvirt instance bool [System.Runtime]System.Collections.
IEnumerator::MoveNext()
      IL_0055: brtrue.s IL_004a
```

```
    // end loop

  IL_0057: leave.s IL_0065
} // end .try
finally
{
  IL_0059: ldloc.s 4
  IL_005b: brfalse.s IL_0064

  IL_005d: ldloc.s 4
  IL_005f: callvirt instance void [System.Runtime]System.
IDisposable::Dispose()

  IL_0064: endfinally
} // end handler

IL_0065: ldloc.3
IL_0066: ret
} // end of method Enumerable::Count
```

> **Good Practice:** The IL code is not especially useful unless you get very advanced with C# and .NET development, when knowing how the C# compiler translates your source code into IL code can be important. The much more useful edit windows contain the equivalent C# source code written by Microsoft experts. You can learn a lot of good practices from seeing how professionals implement types. For example, the Count method shows how to check arguments for null.

20. Close ILSpy.

> You can learn how to use the ILSpy extension for Visual Studio Code at the following link: `https://github.com/markjprice/cs11dotnet7/blob/main/docs/code-editors/vscode.md#decompiling-using-the-ilspy-extension-for-visual-studio-code`.

Viewing source links with Visual Studio 2022

Instead of decompiling, Visual Studio 2022 has a feature that allows you to view the original source code using source links. Let's see how it works:

1. Use your preferred code editor to add a new **Console App**/console project to the Chapter07 solution/workspace named SourceLinks.

2. In Program.cs, delete the existing statements. Add statements to declare a string variable and then output its value and the number of characters it has, as shown in the following code:

```
string name = "Timothée Chalamet";
int length = name.Count();
```

```
Console.WriteLine($"{name} has {length} characters.");
```

3. Right-click in the Count method and select **Go To Implementation**.

4. Note the source code file is named Count.cs and it defines a partial Enumerable class with implementations of five count-related methods, as shown in *Figure 7.6*:

Figure 7.6: Viewing the original source file for LINQ's Count method implementation

You can learn more from viewing source links than decompiling because they show best practices for situations like how to divide up a class into partial classes for easier management. When we used the ILSpy compiler, all it could do was show all the hundreds of methods of the Enumerable class.

> You can learn more about how source links work and how any NuGet package can support them at the following link: https://learn.microsoft.com/en-us/dotnet/standard/library-guidance/sourcelink.

No, you cannot technically prevent decompilation

I sometimes get asked if there is a way to protect compiled code to prevent decompilation. The quick answer is no, and if you think about it, you'll see why this must be the case. You can make it harder using obfuscation tools like **Dotfuscator**, but ultimately you cannot completely prevent it.

All compiled applications contain instructions to the platform, operating system, and hardware on which it runs. Those instructions must be functionally the same as the original source code but are just harder for a human to read. Those instructions must be readable to execute your code; they therefore must be readable to be decompiled. If you were to protect your code from decompilation using some custom technique, then you would also prevent your code from running!

Virtual machines simulate hardware and so can capture all interaction between your running application and the software and hardware that it thinks it is running on.

If you could protect your code, then you would also prevent attaching to it with a debugger and stepping through it. If the compiled application has a pdb file, then you can attach a debugger and step through the statements line-by-line. Even without the pdb file, you can still attach a debugger and get some idea of how the code works.

This is true for all programming languages. Not just .NET languages like C#, Visual Basic, and F#, but also C, C++, Delphi, and assembly language: all can be attached to for debugging or to be disassembled or decompiled. Some tools used by professionals are shown in the following table:

Type	Product	Description
Virtual Machine	VMware	Professionals like malware analysts always run software inside a VM.
Debugger	SoftICE	Runs underneath the operating system, usually in a VM.
Debugger	WinDbg	Useful for understanding Windows internals because it knows more about Windows data structures than other debuggers.
Disassembler	IDA Pro	Used by professional malware analysts.
Decompiler	HexRays	Decompiles C apps. Plugin for IDA Pro.
Decompiler	DeDe	Decompiles Delphi apps.
Decompiler	dotPeek	.NET decompiler from JetBrains.

 Good Practice: Debugging, disassembling, and decompiling someone else's software is likely against its license agreement and illegal in many jurisdictions. Instead of trying to protect your intellectual property with a technical solution, the law is sometimes your only recourse.

Packaging your libraries for NuGet distribution

Before we learn how to create and package our own libraries, we will review how a project can use an existing package.

Referencing a NuGet package

Let's say that you want to add a package created by a third-party developer, for example, Newtonsoft. Json, a popular package for working with the **JavaScript Object Notation (JSON)** serialization format:

1. In the AssembliesAndNamespaces project, add a reference to the Newtonsoft.Json NuGet package, either using the GUI for Visual Studio 2022 or the dotnet add package command for Visual Studio Code.

2. Open the AssembliesAndNamespaces.csproj file and note that a package reference has been added, as shown in the following markup:

```
<ItemGroup>
  <PackageReference Include="newtonsoft.json" Version="13.0.1" />
</ItemGroup>
```

If you have a more recent version of the `newtonsoft.json` package, then it has been updated since this chapter was written.

Fixing dependencies

To consistently restore packages and write reliable code, it's important that you **fix dependencies**. Fixing dependencies means you are using the same family of packages released for a specific version of .NET, for example, SQLite for .NET 7.0, as shown highlighted in the following markup:

```
<Project Sdk="Microsoft.NET.Sdk">

  <PropertyGroup>
    <OutputType>Exe</OutputType>
    <TargetFramework>net7.0</TargetFramework>
    <Nullable>enable</Nullable>
    <ImplicitUsings>enable</ImplicitUsings>
  </PropertyGroup>

  <ItemGroup>
    <PackageReference
      Include="Microsoft.EntityFrameworkCore.Sqlite"
      Version="7.0.0" />
  </ItemGroup>

</Project>
```

To fix dependencies, every package should have a single version with no additional qualifiers. Additional qualifiers include betas (`beta1`), release candidates (`rc4`), and wildcards (`*`).

Wildcards allow future versions to be automatically referenced and used because they always represent the most recent release. But wildcards are therefore dangerous because they could result in the use of future incompatible packages that break your code.

This can be worth the risk while writing a book where new preview versions are released every month and you do not want to keep updating the package references, as I did during 2022, and as shown in the following markup:

```
<PackageReference
  Include="Microsoft.EntityFrameworkCore.Sqlite"
  Version="7.0.0-preview.*" />
```

If you use the `dotnet add package` command, or Visual Studio's **Manage NuGet Packages**, then it will by default use the latest specific version of a package. But if you copy and paste configuration from a blog article or manually add a reference yourself, you might include wildcard qualifiers.

The following dependencies are examples of NuGet package references that are *not* fixed and therefore should be avoided unless you know the implications:

```
<PackageReference Include="System.Net.Http" Version="4.1.0-*" />
<PackageReference Include="Newtonsoft.Json" Version="13.0.2-beta1" />
```

 Good Practice: Microsoft guarantees that if you fixed your dependencies to what ships with a specific version of .NET, for example, 6.0.0, those packages will all work together. Almost always fix your dependencies.

Packaging a library for NuGet

Now, let's package the SharedLibrary project that you created earlier:

1. In the SharedLibrary project, rename the Class1.cs file to StringExtensions.cs.

2. Modify its contents to provide some useful extension methods for validating various text values using regular expressions, remembering that we are targeting .NET Standard 2.0 so the compiler is C# 8.0 by default and therefore we use older syntax for namespaces and so on, as shown in the following code:

```csharp
using System.Text.RegularExpressions;

namespace Packt.Shared
{
  public static class StringExtensions
  {
    public static bool IsValidXmlTag(this string input)
    {
      return Regex.IsMatch(input,
        @"^<([a-z]+)([^<]+)*(?:>(.*)<\/\1>|\s+\/>)$");
    }

    public static bool IsValidPassword(this string input)
    {
      // minimum of eight valid characters
      return Regex.IsMatch(input, "^[a-zA-Z0-9_-]{8,}$");
    }

    public static bool IsValidHex(this string input)
    {
      // three or six valid hex number characters
      return Regex.IsMatch(input,
        "^#?([a-fA-F0-9]{3}|[a-fA-F0-9]{6})$");
    }
  }
}
```

You will learn how to write regular expressions in *Chapter 8, Working with Common .NET Types.*

3. In `SharedLibrary.csproj`, modify its contents, as shown highlighted in the following markup, and note the following:

    •   `PackageId` must be globally unique, so you must use a different value if you want to publish this NuGet package to the `https://www.nuget.org/` public feed for others to reference and download.

    •   `PackageLicenseExpression` must be a value from `https://spdx.org/licenses/`, or you could specify a custom license.

    •   All the other elements are self-explanatory:

```xml
<Project Sdk="Microsoft.NET.Sdk">

  <PropertyGroup>
    <TargetFramework>netstandard2.0</TargetFramework>
    <GeneratePackageOnBuild>true</GeneratePackageOnBuild>
    <PackageId>Packt.CSdotnet.SharedLibrary</PackageId>
    <PackageVersion>7.0.0.0</PackageVersion>
    <Title>C# 11 and .NET 7 Shared Library</Title>
    <Authors>Mark J Price</Authors>
    <PackageLicenseExpression>
      MS-PL
    </PackageLicenseExpression>
    <PackageProjectUrl>
      https://github.com/markjprice/cs11dotnet7
    </PackageProjectUrl>
    <PackageIcon>packt-csdotnet-sharedlibrary.png</PackageIcon>
    <PackageRequireLicenseAcceptance>true</PackageRequireLicenseAcceptance>
    <PackageReleaseNotes>
      Example shared library packaged for NuGet.
    </PackageReleaseNotes>
    <Description>
      Three extension methods to validate a string value.
    </Description>
    <Copyright>
      Copyright © 2016-2022 Packt Publishing Limited
    </Copyright>
```

```xml
      <PackageTags>string extensions packt csharp dotnet</
PackageTags>
   </PropertyGroup>

   <ItemGroup>
     <None Include="packt-csdotnet-sharedlibrary.png">
       <Pack>True</Pack>
       <PackagePath></PackagePath>
     </None>
   </ItemGroup>

</Project>
```

 Good Practice: Configuration property values that are true or false values cannot have any whitespace, so the `<PackageRequireLicenseAcceptance>` entry cannot have a carriage return and indentation as shown in the preceding markup.

4. Download the icon file and save it in the SharedLibrary folder from the following link: https:// github.com/markjprice/cs11dotnet7/blob/main/vs4win/Chapter07/SharedLibrary/packt-csdotnet-sharedlibrary.png.

5. Build the release assembly:

    -   In Visual Studio 2022, select **Release** in the toolbar, and then navigate to **Build** | **Build SharedLibrary**.

    -   In Visual Studio Code, in **Terminal**, enter dotnet build -c Release.

If we had not set `<GeneratePackageOnBuild>` to true in the project file, then we would have to create a NuGet package manually using the following additional steps:

    -   In Visual Studio 2022, navigate to **Build** | **Pack SharedLibrary**.

    -   In Visual Studio Code, in **Terminal**, enter dotnet pack -c Release.

Publishing a package to a public NuGet feed

If you want everyone to be able to download and use your NuGet package, then you must upload it to a public NuGet feed like Microsoft's:

1. Start your favorite browser and navigate to the following link: https://www.nuget.org/packages/manage/upload.

2. You will need to sign up for, and then sign in with, a Microsoft account at `https://www.nuget.org/` if you want to upload a NuGet package for other developers to reference as a dependency package.

3. Click the **Browse...** button and select the `.nupkg` file that was created by generating the NuGet package. The folder path should be `cs11dotnet7\Chapter07\SharedLibrary\bin\Release` and the file is named `Packt.CSdotnet.SharedLibrary.7.0.0.nupkg`.

4. Verify that the information you entered in the `SharedLibrary.csproj` file has been correctly filled in, and then click **Submit**.

5. Wait a few seconds, and you will see a success message showing that your package has been uploaded, as shown in *Figure 7.7*:

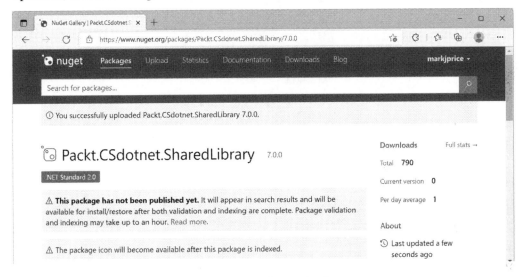

Figure 7.7: A NuGet package upload message

 Good Practice: If you get an error, then review the project file for mistakes, or read more information about the `PackageReference` format at `https://docs.microsoft.com/en-us/nuget/reference/msbuild-targets`.

6. Click the **Frameworks** tab, and note that because we targeted .NET Standard 2.0, our class library can be used by every .NET platform, as shown in *Figure 7.8*:

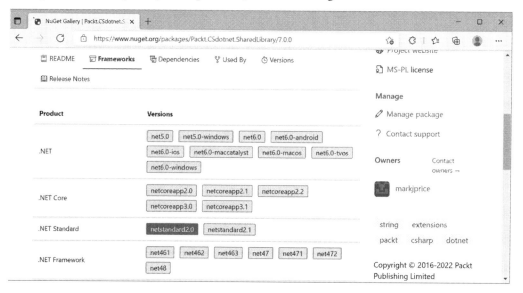

Figure 7.8: .NET Standard 2.0 class library NuGet packages can be used by all .NET platforms

Publishing a package to a private NuGet feed

Organizations can host their own private NuGet feeds. This can be a handy way for many developer teams to share work. You can read more at the following link:

https://docs.microsoft.com/en-us/nuget/hosting-packages/overview

Exploring NuGet packages with a tool

A handy tool named **NuGet Package Explorer** for opening and reviewing more details about a NuGet package was created by Uno Platform. As well as being a website, it can be installed as a cross-platform app. Let's see what it can do:

1. Start your favorite browser and navigate to the following link: https://nuget.info.
2. In the search box, enter Packt.CSdotnet.SharedLibrary.
3. Select the package **v7.0.0** published by **Mark J Price** and then click the **Open** button.
4. In the **Contents** section, expand the lib folder and the netstandard2.0 folder.

5. Select `SharedLibrary.dll`, and note the details, as shown in *Figure 7.9*:

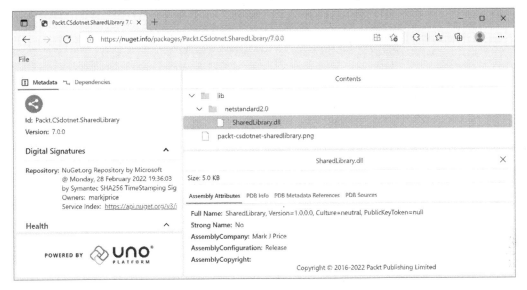

Figure 7.9: Exploring my package using NuGet Package Explorer from Uno Platform

6. If you want to use this tool locally in the future, click the install button in your browser.

7. Close your browser.

Not all browsers support installing web apps like this. I recommend Chrome for testing and development.

Testing your class library package

You will now test your uploaded package by referencing it in the `AssembliesAndNamespaces` project:

1. In the `AssembliesAndNamespaces` project, add a reference to your (or my) package, as shown highlighted in the following markup:

```
<ItemGroup>
  <PackageReference Include="newtonsoft.json" Version="13.0.1" />
  <PackageReference Include="packt.csdotnet.sharedlibrary"
    Version="7.0.0" />
</ItemGroup>
```

2. Build the `AssembliesAndNamespaces` console app.

3. In `Program.cs`, import the `Packt.Shared` namespace.

4. In `Program.cs`, prompt the user to enter some `string` values, and then validate them using the extension methods in the package, as shown in the following code:

```
Write("Enter a color value in hex: ");
string? hex = ReadLine(); // or "00ffc8"
```

```
WriteLine("Is {0} a valid color value? {1}",
  arg0: hex, arg1: hex.IsValidHex());

Write("Enter a XML element: ");
string? xmlTag = ReadLine(); // or "<h1 class=\"<\" />"
WriteLine("Is {0} a valid XML element? {1}",
  arg0: xmlTag, arg1: xmlTag.IsValidXmlTag());

Write("Enter a password: ");
string? password = ReadLine(); // or "secretsauce"
WriteLine("Is {0} a valid password? {1}",
  arg0: password, arg1: password.IsValidPassword());
```

5. Run the console app, enter some values as prompted, and view the results, as shown in the following output:

```
Enter a color value in hex: 00ffc8
Is 00ffc8 a valid color value? True
Enter an XML element: <h1 class="<" />
Is <h1 class="<" /> a valid XML element? False
Enter a password: secretsauce
Is secretsauce a valid password? True
```

Porting from .NET Framework to modern .NET

If you are an existing .NET Framework developer, then you may have existing applications that you think you should port to modern .NET. But you should carefully consider if porting is the right choice for your code, because sometimes, the best choice is not to port.

For example, you might have a complex website project that runs on .NET Framework 4.8 but is only visited by a small number of users. If it works and handles the visitor traffic on minimal hardware, then potentially spending months porting it to a modern .NET platform could be a waste of time. But if the website currently requires many expensive Windows servers, then the cost of porting could eventually pay off if you can migrate to fewer, less costly Linux servers.

Could you port?

Modern .NET has great support for the following types of applications on Windows, macOS, and Linux, so they are good candidates for porting:

*   **ASP.NET Core** websites, including Razor Pages and MVC
*   **ASP.NET Core** web services (**REST/HTTP**), including **Web APIs**, **Minimal APIs**, and **OData**
*   **ASP.NET Core-hosted** services, including **gRPC**, **GraphQL**, and **SignalR**
*   **Console App** command-line interfaces

Modern .NET has decent support for the following types of applications on Windows, so they are potential candidates for porting:

- **Windows Forms** applications
- **Windows Presentation Foundation (WPF)** applications

Modern .NET has good support for the following types of applications on cross-platform desktop and mobile devices:

- **Xamarin** apps for mobile iOS and Android
- **.NET MAUI** for desktop Windows and macOS, or mobile iOS and Android

Modern .NET does not support the following types of legacy Microsoft projects:

- **ASP.NET Web Forms** websites. These might be best reimplemented using **ASP.NET Core Razor Pages** or Blazor.
- **Windows Communication Foundation (WCF)** services (but there is an open-source project named **CoreWCF** that you might be able to use depending on requirements). WCF services might be better reimplemented using **ASP.NET Core gRPC** services.
- **Silverlight** applications. These might be best reimplemented using **Blazor** or **.NET MAUI**.

Silverlight and ASP.NET Web Forms applications will never be able to be ported to modern .NET, but existing Windows Forms and WPF applications could be ported to .NET on Windows to benefit from the new APIs and faster performance.

Legacy ASP.NET MVC web applications and ASP.NET Web API web services currently on .NET Framework could be ported to modern .NET and then be hosted on Windows, Linux, or macOS.

Should you port?

Even if you *could* port, *should* you? What benefits do you gain? Some common benefits include the following:

- **Deployment to Linux, Docker, or Kubernetes for websites and web services:** These OSes are lightweight and cost-effective as website and web service platforms, especially when compared to the more costly Windows Server.
- **Removal of dependency on IIS and System.Web.dll:** Even if you continue to deploy to Windows Server, ASP.NET Core can be hosted on lightweight, higher-performance Kestrel (or other) web servers.
- **Command-line tools:** Tools that developers and administrators use to automate their tasks are often built as console applications. The ability to run a single tool cross-platform is very useful.

Differences between .NET Framework and modern .NET

There are three key differences, as shown in the following table:

Modern .NET	.NET Framework
Distributed as NuGet packages, so each application can be deployed with its own app-local copy of the version of .NET that it needs.	Distributed as a system-wide, shared set of assemblies (literally, in the **Global Assembly Cache (GAC)**).
Split into small, layered components, so a minimal deployment can be performed.	Single, monolithic deployment.
Removes older technologies, such as ASP.NET Web Forms, and non-cross-platform features, such as AppDomains, .NET Remoting, and binary serialization.	As well as some similar technologies to those in modern .NET like ASP.NET Core MVC, it also retains some older technologies, such as ASP.NET Web Forms.

.NET Portability Analyzer

Microsoft has a useful tool that you can run against your existing applications to generate a report for porting. You can watch a demonstration of the tool at the following link: `https://learn.microsoft.com/en-us/shows/seth-juarez/brief-look-net-portability-analyzer`.

.NET Upgrade Assistant

Microsoft's latest tool for upgrading legacy projects to modern .NET is the **.NET Upgrade Assistant**.

For my day job, I used to work for a company named Optimizely. They have an enterprise-scale **Digital Experience Platform (DXP)** based on .NET comprising a **Content Management System (CMS)** and a Digital Commerce platform. Microsoft needed a challenging migration project to design and test the .NET Upgrade Assistant with, so we worked with them to build a great tool.

Currently, it supports the following .NET Framework project types and more will be added later:

- ASP.NET MVC
- Windows Forms
- WPF
- Console Application
- Class Library

It is installed as a global `dotnet` tool, as shown in the following command:

```
dotnet tool install -g upgrade-assistant
```

You can read more about this tool and how to use it at the following link:

`https://docs.microsoft.com/en-us/dotnet/core/porting/upgrade-assistant-overview`

Using non-.NET Standard libraries

Most existing NuGet packages can be used with modern .NET, even if they are not compiled for .NET Standard or a modern version like .NET 7. If you find a package that does not officially support .NET Standard, as shown on its nuget.org web page, you do not have to give up. You should try it and see if it works.

For example, there is a package of custom collections for handling matrices created by Dialect Software LLC, documented at the following link:

https://www.nuget.org/packages/DialectSoftware.Collections.Matrix/

This package was last updated in 2013, which was long before .NET Core or .NET 7 existed, so this package was built for .NET Framework. If an assembly package like this only uses APIs available in .NET Standard, it can be used in a modern .NET project.

Let's try using it and see if it works:

1. In the AssembliesAndNamespaces project, add a package reference for Dialect Software's package, as shown in the following markup:

```
<PackageReference
  Include="dialectsoftware.collections.matrix"
  Version="1.0.0" />
```

2. Build the AssembliesAndNamespaces project to restore packages.

3. In Program.cs, add statements to import the DialectSoftware.Collections and DialectSoftware.Collections.Generics namespaces.

4. Add statements to create instances of Axis and Matrix<T>, populate them with values, and output them, as shown in the following code:

```
Axis x = new("x", 0, 10, 1);
Axis y = new("y", 0, 4, 1);
Matrix<long> matrix = new(new[] { x, y });

for (int i = 0; i < matrix.Axes[0].Points.Length; i++)
{
  matrix.Axes[0].Points[i].Label = "x" + i.ToString();
}

for (int i = 0; i < matrix.Axes[1].Points.Length; i++)
{
  matrix.Axes[1].Points[i].Label = "y" + i.ToString();
}

foreach (long[] c in matrix)
{
  matrix[c] = c[0] + c[1];
}
```

```
foreach (long[] c in matrix)
{
  WriteLine("{0},{1} ({2},{3}) = {4}",
    matrix.Axes[0].Points[c[0]].Label,
    matrix.Axes[1].Points[c[1]].Label,
    c[0], c[1], matrix[c]);
}
```

5. Run the code, noting the warning message and the results, as shown in the following output:

```
warning NU1701: Package 'DialectSoftware.Collections.Matrix
1.0.0' was restored using '.NETFramework,Version=v4.6.1,
.NETFramework,Version=v4.6.2, .NETFramework,Version=v4.7,
.NETFramework,Version=v4.7.1, .NETFramework,Version=v4.7.2,
.NETFramework,Version=v4.8' instead of the project target framework
'net7.0'. This package may not be fully compatible with your project.
x0,y0 (0,0) = 0
x0,y1 (0,1) = 1
x0,y2 (0,2) = 2
x0,y3 (0,3) = 3
...
```

Even though this package was created before modern .NET existed, and the compiler and runtime have no way of knowing if it will work and therefore show warnings, because it happens to only call .NET Standard-compatible APIs, it works.

Working with preview features

It is a challenge for Microsoft to deliver some new features that have cross-cutting effects across many parts of .NET like the runtime, language compilers, and API libraries. It is the classic chicken and egg problem. What do you do first?

From a practical perspective, it means that although Microsoft might have completed most of the work needed for a feature, the whole thing might not be ready until very late in their now annual cycle of .NET releases, too late for proper testing in "the wild."

So, from .NET 6 onward, Microsoft will include preview features in **general availability** (GA) releases. Developers can opt into these preview features and provide Microsoft with feedback. In a later GA release, they can be enabled for everyone.

It is important to note that this topic is about *preview features*. This is different from a preview version of .NET or a preview version of Visual Studio 2022. Microsoft releases preview versions of Visual Studio and .NET while developing them to get feedback from developers and then do a final GA release. At GA, the feature is available for everyone. Before GA, the only way to get the new functionality is to install a preview version. *Preview features* are different because they are installed with GA releases and must be optionally enabled.

For example, when Microsoft released .NET SDK 6.0.200 in February 2022, it included the C# 11 compiler as a preview feature. This meant that .NET 6 developers could optionally set the language version to preview, and then start exploring C# 11 features like raw string literals and the required keyword.

 Good Practice: Preview features are not supported in production code. Preview features are likely to have breaking changes before the final release. Enable preview features at your own risk.

Requiring preview features

The [RequiresPreviewFeatures] attribute is used to indicate assemblies, types, or members that use and therefore require warnings about preview features. A code analyzer then scans for this assembly and generates warnings if needed. If your code does not use any preview features, you will not see any warnings. If you use any preview features, then your code should warn consumers of your code that you use preview features.

Enabling preview features

In the project file, add an element to enable preview features and an element to enable preview language features, as shown highlighted in the following markup:

```
<Project Sdk="Microsoft.NET.Sdk">

  <PropertyGroup>
    <OutputType>Exe</OutputType>
    <TargetFramework>net7.0</TargetFramework>
    <Nullable>enable</Nullable>
    <ImplicitUsings>enable</ImplicitUsings>
    <EnablePreviewFeatures>true</EnablePreviewFeatures>
    <LangVersion>preview</LangVersion>
  </PropertyGroup>

</Project>
```

Practicing and exploring

Test your knowledge and understanding by answering some questions, getting some hands-on practice, and exploring with deeper research into topics of this chapter.

Exercise 7.1 — Test your knowledge

Answer the following questions:

1. What is the difference between a namespace and an assembly?
2. How do you reference another project in a .csproj file?

3. What is the benefit of a tool like ILSpy?

4. Which .NET type does the C# `float` alias represent?

5. When porting an application from .NET Framework to modern .NET, what tool should you run before porting, and what tool could you run to perform much of the porting work?

6. What is the difference between framework-dependent and self-contained deployments of .NET applications?

7. What is a RID?

8. What is the difference between the `dotnet pack` and `dotnet publish` commands?

9. What types of applications written for .NET Framework can be ported to modern .NET?

10. Can you use packages written for .NET Framework with modern .NET?

Exercise 7.2 — Explore topics

Use the links on the following page to learn more detail about the topics covered in this chapter:

```
https://github.com/markjprice/cs11dotnet7/blob/main/book-links.md#chapter-7---
packaging-and-distributing-net-types
```

Exercise 7.3 — Explore PowerShell

PowerShell is Microsoft's scripting language for automating tasks on every operating system. Microsoft recommends Visual Studio Code with the PowerShell extension for writing PowerShell scripts.

Since PowerShell is its own extensive language, there is not enough space in this book to cover it. Instead, I have created some supplementary pages on the book's GitHub repository to introduce you to some key concepts and show some examples:

```
https://github.com/markjprice/cs11dotnet7/tree/main/docs/powershell
```

Summary

In this chapter, we:

- Reviewed the journey to .NET 7 for Base Class Library functionality.
- Explored the relationship between assemblies and namespaces.
- Learned how to decompile .NET assemblies for educational purposes.
- Saw options for publishing an app for distribution to multiple operating systems.
- Packaged and distributed a class library.
- Discussed options for porting existing .NET Framework code bases.
- Learned how to activate preview features.

In the next chapter, you will learn about some common Base Class Library types that are included with modern .NET.

8

Working with Common .NET Types

This chapter is about some common types that are included with .NET. These include types for manipulating numbers, text, and collections, improving working with spans, indexes, and ranges, and network access.

This chapter covers the following topics:

- Working with numbers
- Working with text
- Pattern matching with regular expressions
- Storing multiple objects in collections
- Working with spans, indexes, and ranges
- Working with network resources

Working with numbers

One of the most common types of data is numbers. The most common types in .NET for working with numbers are shown in the following table:

Namespace	Example type(s)	Description
System	SByte, Int16, Int32, Int64	Integers; that is, zero, and positive and negative whole numbers
System	Byte, UInt16, UInt32, UInt64	Cardinals; that is, zero, and positive whole numbers, aka unsigned hence the U
System	Half, Single, Double	Reals; that is, floating-point numbers

System	Decimal	Accurate reals; that is, for use in science, engineering, or financial scenarios
System.Numerics	BigInteger, Complex, Quaternion	Arbitrarily large integers, complex numbers, and quaternion numbers

.NET has had the 32-bit float and 64-bit double types since .NET Framework 1.0. The IEEE 754 specification also defines a 16-bit floating-point standard. Machine learning and other algorithms would benefit from this smaller, lower-precision number type so Microsoft introduced the System.Half type with .NET 5 and later.

Currently, the C# language does not define a half alias so you must use the .NET type System.Half. This might change in the future.

Working with big integers

The largest whole number that can be stored in .NET types that have a C# alias is about eighteen and a half quintillion, stored in an unsigned ulong integer. But what if you need to store numbers larger than that?

Let's explore numerics:

1. Use your preferred code editor to create a new project, as defined in the following list:

    •   Project template: **Console App**/console
    •   Project file and folder: WorkingWithNumbers
    •   Workspace/solution file and folder: Chapter08

2. In the project file, add an element to statically and globally import the System.Console class.

3. In Program.cs, delete the existing statements and then add a statement to import System.Numerics, as shown in the following code:

    ```
    using System.Numerics;
    ```

4. Add statements to output the maximum value of the ulong type, and a number with 30 digits using BigInteger, as shown in the following code:

    ```
    WriteLine("Working with large integers:");
    WriteLine("--------------------------------------");

    ulong big = ulong.MaxValue;
    WriteLine($"{big,40:N0}");

    BigInteger bigger =
      BigInteger.Parse("123456789012345678901234567890");
    WriteLine($"{bigger,40:N0}");
    ```

The **40** in the format code means "right-align 40 characters," so both numbers are lined up to the right-hand edge. The **N0** means "use thousand separators and zero decimal places."

5.   Run the code and view the result, as shown in the following output:

```
Working with large integers:
----------------------------------------
              18,446,744,073,709,551,615
   123,456,789,012,345,678,901,234,567,890
```

Working with complex numbers

A complex number can be expressed as $a + bi$, where a and b are real numbers and i is an imaginary unit, where $i^2 = -1$. If the real part a is zero, it is a pure imaginary number. If the imaginary part b is zero, it is a real number.

Complex numbers have practical applications in many **STEM (science, technology, engineering, and mathematics)** fields of study. They are added by separately adding the real and imaginary parts of the summands; consider this:

```
(a + bi) + (c + di) = (a + c) + (b + d)i
```

Let's explore complex numbers:

1.   In `Program.cs`, add statements to add two complex numbers, as shown in the following code:

```
WriteLine("Working with complex numbers:");

Complex c1 = new(real: 4, imaginary: 2);
Complex c2 = new(real: 3, imaginary: 7);
Complex c3 = c1 + c2;

// output using default ToString implementation
WriteLine($"{c1} added to {c2} is {c3}");

// output using custom format
WriteLine("{0} + {1}i added to {2} + {3}i is {4} + {5}i",
  c1.Real, c1.Imaginary,
  c2.Real, c2.Imaginary,
  c3.Real, c3.Imaginary);
```

2.   Run the code and view the result, as shown in the following output:

```
Working with complex numbers:
(4, 2) added to (3, 7) is (7, 9)
4 + 2i added to 3 + 7i is 7 + 9i
```

Understanding quaternions

Quaternions are a number system that extends complex numbers. They form a four-dimensional associative normed division algebra over the real numbers, and therefore also a domain.

Huh? Yes, I know. I don't understand that either. Don't worry; we're not going to write any code using them! Suffice to say, they are good at describing spatial rotations, so video game engines use them, as do many computer simulations and flight control systems.

Generating random numbers for games and similar apps

In scenarios that don't need truly random numbers like games, you can create an instance of the Random class, as shown in the following code example:

```
Random r = new();
```

Random has a constructor with a parameter for specifying a seed value used to initialize its pseudo-random number generator, as shown in the following code:

```
Random r = new(Seed: 46378);
```

As you learned in *Chapter 2, Speaking C#*, parameter names should use camel case. The developer who defined the constructor for the Random class broke this convention! The parameter name should be seed, not Seed.

 Good Practice: Shared seed values act as a secret key, so if you use the same random number generation algorithm with the same seed value in two applications, then they can generate the same "random" sequences of numbers. Sometimes this is necessary, for example, when synchronizing a GPS receiver with a satellite, or when a game needs to randomly generate the same level. But usually, you want to keep your seed secret.

To avoid allocating more memory, .NET 6 introduced a shared static instance of Random, as shown in the following code:

```
Random r = Random.Shared;
```

Once you have a Random object, you can call its methods to generate random numbers, as shown in the following code examples:

```
// minValue is an inclusive lower bound i.e. 1 is a possible value
// maxValue is an exclusive upper bound i.e. 7 is not a possible value
int dieRoll = r.Next(minValue: 1, maxValue: 7); // returns 1 to 6

double randomReal = r.NextDouble(); // returns 0.0 to less than 1.0

byte[] arrayOfBytes = new byte[256];
r.NextBytes(arrayOfBytes); // 256 random bytes in an array
```

The Next method takes two parameters: minValue and maxValue. But maxValue is not the maximum value that the method returns! It is an *exclusive upper bound,* meaning it is one more than the maximum value. In a similar way, the value returned by the NextDouble method is greater than or equal to 0.0 and less than 1.0. NextBytes populates an array of any size with random byte (0 to 255) values.

 In scenarios that do need truly random numbers like cryptography, there are specialized types for that, like RandomNumberGenerator. I cover this and other cryptographic types in the companion book, *Apps and Services with .NET 7.*

Working with text

One of the other most common types of data for variables is text. The most common types in .NET for working with text are shown in the following table:

Namespace	Type	Description
System	Char	Storage for a single text character
System	String	Storage for multiple text characters
System.Text	StringBuilder	Efficiently manipulates strings
System.Text.RegularExpressions	Regex	Efficiently pattern-matches strings

Getting the length of a string

Let's explore some common tasks when working with text; for example, sometimes you need to find out the length of a piece of text stored in a string variable:

1. Use your preferred code editor to add a new **Console App**/console project named WorkingWithText to the Chapter08 solution/workspace:

    *   In Visual Studio, set the startup project for the solution to the current selection.
    *   In Visual Studio Code, select WorkingWithText as the active OmniSharp project.

2. In the WorkingWithText project, in Program.cs, delete the existing statements and then add statements to define a variable to store the name of the city London, and then write its name and length to the console, as shown in the following code:

```
string city = "London";
WriteLine($"{city} is {city.Length} characters long.");
```

3. Run the code and view the result, as shown in the following output:

```
London is 6 characters long.
```

Getting the characters of a string

The string class uses an array of char internally to store the text. It also has an indexer, which means that we can use the array syntax to read its characters. Array indexes start at zero, so the third character will be at index 2.

Let's see this in action:

1. Add a statement to write the characters at the first and fourth positions in the string variable, as shown in the following code:

    ```
    WriteLine($"First char is {city[0]} and fourth is {city[3]}.");
    ```

2. Run the code and view the result, as shown in the following output:

    ```
    First char is L and fourth is d.
    ```

Splitting a string

Sometimes, you need to split some text wherever there is a character, such as a comma:

1. Add statements to define a single string variable containing comma-separated city names, then use the Split method and specify that you want to treat commas as the separator, and then enumerate the returned array of string values, as shown in the following code:

    ```
    string cities = "Paris,Tehran,Chennai,Sydney,New York,Medellín";

    string[] citiesArray = cities.Split(',');

    WriteLine($"There are {citiesArray.Length} items in the array:");

    foreach (string item in citiesArray)
    {
      WriteLine(item);
    }
    ```

2. Run the code and view the result, as shown in the following output:

    ```
    There are 6 items in the array:
    Paris
    Tehran
    Chennai
    Sydney
    New York
    Medellín
    ```

Later in this chapter, you will learn how to handle more complex scenarios.

Getting part of a string

Sometimes, you need to get part of some text. The IndexOf method has nine overloads that return the index position of a specified char or string within a string.

The Substring method has two overloads, as shown in the following list:

- Substring(startIndex, length): Returns part of a string starting at startIndex and containing the next length characters.
- Substring(startIndex): Returns part of a string starting at startIndex and containing all characters up to the end of the string.

Let's explore a simple example:

1. Add statements to store a person's full name in a string variable with a space character between the first and last names, find the position of the space, and then extract the first name and last name as two parts so that they can be recombined in a different order, as shown in the following code:

```
string fullName = "Alan Shore";

int indexOfTheSpace = fullName.IndexOf(' ');

string firstName = fullName.Substring(
  startIndex: 0, length: indexOfTheSpace);

string lastName = fullName.Substring(
  startIndex: indexOfTheSpace + 1);

WriteLine($"Original: {fullName}");
WriteLine($"Swapped: {lastName}, {firstName}");
```

2. Run the code and view the result, as shown in the following output:

```
Original: Alan Shore
Swapped: Shore, Alan
```

If the format of the initial full name was different, for example, "LastName, FirstName", then the code would need to be different. As an optional exercise, try writing some statements that would change the input "Shore, Alan" into "Alan Shore".

Checking a string for content

Sometimes, you need to check whether a piece of text starts or ends with some characters or contains some characters.

You can achieve this with methods named StartsWith, EndsWith, and Contains:

1. Add statements to store a string value and then check if it starts with or contains a couple of different string values, as shown in the following code:

```
string company = "Microsoft";
bool startsWithM = company.StartsWith("M");
bool containsN = company.Contains("N");
```

```
WriteLine($"Text: {company}");
WriteLine($"Starts with M: {startsWithM}, contains an N: {containsN}");
```

2. Run the code and view the result, as shown in the following output:

```
Text: Microsoft
Starts with M: True, contains an N: False
```

Joining, formatting, and other string members

There are many other `string` members, as shown in the following table:

Member	Description
Trim, TrimStart, TrimEnd	These methods trim whitespace characters such as space, tab, and carriage return from the beginning and/or end.
ToUpper, ToLower	These convert all the characters into uppercase or lowercase.
Insert, Remove	These methods insert or remove some text.
Replace	This replaces some text with other text.
string.Empty	This can be used instead of allocating memory each time you use a literal string value using an empty pair of double quotes ("").
string.Concat	This concatenates two string variables. The + operator does the equivalent when used between string operands.
string.Join	This concatenates one or more string variables with a character in between each one.
string.IsNullOrEmpty	This checks whether a string variable is null or empty.
string.IsNullOrWhitespace	This checks whether a string variable is null or whitespace; that is, a mix of any number of horizontal and vertical spacing characters, for example, tab, space, carriage return, line feed, and so on.
string.Format	An alternative method to string interpolation for outputting formatted string values, which uses positioned instead of named parameters.

Some of the preceding methods are `static` methods. This means that the method can only be called from the type, not from a variable instance. In the preceding table, I indicated the static methods by prefixing them with `string.`, as in `string.Format`.

Let's explore some of these methods:

1. Add statements to take an array of `string` values and combine them back together into a single `string` variable with separators using the `Join` method, as shown in the following code:

```
string recombined = string.Join(" => ", citiesArray);
WriteLine(recombined);
```

2. Run the code and view the result, as shown in the following output:

```
Paris => Tehran => Chennai => Sydney => New York => Medellín
```

3. Add statements to use positioned parameters and interpolated `string` formatting syntax to output the same three variables twice, as shown in the following code:

```
string fruit = "Apples";
decimal price = 0.39M;
DateTime when = DateTime.Today;

WriteLine($"Interpolated:  {fruit} cost {price:C} on {when:dddd}.");
WriteLine(string.Format("string.Format: {0} cost {1:C} on {2:dddd}.",
  arg0: fruit, arg1: price, arg2: when));
```

4. Run the code and view the result, as shown in the following output:

```
Interpolated:  Apples cost £0.39 on Thursday.
string.Format: Apples cost £0.39 on Thursday.
```

Note that we could have simplified the second statement because `Console.WriteLine` supports the same format codes as `string.Format`, as shown in the following code:

```
WriteLine("WriteLine: {0} cost {1:C} on {2:dddd}.",
  arg0: fruit, arg1: price, arg2: when);
```

Building strings efficiently

You can concatenate two strings to make a new `string` using the `String.Concat` method or simply by using the `+` operator. But both choices are bad practice because .NET must create a completely new string in memory.

This might not be noticeable if you are only adding two `string` values, but if you concatenate inside a loop with many iterations, it can have a significant negative impact on performance and memory use.

You can concatenate `string` variables more efficiently using the `StringBuilder` type, which you can read more about at the following link:

```
https://docs.microsoft.com/en-us/dotnet/api/system.text.stringbuilder#examples
```

Pattern matching with regular expressions

Regular expressions are useful for validating input from the user. They are very powerful and can get very complicated. Almost all programming languages have support for regular expressions and use a common set of special characters to define them.

Let's try out some example regular expressions:

1. Use your preferred code editor to add a new **Console App**/console project named WorkingWithRegularExpressions to the Chapter08 solution/workspace:

    *   In Visual Studio Code, select WorkingWithRegularExpressions as the active OmniSharp project.

2. In Program.cs, delete the existing statements and then import the following namespace:

    ```
    using System.Text.RegularExpressions; // Regex
    ```

Checking for digits entered as text

We will start by implementing the common example of validating number input:

1. In Program.cs, add statements to prompt the user to enter their age and then check that it is valid using a regular expression that looks for a digit character, as shown in the following code:

    ```
    Write("Enter your age: ");
    string input = ReadLine()!; // null-forgiving

    Regex ageChecker = new(@"\d");

    if (ageChecker.IsMatch(input))
    {
      WriteLine("Thank you!");
    }
    else
    {
      WriteLine($"This is not a valid age: {input}");
    }
    ```

    Note the following about the code:

    *   The @ character switches off the ability to use escape characters in the string. Escape characters are prefixed with a backslash. For example, \t means a tab and \n means a new line. When writing regular expressions, we need to disable this feature. To paraphrase the television show *The West Wing*, "Let backslash be backslash."
    *   Once escape characters are disabled with @, then they can be interpreted by a regular expression. For example, \d means digit. You will learn about more regular expressions that are prefixed with a backslash later in this topic.

2. Run the code, enter a whole number such as 34 for the age, and view the result, as shown in the following output:

```
Enter your age: 34
Thank you!
```

3. Run the code again, enter carrots, and view the result, as shown in the following output:

```
Enter your age: carrots
This is not a valid age: carrots
```

4. Run the code again, enter bob30smith, and view the result, as shown in the following output:

```
Enter your age: bob30smith
Thank you!
```

The regular expression we used is \d, which means *one digit*. However, it does not specify what can be entered before and after that one digit. This regular expression could be described in English as "Enter any characters you want as long as you enter at least one digit character."

In regular expressions, you indicate the start of some input with the caret ^ symbol and the end of some input with the dollar $ symbol. Let's use these symbols to indicate that we expect nothing else between the start and end of the input except for a digit.

5. Change the regular expression to ^\d$, as shown in the following code:

```
Regex ageChecker = new(@"^\d$");
```

6. Run the code again and note that it rejects any input except a single digit. We want to allow one or more digits. To do this, we add a + after the \d expression to modify the meaning to one or more.

7. Change the regular expression, as shown in the following code:

```
Regex ageChecker = new(@"^\d+$");
```

8. Run the code again and note the regular expression only allows zero or positive whole numbers of any length.

Regular expression performance improvements

The .NET types for working with regular expressions are used throughout the .NET platform and many of the apps built with it. As such, they have a significant impact on performance, but until now, they have not received much optimization attention from Microsoft.

With .NET 5 and later, the System.Text.RegularExpressions namespace has rewritten internals to squeeze out maximum performance. Common regular expression benchmarks using methods like IsMatch are now five times faster. And the best thing is, you do not have to change your code to get the benefits!

With .NET 7 and later, the IsMatch method of the Regex class now has an overload for a ReadOnlySpan<char> as its input, which gives even better performance.

Understanding the syntax of a regular expression

Here are some common regular expression symbols that you can use in regular expressions:

Symbol	Meaning	Symbol	Meaning
^	Start of input	$	End of input
\d	A single digit	\D	A single *non*-digit
\s	Whitespace	\S	*Non*-whitespace
\w	Word characters	\W	*Non*-word characters
[A-Za-z0-9]	Range(s) of characters	\^	^ (caret) character
[aeiou]	Set of characters	[^aeiou]	*Not* in a set of characters
.	Any single character	\.	. (dot) character

In addition, here are some regular expression quantifiers that affect the previous symbols in a regular expression:

Symbol	Meaning	Symbol	Meaning
+	One or more	?	One or none
{3}	Exactly three	{3,5}	Three to five
{3,}	At least three	{,3}	Up to three

Examples of regular expressions

Here are some examples of regular expressions with descriptions of their meaning:

Expression	Meaning
\d	A single digit somewhere in the input.
a	The character "a" somewhere in the input.
Bob	The word "Bob" somewhere in the input.
^Bob	The word "Bob" at the start of the input.
Bob$	The word "Bob" at the end of the input.
^\d{2}$	Exactly two digits.
^[0-9]{2}$	Exactly two digits.
^[A-Z]{4,}$	At least four uppercase English letters in the ASCII character set only.
^[A-Za-z]{4,}$	At least four upper or lowercase English letters in the ASCII character set only.
^[A-Z]{2}\d{3}$	Two uppercase English letters in the ASCII character set and three digits only.

`^[A-Za-z\u00c0-\u017e]+$`	At least one uppercase or lowercase English letter in the ASCII character set or European letters in the Unicode character set, as shown in the following list: ÀÁÂÃÄÅÆÇÈÉÊËÌÍÎÏÐÑÒÓÔÕÖ×ØÙÚÛÜÝ Þßàáâãäåæçèéêëìíîïðñòóôõö÷øùúûüýþÿıŒœŠšŸŽž
`^d.g$`	The letter d, then any character, and then the letter g, so it would match both dig and dog or any single character between the d and g.
`^d\.g$`	The letter d, then a dot ., and then the letter g, so it would match d.g only.

Good Practice: Use regular expressions to validate input from the user. The same regular expressions can be reused in other languages such as JavaScript and Python.

Splitting a complex comma-separated string

Earlier in this chapter, you learned how to split a simple comma-separated string variable. But what about the following example of film titles?

```
"Monsters, Inc.","I, Tonya","Lock, Stock and Two Smoking Barrels"
```

The `string` value uses double quotes around each film title. We can use these to identify whether we need to split on a comma (or not). The `Split` method is not powerful enough, so we can use a regular expression instead.

Good Practice: You can read a fuller explanation in the Stack Overflow article that inspired this task at the following link: `https://stackoverflow.com/questions/18144431/regex-to-split-a-csv`.

To include double quotes inside a `string` value, we prefix them with a backslash, or we could use the raw string literal feature in C# 11 or later:

1. Add statements to store a complex comma-separated `string` variable, and then split it in a dumb way using the `Split` method, as shown in the following code:

```
// C# 1 to 10: Use escaped double-quote characters \"
// string films = "\"Monsters, Inc.\",\"I, Tonya\",\"Lock, Stock and Two
Smoking Barrels\"";

// C# 11 or later: Use """ to start and end a raw string literal
string films = """
"Monsters, Inc.","I, Tonya","Lock, Stock and Two Smoking Barrels"
""";
```

```
WriteLine($"Films to split: {films}");

string[] filmsDumb = films.Split(',');

WriteLine("Splitting with string.Split method:");
foreach (string film in filmsDumb)
{
  WriteLine(film);
}
```

2. Add statements to define a regular expression to split and write the film titles in a smart way, as shown in the following code:

```
Regex csv = new(
  "(?:^|,)(?=[^\"]|(\")?)\"?((?(1)[^\"]*|[^,\"]*))\"?(?=,|$)");

MatchCollection filmsSmart = csv.Matches(films);

WriteLine("Splitting with regular expression:");
foreach (Match film in filmsSmart)
{
  WriteLine(film.Groups[2].Value);
}
```

 In a later section, you will see how you can get a source generator to auto-generate XML comments for a regular expression to explain how it works. This is really useful for regular expressions that you might have copied from a website.

3. Run the code and view the result, as shown in the following output:

```
Splitting with string.Split method:
"Monsters
 Inc."
"I
 Tonya"
"Lock
 Stock and Two Smoking Barrels"
Splitting with regular expression:
Monsters, Inc.
I, Tonya
Lock, Stock and Two Smoking Barrels
```

Activating regular expression syntax coloring

If you use Visual Studio 2022 as your code editor, then you probably noticed that when passing a string value to the Regex constructor, you see color syntax highlighting, as shown in *Figure 8.1*:

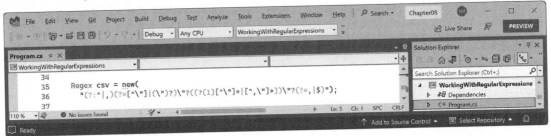

Figure 8.1: Regular expression color syntax highlighting when using the Regex constructor

 This would be a good time to remind print book readers who will only see the preceding figure in grayscale that they can see all figures in full color as a PDF at the following link: `https://static.packt-cdn.com/downloads/9781803237800_ColorImages.pdf`.

Why does this string get syntax coloring for regular expressions when most string values do not? Let's find out:

1. Right-click in the new constructor, select **Go To Implementation**, and note the string parameter named pattern is decorated with an attribute named StringSyntax that has the string constant Regex value passed to it, as shown highlighted in the following code:

```
public Regex([StringSyntax(StringSyntaxAttribute.Regex)] string pattern)
:
  this(pattern, culture: null)
{
}
```

2. Right-click in the StringSyntax attribute, select **Go To Implementation**, and note there are 12 recognized string syntax formats that you can choose from as well as Regex, as shown in the following partial code:

```
[AttributeUsage(AttributeTargets.Property | AttributeTargets.Field |
AttributeTargets.Parameter, AllowMultiple = false, Inherited = false)]
public sealed class StringSyntaxAttribute : Attribute
{
  public const string CompositeFormat = "CompositeFormat";
  public const string DateOnlyFormat = "DateOnlyFormat";
  public const string DateTimeFormat = "DateTimeFormat";
  public const string EnumFormat = "EnumFormat";
```

```
public const string GuidFormat = "GuidFormat";
public const string Json = "Json";
public const string NumericFormat = "NumericFormat";
public const string Regex = "Regex";
public const string TimeOnlyFormat = "TimeOnlyFormat";
public const string TimeSpanFormat = "TimeSpanFormat";
public const string Uri = "Uri";
public const string Xml = "Xml";
...
}
```

3. In the `WorkingWithRegularExpressions` project, add a new class file named `Program.Strings.cs`, and modify its content to define some `string` constants, as shown in the following code:

```
partial class Program
{
  const string digitsOnlyText = @"^\d+$";

  const string commaSeparatorText =
    "(?:^|,)(?=[^\"]|(\")?)\"?((?(1)[^\"]*|[^,\"]*))\"?(?=,|$)";
}
```

 Note that the two `string` constants do not have any color syntax highlighting yet.

4. In `Program.cs`, replace the literal `string` with the `string` constant for the digits-only regular expression, as shown highlighted in the following code:

```
Regex ageChecker = new(digitsOnlyText);
```

5. In `Program.cs`, replace the literal `string` with the `string` constant for the comma separator regular expression, as shown highlighted in the following code:

```
Regex csv = new(commaSeparatorText);
```

6. Run the console app and confirm that the regular expression behavior is as before.

7. In `Program.Strings.cs`, import the namespace for the [StringSyntax] attribute and then decorate both `string` constants with it, as shown highlighted in the following code:

```
using System.Diagnostics.CodeAnalysis; // [StringSyntax]

partial class Program
{
  [StringSyntax(StringSyntaxAttribute.Regex)]
  const string digitsOnlyText = @"^\d+$";
```

```
[StringSyntax(StringSyntaxAttribute.Regex)]
const string commaSeparatorText =
  "(?:^|,)(?=[^\"]|(\")?)\"?((?(1)[^\"]*|[^,\"]*))\"?(?=,|$)";
}
```

8. In `Program.Strings.cs`, add another `string` constant for formatting a date, as shown in the following code:

```
[StringSyntax(StringSyntaxAttribute.DateTimeFormat)]
const string fullDateTime = "";
```

9. Click inside the empty string, type a letter d, and note the IntelliSense, as shown in *Figure 8.2*:

Figure 8.2: IntelliSense activated due to the StringSyntax attribute

10. Finish entering the date format and as you type note the IntelliSense: `dddd, d MMMM yyyy`.

11. Add at the end of the `digitsOnlyText` string literal, add a `\`, and note the IntelliSense to help you write a valid regular expression, as shown in *Figure 8.3*:

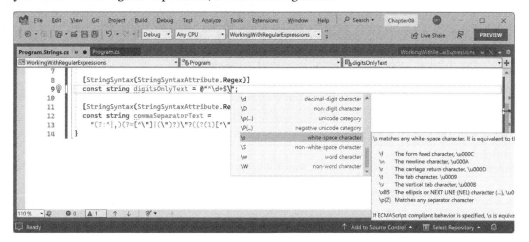

Figure 8.3: IntelliSense for writing a regular expression

The [StringSyntax] attribute is a new feature introduced in .NET 7. It is up to your code editor to recognize it. .NET 7 libraries have more than 350 parameters, properties, and fields that are now decorated with this attribute.

Improving regular expression performance with source generators

When you pass a string literal or string constant to the constructor of Regex, the class parses the string and transforms it into an internal tree structure that represents the expression in an optimized way that can be executed efficiently by a regular expression interpreter.

You can also compile regular expressions by specifying a RegexOption, as shown in the following code:

```
Regex ageChecker = new(digitsOnlyText, RegexOptions.Compiled);
```

Unfortunately, compiling has the negative affect of slowing down the initial creation of the regular expression. After creating the tree structure that would then be executed by the interpreter, the compiler then has to convert the tree into IL code, and then that IL code needs to be JIT compiled into native code. If you only run the regular expression a few times, it is not worth compiling it, which is why it is not the default behavior.

.NET 7 introduces a source generator for regular expressions which recognizes if you decorate a partial method that returns Regex with the [GeneratedRegex] attribute. It generates an implementation of that method which implements the logic for the regular expression.

Let's see it in action:

1. In the WorkingWithRegularExpressions project, add a new class file named Program.Regexs. cs, and modify its content to define some partial methods, as shown in the following code:

    ```
    using System.Text.RegularExpressions; // [GeneratedRegex]

    partial class Program
    {
      [GeneratedRegex(digitsOnlyText, RegexOptions.IgnoreCase)]
      private static partial Regex DigitsOnly();

      [GeneratedRegex(commaSeparatorText, RegexOptions.IgnoreCase)]
      private static partial Regex CommaSeparator();
    }
    ```

2. In Program.cs, replace the new constructor with a call to the partial method that returns the digits-only regular expression, as shown highlighted in the following code:

    ```
    Regex ageChecker = DigitsOnly();
    ```

3. In `Program.cs`, replace the new constructor with a call to the partial method that returns the comma separator regular expression, as shown highlighted in the following code:

```
Regex csv = CommaSeparator();
```

4. Hover your mouse pointer over the partial methods and note that the tooltip describes the behavior of the regular expression, as shown in *Figure 8.4*:

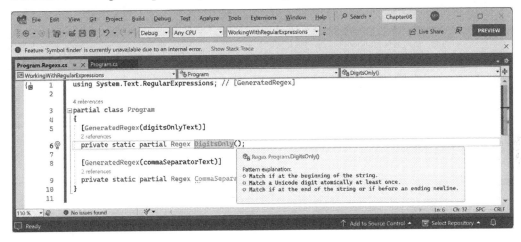

Figure 8.4: Tooltip for a partial method shows a description of the regular expression

5. Right-click the `DigitsOnly` partial method, select **Go To Definition**, and note that you can review the implementation of the auto-generated partial methods, as shown in *Figure 8.5*:

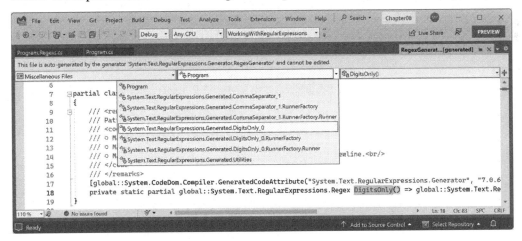

Figure 8.5: The auto-generated source code for the regular expression

6. Run the console app and confirm that the functionality is the same as before.

 You can learn more about the improvements to regular expressions with .NET 7 at the following link: https://devblogs.microsoft.com/dotnet/regular-expression-improvements-in-dotnet-7.

Storing multiple objects in collections

Another of the most common types of data is collections. If you need to store multiple values in a variable, then you can use a collection.

A collection is a data structure in memory that can manage multiple items in different ways, although all collections have some shared functionality.

The most common types in .NET for working with collections are shown in the following table:

Namespace	Example type(s)	Description
System .Collections	IEnumerable, IEnumerable<T>	Interfaces and base classes used by collections.
System .Collections .Generic	List<T>, Dictionary<T>, Queue<T>, Stack<T>	Introduced in C# 2.0 with .NET Framework 2.0. These collections allow you to specify the type you want to store using a generic type parameter (which is safer, faster, and more efficient).
System .Collections .Concurrent	BlockingCollection, ConcurrentDictionary, ConcurrentQueue	These collections are safe to use in multithreaded scenarios.
System .Collections .Immutable	ImmutableArray, ImmutableDictionary, ImmutableList, ImmutableQueue	Designed for scenarios where the contents of the original collection will never change, although they can create modified collections as a new instance.

Common features of all collections

All collections implement the ICollection interface; this means that they must have a Count property to tell you how many objects are in them, as shown in the following code:

```
namespace System.Collections;

public interface ICollection : IEnumerable
{
  int Count { get; }
  bool IsSynchronized { get; }
  object SyncRoot { get; }
  void CopyTo(Array array, int index);
}
```

For example, if we had a collection named passengers, we could do this:

```
int howMany = passengers.Count;
```

All collections implement the IEnumerable interface, which means that they can be iterated using the foreach statement. They must have a GetEnumerator method that returns an object that implements IEnumerator; this means that the returned object must have MoveNext and Reset methods for navigating through the collection and a Current property containing the current item in the collection, as shown in the following code:

```
namespace System.Collections;

public interface IEnumerable
{
  IEnumerator GetEnumerator();
}

public interface IEnumerator
{
  object Current { get; }
  bool MoveNext();
  void Reset();
}
```

For example, to perform an action on each object in the passengers collection, we could write the following code:

```
foreach (Passenger p in passengers)
{
  // perform an action on each passenger
}
```

As well as object-based collection interfaces, there are also generic interfaces and classes, where the generic type defines the type stored in the collection, as shown in the following code:

```
namespace System.Collections.Generic;

public interface ICollection<T> : IEnumerable<T>, IEnumerable
{
  int Count { get; }
  bool IsReadOnly { get; }
  void Add(T item);
  void Clear();
  bool Contains(T item);
  void CopyTo(T[] array, int index);
  bool Remove(T item);
}
```

Improving performance by ensuring the capacity of a collection

Since .NET 1.1, types like StringBuilder have had a method named EnsureCapacity that can pre-size its internal storage array to the expected final size of the string. This improves performance because it does not have to repeatedly increment the size of the array as more characters are appended.

Since .NET Core 2.1, types like Dictionary<T> and HashSet<T> have also had EnsureCapacity.

In .NET 6 and later, collections like List<T>, Queue<T>, and Stack<T> now have an EnsureCapacity method too, as shown in the following code:

```
List<string> names = new();
names.EnsureCapacity(10_000);
// Load ten thousand names into the list
```

Understanding collection choices

There are several different choices of collection that you can use for different purposes: lists, dictionaries, stacks, queues, sets, and many other more specialized collections.

Lists

Lists, that is, a type that implements IList<T>, are **ordered collections**, as shown in the following code:

```
namespace System.Collections.Generic;


[DefaultMember("Item")] // aka this indexer
public interface IList<T> : ICollection<T>, IEnumerable<T>, IEnumerable
{
  T this[int index] { get; set; }
  int IndexOf(T item);
  void Insert(int index, T item);
  void RemoveAt(int index);
}
```

IList<T> derives from ICollection<T> so it has a Count property, and an Add method to put an item at the end of the collection, as well as an Insert method to put an item in the list at a specified position, and RemoveAt to remove an item at a specified position.

Lists are a good choice when you want to manually control the order of items in a collection. Each item in a list has a unique index (or position) that is automatically assigned. Items can be any type defined by T and items can be duplicated. Indexes are int types and start from 0, so the first item in a list is at index 0, as shown in the following table:

Index	Item
0	London
1	Paris

2	London
3	Sydney

If a new item (for example, Santiago) is inserted between London and Sydney, then the index of Sydney is automatically incremented. Therefore, you must be aware that an item's index can change after inserting or removing items, as shown in the following table:

Index	Item
0	London
1	Paris
2	London
3	Santiago
4	Sydney

 Good Practice: Some developers can get into a poor habit of using List<T> and other collections when an array would be better. Use arrays instead of collections if the data will not change size after instantiation.

Dictionaries

Dictionaries are a good choice when each **value** (or object) has a unique sub-value (or a made-up value) that can be used as a **key** to quickly find a value in the collection later. The key must be unique. For example, if you are storing a list of people, you could choose to use a government-issued identity number as the key. Dictionaries are called **hashmaps** in other languages like Python and Java.

Think of the key as being like an index entry in a real-world dictionary. It allows you to quickly find the definition of a word because the words (in other words, keys) are kept sorted, and if we know we're looking for the definition of *manatee*, we will jump to the middle of the dictionary to start looking, because the letter *M* is in the middle of the alphabet.

Dictionaries in programming are similarly smart when looking something up. They must implement the interface IDictionary<TKey, TValue>, as shown in the following code:

```
namespace System.Collections.Generic;


[DefaultMember("Item")] // aka this indexer
public interface IDictionary<TKey, TValue>
  : ICollection<KeyValuePair<TKey, TValue>>,
    IEnumerable<KeyValuePair<TKey, TValue>>, IEnumerable
{
  TValue this[TKey key] { get; set; }
  ICollection<TKey> Keys { get; }
  ICollection<TValue> Values { get; }
```

```
    void Add(TKey key, TValue value);
    bool ContainsKey(TKey key);
    bool Remove(TKey key);
    bool TryGetValue(TKey key, [MaybeNullWhen(false)] out TValue value);
}
```

Items in a dictionary are instances of the struct, aka the value type, KeyValuePair<TKey, TValue>, where TKey is the type of the key and TValue is the type of the value, as shown in the following code:

```
namespace System.Collections.Generic;

public readonly struct KeyValuePair<TKey, TValue>
{
  public KeyValuePair(TKey key, TValue value);
  public TKey Key { get; }
  public TValue Value { get; }
  [EditorBrowsable(EditorBrowsableState.Never)]
  public void Deconstruct(out TKey key, out TValue value);
  public override string ToString();
}
```

An example Dictionary<string, Person> uses a string as the key and a Person instance as the value. Dictionary<string, string> uses string values for both, as shown in the following table:

Key	Value
BSA	Bob Smith
MW	Max Williams
BSB	Bob Smith
AM	Amir Mohammed

Stacks

Stacks are a good choice when you want to implement **last-in, first-out (LIFO)** behavior. With a stack, you can only directly access or remove the one item at the top of the stack, although you can enumerate to read through the whole stack of items. You cannot, for example, directly access the second item in a stack.

For example, word processors use a stack to remember the sequence of actions you have recently performed, and then when you press *Ctrl* + *Z*, it will undo the last action in the stack, and then the next-to-last action, and so on.

Queues

Queues are a good choice when you want to implement the **first-in, first-out (FIFO)** behavior. With a queue, you can only directly access or remove the one item at the front of the queue, although you can enumerate to read through the whole queue of items. You cannot, for example, directly access the second item in a queue.

For example, background processes use a queue to process work items in the order that they arrive, just like people standing in line at the post office.

.NET 6 introduced the `PriorityQueue`, where each item in the queue has a priority value assigned, as well as its position in the queue.

Sets

Sets are a good choice when you want to perform set operations between two collections. For example, you may have two collections of city names, and you want to know which names appear in both sets (known as the *intersect* between the sets). Items in a set must be unique.

Collection methods summary

Each collection has a different set of methods for adding and removing items, as shown in the following table:

Collection	Add methods	Remove methods	Description
List	Add, Insert	Remove, RemoveAt	Lists are ordered so items have an integer index position. Add will add a new item at the end of the list. Insert will add a new item at the index position specified.
Dictionary	Add	Remove	Dictionaries are not ordered so items do not have integer index positions. You can check if a key has been used by calling the ContainsKey method.
Stack	Push	Pop	Stacks always add a new item at the top of the stack using the Push method. The first item is at the bottom. Items are always removed from the top of the stack using the Pop method. Call the Peek method to see this value without removing it.
Queue	Enqueue	Dequeue	Queues always add a new item at the end of the queue using the Enqueue method. The first item is at the front of the queue. Items are always removed from the front of the queue using the Dequeue method. Call the Peek method to see this value without removing it.

Working with lists

Let's explore lists:

1. Use your preferred code editor to add a new **Console App**/console project named WorkingWithCollections to the Chapter08 solution/workspace:

   - In Visual Studio Code, select WorkingWithCollections as the active OmniSharp project.

2. Add a new class file named Program.Helpers.cs.

3. In Program.Helpers.cs, define a partial Program class with a method to output a collection of string values with a title, as shown in the following code:

```
partial class Program
{
  static void Output(string title, IEnumerable<string> collection)
  {
    WriteLine(title);
    foreach (string item in collection)
    {
      WriteLine($"  {item}");
    }
  }
}
```

4. In Program.cs, delete the existing statements and then add some statements to illustrate some of the common ways of defining and working with lists, as shown in the following code:

```
// Simple syntax for creating a list and adding three items
List<string> cities = new();
cities.Add("London");
cities.Add("Paris");
cities.Add("Milan");

/* Alternative syntax that is converted by the compiler into
   the three Add method calls above
List<string> cities = new()
  { "London", "Paris", "Milan" }; */

/* Alternative syntax that passes an
   array of string values to AddRange method
List<string> cities = new();
cities.AddRange(new[] { "London", "Paris", "Milan" }); */

Output("Initial list", cities);
WriteLine($"The first city is {cities[0]}.");
WriteLine($"The last city is {cities[cities.Count - 1]}.");

cities.Insert(0, "Sydney");
```

```
Output("After inserting Sydney at index 0", cities);

cities.RemoveAt(1);
cities.Remove("Milan");
Output("After removing two cities", cities);
```

5. Run the code and view the result, as shown in the following output:

```
Initial list
  London
  Paris
  Milan
The first city is London.
The last city is Milan.
After inserting Sydney at index 0
  Sydney
  London
  Paris
  Milan
After removing two cities
  Sydney
  Paris
```

Working with dictionaries

Let's explore dictionaries:

1. In `Program.cs`, add some statements to illustrate some of the common ways of working with dictionaries, for example, looking up word definitions, as shown in the following code:

```
Dictionary<string, string> keywords = new();

// add using named parameters
keywords.Add(key: "int", value: "32-bit integer data type");

// add using positional parameters
keywords.Add("long", "64-bit integer data type");
keywords.Add("float", "Single precision floating point number");

/* Alternative syntax; compiler converts this to calls to Add method
Dictionary<string, string> keywords = new()
{
  { "int", "32-bit integer data type" },
  { "long", "64-bit integer data type" },
  { "float", "Single precision floating point number" },
}; */

/* Alternative syntax; compiler converts this to calls to Add method
```

```
Dictionary<string, string> keywords = new()
{
    ["int"] = "32-bit integer data type",
    ["long"] = "64-bit integer data type",
    ["float"] = "Single precision floating point number", // last comma is
optional
}; */

Output("Dictionary keys:", keywords.Keys);
Output("Dictionary values:", keywords.Values);

WriteLine("Keywords and their definitions");
foreach (KeyValuePair<string, string> item in keywords)
{
    WriteLine($"  {item.Key}: {item.Value}");
}

// look up a value using a key
string key = "long";
WriteLine($"The definition of {key} is {keywords[key]}");
```

2. Run the code and view the result, as shown in the following output:

```
Dictionary keys:
  int
  long
  float
Dictionary values:
  32-bit integer data type
  64-bit integer data type
  Single precision floating point number
Keywords and their definitions
  int: 32-bit integer data type
  long: 64-bit integer data type
  float: Single precision floating point number
The definition of long is 64-bit integer data type
```

Working with queues

Let's explore queues:

1. In `Program.cs`, add some statements to illustrate some of the common ways of working with queues, for example, handling customers in a queue for coffee, as shown in the following code:

```
Queue<string> coffee = new();

coffee.Enqueue("Damir"); // front of queue
```

```
coffee.Enqueue("Andrea");
coffee.Enqueue("Ronald");
coffee.Enqueue("Amin");
coffee.Enqueue("Irina"); // back of queue

Output("Initial queue from front to back", coffee);

// server handles next person in queue
string served = coffee.Dequeue();
WriteLine($"Served: {served}.");

// server handles next person in queue
served = coffee.Dequeue();
WriteLine($"Served: {served}.");
Output("Current queue from front to back", coffee);

WriteLine($"{coffee.Peek()} is next in line.");
Output("Current queue from front to back", coffee);
```

2. Run the code and view the result, as shown in the following output:

```
Initial queue from front to back
  Damir
  Andrea
  Ronald
  Amin
  Irina
Served: Damir.
Served: Andrea.
Current queue from front to back
  Ronald
  Amin
  Irina
Ronald is next in line.
Current queue from front to back
  Ronald
  Amin
  Irina
```

3. In `Program.Helpers.cs`, in the partial `Program` class, add a static method named `OutputPQ`, as shown in the following code:

```
static void OutputPQ<TElement, TPriority>(string title,
  IEnumerable<(TElement Element, TPriority Priority)> collection)
{
  WriteLine(title);
```

```
        foreach ((TElement, TPriority) item in collection)
        {
          WriteLine($"  {item.Item1}: {item.Item2}");
        }
      }
    }
```

 Note that the `OutputPQ` method is generic. You can specify the two types used in
the tuples that are passed in as `collection`.

4. In `Program.cs`, add some statements to illustrate some of the common ways of working with
    priority queues, as shown in the following code:

```
    PriorityQueue<string, int> vaccine = new();

    // add some people
    // 1 = high priority people in their 70s or poor health
    // 2 = medium priority e.g. middle-aged
    // 3 = low priority e.g. teens and twenties

    vaccine.Enqueue("Pamela", 1);  // my mum (70s)
    vaccine.Enqueue("Rebecca", 3); // my niece (teens)
    vaccine.Enqueue("Juliet", 2);  // my sister (40s)
    vaccine.Enqueue("Ian", 1);     // my dad (70s)

    OutputPQ("Current queue for vaccination:", vaccine.UnorderedItems);

    WriteLine($"{vaccine.Dequeue()} has been vaccinated.");
    WriteLine($"{vaccine.Dequeue()} has been vaccinated.");
    OutputPQ("Current queue for vaccination:", vaccine.UnorderedItems);

    WriteLine($"{vaccine.Dequeue()} has been vaccinated.");

    WriteLine("Adding Mark to queue with priority 2");
    vaccine.Enqueue("Mark", 2); // me (40s)

    WriteLine($"{vaccine.Peek()} will be next to be vaccinated.");
    OutputPQ("Current queue for vaccination:", vaccine.UnorderedItems);
```

5. Run the code and view the result, as shown in the following output:

```
Current queue for vaccination:
  Pamela: 1
  Rebecca: 3
  Juliet: 2
```

```
    Ian: 1
Pamela has been vaccinated.
Ian has been vaccinated.
Current queue for vaccination:
    Juliet: 2
    Rebecca: 3
Juliet has been vaccinated.
Adding Mark to queue with priority 2
Mark will be next to be vaccinated.
Current queue for vaccination:
    Mark: 2
    Rebecca: 3
```

Sorting collections

A List<T> class can be sorted by manually calling its Sort method (but remember that the indexes of each item will change). Manually sorting a list of string values or other built-in types will work without extra effort on your part, but if you create a collection of your own type, then that type must implement an interface named IComparable. You learned how to do this in *Chapter 6, Implementing Interfaces and Inheriting Classes.*

A Stack<T> or Queue<T> collection cannot be sorted because you wouldn't usually want that functionality; for example, you would probably never sort a queue of guests checking into a hotel. But sometimes, you might want to sort a dictionary or a set.

Sometimes it would be useful to have an automatically sorted collection, that is, one that maintains the items in a sorted order as you add and remove them.

There are multiple auto-sorting collections to choose from. The differences between these sorted collections are often subtle but can have an impact on the memory requirements and performance of your application, so it is worth putting effort into picking the most appropriate option for your requirements.

Some common auto-sorting collections are shown in the following table:

Collection	Description
SortedDictionary<TKey, TValue>	This represents a collection of key/value pairs that are sorted by key.
SortedList<TKey, TValue>	This represents a collection of key/value pairs that are sorted by key.
SortedSet<T>	This represents a collection of unique objects that are maintained in a sorted order.

More specialized collections

There are a few other collections for special situations.

Working with a compact array of bit values

The `System.Collections.BitArray` collection manages a compact array of bit values, which are represented as Booleans, where `true` indicates that the bit is on (value is 1) and `false` indicates that the bit is off (value is 0).

Working with efficient lists

The `System.Collections.Generics.LinkedList<T>` collection represents a doubly linked list where every item has a reference to its previous and next items. They provide better performance compared to `List<T>` for scenarios where you will frequently insert and remove items from the middle of the list. In a `LinkedList<T>` the items do not have to be rearranged in memory.

Working with immutable collections

Sometimes you need to make a collection immutable, meaning that its members cannot change; that is, you cannot add or remove them.

If you import the `System.Collections.Immutable` namespace, then any collection that implements `IEnumerable<T>` is given six extension methods to convert it into an immutable list, dictionary, hash set, and so on.

Let's see a simple example:

1. In the `WorkingWithCollections` project, in `Program.cs`, import the `System.Collections.Immutable` namespace.

2. In `Program.cs`, add statements to convert the cities list into an immutable list and then add a new city to it, as shown in the following code:

    ```
    ImmutableList<string> immutableCities = cities.ToImmutableList();
    ImmutableList<string> newList = immutableCities.Add("Rio");
    Output("Immutable list of cities:", immutableCities);
    Output("New list of cities:", newList);
    ```

3. Run the code, view the result, and note that the immutable list of cities does not get modified when you call the `Add` method on it; instead, it returns a new list with all the existing cities plus the newly added city, as shown in the following output:

    ```
    Immutable list of cities:
      Sydney
      Paris
    New list of cities:
      Sydney
      Paris
      Rio
    ```

Good Practice: To improve performance, many applications store a shared copy of commonly accessed objects in a central cache. To safely allow multiple threads to work with those objects knowing they won't change, you should make them immutable or use a concurrent collection type that you can read about at the following link: `https://docs.microsoft.com/en-us/dotnet/api/system.collections.concurrent`.

Good practice with collections

Let's say you need to create a method to process a collection. For maximum flexibility, you could declare the input parameter to be `IEnumerable<T>` and make the method generic, as shown in the following code:

```
void ProcessCollection<T>(IEnumerable<T> collection)
{
  // process the items in the collection,
  // perhaps using a foreach statement
}
```

I could pass an array, a list, a queue, or a stack, containing any type like `int` or `string` or `Person`, or anything else that implements `IEnumerable<T>`, into this method and it will process the items. However, the flexibility to pass any collection to this method comes at a performance cost.

One of the performance problems with `IEnumerable<T>` is also one of its benefits: deferred execution, also known as lazy loading. Types that implement this interface do not have to implement deferred execution, but many do.

But the worst performance problem with `IEnumerable<T>` is that the iteration must allocate an object on the heap. To avoid this memory allocation, you should define your method using a concrete type, as shown highlighted in the following code:

```
void ProcessCollection<T>(List<T> collection)
{
  // process the items in the collection,
  // perhaps using a foreach statement
}
```

This will use the `List<T>.Enumerator GetEnumerator()` method, which returns a `struct`, instead of the `IEnumerator<T> GetEnumerator()` method, which returns a reference type. Your code will be two to three times faster and require less memory. As with all recommendations related to performance, you should confirm the benefit by running performance tests on your actual code in a product environment.

Working with spans, indexes, and ranges

One of Microsoft's goals with .NET Core 2.1 was to improve performance and resource usage. A key .NET feature that enables this is the `Span<T>` type.

Using memory efficiently using spans

When manipulating arrays, you will often create new copies of subsets of existing ones so that you can process just the subset. This is not efficient because duplicate objects must be created in memory.

If you need to work with a subset of an array, use a **span** because it is like a window into the original array. This is more efficient in terms of memory usage and improves performance. Spans only work with arrays, not collections, because the memory must be contiguous.

Before we look at spans in more detail, we need to understand some related objects: indexes and ranges.

Identifying positions with the Index type

C# 8.0 introduced two features for identifying an item's index position within an array and a range of items using two indexes.

You learned in the previous section that objects in a list can be accessed by passing an integer into their indexer, as shown in the following code:

```
int index = 3;
Person p = people[index]; // fourth person in array
char letter = name[index]; // fourth letter in name
```

The Index value type is a more formal way of identifying a position, and supports counting from the end, as shown in the following code:

```
// two ways to define the same index, 3 in from the start
Index i1 = new(value: 3); // counts from the start
Index i2 = 3; // using implicit int conversion operator

// two ways to define the same index, 5 in from the end
Index i3 = new(value: 5, fromEnd: true);
Index i4 = ^5; // using the caret operator
```

Identifying ranges with the Range type

The Range value type uses Index values to indicate the start and end of its range, using its constructor, C# syntax, or its static methods, as shown in the following code:

```
Range r1 = new(start: new Index(3), end: new Index(7));
Range r2 = new(start: 3, end: 7); // using implicit int conversion
Range r3 = 3..7; // using C# 8.0 or later syntax
Range r4 = Range.StartAt(3); // from index 3 to last index
Range r5 = 3..; // from index 3 to last index
Range r6 = Range.EndAt(3); // from index 0 to index 3
Range r7 = ..3; // from index 0 to index 3
```

Extension methods have been added to `string` values (which internally use an array of char), `int` arrays, and spans to make ranges easier to work with. These extension methods accept a range as a parameter and return a `Span<T>`. This makes them very memory-efficient.

Using indexes, ranges, and spans

Let's explore using indexes and ranges to return spans:

1. Use your preferred code editor to add a new **Console App**/console project named `WorkingWithRanges` to the `Chapter08` solution/workspace:

    - In Visual Studio Code, select `WorkingWithRanges` as the active OmniSharp project.

2. In `Program.cs`, delete the existing statements and then add statements to compare using the `string` type's `Substring` method with ranges to extract parts of someone's name, as shown in the following code:

```csharp
string name = "Samantha Jones";

// getting the lengths of the first and last names

int lengthOfFirst = name.IndexOf(' ');
int lengthOfLast = name.Length - lengthOfFirst - 1;

// Using Substring

string firstName = name.Substring(
  startIndex: 0,
  length: lengthOfFirst);

string lastName = name.Substring(
  startIndex: name.Length - lengthOfLast,
  length: lengthOfLast);

WriteLine($"First name: {firstName}, Last name: {lastName}");

// Using spans

ReadOnlySpan<char> nameAsSpan = name.AsSpan();
ReadOnlySpan<char> firstNameSpan = nameAsSpan[0..lengthOfFirst];
ReadOnlySpan<char> lastNameSpan = nameAsSpan[^lengthOfLast..^0];

WriteLine("First name: {0}, Last name: {1}",
  arg0: firstNameSpan.ToString(),
  arg1: lastNameSpan.ToString());
```

3. Run the code and view the result, as shown in the following output:

```
First name: Samantha, Last name: Jones
First name: Samantha, Last name: Jones
```

Working with network resources

Sometimes you will need to work with network resources. The most common types in .NET for working with network resources are shown in the following table:

Namespace	Example type(s)	Description
System.Net	Dns, Uri, Cookie, WebClient, IPAddress	These are for working with DNS servers, URIs, IP addresses, and so on.
System.Net	FtpStatusCode, FtpWebRequest, FtpWebResponse	These are for working with FTP servers.
System.Net	HttpStatusCode, HttpWebRequest, HttpWebResponse	These are for working with HTTP servers; that is, websites and services. Types from System.Net.Http are easier to use.
System.Net.Http	HttpClient, HttpMethod, HttpRequestMessage, HttpResponseMessage	These are for working with HTTP servers; that is, websites and services. You will learn how to use these in *Chapter 15, Building and Consuming Web Services*.
System.Net.Mail	Attachment, MailAddress, MailMessage, SmtpClient	These are for working with SMTP servers; that is, sending email messages.
System.Net .NetworkInformation	IPStatus, NetworkChange, Ping, TcpStatistics	These are for working with low-level network protocols.

Working with URIs, DNS, and IP addresses

Let's explore some common types for working with network resources:

1. Use your preferred code editor to add a new **Console App**/console project named WorkingWithNetworkResources to the Chapter08 solution/workspace:

   - In Visual Studio Code, select WorkingWithNetworkResources as the active OmniSharp project.

2. In `Program.cs`, delete the existing statements and then import the namespace for working with a network, as shown in the following code:

```
using System.Net; // IPHostEntry, Dns, IPAddress
```

3. In `Program.cs`, add statements to prompt the user to enter a website address, and then use the `Uri` type to break it down into its parts, including the scheme (HTTP, FTP, and so on), port number, and host, as shown in the following code:

```
Write("Enter a valid web address (or press Enter): ");
string? url = ReadLine();

if (string.IsNullOrWhiteSpace(url)) // if they enter nothing...
{
  // ... set a default URL
  url = "https://stackoverflow.com/search?q=securestring";
}

Uri uri = new(url);
WriteLine($"URL: {url}");
WriteLine($"Scheme: {uri.Scheme}");
WriteLine($"Port: {uri.Port}");
WriteLine($"Host: {uri.Host}");
WriteLine($"Path: {uri.AbsolutePath}");
WriteLine($"Query: {uri.Query}");
```

4. Run the code, enter a valid website address or press *Enter*, and view the result, as shown in the following output:

```
Enter a valid web address (or press Enter):
URL: https://stackoverflow.com/search?q=securestring
Scheme: https
Port: 443
Host: stackoverflow.com
Path: /search
Query: ?q=securestring
```

5. In `Program.cs`, add statements to get the IP address for the entered website, as shown in the following code:

```
IPHostEntry entry = Dns.GetHostEntry(uri.Host);
WriteLine($"{entry.HostName} has the following IP addresses:");
foreach (IPAddress address in entry.AddressList)
{
  WriteLine($"  {address} ({address.AddressFamily})");
}
```

6. Run the code, enter a valid website address or press *Enter*, and view the result, as shown in the following output:

```
stackoverflow.com has the following IP addresses:
    151.101.1.69 (InterNetwork)
    151.101.65.69 (InterNetwork)
    151.101.129.69 (InterNetwork)
    151.101.193.69 (InterNetwork)
```

Pinging a server

Now you will add code to ping a web server to check its health:

1. In `Program.cs`, import the namespace to get more information about networks, as shown in the following code:

    ```
    using System.Net.NetworkInformation; // Ping, PingReply, IPStatus
    ```

2. Add statements to ping the entered website, as shown in the following code:

    ```
    try
    {
      Ping ping = new();

      WriteLine("Pinging server. Please wait...");
      PingReply reply = ping.Send(uri.Host);
      WriteLine($"{uri.Host} was pinged and replied: {reply.Status}.");

      if (reply.Status == IPStatus.Success)
      {
        WriteLine("Reply from {0} took {1:N0}ms",
          arg0: reply.Address,
          arg1: reply.RoundtripTime);
      }
    }
    catch (Exception ex)
    {
      WriteLine($"{ex.GetType().ToString()} says {ex.Message}");
    }
    ```

3. Run the code, press *Enter*, and view the result, as shown in the following output:

    ```
    Pinging server. Please wait...
    stackoverflow.com was pinged and replied: Success.
    Reply from 151.101.193.69 took 9ms
    ```

4. Run the code again but this time enter `http://google.com`, as shown in the following output:

    ```
    Enter a valid web address (or press Enter): http://google.com
    URL: http://google.com
    ```

```
Scheme: http
Port: 80
Host: google.com
Path: /
Query:
google.com has the following IP addresses:
  2a00:1450:4009:822::200e (InterNetworkV6)
  142.250.180.14 (InterNetwork)
Pinging server. Please wait...
google.com was pinged and replied: Success.
Reply from 2a00:1450:4009:822::200e took 9ms
```

Practicing and exploring

Test your knowledge and understanding by answering some questions, getting some hands-on practice, and exploring with deeper research into the topics in this chapter.

Exercise 8.1 — Test your knowledge

Use the web to answer the following questions:

1. What is the maximum number of characters that can be stored in a string variable?

2. When and why should you use a SecureString type?

3. When is it appropriate to use a StringBuilder class?

4. When should you use a LinkedList<T> class?

5. When should you use a SortedDictionary<T> class rather than a SortedList<T> class?

6. In a regular expression, what does $ mean?

7. In a regular expression, how can you represent digits?

8. Why should you *not* use the official standard for email addresses to create a regular expression to validate a user's email address?

9. What characters are output when the following code runs?

```
string city = "Aberdeen";
ReadOnlySpan<char> citySpan = city.AsSpan()[^5..^0];
WriteLine(citySpan.ToString());
```

10. How could you check that a web service is available before calling it?

Exercise 8.2 — Practice regular expressions

In the Chapter08 solution/workspace, create a console app named Ch08Ex02RegularExpressions that prompts the user to enter a regular expression and then prompts the user to enter some input, and compare the two for a match until the user presses *Esc*, as shown in the following output:

```
The default regular expression checks for at least one digit.
Enter a regular expression (or press ENTER to use the default): ^[a-z]+$
Enter some input: apples
```

```
apples matches ^[a-z]+$? True
Press ESC to end or any key to try again.
Enter a regular expression (or press ENTER to use the default): ^[a-z]+$
Enter some input: abc123xyz
abc123xyz matches ^[a-z]+$? False
Press ESC to end or any key to try again.
```

Exercise 8.3 – Practice writing extension methods

In the Chapter08 solution/workspace, create a class library named Ch08Ex03NumbersAsWordsLib and projects to test it. It should define extension methods that extend number types such as BigInteger and int with a method named ToWords that returns a string describing the number.

For example, 18,000,000 would be eighteen million, and 18,456,002,032,011,000,007 would be eighteen quintillion, four hundred and fifty-six quadrillion, two trillion, thirty-two billion, eleven million, and seven.

You can read more about names for large numbers at the following link: https://en.wikipedia.org/wiki/Names_of_large_numbers.

Exercise 8.4 – Explore topics

Use the links on the following page to learn more detail about the topics covered in this chapter:

https://github.com/markjprice/cs11dotnet7/blob/main/book-links.md#chapter-8---working-with-common-net-types

Summary

In this chapter, you explored:

- Choices for types to store and manipulate numbers.
- Handling text, including using regular expressions for validating input.
- Collections to use for storing multiple items.
- Working with indexes, ranges, and spans.
- Using some types for interacting with network resources.

In the next chapter, we will manage files and streams, encode and decode text, and perform serialization.

9

Working with Files, Streams, and Serialization

This chapter is about reading and writing to files and streams, text encoding, and serialization.

We will cover the following topics:

- Managing the filesystem
- Reading and writing with streams
- Encoding and decoding text
- Reading and writing with random access handles
- Serializing object graphs

Managing the filesystem

Your applications will often need to perform input and output operations with files and directories in different environments. The System and System.IO namespaces contain classes for this purpose.

Handling cross-platform environments and filesystems

Let's explore how to handle cross-platform environments and the differences between Windows and Linux or macOS. Paths are different for Windows, macOS, and Linux, so we will start by exploring how .NET handles this:

1. Use your preferred code editor to create a new project, as defined in the following list:

    - Project template: **Console App**/console
    - Project file and folder: WorkingWithFileSystems
    - Workspace/solution file and folder: Chapter09

2. In the project file, add an element to statically and globally import the System.Console class.

3. Add a new class file named Program.Helpers.cs.

4. In `Program.Helpers.cs`, add a partial `Program` class with a `SectionTitle` method, as shown in the following code:

```
partial class Program
{
  static void SectionTitle(string title)
  {
    ConsoleColor previousColor = ForegroundColor;
    ForegroundColor = ConsoleColor.Yellow;
    WriteLine("*");
    WriteLine($"* {title}");
    WriteLine("*");
    ForegroundColor = previousColor;
  }
}
```

5. In `Program.cs`, delete the existing statements and then add statements to statically import the `System.IO.Directory`, `System.Environment`, and `System.IO.Path` types, as shown in the following code:

```
using static System.IO.Directory;
using static System.IO.Path;
using static System.Environment;
```

6. In `Program.cs`, add statements to do the following:

    *   Output the path and directory separation characters.

    *   Output the path of the current directory.

    *   Output some special paths for system files, temporary files, and documents:

```
SectionTitle("* Handling cross-platform environments and
filesystems");
WriteLine("{0,-33} {1}", arg0: "Path.PathSeparator",
  arg1: PathSeparator);
WriteLine("{0,-33} {1}", arg0: "Path.DirectorySeparatorChar",
  arg1: DirectorySeparatorChar);
WriteLine("{0,-33} {1}", arg0: "Directory.GetCurrentDirectory()",
  arg1: GetCurrentDirectory());
WriteLine("{0,-33} {1}", arg0: "Environment.CurrentDirectory",
  arg1: CurrentDirectory);
WriteLine("{0,-33} {1}", arg0: "Environment.SystemDirectory",
  arg1: SystemDirectory);
WriteLine("{0,-33} {1}", arg0: "Path.GetTempPath()",
  arg1: GetTempPath());
WriteLine("GetFolderPath(SpecialFolder");
WriteLine("{0,-33} {1}", arg0: " .System)",
  arg1: GetFolderPath(SpecialFolder.System));
WriteLine("{0,-33} {1}", arg0: " .ApplicationData)",
```

```
    arg1: GetFolderPath(SpecialFolder.ApplicationData));
WriteLine("{0,-33} {1}", arg0: " .MyDocuments)",
    arg1: GetFolderPath(SpecialFolder.MyDocuments));
WriteLine("{0,-33} {1}", arg0: " .Personal)",
    arg1: GetFolderPath(SpecialFolder.Personal));
```

 The `Environment` type has many other useful members that we did not use in this code, including the `GetEnvironmentVariables` method and the `OSVersion` and `ProcessorCount` properties.

7. Run the code and view the result, as shown in *Figure 9.1*:

Figure 9.1: Running your application to show filesystem information on Windows with Visual Studio 2022

When running the console app using dotnet run with Visual Studio Code, the `CurrentDirectory` will be the project folder, not a folder inside bin, as shown in the following output:

```
Path.PathSeparator                   ;
Path.DirectorySeparatorChar          \
Directory.GetCurrentDirectory()      C:\cs11dotnet7\Chapter09\
WorkingWithFileSystems
Environment.CurrentDirectory         C:\cs11dotnet7\Chapter09\
WorkingWithFileSystems
Environment.SystemDirectory          C:\WINDOWS\system32
Path.GetTempPath()                   C:\Users\markj\AppData\Local\Temp\
GetFolderPath(SpecialFolder
 .System)                            C:\WINDOWS\system32
 .ApplicationData)                   C:\Users\markj\AppData\Roaming
 .MyDocuments)                       C:\Users\markj\OneDrive\Documents
 .Personal)                          C:\Users\markj\OneDrive\Documents
```

Good Practice: Windows uses a backslash \ for the directory separator character. macOS and Linux use a forward slash / for the directory separator character. Do not assume what character is used in your code when combining paths.

Managing drives

To manage drives, use the `DriveInfo` type, which has a static method that returns information about all the drives connected to your computer. Each drive has a drive type.

Let's explore drives:

1. In `Program.cs`, write statements to get all the drives and output their name, type, size, available free space, and format, but only if the drive is ready, as shown in the following code:

    ```
    SectionTitle("Managing drives");
    WriteLine("{0,-30} | {1,-10} | {2,-7} | {3,18} | {4,18}",
      "NAME", "TYPE", "FORMAT", "SIZE (BYTES)", "FREE SPACE");

    foreach (DriveInfo drive in DriveInfo.GetDrives())
    {
      if (drive.IsReady)
      {
        WriteLine(
          "{0,-30} | {1,-10} | {2,-7} | {3,18:N0} | {4,18:N0}",
          drive.Name, drive.DriveType, drive.DriveFormat,
          drive.TotalSize, drive.AvailableFreeSpace);
      }
      else
      {
        WriteLine("{0,-30} | {1,-10}", drive.Name, drive.DriveType);
      }
    }
    ```

 Good Practice: Check that a drive is ready before reading properties such as `TotalSize` or you will see an exception thrown with removable drives.

2. Run the code and view the result, as shown in *Figure 9.2*:

Figure 9.2: Showing drive information on Windows

Managing directories

To manage directories, use the `Directory`, `Path`, and `Environment` static classes. These types include many members for working with the filesystem.

When constructing custom paths, you must be careful to write your code so that it makes no assumptions about the platform, for example, what to use for the directory separator character:

1. In `Program.cs`, write statements to do the following:

    -   Define a custom path under the user's home directory by creating an array of strings for the directory names, and then properly combining them with the `Path` type's `Combine` method.

    -   Check for the existence of the custom directory path using the `Exists` method of the `Directory` class.

    -   Create and then delete the directory, including files and subdirectories within it, using the `CreateDirectory` and `Delete` methods of the `Directory` class:

    ```
    SectionTitle("Managing directories");

    // define a directory path for a new folder
    // starting in the user's folder
    string newFolder = Combine(
      GetFolderPath(SpecialFolder.Personal), "NewFolder");

    WriteLine($"Working with: {newFolder}");

    // check if it exists
    WriteLine($"Does it exist? {Path.Exists(newFolder)}");

    // create directory
    WriteLine("Creating it...");
    CreateDirectory(newFolder);
    WriteLine($"Does it exist? {Path.Exists(newFolder)}");
    Write("Confirm the directory exists, and then press ENTER: ");
    ReadLine();

    // delete directory
    WriteLine("Deleting it...");
    Delete(newFolder, recursive: true);
    WriteLine($"Does it exist? {Path.Exists(newFolder)}");
    ```

2. Run the code and view the result, and use your favorite file management tool to confirm that the directory has been created before pressing *Enter* to delete it, as shown in the following output:

    ```
    Working with: C:\Users\markj\OneDrive\Documents\NewFolder
    Does it exist? False
    Creating it...
    Does it exist? True
    Confirm the directory exists, and then press ENTER:
    Deleting it...
    Does it exist? False
    ```

Managing files

When working with files, you could statically import the file type, just as we did for the directory type, but, for the next example, we will not, because it has some of the same methods as the directory type and they would conflict. The file type has a short enough name not to matter in this case. The steps are as follows:

1. In `Program.cs`, write statements to do the following:

    1. Check for the existence of a file.
    2. Create a text file.
    3. Write a line of text to the file.
    4. Close the file to release system resources and file locks (this would normally be done inside a `try-finally` statement block to ensure that the file is closed even if an exception occurs when writing to it).
    5. Copy the file to a backup.
    6. Delete the original file.
    7. Read the backup file's contents and then close it:

        ```
        SectionTitle("Managing files");

        // define a directory path to output files
        // starting in the user's folder
        string dir = Combine(
          GetFolderPath(SpecialFolder.Personal), "OutputFiles");

        CreateDirectory(dir);

        // define file paths
        string textFile = Combine(dir, "Dummy.txt");
        string backupFile = Combine(dir, "Dummy.bak");
        WriteLine($"Working with: {textFile}");

        // check if a file exists
        WriteLine($"Does it exist? {File.Exists(textFile)}");

        // create a new text file and write a line to it
        StreamWriter textWriter = File.CreateText(textFile);
        textWriter.WriteLine("Hello, C#!");
        textWriter.Close(); // close file and release resources
        WriteLine($"Does it exist? {File.Exists(textFile)}");

        // copy the file, and overwrite if it already exists
        File.Copy(sourceFileName: textFile,
          destFileName: backupFile, overwrite: true);
        ```

```
WriteLine(
  $"Does {backupFile} exist? {File.Exists(backupFile)}");

Write("Confirm the files exist, and then press ENTER: ");
ReadLine();

// delete file
File.Delete(textFile);
WriteLine($"Does it exist? {File.Exists(textFile)}");

// read from the text file backup
WriteLine($"Reading contents of {backupFile}:");
StreamReader textReader = File.OpenText(backupFile);
WriteLine(textReader.ReadToEnd());
textReader.Close();
```

2. Run the code and view the result, as shown in the following output:

```
Working with: C:\Users\markj\OneDrive\Documents\OutputFiles\Dummy.txt
Does it exist? False
Does it exist? True
Does C:\Users\markj\OneDrive\Documents\OutputFiles\Dummy.bak exist? True
Confirm the files exist, and then press ENTER:
Does it exist? False
Reading contents of C:\Users\markj\OneDrive\Documents\OutputFiles\Dummy.
bak:
Hello, C#!
```

Managing paths

Sometimes, you need to work with parts of a path; for example, you might want to extract just the folder name, the filename, or the extension. Sometimes, you need to generate temporary folders and filenames. You can do this with static methods of the Path class:

1. In Program.cs, add the following statements:

```
SectionTitle("Managing paths");

WriteLine($"Folder Name: {GetDirectoryName(textFile)}");
WriteLine($"File Name: {GetFileName(textFile)}");
WriteLine("File Name without Extension: {0}",
GetFileNameWithoutExtension(textFile));
WriteLine($"File Extension: {GetExtension(textFile)}");
WriteLine($"Random File Name: {GetRandomFileName()}");
WriteLine($"Temporary File Name: {GetTempFileName()}");
```

2. Run the code and view the result, as shown in the following output:

```
Folder Name: C:\Users\markj\OneDrive\Documents\OutputFiles
File Name: Dummy.txt
File Name without Extension: Dummy
File Extension: .txt
Random File Name: u45w1zki.co3
Temporary File Name:
/var/folders/tz/xx0y_wld5sx0nv0fjtq4tnpc0000gn/T/tmpyqrepP.tmp
```

 GetTempFileName creates a zero-byte file and returns its name, ready for you to use. GetRandomFileName just returns a filename; it doesn't create the file.

Getting file information

To get more information about a file or directory, for example, its size or when it was last accessed, you can create an instance of the FileInfo or DirectoryInfo class.

FileInfo and DirectoryInfo both inherit from FileSystemInfo, so they both have members such as LastAccessTime and Delete, as well as extra members specific to themselves, as shown in the following table:

Class	Members
FileSystemInfo	Fields: FullPath, OriginalPath Properties: Attributes, CreationTime, CreationTimeUtc, Exists, Extension, FullName, LastAccessTime, LastAccessTimeUtc, LastWriteTime, LastWriteTimeUtc, Name Methods: Delete, GetObjectData, Refresh
DirectoryInfo	Properties: Parent, Root Methods: Create, CreateSubdirectory, EnumerateDirectories, EnumerateFiles, EnumerateFileSystemInfos, GetAccessControl, GetDirectories, GetFiles, GetFileSystemInfos, MoveTo, SetAccessControl
FileInfo	Properties: Directory, DirectoryName, IsReadOnly, Length Methods: AppendText, CopyTo, Create, CreateText, Decrypt, Encrypt, GetAccessControl, MoveTo, Open, OpenRead, OpenText, OpenWrite, Replace, SetAccessControl

Let's write some code that uses a FileInfo instance for efficiently performing multiple actions on a file:

1. In Program.cs, add statements to create an instance of FileInfo for the backup file and write information about it to the console, as shown in the following code:

```
SectionTitle("Getting file information");
```

```
FileInfo info = new(backupFile);
WriteLine($"{backupFile}:");
WriteLine($"Contains {info.Length} bytes");
WriteLine($"Last accessed {info.LastAccessTime}");
WriteLine($"Has readonly set to {info.IsReadOnly}");
```

2. Run the code and view the result, as shown in the following output:

```
C:\Users\markj\OneDrive\Documents\OutputFiles\Dummy.bak:
Contains 12 bytes
Last accessed 26/10/2022 09:08:26
Has readonly set to False
```

The number of bytes might be different on your operating system because different operating systems can use different line endings.

Controlling how you work with files

When working with files, you often need to control how they are opened. The File.Open method has overloads to specify additional options using enum values.

The enum types are as follows:

- FileMode: This controls what you want to do with the file, like CreateNew, OpenOrCreate, or Truncate.
- FileAccess: This controls what level of access you need, like ReadWrite.
- FileShare: This controls locks on the file to allow other processes the specified level of access, like Read.

You might want to open a file and read from it, and allow other processes to read it too, as shown in the following code:

```
FileStream file = File.Open(pathToFile,
  FileMode.Open, FileAccess.Read, FileShare.Read);
```

There is also an enum for attributes of a file as follows:

- FileAttributes: This is to check a FileSystemInfo-derived type's Attributes property for values like Archive and Encrypted.

You could check a file or directory's attributes, as shown in the following code:

```
FileInfo info = new(backupFile);
WriteLine("Is the backup file compressed? {0}",
  info.Attributes.HasFlag(FileAttributes.Compressed));
```

Reading and writing with streams

A **stream** is a sequence of bytes that can be read from and written to. Although files can be processed rather like arrays, with random access provided by knowing the position of a byte within the file, it can be useful to process files as a stream in which the bytes can be accessed in sequential order.

Streams can also be used to process terminal input and output and networking resources such as sockets and ports that do not provide random access and cannot seek (that is, move) to a position. You can write code to process some arbitrary bytes without knowing or caring where they come from. Your code simply reads or writes to a stream, and another piece of code handles where the bytes are actually stored.

Understanding abstract and concrete streams

There is an `abstract` class named `Stream` that represents any type of stream. Remember that an `abstract` class cannot be instantiated using `new`; it can only be inherited.

There are many concrete classes that inherit from this base class, including `FileStream`, `MemoryStream`, `BufferedStream`, `GZipStream`, and `SslStream`, so they all work the same way. All streams implement `IDisposable`, so they have a `Dispose` method to release unmanaged resources.

Some of the common members of the `Stream` class are described in the following table:

Member	Description
CanRead, CanWrite	These properties determine if you can read from and write to the stream.
Length, Position	These properties determine the total number of bytes and the current position within the stream. These properties may throw an exception for some types of streams.
Dispose	This method closes the stream and releases its resources.
Flush	If the stream has a buffer, then this method writes the bytes in the buffer to the stream and the buffer is cleared.
CanSeek	This property determines if the Seek method can be used.
Seek	This method moves the current position to the one specified in its parameter.
Read, ReadAsync	These methods read a specified number of bytes from the stream into a byte array and advance the position.
ReadByte	This method reads the next byte from the stream and advances the position.
Write, WriteAsync	These methods write the contents of a byte array into the stream.
WriteByte	This method writes a byte to the stream.

Understanding storage streams

Some storage streams that represent a location where the bytes will be stored are described in the following table:

Namespace	Class	Description
System.IO	FileStream	Bytes stored in the filesystem.
System.IO	MemoryStream	Bytes stored in memory in the current process.
System.Net.Sockets	NetworkStream	Bytes stored at a network location.

 FileStream was rewritten in .NET 6 to have much higher performance and reliability on Windows. You can read more about this at the following link: https://devblogs. microsoft.com/dotnet/file-io-improvements-in-dotnet-6/.

Understanding function streams

Some function streams that cannot exist on their own, but can only be "plugged onto" other streams to add functionality, are described in the following table:

Namespace	Class	Description
System.Security.Cryptography	CryptoStream	This encrypts and decrypts the stream.
System.IO.Compression	GZipStream, DeflateStream	These compress and decompress the stream.
System.Net.Security	AuthenticatedStream	This sends credentials across the stream.

Understanding stream helpers

Although there will be occasions where you need to work with streams at a low level, most often, you can plug helper classes into the chain to make things easier. All the helper types for streams implement IDisposable, so they have a Dispose method to release unmanaged resources.

Some helper classes to handle common scenarios are described in the following table:

Namespace	Class	Description
System.IO	StreamReader	This reads from the underlying stream as plain text.
System.IO	StreamWriter	This writes to the underlying stream as plain text.
System.IO	BinaryReader	This reads from streams as .NET types. For example, the ReadDecimal method reads the next 16 bytes from the underlying stream as a decimal value and the ReadInt32 method reads the next 4 bytes as an int value.

System.IO	BinaryWriter	This writes to streams as .NET types. For example, the Write method with a decimal parameter writes 16 bytes to the underlying stream and the Write method with an int parameter writes 4 bytes.
System.Xml	XmlReader	This reads from the underlying stream using XML format.
System.Xml	XmlWriter	This writes to the underlying stream using XML format.

Writing to text streams

Let's type some code to write text to a stream:

1. Use your preferred code editor to add a new **Console App**/console project named WorkingWithStreams to the Chapter09 solution/workspace.

    - In Visual Studio, set the startup project for the solution to the current selection.
    - In Visual Studio Code, select WorkingWithStreams as the active OmniSharp project.

2. In the project file, add an element to statically and globally import the System.Console class.

3. Add a new class file named Program.Helpers.cs.

4. In Program.Helpers.cs, add a partial Program class with a SectionTitle method, as shown in the following code:

    ```
    partial class Program
    {
      static void SectionTitle(string title)
      {
        ConsoleColor previousColor = ForegroundColor;
        ForegroundColor = ConsoleColor.Yellow;
        WriteLine("*");
        WriteLine($"* {title}");
        WriteLine("*");
        ForegroundColor = previousColor;
      }
    }
    ```

5. Add a new class file named Viper.cs.

6. In Viper.cs, define a static class named Viper with a static array of string values named Callsigns, as shown in the following code:

    ```
    static class Viper
    {
      // define an array of Viper pilot call signs
      public static string[] Callsigns = new[]
      {
        "Husker", "Starbuck", "Apollo", "Boomer",
        "Bulldog", "Athena", "Helo", "Racetrack"
      };
    ```

```
}
```

7. In `Program.cs`, delete the existing statements and then import the `System.Xml` namespace and statically import the `System.Environment` and `System.IO.Path` types.

8. In `Program.cs`, add statements to enumerate the Viper call signs, writing each one on its own line in a single text file, as shown in the following code:

```
SectionTitle("Writing to text streams");

// define a file to write to
string textFile = Combine(CurrentDirectory, "streams.txt");

// create a text file and return a helper writer
StreamWriter text = File.CreateText(textFile);

// enumerate the strings, writing each one
// to the stream on a separate line
foreach (string item in Viper.Callsigns)
{
  text.WriteLine(item);
}
text.Close(); // release resources

// output the contents of the file
WriteLine("{0} contains {1:N0} bytes.",
  arg0: textFile,
  arg1: new FileInfo(textFile).Length);

WriteLine(File.ReadAllText(textFile));
```

9. Run the code and view the result, as shown in the following output:

```
C:\cs11dotnet7\Chapter09\WorkingWithStreams\bin\Debug\net7.0\streams.txt
contains 68 bytes.
Husker
Starbuck
Apollo
Boomer
Bulldog
Athena
Helo
Racetrack
```

10. Open the file that was created and check that it contains the list of call signs.

Writing to XML streams

There are two ways to write an XML element, as follows:

- `WriteStartElement` and `WriteEndElement`: Use this pair when an element might have child elements.

- `WriteElementString`: Use this when an element does not have children.

When you open a file to read or write to it, you are using resources outside of .NET. These are called **unmanaged resources** and must be disposed of when you are done working with them.

To deterministically control when they are disposed of, we can call the `Dispose` method inside a `finally` block.

Now, let's try storing the Viper pilot call signs array of `string` values in an XML file:

1. In `Program.cs`, add statements that enumerate the call signs, writing each one as an element in a single XML file, as shown in the following code:

```
SectionTitle("Writing to XML streams");

// define a file path to write to
string xmlFile = Combine(CurrentDirectory, "streams.xml");

// declare variables for the filestream and XML writer
FileStream? xmlFileStream = null;
XmlWriter? xml = null;

try
{
  // create a file stream
  xmlFileStream = File.Create(xmlFile);

  // wrap the file stream in an XML writer helper
  // and automatically indent nested elements
  xml = XmlWriter.Create(xmlFileStream,
    new XmlWriterSettings { Indent = true });

  // write the XML declaration
  xml.WriteStartDocument();

  // write a root element
  xml.WriteStartElement("callsigns");

  // enumerate the strings, writing each one to the stream
  foreach (string item in Viper.Callsigns)
  {
    xml.WriteElementString("callsign", item);
  }
```

```
  // write the close root element
  xml.WriteEndElement();

  // close helper and stream
  xml.Close();
  xmlFileStream.Close();
}
catch (Exception ex)
{
  // if the path doesn't exist the exception will be caught
  WriteLine($"{ex.GetType()} says {ex.Message}");
}
finally
{
  if (xml != null)
  {
    xml.Dispose();
    WriteLine("The XML writer's unmanaged resources have been
    disposed.");
  }

  if (xmlFileStream != null)
  {
    xmlFileStream.Dispose();
    WriteLine("The file stream's unmanaged resources have been
    disposed.");
  }
}

// output all the contents of the file
WriteLine("{0} contains {1:N0} bytes.",
  arg0: xmlFile,
  arg1: new FileInfo(xmlFile).Length);
WriteLine(File.ReadAllText(xmlFile));
```

2. Run the code and view the result, as shown in the following output:

```
The XML writer's unmanaged resources have been disposed.
The file stream's unmanaged resources have been disposed.
C:\cs11dotnet7\Chapter09\WorkingWithStreams\streams.xml contains
320 bytes.
<?xml version="1.0" encoding="utf-8"?>
<callsigns>
  <callsign>Husker</callsign>
  <callsign>Starbuck</callsign>
  <callsign>Apollo</callsign>
```

```
    <callsign>Boomer</callsign>
    <callsign>Bulldog</callsign>
    <callsign>Athena</callsign>
    <callsign>Helo</callsign>
    <callsign>Racetrack</callsign>
  </callsigns>
```

 Good Practice: Before calling the `Dispose` method, check that the object is not null.

Simplifying disposal by using the using statement

You can simplify the code that needs to check for a `null` object and then call its `Dispose` method by using the `using` statement. Generally, I would recommend using `using` rather than manually calling `Dispose` unless you need a greater level of control.

Confusingly, there are two uses for the `using` keyword: importing a namespace and generating a `finally` statement that calls `Dispose` on an object that implements `IDisposable`.

The compiler changes a `using` statement block into a `try-finally` statement without a `catch` statement. You can use nested `try` statements; so, if you do want to catch any exceptions, you can, as shown in the following code example:

```csharp
using (FileStream file2 = File.OpenWrite(
  Path.Combine(path, "file2.txt")))
{
  using (StreamWriter writer2 = new StreamWriter(file2))
  {
    try
    {
      writer2.WriteLine("Welcome, .NET!");
    }
    catch(Exception ex)
    {
      WriteLine($"{ex.GetType()} says {ex.Message}");
    }
  } // automatically calls Dispose if the object is not null
} // automatically calls Dispose if the object is not null
```

You can even simplify the code further by not explicitly specifying the braces and indentation for the `using` statements, as shown in the following code:

```csharp
using FileStream file2 = File.OpenWrite(Path.Combine(path, "file2.txt"));
using StreamWriter writer2 = new(file2);
```

```
try
{
  writer2.WriteLine("Welcome, .NET!");
}
catch(Exception ex)
{
  WriteLine($"{ex.GetType()} says {ex.Message}");
}
```

Compressing streams

XML is relatively verbose, so it takes up more space in bytes than plain text. Let's see how we can squeeze the XML using a common compression algorithm known as GZIP.

In .NET Core 2.1, Microsoft introduced an implementation of the Brotli compression algorithm. In performance, Brotli is like the algorithm used in DEFLATE and GZIP, but the output is about 20% denser.

Let's compare the two compression algorithms:

1. Add a new class file named `Program.Compress.cs`.
2. In `Program.Compress.cs`, write statements to use instances of `GZipStream` or `BrotliStream` to create a compressed file containing the same XML elements as before, and then decompress it while reading it and outputting to the console, as shown in the following code:

```csharp
using System.IO.Compression; // BrotliStream, GZipStream, CompressionMode
using System.Xml; // XmlWriter, XmlReader

using static System.Environment; // CurrentDirectory
using static System.IO.Path; // Combine

partial class Program
{
  static void Compress(string algorithm = "gzip")
  {
    // define a file path using algorithm as file extension
    string filePath = Combine(
      CurrentDirectory, $"streams.{algorithm}");

    FileStream file = File.Create(filePath);
    Stream compressor;
    if (algorithm == "gzip")
    {
      compressor = new GZipStream(file, CompressionMode.Compress);
    }
```

```
    else
    {
      compressor = new BrotliStream(file, CompressionMode.Compress);
    }

    using (compressor)
    {
      using (XmlWriter xml = XmlWriter.Create(compressor))
      {
        xml.WriteStartDocument();
        xml.WriteStartElement("callsigns");
        foreach (string item in Viper.Callsigns)
        {
          xml.WriteElementString("callsign", item);
        }
      }
    } // also closes the underlying stream

    // output all the contents of the compressed file
    WriteLine("{0} contains {1:N0} bytes.",
      filePath, new FileInfo(filePath).Length);

    WriteLine($"The compressed contents:");
    WriteLine(File.ReadAllText(filePath));

    // read a compressed file
    WriteLine("Reading the compressed XML file:");
    file = File.Open(filePath, FileMode.Open);
    Stream decompressor;
    if (algorithm == "gzip")
    {
      decompressor = new GZipStream(
        file, CompressionMode.Decompress);
    }
    else
    {
      decompressor = new BrotliStream(
        file, CompressionMode.Decompress);
    }

    using (decompressor)

    using (XmlReader reader = XmlReader.Create(decompressor))

    while (reader.Read())
```

```
{
  // check if we are on an element node named callsign
  if ((reader.NodeType == XmlNodeType.Element)
    && (reader.Name == "callsign"))
  {
    reader.Read(); // move to the text inside element
    WriteLine($"{reader.Value}"); // read its value
  }
}
}
}
}
```

3. In `Program.cs`, add calls to `Compress` with parameters to use `gzip` and `brotli` algorithms, as shown in the following code:

```
SectionTitle("Compressing streams");
Compress(algorithm: "gzip");
Compress(algorithm: "brotli");
```

4. Run the code and compare the sizes of the XML file and the compressed XML file using `gzip` and `brotli` algorithms, as shown in the following edited output:

```
C:\cs11dotnet7\Chapter09\WorkingWithStreams\bin\Debug\net7.0\streams.gzip
contains 151 bytes.
The compressed contents:
▼?
z?{??}En?BYjQqf~??????Bj^r~Jf^??RiI??????MrbNNqfz^1?i?QZ??Zd?‡@
H♣?$~%?&gc?t,?????*????H?????t?&?d??%b??H?aUPbrjIQ"??b;??♥??9→L☺
C:\cs11dotnet7\Chapter09\WorkingWithStreams\bin\Debug\net7.0\streams.
brotli contains 118 bytes.
The compressed contents:
??L      vl?9?L'??w?????.??lt???k?♥?L♥?-I‡hQ☻?^~{}?}?a{Ln?4xG?eX??V?#?Fp?P
??w>0→♪?W?U??{???02/???y?? Zo??|????M?♥
```

 The compressed files are less than half the size of the same XML without compression, which was 320 bytes.

Working with tar archives

A file with the extension `.tar` has been created using the Unix-based archival application tar. A file with the extension `.tar.gz` has been created using tar and then compressed using the GZIP compression algorithm.

.NET 7 introduces the `System.Formats.Tar` assembly, which has APIs for reading, writing, archiving, and extracting tar archives.

The `TarFile` class has static public members, as shown in the following table:

Member	Description
`CreateFromDirectory` and `CreateFromDirectoryAsync`	Creates a tar stream that contains all the filesystem entries from the specified directory.
`ExtractToDirectory` and `ExtractToDirectoryAsync`	Extracts the contents of a stream that represents a tar archive into the specified directory.
`DefaultCapacity`	Windows' `MAX_PATH` (260) is used as an arbitrary default capacity.

Let's see some example code in action:

1. Use your preferred code editor to add a new **Console App**/console project named `WorkingWithTarArchives` to the `Chapter09` solution/workspace.

   • In Visual Studio Code, select `WorkingWithTarArchives` as the active OmniSharp project.

2. In the project file, add an element to statically and globally import the `System.Console` class.

3. In `Program.Helpers.cs`, add a partial `Program` class with three methods to output errors, warnings, and information messages to the console in appropriate colors, as shown in the following code:

```
partial class Program
{
  static void WriteError(string message)
  {
    ConsoleColor previousColor = ForegroundColor;
    ForegroundColor = ConsoleColor.Red;
    WriteLine($"FAIL: {message}");
    ForegroundColor = previousColor;
  }

  static void WriteWarning(string message)
  {
    ConsoleColor previousColor = ForegroundColor;
    ForegroundColor = ConsoleColor.DarkYellow;
    WriteLine($"WARN: {message}");
    ForegroundColor = previousColor;
  }

  static void WriteInformation(string message)
  {
    ConsoleColor previousColor = ForegroundColor;
    ForegroundColor = ConsoleColor.Blue;
    WriteLine($"INFO: {message}");
    ForegroundColor = previousColor;
  }
}
```

4. In the `WorkingWithTarArchives` project, create a folder named `images` and copy some images into it.

 • If you are using Visual Studio 2022, then select all the image files, view **Properties**, and set **Copy to Output Directory** to **Copy always**.

 You can download some images from the following link: `https://github.com/markjprice/cs11dotnet7/tree/main/vs4win/Chapter09/WorkingWithTarArchives/images`.

5. In `Program.cs`, delete the existing statements and then add statements to archive the contents of a specified folder into a tar archive file and then extract it into a new folder, as shown in the following code:

```csharp
using System.Formats.Tar; // TarFile

try
{
  string current = Environment.CurrentDirectory;
  WriteInformation($"Current directory:   {current}");

  string sourceDirectory = Path.Combine(current, "images");
  string destinationDirectory = Path.Combine(current, "extracted");
  string tarFile = Path.Combine(current, "images-archive.tar");

  if (!Directory.Exists(sourceDirectory))
  {
    WriteError($"The {sourceDirectory} directory must exist. Please
create it and add some files to it.");
    return;
  }

  if (File.Exists(tarFile))
  {
    // If the Tar archive file already exists then we must delete it.
    File.Delete(tarFile);
    WriteWarning($"{tarFile} already existed so it was deleted.");
  }

  WriteInformation(
    $"Archiving directory: {sourceDirectory}\n       To .tar file:
{tarFile}");

  TarFile.CreateFromDirectory(
    sourceDirectoryName: sourceDirectory,
    destinationFileName: tarFile,
```

```
        includeBaseDirectory: true);

    WriteInformation($"Does {tarFile} exist? {File.Exists(tarFile)}.");

    if (!Directory.Exists(destinationDirectory))
    {
      // If the destination directory does not exist then we must create
      // it before extracting a Tar archive to it.
      Directory.CreateDirectory(destinationDirectory);
      WriteWarning($"{destinationDirectory} did not exist so it was
created.");
    }

    WriteInformation(
      $"Extracting archive:  {tarFile}\n      To directory:
{destinationDirectory}");

    TarFile.ExtractToDirectory(
      sourceFileName: tarFile,
      destinationDirectoryName: destinationDirectory,
      overwriteFiles: true);

    if (Directory.Exists(destinationDirectory))
    {
      foreach (string dir in Directory.
GetDirectories(destinationDirectory))
      {
        WriteInformation(
          $"Extracted directory {dir} containing these files: " +
          string.Join(',', Directory.EnumerateFiles(dir)
            .Select(file => Path.GetFileName(file))));
      }
    }
}
catch (Exception ex)
{
  WriteError(ex.Message);
}
```

6. Run the console app and note the messages, as shown in the following output:

```
INFO: Current directory:    C:\cs11dotnet7\Chapter09\
WorkingWithTarArchives\bin\Debug\net7.0
INFO: Archiving directory: C:\cs11dotnet7\Chapter09\
WorkingWithTarArchives\bin\Debug\net7.0\images
      To .tar file:        C:\cs11dotnet7\Chapter09\
WorkingWithTarArchives\bin\Debug\net7.0\images-archive.tar
```

```
INFO: Does C:\cs11dotnet7\Chapter09\WorkingWithTarArchives\bin\Debug\
net7.0\images-archive.tar exist? True.
WARN: C:\cs11dotnet7\Chapter09\WorkingWithTarArchives\bin\Debug\net7.0\
extracted did not exist so it was created.
INFO: Extracting archive:  C:\cs11dotnet7\Chapter09\
WorkingWithTarArchives\bin\Debug\net7.0\images-archive.tar
        To directory:        C:\cs11dotnet7\Chapter09\
WorkingWithTarArchives\bin\Debug\net7.0\extracted
INFO: Extracted directory C:\cs11dotnet7\Chapter09\
WorkingWithTarArchives\bin\Debug\net7.0\extracted\images containing
these files: category1.jpeg,category2.jpeg,category3.jpeg,category4.
jpeg,category5.jpeg,category6.jpeg,category7.jpeg,category8.jpeg
```

7. If you have software that can view the contents of a tar archive like 7-Zip, then use it to review
    the contents of the `images-archive.tar` file, as shown in *Figure 9.3*:

Figure 9.3: Opening a tar archive file on Windows using 7-Zip

You can download and install the free and open-source 7-Zip at the following link: `https://www.7-zip.org/`.

Reading and writing tar entries

As well as the `TarFile` class, there are classes for reading and writing individual entries in a tar archive, named `TarEntry`, `TarEntryFormat`, `TarReader`, and `TarWriter`. These can be combined with
`GzipStream` to compress or decompress entries as they are written and read.

You can learn more about .NET tar support at the following link: `https://learn.microsoft.com/en-us/dotnet/api/system.formats.tar`.

Encoding and decoding text

Text characters can be represented in different ways. For example, the alphabet can be encoded using
Morse code into a series of dots and dashes for transmission over a telegraph line.

In a similar way, text inside a computer is stored as bits (ones and zeros) representing a code point within a code space. Most code points represent a single character, but they can also have other meanings, such as formatting.

For example, ASCII has a code space with 128 code points. .NET uses a standard called **Unicode** to encode text internally. Unicode has more than one million code points.

Sometimes, you will need to move text outside .NET for use by systems that do not use Unicode or use a variation of Unicode, so it is important to learn how to convert between encodings.

The following table lists some alternative text encodings commonly used by computers:

Encoding	Description
ASCII	This encodes a limited range of characters using the lower seven bits of a byte.
UTF-8	This represents each Unicode code point as a sequence of one to four bytes.
UTF-7	This is designed to be more efficient over 7-bit channels than UTF-8 but it has security and robustness issues, so UTF-8 is recommended over UTF-7.
UTF-16	This represents each Unicode code point as a sequence of one or two 16-bit integers.
UTF-32	This represents each Unicode code point as a 32-bit integer and is therefore a fixed-length encoding unlike the other Unicode encodings, which are all variable-length encodings.
ANSI/ISO encodings	This provides support for a variety of code pages that are used to support a specific language or group of languages.

> **Good Practice:** In most cases today, UTF-8 is a good default, which is why it is literally the default encoding, that is, `Encoding.Default`. You should avoid using `Encoding.UTF7` because it is unsecure. Due to this, the C# compiler will warn you when you try to use UTF-7. Of course, you might need to generate text using that encoding for compatibility with another system, so it needs to remain an option in .NET.

Encoding strings as byte arrays

Let's explore text encodings:

1. Use your preferred code editor to add a new **Console App**/console project named WorkingWithEncodings to the Chapter09 solution/workspace.

    *   In Visual Studio Code, select WorkingWithEncodings as the active OmniSharp project.

2. In the project file, add an element to statically and globally import the System.Console class.

3. In Program.cs, delete the existing statements, import the System.Text namespace, and then add statements to encode a string using an encoding chosen by the user, loop through each byte, and then decode it back into a string and output it, as shown in the following code:

    ```
    using System.Text;
    ```

```csharp
WriteLine("Encodings");
WriteLine("[1] ASCII");
WriteLine("[2] UTF-7");
WriteLine("[3] UTF-8");
WriteLine("[4] UTF-16 (Unicode)");
WriteLine("[5] UTF-32");
WriteLine("[6] Latin1");
WriteLine("[any other key] Default encoding");
WriteLine();

// choose an encoding
Write("Press a number to choose an encoding.");
ConsoleKey number = ReadKey(intercept: true).Key;
WriteLine(); WriteLine();

Encoding encoder = number switch
{
  ConsoleKey.D1 or ConsoleKey.NumPad1 => Encoding.ASCII,
  ConsoleKey.D2 or ConsoleKey.NumPad2 => Encoding.UTF7,
  ConsoleKey.D3 or ConsoleKey.NumPad3 => Encoding.UTF8,
  ConsoleKey.D4 or ConsoleKey.NumPad4 => Encoding.Unicode,
  ConsoleKey.D5 or ConsoleKey.NumPad5 => Encoding.UTF32,
  ConsoleKey.D6 or ConsoleKey.NumPad6 => Encoding.Latin1,
  _                                   => Encoding.Default
};

// define a string to encode
string message = "Café £4.39";
WriteLine($"Text to encode: {message}  Characters: {message.Length}");

// encode the string into a byte array
byte[] encoded = encoder.GetBytes(message);

// check how many bytes the encoding needed
WriteLine("{0} used {1:N0} bytes.", encoder.GetType().Name,
encoded.Length);
WriteLine();

// enumerate each byte
WriteLine($"BYTE | HEX | CHAR");
foreach (byte b in encoded)
{
  WriteLine($"{b,4} | {b.ToString("X"),3} | {(char)b,4}");
}

// decode the byte array back into a string and display it
```

```
string decoded = encoder.GetString(encoded);
WriteLine(decoded);
```

4. Run the code, press *1* to choose ASCII, and note that when outputting the bytes, the pound sign (£) and accented e (é) cannot be represented in ASCII, so it uses a question mark instead:

```
Text to encode: Café £4.39  Characters: 10
ASCIIEncodingSealed used 10 bytes.

BYTE | HEX | CHAR
  67 |  43 |   C
  97 |  61 |   a
 102 |  66 |   f
  63 |  3F |   ?
  32 |  20 |
  63 |  3F |   ?
  52 |  34 |   4
  46 |  2E |   .
  51 |  33 |   3
  57 |  39 |   9
Caf? ?4.39
```

5. Rerun the code and press *3* to choose UTF-8. Note that UTF-8 requires 2 extra bytes for the two characters that need 2 bytes each (12 bytes instead of 10 bytes in total) but it can encode and decode the é and £ characters:

```
Text to encode: Café £4.39  Characters: 10
UTF8EncodingSealed used 12 bytes.

BYTE | HEX | CHAR
  67 |  43 |   C
  97 |  61 |   a
 102 |  66 |   f
 195 |  C3 |   Ã
 169 |  A9 |   ©
  32 |  20 |
 194 |  C2 |   Â
 163 |  A3 |   £
  52 |  34 |   4
  46 |  2E |   .
  51 |  33 |   3
  57 |  39 |   9
Café £4.39
```

6. Rerun the code and press *4* to choose Unicode (UTF-16). Note that UTF-16 requires 2 bytes for every character, so 20 bytes in total, and it can encode and decode the é and £ characters. This encoding is used internally by .NET to store char and string values.

Encoding and decoding text in files

When using stream helper classes, such as `StreamReader` and `StreamWriter`, you can specify the encoding you want to use. As you write to the helper, the text will automatically be encoded, and as you read from the helper, the bytes will be automatically decoded.

To specify an encoding, pass the encoding as a second parameter to the helper type's constructor, as shown in the following code:

```
StreamReader reader = new(stream, Encoding.UTF8);
StreamWriter writer = new(stream, Encoding.UTF8);
```

> **Good Practice:** Often, you won't have the choice of which encoding to use, because you will be generating a file for use by another system. However, if you do, pick one that uses the fewest number of bytes but can store every character you need.

Reading and writing with random access handles

With .NET 6 and later, there is a new API for working with files without needing a file stream.

First, you must get a handle to the file, as shown in the following code:

```
using Microsoft.Win32.SafeHandles; // SafeFileHandle
using System.Text; // Encoding

using SafeFileHandle handle =
  File.OpenHandle(path: "coffee.txt",
    mode: FileMode.OpenOrCreate,
    access: FileAccess.ReadWrite);
```

You can then write some text encoded as a byte array and then stored in a read-only memory buffer to the file, as shown in the following code:

```
string message = "Café £4.39";
ReadOnlyMemory<byte> buffer = new(Encoding.UTF8.GetBytes(message));
await RandomAccess.WriteAsync(handle, buffer, fileOffset: 0);
```

To read from the file, get the length of the file, allocate a memory buffer for the contents using that length, and then read the file, as shown in the following code:

```
long length = RandomAccess.GetLength(handle);
Memory<byte> contentBytes = new(new byte[length]);
await RandomAccess.ReadAsync(handle, contentBytes, fileOffset: 0);
string content = Encoding.UTF8.GetString(contentBytes.ToArray());
WriteLine($"Content of file: {content}");
```

Serializing object graphs

An **object graph** is multiple objects that are related to each other either through a direct reference or indirectly through a chain of references.

Serialization is the process of converting a live object graph into a sequence of bytes using a specified format. **Deserialization** is the reverse process. You would do this to save the current state of a live object so that you can recreate it in the future, for example, saving the current state of a game so that you can continue at the same place tomorrow. Serialized objects are usually stored in a file or database.

There are dozens of formats you can specify, but the two most common ones are **eXtensible Markup Language** (**XML**) and **JavaScript Object Notation** (**JSON**).

> **Good Practice:** JSON is more compact and is best for web and mobile applications. XML is more verbose but is better supported in more legacy systems. Use JSON to minimize the size of serialized object graphs. JSON is also a good choice when sending object graphs to web applications and mobile applications because JSON is the native serialization format for JavaScript, and mobile apps often make calls over limited bandwidth, so the number of bytes is important.

.NET has multiple classes that will serialize to and from XML and JSON. We will start by looking at `XmlSerializer` and `JsonSerializer`.

Serializing as XML

Let's start by looking at XML, probably the world's most used serialization format (for now). To show a typical example, we will define a custom class to store information about a person and then create an object graph using a list of `Person` instances with nesting:

1. Use your preferred code editor to add a new **Console App**/console project named `WorkingWithSerialization` to the `Chapter09` solution/workspace.

    *   In Visual Studio Code, select `WorkingWithSerialization` as the active OmniSharp project.

2. Add a new class file named `Person.cs` to define a `Person` class with a `Salary` property that is `protected`, meaning it is only accessible to itself and derived classes. To populate the salary, the class has a constructor with a single parameter to set the initial salary, as shown in the following code:

    ```
    namespace Packt.Shared;

    public class Person
    {
      public Person(decimal initialSalary)
      {
        Salary = initialSalary;
      }
    ```

```
    public string? FirstName { get; set; }
    public string? LastName { get; set; }
    public DateTime DateOfBirth { get; set; }
    public HashSet<Person>? Children { get; set; }
    protected decimal Salary { get; set; }
}
```

3. In `Program.cs`, delete the existing statements. Import namespaces for working with XML serial-
    ization and statically import the `Environment` and `Path` classes, as shown in the following code:

```
using System.Xml.Serialization; // XmlSerializer
using Packt.Shared; // Person

using static System.Environment;
using static System.IO.Path;
```

4. In `Program.cs`, add statements to create an object graph of `Person` instances, as shown in the
    following code:

```
// create an object graph
List<Person> people = new()
{
  new(30000M)
  {
    FirstName = "Alice",
    LastName = "Smith",
    DateOfBirth = new(year: 1974, month: 3, day: 14)
  },
  new(40000M)
  {
    FirstName = "Bob",
    LastName = "Jones",
    DateOfBirth = new(year: 1969, month: 11, day: 23)
  },
  new(20000M)
  {
    FirstName = "Charlie",
    LastName = "Cox",
    DateOfBirth = new(year: 1984, month: 5, day: 4),
    Children = new()
    {
      new(0M)
      {
        FirstName = "Sally",
        LastName = "Cox",
        DateOfBirth = new(year: 2012, month: 7, day: 12)
      }
```

```
      }
    }
};

// create object that will format a List of Persons as XML
XmlSerializer xs = new(type: people.GetType());

// create a file to write to
string path = Combine(CurrentDirectory, "people.xml");

using (FileStream stream = File.Create(path))
{
    // serialize the object graph to the stream
    xs.Serialize(stream, people);
}

WriteLine("Written {0:N0} bytes of XML to {1}",
    arg0: new FileInfo(path).Length,
    arg1: path);
WriteLine();

// Display the serialized object graph
WriteLine(File.ReadAllText(path));
```

5. Run the code, view the result, and note that an exception is thrown, as shown in the following output:

```
Unhandled Exception: System.InvalidOperationException: Packt.Shared.
Person cannot be serialized because it does not have a parameterless
constructor.
```

6. In `Person.cs`, add a statement to define a parameterless constructor, as shown in the following code:

```
public Person() { }
```

 The constructor does not need to do anything, but it must exist so that the `XmlSerializer` can call it to instantiate new `Person` instances during the deserialization process.

7. Run the code and view the result, and note that the object graph is serialized as XML elements like `<FirstName>Bob</FirstName>` and that the `Salary` property is not included because it is not a `public` property, as shown in the following output:

```
Written 656 bytes of XML to C:\cs11dotnet7\Chapter09\
WorkingWithSerialization\bin\Debug\net7.0\people.xml
```

```
<?xml version="1.0" encoding="utf-8"?><ArrayOfPerson xmlns:xsi="http://
www.w3.org/2001/XMLSchema-instance" xmlns:xsd="http://
www.w3.org/2001/XMLSchema"><Person><FirstName>Alice</
FirstName><LastName>Smith</LastName><DateOfBirth>1974-03-
14T00:00:00</DateOfBirth></Person><Person><FirstName>Bob</
FirstName><LastName>Jones</LastName><DateOfBirth>1969-11-
23T00:00:00</DateOfBirth></Person><Person><FirstName>Charlie</
FirstName><LastName>Cox</LastName><DateOfBirth>1984-05-04T00:00:00</
DateOfBirth><Children><Person><FirstName>Sally</FirstName><LastName>Cox</
LastName><DateOfBirth>2012-07-12T00:00:00</DateOfBirth></Person></
Children></Person></ArrayOfPerson>
```

Generating compact XML

We could make the XML more compact using attributes instead of elements for some fields:

1. In `Person.cs`, import the `System.Xml.Serialization` namespace so that you can decorate some properties with the `[XmlAttribute]` attribute, as shown in the following code:

    ```
    using System.Xml.Serialization; // [XmlAttribute]
    ```

2. In `Person.cs`, decorate the first name, last name, and date of birth properties with the `[XmlAttribute]` attribute, and set a short name for each property, as shown highlighted in the following code:

    ```
    [XmlAttribute("fname")]
    public string? FirstName { get; set; }

    [XmlAttribute("lname")]
    public string? LastName { get; set; }

    [XmlAttribute("dob")]
    public DateTime DateOfBirth { get; set; }
    ```

3. Run the code and note that the size of the file has been reduced from 656 to 451 bytes, a space-saving of more than a third, by outputting property values as XML attributes, as shown in the following output:

    ```
    Written 451 bytes of XML to C:\cs11dotnet7\Chapter09\
    WorkingWithSerialization\bin\Debug\net7.0\people.xml

    <?xml version="1.0" encoding="utf-8"?><ArrayOfPerson xmlns:xsi="http://
    www.w3.org/2001/XMLSchema-instance" xmlns:xsd="http://www.w3.org/2001/
    XMLSchema"><Person fname="Alice" lname="Smith" dob="1974-03-14T00:00:00"
    /><Person fname="Bob" lname="Jones" dob="1969-11-23T00:00:00" /><Person
    fname="Charlie" lname="Cox" dob="1984-05-04T00:00:00"><Children><Person
    fname="Sally" lname="Cox" dob="2012-07-12T00:00:00" /></Children></
    Person></ArrayOfPerson>
    ```

Deserializing XML files

Now, let's try deserializing the XML file back into live objects in memory:

1. In `Program.cs`, add statements to open the XML file and then deserialize it, as shown in the following code:

```
WriteLine();
WriteLine("* Deserializing XML files");

using (FileStream xmlLoad = File.Open(path, FileMode.Open))
{
  // deserialize and cast the object graph into a List of Person
  List<Person>? loadedPeople =
    xs.Deserialize(xmlLoad) as List<Person>;

  if (loadedPeople is not null)
  {
    foreach (Person p in loadedPeople)
    {
      WriteLine("{0} has {1} children.",
        p.LastName, p.Children?.Count ?? 0);
    }
  }
}
```

2. Run the code and note that the people are loaded successfully from the XML file and then enumerated, as shown in the following output:

```
* Deserializing XML files
Smith has 0 children.
Jones has 0 children.
Cox has 1 children.
```

There are many other attributes that can be used to control the XML generated.

If you don't use any annotations, `XmlSerializer` performs a case-insensitive match using the property name when deserializing.

 Good Practice: When using `XmlSerializer`, remember that only the public fields and properties are included, and the type must have a parameterless constructor. You can customize the output with attributes.

Serializing with JSON

One of the most popular .NET libraries for working with the JSON serialization format is **Newtonsoft. Json**, known as **Json.NET**. It is mature and powerful.

Newtonsoft.Json is so popular that it overflowed the bounds of the 32-bit integer used for the download count in the NuGet package manager, as shown in the following tweet in *Figure 9.4*:

Figure 9.4: Negative 2 billion downloads for Newtonsoft.Json in August 2022

Let's see it in action:

1. In the `WorkingWithSerialization` project, add a package reference for the latest version of `Newtonsoft.Json`, as shown in the following markup:

```
<ItemGroup>
  <PackageReference Include="Newtonsoft.Json" Version="13.0.1" />
</ItemGroup>
```

2. Build the `WorkingWithSerialization` project to restore packages.

3. In `Program.cs`, add statements to create a text file and then serialize the people into the file as JSON, as shown in the following code:

```
// create a file to write to
string jsonPath = Combine(CurrentDirectory, "people.json");

using (StreamWriter jsonStream = File.CreateText(jsonPath))
{
  // create an object that will format as JSON
  Newtonsoft.Json.JsonSerializer jss = new();

  // serialize the object graph into a string
  jss.Serialize(jsonStream, people);
}

WriteLine();
WriteLine("Written {0:N0} bytes of JSON to: {1}",
  arg0: new FileInfo(jsonPath).Length,
```

```
      arg1: jsonPath);

  // display the serialized object graph
  WriteLine(File.ReadAllText(jsonPath));
```

4. Run the code and note that JSON requires fewer than half the number of bytes compared to XML with elements. It's even smaller than the XML file, which uses attributes, as shown in the following output:

```
Written 366 bytes of JSON to: C:\cs11dotnet7\Chapter09\
WorkingWithSerialization\bin\Debug\net7.0\people.json
[{"FirstName":"Alice","LastName":"Smith","DateOfBirth":"1974-03-
14T00:00:00","Children":null},{"FirstName":"Bob","LastName":"Jones","Date
OfBirth":"1969-11-23T00:00:00","Children":null},{"FirstName":"Charlie","L
astName":"Cox","DateOfBirth":"1984-05-04T00:00:00","Children":[{"FirstNam
e":"Sally","LastName":"Cox","DateOfBirth":"2012-07-12T00:00:00","Children
":null}]}]
```

High-performance JSON processing

.NET Core 3.0 introduced a new namespace for working with JSON, `System.Text.Json`, which is optimized for performance by leveraging APIs like `Span<T>`.

Also, older libraries like Json.NET are implemented by reading UTF-16. It would be more performant to read and write JSON documents using UTF-8 because most network protocols, including HTTP, use UTF-8 and you can avoid transcoding UTF-8 to and from Json.NET's Unicode `string` values.

With the new API, Microsoft achieved between 1.3x and 5x improvement, depending on the scenario.

The original author of Json.NET, James Newton-King, joined Microsoft and has been working with them to develop their new JSON types. As he says in a comment discussing the new JSON APIs, "Json. NET isn't going away", as shown in *Figure 9.5*:

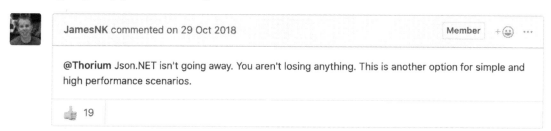

Figure 9.5: A comment by the original author of Json.NET

Let's see how to use the new JSON APIs to deserialize a JSON file:

1. In the `WorkingWithSerialization` project, at the top of `Program.cs`, import the new JSON class for performing serialization using an alias to avoid conflicting names with the Json.NET one we used before, as shown in the following code:

```
using FastJson = System.Text.Json.JsonSerializer;
```

2. In `Program.cs`, add statements to open the JSON file, deserialize it, and output the names and counts of the children of the people, as shown in the following code:

```
WriteLine();
WriteLine("* Deserializing JSON files");

using (FileStream jsonLoad = File.Open(jsonPath, FileMode.Open))
{
  // deserialize object graph into a List of Person
  List<Person>? loadedPeople =
    await FastJson.DeserializeAsync(utf8Json: jsonLoad,
      returnType: typeof(List<Person>)) as List<Person>;

  if (loadedPeople is not null)
  {
    foreach (Person p in loadedPeople)
    {
      WriteLine("{0} has {1} children.",
        p.LastName, p.Children?.Count ?? 0);
    }
  }
}
```

3. Run the code and view the result, as shown in the following output:

```
* Deserializing JSON files
Smith has 0 children.
Jones has 0 children.
Cox has 1 children.
```

> **Good Practice:** Choose Json.NET for developer productivity and a large feature set, or `System.Text.Json` for performance. You can review a list of the differences at the following link: `https://docs.microsoft.com/en-us/dotnet/standard/serialization/system-text-json-migrate-from-newtonsoft-how-to?pivots=dotnet-7-0#table-of-differences-between-newtonsoftjson-and-systemtextjson`.

Controlling JSON processing

There are many options for taking control of how JSON is processed, as shown in the following list:

- Including and excluding fields.
- Setting a casing policy.
- Selecting a case-sensitivity policy.
- Choosing between compact and prettified whitespace.

Let's see some in action:

1. Use your preferred code editor to add a new **Console App**/console project named WorkingWithJson to the Chapter09 solution/workspace.

   - In Visual Studio Code, select WorkingWithJson as the active OmniSharp project.

2. In the WorkingWithJson project, in Program.cs, delete the existing statements, import the main namespace for working with high-performance JSON, and then statically import the System.Environment and System.IO.Path types, as shown in the following code:

```
using System.Text.Json; // JsonSerializer

using static System.Environment;
using static System.IO.Path;
```

3. Add a new class file named Book.cs.

4. In Book.cs, define a class named Book, as shown in the following code:

```
using System.Text.Json.Serialization; // [JsonInclude]

public class Book
{
  // constructor to set non-nullable property
  public Book(string title)
  {
    Title = title;
  }

  // properties
  public string Title { get; set; }
  public string? Author { get; set; }

  // fields
  [JsonInclude] // include this field
  public DateTime PublishDate;

  [JsonInclude] // include this field
  public DateTimeOffset Created;

  public ushort Pages;
}
```

5. In Program.cs, add statements to create an instance of the Book class and serialize it to JSON, as shown in the following code:

```
Book mybook = new(title:
  "C# 11 and .NET 7 - Modern Cross-Platform Development Fundamentals")
```

```
{
  Author = "Mark J Price",
  PublishDate = new(year: 2022, month: 11, day: 8),
  Pages = 823,
  Created = DateTimeOffset.UtcNow,
};

JsonSerializerOptions options = new()
{
  IncludeFields = true, // includes all fields
  PropertyNameCaseInsensitive = true,
  WriteIndented = true,
  PropertyNamingPolicy = JsonNamingPolicy.CamelCase,
};

string filePath = Combine(CurrentDirectory, "mybook.json");

using (Stream fileStream = File.Create(filePath))
{
  JsonSerializer.Serialize<Book>(
    utf8Json: fileStream, value: mybook, options);
}

WriteLine("Written {0:N0} bytes of JSON to {1}",
  arg0: new FileInfo(filePath).Length,
  arg1: filePath);
WriteLine();

// display the serialized object graph
WriteLine(File.ReadAllText(filePath));
```

6. Run the code and view the result, as shown in the following output:

```
Written 222 bytes of JSON to C:\cs11dotnet7\Chapter09\WorkingWithJson\
bin\Debug\net7.0\mybook.json

{
  "title": "C# 11 and .NET 7 - Modern Cross-Platform Development
Fundamentals",
  "author": "Mark J Price",
  "publishDate": "2022-11-08T00:00:00",
  "created": "2022-03-04T08:16:38.1823225+00:00",
  "pages": 823
}
```

Note the following:

- The JSON file is 222 bytes.
- The member names use camelCasing, for example, `publishDate`. This is best for subsequent processing in a browser with JavaScript.
- All fields are included due to the options set, including `pages`.
- JSON is prettified for easier human legibility.
- `DateTime` and `DateTimeOffset` values are stored as a single standard `string` format.

7. In `Program.cs`, when setting the `JsonSerializerOptions`, comment out the setting of casing policy, write indented, and include fields.

8. Run the code and view the result, as shown in the following output:

```
Written 183 bytes of JSON to C:\cs11dotnet7\Chapter09\WorkingWithJson\
bin\Debug\net7.0\mybook.json

{"Title":"C# 11 and .NET 7 - Modern Cross-Platform Development
Fundamentals","Author":"Mark J Price","PublishDate":"2022-11-
08T00:00:00","Created":"2022-03-04T08:20:15.0989884+00:00"}
```

Note the following:

- The JSON file is 183 bytes, a more than 20% reduction.
- The member names use normal casing, for example, `PublishDate`.
- The `Pages` field is missing. The other fields are included due to the `[JsonInclude]` attribute on the `PublishDate` and `Created` fields.

New JSON extension methods for working with HTTP responses

In .NET 5, Microsoft added refinements to the types in the `System.Text.Json` namespace like extension methods for `HttpResponse`, which you will see in *Chapter 15, Building and Consuming Web Services*.

Migrating from Newtonsoft to new JSON

If you have existing code that uses the Newtonsoft Json.NET library and you want to migrate to the new `System.Text.Json` namespace, then Microsoft has specific documentation for that, which you will find at the following link:

https://docs.microsoft.com/en-us/dotnet/standard/serialization/system-text-json-migrate-from-newtonsoft-how-to

Practicing and exploring

Test your knowledge and understanding by answering some questions, getting some hands-on practice, and exploring this chapter's topics with more in-depth research.

Exercise 9.1 – Test your knowledge

Answer the following questions:

1. What is the difference between using the `File` class and the `FileInfo` class?
2. What is the difference between the `ReadByte` method and the `Read` method of a stream?
3. When would you use the `StringReader`, `TextReader`, and `StreamReader` classes?
4. What does the `DeflateStream` type do?
5. How many bytes per character does UTF-8 encoding use?
6. What is an object graph?
7. What is the best serialization format to choose for minimizing space requirements?
8. What is the best serialization format to choose for cross-platform compatibility?
9. Why is it bad to use a `string` value like `"\Code\Chapter01"` to represent a path, and what should you do instead?
10. Where can you find information about NuGet packages and their dependencies?

Exercise 9.2 – Practice serializing as XML

In the `Chapter09` solution/workspace, create a console app named `Ch09Ex02SerializingShapes` that creates a list of shapes, uses serialization to save it to the filesystem using XML, and then deserializes it back:

```
// create a List of Shapes to serialize
List<Shape> listOfShapes = new()
{
  new Circle { Colour = "Red", Radius = 2.5 },
  new Rectangle { Colour = "Blue", Height = 20.0, Width = 10.0 },
  new Circle { Colour = "Green", Radius = 8.0 },
  new Circle { Colour = "Purple", Radius = 12.3 },
  new Rectangle { Colour = "Blue", Height = 45.0, Width = 18.0 }
};
```

Shapes should have a read-only property named `Area` so that when you deserialize, you can output a list of shapes, including their areas, as shown here:

```
List<Shape> loadedShapesXml =
  serializerXml.Deserialize(fileXml) as List<Shape>;

foreach (Shape item in loadedShapesXml)
{
  WriteLine("{0} is {1} and has an area of {2:N2}",
    item.GetType().Name, item.Colour, item.Area);
}
```

This is what your output should look like when you run your console application:

```
Loading shapes from XML:
Circle is Red and has an area of 19.63
Rectangle is Blue and has an area of 200.00
Circle is Green and has an area of 201.06
Circle is Purple and has an area of 475.29
Rectangle is Blue and has an area of 810.00
```

Exercise 9.3 – Explore topics

Use the links on the following page to learn more detail about the topics covered in this chapter:

```
https://github.com/markjprice/cs11dotnet7/blob/main/book-links.md#chapter-9---working-
with-files-streams-and-serialization
```

Summary

In this chapter, you learned how to:

- Read from and write to text files.
- Read from and write to XML files.
- Compress and decompress files.
- Encode and decode text.
- Serialize an object graph into JSON and XML.
- Deserialize an object graph from JSON and XML.

In the next chapter, you will learn how to work with databases using Entity Framework Core.

10

Working with Data Using Entity Framework Core

This chapter is about reading and writing to relational data stores, such as SQLite and SQL Server, by using the object-to-data store mapping technology named **Entity Framework Core (EF Core)**.

This chapter will cover the following topics:

- Understanding modern databases
- Setting up EF Core
- Defining EF Core models
- Querying EF Core models
- Loading patterns with EF Core
- Modifying data with EF Core
- Working with transactions
- Code First EF Core models (online section)

Understanding modern databases

Two of the most common places to store data are in a **Relational Database Management System (RDBMS)** such as SQL Server, PostgreSQL, MySQL, and SQLite, or in a **NoSQL** database such as Azure Cosmos DB, Redis, MongoDB, and Apache Cassandra.

Relational databases were invented in the 1970s. They are queried with **Structured Query Language (SQL)**. At the time, data storage costs were high, so they reduce data duplication as much as possible. Data is stored in tabular structures with rows and columns that are tricky to refactor once in production. They can be difficult and expensive to scale.

NoSQL databases do not just mean "no SQL"; they can also mean "not only SQL." They were invented in the 2000s, after the Internet and the Web had become popular and adopted many of the learnings from that era of software.

They are designed for massive scalability, high performance, and to make programming easier by providing maximum flexibility and allowing schema changes at any time because they do not enforce a structure.

Understanding legacy Entity Framework

Entity Framework (**EF**) was first released as part of .NET Framework 3.5 with Service Pack 1 back in late 2008. Since then, Entity Framework has evolved, as Microsoft has observed how programmers use an **object-relational mapping** (**ORM**) tool in the real world.

ORMs use a mapping definition to associate columns in tables to properties in classes. Then, a programmer can interact with objects of different types in a way that they are familiar with, instead of having to deal with knowing how to store the values in a relational table or another structure provided by a NoSQL data store.

The version of EF included with .NET Framework is **Entity Framework 6** (**EF6**). It is mature, stable, and supports an EDMX (XML file) way of defining the model, as well as complex inheritance models and a few other advanced features.

EF 6.3 and later have been extracted from .NET Framework as a separate package, so it can be supported on .NET Core 3.0 and later. This enables existing projects like web applications and services to be ported and run cross-platform. However, EF6 should be considered a legacy technology because it has some limitations when running cross-platform and no new features will be added to it.

Using the legacy Entity Framework 6.3 or later

To use the legacy Entity Framework in a .NET Core 3.0 or later project, you must add a package reference to it in your project file, as shown in the following markup:

```
<PackageReference Include="EntityFramework" Version="6.4.4" />
```

Good Practice: Only use legacy EF6 if you must; for example, when migrating a WPF app that uses it. This book is about modern cross-platform development, so in the rest of this chapter, I will only cover the modern Entity Framework Core. You will not need to reference the legacy EF6 package as shown above in the projects for this chapter.

Understanding Entity Framework Core

The truly cross-platform version, **EF Core**, is different from the legacy Entity Framework. Although EF Core has a similar name, you should be aware of how it varies from EF6. The latest EF Core is version 7, to match .NET 7.

EF Core 5 and later only support .NET 5 and later. EF Core 3.0 and later only work with platforms that support .NET Standard 2.1, meaning .NET Core 3.0 and later. EF Core 3.0 and later does not support .NET Standard 2.0 platforms like .NET Framework 4.8.

EF Core 7 targets .NET 6 or later. This means that you can use all the new features of EF Core 7 with either .NET 6 or .NET 7. I expect many developers who have to use .NET 6 for its Long Term Support to upgrade the EF Core packages that they reference to version 7.

As well as traditional RDBMSs, EF Core supports modern cloud-based, nonrelational, schema-less data stores, such as Azure Cosmos DB and MongoDB, sometimes with third-party providers.

EF Core has so many improvements that this chapter cannot cover them all. For example, a new feature introduced with EF Core 7 is support for JSON columns, meaning that a database that allows columns to store JSON documents can query into those documents and use elements of those documents in filters and ordering expressions. But, in EF Core 7, the JSON column feature is only implemented for SQL Server. Future EF Core versions will add support for other databases like SQLite and at that point I might add coverage of the feature. In this chapter, I will focus on the fundamentals that all .NET developers should know and some of the most useful new features.

Understanding Database First and Code First

There are two approaches to working with EF Core:

1. **Database First**: A database already exists, so you build a model that matches its structure and features.
2. **Code First**: No database exists, so you build a model and then use EF Core to create a database that matches its structure and features.

We will start by using EF Core with an existing database.

Performance improvements in EF Core 7

The EF Core team continues to work hard on improving the performance of EF Core. For example, if EF Core 7 identifies that only a single statement will be executed against the database when SaveChanges is called, then it does not create an explicit transaction as earlier versions do. That gives a 25% performance improvement to a common scenario.

There is too much detail about all the recent improvements to cover in this chapter, and you get all the benefits without needing to know how they work anyway. If you are interested (and it is fascinating what they looked at and how they took advantage of some cool SQL Server features in particular) then I recommend that you read the following posts from the EF Core team:

- Announcing Entity Framework Core 7 Preview 6: Performance Edition: `https://devblogs.microsoft.com/dotnet/announcing-ef-core-7-preview6-performance-optimizations/`
- Announcing Entity Framework Core 6.0 Preview 4: Performance Edition: `https://devblogs.microsoft.com/dotnet/announcing-entity-framework-core-6-0-preview-4-performance-edition/`

Creating a console app for working with EF Core

First, we will create a console app project for this chapter:

1. Use your preferred code editor to create a new project, as defined in the following list:

   - Project template: **Console App**/console

   - Project file and folder: WorkingWithEFCore

   - Workspace/solution file and folder: Chapter10

Using a sample relational database

To learn how to manage an RDBMS using .NET, it would be useful to have a sample one so that you can practice on one that has a medium complexity and a decent number of sample records. Microsoft offers several sample databases, most of which are too complex for our needs, so instead, we will use a database that was first created in the early 1990s known as **Northwind**.

Let's take a minute to look at a diagram of the Northwind database. You can use the following diagram to refer to as we write code and queries throughout this book:

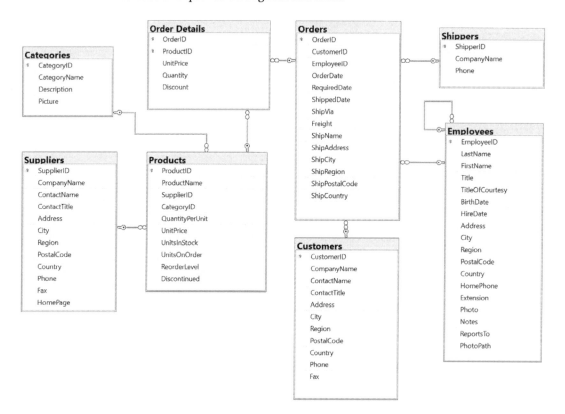

Figure 10.1: The Northwind database tables and relationships

You will write code to work with the `Categories` and `Products` tables later in this chapter, and other tables in later chapters. But before we do, note that:

- Each category has a unique identifier, name, description, and picture.
- Each product has a unique identifier, name, unit price, units in stock, and other fields.
- Each product is associated with a category by storing the category's unique identifier.
- The relationship between `Categories` and `Products` is one-to-many, meaning each category can have zero or more products. This is indicated in *Figure 10.1* by an infinity symbol at one end (meaning many) and a yellow key at the other end (meaning one).

Using SQLite

SQLite is a small, cross-platform, self-contained RDBMS that is available in the public domain. It's the most common RDBMS for mobile platforms such as iOS (iPhone and iPad) and Android.

> I decided to demonstrate using only SQLite for the 7th edition, since the important themes are cross-platform development and fundamental skills which only need basic database capabilities. I have created a large chapter about SQL Server and its more powerful capabilities in my new companion book. Although you can use SQL Server for the coding tasks in this book, to learn more about SQL Server, I recommend looking at *Apps and Services with .NET 7*.

Setting up SQLite for Windows

On Windows, we need to add the folder for SQLite to the system path so it will be found when we enter commands at a command prompt or terminal:

1. Start your favorite browser and navigate to the following link: `https://www.sqlite.org/download.html`.
2. Scroll down the page to the **Precompiled Binaries for Windows** section.
3. Click **sqlite-tools-win32-x86-3380000.zip**. Note that the file might have a higher version number after this book is published, as shown in the following screenshot:

Figure 10.2: Downloading SQLite for Windows

4. Extract the ZIP file into a folder named `C:\Sqlite\`. Make sure that the extracted `sqlite3.exe` file is directly inside the `C:\SQLite` folder or the executable will not be found later when you try to use it.

5. In the Windows **Start** menu, navigate to **Settings**.

6. Search for `environment` and choose **Edit the system environment variables**. On non-English versions of Windows, please search for the equivalent word in your local language to find the setting.

7. Click the **Environment Variables** button.

8. In **System variables**, select **Path** in the list, and then click **Edit....**

9. If `C:\SQLite` is not already in the path, then click **New**, enter `C:\Sqlite`, and press *Enter*.

10. Click **OK**, click **OK**, click **OK**, and then close **Settings**.

Setting up SQLite for macOS

SQLite is included in macOS in the `/usr/bin/` directory as a command-line application named `sqlite3`.

Setting up SQLite for other OSes

SQLite can be downloaded and installed for other OSes from the following link: `https://www.sqlite.org/download.html`.

Creating the Northwind sample database for SQLite

Now we can create the Northwind sample database for SQLite using an SQL script:

1. If you have not previously cloned the GitHub repository for this book, then do so now using the following link: `https://github.com/markjprice/cs11dotnet7`.

2. Copy the script to create the Northwind database for SQLite from the following path in your local Git repository: `/sql-scripts/Northwind4SQLite.sql` into the `WorkingWithEFCore` folder.

3. Start a command line with administrator access level in the `WorkingWithEFCore` folder:

    *   On Windows, start **File Explorer**, right-click the `WorkingWithEFCore` folder, and select **New Command Prompt at Folder** or **Open in Windows Terminal**.

    *   On macOS, start **Finder**, right-click the `WorkingWithEFCore` folder, and select **New Terminal at Folder**.

4. Enter the command to execute the SQL script using SQLite and create the `Northwind.db` database, as shown in the following command:

    ```
    sqlite3 Northwind.db -init Northwind4SQLite.sql
    ```

5. Be patient because this command might take a while to create the database structure. Eventually, you will see the SQLite command prompt, as shown in the following output:

    ```
    -- Loading resources from Northwind4SQLite.sql
    SQLite version 3.38.0 2022-02-22 18:58:40
    ```

```
Enter ".help" for usage hints.
sqlite>
```

6. To exit SQLite command mode:

    - On Windows, press *Ctrl + C*
    - On macOS, press *Ctrl + D*

7. Leave your terminal or command prompt window open because you will use it again soon.

If you are using Visual Studio 2022

If you are using Visual Studio Code and the dotnet run command, then the compiled application executes in the WorkingWithEFCore folder so it will find the database file stored there.

But if you are using Visual Studio 2022 for Windows or Mac, then the compiled application executes in the WorkingWithEFCore\bin\Debug\net7.0 folder, so it will not find the database file because it is not in that directory.

Let's tell Visual Studio 2022 to copy the database file to the directory that it runs the code in so that it can find the file, but only if the database file is newer or is missing:

1. In **Solution Explorer**, right-click the Northwind.db file and select **Properties**.

2. In **Properties**, set **Copy to Output Directory** to **Copy if newer**.

3. In WorkingWithEFCore.csproj, note the new elements, as shown in the following markup:

    ```
    <ItemGroup>
      <None Update="Northwind.db">
        <CopyToOutputDirectory>PreserveNewest</CopyToOutputDirectory>
      </None>
    </ItemGroup>
    ```

 If you prefer to overwrite the data changes every time you start the project, then set CopyToOutputDirectory to Always.

Managing the Northwind sample database with SQLiteStudio

You can use a cross-platform graphical database manager named **SQLiteStudio** to easily manage SQLite databases:

1. Navigate to the following link, https://sqlitestudio.pl, and download and extract the application to your preferred location.

2. Start **SQLiteStudio**.

3. On the **Database** menu, choose **Add a database**.

4. In the **Database** dialog, in the **File** section, click on the yellow folder button to browse for an existing database file on the local computer, select the Northwind.db file in the WorkingWithEFCore folder, and then click **OK**, as shown in *Figure 10.3*:

Figure 10.3: Adding the Northwind.db database file to SQLiteStudio

5. Right-click on the **Northwind** database and choose **Connect to the database.** You will see the 10 tables that were created by the script. (The script for SQLite is simpler than the one for SQL Server; it does not create as many tables or other database objects.)

6. Right-click on the **Products** table and choose **Edit the table.**

7. In the table editor window, note the structure of the Products table, including column names, data types, keys, and constraints, as shown in *Figure 10.4*:

Figure 10.4: The table editor in SQLiteStudio showing the structure of the Products table

8. In the table editor window, click the **Data** tab, and you will see 77 products, as shown in *Figure 10.5*:

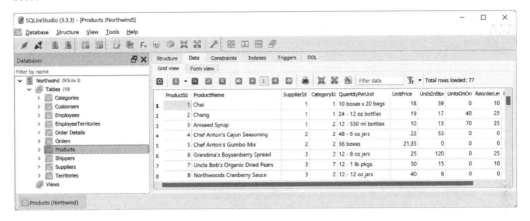

Figure 10.5: The Data tab showing the rows in the Products table

9. In the **Database** window, right-click **Northwind** and select **Disconnect from the database**.

10. Exit SQLiteStudio.

Using the lightweight ADO.NET provider for SQLite

Before Entity Framework, there was **ADO.NET**. This is a simpler and more efficient API for working with databases. It provides abstract classes like DbConnection, DbCommand, and DbReader, and provider-specific implementations of them like SqliteConnection and SqliteCommand.

The Entity Framework Core provider for SQLite is built on top of this library, but it can also be used independently for better performance. This book does not cover using this library, but you can learn more about it at the following link:

https://docs.microsoft.com/en-us/dotnet/standard/data/sqlite/

Using SQL Server for Windows

If you are using Windows and would prefer to use SQL Server (because enterprises that standardize on Windows tend to also use SQL Server as their database), please see the online instructions at the following link:

https://github.com/markjprice/cs11dotnet7/blob/main/docs/sql-server/README.md

Setting up EF Core

Before we dive into the practicalities of managing data using EF Core, let's briefly talk about choosing between EF Core database providers.

Choosing an EF Core database provider

To manage data in a specific database, we need classes that know how to efficiently talk to that database.

EF Core database providers are sets of classes that are optimized for a specific data store. There is even a provider for storing the data in the memory of the current process, which can be useful for high-performance unit testing since it avoids hitting an external system.

They are distributed as NuGet packages, as shown in the following table:

To manage this data store	Install this NuGet package
SQL Server 2012 or later	`Microsoft.EntityFrameworkCore.SqlServer`
SQLite 3.7 or later	`Microsoft.EntityFrameworkCore.SQLite`
In-memory	`Microsoft.EntityFrameworkCore.InMemory`
Azure Cosmos DB SQL API	`Microsoft.EntityFrameworkCore.Cosmos`
MySQL	`MySQL.EntityFrameworkCore`
Oracle DB 11.2	`Oracle.EntityFrameworkCore`
PostgreSQL	`Npgsql.EntityFrameworkCore.PostgreSQL`

You can install as many EF Core database providers in the same project as you need. Each package includes the shared types as well as provider-specific types.

Connecting to a database

To connect to a SQLite database, we just need to know the database filename, set using the parameter `Filename`. We specify this information in a **connection string**.

Defining the Northwind database context class

The `Northwind` class will be used to represent the database. To use EF Core, the class must inherit from `DbContext`. This class understands how to communicate with databases and dynamically generate SQL statements to query and manipulate data.

Your `DbContext`-derived class should have an overridden method named `OnConfiguring`, which will set the database connection string.

We will create a project that uses SQLite, but feel free to use SQL Server instead:

1. In the `WorkingWithEFCore` project, add a package reference to the EF Core provider for SQLite and globally and statically import the `System.Console` class for all C# files, as shown in the following markup:

    ```xml
    <ItemGroup>
      <Using Include="System.Console" Static="true" />
    </ItemGroup>
    <ItemGroup>
      <PackageReference
    ```

```
        Include="Microsoft.EntityFrameworkCore.Sqlite"
        Version="7.0.0" />
  </ItemGroup>
```

2.   Build the WorkingWithEFCore project to restore packages.

3.   Add a new class file named Northwind.cs.

4.   In Northwind.cs, import the main namespace for EF Core, define a class named Northwind, and make the class inherit from DbContext. Then, in an OnConfiguring method, configure the options builder to use SQLite, as shown in the following code:

```
using Microsoft.EntityFrameworkCore; // DbContext,
DbContextOptionsBuilder

namespace Packt.Shared;

// this manages the connection to the database
public class Northwind : DbContext
{
  protected override void OnConfiguring(
    DbContextOptionsBuilder optionsBuilder)
  {
    string path = Path.Combine(
      Environment.CurrentDirectory, "Northwind.db");

    string connection = $"Filename={path}";

    ConsoleColor previousColor = ForegroundColor;
    ForegroundColor = ConsoleColor.DarkYellow;
    WriteLine($"Connection: {connection}");
    ForegroundColor = previousColor;

    optionsBuilder.UseSqlite(connection);
  }
}
```

5.   In Program.cs, delete the existing statements. Then, import the Packt.Shared namespace and output the database provider, as shown in the following code:

```
using Packt.Shared;

Northwind db = new();
WriteLine($"Provider: {db.Database.ProviderName}");
```

6.   Run the console app and note the output showing the database connection string and which database provider you are using, as shown in the following output:

```
Connection: Filename=C:\cs11dotnet7\Chapter10\WorkingWithEFCore\bin\
Debug\net7.0\Northwind.db
Provider: Microsoft.EntityFrameworkCore.Sqlite
```

Defining EF Core models

EF Core uses a combination of **conventions, annotation attributes,** and **Fluent API** statements to build an **entity model** at runtime so that any actions performed on the classes can later be automatically translated into actions performed on the actual database. An **entity class** represents the structure of a table, and an instance of the class represents a row in that table.

First, we will review the three ways to define a model, with code examples, and then we will create some classes that implement those techniques.

Using EF Core conventions to define the model

The code we will write will use the following conventions:

- The name of a table is assumed to match the name of a `DbSet<T>` property in the `DbContext` class, for example, `Products`.
- The names of the columns are assumed to match the names of properties in the entity model class, for example, `ProductId`.
- The `string` .NET type is assumed to be a `nvarchar` type in the database.
- The `int` .NET type is assumed to be an `int` type in the database.
- The primary key is assumed to be a property that is named `Id` or `ID`, or when the entity model class is named `Product`, then the property can be named `ProductId` or `ProductID`. If this property is an integer type or the `Guid` type, then it is also assumed to be an `IDENTITY` column (a column type that automatically assigns a value when inserting).

 Good Practice: There are many other conventions that you should know, and you can even define your own, but that is beyond the scope of this book. You can read about them at the following link: `https://docs.microsoft.com/en-us/ef/core/modeling/`.

Using EF Core annotation attributes to define the model

Conventions often aren't enough to completely map the classes to the database objects. A simple way of adding more smarts to your model is to apply annotation attributes.

Some common attributes are shown in the following table:

Attribute	Description
`[Required]`	Ensures the value is not null.
`[StringLength(50)]`	Ensures the value is up to 50 characters in length.
`[RegularExpression(expression)]`	Ensures the value matches the specified regular expression.
`[Column(TypeName = "money",` `  Name = "UnitPrice")]`	Specifies the column type and column name used in the table.

For example, in the database, the maximum length of a product name is 40, and the value cannot be null, as shown highlighted in the following **Data Definition Language (DDL)** code that defines how to create a table named `Products` with its columns, data types, keys, and other constraints:

```
CREATE TABLE Products (
    ProductId       INTEGER       PRIMARY KEY,
    ProductName     NVARCHAR (40) NOT NULL,
    SupplierId      "INT",
    CategoryId      "INT",
    QuantityPerUnit NVARCHAR (20),
    UnitPrice       "MONEY"       CONSTRAINT DF_Products_UnitPrice DEFAULT (0),
    UnitsInStock    "SMALLINT"    CONSTRAINT DF_Products_UnitsInStock DEFAULT (0),
    UnitsOnOrder    "SMALLINT"    CONSTRAINT DF_Products_UnitsOnOrder DEFAULT (0),
    ReorderLevel    "SMALLINT"    CONSTRAINT DF_Products_ReorderLevel DEFAULT (0),
    Discontinued    "BIT"         NOT NULL
                                  CONSTRAINT DF_Products_Discontinued DEFAULT (0),
    CONSTRAINT FK_Products_Categories FOREIGN KEY (
        CategoryId
    )
    REFERENCES Categories (CategoryId),
    CONSTRAINT FK_Products_Suppliers FOREIGN KEY (
        SupplierId
    )
    REFERENCES Suppliers (SupplierId),
    CONSTRAINT CK_Products_UnitPrice CHECK (UnitPrice >= 0),
    CONSTRAINT CK_ReorderLevel CHECK (ReorderLevel >= 0),
    CONSTRAINT CK_UnitsInStock CHECK (UnitsInStock >= 0),
    CONSTRAINT CK_UnitsOnOrder CHECK (UnitsOnOrder >= 0)
);
```

In a `Product` class, we could apply attributes to specify this, as shown in the following code:

```
[Required]
[StringLength(40)]
public string ProductName { get; set; }
```

When there isn't an obvious map between .NET types and database types, an attribute can be used.

For example, in the database, the column type of `UnitPrice` for the `Products` table is money. .NET does not have a money type, so it should use `decimal` instead, as shown in the following code:

```
[Column(TypeName = "money")]
public decimal? UnitPrice { get; set; }
```

Using the EF Core Fluent API to define the model

The last way that the model can be defined is by using the Fluent API. This API can be used instead of attributes, as well as being used in addition to them. For example, to define the `ProductName` property, instead of decorating the property with two attributes, an equivalent Fluent API statement could be written in the `OnModelCreating` method of the database context class, as shown in the following code:

```
modelBuilder.Entity<Product>()
    .Property(product => product.ProductName)
    .IsRequired()
    .HasMaxLength(40);
```

This keeps the entity model class simpler.

Understanding data seeding with the Fluent API

Another benefit of the Fluent API is to provide initial data to populate a database. EF Core automatically works out what insert, update, or delete operations must be executed.

For example, if we wanted to make sure that a new database has at least one row in the `Product` table, then we would call the `HasData` method, as shown in the following code:

```
modelBuilder.Entity<Product>()
    .HasData(new Product
    {
        ProductId = 1,
        ProductName = "Chai",
        UnitPrice = 8.99M
    });
```

Our model will map to an existing database that is already populated with data, so we will not need to use this technique in our code.

Building EF Core models for the Northwind tables

Now that you've learned about ways to define EF Core models, let's build models to represent two of the tables in the `Northwind` database.

The two entity classes will refer to each other, so to avoid compiler errors, we will create the classes without any members first:

1. In the `WorkingWithEFCore` project, add two class files named `Category.cs` and `Product.cs`.
2. In `Category.cs`, define a class named `Category`, as shown in the following code:

    ```
    namespace Packt.Shared;

    public class Category
    {
    }
    ```

3. In `Product.cs`, define a class named `Product`, as shown in the following code:

```
namespace Packt.Shared;

public class Product
{
}
```

Defining the Category and Product entity classes

The `Category` class, also known as an entity model, will be used to represent a row in the `Categories` table. This table has four columns, as shown in the following DDL:

```
CREATE TABLE Categories (
    CategoryId    INTEGER         PRIMARY KEY,
    CategoryName NVARCHAR (15) NOT NULL,
    Description  "NTEXT",
    Picture      "IMAGE"
);
```

We will use conventions to define:

- Three of the four properties (we will not map the `Picture` column).
- The primary key.
- The one-to-many relationship to the `Products` table.

To map the `Description` column to the correct database type, we will need to decorate the `string` property with the `Column` attribute.

Later in this chapter, we will use the Fluent API to define that `CategoryName` cannot be null and is limited to a maximum of 15 characters.

Let's go:

1. Modify the `Category` entity model class, as shown in the following code:

```
using System.ComponentModel.DataAnnotations.Schema; // [Column]

namespace Packt.Shared;

public class Category
{
    // these properties map to columns in the database
    public int CategoryId { get; set; }

    public string? CategoryName { get; set; }

    [Column(TypeName = "ntext")]
    public string? Description { get; set; }
```

```
      // defines a navigation property for related rows
      public virtual ICollection<Product> Products { get; set; }

      public Category()
      {
        // to enable developers to add products to a Category, we must
        // initialize the navigation property to an empty collection
        Products = new HashSet<Product>();
      }
    }
```

Note the following:

- The `Product` class will be used to represent a row in the `Products` table, which has ten columns.

- You do not need to include all columns from a table as properties of a class. We will only map six properties: `ProductId`, `ProductName`, `UnitPrice`, `UnitsInStock`, `Discontinued`, and `CategoryId`.

- Columns that are not mapped to properties cannot be read or set using the class instances. If you use the class to create a new object, then the new row in the table will have `NULL` or some other default value for the unmapped column values in that row. You must make sure that those missing columns are optional or have default values set by the database or an exception will be thrown at runtime. In this scenario, the rows already have data values and I have decided that I do not need to read those values in this application.

- We can rename a column by defining a property with a different name, like `Cost`, and then decorating the property with the `[Column]` attribute and specifying its column name, like `UnitPrice`.

- The final property, `CategoryId`, is associated with a `Category` property that will be used to map each product to its parent category.

2. Modify the `Product` class, as shown in the following code:

```
using System.ComponentModel.DataAnnotations; // [Required], [StringLength]
using System.ComponentModel.DataAnnotations.Schema; // [Column]

namespace Packt.Shared;

public class Product
{
  public int ProductId { get; set; } // primary key

  [Required]
```

```
    [StringLength(40)]
    public string ProductName { get; set; } = null!;

    [Column("UnitPrice", TypeName = "money")]
    public decimal? Cost { get; set; } // property name != column name

    [Column("UnitsInStock")]
    public short? Stock { get; set; }

    public bool Discontinued { get; set; }

    // these two define the foreign key relationship
    // to the Categories table
    public int CategoryId { get; set; }
    public virtual Category Category { get; set; } = null!;
}
```

The two properties that relate the two entities, `Category.Products` and `Product.Category`, are both marked as `virtual`. This allows EF Core to inherit and override the properties to provide extra features, such as lazy loading.

Adding tables to the Northwind database context class

Inside your `DbContext`-derived class, you must define at least one property of the `DbSet<T>` type. These properties represent the tables. To tell EF Core what columns each table has, the `DbSet<T>` properties use generics to specify a class that represents a row in the table. That entity model class has properties that represent its columns.

The `DbContext`-derived class can optionally have an overridden method named `OnModelCreating`. This is where you can write Fluent API statements as an alternative to decorating your entity classes with attributes.

Let's write the code:

- Modify the `Northwind` class to add statements to define two properties for the two tables and an `OnModelCreating` method, as shown highlighted in the following code:

```
public class Northwind : DbContext
{
    // these properties map to tables in the database
    public DbSet<Category>? Categories { get; set; }
    public DbSet<Product>? Products { get; set; }

    protected override void OnConfiguring(
      DbContextOptionsBuilder optionsBuilder)
    {
      ...
    }
```

```
protected override void OnModelCreating(
  ModelBuilder modelBuilder)
{
  // example of using Fluent API instead of attributes
  // to limit the length of a category name to 15
  modelBuilder.Entity<Category>()
    .Property(category => category.CategoryName)
    .IsRequired() // NOT NULL
    .HasMaxLength(15);

  if (Database.ProviderName?.Contains("Sqlite") ?? false)
  {
    // added to "fix" the lack of decimal support in SQLite
    modelBuilder.Entity<Product>()
      .Property(product => product.Cost)
      .HasConversion<double>();
  }
}
}
```

In EF Core 3.0 and later, the decimal type is not supported by the SQLite database provider for sorting and other operations. We can fix this by telling the model that decimal values can be converted into double values when using the SQLite database provider. This does not actually perform any conversion at runtime.

Now that you have seen some examples of defining an entity model manually, let's see a tool that can do some of the work for you.

Setting up the dotnet-ef tool

The .NET CLI tool named dotnet can be extended with capabilities useful for working with EF Core. It can perform design-time tasks like creating and applying migrations from an older model to a newer model and generating code for a model from an existing database.

The dotnet ef command-line tool is not automatically installed. You must install this package as either a **global** or **local tool**. If you have already installed an older version of the tool, then you should uninstall any existing version:

1. At a command prompt or terminal, check if you have already installed dotnet-ef as a global tool, as shown in the following command:

   ```
   dotnet tool list --global
   ```

2. Check in the list if an older version of the tool has been installed, like the one for .NET Core 3.1, as shown in the following output:

   ```
   Package Id        Version      Commands
   ------------------------------------------
   ```

```
dotnet-ef        3.1.0        dotnet-ef
```

3. If an old version is already installed, then uninstall the tool, as shown in the following command:

```
dotnet tool uninstall --global dotnet-ef
```

4. Install the latest version, as shown in the following command:

```
dotnet tool install --global dotnet-ef
```

 If necessary, follow any OS-specific instructions to add the dotnet tools directory to your PATH environment variable, as described in the output of installing the dotnet-ef tool.

Scaffolding models using an existing database

Scaffolding is the process of using a tool to create classes that represent the model of an existing database using reverse engineering. A good scaffolding tool allows you to extend the automatically generated classes and then regenerate those classes without losing your extended classes.

If you know that you will never regenerate the classes using the tool, then feel free to change the code for the automatically generated classes as much as you want. The code generated by the tool is just the best approximation.

 Good Practice: Do not be afraid to overrule a tool when you know better.

Let's see if the tool generates the same model as we did manually:

1. Add the latest version of the Microsoft.EntityFrameworkCore.Design package to the WorkingWithEFCore project.

2. At a command prompt or terminal in the WorkingWithEFCore folder, generate a model for the Categories and Products tables in a new folder named AutoGenModels, as shown in the following command:

```
dotnet ef dbcontext scaffold "Filename=Northwind.db" Microsoft.
EntityFrameworkCore.Sqlite --table Categories --table Products --output-
dir AutoGenModels --namespace WorkingWithEFCore.AutoGen --data-
annotations --context Northwind
```

Note the following:

-   The command action: dbcontext scaffold
-   The connection string: "Filename=Northwind.db"
-   The database provider: Microsoft.EntityFrameworkCore.Sqlite

- The tables to generate models for: `--table Categories --table Products`
- The output folder: `--output-dir AutoGenModels`
- The namespace: `--namespace WorkingWithEFCore.AutoGen`
- To use data annotations as well as the Fluent API: `--data-annotations`
- To rename the context from `[database_name]Context`: `--context Northwind`

3. Note the build messages and warnings, as shown in the following output:

```
Build started...
Build succeeded.
To protect potentially sensitive information in your connection string,
you should move it out of source code. You can avoid scaffolding the
connection string by using the Name= syntax to read it from configuration
- see https://go.microsoft.com/fwlink/?linkid=2131148. For more
guidance on storing connection strings, see http://go.microsoft.com/
fwlink/?LinkId=723263.
Skipping foreign key with identity '0' on table 'Products' since
principal table 'Suppliers' was not found in the model. This usually
happens when the principal table was not included in the selection set.
```

4. Open the `AutoGenModels` folder and note the three class files that were automatically generated: `Category.cs`, `Northwind.cs`, and `Product.cs`.

5. Open `Category.cs` and note the differences compared to the one you created manually, as shown in the following code:

```csharp
using System;
using System.Collections.Generic;
using System.ComponentModel.DataAnnotations;
using System.ComponentModel.DataAnnotations.Schema;
using Microsoft.EntityFrameworkCore;

namespace WorkingWithEFCore.AutoGen
{
  [Index("CategoryName", Name = "CategoryName")]
  public partial class Category
  {
    public Category()
    {
      Products = new HashSet<Product>();
    }

    [Key]
    public long CategoryId { get; set; }
    [Column(TypeName = "nvarchar (15)")]
    public string CategoryName { get; set; }
    [Column(TypeName = "ntext")]
    public string? Description { get; set; }
    [Column(TypeName = "image")]
    public byte[]? Picture { get; set; }
```

```
        [InverseProperty("Category")]
        public virtual ICollection<Product> Products { get; set; }
    }
}
```

Note the following:

- It decorates the entity class with the [Index] attribute that was introduced in EF Core 5.0. This indicates properties that should have an index. In earlier versions, only the Fluent API was supported for defining indexes. Since we are working with an existing database, this is not needed. But if we wanted to recreate a new empty database from our code, then this information would be needed.

- The table name in the database is Categories but the dotnet-ef tool uses the **Humanizer** third-party library to automatically singularize the class name to Category, which is a more natural name when creating a single entity.

- The entity class is declared using the partial keyword so that you can create a matching partial class for adding additional code. This allows you to rerun the tool and regenerate the entity class without losing that extra code.

- The CategoryId property is decorated with the [Key] attribute to indicate that it is the primary key for this entity. The data type for this property is int for SQL Server and long for SQLite.

- The Products property uses the [InverseProperty] attribute to define the foreign key relationship to the Category property on the Product entity class.

6. Open Product.cs and note the differences compared to the one you created manually.

7. Open Northwind.cs and note the differences compared to the one you created manually, as shown in the following edited-for-space code:

```
using Microsoft.EntityFrameworkCore;

namespace WorkingWithEFCore.AutoGen
{
  public partial class Northwind : DbContext
  {
    public Northwind()
    {
    }

    public Northwind(DbContextOptions<Northwind> options)
      : base(options)
    {
    }

    public virtual DbSet<Category> Categories { get; set; } = null!;
    public virtual DbSet<Product> Products { get; set; } = null!;
```

```
    protected override void OnConfiguring(
      DbContextOptionsBuilder optionsBuilder)
    {
      if (!optionsBuilder.IsConfigured)
      {
#warning To protect potentially sensitive information in your connection
string, you should move it out of source code. You can avoid scaffolding
the connection string by using the Name= syntax to read it from
configuration - see https://go.microsoft.com/fwlink/?linkid=2131148. For
more guidance on storing connection strings, see http://go.microsoft.com/
fwlink/?LinkId=723263.
        optionsBuilder.UseSqlite("Filename=Northwind.db");
      }
    }

    protected override void OnModelCreating(ModelBuilder modelBuilder)
    {
      modelBuilder.Entity<Category>(entity =>
      {
        ...
      });
      modelBuilder.Entity<Product>(entity =>
      {
        ...
      });
      OnModelCreatingPartial(modelBuilder);
    }
    partial void OnModelCreatingPartial(ModelBuilder modelBuilder);
  }
}
```

Note the following:

- The Northwind data context class is partial to allow you to extend it and regenerate it in the future.

- It has two constructors: a default parameter-less one and one that allows options to be passed in. This is useful in apps where you want to specify the connection string at runtime.

- The two DbSet<T> properties that represent the Categories and Products tables are set to the null-forgiving value to prevent static compiler analysis warnings at compile time. It has no effect at runtime.

- In the OnConfiguring method, if options have not been specified in the constructor, then it defaults to using a connection string that looks for the database file in the current folder. It has a compiler warning to remind you that you should not hardcode security information in this connection string.

- In the `OnModelCreating` method, the Fluent API is used to configure the two entity classes, and then a partial method named `OnModelCreatingPartial` is invoked. This allows you to implement that partial method in your own partial `Northwind` class to add your own Fluent API configuration that will not be lost if you regenerate the model classes.

8. Close the automatically generated class files.

Customizing the reverse engineering templates

One of the new features introduced with EF Core 7 is the ability to customize the code that is automatically generated by the `dotnet-ef` scaffolding tool. This is an advanced technique, so I do not cover it in this book. Usually, it is easier to just modify the code that is generated by default anyway.

If you would like to learn how to modify the T4 templates used by the `dotnet-ef` scaffolding tool, then you can find that information at the following link:

`https://learn.microsoft.com/en-us/ef/core/managing-schemas/scaffolding/templates`

Configuring preconvention models

Along with support for the `DateOnly` and `TimeOnly` types for use with the SQLite database provider, one of the new features introduced with EF Core 6 was configuring preconvention models.

As models become more complex, relying on conventions to discover entity types and their properties and successfully map them to tables and columns becomes harder. It would be useful if you could configure the conventions themselves before they are used to analyze and build a model.

For example, you might want to define a convention to say that all `string` properties should have a maximum length of 50 characters as a default, or any property types that implement a custom interface should not be mapped, as shown in the following code:

```
protected override void ConfigureConventions(
  ModelConfigurationBuilder configurationBuilder)
{
  configurationBuilder.Properties<string>().HaveMaxLength(50);
  configurationBuilder.IgnoreAny<IDoNotMap>();
}
```

In the rest of this chapter, we will use the classes that you manually created.

Querying EF Core models

Now that we have a model that maps to the Northwind database and two of its tables, we can write some simple LINQ queries to fetch data. You will learn much more about writing LINQ queries in *Chapter 11, Querying and Manipulating Data Using LINQ*.

For now, just write the code and view the results:

1. Add a new class file named `Program.Helpers.cs`.

2. In `Program.Helpers.cs`, add a partial `Program` class with a `SectionTitle` method, as shown in the following code:

```
partial class Program
{
  static void SectionTitle(string title)
  {
    ConsoleColor previousColor = ForegroundColor;
    ForegroundColor = ConsoleColor.Yellow;
    WriteLine("*");
    WriteLine($"* {title}");
    WriteLine("*");
    ForegroundColor = previousColor;
  }

  static void Fail(string message)
  {
    ConsoleColor previousColor = ForegroundColor;
    ForegroundColor = ConsoleColor.Red;
    WriteLine($"Fail > {message}");
    ForegroundColor = previousColor;
  }

  static void Info(string message)
  {
    ConsoleColor previousColor = ForegroundColor;
    ForegroundColor = ConsoleColor.Cyan;
    WriteLine($"Info > {message}");
    ForegroundColor = previousColor;
  }
}
```

3. Add a new class file named `Program.Queries.cs`.

4. In `Program.Queries.cs`, define a partial `Program` class with a `QueryingCategories` method, and add statements to do these tasks, as shown in the following code:

    *   Create an instance of the `Northwind` class that will manage the database. Database context instances are designed for short lifetimes in a unit of work. They should be disposed of as soon as possible, so we will wrap it in a using statement. In *Chapter 13, Building Websites Using ASP.NET Core Razor Pages*, you will learn how to get a database context using dependency injection.

    *   Create a query for all categories that includes their related products. `Include` is an extension method that requires you to import the `Microsoft.EntityFrameworkCore` namespace.

- Enumerate through the categories, outputting the name and number of products for each one:

```
using Microsoft.EntityFrameworkCore; // Include extension method
using Packt.Shared; // Northwind, Category, Product

partial class Program
{
  static void QueryingCategories()
  {
    using (Northwind db = new())
    {
      SectionTitle("Categories and how many products they have:");

      // a query to get all categories and their related products
      IQueryable<Category>? categories = db.Categories?
        .Include(c => c.Products);

      if ((categories is null) || (!categories.Any()))
      {
        Fail("No categories found.");
        return;
      }

      // execute query and enumerate results
      foreach (Category c in categories)
      {
        WriteLine($"{c.CategoryName} has {c.Products.Count}
products.");
      }
    }
  }
}
```

 Note that the order of the clauses in the `if` statement is important. We must check that `categories` is `null` first. If this is `true`, then the code will never execute the second clause and therefore won't throw a `NullReferenceException` when accessing the `Any()` member.

5. In `Program.cs`, comment out the two statements that create a Northwind instance and output the database provider name, and then call the `QueryingCategories` method, as shown in the following code:

```
QueryingCategories();
```

6. Run the code and view the result (if run with Visual Studio 2022 for Windows using the SQLite database provider), as shown in the following partial output:

```
Beverages has 12 products.
Condiments has 12 products.
Confections has 13 products.
Dairy Products has 10 products.
Grains/Cereals has 7 products.
Meat/Poultry has 6 products.
Produce has 5 products.
Seafood has 12 products.
```

If you run with Visual Studio Code using the SQLite database provider, then the path will be the WorkingWithEFCore folder.

Warning! If you see the following exception when using SQLite with Visual Studio 2022, the most likely problem is that the Northwind.db file is not being copied to the output directory. Make sure **Copy to Output Directory** is set to **Copy if newer:**

```
Unhandled exception. Microsoft.Data.Sqlite.SqliteException
(0x80004005): SQLite Error 1: 'no such table: Categories'.
```

Filtering included entities

EF Core 5 introduced **filtered includes**, which means you can specify a lambda expression in the Include method call to filter which entities are returned in the results:

1. In Program.Queries.cs, define a FilteredIncludes method, and add statements to do these tasks, as shown in the following code:

    •   Create an instance of the Northwind class that will manage the database.

    •   Prompt the user to enter a minimum value for units in stock.

    •   Create a query for categories that have products with that minimum number of units in stock.

    •   Enumerate through the categories and products, outputting the name and units in stock for each one:

    ```
    static void FilteredIncludes()
    {
      using (Northwind db = new())
      {
        SectionTitle("Products with a minimum number of units in
    stock.");

        string? input;
        int stock;

        do
    ```

```
        {
          Write("Enter a minimum for units in stock: ");
          input = ReadLine();
        } while (!int.TryParse(input, out stock));

        IQueryable<Category>? categories = db.Categories?
          .Include(c => c.Products.Where(p => p.Stock >= stock));

        if ((categories is null) || (!categories.Any()))
        {
          Fail("No categories found.");
          return;
        }

        foreach (Category c in categories)
        {
          WriteLine($"{c.CategoryName} has {c.Products.Count} products
          with a minimum of {stock} units in stock.");

          foreach(Product p in c.Products)
          {
            WriteLine($"  {p.ProductName} has {p.Stock} units in
            stock.");
          }
        }
      }
    }
```

2. In `Program.cs`, call the `FilteredIncludes` method, as shown in the following code:

```
FilteredIncludes();
```

3. Run the code, enter a minimum for units in stock like `100`, and view the result, as shown in the following partial output:

```
Enter a minimum for units in stock: 100
Beverages has 2 products with a minimum of 100 units in stock.
  Sasquatch Ale has 111 units in stock.
  Rhönbräu Klosterbier has 125 units in stock.
Condiments has 2 products with a minimum of 100 units in stock.
  Grandma's Boysenberry Spread has 120 units in stock.
  Sirop d'érable has 113 units in stock.
Confections has 0 products with a minimum of 100 units in stock.
Dairy Products has 1 products with a minimum of 100 units in stock.
  Geitost has 112 units in stock.
Grains/Cereals has 1 products with a minimum of 100 units in stock.
  Gustaf's Knäckebröd has 104 units in stock.
Meat/Poultry has 1 products with a minimum of 100 units in stock.
  Pâté chinois has 115 units in stock.
```

```
Produce has 0 products with a minimum of 100 units in stock.
Seafood has 3 products with a minimum of 100 units in stock.
 Inlagd Sill has 112 units in stock.
 Boston Crab Meat has 123 units in stock.
 Röd Kaviar has 101 units in stock.
```

Unicode characters in the Windows console: There is a limitation with the console provided by Microsoft on versions of Windows before the Windows 10 Fall Creators Update. By default, the console cannot display Unicode characters, for example, in the name Rhönbräu.

If you have this issue, then you can temporarily change the code page (also known as the character set) in a console to Unicode UTF-8 by entering the following command at the prompt before running the app:

```
chcp 65001
```

Filtering and sorting products

Let's explore a more complex query that will filter and sort data:

1. In `Program.Queries.cs`, define a `QueryingProducts` method, and add statements to do the following, as shown in the following code:

    *   Create an instance of the `Northwind` class that will manage the database.
    *   Prompt the user for a price for products.
    *   Create a query for products that cost more than the price using LINQ.
    *   Loop through the results, outputting the ID, name, cost (formatted in US dollars), and the number of units in stock:

    ```
    static void QueryingProducts()
    {
      using (Northwind db = new())
      {
        SectionTitle("Products that cost more than a price, highest at
    top.");

        string? input;
        decimal price;

        do
        {
          Write("Enter a product price: ");
          input = ReadLine();
    ```

```
    } while (!decimal.TryParse(input, out price));

    IQueryable<Product>? products = db.Products?
      .Where(product => product.Cost > price)
      .OrderByDescending(product => product.Cost);

    if ((products is null) || (!products.Any()))
    {
      Fail("No products found.");
      return;
    }

    foreach (Product p in products)
    {
      WriteLine(
        "{0}: {1} costs {2:$#,##0.00} and has {3} in stock.",
        p.ProductId, p.ProductName, p.Cost, p.Stock);
    }
  }
}
```

 Checking for "not any" by calling !products.Any() is more efficient than checking for a count of zero as shown in the following code: products.Count() == 0.

2. In Program.cs, call the QueryingProducts method.

3. Run the code, enter 50 when prompted to enter a product price, and view the result, as shown in the following partial output:

```
Enter a product price: 50
38: Côte de Blaye costs $263.50 and has 17 in stock.
29: Thüringer Rostbratwurst costs $123.79 and has 0 in stock.
9: Mishi Kobe Niku costs $97.00 and has 29 in stock.
20: Sir Rodney's Marmalade costs $81.00 and has 40 in stock.
18: Carnarvon Tigers costs $62.50 and has 42 in stock.
59: Raclette Courdavault costs $55.00 and has 79 in stock.
51: Manjimup Dried Apples costs $53.00 and has 20 in stock.
```

4. Run the code, enter 500 when prompted to enter a product price, and view the result, as shown in the following output:

```
Fail > No products found.
```

Getting the generated SQL

You might be wondering how well written the SQL statements are that are generated from the C# queries we write. EF Core 5 introduced a quick and easy way to see the SQL generated:

1. In the `FilteredIncludes` method, before using the `foreach` statement to enumerate the query, add a statement to output the generated SQL, as shown in the following code:

   ```
   Info($"ToQueryString: {categories.ToQueryString()}");
   ```

2. In the `QueryingProducts` method, before using the `foreach` statement to enumerate the query, add a statement to output the generated SQL, as shown in the following code:

   ```
   Info($"ToQueryString: {products.ToQueryString()}");
   ```

3. Run the code, enter a minimum for units in stock like 99, and view the result, as shown in the following partial output:

```
Enter a minimum for units in stock: 99
Connection: Filename=C:\cs11dotnet7\Chapter10\WorkingWithEFCore\bin\
Debug\net7.0\Northwind.db
Info > ToQueryString: .param set @__stock_0 99
SELECT "c"."CategoryId", "c"."CategoryName", "c"."Description",
"t"."ProductId", "t"."CategoryId", "t"."UnitPrice", "t"."Discontinued",
"t"."ProductName", "t"."UnitsInStock"
FROM "Categories" AS "c"
LEFT JOIN (
    SELECT "p"."ProductId", "p"."CategoryId", "p"."UnitPrice",
"p"."Discontinued", "p"."ProductName", "p"."UnitsInStock"
    FROM "Products" AS "p"
    WHERE "p"."UnitsInStock" >= @__stock_0
) AS "t" ON "c"."CategoryId" = "t"."CategoryId"
ORDER BY "c"."CategoryId"
Beverages has 2 products with a minimum of 99 units in stock.
  Sasquatch Ale has 111 units in stock.
  Rhönbräu Klosterbier has 125 units in stock.
...
```

Note the SQL parameter named *@__stock_0* has been set to a minimum stock value of 99.

If you had used SQL Server, the generated SQL is slightly different. For example, it uses square brackets instead of double quotes around object names, as shown in the following output:

```
Info > ToQueryString: DECLARE @__stock_0 smallint = CAST(99 AS smallint);

SELECT [c].[CategoryId], [c].[CategoryName], [c].[Description], [t].
[ProductId], [t].[CategoryId], [t].[UnitPrice], [t].[Discontinued], [t].
[ProductName], [t].[UnitsInStock]
FROM [Categories] AS [c]
LEFT JOIN (
```

```
    SELECT [p].[ProductId], [p].[CategoryId], [p].[UnitPrice], [p].
[Discontinued], [p].[ProductName], [p].[UnitsInStock]
    FROM [Products] AS [p]
    WHERE [p].[UnitsInStock] >= @__stock_0
) AS [t] ON [c].[CategoryId] = [t].[CategoryId]
ORDER BY [c].[CategoryId]
```

Logging EF Core

To monitor the interaction between EF Core and the database, we can enable logging. Logging could be to the console, to Debug or Trace, or to a file.

By default, EF Core logging will exclude any data in case it is sensitive. You can include this data by calling the EnableSensitiveDataLogging method, especially during development. You should disable it again before deploying to production.

Let's see an example of this in action:

1. In Northwind.cs, at the bottom of the OnConfiguring method, add a statement to log to the console, as shown in the following code:

    ```
    optionsBuilder.LogTo(WriteLine) // Console
        .EnableSensitiveDataLogging();
    ```

    > LogTo requires an Action<string> delegate. EF Core will call this delegate, passing a string value for each log message. Passing the Console class WriteLine method, therefore, tells the logger to write each method to the console.

2. Run the code and view the log messages, which are partially shown in the following output:

    ```
    ...
    dbug: 05/03/2022 12:36:11.702 RelationalEventId.ConnectionOpening[20000]
    (Microsoft.EntityFrameworkCore.Database.Connection)
          Opening connection to database 'main' on server 'C:\cs11dotnet7\
    Chapter10\WorkingWithEFCore\bin\Debug\net7.0\Northwind.db'.
    dbug: 05/03/2022 12:36:11.718 RelationalEventId.ConnectionOpened[20001]
    (Microsoft.EntityFrameworkCore.Database.Connection)
          Opened connection to database 'main' on server 'C:\cs11dotnet7\
    Chapter10\WorkingWithEFCore\bin\Debug\net7.0\Northwind.db'.
    dbug: 05/03/2022 12:36:11.721 RelationalEventId.CommandExecuting[20100]
    (Microsoft.EntityFrameworkCore.Database.Command)

          Executing DbCommand [Parameters=[], CommandType='Text',
    CommandTimeout='30']
          SELECT "c"."CategoryId", "c"."CategoryName", "c"."Description",
    "p"."ProductId", "p"."CategoryId", "p"."UnitPrice", "p"."Discontinued",
    "p"."ProductName", "p"."UnitsInStock"
          FROM "Categories" AS "c"
    ```

```
        LEFT JOIN "Products" AS "p" ON "c"."CategoryId" = "p"."CategoryId"
        ORDER BY "c"."CategoryId"
    ...
```

Your logs might vary from those shown above based on your chosen database provider and code editor, and future improvements to EF Core. For now, note that different events like opening a connection or executing a command have different event IDs, as shown in the following list:

- 20000 `RelationalEventId.ConnectionOpening`: Includes the database file path.
- 20001 `RelationalEventId.ConnectionOpened`: Includes the database file path.
- 20100 `RelationalEventId.CommandExecuting`: Includes the SQL statement.

Filtering logs by provider-specific values

The event ID values and what they mean will be specific to the EF Core provider. If we want to know how the LINQ query has been translated into SQL statements and is executing, then the event ID to output has an `Id` value of `20100`:

1. Modify the `LogTo` method call to only output events with an `Id` of `20100`, as shown highlighted in the following code:

```
optionsBuilder.LogTo(WriteLine, // Console
  new[] { RelationalEventId.CommandExecuting })
  .EnableSensitiveDataLogging();
```

2. Run the code, and note the following SQL statements that were logged, as shown in the following output that has been edited for space:

```
dbug: 05/03/2022 12:48:43.153 RelationalEventId.CommandExecuting[20100]
(Microsoft.EntityFrameworkCore.Database.Command)
      Executing DbCommand [Parameters=[], CommandType='Text',
CommandTimeout='30']
      SELECT "c"."CategoryId", "c"."CategoryName", "c"."Description",
"p"."ProductId", "p"."CategoryId", "p"."UnitPrice", "p"."Discontinued",
"p"."ProductName", "p"."UnitsInStock"
      FROM "Categories" AS "c"
      LEFT JOIN "Products" AS "p" ON "c"."CategoryId" = "p"."CategoryId"
      ORDER BY "c"."CategoryId"
Beverages has 12 products.
Condiments has 12 products.
Confections has 13 products.
Dairy Products has 10 products.
Grains/Cereals has 7 products.
Meat/Poultry has 6 products.
Produce has 5 products.
Seafood has 12 products.
```

Logging with query tags

When logging LINQ queries, it can be tricky to correlate log messages in complex scenarios. EF Core 2.2 introduced the query tags feature to help by allowing you to add SQL comments to the log.

You can annotate a LINQ query using the `TagWith` method, as shown in the following code:

```
IQueryable<Product>? products = db.Products?
  .TagWith("Products filtered by price and sorted.")
  .Where(product => product.Cost > price)
  .OrderByDescending(product => product.Cost);
```

This will add a SQL comment to the log, as shown in the following output:

```
-- Products filtered by price and sorted.
```

Pattern matching with Like

EF Core supports common SQL statements including `Like` for pattern matching:

1. In `Program.Queries.cs`, add a method named `QueryingWithLike`, as shown in the following code, and note:

    - We have enabled logging.
    - We prompt the user to enter part of a product name and then use the `EF.Functions.Like` method to search anywhere in the `ProductName` property.
    - For each matching product, we output its name, stock, and if it is discontinued:

    ```csharp
    static void QueryingWithLike()
    {
      using (Northwind db = new())
      {
        SectionTitle("Pattern matching with LIKE.");

        Write("Enter part of a product name: ");
        string? input = ReadLine();

        if (string.IsNullOrWhiteSpace(input))
        {
          Fail("You did not enter part of a product name.");
          return;
        }

        IQueryable<Product>? products = db.Products?
          .Where(p => EF.Functions.Like(p.ProductName, $"%{input}%"));

        if ((products is null) || (!products.Any()))
    ```

```
        {
            Fail("No products found.");
            return;
        }

        foreach (Product p in products)
        {
            WriteLine("{0} has {1} units in stock. Discontinued? {2}",
                p.ProductName, p.Stock, p.Discontinued);
        }
    }
}
```

2. In `Program.cs`, comment out the existing methods, and call `QueryingWithLike`.

3. Run the code, enter a partial product name such as `che`, and view the result, as shown in the following edited output:

```
Enter part of a product name: che
dbug: 05/03/2022 13:03:42.793 RelationalEventId.CommandExecuting[20100]
(Microsoft.EntityFrameworkCore.Database.Command)
        Executing DbCommand [Parameters=[@__Format_1='%che%' (Size = 5)],
CommandType='Text', CommandTimeout='30']
        SELECT "p"."ProductId", "p"."CategoryId", "p"."UnitPrice",
"p"."Discontinued", "p"."ProductName", "p"."UnitsInStock"
        FROM "Products" AS "p"
        WHERE "p"."ProductName" LIKE @__Format_1
Chef Anton's Cajun Seasoning has 53 units in stock. Discontinued? False
Chef Anton's Gumbo Mix has 0 units in stock. Discontinued? True
Queso Manchego La Pastora has 86 units in stock. Discontinued? False
Gumbär Gummibärchen has 15 units in stock. Discontinued? False
```

Generating a random number in queries

EF Core 6 introduced a useful function, `EF.Functions.Random`, that maps to a database function returning a pseudo-random number between 0 and 1 exclusive. For example, you could multiply the random number by the count of rows in a table to select one random row from that table:

1. In `Program.Queries.cs`, add a method named `GetRandomProduct`, as shown in the following code:

```
static void GetRandomProduct()
{
    using (Northwind db = new())
    {
        SectionTitle("Get a random product.");

        int? rowCount = db.Products?.Count();
```

```
      if (rowCount == null)
      {
        Fail("Products table is empty.");
        return;
      }

      Product? p = db.Products?.FirstOrDefault(
        p => p.ProductId == (int)(EF.Functions.Random() * rowCount));

      if (p == null)
      {
        Fail("Product not found.");
        return;
      }

      WriteLine($"Random product: {p.ProductId} {p.ProductName}");
    }
  }
```

2. In `Program.cs`, call `GetRandomProduct`.

3. Run the code and view the result, as shown in the following output:

```
dbug: 05/03/2022 13:19:01.783 RelationalEventId.CommandExecuting[20100]
(Microsoft.EntityFrameworkCore.Database.Command)
      Executing DbCommand [Parameters=[], CommandType='Text',
CommandTimeout='30']
      SELECT COUNT(*)
      FROM "Products" AS "p"
dbug: 05/03/2022 13:19:01.848 RelationalEventId.CommandExecuting[20100]
(Microsoft.EntityFrameworkCore.Database.Command)
      Executing DbCommand [Parameters=[@__p_1='77' (Nullable = true)],
CommandType='Text', CommandTimeout='30']
      SELECT "p"."ProductId", "p"."CategoryId", "p"."UnitPrice",
"p"."Discontinued", "p"."ProductName", "p"."UnitsInStock"
      FROM "Products" AS "p"
      WHERE "p"."ProductId" = CAST((abs(random() /
9.2233720368547799E+18) * @__p_1) AS INTEGER)
      LIMIT 1
Random product: 42 Singaporean Hokkien Fried Mee
```

Defining global filters

Northwind products can be discontinued, so it might be useful to ensure that discontinued products are never returned in results, even if the programmer does not use `Where` to filter them out in their queries:

1. In `Northwind.cs`, at the bottom of the `OnModelCreating` method, add a global filter to remove discontinued products, as shown in the following code:

```
// global filter to remove discontinued products
```

```
modelBuilder.Entity<Product>()
    .HasQueryFilter(p => !p.Discontinued);
```

2. In `Program.cs`, uncomment the call to `QueryingWithLike`, and comment out all the other method calls.

3. Run the code, enter the partial product name `che`, view the result, and note that **Chef Anton's Gumbo Mix** is now missing, because the SQL statement generated includes a filter for the `Discontinued` column, as shown highlighted in the following output:

```
Enter part of a product name: che
dbug: 05/03/2022 13:34:27.290 RelationalEventId.CommandExecuting[20100]
(Microsoft.EntityFrameworkCore.Database.Command)
      Executing DbCommand [Parameters=[@__Format_1='%che%' (Size = 5)],
CommandType='Text', CommandTimeout='30']
      SELECT "p"."ProductId", "p"."CategoryId", "p"."UnitPrice",
"p"."Discontinued", "p"."ProductName", "p"."UnitsInStock"
      FROM "Products" AS "p"
      WHERE NOT ("p"."Discontinued") AND ("p"."ProductName" LIKE @__
Format_1)
Chef Anton's Cajun Seasoning has 53 units in stock. Discontinued? False
Queso Manchego La Pastora has 86 units in stock. Discontinued? False
Gumbär Gummibärchen has 15 units in stock. Discontinued? False
```

Loading patterns with EF Core

There are three loading patterns that are commonly used with EF Core:

*   **Eager loading:** Load data early.
*   **Lazy loading:** Load data automatically just before it is needed.
*   **Explicit loading:** Load data manually.

In this section, we're going to introduce each of them.

Eager loading entities using the Include extension method

In the `QueryingCategories` method, the code currently uses the `Categories` property to loop through each category, outputting the category name and the number of products in that category.

This works because when we wrote the query, we enabled eager loading by calling the `Include` method for the related products.

Let's see what happens if we do not call `Include`:

1. Modify the query to comment out the `Include` method call, as shown in the following code:

```
IQueryable<Category>? categories = db.Categories;
//.Include(c => c.Products);
```

2. In `Program.cs`, comment out all methods except `QueryingCategories`.

3. Run the code and view the result, as shown in the following partial output:

```
Beverages has 0 products.
Condiments has 0 products.
Confections has 0 products.
Dairy Products has 0 products.
Grains/Cereals has 0 products.
Meat/Poultry has 0 products.
Produce has 0 products.
Seafood has 0 products.
```

Each item in `foreach` is an instance of the `Category` class, which has a property named `Products`, that is, the list of products in that category. Since the original query is only selected from the `Categories` table, this property is empty for each category.

Enabling lazy loading

Lazy loading was introduced in EF Core 2.1, and it can automatically load missing related data. To enable lazy loading, developers must:

- Reference a NuGet package for proxies.
- Configure lazy loading to use a proxy.

Let's see this in action:

1. In the `WorkingWithEFCore` project, add a package reference for EF Core proxies, as shown in the following markup:

```
<PackageReference
  Include="Microsoft.EntityFrameworkCore.Proxies"
  Version="7.0.0" />
```

2. Build the project to restore packages.

3. Open `Northwind.cs` and, at the bottom of the `OnConfiguring` method, call an extension method to use lazy loading proxies, as shown in the following code:

```
optionsBuilder.UseLazyLoadingProxies();
```

Now, every time the loop enumerates, and an attempt is made to read the `Products` property, the lazy loading proxy will check if they are loaded. If not, it will load them for us "lazily" by executing a `SELECT` statement to load just that set of products for the current category, and then the correct count will be returned to the output.

4. Run the code and note that the product counts are now correct. But you will see that the problem with lazy loading is that multiple round trips to the database server are required to eventually fetch all the data. For example, getting all the categories and then getting the products for the first category, Beverages, requires the execution of two SQL commands, as shown in the following partial output:

```
dbug: 05/03/2022 13:41:40.221 RelationalEventId.CommandExecuting[20100]
(Microsoft.EntityFrameworkCore.Database.Command)
      Executing DbCommand [Parameters=[], CommandType='Text',
CommandTimeout='30']
      SELECT "c"."CategoryId", "c"."CategoryName", "c"."Description"
      FROM "Categories" AS "c"
dbug: 05/03/2022 13:41:40.331 RelationalEventId.CommandExecuting[20100]
(Microsoft.EntityFrameworkCore.Database.Command)
      Executing DbCommand [Parameters=[@__p_0='1'], CommandType='Text',
CommandTimeout='30']
      SELECT "p"."ProductId", "p"."CategoryId", "p"."UnitPrice",
"p"."Discontinued", "p"."ProductName", "p"."UnitsInStock"
      FROM "Products" AS "p"
      WHERE NOT ("p"."Discontinued") AND "p"."CategoryId" = @__p_0
Beverages has 11 products.
```

Explicit loading entities using the Load method

Another type of loading is explicit loading. It works in a similar way to lazy loading, with the difference being that you are in control of exactly what related data is loaded and when:

1. At the top of `Program.Queries.cs`, import the change tracking namespace to enable us to use the `CollectionEntry` class to manually load related entities, as shown in the following code:

   ```
   using Microsoft.EntityFrameworkCore.ChangeTracking; //CollectionEntry
   ```

2. In `QueryingCategories`, modify the statements to disable lazy loading and then prompt the user as to whether they want to enable eager loading and explicit loading, as shown in the following code:

   ```
   IQueryable<Category>? categories;
     // = db.Categories;
     // .Include(c => c.Products);

   db.ChangeTracker.LazyLoadingEnabled = false;

   Write("Enable eager loading? (Y/N): ");
   bool eagerLoading = (ReadKey(intercept: true).Key == ConsoleKey.Y);
   bool explicitLoading = false;
   WriteLine();

   if (eagerLoading)
   ```

```
{
  categories = db.Categories?.Include(c => c.Products);
}
else
{
  categories = db.Categories;
  Write("Enable explicit loading? (Y/N): ");
  explicitLoading = (ReadKey(intercept: true).Key == ConsoleKey.Y);
  WriteLine();
}
```

3. In the `foreach` loop, before the `WriteLine` method call, add statements to check if explicit loading is enabled, and if so, prompt the user as to whether they want to explicitly load each individual category, as shown in the following code:

```
if (explicitLoading)
{
  Write($"Explicitly load products for {c.CategoryName}? (Y/N): ");
  ConsoleKeyInfo key = ReadKey(intercept: true);
  WriteLine();

  if (key.Key == ConsoleKey.Y)
  {
    CollectionEntry<Category, Product> products =
      db.Entry(c).Collection(c2 => c2.Products);

    if (!products.IsLoaded) products.Load();
  }
}
```

4. Run the code:

   1. Press *N* to disable eager loading.
   2. Then, press *Y* to enable explicit loading.
   3. For each category, press *Y* or *N* to load its products as you wish.

I chose to load products for only two of the eight categories, `Beverages` and `Seafood`, as shown in the following output that has been edited for space:

```
Enable eager loading? (Y/N):
Enable explicit loading? (Y/N):
dbug: 05/03/2022 13:48:48.541 RelationalEventId.CommandExecuting[20100]
(Microsoft.EntityFrameworkCore.Database.Command)
      Executing DbCommand [Parameters=[], CommandType='Text',
CommandTimeout='30']
      SELECT "c"."CategoryId", "c"."CategoryName", "c"."Description"
      FROM "Categories" AS "c"
Explicitly load products for Beverages? (Y/N):
```

```
dbug: 05/03/2022 13:49:07.416 RelationalEventId.CommandExecuting[20100]
(Microsoft.EntityFrameworkCore.Database.Command)
      Executing DbCommand [Parameters=[@__p_0='1'], CommandType='Text',
CommandTimeout='30']
      SELECT "p"."ProductId", "p"."CategoryId", "p"."UnitPrice",
"p"."Discontinued", "p"."ProductName", "p"."UnitsInStock"
      FROM "Products" AS "p"
      WHERE NOT ("p"."Discontinued") AND "p"."CategoryId" = @__p_0
Beverages has 11 products.
Explicitly load products for Condiments? (Y/N):
Condiments has 0 products.
Explicitly load products for Confections? (Y/N):
Confections has 0 products.
Explicitly load products for Dairy Products? (Y/N):
Dairy Products has 0 products.
Explicitly load products for Grains/Cereals? (Y/N):
Grains/Cereals has 0 products.
Explicitly load products for Meat/Poultry? (Y/N):
Meat/Poultry has 0 products.
Explicitly load products for Produce? (Y/N):
Produce has 0 products.
Explicitly load products for Seafood? (Y/N):
dbug: 05/03/2022 13:49:16.682 RelationalEventId.CommandExecuting[20100]
(Microsoft.EntityFrameworkCore.Database.Command)
      Executing DbCommand [Parameters=[@__p_0='8'], CommandType='Text',
CommandTimeout='30']
      SELECT "p"."ProductId", "p"."CategoryId", "p"."UnitPrice",
"p"."Discontinued", "p"."ProductName", "p"."UnitsInStock"
      FROM "Products" AS "p"
      WHERE NOT ("p"."Discontinued") AND "p"."CategoryId" = @__p_0
Seafood has 12 products.
```

Good Practice: Carefully consider which loading pattern is best for your code. Lazy loading could literally make you a lazy database developer! Read more about loading patterns at the following link: https://docs.microsoft.com/en-us/ef/core/querying/related-data.

Modifying data with EF Core

Inserting, updating, and deleting entities using EF Core is an easy task to accomplish.

DbContext maintains change tracking automatically, so the local entities can have multiple changes tracked, including adding new entities, modifying existing entities, and removing entities.

When you are ready to send those changes to the underlying database, call the SaveChanges method. The number of entities successfully changed will be returned.

Inserting entities

Let's start by looking at how to add a new row to a table:

1. Add a new class file named `Program.Modifications.cs`.

2. In `Program.Modifications.cs`, create a partial `Program` class with a method named `ListProducts` that outputs the ID, name, cost, stock, and discontinued properties of each product sorted with the costliest first, and highlights any that match an array of `int` values that can be optionally passed to the method, as shown in the following code:

```
using Microsoft.EntityFrameworkCore; // ExecuteUpdate, ExecuteDelete
using Microsoft.EntityFrameworkCore.ChangeTracking; // EntityEntry<T>
using Packt.Shared; // Northwind, Product

partial class Program
{
  static void ListProducts(int[]? productIdsToHighlight = null)
  {
    using (Northwind db = new())
    {
      if ((db.Products is null) || (!db.Products.Any()))
      {
        Fail("There are no products.");
        return;
      }

      WriteLine("| {0,-3} | {1,-35} | {2,8} | {3,5} | {4} |",
        "Id", "Product Name", "Cost", "Stock", "Disc.");

      foreach (Product p in db.Products)
      {
        ConsoleColor previousColor = ForegroundColor;

        if ((productIdsToHighlight is not null) &&
          productIdsToHighlight.Contains(p.ProductId))
        {
          ForegroundColor = ConsoleColor.Green;
        }

        WriteLine("| {0:000} | {1,-35} | {2,8:$#,##0.00} | {3,5} | {4} |",
          p.ProductId, p.ProductName, p.Cost, p.Stock, p.Discontinued);

        ForegroundColor = previousColor;
      }
    }
  }
}
```

Remember that `1,-35` means left-align argument 1 within a 35-character-wide column, and `3,5` means right-align argument 3 within a 5-character-wide column.

3. In `Program.Modifications.cs`, add a method named `AddProduct`, as shown in the following code:

```
static (int affected, int productId) AddProduct(
  int categoryId, string productName, decimal? price)
{
  using (Northwind db = new())
  {
    if (db.Products is null) return (0, 0);

    Product p = new()
    {
      CategoryId = categoryId,
      ProductName = productName,
      Cost = price,
      Stock = 72
    };

    // set product as added in change tracking
    EntityEntry<Product> entity = db.Products.Add(p);
    WriteLine($"State: {entity.State}, ProductId: {p.ProductId}");

    // save tracked change to database
    int affected = db.SaveChanges();
    WriteLine($"State: {entity.State}, ProductId: {p.ProductId}");

    return (affected, p.ProductId);
  }
}
```

4. In `Program.cs`, comment out previous method calls, and then call `AddProduct` and `ListProducts`, as shown in the following code:

```
var resultAdd = AddProduct(categoryId: 6,
  productName: "Bob's Burgers", price: 500M);

if (resultAdd.affected == 1)
{
  WriteLine($"Add product successful with ID: {resultAdd.productId}.");
}
```

```
ListProducts(productIdToHighlight: resultAdd.productId);
```

5. Run the code, view the result, and note the new product has been added, as shown in the
   following partial output:

```
State: Added, ProductId: 0
dbug: 05/03/2022 14:21:37.818 RelationalEventId.CommandExecuting[20100]
(Microsoft.EntityFrameworkCore.Database.Command)
      Executing DbCommand [Parameters=[@p0='6', @p1='500' (Nullable =
true), @p2='False', @p3='Bob's Burgers' (Nullable = false) (Size = 13), @
p4=NULL (DbType = Int16)], CommandType='Text', CommandTimeout='30']
      INSERT INTO "Products" ("CategoryId", "UnitPrice", "Discontinued",
"ProductName", "UnitsInStock")
      VALUES (@p0, @p1, @p2, @p3, @p4);
      SELECT "ProductId"
      FROM "Products"
      WHERE changes() = 1 AND "rowid" = last_insert_rowid();
State: Unchanged, ProductId: 78
Add product successful with ID: 78.
| Id  | Product Name                            |     Cost | Stock | Disc. |
| 001 | Chai                                    |  $18.00  |    39 | False |
| 002 | Chang                                   |  $19.00  |    17 | False |
...
| 078 | Bob's Burgers                           | $500.00  |    72 | False |
```

When the new product is first created in memory and being tracked by the EF Core change
tracker, it has a state of Added and its ID is 0. After the call to SaveChanges, it has a state
of Unchanged and its ID is 78, the value assigned by the database.

Updating entities

Now, let's modify an existing row in a table.

We will find a product to update by specifying the start of a product name and only return the first
match. In a real application, if you need to update a specific product then you must use a unique
identifier like ProductId.

I cannot know what the product ID will be for the products that you add. I do know that
there are no products that start with "Bob" in the existing Northwind database. Finding a
product to update using its name avoids having to tell you to first discover what the product ID is for a product that you've added. It is likely to be 78 because there are already 77
products in the table, but once you've added that and then deleted it, the next product to
be added would be 79 and it all gets out of sync.

Let's go:

1. In `Program.Modifications.cs`, add a method to increase the price of the first product with a name that begins with a specified value (we'll use `Bob` in our example) by a specified amount like $20, as shown in the following code:

    ```
    static (int affected, int productId) IncreaseProductPrice(
      string productNameStartsWith, decimal amount)
    {
      using (Northwind db = new())
      {
        if (db.Products is null) return (0, 0);

        // Get the first product whose name starts with the parameter value.
        Product updateProduct = db.Products.First(
          p => p.ProductName.StartsWith(productNameStartsWith));

        updateProduct.Cost += amount;

        int affected = db.SaveChanges();

        return (affected, updateProduct.ProductId);
      }
    }
    ```

2. In `Program.cs`, add statements to call `IncreaseProductPrice` and then `ListProducts`, as shown in the following code:

    ```
    var resultUpdate = IncreaseProductPrice(
      productNameStartsWith: "Bob", amount: 20M);

    if (resultUpdate.affected == 1)
    {
      WriteLine("Increase price success for ID: {resultUpdate.productId}.");
    }

    ListProducts(productIdsToHighlight: new[] { resultUpdate.productId });
    ```

3. Run the code, view the result, and note that the existing entity for Bob's Burgers has increased in price by $20, as shown in the following partial output:

    ```
    dbug: 05/03/2022 14:44:47.024 RelationalEventId.CommandExecuting[20100]
    (Microsoft.EntityFrameworkCore.Database.Command)

          Executing DbCommand [Parameters=[@__productNameStartsWith_0='Bob'
    (Size = 3)], CommandType='Text', CommandTimeout='30']
          SELECT "p"."ProductId", "p"."CategoryId", "p"."UnitPrice",
    "p"."Discontinued", "p"."ProductName", "p"."UnitsInStock"
    ```

```
      FROM "Products" AS "p"
      WHERE NOT ("p"."Discontinued") AND (@__productNameStartsWith_0 =
'' OR (("p"."ProductName" LIKE @__productNameStartsWith_0 || '%') AND
substr("p"."ProductName", 1, length(@__productNameStartsWith_0)) = @__
productNameStartsWith_0) OR @__productNameStartsWith_0 = '')
      LIMIT 1
dbug: 05/03/2022 14:44:47.028 RelationalEventId.CommandExecuting[20100]
(Microsoft.EntityFrameworkCore.Database.Command)

      Executing DbCommand [Parameters=[@p1='78', @p0='520' (Nullable =
true)], CommandType='Text', CommandTimeout='30']
      UPDATE "Products" SET "UnitPrice" = @p0
      WHERE "ProductId" = @p1;
      SELECT changes();
Increase price success for ID: 78.
| Id  | Product Name          |         |   Cost  | Stock | Disc. |
| 001 | Chai                  |         | $18.00  |    39 | False |
...
| 078 | Bob's Burgers         |         | $520.00 |    72 | False |
```

Deleting entities

You can remove individual entities with the `Remove` method. `RemoveRange` is more efficient when you want to delete multiple entities.

Let's see how to delete rows from a table:

1. In `Program.Modifications.cs`, add a method to delete all products with a name that begins with a specified value (`Bob` in our example), as shown in the following code:

```
static int DeleteProducts(string productNameStartsWith)
{
  using (Northwind db = new())
  {
    IQueryable<Product>? products = db.Products?.Where(
      p => p.ProductName.StartsWith(productNameStartsWith));

    if ((products is null) || (!products.Any()))
    {
      WriteLine("No products found to delete.");
      return 0;
    }
    else
    {
      if (db.Products is null) return 0;
```

```
            db.Products.RemoveRange(products);
        }

        int affected = db.SaveChanges();
        return affected;
    }
}
```

2. In `Program.cs`, add statements to call `DeleteProducts`, as shown in the following code:

```
WriteLine("About to delete all products whose name starts with Bob.");
Write("Press Enter to continue or any other key to exit: ");
if (ReadKey(intercept: true).Key == ConsoleKey.Enter)
{
    int deleted = DeleteProducts(productNameStartsWith: "Bob");
    WriteLine($"{deleted} product(s) were deleted.");
}
else
{
    WriteLine("Delete was canceled.");
}
```

3. Run the code, press *Enter*, and view the result, as shown in the following partial output:

```
1 product(s) were deleted.
```

If multiple product names started with Bob, then they would all be deleted. As an optional challenge, modify the statements to add three new products that start with Bob and then delete them.

More efficient updates and deletes

You have now seen the traditional way of modifying data using EF Core, as summarized in the following steps:

1. Create a database context. Change tracking is enabled by default.

2. To insert, create a new instance of an entity class and then pass it as an argument to the `Add` method of the appropriate collection, for example, `db.Products.Add(product)`.

3. To update, retrieve the entities that you want to modify and then change their properties.

4. To delete, retrieve the entities that you want to remove and then pass them as an argument to the `Remove` or `RemoveRange` methods of the appropriate collection, for example, `db.Products.Remove(product)`.

5. Call the `SaveChanges` method of the database context. This uses the change tracker to generate SQL statements to perform the needed inserts, updates, and deletes, and then returns the number of entities affected.

EF Core 7 introduces two methods that can make updates and deletes more efficient because they do not require entities to be loaded into memory and have their changes tracked. The methods are named `ExecuteDelete` and `ExecuteUpdate` (and their `Async` equivalents). They are called on a LINQ query and affect the entities in the query result, although the query is not used to retrieve entities so no entities are loaded into the data context.

For example, to delete all rows in a table, call the `ExecuteDelete` or `ExecuteDeleteAsync` method on any `DbSet` property, as shown in the following code:

```
await db.Products.ExecuteDeleteAsync();
```

The preceding code would execute an SQL statement in the database, as shown in the following code:

```
DELETE FROM Products
```

To delete all products that have a unit price greater than 50, as shown in the following code:

```
await db.Products
  .Where(product => product.UnitPrice > 50)
  .ExecuteDeleteAsync();
```

The preceding code would execute an SQL statement in the database, as shown in the following code:

```
DELETE FROM Products p WHERE p.UnitPrice > 50
```

> `ExecuteUpdate` and `ExecuteDelete` can only act on a single table, so although you can write quite complex LINQ queries, they can only update or delete from a single table.

To update all products that are not discontinued to increase their unit price by 10% due to inflation, as shown in the following code:

```
await db.Products
  .Where(product => !product.Discontinued)
  .ExecuteUpdateAsync(s => s.SetProperty(
    p => p.UnitPrice, // Selects the property to update.
    p => p.UnitPrice * 0.1)); // Sets the value to update it to.
```

> You can chain multiple calls to `SetProperty` in the same query to update multiple properties in one command.

Let's see some examples:

1. In `Program.Modifications.cs`, add a method to update all products with a name that begins with a specified value using `ExecuteUpdate`, as shown in the following code:

```
static (int affected, int[]? productIds) IncreaseProductPricesBetter(
  string productNameStartsWith, decimal amount)
{
  using (Northwind db = new())
  {
    if (db.Products is null) return (0, null);

    // Get products whose name starts with the parameter value.
    IQueryable<Product>? products = db.Products.Where(
      p => p.ProductName.StartsWith(productNameStartsWith));

    int affected = products.ExecuteUpdate(s => s.SetProperty(
      p => p.Cost, // Property selector lambda expression.
      p => p.Cost + amount)); // Value to update to lambda expression.

    int[] productIds = products.Select(p => p.ProductId).ToArray();

    return (affected, productIds);
  }
}
```

2. In `Program.cs`, add statements to call `IncreaseProductPricesBetter`, as shown in the following code:

```
var resultUpdateBetter = IncreaseProductPricesBetter(
  productNameStartsWith: "Bob", amount: 20M);

if (resultUpdateBetter.affected > 0)
{
  WriteLine("Increase product price successful.");
}

ListProducts(productIdsToHighlight: resultUpdateBetter.productIds);
```

3. Uncomment the statements that add a new product.

4. Run the console app multiple times and note that, each time, the existing products with the "Bob" prefix are each updated with an incrementing cost, as shown in the following output:

```
...
| 078 | Bob's Burgers                    |  $560.00 |    72 | False |
| 079 | Bob's Burgers                    |  $540.00 |    72 | False |
| 080 | Bob's Burgers                    |  $520.00 |    72 | False |
```

5. In `Program.Modifications.cs`, add a method to delete any products with a name that begins
    with a specified value using `ExecuteDelete`, as shown in the following code:

```
static int DeleteProductsBetter(string productNameStartsWith)
{
  using (Northwind db = new())
  {
    int affected = 0;

    IQueryable<Product>? products = db.Products?.Where(
      p => p.ProductName.StartsWith(productNameStartsWith));

    if ((products is null) || (!products.Any()))
    {
      WriteLine("No products found to delete.");
      return 0;
    }
    else
    {
      affected = products.ExecuteDelete();
    }
    return affected;
  }
}
```

6. In `Program.cs`, add statements to call `DeleteProductsBetter`, as shown in the following code:

```
WriteLine("About to delete all products whose name starts with Bob.");
Write("Press Enter to continue or any other key to exit: ");
if (ReadKey(intercept: true).Key == ConsoleKey.Enter)
{
  int deleted = DeleteProductsBetter(productNameStartsWith: "Bob");
  WriteLine($"{deleted} product(s) were deleted.");
}
else
{
  WriteLine("Delete was canceled.");
}
```

7. Run the console app and confirm that the products are deleted, as shown in the following output:

```
3 product(s) were deleted.
```

Warning! If you mix traditional tracked changes with the `ExecuteUpdate` and
`ExecuteDelete` methods, then note that they are not kept synchronized. The change
tracker will not know what you have updated and deleted using those methods.

Pooling database contexts

The DbContext class is disposable and is designed following the single-unit-of-work principle. In the previous code examples, we created all the DbContext-derived Northwind instances in a using block so that Dispose is properly called at the end of each unit of work.

A feature of ASP.NET Core that is related to EF Core is that it makes your code more efficient by pooling database contexts when building websites and services. This allows you to create and dispose of as many DbContext-derived objects as you want, knowing that your code is still as efficient as possible.

Working with transactions

Every time you call the SaveChanges method, an **implicit transaction** is started so that if something goes wrong, it will automatically roll back all the changes. If the multiple changes within the transaction succeed, then the transaction and all changes are committed.

Transactions maintain the integrity of your database by applying locks to prevent reads and writes while a sequence of changes is occurring.

Transactions are **ACID**, which is an acronym explained in the following list:

- **A is for atomic.** Either all the operations in the transaction commit, or none of them do.
- **C is for consistent.** The state of the database before and after a transaction is consistent. This is dependent on your code logic; for example, when transferring money between bank accounts, it is up to your business logic to ensure that if you debit $100 from one account, you credit $100 to the other account.
- **I is for isolated.** During a transaction, changes are hidden from other processes. There are multiple isolation levels that you can pick from (refer to the following table). The stronger the level, the better the integrity of the data. However, more locks must be applied, which will negatively affect other processes. Snapshot is a special case because it creates multiple copies of rows to avoid locks, but this will increase the size of your database while transactions occur.
- **D is for durable.** If a failure occurs during a transaction, it can be recovered. This is often implemented as a two-phase commit and transaction logs. Once the transaction is committed, it is guaranteed to endure even if there are subsequent errors. The opposite of durable is volatile.

Controlling transactions using isolation levels

A developer can control transactions by setting an **isolation level**, as described in the following table:

Isolation level	Lock(s)	Integrity problems allowed
ReadUncommitted	None	Dirty reads, non-repeatable reads, and phantom data
ReadCommitted	When editing, it applies read lock(s) to block other users from reading the record(s) until the transaction ends	Non-repeatable reads and phantom data

	When reading, it applies edit lock(s) to block	
`RepeatableRead`	other users from editing the record(s) until the	Phantom data
	transaction ends	
	It applies key-range locks to prevent any	
`Serializable`	action that would affect the results, including	None
	inserts and deletes	
`Snapshot`	None	None

Defining an explicit transaction

You can control explicit transactions using the `Database` property of the database context:

1. In `Program.Modifications.cs`, import the EF Core storage namespace to use the `IDbContextTransaction` interface, as shown in the following code:

```
using Microsoft.EntityFrameworkCore.Storage; // IDbContextTransaction
```

2. In the `DeleteProducts` method, after the instantiation of the db variable, add statements to start an explicit transaction and output its isolation level. At the bottom of the method, commit the transaction, and close the brace, as shown highlighted in the following code:

```
static int DeleteProducts(string productNameStartsWith)
{
  using (Northwind db = new())
  {
    using (IDbContextTransaction t = db.Database.BeginTransaction())
    {
      WriteLine("Transaction isolation level: {0}",
        arg0: t.GetDbTransaction().IsolationLevel);

      IQueryable<Product>? products = db.Products?.Where(
        p => p.ProductName.StartsWith(productNameStartsWith));

      if ((products is null) || (!products.Any()))
      {
        WriteLine("No products found to delete.");
        return 0;
      }
      else
      {
        db.Products.RemoveRange(products);
      }

      int affected = db.SaveChanges();
      t.Commit();
      return affected;
```

```
      }
    }
  }
```

3. Run the code and view the result using SQLite, as shown in the following output:

```
Transaction isolation level: Serializable
```

 If you were to use SQL Server, you would see the following output:

```
Transaction isolation level: ReadCommitted
```

Defining Code First EF Core models

This is a bonus section for the chapter that is available online at `https://github.com/markjprice/cs11dotnet7/blob/main/docs/bonus/code-first-models.md`

Practicing and exploring

Test your knowledge and understanding by answering some questions, getting some hands-on practice, and exploring this chapter's topics with deeper research.

Exercise 10.1 – Test your knowledge

Answer the following questions:

1. What type would you use for the property that represents a table, for example, the Products property of a database context?

2. What type would you use for the property that represents a one-to-many relationship, for example, the Products property of a Category entity?

3. What is the EF Core convention for primary keys?

4. When might you use an annotation attribute in an entity class?

5. Why might you choose the Fluent API in preference to annotation attributes?

6. What does a transaction isolation level of Serializable mean?

7. What does the DbContext.SaveChanges() method return?

8. What is the difference between eager loading and explicit loading?

9. How should you define an EF Core entity class to match the following table?

```
CREATE TABLE Employees(
  EmpId INT IDENTITY,
  FirstName NVARCHAR(40) NOT NULL,
  Salary MONEY
)
```

10. What benefit do you get from declaring entity navigation properties as virtual?

Exercise 10.2 – Practice exporting data using different serialization formats

In the Chapter10 solution/workspace, create a console app named Ch10Ex02DataSerialization that queries the Northwind database for all the categories and products, and then serializes the data using at least three formats of serialization available to .NET. Which format of serialization uses the least number of bytes?

Exercise 10.3 – Explore topics

Use the links on the following page to learn more detail about the topics covered in this chapter:

https://github.com/markjprice/cs11dotnet7/blob/main/book-links.md#chapter-10---working-with-data-using-entity-framework-core

Exercise 10.4 – Explore NoSQL databases

This chapter focused on RDBMSs such as SQL Server and SQLite. If you wish to learn more about NoSQL databases, such as Cosmos DB and MongoDB, and how to use them with EF Core, then I recommend the following links:

- **Welcome to Azure Cosmos DB:** https://docs.microsoft.com/en-us/azure/cosmos-db/introduction
- **Use NoSQL databases as a persistence infrastructure:** https://docs.microsoft.com/en-us/dotnet/standard/microservices-architecture/microservice-ddd-cqrs-patterns/nosql-database-persistence-infrastructure
- **Document Database Providers for Entity Framework Core:** https://github.com/BlueshiftSoftware/EntityFrameworkCore

Summary

In this chapter, you learned how to:

- Connect to and build entity data models for an existing database.
- Execute a simple LINQ query and process the results.
- Use filtered includes.
- Add, modify, and delete data.
- Define a Code First model and use it to create a new database and populate it with data.

In the next chapter, you will learn how to write more advanced LINQ queries to select, filter, sort, join, and group.

11

Querying and Manipulating Data Using LINQ

This chapter is about **Language INtegrated Query (LINQ)** expressions. LINQ is a set of language extensions that add the ability to work with sequences of data and then filter, sort, and project them into different outputs.

This chapter will cover the following topics:

- Why LINQ?
- Writing LINQ expressions
- Using LINQ with EF Core
- Sweetening LINQ syntax with syntactic sugar
- Using multiple threads with parallel LINQ (online section)
- Creating your own LINQ extension methods
- Working with LINQ to XML

Why LINQ?

The first question we need to answer is a fundamental one: why LINQ?

Comparing imperative and declarative language features

LINQ was introduced in 2008 with C# 3.0 and .NET Framework 3.0. Before that, if a C# and .NET programmer wanted to process a sequence of items, they had to use procedural, aka imperative, code statements. For example, a loop:

1. Set the current position to the first item.
2. Check if the item is one that should be processed by comparing one or more properties against specified values. For example, is the unit price greater than 50 or is the country equal to Belgium?

3. If a match, process that item. For example, output one or more of its properties to the user, update one or more properties to new values, delete the item, or perform an aggregate calculation like counting or summing values.

4. Move to the next item. Repeat until all items have been processed.

Procedural, aka imperative, code tells the compiler *how* to achieve a goal. Do this. Then do that. Since the compiler does not know what you are trying to achieve, it cannot help you as much. You are 100% responsible for ensuring that every *how-to* step is exactly correct.

LINQ makes these common tasks much easier with less opportunity to introduce bugs. Instead of needing to explicitly state each individual action, like move, read, update, and so on, LINQ enables the programmer to use a declarative or functional style of writing statements.

Declarative code tells the compiler *what* goal to achieve. The compiler works out the best way to achieve the goal. The statements also tend to be more concise.

> **Good Practice:** If you do not fully understand how LINQ works, then the statements you write can introduce their own subtle bugs! A code teaser doing the rounds recently involves a sequence of tasks and understanding when they are executed (`https://twitter.com/amantinband/status/1559187912218099714`). Most experienced developers got it wrong! To be fair, it is the combination of LINQ behavior with multi-threading behavior that confused most of them. But by the end of this chapter, you will be better informed to understand why the code was dangerous due to LINQ behavior.

Writing LINQ expressions

Although we wrote a few LINQ expressions in *Chapter 10, Working with Data Using Entity Framework Core*, they weren't the focus, and so I didn't properly explain how LINQ works. Let's now take time to properly understand LINQ expressions.

What makes LINQ?

LINQ has several parts; some are required, and some are optional:

*   **Extension methods (required):** These include examples such as `Where`, `OrderBy`, and `Select`. These are what provide the functionality of LINQ.

*   **LINQ providers (required):** These include **LINQ to Objects** for processing in-memory objects, **LINQ to Entities** for processing data stored in external databases and modeled with EF Core, and **LINQ to XML** for processing data stored as XML. These providers are what execute LINQ expressions in a way specific to different types of data.

*   **Lambda expressions (optional):** These can be used instead of named methods to simplify LINQ queries, for example, for the conditional logic of the `Where` method for filtering.

*   **LINQ query comprehension syntax (optional):** These include C# keywords like `from`, `in`, `where`, `orderby`, `descending`, and `select`. These are aliases for some of the LINQ extension methods, and their use can simplify the queries you write, especially if you already have experience with other query languages, such as **Structured Query Language (SQL)**.

When programmers are first introduced to LINQ, they often believe that LINQ query comprehension syntax is LINQ but, ironically, that is one of the parts of LINQ that is optional!

Building LINQ expressions with the Enumerable class

The LINQ extension methods, such as `Where` and `Select`, are appended by the `Enumerable` static class to any type, known as a **sequence**, that implements `IEnumerable<T>`.

For example, an array of any type implements the `IEnumerable<T>` class, where `T` is the type of item in the array. This means that all arrays support LINQ to query and manipulate them.

All generic collections, such as `List<T>`, `Dictionary<TKey, TValue>`, `Stack<T>`, and `Queue<T>`, implement `IEnumerable<T>`, so they can be queried and manipulated with LINQ too.

`Enumerable` defines more than 50 extension methods, as summarized in the following table:

 This table will be useful for you for future reference, but for now, you might want to briefly scan it to get a feel for what extension methods exist and come back later to review it properly.

Method(s)	Description
`First, FirstOrDefault, Last, LastOrDefault`	Get the first or last item in the sequence or throw an exception, or return the default value for the type, for example, 0 for an int and null for a reference type, if there is not a first or last item.
`Where`	Return a sequence of items that match a specified filter.
`Single, SingleOrDefault`	Return an item that matches a specified filter or throw an exception, or return the default value for the type if there is not exactly one match.
`ElementAt, ElementAtOrDefault`	Return an item at a specified index position or throw an exception, or return the default value for the type if there is not an item at that position. Introduced in .NET 6 are overloads that can be passed an `Index` instead of an int, which is more efficient when working with `Span<T>` sequences.
`Select, SelectMany`	Project items into a different shape, that is, a different type, and flatten a nested hierarchy of items.
`OrderBy, OrderByDescending, ThenBy, ThenByDescending`	Sort items by a specified field or property.
`Order, OrderDescending`	Sort items by the item itself. Introduced in .NET 7.
`Reverse`	Reverse the order of the items.
`GroupBy, GroupJoin, Join`	Group and/or join two sequences.

Skip, SkipWhile	Skip a number of items, or skip while an expression is true.
Take, TakeWhile	Take a number of items, or take while an expression is true. Introduced in .NET 6 is an overload that can be passed a Range, for example, Take(range: 3..^5) meaning take a subset starting 3 items in from the start and ending 5 items in from the end, or instead of Skip(4) you could use Take(4..).
Aggregate, Average, Count, LongCount, Max, Min, Sum	Calculate aggregate values.
TryGetNonEnumeratedCount	Count() checks if a Count property is implemented on the sequence and returns its value, or it enumerates the entire sequence to count its items. Introduced in .NET 6 is this method, which only checks for Count; if it is missing, it returns false and sets the out parameter to 0 to avoid a potentially poor-performing operation.
All, Any, Contains	Return true if all or any of the items match the filter, or if the sequence contains a specified item.
Cast<T>	Cast items into a specified type. It is useful to convert non-generic objects to a generic type in scenarios where the compiler would otherwise complain.
OfType<T>	Remove items that do not match a specified type.
Distinct	Remove duplicate items.
Except, Intersect, Union	Perform operations that return sets. Sets cannot have duplicate items. Although the inputs can be any sequence and so the inputs can have duplicates, the result is always a set.
DistinctBy, ExceptBy, IntersectBy, UnionBy, MinBy, MaxBy	Allow the comparison to be performed on a subset of the item rather than the entire item. For example, instead of removing duplicates with Distinct by comparing an entire Person object, you could remove duplicates with DistinctBy by comparing just their LastName and DateOfBirth.
Chunk	Divide a sequence into sized batches.
Append, Concat, Prepend	Perform sequence-combining operations.
Zip	Perform a match operation on two or three sequences based on the position of items, for example, the item at position 1 in the first sequence matches the item at position 1 in the second sequence.
ToArray, ToList, ToDictionary, ToHashSet, ToLookup	Convert the sequence into an array or collection. These are the only extension methods that force the execution of a LINQ expression immediately rather than wait for deferred execution, which you will learn about shortly.

The `Enumerable` class also has some methods that are not extension methods, as shown in the following table:

Method	Description
`Empty<T>`	Returns an empty sequence of the specified type `T`. It is useful for passing an empty sequence to a method that requires an `IEnumerable<T>`.
`Range`	Returns a sequence of integers from the `start` value with count items. For example, `Enumerable.Range(start: 5, count: 3)` would contain the integers 5, 6, and 7.
`Repeat`	Returns a sequence that contains the same element repeated count times. For example, `Enumerable.Repeat(element: "5", count: 3)` would contain the string values "5", "5", and "5".

Understanding deferred execution

LINQ uses **deferred execution**. It is important to understand that calling most of the above extension methods does not execute the query and get the results. Most of these extension methods return a LINQ expression that represents a *question*, not an *answer*. Let's explore:

1. Use your preferred code editor to create a new project, as defined in the following list:

    - Project template: **Console App**/`console`
    - Project file and folder: `LinqWithObjects`
    - Workspace/solution file and folder: `Chapter11`

2. In the project file, globally and statically import the `System.Console` class.

3. Add a new class file name `Program.Helpers.cs`.

4. In `Program.Helpers.cs`, define a partial `Program` class with a method to output a section title, as shown in the following code:

    ```
    partial class Program
    {
      static void SectionTitle(string title)
      {
        ConsoleColor previousColor = ForegroundColor;
        ForegroundColor = ConsoleColor.DarkYellow;
        WriteLine("*");
        WriteLine($"* {title}");
        WriteLine("*");
        ForegroundColor = previousColor;
      }
    }
    ```

5. In `Program.cs`, delete the existing statements and then add statements to define a sequence of string values for people who work in an office, as shown in the following code:

    ```
    // a string array is a sequence that implements IEnumerable<string>
    string[] names = new[] { "Michael", "Pam", "Jim", "Dwight",
    ```

```
    "Angela", "Kevin", "Toby", "Creed" };

SectionTitle("Deferred execution");

// Question: Which names end with an M?
// (written using a LINQ extension method)
var query1 = names.Where(name => name.EndsWith("m"));

// Question: Which names end with an M?
// (written using LINQ query comprehension syntax)
var query2 = from name in names where name.EndsWith("m") select name;
```

6. To get the answer, i.e. execute the query, you must **materialize** it by either calling one of the "To" methods like ToArray or ToLookup or by enumerating the query, as shown in the following code:

```
// Answer returned as an array of strings containing Pam and Jim
string[] result1 = query1.ToArray();

// Answer returned as a list of strings containing Pam and Jim
List<string> result2 = query2.ToList();

// Answer returned as we enumerate over the results
foreach (string name in query1)
{
  WriteLine(name); // outputs Pam
  names[2] = "Jimmy"; // change Jim to Jimmy
  // on the second iteration Jimmy does not end with an m
}
```

7. Run the console app and note the result, as shown in the following output:

```
Pam
```

Due to deferred execution, after outputting the first result, Pam, if the original array values change, then by the time we loop back around, there are no more matches because Jim has become Jimmy and does not end with an m, so only Pam is outputted.

Before we get too deep into the weeds, let's slow down and look at some common LINQ extension methods and how to use them, one at a time.

Filtering entities with Where

The most common reason for using LINQ is to filter items in a sequence using the Where extension method. Let's explore filtering by defining a sequence of names and then applying LINQ operations to it:

1. In the project file, add an element to remove the System.Linq namespace from automatically being imported globally, as shown highlighted in the following markup:

```
<ItemGroup>
  <Using Include="System.Console" Static="true" />
```

```
    <Using Remove="System.Linq" />
  </ItemGroup>
```

2. In `Program.cs`, attempt to call the `Where` extension method on the array of names, as shown in the following code:

```
SectionTitle("Writing queries");

var query = names.W
```

3. As you try to type the `Where` method, note that it is missing from the IntelliSense list of members of a `string` array, as shown in *Figure 11.1*:

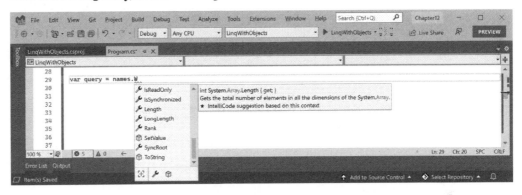

Figure 11.1: IntelliSense with the Where extension method missing

This is because `Where` is an extension method. It does not exist on the array type. To make the `Where` extension method available, we must import the `System.Linq` namespace. This is implicitly imported by default in new .NET 6 and later projects, but we removed it.

4. In the project file, comment out the element that removed `System.Linq`, as shown in the following code:

```
<!--<Using Remove="System.Linq" />-->
```

5. Retype the `Where` method and note that the IntelliSense list now includes the extension methods added by the `Enumerable` class, as shown in *Figure 11.2*:

Figure 11.2: IntelliSense showing LINQ Enumerable extension methods now

6. As you type the parentheses for the Where method, IntelliSense tells us that to call Where, we must pass in an instance of a Func<string, bool> delegate.

7. Enter an expression to create a new instance of a Func<string, bool> delegate, and for now, note that we have not yet supplied a method name because we will define it in the next step, as shown in the following code:

```
var query = names.Where(new Func<string, bool>( ))
```

The Func<string, bool> delegate tells us that for each string variable passed to the method, the method must return a bool value. If the method returns true, it indicates that we should include the string in the results, and if the method returns false, it indicates that we should exclude it.

Targeting a named method

Let's define a method that only includes names that are longer than four characters:

1. Add a new class named Program.Functions.cs.

2. In Program.Functions.cs, define a partial Program class with a method that will include only names longer than four characters, as shown in the following code:

```
partial class Program
{
  static bool NameLongerThanFour(string name)
  {
    return name.Length > 4;
  }
}
```

3. In Program.cs, pass the method's name into the Func<string, bool> delegate, as shown highlighted in the following code:

```
var query = names.Where(
  new Func<string, bool>(NameLongerThanFour));
```

4. Remove the code that modified Jim to Jimmy and any excess comments, as shown in the following code:

```
foreach (string item in query)
{
  WriteLine(item);
}
```

5. Run the code and view the results, noting that only names longer than four letters are listed, as shown in the following output:

```
Michael
Dwight
Angela
Kevin
Creed
```

Simplifying the code by removing the explicit delegate instantiation

We can simplify the code by deleting the explicit instantiation of the Func<string, bool> delegate because the C# compiler can instantiate the delegate for us:

1. To help you learn by seeing progressively improved code, copy and paste the query.

2. Comment out the first example, as shown in the following code:

```
// var query = names.Where(
// new Func<string, bool>(NameLongerThanFour));
```

3. Modify the copy to remove the explicit instantiation of the delegate, as shown in the following code:

```
var query = names.Where(NameLongerThanFour);
```

4. Run the code and note that it has the same behavior.

Targeting a lambda expression

We can simplify our code even further using a **lambda expression** in place of a named method.

Although it can look complicated at first, a lambda expression is simply a *nameless function*. It uses the => symbol (read as "goes to") to indicate the return value:

1. Copy and paste the query, comment the second example, and modify the query, as shown in the following code:

```
var query = names.Where(name => name.Length > 4);
```

Note that the syntax for a lambda expression includes all the important parts of the NameLongerThanFour method, but nothing more. A lambda expression only needs to define the following:

- The names of input parameters: name
- A return value expression: name.Length > 4

The type of the name input parameter is inferred from the fact that the sequence contains string values, and the return type must be a bool value as defined by the delegate for Where to work, so the expression after the => symbol must return a bool value.

The compiler does most of the work for us, so our code can be as concise as possible.

2. Run the code and note that it has the same behavior.

Sorting entities

Other commonly used extension methods are OrderBy and ThenBy, used for sorting a sequence.

Extension methods can be chained if the previous method returns another sequence, that is, a type that implements the IEnumerable<T> interface.

Sorting by a single property using OrderBy

Let's continue working with the current project to explore sorting:

1. Append a call to OrderBy to the end of the existing query, as shown in the following code:

    ```
    var query = names
      .Where(name => name.Length > 4)
      .OrderBy(name => name.Length);
    ```

     Good Practice: Format the LINQ statement so that each extension method call happens on its own line, to make it easier to read.

2. Run the code and note that the names are now sorted by shortest first, as shown in the following output:

    ```
    Kevin
    Creed
    Dwight
    Angela
    Michael
    ```

To put the longest name first, you would use OrderByDescending.

Sorting by a subsequent property using ThenBy

We might want to sort by more than one property, for example, to sort names of the same length in alphabetical order:

1. Add a call to the ThenBy method at the end of the existing query, as shown highlighted in the following code:

    ```
    var query = names
      .Where(name => name.Length > 4)
      .OrderBy(name => name.Length)
      .ThenBy(name => name);
    ```

2. Run the code and note the slight difference in the following sort order. Within a group of names of the same length, the names are sorted alphabetically by the full value of the string, so Creed comes before Kevin, and Angela comes before Dwight, as shown in the following output:

    ```
    Creed
    Kevin
    Angela
    Dwight
    Michael
    ```

Sorting by the item itself

Introduced in .NET 7 are the Order and OrderDescending extension methods. These simplify ordering by the item itself. For example, if you have a sequence of string values, then before .NET 7 you would have to call the OrderBy method and pass a lambda that selects the items themselves, as shown in the following code:

```
var query = names.OrderBy(name => name);
```

With .NET 7 or later, we can simplify the statement, as shown in the following code:

```
var query = names.Order();
```

OrderDescending does a similar thing but in descending order.

Declaring a query using var or a specified type

While writing a LINQ expression, it is convenient to use var to declare the query object. This is because the type frequently changes as you work on the LINQ expression. For example, our query started as an IEnumerable<string> and is currently an IOrderedEnumerable<string>:

1. Hover your mouse over the var keyword and note that its type is IOrderedEnumerable<string>.
2. Replace var with the actual type, as shown highlighted in the following code:

```
IOrderedEnumerable<string> query = names
  .Where(name => name.Length > 4)
  .OrderBy(name => name.Length)
  .ThenBy(name => name);
```

 Good Practice: Once you have finished working on a query, you could change the declared type from var to the actual type to make it clearer what the type is. This is easy because your code editor can tell you what it is.

Filtering by type

The Where extension method is great for filtering by values, such as text and numbers. But what if the sequence contains multiple types, and you want to filter by a specific type and respect any inheritance hierarchy?

Imagine that you have a sequence of exceptions. There are hundreds of exception types that form a complex hierarchy, as partially shown in *Figure 11.3*:

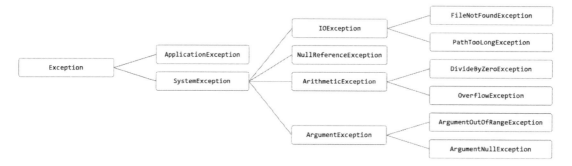

Figure 11.3: A partial exception inheritance hierarchy

Let's explore filtering by type:

1. In `Program.cs`, define a list of exception-derived objects, as shown in the following code:

    ```
    SectionTitle("Filtering by type");

    List<Exception> exceptions = new()
    {
      new ArgumentException(),
      new SystemException(),
      new IndexOutOfRangeException(),
      new InvalidOperationException(),
      new NullReferenceException(),
      new InvalidCastException(),
      new OverflowException(),
      new DivideByZeroException(),
      new ApplicationException()
    };
    ```

2. Write statements using the `OfType<T>` extension method to remove exceptions that are not arithmetic exceptions and write only the arithmetic exceptions to the console, as shown in the following code:

    ```
    IEnumerable<ArithmeticException> arithmeticExceptionsQuery =
      exceptions.OfType<ArithmeticException>();

    foreach (ArithmeticException exception in arithmeticExceptionsQuery)
    {
      WriteLine(exception);
    }
    ```

3. Run the code and note that the results only include exceptions of the `ArithmeticException` type, or the `ArithmeticException`-derived types, as shown in the following output:

```
System.OverflowException: Arithmetic operation resulted in an overflow.
System.DivideByZeroException: Attempted to divide by zero.
```

Working with sets and bags using LINQ

Sets are one of the most fundamental concepts in mathematics. A **set** is a collection of one or more distinct objects. A **multiset**, aka **bag**, is a collection of one or more objects that can have duplicates.

You might remember being taught about Venn diagrams in school. Common set operations include the **intersect** or **union** between sets.

Let's write some code that will define three arrays of `string` values for cohorts of apprentices and then perform some common set and multiset operations on them:

1. In `Program.Helpers.cs`, add the following method that outputs any sequence of `string` variables as a comma-separated single `string` to the console output, along with an optional description, as shown in the following code:

```
static void Output(IEnumerable<string> cohort, string description = "")
{
  if (!string.IsNullOrEmpty(description))
  {
    WriteLine(description);
  }
  Write(" ");
  WriteLine(string.Join(", ", cohort.ToArray()));
  WriteLine();
}
```

2. In `Program.cs`, add statements to define three arrays of names, output them, and then perform various set operations on them, as shown in the following code:

```
string[] cohort1 = new[]
  { "Rachel", "Gareth", "Jonathan", "George" };

string[] cohort2 = new[]
  { "Jack", "Stephen", "Daniel", "Jack", "Jared" };

string[] cohort3 = new[]
  { "Declan", "Jack", "Jack", "Jasmine", "Conor" };

SectionTitle("The cohorts");

Output(cohort1, "Cohort 1");
Output(cohort2, "Cohort 2");
Output(cohort3, "Cohort 3");
```

```
SectionTitle("Set operations");

Output(cohort2.Distinct(), "cohort2.Distinct()");
Output(cohort2.DistinctBy(name => name.Substring(0, 2)),
  "cohort2.DistinctBy(name => name.Substring(0, 2)):");
Output(cohort2.Union(cohort3), "cohort2.Union(cohort3)");
Output(cohort2.Concat(cohort3), "cohort2.Concat(cohort3)");
Output(cohort2.Intersect(cohort3), "cohort2.Intersect(cohort3)");
Output(cohort2.Except(cohort3), "cohort2.Except(cohort3)");
Output(cohort1.Zip(cohort2,(c1, c2) => $"{c1} matched with {c2}"),
  "cohort1.Zip(cohort2)");
```

3. Run the code and view the results, as shown in the following output:

```
Cohort 1
  Rachel, Gareth, Jonathan, George
Cohort 2
  Jack, Stephen, Daniel, Jack, Jared
Cohort 3
  Declan, Jack, Jack, Jasmine, Conor

cohort2.Distinct()
  Jack, Stephen, Daniel, Jared
cohort2.DistinctBy(name => name.Substring(0, 2)):
  Jack, Stephen, Daniel
cohort2.Union(cohort3)
  Jack, Stephen, Daniel, Jared, Declan, Jasmine, Conor
cohort2.Concat(cohort3)
  Jack, Stephen, Daniel, Jack, Jared, Declan, Jack, Jack, Jasmine, Conor
cohort2.Intersect(cohort3)
  Jack
cohort2.Except(cohort3)
  Stephen, Daniel, Jared
cohort1.Zip(cohort2)
  Rachel matched with Jack, Gareth matched with Stephen, Jonathan matched
with Daniel, George matched with Jack
```

With `Zip`, if there are unequal numbers of items in the two sequences, then some items will not have a matching partner. Those without a partner, like `Jared`, will not be included in the result.

For the `DistinctBy` example, instead of removing duplicates by comparing the whole name, we define a lambda key selector to remove duplicates by comparing the first two characters, so `Jared` is removed because `Jack` already is a name that starts with `Ja`.

So far, we have used the LINQ to Objects provider to work with in-memory objects. Next, we will use the LINQ to Entities provider to work with entities stored in a database.

Using LINQ with EF Core

We have looked at LINQ queries that filter and sort, but none that change the shape of the items in the sequence. This is called **projection** because it's about projecting items of one shape into another shape. To learn about projection, it is best to have some more complex types to work with, so in the next project, instead of using `string` sequences, we will use sequences of entities from the Northwind sample database that you were introduced to in *Chapter 10, Working with Data Using Entity Framework Core*.

I will give instructions to use SQLite because it is cross-platform, but if you prefer to use SQL Server then feel free to do so. I have included some commented code to enable SQL Server if you choose.

Building an EF Core model

We must define an EF Core model to represent the database and tables that we will work with. We will define the model manually to take complete control and to prevent a relationship from being automatically defined between the `Categories` and `Products` tables. Later, you will use LINQ to join the two entity sets:

1. Use your preferred code editor to add a new **Console App**/`console` project named `LinqWithEFCore` to the `Chapter11` solution/workspace.

    *   In Visual Studio Code, select `LinqWithEFCore` as the active OmniSharp project.

2. In the `LinqWithEFCore` project, add a package reference to the EF Core provider for SQLite and/or SQL Server, as shown in the following markup:

    ```
    <ItemGroup>
      <PackageReference
        Include="Microsoft.EntityFrameworkCore.Sqlite"
        Version="7.0.0" />
      <PackageReference
        Include="Microsoft.EntityFrameworkCore.SqlServer"
        Version="7.0.0" />
    </ItemGroup>
    ```

3. Build the project to restore packages.

4. Copy the `Northwind4Sqlite.sql` file into the `LinqWithEFCore` folder.

5. At a command prompt or terminal, create the Northwind database by executing the following command:

    ```
    sqlite3 Northwind.db -init Northwind4Sqlite.sql
    ```

6. Be patient because this command might take a while to create the database structure. Eventually, you will see the SQLite command prompt, as shown in the following output:

    ```
    -- Loading resources from Northwind4Sqlite.sql
    SQLite version 3.38.0 2022-02-22 15:20:15
    Enter ".help" for usage hints.
    sqlite>
    ```

7. To exit SQLite command mode, press *Ctrl + C* on Windows or *cmd + D* on macOS.

8. Add three class files to the project, named `Northwind.cs`, `Category.cs`, and `Product.cs`.

9. Modify the class file named `Northwind.cs`, as shown in the following code:

```csharp
using Microsoft.EntityFrameworkCore; // DbContext, DbSet<T>

namespace Packt.Shared;

public class Northwind : DbContext
{
  public DbSet<Category> Categories { get; set; } = null!;
  public DbSet<Product> Products { get; set; } = null!;

  protected override void OnConfiguring(
    DbContextOptionsBuilder optionsBuilder)
  {
    string path = Path.Combine(
      Environment.CurrentDirectory, "Northwind.db");

    optionsBuilder.UseSqlite($"Filename={path}");

    /*
    string connection = "Data Source=.;" +
        "Initial Catalog=Northwind;" +
        "Integrated Security=true;" +
        "MultipleActiveResultSets=true;";

    optionsBuilder.UseSqlServer(connection);
    */
  }

  protected override void OnModelCreating(
    ModelBuilder modelBuilder)
  {
    if ((Database.ProviderName is not null)
      && (Database.ProviderName.Contains("Sqlite")))
    {
      modelBuilder.Entity<Product>()
        .Property(product => product.UnitPrice)
        .HasConversion<double>();
    }
  }
}
```

10. Modify the class file named `Category.cs`, as shown in the following code:

```
using System.ComponentModel.DataAnnotations;

namespace Packt.Shared;

public class Category
{
  public int CategoryId { get; set; }

  [Required]
  [StringLength(15)]
  public string CategoryName { get; set; } = null!;

  public string? Description { get; set; }
}
```

11. Modify the class file named `Product.cs`, as shown in the following code:

```
using System.ComponentModel.DataAnnotations;
using System.ComponentModel.DataAnnotations.Schema;

namespace Packt.Shared;

public class Product
{
  public int ProductId { get; set; }

  [Required]
  [StringLength(40)]
  public string ProductName { get; set; } = null!;

  public int? SupplierId { get; set; }
  public int? CategoryId { get; set; }

  [StringLength(20)]
  public string? QuantityPerUnit { get; set; }

  [Column(TypeName = "money")] // required for SQL Server provider
  public decimal? UnitPrice { get; set; }

  public short? UnitsInStock { get; set; }
  public short? UnitsOnOrder { get; set; }
  public short? ReorderLevel { get; set; }
  public bool Discontinued { get; set; }
}
```

12. Build the project and fix any compiler errors.

Using Visual Studio 2022 with SQLite databases

If you are using Visual Studio 2022 for Windows or Mac with SQLite, then the compiled application executes in the `LinqWithEFCore\bin\Debug\net7.0` folder, so it will not find the database file unless we indicate that it should be copied to the output directory:

1. In **Solution Explorer**, right-click the `Northwind.db` file and select **Properties**.

2. In **Properties**, set **Copy to Output Directory** to **Copy if newer**.

Filtering and sorting sequences

Now let's write statements to filter and sort sequences of rows from the tables:

1. In the `LinqWithEFCore` project, add a new class file name `Program.Helpers.cs`.

2. In `Program.Helpers.cs`, define a partial `Program` class with a method to output a section title, as shown in the following code:

```
partial class Program
{
  static void SectionTitle(string title)
  {
    ConsoleColor previousColor = ForegroundColor;
    ForegroundColor = ConsoleColor.DarkYellow;
    WriteLine("*");
    WriteLine($"* {title}");
    WriteLine("*");
    ForegroundColor = previousColor;
  }
}
```

3. In the `LinqWithEFCore` project, add a new class file named `Program.Functions.cs`.

4. In `Program.Functions.cs`, define a partial `Program` class and add a method to filter and sort products, as shown in the following code:

```
using Packt.Shared; // Northwind, Category, Product
using Microsoft.EntityFrameworkCore; // DbSet<T>

partial class Program
{
  static void FilterAndSort()
  {
    SectionTitle("Filter and sort");

    using (Northwind db = new())
    {
      DbSet<Product> allProducts = db.Products;
```

```
        IQueryable<Product> filteredProducts =
          allProducts.Where(product => product.UnitPrice < 10M);

        IOrderedQueryable<Product> sortedAndFilteredProducts =
          filteredProducts.OrderByDescending(product => product.UnitPrice);

        WriteLine("Products that cost less than $10:");

        foreach (Product p in sortedAndFilteredProducts)
        {
          WriteLine("{0}: {1} costs {2:$#,##0.00}",
            p.ProductId, p.ProductName, p.UnitPrice);
        }
        WriteLine();
      }
    }
}
```

Note the following about the preceding code:

- `DbSet<T>` implements `IEnumerable<T>`, so LINQ can be used to query and manipulate sequences of entities in models built for EF Core.

  (Actually, I should say `TEntity` instead of `T`, but the name of this generic type has no functional effect. The only requirement is that the type is a `class`. The name just indicates the class is expected to be an entity model.)

- The sequences implement `IQueryable<T>` (or `IOrderedQueryable<T>` after a call to an ordering LINQ method) instead of `IEnumerable<T>` or `IOrderedEnumerable<T>`. This is an indication that we are using a LINQ provider that builds the query using expression trees. They represent code in a tree-like data structure and enable the creation of dynamic queries, which is useful for building LINQ queries for external data providers like SQLite.

- The LINQ expression will be converted into another query language, such as SQL. Enumerating the query with `foreach` or calling a method such as `ToArray` will force the execution of the query and materialize the results.

5. In `Program.cs`, call the `FilterAndSort` method.

6. Run the code and view the result, as shown in the following output:

```
Products that cost less than $10:
41: Jack's New England Clam Chowder costs $9.65
45: Rogede sild costs $9.50
47: Zaanse koeken costs $9.50
19: Teatime Chocolate Biscuits costs $9.20
23: Tunnbröd costs $9.00
75: Rhönbräu Klosterbier costs $7.75
```

```
54: Tourtière costs $7.45
52: Filo Mix costs $7.00
13: Konbu costs $6.00
24: Guaraná Fantástica costs $4.50
33: Geitost costs $2.50
```

Although this query outputs the information we want, it does so inefficiently because it gets all columns from the Products table instead of just the three columns we need. Let's log the generated SQL:

1. In the FilterAndSort method, after defining the query, add a statement to output the SQL, as
    shown in the following code:

    ```
    WriteLine(sortedAndFilteredProducts.ToQueryString());
    ```

2. Run the code and view the result that shows the SQL executed before the product details, as
    shown in the following partial output:

    ```
    SELECT "p"."ProductId", "p"."CategoryId", "p"."Discontinued",
    "p"."ProductName", "p"."QuantityPerUnit", "p"."ReorderLevel",
    "p"."SupplierId", "p"."UnitPrice", "p"."UnitsInStock", "p"."UnitsOnOrder"
    FROM "Products" AS "p"
    WHERE "p"."UnitPrice" < 10.0
    ORDER BY "p"."UnitPrice" DESC
    Products that cost less than $10:
    ...
    ```

Projecting sequences into new types

Before we look at projection, we need to review object initialization syntax. If you have a class defined,
then you can instantiate an object using the class name, new(), and curly braces to set initial values
for fields and properties, as shown in the following code:

```
// Person.cs
public class Person
{
  public string Name { get; set; }
  public DateTime DateOfBirth { get; set; }
}

// Program.cs
Person knownTypeObject = new()
{
  Name = "Boris Johnson",
  DateOfBirth = new(year: 1964, month: 6, day: 19)
};
```

C# 3.0 and later allow instances of **anonymous types** to be instantiated using the var keyword, as shown in the following code:

```
var anonymouslyTypedObject = new
{
  Name = "Boris Johnson",
  DateOfBirth = new DateTime(year: 1964, month: 6, day: 19)
};
```

Although we did not specify a type, the compiler can infer an anonymous type from the setting of two properties named Name and DateOfBirth. The compiler can infer the types of the two properties from the values assigned: a literal string and a new instance of a date/time value.

This capability is especially useful when writing LINQ queries to project an existing type into a new type without having to explicitly define the new type. Since the type is anonymous, this can only work with var-declared local variables.

Let's make the SQL command executed against the database table more efficient by adding a call to the Select method to project instances of the Product class into instances of a new anonymous type with only three properties:

1. In Program.Functions.cs, in the FilterAndSort method, add a statement to extend the LINQ query to use the Select method to return only the three properties (that is, table columns) that we need, and modify the foreach statement to use the var keyword and the projection LINQ expression, as shown highlighted in the following code:

```
IOrderedQueryable<Product> sortedAndFilteredProducts =
    filteredProducts.OrderByDescending(product => product.UnitPrice);

var projectedProducts = sortedAndFilteredProducts
  .Select(product => new // anonymous type
  {
    product.ProductId,
    product.ProductName,
    product.UnitPrice
  });

WriteLine(projectedProducts.ToQueryString());

WriteLine("Products that cost less than $10:");
foreach (var p in projectedProducts)
  {
```

2. Hover your mouse over the new keyword in the Select method call and the var keyword in the foreach statement and note that it is an anonymous type, as shown in *Figure 11.4*:

Figure 11.4: An anonymous type used during LINQ projection

3. Run the code and confirm that the output is the same as before and the generated SQL is more efficient, as shown in the following output:

```
SELECT "p"."ProductId", "p"."ProductName", "p"."UnitPrice"
FROM "Products" AS "p"
WHERE "p"."UnitPrice" < 10.0
ORDER BY "p"."UnitPrice" DESC
```

Joining and grouping sequences

There are two extension methods for joining and grouping:

*   Join: This method has four parameters: the sequence that you want to join with, the property or properties on the *left* sequence to match on, the property or properties on the *right* sequence to match on, and a projection.

*   GroupJoin: This method has the same parameters, but it combines the matches into a group object with a Key property for the matching value and an IEnumerable<T> type for the multiple matches.

Joining sequences

Let's explore these methods when working with two tables, Categories and Products:

1. In Program.Functions.cs, add a method to select categories and products, join them, and output them, as shown in the following code:

```
static void JoinCategoriesAndProducts()
{
    SectionTitle("Join categories and products");

    using (Northwind db = new())
    {
```

```
// join every product to its category to return 77 matches
var queryJoin = db.Categories.Join(
  inner: db.Products,
  outerKeySelector: category => category.CategoryId,
  innerKeySelector: product => product.CategoryId,
  resultSelector: (c, p) =>
    new { c.CategoryName, p.ProductName, p.ProductId });

foreach (var item in queryJoin)
{
  WriteLine("{0}: {1} is in {2}.",
    arg0: item.ProductId,
    arg1: item.ProductName,
    arg2: item.CategoryName);
}
}
}
```

 In a join, there are two sequences, outer and inner. In the preceding example, categories is the outer sequence and products is the inner sequence.

2. In `Program.cs`, call the `JoinCategoriesAndProducts` method.

3. Run the code and view the results. Note that there is a single line of output for each of the 77 products, as shown in the following output (edited to only include the first four items):

```
1: Chai is in Beverages.
2: Chang is in Beverages.
3: Aniseed Syrup is in Condiments.
4: Chef Anton's Cajun Seasoning is in Condiments.
...
```

4. At the end of the existing query, call the `OrderBy` method to sort by `CategoryName`, as shown highlighted in the following code:

```
var queryJoin = db.Categories.Join(
  inner: db.Products,
  outerKeySelector: category => category.CategoryId,
  innerKeySelector: product => product.CategoryId,
  resultSelector: (c, p) =>
    new { c.CategoryName, p.ProductName, p.ProductId })
  .OrderBy(cp => cp.CategoryName);
```

5.   Run the code and view the results. Note that there is a single line of output for each of the 77
     products, and the results show all products in the Beverages category first, then the Condiments
     category, and so on, as shown in the following partial output:

```
1: Chai is in Beverages.
2: Chang is in Beverages.
24: Guaraná Fantástica is in Beverages.
34: Sasquatch Ale is in Beverages.
...
```

Group-joining sequences

Let's explore group-joining when working with the same two tables as we used to explore joining,
Categories and Products, so we can compare the subtle differences:

1.   In Program.Functions.cs, add a method to group and join, show the group name, and then
     show all the items within each group, as shown in the following code:

```csharp
static void GroupJoinCategoriesAndProducts()
{
  SectionTitle("Group join categories and products");

  using (Northwind db = new())
  {
    // group all products by their category to return 8 matches
    var queryGroup = db.Categories.AsEnumerable().GroupJoin(
      inner: db.Products,
      outerKeySelector: category => category.CategoryId,
      innerKeySelector: product => product.CategoryId,
      resultSelector: (c, matchingProducts) => new
      {
        c.CategoryName,
        Products = matchingProducts.OrderBy(p => p.ProductName)
      });

    foreach (var category in queryGroup)
    {
      WriteLine("{0} has {1} products.",
        arg0: category.CategoryName,
        arg1: category.Products.Count());

      foreach (var product in category.Products)
      {
        WriteLine($" {product.ProductName}");
      }
    }
  }
}
```

If we had not called the AsEnumerable method, then a runtime exception would have been thrown, as shown in the following output:

```
Unhandled exception. System.ArgumentException:  Argument type 'System.
Linq.IOrderedQueryable'1[Packt.Shared.Product]' does not match the
corresponding member type 'System.Linq.IOrderedEnumerable'1[Packt.Shared.
Product]' (Parameter 'arguments[1]')
```

This is because not all LINQ extension methods can be converted from expression trees into some other query syntax like SQL. In these cases, we can convert from IQueryable<T> to IEnumerable<T> by calling the AsEnumerable method, which forces query processing to use LINQ to EF Core only to bring the data into the application, and then use LINQ to Objects to execute more complex processing in memory. But, often, this is less efficient.

2. In Program.cs, call the GroupJoinCategoriesAndProducts method.

3. Run the code, view the results, and note that the products inside each category have been sorted by their name, as defined in the query, and as shown in the following partial output:

```
Beverages has 12 products.
  Chai
  Chang
  ...
Condiments has 12 products.
  Aniseed Syrup
  Chef Anton's Cajun Seasoning
  ...
```

Aggregating sequences

There are LINQ extension methods to perform aggregation functions, such as Average and Sum. Let's write some code to see some of these methods in action, aggregating information from the Products table:

1. In Program.Functions.cs, add a method to show the use of the aggregation extension methods, as shown in the following code:

```
static void AggregateProducts()
{
  SectionTitle("Aggregate products");

  using (Northwind db = new())
  {
    // Try to get an efficient count from EF Core DbSet<T>.
    if (db.Products.TryGetNonEnumeratedCount(out int countDbSet))
    {
      WriteLine("{0,-25} {1,10}",
        arg0: "Product count from DbSet:",
        arg1: countDbSet);
    }
```

```
    else
    {
      WriteLine("Products DbSet does not have a Count property.");
    }

    // Try to get an efficient count from a List<T>.
    List<Product> products = db.Products.ToList();

    if (products.TryGetNonEnumeratedCount(out int countList))
    {
      WriteLine("{0,-25} {1,10}",
        arg0: "Product count from list:",
        arg1: countList);
    }
    else
    {
      WriteLine("Products list does not have a Count property.");
    }

WriteLine("{0,-25} {1,10}",
    arg0: "Product count:",
    arg1: db.Products.Count());

WriteLine("{0,-27} {1,8}", // Note the different column widths.
    arg0: "Discontinued product count:",
    arg1: db.Products.Count(product => product.Discontinued));

WriteLine("{0,-25} {1,10:$#,##0.00}",
    arg0: "Highest product price:",
    arg1: db.Products.Max(p => p.UnitPrice));

WriteLine("{0,-25} {1,10:N0}",
    arg0: "Sum of units in stock:",
    arg1: db.Products.Sum(p => p.UnitsInStock));

WriteLine("{0,-25} {1,10:N0}",
    arg0: "Sum of units on order:",
    arg1: db.Products.Sum(p => p.UnitsOnOrder));

WriteLine("{0,-25} {1,10:$#,##0.00}",
    arg0: "Average unit price:",
    arg1: db.Products.Average(p => p.UnitPrice));

WriteLine("{0,-25} {1,10:$#,##0.00}",
    arg0: "Value of units in stock:",
    arg1: db.Products
```

```
        .Sum(p => p.UnitPrice * p.UnitsInStock));
  }
}
```

Good Practice: Getting a count can seem like a simple operation, but it can be costly. A DbSet<T> like Products does not have a Count property so TryGetNonEnumeratedCount returns false. A List<T> like products does have a Count property because it implements ICollection, so TryGetNonEnumeratedCount returns true. (In this case, we had to instantiate a list which is itself a costly operation, but if you already have a list and need to know the number of items then this would be efficient.) You can always call Count() on a DbSet<T>, but it can be slow because it has to enumerate the sequence. You can pass a lambda expression to Count() to filter which items in the sequence should be counted.

2.   In Program.cs, call the AggregateProducts method.

3.   Run the code and view the result, as shown in the following output:

```
Products DbSet does not have a Count property.
Product count from list:         77
Product count:                   77
Discontinued product count:       8
Highest product price:      $263.50
Sum of units in stock:        3,119
Sum of units on order:          780
Average unit price:          $28.87
Value of units in stock:  $74,050.85
```

Be careful with Count!

Amichai Mantinband is a software engineer at Microsoft, and he does a great job of highlighting interesting parts of the C# and .NET developer stack.

Recently, he posted a code teaser on Twitter, LinkedIn, and YouTube, with a poll to find out what developers thought the code would do.

Here's the code:

```
IEnumerable<Task> tasks = Enumerable.Range(0, 2)
  .Select(_ => Task.Run(() => Console.WriteLine("*")));

await Task.WhenAll(tasks);

Console.WriteLine($"{tasks.Count()} stars!");
```

What will the output be?

1. **2 stars!
2. **2 stars!**
3. ****2 stars!
4. Something else

Most got it wrong, as shown in *Figure 11.5*:

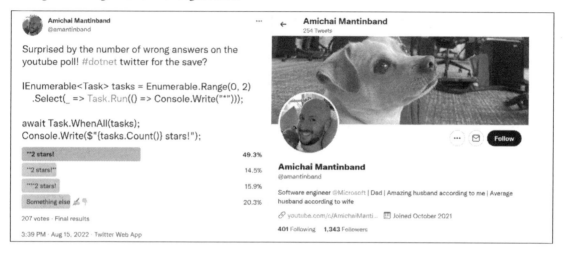

Figure 11.5: A tricky LINQ and Task code teaser from Amichai Mantinband

By this point in this chapter, I would hope that you would understand the LINQ parts of this tricky question. Don't worry! I would not expect you to understand the subtleties of multi-threading with tasks. It is still worth breaking down the code to make sure you understand the LINQ parts:

Code	Description
`Enumerable.Range(0, 2)`	Returns a sequence of two integers, 0 and 1. Personally, I would have added named parameters to make this clearer, as shown in the following code: `Enumerable.Range(start: 0, count: 2)`.
`Select(_ => Task.Run(...)`	Creates a task with its own thread for each of the two numbers. The `_` parameter discards the number value. Each task outputs a star * to the console.
`await Task.WhenAll(tasks);`	Blocks the main thread until both of the two tasks have completed. So, at this point, we know that two stars ** have been output to the console.
`tasks.Count()`	For the LINQ `Count()` extension method to work in this scenario, it must *enumerate the sequence*. This triggers the two tasks to execute again! But we do not know when those two tasks will execute. The value 2 is returned from the method call.
`Console.WriteLine($"... stars!");`	`2 stars!` is output to the console.

So, we know that ** is output to the console first, then one or both tasks might output their star, then 2 stars! is output, and finally, one or both tasks might output their star if they did not have time to do so before, or the main thread might end, terminating the console app before either task can output their star:

```
**[each task could output * here]2 stars![each task could output * here]
```

So, the best answer to Amichai's teaser is "Something else".

Good Practice: Be careful when calling LINQ extension methods like Count that need to enumerate over the sequence to calculate their return value. Even if you are not working with a sequence of executable objects like tasks, re-enumerating the sequence is likely to be inefficient.

Paging with LINQ

Let's see how we could implement paging using the Skip and Take extension methods:

1. In Program.Functions.cs, add a method to output to the console a table of products passed as an array, as shown in the following code:

```
static void OutputTableOfProducts(Product[] products,
  int currentPage, int totalPages)
{
  string line = new('-', count: 73);
  string lineHalf = new('-', count: 30);

  WriteLine(line);
  WriteLine("{0,4} {1,-40} {2,12} {3,-15}",
    "ID", "Product Name", "Unit Price", "Discontinued");
  WriteLine(line);

  foreach (Product p in products)
  {
    WriteLine("{0,4} {1,-40} {2,12:C} {3,-15}",
      p.ProductId, p.ProductName, p.UnitPrice, p.Discontinued);
  }
  WriteLine("{0} Page {1} of {2} {3}",
    lineHalf, currentPage + 1, totalPages + 1, lineHalf);
}
```

As usual in computing, our code we will start counting from zero, so we need to add one to both the currentPage count and totalPages count before showing these values in a user interface.

2. In `Program.Functions.cs`, add a method to create a LINQ query that creates a page of products, outputs the SQL generated from it, and then passes the results as an array of products to the method that outputs a table of products, as shown in the following code:

```
static void OutputPageOfProducts(IQueryable<Product> products,
    int pageSize, int currentPage, int totalPages)
{
    // We must order data before skipping and taking to ensure
    // the data is not randomly sorted in each page.
    var pagingQuery = products.OrderBy(p => p.ProductId)
        .Skip(currentPage * pageSize).Take(pageSize);

    SectionTitle(pagingQuery.ToQueryString());

    OutputTableOfProducts(pagingQuery.ToArray(),
        currentPage, totalPages);
}
```

3. In `Program.Functions.cs`, add a method to loop while the user presses either left or right arrows to page through the products in the database, showing one page at a time, as shown in the following code:

```
static void PagingProducts()
{
    SectionTitle("Paging products");

    using (Northwind db = new())
    {
        int pageSize = 10;
        int currentPage = 0;
        int productCount = db.Products.Count();
        int totalPages = productCount / pageSize;

        while (true)
        {
            OutputPageOfProducts(db.Products, pageSize, currentPage, totalPages);

            Write("Press <- to page back, press -> to page forward, any key to
            exit.");
            ConsoleKey key = ReadKey().Key;

            if (key == ConsoleKey.LeftArrow)
                if (currentPage == 0)
                    currentPage = totalPages;
                else
                    currentPage--;
```

```
        else if (key == ConsoleKey.RightArrow)
          if (currentPage == totalPages)
            currentPage = 0;
          else
            currentPage++;
        else
          break; // out of the while loop.

        WriteLine();
      }
    }
}
```

4. In `Program.cs`, comment out any other methods and then call the `PagingProducts` method.

5. Run the code and view the result, as shown in the following output:

```
-----------------------------------------------------------
ID Product Name                        Unit Price Discontinued
-----------------------------------------------------------
1 Chai                                   £18.00 False
2 Chang                                  £19.00 False
3 Aniseed Syrup                          £10.00 False
4 Chef Anton's Cajun Seasoning           £22.00 False
5 Chef Anton's Gumbo Mix                 £21.35 True
6 Grandma's Boysenberry Spread           £25.00 False
7 Uncle Bob's Organic Dried Pears        £30.00 False
8 Northwoods Cranberry Sauce             £40.00 False
9 Mishi Kobe Niku                        £97.00 True
10 Ikura                                 £31.00 False
--------------------------- Page 1 of 8 ----------------
Press <- to page back, press -> to page forward.
```

The preceding output excludes the SQL statement used to efficiently get the page of products by using ORDER BY, LIMIT, and OFFSET, as shown in the following code:

```
.param set @__p_1 10
.param set @__p_0 0


SELECT "p"."ProductId", "p"."CategoryId",
"p"."Discontinued", "p"."ProductName",
"p"."QuantityPerUnit", "p"."ReorderLevel",
"p"."SupplierId", "p"."UnitPrice", "p"."UnitsInStock",
"p"."UnitsOnOrder"
FROM "Products" AS "p"
ORDER BY "p"."ProductId"
LIMIT @__p_1 OFFSET @__p_0
```

6. Press the right arrow and note the second page of results, as shown in the following output:

```
------------------------------------------------------------
ID Product Name                        Unit Price Discontinued
------------------------------------------------------------
11 Queso Cabrales                         £21.00 False
12 Queso Manchego La Pastora              £38.00 False
13 Konbu                                   £6.00 False
14 Tofu                                   £23.25 False
15 Genen Shouyu                           £15.50 False
16 Pavlova                                £17.45 False
17 Alice Mutton                           £39.00 True
18 Carnarvon Tigers                       £62.50 False
19 Teatime Chocolate Biscuits             £9.20 False
20 Sir Rodney's Marmalade                 £81.00 False
--------------------------- Page 2 of 8 ----------------
Press <- to page back, press -> to page forward.
```

7. Press the left arrow twice and note that it loops around to the last page of results, as shown in the following output:

```
------------------------------------------------------------
ID Product Name                        Unit Price Discontinued
------------------------------------------------------------
71 Flotemysost                            £21.50 False
72 Mozzarella di Giovanni                 £34.80 False
73 Röd Kaviar                             £15.00 False
74 Longlife Tofu                          £10.00 False
75 Rhönbräu Klosterbier                    £7.75 False
76 Lakkalikööri                           £18.00 False
77 Original Frankfurter grüne Soße        £13.00 False
--------------------------- Page 8 of 8 ----------------
Press <- to page back, press -> to page forward.
```

8. Press any other key to end the loop.

9. In `Program.Functions.cs`, comment out the statement to output the SQL used, as shown highlighted in the following code:

```
// SectionTitle(pagingQuery.ToQueryString());
```

 As an optional task, explore how you might use the `Chunk` method to output pages of products.

Good Practice: You should always order data before calling `Skip` and `Take` if you want to implement paging. This is because each time you execute a query, the LINQ provider does not have to guarantee to return the data is in the same order unless you have specified it. Therefore, if the SQLite provider wanted to, the first time you request a page of products they might be in `ProductId` order, but the next time you request a page of products they might be in `UnitPrice` order, or a random order, and that would confuse users! In practice, at least for relational databases, the default order is usually by its index on the primary key.

Sweetening LINQ syntax with syntactic sugar

C# 3.0 introduced some new language keywords in 2008 to make it easier for programmers with experience with SQL to write LINQ queries. This syntactic sugar is officially called the **LINQ query comprehension syntax**.

Consider the following array of `string` values:

```
string[] names = new[] { "Michael", "Pam", "Jim", "Dwight",
  "Angela", "Kevin", "Toby", "Creed" };
```

To filter and sort the names, you could use extension methods and lambda expressions, as shown in the following code:

```
var query = names
  .Where(name => name.Length > 4)
  .OrderBy(name => name.Length)
  .ThenBy(name => name);
```

Or you could achieve the same results by using query comprehension syntax, as shown in the following code:

```
var query = from name in names
  where name.Length > 4
  orderby name.Length, name
  select name;
```

The compiler changes the query comprehension syntax to the equivalent extension methods and lambda expressions for you.

The `select` keyword is always required for LINQ query comprehension syntax. The `Select` extension method is optional when using extension methods and lambda expressions because if you do not call `Select`, then the whole item is implicitly selected.

Not all extension methods have a C# keyword equivalent, for example, the `Skip` and `Take` extension methods, which are commonly used to implement paging for lots of data.

A query that skips and takes cannot be written using only the query comprehension syntax, so we could write the query using all extension methods, as shown in the following code:

```
var query = names
  .Where(name => name.Length > 4)
  .Skip(80)
  .Take(10);
```

Or we could wrap query comprehension syntax in parentheses and then switch to using extension methods, as shown in the following code:

```
var query = (from name in names
  where name.Length > 4
  select name)
  .Skip(80)
  .Take(10);
```

Using multiple threads with parallel LINQ

This is a bonus section for the chapter that is available online at `https://github.com/markjprice/cs11dotnet7/blob/main/docs/bonus/plinq.md`

Creating your own LINQ extension methods

In *Chapter 6, Implementing Interfaces and Inheriting Classes*, you learned how to create your own extension methods. To create LINQ extension methods, all you must do is extend the `IEnumerable<T>` type.

 Good Practice: Put your own extension methods in a separate class library so that they can be easily deployed as their own assembly or NuGet package.

We will improve the `Average` extension method as an example. A well-educated school child will tell you that *average* can mean one of three things:

- **Mean:** Sum the numbers and divide by the count.
- **Mode:** The most common number.
- **Median:** The number in the middle of the numbers when ordered.

Microsoft's implementation of the `Average` extension method calculates the *mean*. We might want to define our own extension methods for `Mode` and `Median`:

1. In the `LinqWithEFCore` project, add a new class file named `MyLinqExtensions.cs`.
2. Modify the class, as shown in the following code:

```
namespace System.Linq; // extend Microsoft's namespace

public static class MyLinqExtensions
```

```
{
  // this is a chainable LINQ extension method
  public static IEnumerable<T> ProcessSequence<T>(
    this IEnumerable<T> sequence)
  {
    // you could do some processing here
    return sequence;
  }

  public static IQueryable<T> ProcessSequence<T>(
    this IQueryable<T> sequence)
  {
    // you could do some processing here
    return sequence;
  }

  // these are scalar LINQ extension methods
  public static int? Median(
    this IEnumerable<int?> sequence)
  {
    var ordered = sequence.OrderBy(item => item);
    int middlePosition = ordered.Count() / 2;
    return ordered.ElementAt(middlePosition);
  }

  public static int? Median<T>(
    this IEnumerable<T> sequence, Func<T, int?> selector)
  {
    return sequence.Select(selector).Median();
  }

  public static decimal? Median(
    this IEnumerable<decimal?> sequence)
  {
    var ordered = sequence.OrderBy(item => item);
    int middlePosition = ordered.Count() / 2;
    return ordered.ElementAt(middlePosition);
  }

  public static decimal? Median<T>(
    this IEnumerable<T> sequence, Func<T, decimal?> selector)
  {
    return sequence.Select(selector).Median();
  }

  public static int? Mode(
```

```
    this IEnumerable<int?> sequence)
  {
    var grouped = sequence.GroupBy(item => item);
    var orderedGroups = grouped.OrderByDescending(
      group => group.Count());
    return orderedGroups.FirstOrDefault()?.Key;
  }

  public static int? Mode<T>(
    this IEnumerable<T> sequence, Func<T, int?> selector)
  {
    return sequence.Select(selector)?.Mode();
  }

  public static decimal? Mode(
    this IEnumerable<decimal?> sequence)
  {
    var grouped = sequence.GroupBy(item => item);
    var orderedGroups = grouped.OrderByDescending(
      group => group.Count());
    return orderedGroups.FirstOrDefault()?.Key;
  }

  public static decimal? Mode<T>(
    this IEnumerable<T> sequence, Func<T, decimal?> selector)
  {
    return sequence.Select(selector).Mode();
  }
}
```

If this class was in a separate class library, to use your LINQ extension methods, you would simply need to reference the class library assembly because the System.Linq namespace is already implicitly imported.

 Warning! All but one of the above extension methods cannot be used with IQueryable sequences like those used by LINQ to SQLite or LINQ to SQL Server, because we have not implemented a way to translate our code into the underlying query language like SQL.

Trying the chainable extension method

First, we will try chaining the ProcessSequence method with other extension methods:

1. In Program.Functions.cs, in the FilterAndSort method, modify the LINQ query for Products to call your custom chainable extension method, as shown highlighted in the following code:

    ```
    DbSet<Product> allProducts = db.Products;
    ```

```
IQueryable<Product> processedProducts = allProducts.ProcessSequence();

IQueryable<Product> filteredProducts = processedProducts
  .Where(product => product.UnitPrice < 10M);
```

2. In `Program.cs`, uncomment the `FilterAndSort` method and comment out any calls to other methods.

3. Run the code and note that you see the same output as before because your method doesn't modify the sequence. But you now know how to extend a LINQ expression with your own functionality.

Trying the mode and median methods

Second, we will try using the `Mode` and `Median` methods to calculate other kinds of averages:

1. In `Program.Functions.cs`, add a method to output the mean, median, and mode for the `UnitsInStock` and `UnitPrice` for products, using your custom extension methods and the built-in `Average` extension method, as shown in the following code:

```
static void CustomExtensionMethods()
{
  SectionTitle("Custom aggregate extension methods");

  using (Northwind db = new())
  {
    WriteLine("{0,-25} {1,10:N0}",
      "Mean units in stock:",
      db.Products.Average(p => p.UnitsInStock));

    WriteLine("{0,-25} {1,10:$#,##0.00}",
      "Mean unit price:",
      db.Products.Average(p => p.UnitPrice));

    WriteLine("{0,-25} {1,10:N0}",
      "Median units in stock:",
      db.Products.Median(p => p.UnitsInStock));

    WriteLine("{0,-25} {1,10:$#,##0.00}",
      "Median unit price:",
      db.Products.Median(p => p.UnitPrice));

    WriteLine("{0,-25} {1,10:N0}",
      "Mode units in stock:",
      db.Products.Mode(p => p.UnitsInStock));

    WriteLine("{0,-25} {1,10:$#,##0.00}",
      "Mode unit price:",
      db.Products.Mode(p => p.UnitPrice));
```

```
      }
    }
```

2. In `Program.cs`, call the `CustomExtensionMethods` method.

3. Run the code and view the result, as shown in the following output:

```
Mean units in stock:                    41
Mean unit price:                    $28.87
Median units in stock:                  26
Median unit price:                  $19.50
Mode units in stock:                     0
Mode unit price:                    $18.00
```

There are four products with a unit price of $18.00. There are five products with 0 units in stock.

Working with LINQ to XML

LINQ to XML is a LINQ provider that allows you to query and manipulate XML.

Generating XML using LINQ to XML

Let's create a method to convert the `Products` table into XML:

1. In the `LinqWithEFCore` project, in `Program.Functions.cs`, import the `System.Xml.Linq` name-space.

2. In `Program.Functions.cs`, add a method to output the products in XML format, as shown in the following code:

```
static void OutputProductsAsXml()
{
  SectionTitle("Output products as XML");

  using (Northwind db = new())
  {
    Product[] productsArray = db.Products.ToArray();

    XElement xml = new("products",
      from p in productsArray
      select new XElement("product",
        new XAttribute("id", p.ProductId),
        new XAttribute("price", p.UnitPrice),
        new XElement("name", p.ProductName)));

    WriteLine(xml.ToString());
  }
}
```

3. In `Program.cs`, call the `OutputProductsAsXml` method.

4. Run the code, view the result, and note that the structure of the XML generated matches the elements and attributes that the LINQ to XML statement declaratively described in the preceding code, as shown in the following partial output:

```
<products>
  <product id="1" price="18">
    <name>Chai</name>
  </product>
  <product id="2" price="19">
    <name>Chang</name>
  </product>
  ...
```

Reading XML using LINQ to XML

You might want to use LINQ to XML to easily query or process XML files:

1. In the `LinqWithEFCore` project, add a file named `settings.xml`.

2. Modify its contents, as shown in the following markup:

```
<?xml version="1.0" encoding="utf-8" ?>
<appSettings>
  <add key="color" value="red" />
  <add key="size" value="large" />
  <add key="price" value="23.99" />
</appSettings>
```

 If you are using Visual Studio 2022, then the compiled application executes in the `LinqWithEFCore\bin\Debug\net7.0` folder so it will not find the `settings.xml` file unless we indicate that it should always be copied to the output directory. Select the `settings.xml` file and set its **Copy to Output Directory** property to **Copy always**.

3. In `Program.Functions.cs`, add a method to complete these tasks, as shown in the following code:

- Load the XML file.
- Use LINQ to XML to search for an element named `appSettings` and its descendants named `add`.
- Project the XML into an array of an anonymous type with `Key` and `Value` properties.
- Enumerate through the array to show the results:

```
static void ProcessSettings()
{
  string path = Path.Combine(
```

```
       Environment.CurrentDirectory, "settings.xml");

    WriteLine($"Settings file path: {path}");
    XDocument doc = XDocument.Load(path);
    var appSettings = doc.Descendants("appSettings")
      .Descendants("add")
      .Select(node => new
      {
        Key = node.Attribute("key")?.Value,
        Value = node.Attribute("value")?.Value
      }).ToArray();

    foreach (var item in appSettings)
    {
      WriteLine($"{item.Key}: {item.Value}");
    }
  }
}
```

4. In `Program.cs`, call the `ProcessSettings` method.

5. Run the console app and view the result, as shown in the following output:

```
Settings file path: C:\cs11dotnet7\Chapter11\LinqWithEFCore\bin\Debug\
net7.0\settings.xml
color: red
size: large
price: 23.99
```

Practicing and exploring

Test your knowledge and understanding by answering some questions, getting some hands-on practice, and exploring with deeper research into the topics covered in this chapter.

Exercise 11.1 – Test your knowledge

Answer the following questions:

1. What are the two required parts of LINQ?

2. Which LINQ extension method would you use to return a subset of properties from a type?

3. Which LINQ extension method would you use to filter a sequence?

4. List five LINQ extension methods that perform aggregation.

5. What is the difference between the `Select` and `SelectMany` extension methods?

6. What is the difference between `IEnumerable<T>` and `IQueryable<T>`? How do you switch between them?

7. What does the last type parameter `T` in generic `Func` delegates like `Func<T1, T2, T>` represent?

8. What is the benefit of a LINQ extension method that ends with `OrDefault`?

9.   Why is query comprehension syntax optional?

10. How can you create your own LINQ extension methods?

Exercise 11.2 – Practice querying with LINQ

In the Chapter11 solution/workspace, create a console application, named Ch11Ex02LinqQueries, that prompts the user for a city and then lists the company names for Northwind customers in that city, as shown in the following output:

```
Enter the name of a city: London
There are 6 customers in London:
  Around the Horn
  B's Beverages
  Consolidated Holdings
  Eastern Connection
  North/South
  Seven Seas Imports
```

Then, enhance the application by displaying a list of all unique cities that customers already reside in as a prompt to the user before they enter their preferred city, as shown in the following output:

```
Aachen, Albuquerque, Anchorage, Århus, Barcelona, Barquisimeto, Bergamo,
Berlin, Bern, Boise, Bräcke, Brandenburg, Bruxelles, Buenos Aires, Butte,
Campinas, Caracas, Charleroi, Cork, Cowes, Cunewalde, Elgin, Eugene, Frankfurt
a.M., Genève, Graz, Helsinki, I. de Margarita, Kirkland, Kobenhavn, Köln,
Lander, Leipzig, Lille, Lisboa, London, Luleå, Lyon, Madrid, Mannheim,
Marseille, México D.F., Montréal, München, Münster, Nantes, Oulu, Paris,
Portland, Reggio Emilia, Reims, Resende, Rio de Janeiro, Salzburg, San
Cristóbal, San Francisco, Sao Paulo, Seattle, Sevilla, Stavern, Strasbourg,
Stuttgart, Torino, Toulouse, Tsawassen, Vancouver, Versailles, Walla Walla,
Warszawa
```

Exercise 11.3 – Explore topics

Use the links on the following page to learn more details about the topics covered in this chapter:

https://github.com/markjprice/cs11dotnet7/blob/main/book-links.md#chapter-11---querying-and-manipulating-data-using-linq

Summary

In this chapter, you learned how to write LINQ queries to perform common tasks like:

- Selecting just the properties of an item that you need.

- Projecting items into different types.

- Filtering items based on conditions.

- Sorting items.

- Joining and grouping items.

- Manipulating items in different formats, including XML.

In the next chapter, you will be introduced to web development using ASP.NET Core. In the remaining chapters, you will learn how to implement the major components of ASP.NET Core like Razor Pages, MVC, Web API, and Blazor.

Join our book's Discord space

Join the book's Discord workspace for *Ask me Anything* sessions with the author.

https://packt.link/csharp11dotnet7

12

Introducing Web Development Using ASP.NET Core

The third and final part of this book is about web development using ASP.NET Core. You will learn how to build cross-platform projects such as websites, web services, and web browser apps.

Microsoft calls platforms for building applications **app models** or **workloads**.

I recommend that you work through this and subsequent chapters sequentially because later chapters will reference projects in earlier chapters, and you will build up sufficient knowledge and skills to tackle the trickier problems in later chapters.

In this chapter, we will cover the following topics:

- Understanding ASP.NET Core
- New features in ASP.NET Core
- Structuring projects
- Building an entity model for use in the rest of the book
- Understanding web development

Understanding ASP.NET Core

Since this book is about C# and .NET, we will learn about app models that use them to build the practical applications that we will encounter in the remaining chapters of this book.

 Learn More: Microsoft has extensive guidance for implementing app models in its .NET Application Architecture Guidance documentation, which you can read at the following link: https://www.microsoft.com/net/learn/architecture.

Microsoft ASP.NET Core is part of a history of Microsoft technologies used to build websites and services that have evolved over the years:

- **Active Server Pages** (**ASP**) was released in 1996 and was Microsoft's first attempt at a platform for dynamic server-side execution of website code. ASP files contain a mix of HTML and code that executes on the server written in the VBScript language.

- **ASP.NET Web Forms** was released in 2002 with the .NET Framework and was designed to enable non-web developers, such as those familiar with Visual Basic, to quickly create websites by dragging and dropping visual components and writing event-driven code in Visual Basic or C#. Web Forms should be avoided for new .NET Framework web projects in favor of ASP.NET MVC.

- **Windows Communication Foundation** (**WCF**) was released in 2006 and enables developers to build SOAP and REST services. SOAP is powerful but complex, so it should be avoided unless you need advanced features, such as distributed transactions and complex messaging topologies.

- **ASP.NET MVC** was released in 2009 to cleanly separate the concerns of web developers between the **models**, which temporarily store the data; the **views**, which present the data using various formats in the UI; and the **controllers**, which fetch the model and pass it to a view. This separation enables improved reuse and unit testing.

- **ASP.NET Web API** was released in 2012 and enables developers to create HTTP services (aka REST services) that are simpler and more scalable than SOAP services.

- **ASP.NET SignalR** was released in 2013 and enables real-time communication in websites by abstracting underlying technologies and techniques, such as WebSockets and long polling. This enables website features such as live chat or updates to time-sensitive data such as stock prices across a wide variety of web browsers, even when they do not support an underlying technology such as WebSockets.

- **ASP.NET Core** was released in 2016 and combines modern implementations of .NET Framework technologies such as MVC, Web API, and SignalR, with newer technologies such as Razor Pages, gRPC, and Blazor, all running on modern .NET. Therefore, it can execute cross-platform. ASP.NET Core has many project templates to get you started with its supported technologies.

 Good Practice: Choose ASP.NET Core to develop websites and web services because it includes web-related technologies that are modern and cross-platform.

Classic ASP.NET versus modern ASP.NET Core

Until modern .NET, ASP.NET was built on top of a large assembly in .NET Framework named System. Web.dll and it was tightly coupled to Microsoft's Windows-only web server named **Internet Information Services** (**IIS**). Over the years, this assembly has accumulated a lot of features, many of which are not suitable for modern cross-platform development.

ASP.NET Core is a major redesign of ASP.NET. It removes the dependency on the System.Web.dll assembly and IIS and is composed of modular lightweight packages, just like the rest of modern .NET. Using IIS as the web server is still supported by ASP.NET Core, but there is a better option.

You can develop and run ASP.NET Core applications cross-platform on Windows, macOS, and Linux. Microsoft has even created a cross-platform, super-performant web server named **Kestrel**, and the entire stack is open source.

ASP.NET Core 2.2 or later projects default to the new in-process hosting model. This gives a 400% performance improvement when hosting in Microsoft IIS, but Microsoft still recommends using Kestrel for even better performance.

Building websites using ASP.NET Core

Websites are made up of multiple web pages loaded statically from the filesystem or generated dynamically by a server-side technology such as ASP.NET Core. A web browser makes GET requests using **Uniform Resource Locators** (**URLs**) that identify each page and can manipulate data stored on the server using POST, PUT, and DELETE requests.

With many websites, the web browser is treated as a presentation layer, with almost all the processing performed on the server side. Some JavaScript might be used on the client side to implement form validation warnings and some presentation features, such as carousels.

ASP.NET Core provides multiple technologies for building websites:

- **ASP.NET Core Razor Pages** and **Razor class libraries** are ways to dynamically generate HTML for simple websites. You will learn about them in detail in *Chapter 13, Building Websites Using ASP.NET Core Razor Pages*.
- **ASP.NET Core MVC** is an implementation of the **Model-View-Controller** (**MVC**) design pattern that is popular for developing complex websites. You will learn about it in detail in *Chapter 14, Building Websites Using the Model-View-Controller Pattern*.
- **Blazor** lets you build user interface components using C# and .NET instead of a JavaScript-based UI framework like Angular, React, and Vue. **Blazor WebAssembly** runs your code in the browser like a JavaScript-based framework would. **Blazor Server** runs your code on the server and updates the web page dynamically. You will learn about Blazor in detail in *Chapter 16, Building User Interfaces Using Blazor*. Blazor is not just for building websites; it can also be used to create hybrid mobile and desktop apps by being hosted inside a .NET MAUI app.

Building websites using a content management system

Most websites have a lot of content, and if developers had to be involved every time some content needed to be changed, that would not scale well. A **Content Management System** (**CMS**) enables developers to define content structure and templates to provide consistency and good design while making it easy for a non-technical content owner to manage the actual content. They can create new pages or blocks of content, and update existing content, knowing it will look great for visitors with minimal effort.

There is a multitude of CMSs available for all web platforms, like WordPress for PHP or Django CMS for Python. CMSs that support modern .NET include Optimizely Content Cloud, Piranha CMS, and Orchard Core.

The key benefit of using a CMS is that it provides a friendly content management user interface. Content owners log in to the website and manage the content themselves. The content is then rendered and returned to visitors using ASP.NET Core MVC controllers and views, or via web service endpoints, known as a **headless CMS,** to provide that content to "heads" implemented as mobile or desktop apps, in-store touchpoints, or clients built with JavaScript frameworks or Blazor.

This book does not cover .NET CMSs, so I have included links where you can learn more about them in the GitHub repository:

```
https://github.com/markjprice/cs11dotnet7/blob/main/book-links.md#net-content-
management-systems
```

Building web applications using SPA frameworks

Web applications are often built using technologies known as **Single-Page Applications (SPAs)** frameworks, such as Blazor WebAssembly, Angular, React, Vue, or a proprietary JavaScript library. They can make requests to a backend web service for getting more data when needed and posting updated data using common serialization formats such as XML and JSON. The canonical examples are Google web apps like Gmail, Maps, and Docs.

With a web application, the client side uses JavaScript frameworks or Blazor WebAssembly to implement sophisticated user interactions, but most of the important processing and data access still happens on the server side, because the web browser has limited access to local system resources.

JavaScript is loosely typed and is not designed for complex projects, so most JavaScript libraries these days use TypeScript, which adds strong typing to JavaScript and is designed with many modern language features for handling complex implementations.

.NET SDK has project templates for JavaScript and TypeScript-based SPAs, but we will not spend any time learning how to build JavaScript- and TypeScript-based SPAs in this book, even though they are commonly used with ASP.NET Core as the backend, because this book is about C#; it is not about other languages.

In summary, C# and .NET can be used on both the server side and the client side to build websites, as shown in *Figure 12.1*:

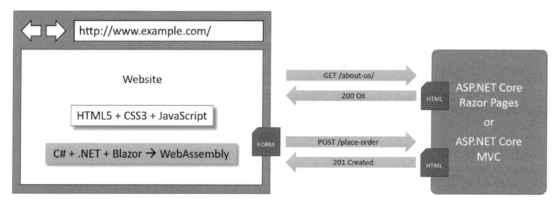

Figure 12.1: The use of C# and .NET to build websites on both the server side and the client side

Building web and other services

Although we will not learn about JavaScript- and TypeScript-based SPAs, we will learn how to build a web service using the **ASP.NET Core Web API**, and then call that web service from the server-side code in our ASP.NET Core websites. Later, we will call that web service from Blazor WebAssembly components and cross-platform mobile and desktop apps.

There are no formal definitions, but services are sometimes described based on their complexity:

- **Service:** All functionality needed by a client app in one monolithic service.
- **Microservice:** Multiple services that each focus on a smaller set of functionalities.
- **Nanoservice:** A single function provided as a service. Unlike services and microservices that are hosted 24/7/365, nanoservices are often inactive until called upon to reduce resources and costs.

New features in ASP.NET Core

Over the past few years, Microsoft has rapidly expanded the capabilities of ASP.NET Core. You should note which .NET platforms are supported, as shown in the following list:

- ASP.NET Core 1.0 to 2.2 runs on either .NET Core or .NET Framework.
- ASP.NET Core 3.0 or later only runs on .NET Core 3.0 or later.

ASP.NET Core 1.0

ASP.NET Core 1.0 was released in June 2016 and focused on implementing a minimum API suitable for building modern cross-platform web apps and services for Windows, macOS, and Linux.

ASP.NET Core 1.1

ASP.NET Core 1.1 was released in November 2016 and focused on bug fixes and general improvements to features and performance.

ASP.NET Core 2.0

ASP.NET Core 2.0 was released in August 2017 and focused on adding new features such as Razor Pages, bundling assemblies into a `Microsoft.AspNetCore.All` metapackage, targeting .NET Standard 2.0, providing a new authentication model and performance improvements.

The biggest new features introduced with ASP.NET Core 2.0 are ASP.NET Core Razor Pages, which is covered in *Chapter 13, Building Websites Using ASP.NET Core Razor Pages*, and ASP.NET Core OData support. OData is covered in my other book, *Apps and Services with .NET 7*.

ASP.NET Core 2.1

ASP.NET Core 2.1 was released in May 2018 and was a **Long Term Support** (**LTS**) release, meaning it was supported for three years until August 21, 2021 (LTS designation was not officially assigned to it until August 2018 with version 2.1.3).

It focused on adding new features such as **SignalR** for real-time communication, **Razor class libraries** for reusing web components, **ASP.NET Core Identity** for authentication, and better support for HTTPS and the European Union's **General Data Protection Regulation (GDPR)**, including the topics listed in the following table:

Feature	Chapter	Topic
Razor class libraries	13	Using Razor class libraries
GDPR support	14	Creating and exploring an ASP.NET Core MVC website
Identity UI library and scaffolding	14	Exploring an ASP.NET Core MVC website
Integration tests	14	Testing an ASP.NET Core MVC website
`[ApiController]`, `ActionResult<T>`	15	Creating an ASP.NET Core Web API project
Problem details	15	Implementing a Web API controller
`IHttpClientFactory`	15	Configuring HTTP clients using HttpClientFactory

ASP.NET Core 2.2

ASP.NET Core 2.2 was released in December 2018 and focused on improving the building of RESTful HTTP APIs, updating the project templates to Bootstrap 4 and Angular 6, an optimized configuration for hosting in Azure, and performance improvements, including the topics listed in the following table:

Feature	Chapter	Topic
HTTP/2 in Kestrel	13	Classic ASP.NET versus modern ASP.NET Core
In-process hosting model	13	Creating an ASP.NET Core project
Endpoint routing	13	Understanding endpoint routing
Health Checks Middleware	15	Implementing health checks
Open API analyzers	15	Implementing Open API analyzers and conventions

ASP.NET Core 3.0

ASP.NET Core 3.0 was released in September 2019 and focused on fully leveraging .NET Core 3.0 and .NET Standard 2.1, which meant it could not support .NET Framework, and it added useful refinements, including the topics listed in the following table:

Feature	Chapter	Topic
Static assets in Razor class libraries	13	Using Razor class libraries
New options for MVC service registration	14	Understanding ASP.NET Core MVC startup
Blazor Server	16	Building components using Blazor Server

ASP.NET Core 3.1

ASP.NET Core 3.1 was released in December 2019 and is an LTS release, meaning it will be supported until December 13, 2022. It focused on refinements like partial class support for Razor components and a new `<component>` tag helper.

Blazor WebAssembly 3.2

Blazor WebAssembly 3.2 was released in May 2020. It was a Current (now known as Standard) release, meaning that projects had to be upgraded to the .NET 5 version within three months of the .NET 5 release, that is, by February 10, 2021. Microsoft finally delivered on the promise of full-stack web development with .NET, and both Blazor Server and Blazor WebAssembly are covered in *Chapter 16, Building User Interfaces Using Blazor*.

ASP.NET Core 5.0

ASP.NET Core 5.0 was released in November 2020 and focused on bug fixes, performance improvements, using caching for certificate authentication, HPACK dynamic compression of HTTP/2 response headers in Kestrel, nullable annotations for ASP.NET Core assemblies, and a reduction in container image sizes, including the topics listed in the following table:

Feature	Chapter	Topic
Extension method to allow anonymous access to an endpoint	15	Securing web services
JSON extension methods for `HttpRequest` and `HttpResponse`	15	Getting customers as JSON in the controller

ASP.NET Core 6.0

ASP.NET Core 6.0 was released in November 2021 and focused on productivity improvements like minimizing code to implement basic websites and services, support for .NET Hot Reload, and new hosting options for Blazor, like hybrid apps using .NET MAUI, including the topics listed in the following table:

Feature	Chapter	Topic
New empty web project template	13	Understanding the empty web template
Minimal APIs	15	Implementing Minimal Web APIs
Blazor WebAssembly AOT	16	Enabling Blazor WebAssembly ahead-of-time compilation

ASP.NET Core 7.0

ASP.NET Core 7.0 was released in November 2022 and focused on filling well-known gaps in functionality like HTTP/3 support, output caching, and many quality-of-life improvements to Blazor, including the topics listed in the following table:

Feature	Chapter	Topic
HTTP request decompression	13	Enabling request decompression support
HTTP/3 support	13	Enabling HTTP/3 support
Output caching	14	Using a filter to cache output
W3C log additional headers	15	Support for logging additional request headers in W3CLogger
HTTP/3 client support	15	Enabling HTTP/3 support for HttpClient
Blazor Empty templates	16	Comparing Blazor project templates
Location change support	16	Enabling location change event handling

 You can read the full ASP.NET Core Roadmap for .NET 7 at the following link: `https://github.com/dotnet/aspnetcore/issues/39504`.

Structuring projects

How should you structure your projects? So far, we have built small individual console apps to illustrate language or library features. In the rest of this book, we will build multiple projects using different technologies that work together to provide a single solution.

With large, complex solutions, it can be difficult to navigate through all the code. So, the primary reason to structure your projects is to make it easier to find components. It is good to have an overall name for your solution or workspace that reflects the application or solution.

We will build multiple projects for a fictional company named **Northwind**. We will name the solution or workspace `PracticalApps` and use the name `Northwind` as a prefix for all the project names.

There are many ways to structure and name projects and solutions, for example, using a folder hierarchy as well as a naming convention. If you work in a team, make sure you know how your team does it.

Structuring projects in a solution or workspace

It is good to have a naming convention for your projects in a solution or workspace so that any developer can tell what each one does instantly. A common choice is to use the type of project, for example, class library, console app, website, and so on, as shown in the following table:

Name	Description
Northwind.Common	A class library project for common types like interfaces, enums, classes, records, and structs, used across multiple projects.
Northwind.Common.EntityModels	A class library project for common EF Core entity models. Entity models are often used on both the server and client side, so it is best to separate dependencies on specific database providers.
Northwind.Common.DataContext	A class library project for the EF Core database context with dependencies on specific database providers.
Northwind.Web	An ASP.NET Core project for a simple website that uses a mixture of static HTML files and dynamic Razor Pages.
Northwind.Razor.Component	A class library project for Razor Pages used in multiple projects.
Northwind.Mvc	An ASP.NET Core project for a complex website that uses the MVC pattern and can be more easily unit tested.
Northwind.WebApi	An ASP.NET Core project for an HTTP API service. A good choice for integrating with websites because it can use any JavaScript library or Blazor to interact with the service.
Northwind.BlazorServer	An ASP.NET Core Blazor Server project.
Northwind.BlazorWasm.Client	An ASP.NET Core Blazor WebAssembly client-side project.
Northwind.BlazorWasm.Server	An ASP.NET Core Blazor WebAssembly server-side project.

Building an entity model for use in the rest of the book

Practical applications usually need to work with data in a relational database or another data store. In this chapter, we will define an entity data model for the Northwind database stored in SQL Server or SQLite. It will be used in most of the apps that we create in subsequent chapters.

The Northwind4SQLServer.sql and Northwind4SQLite.sql script files are different. The script for SQL Server creates 13 tables as well as related views and stored procedures. The script for SQLite is a simplified version that only creates 10 tables because SQLite does not support as many features. The main projects in this book only need those 10 tables so you can complete every task in this book with either database.

Instructions to install SQLite can be found in *Chapter 10, Working with Data Using Entity Framework Core*. In that chapter, you will also find instructions for installing the dotnet-ef tool, which you will use to scaffold an entity model from an existing database.

Instructions to install SQL Server can be found in the GitHub repository for the book at the following link: https://github.com/markjprice/cs11dotnet7/blob/main/docs/sql-server/README.md.

Good Practice: You should create a separate class library project for your entity data models. This allows easier sharing between backend web servers and frontend desktop, mobile, and Blazor WebAssembly clients.

Creating a class library for entity models using SQLite

You will now define entity data models in a class library so that they can be reused in other types of projects including client-side app models. If you are not using SQL Server, you will need to create this class library for SQLite. If you are using SQL Server, then you can create both a class library for SQLite and one for SQL Server and then switch between them as you choose.

We will automatically generate some entity models using the EF Core command-line tool:

1. Use your preferred code editor to create a new project, as defined in the following list:

    *   Project template: **Class Library**/classlib
    *   Project file and folder: Northwind.Common.EntityModels.Sqlite
    *   Workspace/solution file and folder: PracticalApps

2. In the Northwind.Common.EntityModels.Sqlite project, add package references for the SQLite database provider and EF Core design-time support, as shown in the following markup:

    ```
    <ItemGroup>
      <PackageReference
        Include="Microsoft.EntityFrameworkCore.Sqlite" Version="7.0.0" />
      <PackageReference
        Include="Microsoft.EntityFrameworkCore.Design" Version="7.0.0">
        <PrivateAssets>all</PrivateAssets>
        <IncludeAssets>runtime; build; native; contentfiles; analyzers;
        buildtransitive</IncludeAssets>
      </PackageReference>
    </ItemGroup>
    ```

3. Delete the Class1.cs file.

4. Build the project.

5. Create the Northwind.db file for SQLite by copying the Northwind4SQLite.sql file into the PracticalApps folder (not the project folder!), and then enter the following command at a command prompt or terminal:

    ```
    sqlite3 Northwind.db -init Northwind4SQLite.sql
    ```

6. Be patient because this command might take a while to create the database structure, as shown in the following output:

    ```
    -- Loading resources from Northwind4SQLite.sql
    SQLite version 3.35.5 2022-04-19 14:49:49
    Enter ".help" for usage hints.
    sqlite>
    ```

7. To exit SQLite command mode, press *Ctrl* + *C* on Windows or *Cmd* + *D* on macOS.

8. Open a command prompt or terminal for the `Northwind.Common.EntityModels.Sqlite` folder.

9. At the command line, generate entity class models for all tables, as shown in the following commands:

```
dotnet ef dbcontext scaffold "Filename=../Northwind.db" Microsoft.
EntityFrameworkCore.Sqlite --namespace Packt.Shared --data-annotations
```

Note the following:

- The command to perform: `dbcontext scaffold`
- The connection strings. `"Filename=../Northwind.db"`
- The database provider: `Microsoft.EntityFrameworkCore.Sqlite`
- The namespace: `--namespace Packt.Shared`
- To use data annotations as well as the Fluent API: `--data-annotations`

10. Note the build messages and warnings, as shown in the following output:

```
Build started...
Build succeeded.
To protect potentially sensitive information in your connection string,
you should move it out of source code. You can avoid scaffolding the
connection string by using the Name= syntax to read it from configuration
- see https://go.microsoft.com/fwlink/?linkid=2131148. For more
guidance on storing connection strings, see http://go.microsoft.com/
fwlink/?LinkId=723263.
```

Improving the class-to-table mapping

The `dotnet-ef` command-line tool generates different code for SQL Server and SQLite because they support different levels of functionality.

For example, SQL Server text columns can have limits on the number of characters. SQLite does not support this. So, `dotnet-ef` will generate validation attributes to ensure `string` properties are limited to a specified number of characters for SQL Server but not for SQLite, as shown in the following code:

```
// SQLite database provider-generated code
[Column(TypeName = "nvarchar (15)")]
public string CategoryName { get; set; } = null!;

// SQL Server database provider-generated code
[StringLength(15)]
public string CategoryName { get; set; } = null!;
```

Neither database provider will mark non-nullable `string` properties as required:

```
// no runtime validation of non-nullable property
public string CategoryName { get; set; } = null!;

// nullable property
```

```
public string? Description { get; set; }

// decorate with attribute to perform runtime validation
[Required]
public string CategoryName { get; set; } = null!;
```

We will make some small changes to improve the entity model mapping and validation rules for SQLite.

 Remember that all code is available in the GitHub repository for the book. Although you will learn more by typing code yourself, you never have to. Go to the following link and press . to get a live code editor in your browser: `https://github.com/markjprice/cs11dotnet7`.

First, we will add a regular expression to validate that a `CustomerId` value is exactly five uppercase letters. Second, we will add string length requirements to validate that multiple properties throughout the entity models know the maximum length allowed for their text values:

1. In `Customer.cs`, add a regular expression to validate its primary key value to only allow uppercase Western characters, as shown highlighted in the following code:

    ```
    [Key]
    [Column(TypeName = "nchar (5)")]
    [RegularExpression("[A-Z]{5}")]
    public string CustomerId { get; set; } = null!;
    ```

2. Activate your code editor's find and replace feature (in Visual Studio 2022, navigate to **Edit | Find and Replace | Quick Replace**), toggle on **Use Regular Expressions**, and then type a regular expression in the find box, as shown in *Figure 12.2* and in the following expression:

    ```
    \[Column\(TypeName = "(nchar|nvarchar) \((.*)\)"\)\]
    ```

3. In the replace box, type a replacement regular expression, as shown in the following expression:

    ```
    $&\n    [StringLength($2)]
    ```

    After the newline character, \n, I have included four space characters to indent correctly on my system, which uses two space characters per indentation level. You can insert as many as you wish.

4. Set the find and replace to search files in the current project.

5. Execute the search and replace to replace all, as shown in *Figure 12.2*:

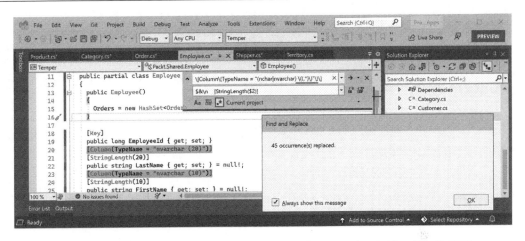

Figure 12.2: Search and replace all matches using regular expressions in Visual Studio 2022

6. Change any date/time properties, for example, in `Employee.cs`, to use a nullable `DateTime` instead of an array of bytes, as shown in the following code:

```
// before
[Column(TypeName = "datetime")]
public byte[]? BirthDate { get; set; }

// after
[Column(TypeName = "datetime")]
public DateTime? BirthDate { get; set; }
```

 Use your code editor's find feature to search for `"datetime"` to find all the properties that need changing.

7. Change any money properties, for example, in `Order.cs`, to use a nullable `decimal` instead of an array of bytes, as shown in the following code:

```
// before
[Column(TypeName =  "money")]
public byte[]? Freight { get; set; }

// after
[Column(TypeName = "money")]
public decimal? Freight { get; set; }
```

Use your code editor's find feature to search for **"money"** to find all the properties that need changing.

8. In `Product.cs`, make the `Discontinued` property a bool instead of an array of bytes and remove the initializer that sets the default value to `null`, as shown in the following code:

```
[Column(TypeName = "bit")]
public bool Discontinued { get; set; }
```

9. In `Category.cs`, make the `CategoryId` property an int, as shown highlighted in the following code:

```
[Key]
public int CategoryId { get; set; }
```

10. In `Category.cs`, make the `CategoryName` property required, as shown highlighted in the following code:

```
[Required]
[Column(TypeName = "nvarchar (15)")]
[StringLength(15)]
public string CategoryName { get; set; }
```

11. In `Customer.cs`, make the `CompanyName` property required, as shown highlighted in the following code:

```
[Required]
[Column(TypeName = "nvarchar (40)")]
[StringLength(40)]
public string CompanyName { get; set; }
```

12. In `Employee.cs`, make the:

   - `EmployeeId` property an int instead of a `long`.
   - `FirstName` and `LastName` properties required.
   - `ReportsTo` property an int? instead of a long?.

13. In `EmployeeTerritory.cs`, make the:

   - `EmployeeId` property an int instead of a `long`.
   - `TerritoryId` property required.

14. In `Order.cs`:

   - Make the `OrderId` property an int instead of a `long`.
   - Decorate the `CustomerId` property with a regular expression to enforce five uppercase characters.

- Make the EmployeeId property an int? instead of a long?.
- Make the ShipVia property an int? instead of a long?.

15. In OrderDetail.cs, make the:

  - OrderId property an int instead of a long.
  - ProductId property an int instead of a long.
  - Quantity property a short instead of a long.

16. In Product.cs, make the:

  - ProductId property an int instead of a long.
  - ProductName property required.
  - SupplierId and CategoryId properties an int? instead of a long?.
  - UnitsInStock, UnitsOnOrder, and ReorderLevel properties a short? instead of a long?.

17. In Shipper.cs, make the:

  - ShipperId property an int instead of a long.
  - CompanyName property required.

18. In Supplier.cs, make the:

  - SupplierId property an int instead of a long.
  - CompanyName property required.

19. In Territory.cs, make the:

  - RegionId property an int instead of a long.
  - TerritoryId and TerritoryDescription properties required.

Now that we have a class library for the entity classes, we can create a class library for the database context.

Creating a class library for a Northwind database context

You will now define a database context class library:

1. Add a new project to the solution/workspace, as defined in the following list:

  - Project template: **Class Library**/classlib
  - Project file and folder: Northwind.Common.DataContext.Sqlite
  - Workspace/solution file and folder: PracticalApps

2. In Visual Studio, set the startup project for the solution to the current selection. In Visual Studio Code, select Northwind.Common.DataContext.Sqlite as the active OmniSharp project.

3. In the `Northwind.Common.DataContext.Sqlite` project, add a project reference to the `Northwind.Common.EntityModels.Sqlite` project and add a package reference to the EF Core data provider for SQLite, as shown in the following markup:

```
<ItemGroup>
  <PackageReference
    Include="Microsoft.EntityFrameworkCore.SQLite" Version="7.0.0" />
</ItemGroup>

<ItemGroup>
  <ProjectReference Include=
    "..\Northwind.Common.EntityModels.Sqlite\Northwind.Common
.EntityModels.Sqlite.csproj" />
</ItemGroup>
```

Warning! The path to the project reference should not have a line break in your project file.

4. In the `Northwind.Common.DataContext.Sqlite` project, delete the `Class1.cs` class file.

5. Build the `Northwind.Common.DataContext.Sqlite` project.

6. Move the `NorthwindContext.cs` file from the `Northwind.Common.EntityModels.Sqlite` project/ folder to the `Northwind.Common.DataContext.Sqlite` project/folder.

In Visual Studio **Solution Explorer**, if you drag and drop a file between projects it will be copied. If you hold down *Shift* while dragging and dropping, it will be moved. In Visual Studio Code **EXPLORER**, if you drag and drop a file between projects it will be moved. If you hold down *Ctrl* while dragging and dropping, it will be copied.

7. In `NorthwindContext.cs`, in the `OnConfiguring` method, remove the compiler `#warning` about the connection string.

Good Practice: We will override the default database connection string in any projects such as websites that need to work with the Northwind database, so the class derived from `DbContext` must have a constructor with a `DbContextOptions` parameter for this to work, and the generated file does this correctly, as shown in the following code:

```
public NorthwindContext(DbContextOptions<NorthwindContext>
options)
  : base(options)
{
}
```

8. In NorthwindContext.cs, in the OnConfiguring method, add statements to check the end of the current directory to adjust for when running in Visual Studio 2022 compared to the command line and Visual Studio Code, as shown highlighted in the following code:

```
protected override void OnConfiguring(DbContextOptionsBuilder
optionsBuilder)
{
  if (!optionsBuilder.IsConfigured)
  {
    string dir = Environment.CurrentDirectory;
    string path = string.Empty;

    if (dir.EndsWith("net7.0"))
    {
      // Running in the <project>\bin\<Debug|Release>\net7.0 directory.
      path = Path.Combine("..", "..", "..", "..", "Northwind.db");
    }
    else
    {
      // Running in the <project> directory.
      path = Path.Combine("..", "Northwind.db");
    }

    optionsBuilder.UseSqlite($"Filename={path}");
  }
}
```

9. In the OnModelCreating method, remove all Fluent API statements that call the ValueGeneratedNever method, like the one shown in the following code. This will configure primary key properties like SupplierId to never generate a value automatically or call the HasDefaultValueSql method:

```
modelBuilder.Entity<Supplier>(entity =>
{
  entity.Property(e => e.SupplierId).ValueGeneratedNever();
});
```

 If we do not remove the configuration like the statements above, then when we add new suppliers, the SupplierId value will always be 0 and we will only be able to add one supplier with that value; all other attempts will throw an exception.

10. For the Product entity, tell SQLite that the UnitPrice can be converted from decimal to double. The OnModelCreating method should now be much simplified, as shown in the following code:

```
protected override void OnModelCreating(ModelBuilder modelBuilder)
{
```

```
  modelBuilder.Entity<OrderDetail>(entity =>
  {
    entity.HasKey(e => new { e.OrderId, e.ProductId });

    entity.HasOne(d => d.Order)
      .WithMany(p => p.OrderDetails)
      .HasForeignKey(d => d.OrderId)
      .OnDelete(DeleteBehavior.ClientSetNull);

    entity.HasOne(d => d.Product)
      .WithMany(p => p.OrderDetails)
      .HasForeignKey(d => d.ProductId)
      .OnDelete(DeleteBehavior.ClientSetNull);
  });
  modelBuilder.Entity<Product>()
    .Property(product => product.UnitPrice)
    .HasConversion<double>();

  OnModelCreatingPartial(modelBuilder);
}
```

11. In the `Northwind.Common.DataContext.Sqlite` project, add a class named `NorthwindContextExtensions.cs`. Modify its contents to define an extension method that adds the Northwind database context to a collection of dependency services, as shown in the following code:

```
using Microsoft.EntityFrameworkCore; // UseSqlite
using Microsoft.Extensions.DependencyInjection; // IServiceCollection

namespace Packt.Shared;

public static class NorthwindContextExtensions
{
  /// <summary>
  /// Adds NorthwindContext to the specified IServiceCollection. Uses the
  Sqlite database provider.
  /// </summary>
  /// <param name="services"></param>
  /// <param name="relativePath">Set to override the default of ".."
  </param>
  /// <returns>An IServiceCollection that can be used to add more services.
  </returns>
  public static IServiceCollection AddNorthwindContext(
    this IServiceCollection services, string relativePath = "..")
  {
    string databasePath = Path.Combine(relativePath, "Northwind.db");
```

```
    services.AddDbContext<NorthwindContext>(options =>
    {
      options.UseSqlite($"Data Source={databasePath}");

      options.LogTo(WriteLine, // Console
        new[] { Microsoft.EntityFrameworkCore
          .Diagnostics.RelationalEventId.CommandExecuting });
    });

    return services;
  }
}
```

12. Build the two class libraries and fix any compiler errors.

Creating a class library for entity models using SQL Server

To use SQL Server, you will not need to do anything if you already set up the Northwind database in *Chapter 10, Working with Data Using Entity Framework Core*. But you will now create the entity models using the dotnet-ef tool:

1. Add a new project, as defined in the following list:

    - Project template: **Class Library**/classlib
    - Project file and folder: Northwind.Common.EntityModels.SqlServer
    - Workspace/solution file and folder: PracticalApps

2. In the Northwind.Common.EntityModels.SqlServer project, add package references for the SQL Server database provider and EF Core design-time support, as shown in the following markup:

```
<ItemGroup>
  <PackageReference
    Include="Microsoft.EntityFrameworkCore.SqlServer" Version="7.0.0" />
  <PackageReference
    Include="Microsoft.EntityFrameworkCore.Design" Version="7.0.0">
    <PrivateAssets>all</PrivateAssets>
    <IncludeAssets>runtime; build; native; contentfiles; analyzers;
    buildtransitive</IncludeAssets>
  </PackageReference>
</ItemGroup>
```

3. Delete the Class1.cs file.
4. Build the project.
5. Open a command prompt or terminal for the Northwind.Common.EntityModels.SqlServer folder.

6. At the command line, generate entity class models for all tables, as shown in the following commands:

```
dotnet ef dbcontext scaffold "Data Source=.;Initial
Catalog=Northwind;Integrated Security=true;" Microsoft.
EntityFrameworkCore.SqlServer --namespace Packt.Shared --data-annotations
```

Note the following:

*   The command to perform: `dbcontext scaffold`
*   The connection strings. `"Data Source=.;Initial Catalog=Northwind;Integrated Security=true;"`
*   The database provider: `Microsoft.EntityFrameworkCore.SqlServer`
*   The namespace: `--namespace Packt.Shared`
*   To use data annotations as well as the Fluent API: `--data-annotations`

7. In `Customer.cs`, add a regular expression to validate its primary key value to only allow uppercase Western characters, as shown highlighted in the following code:

```
[Key]
[StringLength(5)]
[RegularExpression("[A-Z]{5}")]
public string CustomerId { get; set; } = null!;
```

8. In `Customer.cs`, make the `CustomerId` and `CompanyName` properties required.

9. Add a new project, as defined in the following list:

*   Project template: **Class Library**/`classlib`
*   Project file and folder: `Northwind.Common.DataContext.SqlServer`
*   Workspace/solution file and folder: `PracticalApps`
*   In Visual Studio Code, select `Northwind.Common.DataContext.SqlServer` as the active OmniSharp project

10. In the `Northwind.Common.DataContext.SqlServer` project, add a project reference to the `Northwind.Common.EntityModels.SqlServer` project and add a package reference to the EF Core data provider for SQL Server, as shown in the following markup:

```
<ItemGroup>
  <PackageReference
    Include="Microsoft.EntityFrameworkCore.SqlServer" Version="7.0.0" />
</ItemGroup>

<ItemGroup>
  <ProjectReference Include=
    "..\Northwind.Common.EntityModels.SqlServer\Northwind.Common
.EntityModels.SqlServer.csproj" />
</ItemGroup>
```

Warning! The path to the project reference should not have a line break in your project file.

11. In the `Northwind.Common.DataContext.SqlServer` project, delete the `Class1.cs` file.

12. Build the `Northwind.Common.DataContext.SqlServer` project.

13. Move the `NorthwindContext.cs` file from the `Northwind.Common.EntityModels.SqlServer` project/folder to the `Northwind.Common.DataContext.SqlServer` project/folder.

14. In the `Northwind.Common.DataContext.SqlServer` project, in `NorthwindContext.cs`, remove the compiler warning about the connection string.

15. In the `Northwind.Common.DataContext.SqlServer` project, add a class named `NorthwindContextExtensions.cs`. Modify its contents to define an extension method that adds the Northwind database context to a collection of dependency services, as shown in the following code:

```
using Microsoft.EntityFrameworkCore; // UseSqlServer
using Microsoft.Extensions.DependencyInjection; // IServiceCollection

namespace Packt.Shared;

public static class NorthwindContextExtensions
{
  /// <summary>
  /// Adds NorthwindContext to the specified IServiceCollection. Uses the
  SqlServer database provider.
  /// </summary>
  /// <param name="services"></param>
  /// <param name="connectionString">Set to override the default.</param>
  /// <returns>An IServiceCollection that can be used to add more
  services.</returns>
  public static IServiceCollection AddNorthwindContext(
    this IServiceCollection services,
    string connectionString = "Data Source=.;Initial Catalog=Northwind;" +
    "Integrated Security=true;MultipleActiveResultsets=true;Encrypt=false")
  {
    services.AddDbContext<NorthwindContext>(options =>
    {
      options.UseSqlServer(connectionString);

      options.LogTo(WriteLine, // Console
        new[] { Microsoft.EntityFrameworkCore
          .Diagnostics.RelationalEventId.CommandExecuting });
```

```
        });

        return services;
    }
}
```

16. Build the two class libraries and fix any compiler errors.

 Good Practice: We have provided optional arguments for the `AddNorthwindContext` method so that we can override the hardcoded SQLite database filename path or the SQL Server database connection string. This will allow us more flexibility, for example, to load these values from a configuration file.

Testing the class libraries

Now let's build some unit tests to ensure the class libraries are working correctly:

1. Use your preferred coding tool to add a new **xUnit Test Project [C#]**/xunit project named `Northwind.Common.UnitTests` to the `PracticalApps` workspace/solution.

2. In the `Northwind.Common.UnitTests` project, add a project reference to the `Northwind.Common.DataContext` project for either SQLite or SQL Server, as shown highlighted in the following configuration:

```
<ItemGroup>
  <!-- change Sqlite to SqlServer if you prefer -->
  <ProjectReference Include="..\Northwind.Common.DataContext.Sqlite\
Northwind.Common.DataContext.Sqlite.csproj" />
</ItemGroup>
```

 Warning! The project reference must go all on one line with no line break.

3. Build the `Northwind.Common.UnitTests` project.

4. Rename `UnitTest1.cs` to `EntityModelTests.cs`.

5. Modify the contents of the file to define two tests, the first to connect to the database and the second to confirm there are eight categories in the database, as shown in the following code:

```
using Packt.Shared; // NorthwindContext

namespace Northwind.Common.UnitTests
{
    public class EntityModelTests
    {
```

```
[Fact]
public void DatabaseConnectTest()
{
  using (NorthwindContext db = new())
  {
    Assert.True(db.Database.CanConnect());
  }
}

[Fact]
public void CategoryCountTest()
{
  using (NorthwindContext db = new())
  {
    int expected = 8;
    int actual = db.Categories.Count();

    Assert.Equal(expected, actual);
  }
}
```

6. Run the unit tests:

   - If you are using Visual Studio 2022, then navigate to **Test | Run All Tests** in **Test Explorer**.
   - If you are using Visual Studio Code, then in the `Northwind.Common.UnitTests` project's **TERMINAL** window, run the tests, as shown in the following command: `dotnet test`.

7. Note that the results should indicate that two tests ran, and both passed. If either of the two tests fail, then fix the issue. For example, if you are using SQLite then check the `Northwind.db` file is in the solution directory (one up from the project directories.)

Understanding web development

Developing for the web means developing with **Hypertext Transfer Protocol (HTTP)**, so we will start by reviewing this important foundational technology.

Understanding Hypertext Transfer Protocol

To communicate with a web server, the client, also known as the **user agent**, makes calls over the network using HTTP. As such, HTTP is the technical underpinning of the web. So, when we talk about websites and web services, we mean that they use HTTP to communicate between a client (often a web browser) and a server.

A client makes an HTTP request for a resource, such as a page, uniquely identified by a **Uniform Resource Locator (URL)**, and the server sends back an HTTP response, as shown in *Figure 12.3*:

Figure 12.3: An HTTP request and response

You can use Google Chrome and other browsers to record requests and responses.

> **Good Practice:** Google Chrome is currently used by about two thirds of website visitors worldwide, and it has powerful, built-in developer tools, so it is a good first choice for testing your websites. Test your websites with Chrome and at least two other browsers, for example, Firefox and Safari for macOS and iPhone. Microsoft Edge switched from using Microsoft's own rendering engine to using Chromium in 2019, so it is less important to test with it. If Microsoft's Internet Explorer is used at all, it tends to mostly be inside organizations for intranets.

Understanding the components of a URL

A **Uniform Resource Locator (URL)** is made up of several components:

- **Scheme:** `http` (clear text) or `https` (encrypted).
- **Domain:** For a production website or service, the **top-level domain (TLD)** might be `example.com`. You might have subdomains such as `www`, `jobs`, or `extranet`. During development, you typically use `localhost` for all websites and services.
- **Port number:** For a production website or service, `80` for `http`, `443` for `https`. These port numbers are usually inferred from the scheme. During development, other port numbers are commonly used, such as `5000`, `5001`, and so on, to differentiate between websites and services that all use the shared domain `localhost`.
- **Path:** A relative path to a resource, for example, `/customers/germany`.
- **Query string:** A way to pass parameter values, for example, `?country=Germany&searchtext=shoes`.
- **Fragment:** A reference to an element on a web page using its `id`, for example, `#toc`.

URL is a subset of **Uniform Resource Identifier (URI)**. A URL specifies where a resource is located and how to get it. A URI identifies a resource either by URL or **URN (Uniform Resource Name)**.

Assigning port numbers for projects in this book

In this book, we will use the domain `localhost` for all websites and web services, so we will use port numbers to differentiate projects when multiple need to execute at the same time, as shown in the following table:

Project	Description	Port numbers
`Northwind.Web`	ASP.NET Core Razor Pages website	`5000 HTTP, 5001 HTTPS`
`Northwind.Mvc`	ASP.NET Core MVC website	`5000 HTTP, 5001 HTTPS`
`Northwind.WebApi`	ASP.NET Core Web API service	`5002 HTTPS`
`Minimal.WebApi`	ASP.NET Core Web API (minimal)	`5003 HTTPS`
`Northwind.BlazorServer`	ASP.NET Core Blazor Server	`5004 HTTP, 5005 HTTPS`
`Northwind.BlazorWasm`	ASP.NET Core Blazor WebAssembly	`5006 HTTP, 5007 HTTPS`

Using Google Chrome to make HTTP requests

Let's explore how to use Google Chrome to make HTTP requests:

1. Start Google Chrome.
2. Navigate to **More tools** | **Developer tools**.
3. Click the **Network** tab, and Chrome should immediately start recording the network traffic between your browser and any web servers (note the red circle), as shown in *Figure 12.4*:

Figure 12.4: Chrome Developer Tools recording network traffic

4. In Chrome's address box, enter the address of Microsoft's website for learning ASP.NET, as shown in the following URL:

```
https://dotnet.microsoft.com/learn/aspnet
```

5. In **Developer Tools**, in the list of recorded requests, scroll to the top and click on the first entry, the row where the **Type** is **document**, as shown in *Figure 12.5*:

Figure 12.5: Recorded requests in Developer Tools

6. On the right-hand side, click on the **Headers** tab, and you will see details about **Request Headers** and **Response Headers**, as shown in *Figure 12.6*:

Figure 12.6: Request and response headers

Note the following aspects:

- **Request Method** is GET. Other HTTP methods that you could see here include POST, PUT, DELETE, HEAD, and PATCH.
- **Status Code** is 200 OK. This means that the server found the resource that the browser requested and has returned it in the body of the response. Other status codes that you might see in response to a GET request include 301 Moved Permanently, 400 Bad Request, 401 Unauthorized, and 404 Not Found.
- **Request Headers** sent by the browser to the web server include:
- **accept,** which lists what formats the browser accepts. In this case, the browser is saying it understands HTML, XHTML, XML, and some image formats, but it will accept all other files (*/*). Default weightings, also known as quality values, are 1.0. XML is specified with a quality value of 0.9 so it is preferred less than HTML or XHTML. All other file types are given a quality value of 0.8 so are least preferred.
- **accept-encoding,** which lists what compression algorithms the browser understands, in this case, GZIP, DEFLATE, and Brotli.
- **accept-language,** which lists the human languages it would prefer the content to use. In this case, US English, which has a default quality value of 1.0, then any dialect of English that has an explicitly specified quality value of 0.9, and then any dialect of Swedish that has an explicitly specified quality value of 0.8.
- **Response Headers,** content-encoding, which tells me the server has sent back the HTML web page response compressed using the GZIP algorithm because it knows that the client can decompress that format. (This is not visible in *Figure 12.6* because there is not enough space to expand the **Response Headers** section.)

7. Close Chrome.

Understanding client-side web development technologies

When building websites, a developer needs to know more than just C# and .NET. On the client (that is, in the web browser), you will use a combination of the following technologies:

- **HTML5:** This is used for the content and structure of a web page.
- **CSS3:** This is used for the styles applied to elements on the web page.
- **JavaScript:** This is used to code any business logic needed on the web page, for example, validating form input or making calls to a web service to fetch more data needed by the web page.

Although HTML5, CSS3, and JavaScript are the fundamental components of frontend web development, there are many additional technologies that can make frontend web development more productive, including:

- **Bootstrap,** the world's most popular frontend open-source toolkit.
- **SASS** and **LESS,** CSS preprocessors for styling.
- Microsoft's **TypeScript** language for writing more robust code.
- JavaScript libraries such as **Angular, jQuery, React,** and **Vue.**

All these higher-level technologies ultimately translate or compile to the underlying three core technologies, so they work across all modern browsers.

As part of the build and deploy process, you will likely use technologies such as:

- **Node.js**, a framework for server-side development using JavaScript.
- **Node Package Manager** (**npm**) and **Yarn**, both client-side package managers.
- **Webpack**, a popular module bundler, a tool for compiling, transforming, and bundling website source files.

Practicing and exploring

Test your knowledge and understanding by answering some questions and exploring this chapter's topics with deeper research.

Exercise 12.1 – Test your knowledge

Answer the following questions:

1. What was the name of Microsoft first dynamic server-side executed web page technology and why is it still useful to know this history today?
2. What are the names of two Microsoft web servers?
3. What are some differences between a microservice and a nanoservice?
4. What is Blazor?
5. What was the first version of ASP.NET Core that could not be hosted on .NET Framework?
6. What is a user agent?
7. What impact does the HTTP request-response communication model have on web developers?
8. Name and describe four components of a URL.
9. What capabilities does Developer Tools give you?
10. What are the three main client-side web development technologies and what do they do?

Exercise 12.2 – Know your webbreviations

What do the following web abbreviations stand for and what do they do?

1. URI
2. URL
3. WCF
4. TLD
5. API
6. SPA
7. CMS
8. Wasm

9. SASS

10. REST

Exercise 12.3 – Explore topics

Use the links on the following page to learn more detail about the topics covered in this chapter:

```
https://github.com/markjprice/cs11dotnet7/blob/main/book-links.md#chapter-12---
introducing-web-development-using-aspnet-core
```

Summary

In this chapter, you have:

- Been introduced to some of the app models and workloads that you can use to build websites and web services using C# and .NET.
- Created two to four class libraries to define an entity data model for working with the Northwind database using either SQLite or SQL Server or both.

In the following chapters, you will learn the details about how to build the following:

- Simple websites using static HTML pages and dynamic Razor Pages.
- Complex websites using the Model-View-Controller (MVC) design pattern.
- Web services that can be called by any platform that can make an HTTP request, and client websites that call those web services.
- Blazor user interface components that can be hosted on a web server, in the browser, or on hybrid web-native mobile and desktop apps.

13

Building Websites Using ASP.NET Core Razor Pages

This chapter is about building websites with a modern HTTP architecture on the server side using Microsoft ASP.NET Core. You will learn about building simple websites using the ASP.NET Core Razor Pages feature introduced with ASP.NET Core 2.0 and the Razor class library feature introduced with ASP.NET Core 2.1.

This chapter covers the following topics:

- Exploring ASP.NET Core
- Exploring ASP.NET Core Razor Pages
- Using Entity Framework Core with ASP.NET Core
- Using Razor class libraries
- Configuring services and the HTTP request pipeline
- Enabling HTTP/3 support

Exploring ASP.NET Core

We will start by creating an empty ASP.NET Core project and explore how to enable it to serve simple web pages.

Creating an empty ASP.NET Core project

We will create an ASP.NET Core project that will show a list of suppliers from the Northwind database.

The dotnet tool has many project templates that do a lot of work for you, but it can be difficult to know which works best for a given situation, so we will start with the empty website project template and then add features step by step so that you can understand all the pieces:

1. Use your preferred code editor to open the PracticalApps solution/workspace and then add a new project, as defined in the following list:

    •   Project template: **ASP.NET Core Empty [C#]**/web.

    •   Project file and folder: Northwind.Web.

    •   Workspace/solution file and folder: PracticalApps.

    •   For Visual Studio 2022, leave all other options as their defaults, for example, **Configure for HTTPS** selected, **Enable Docker** cleared, and **Do not use top-level statements** cleared.

    •   For Visual Studio Code and the dotnet new web command, the defaults are the options we want. We will not do this, but if you want to change from top-level statements to the old Program class style, then specify the switch --use-program-main.

    In Visual Studio Code, select Northwind.Web as the active OmniSharp project.

2. Build the Northwind.Web project.

3. Open the Northwind.Web.csproj file and note that the project is like a class library except that the SDK is Microsoft.NET.Sdk.Web, as shown highlighted in the following markup:

```
<Project Sdk="Microsoft.NET.Sdk.Web">

  <PropertyGroup>
    <TargetFramework>net7.0</TargetFramework>
    <Nullable>enable</Nullable>
    <ImplicitUsings>enable</ImplicitUsings>
  </PropertyGroup>

</Project>
```

4. Add an element to globally and statically import the System.Console class.

5. If you are using Visual Studio 2022, in **Solution Explorer**, toggle **Show All Files**.

6. Expand the obj folder, expand the Debug folder, expand the net7.0 folder, select the Northwind.Web.GlobalUsings.g.cs file, and note how the implicitly imported namespaces include all the ones for a console app or class library, as well as some ASP.NET Core ones, such as Microsoft.AspNetCore.Builder, as shown in the following code:

```
// <autogenerated />
global using global::Microsoft.AspNetCore.Builder;
global using global::Microsoft.AspNetCore.Hosting;
global using global::Microsoft.AspNetCore.Http;
global using global::Microsoft.AspNetCore.Routing;
global using global::Microsoft.Extensions.Configuration;
```

```
global using global::Microsoft.Extensions.DependencyInjection;
global using global::Microsoft.Extensions.Hosting;
global using global::Microsoft.Extensions.Logging;
global using global::System;
global using global::System.Collections.Generic;
global using global::System.IO;
global using global::System.Linq;
global using global::System.Net.Http;
global using global::System.Net.Http.Json;
global using global::System.Threading;
global using global::System.Threading.Tasks;
global using static global::System.Console;
```

7. Close the file and collapse the obj folder.

8. Open Program.cs and note the following:

    • An ASP.NET Core project is like a top-level console app, with a hidden <Main>$ method as its entry point that has an argument passed using the name args.

    • It calls WebApplication.CreateBuilder, which creates a host for the website using defaults for a web host that is then built.

    • The website will respond to all HTTP GET requests with plain text: Hello World!.

    • The call to the Run method is a blocking call, so the hidden <Main>$ method does not return until the web server stops running.

    The contents of Program.cs are shown in the following code:

```
var builder = WebApplication.CreateBuilder(args);
var app = builder.Build();

app.MapGet("/", () => "Hello World!");

app.Run();
```

9. At the bottom of Program.cs, add a statement to write a message to the console after the call to the Run method and therefore after the web server has stopped, as shown in the following code:

```
WriteLine("This executes after the web server has stopped!");
```

Testing and securing the website

We will now test the functionality of the ASP.NET Core Empty website project. We will also enable encryption of all traffic between the browser and web server for privacy by switching from HTTP to HTTPS. HTTPS is the secure encrypted version of HTTP.

1. For Visual Studio:

   1. In the toolbar, make sure that the **https** profile is selected rather than **http, IIS Express,** or **WSL,** and change **Web Browser (Microsoft Edge)** to **Google Chrome,** as shown in *Figure 13.1*:

   Figure 13.1: Selecting the https profile with its Kestrel web server in Visual Studio

   2. Navigate to **Debug | Start Without Debugging....**

   3. The first time you start a secure website, you will be prompted that your project is configured to use SSL, and to avoid warnings in the browser, you can choose to trust the self-signed certificate that ASP.NET Core has generated. Click **Yes.**

   4. When you see the **Security Warning** dialog box, click **Yes** again.

2. For Visual Studio Code, enter the command to start the project with the https profile, like this: `dotnet run --launch-profile https`. Then start Chrome.

3. In either Visual Studio's command prompt window or Visual Studio Code's terminal, note the Kestrel web server has started listening on random ports for HTTP and HTTPS, you can press *Ctrl + C* to shut down the Kestrel web server, and the hosting environment is Development, as shown in the following output:

```
info: Microsoft.Hosting.Lifetime[14]
   Now listening on: https://localhost:7251
info: Microsoft.Hosting.Lifetime[14]
   Now listening on: http://localhost:5251
info: Microsoft.Hosting.Lifetime[0]
   Application started. Press Ctrl+C to shut down.
info: Microsoft.Hosting.Lifetime[0]
   Hosting environment: Development
info: Microsoft.Hosting.Lifetime[0]
   Content root path: C:\cs11dotnet7\PracticalApps\Northwind.Web
```

Visual Studio 2022 will also start your chosen browser automatically. If you are using Visual Studio Code, you will have to start Chrome manually.

4. Leave the Kestrel web server running.

5. In Chrome, show **Developer Tools,** and click the **Network** tab.

6. Request the home page for the website project:

    •   If you are using Visual Studio 2022 and Chrome launched automatically with the URL already entered for you, then click the **Refresh** button or press *F5.*

    •   If you are using Visual Studio Code and the terminal or command line, then in the Chrome address bar, enter the address `http://localhost:5251/`, or whatever port number was assigned to HTTP.

7. Note the response is **Hello World!** in plain text, from the cross-platform Kestrel web server, as shown in *Figure 13.2*:

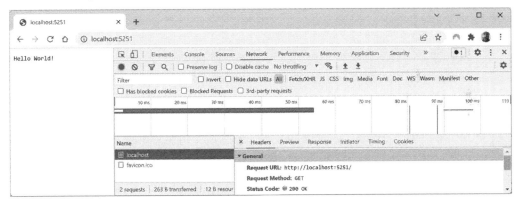

Figure 13.2: Plain text response from the website project

 Browsers like Chrome might also request a `favicon.ico` file to show in their browser window or tab, but this file does not exist in our project so it shows as a **404 Not Found** error. If this annoys you, then you can generate a `favicon.ico` file for free at the following link and put it in the project folder: `https://favicon.io/`. On a web page, you can also specify one in the meta tags, for example, a blank one using Base64 encoding, as shown in the following markup:

```
<link rel="icon" href="data:;base64,iVBORw0KGgo=">
```

8. Enter the address `https://localhost:5001/`, or whatever port number was assigned to HTTPS, and note if you are not using Visual Studio or if you clicked **No** when prompted to trust the SSL certificate, then the response is a privacy error, as shown in *Figure 13.3*:

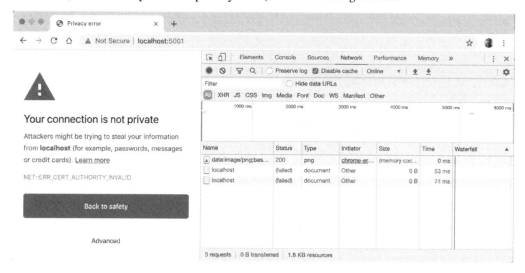

Figure 13.3: Privacy error showing SSL encryption has not been enabled with a certificate

You will see this error when you have not configured a certificate that the browser can trust to encrypt and decrypt HTTPS traffic (and so if you do not see this error, it is because you have already configured a certificate).

In a production environment, you would want to pay a company such as Verisign for an SSL certificate because they provide liability protection and technical support.

 For Linux Developers: If you use a Linux variant that cannot create self-signed certificates or you do not mind reapplying for a new certificate every 90 days, then you can get a free certificate from the following link: `https://letsencrypt.org`.

During development, you can tell your OS to trust a temporary development certificate provided by ASP.NET Core.

9. At the command line or terminal, press *Ctrl + C* to shut down the web server, and note the message that is written, as shown highlighted in the following output:

```
info: Microsoft.Hosting.Lifetime[0]
      Application is shutting down...
This executes after the web server has stopped!
C:\cs11dotnet7\PracticalApps\Northwind.Web\bin\Debug\net7.0\Northwind.
Web.exe (process 19888) exited with code 0.
```

10. If you need to trust a local self-signed SSL certificate, then at the command line or terminal, enter the dotnet dev-certs https --trust command and note the message **Trusting the HTTPS development certificate was requested.** You might be prompted to enter your password and a valid HTTPS certificate may already be present.

Enabling stronger security and redirecting to a secure connection

It is good practice to enable stricter security and automatically redirect requests for HTTP to HTTPS.

Good Practice: HTTP Strict Transport Security (HSTS) is an opt-in security enhancement that you should always enable. If a website specifies it and a browser supports it, then it forces all communication over HTTPS and prevents the visitor from using untrusted or invalid certificates.

Let's do that now:

1. In Program.cs, after the statement that builds the app, add an if statement to enable HSTS when *not* in development, as shown in the following code:

```
if (!app.Environment.IsDevelopment())
{
  app.UseHsts();
}
```

2. Add a statement before the call to MapGet to redirect HTTP requests to HTTPS, as shown in the following code:

```
app.UseHttpsRedirection();
```

3. Start the Northwind.Web website project.

4. If Chrome is still running, close and restart it.

5. In Chrome, show **Developer Tools**, and click the **Network** tab.

6. Enter the address `http://localhost:5251/`, or whatever port number was assigned to HTTP, and note how the server responds with a **307 Temporary Redirect** to `https` and that the certificate is now valid and trusted, as shown in *Figure 13.4*:

Figure 13.4: The connection is now secured using a valid certificate and a 307 redirect

7. Close Chrome and shut down the web server.

  Good Practice: Remember to shut down the Kestrel web server whenever you have finished testing a website.

Controlling the hosting environment

In ASP.NET Core 5 and earlier, the project template set a rule to say that while in development mode, any unhandled exceptions will be shown in the browser window for the developer to see the details of the exception, as shown in the following code:

```
if (app.Environment.IsDevelopment())
{
  app.UseDeveloperExceptionPage();
}
```

With ASP.NET Core 6 and later, this code is executed automatically so it is not included in the project template.

How does ASP.NET Core know when we are running in development mode so that the `IsDevelopment` method returns `true`? Let's find out.

ASP.NET Core can read from settings files and environment variables to determine what hosting environment to use, for example, `DOTNET_ENVIRONMENT` or `ASPNETCORE_ENVIRONMENT`.

You can override these settings during local development:

1. In the Northwind.Web folder, expand the folder named Properties, open the file named launchSettings.json, and note the profiles named https and http that set the environment variable for the hosting environment to Development, as shown highlighted in the following configuration:

```json
{
  "iisSettings": {
    "windowsAuthentication": false,
    "anonymousAuthentication": true,
    "iisExpress": {
      "applicationUrl": "http://localhost:56111",
      "sslPort": 44329
    }
  },
  "profiles": {
    "http": {
      "commandName": "Project",
      "dotnetRunMessages": true,
      "launchBrowser": true,
      "applicationUrl": "http://localhost:5000",
      "environmentVariables": {
        "ASPNETCORE_ENVIRONMENT": "Development"
      }
    },
    "https": {
      "commandName": "Project",
      "dotnetRunMessages": true,
      "launchBrowser": true,
      "applicationUrl": "https://localhost:5001;http://localhost:5000",
      "environmentVariables": {
        "ASPNETCORE_ENVIRONMENT": "Development"
      }
    },
    "IIS Express": {
      "commandName": "IISExpress",
      "launchBrowser": true,
      "environmentVariables": {
        "ASPNETCORE_ENVIRONMENT": "Development"
      }
    }
  }
}
```

2. For both profiles http and https, for their applicationUrl, change the randomly assigned port numbers for HTTP to 5000 and HTTPS to 5001.

3. Change `ASPNETCORE_ENVIRONMENT` to `Production`.

4. If you are using Visual Studio, optionally, change `launchBrowser` to `false` to prevent Visual Studio from automatically launching a browser.

5. Start the website and note the hosting environment is `Production`, as shown in the following output:

```
info: Microsoft.Hosting.Lifetime[0]
    Hosting environment: Production
```

6. Shut down the web server.

7. In `launchSettings.json`, change the environment back to `Development`.

 The `launchSettings.json` file also has a configuration for using IIS as the web server using random port numbers. In this book, we will only be using Kestrel as the web server since it is cross-platform.

Enabling a website to serve static content

A website that only ever returns a single plain text message isn't very useful!

At a minimum, it ought to return static HTML pages, CSS that the web pages will use for styling, and any other static resources, such as images and videos.

By convention, these files should be stored in a directory named `wwwroot` to keep them separate from the dynamically executing parts of your website project.

Creating a folder for static files and a web page

You will now create a folder for your static website resources and a basic index page that uses Bootstrap for styling:

1. In the `Northwind.Web` project/folder, create a folder named `wwwroot`. Note that Visual Studio recognizes it as a special type of folder by giving it a globe icon.

2. Add a new HTML page file to the `wwwroot` folder named `index.html`.

3. In `index.html`, modify its markup to link to CDN-hosted Bootstrap for styling, and use modern good practices such as setting the viewport, as shown in the following markup:

```
<!doctype html>
<html lang="en">
<head>
  <!-- Required meta tags -->
  <meta charset="utf-8" />
  <meta name="viewport" content=
    "width=device-width, initial-scale=1, shrink-to-fit=no" />
  <!-- Bootstrap CSS -->
```

```
    <link href="https://cdn.jsdelivr.net/npm/bootstrap@5.1.3/dist/css/
    bootstrap.min.css" rel="stylesheet" integrity="sha384-1BmE4kWBq78iYhFld
    vKuhfTAU6auU8tT94WrHftjDbrCEXSU1oBoqyl2QvZ6jIW3" crossorigin="anonymous">
    <title>Welcome ASP.NET Core!</title>
  </head>
  <body>
    <div class="container">
      <div class="jumbotron">
        <h1 class="display-3">Welcome to Northwind B2B</h1>
        <p class="lead">We supply products to our customers.</p>
        <hr />
        <h2>This is a static HTML page.</h2>
        <p>Our customers include restaurants, hotels, and cruise lines.</p>
        <p>
          <a class="btn btn-primary"
            href="https://www.asp.net/">Learn more</a>
        </p>
      </div>
    </div>
  </body>
</html>
```

 Good Practice: To get the latest `<link>` element for Bootstrap, copy and paste it from the documentation at the following link: `https://getbootstrap.com/docs/5.1/getting-started/introduction/#starter-template`.

Enabling static and default files

If you were to start the website now and enter `http://localhost:5000/index.html` in the address box, the website would return a `404 Not Found` error saying no web page was found. To enable the website to return static files such as `index.html`, we must explicitly configure that feature.

Even if we enable static files, if you were to start the website and enter `http://localhost:5000/` in the address box, the website would return a `404 Not Found` error because the web server does not know what to return by default if no named file is requested.

You will now enable static files, explicitly configure default files, and change the URL path registered that returns the plain text `Hello World!` response:

1. In `Program.cs`, add statements after enabling HTTPS redirection to enable static files and default files. Also, modify the statement that maps a `GET` request to return the `Hello World!` plain text response to only respond to the URL path `/hello`, as shown highlighted in the following code:

```
app.UseDefaultFiles(); // index.html, default.html, and so on
app.UseStaticFiles();

app.MapGet("/hello", () => "Hello World!");
```

The call to `UseDefaultFiles` must come before the call to `UseStaticFiles`, or it will not work. You will learn more about the ordering of middleware and endpoint routing at the end of this chapter.

2. Start the website.

3. Start Chrome and show **Developer Tools**.

4. In Chrome, enter `http://localhost:5000/` and note that you are redirected to the HTTPS address on port `5001`, and the `index.html` file is now returned over that secure connection because it is one of the possible default files for this website.

5. In **Developer Tools**, note the request for the Bootstrap stylesheet.

6. In Chrome, enter `http://localhost:5000/hello` and note that it returns the plain text **Hello World!** as before.

7. Close Chrome and shut down the web server.

If all web pages are static, that is, they only get changed manually by a web editor, then our website programming work is complete. But almost all websites need dynamic content, which means a web page that is generated at runtime by executing code.

The easiest way to do that is to use a feature of ASP.NET Core named **Razor Pages**.

Exploring ASP.NET Core Razor Pages

ASP.NET Core Razor Pages allow a developer to easily mix C# code statements with HTML markup to make the generated web page dynamic. That is why Razor Pages use the `.cshtml` file extension.

By convention, ASP.NET Core looks for Razor Pages in a folder named `Pages`.

Enabling Razor Pages

You will now copy and change the static HTML page into a dynamic Razor Page, and then add and enable the Razor Pages service:

1. In the `Northwind.Web` project folder, create a folder named `Pages`.

2. Copy the `index.html` file into the `Pages` folder (in Visual Studio, hold down *Ctrl* while dragging and dropping.)

3. For the file in the `Pages` folder, rename the file extension from `.html` to `.cshtml`.

4. In `index.cshtml`, remove the `<h2>` element that says that this is a static HTML page.

5. In `Program.cs`, before the statement that builds the app, add a statement to add ASP.NET Core Razor Pages and its related services, such as model binding, authorization, anti-forgery, views, and tag helpers, as shown in the following code:

    ```
    builder.Services.AddRazorPages();
    ```

6. In `Program.cs`, before the statement that maps an HTTP GET request for the path `/hello`, add a statement to call the `MapRazorPages` method, as shown in the following code:

    ```
    app.MapRazorPages();
    ```

Warning! If you have installed ReSharper, then it might give warnings like "Cannot resolve symbol" in your Razor Pages, Razor views, and Blazor components. This does not always mean there is an actual problem. If the file compiles, then you can ignore ReSharper. Sometimes the poor thing gets confused and needlessly worries developers.

Adding code to a Razor Page

In the HTML markup of a web page, Razor syntax is indicated by the @ symbol. Razor Pages can be described as follows:

- They require the @page directive at the top of the file.
- They can optionally have an @functions section that defines any of the following:
  - Properties for storing data values, like in a class definition. An instance of that class is automatically instantiated, named Model, which can have its properties set in special methods, and you can get the property values in the HTML.
  - Methods named OnGet, OnPost, OnDelete, and so on that execute when HTTP requests are made, such as GET, POST, and DELETE.

Let's now convert the static HTML page into a Razor Page:

1. In the Pages folder, in index.cshtml, make modifications as specified in the following list:
   - Add the @page statement to the top of the file.
   - After the @page statement, add an @functions statement block.
   - Define a property to store the name of the current day as a string value.
   - Define a method to set DayName that executes when an HTTP GET request is made for the page, as shown in the following code:

```
@page
@functions
{
  public string? DayName { get; set; }

  public void OnGet()
  {
    Model.DayName = DateTime.Now.ToString("dddd");
  }
}
```

2. Output the day name inside the second HTML paragraph, as shown highlighted in the following markup:

```
<p>It's @Model.DayName! Our customers include restaurants, hotels, and
cruise lines.</p>
```

3. Start the website.

4.   In Chrome, enter `https://localhost:5001/` and note the current day name is output on the page, as shown in *Figure 13.5*:

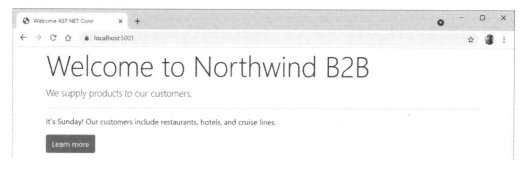

Figure 13.5: Welcome to Northwind page showing the current day

5.   In Chrome, enter `https://localhost:5001/index.html`, which exactly matches the static filename, and note that it returns the static HTML page as before.

6.   In Chrome, enter `https://localhost:5001/hello`, which exactly matches the endpoint route that returns plain text, and note that it returns **Hello World!** as before.

7.   Close Chrome and shut down the web server.

Using shared layouts with Razor Pages

Most websites have more than one page. If every page had to contain all of the boilerplate markup that is currently in `index.cshtml`, that would become a pain to manage. So, ASP.NET Core has a feature named **layouts**.

To use layouts, we must create a Razor file to define the default layout for all Razor Pages (and all MVC views) and store it in a `Shared` folder so that it can be easily found by convention. The name of this file can be anything, because we will specify it, but `_Layout.cshtml` is good practice.

We must also create a specially named file to set the default layout file for all Razor Pages (and all MVC views). This file must be named `_ViewStart.cshtml`.

Let's see layouts in action:

1.   In the `Pages` folder, add a file named `_ViewStart.cshtml`. (The Visual Studio item template is named **Razor View Start**.)

2.   If you are using Visual Studio Code, modify the `_ViewStart.cshtml` file content, as shown in the following markup:

```
@{
    Layout = "_Layout";
}
```

3.   In the `Pages` folder, create a folder named `Shared`.

4.   In the `Shared` folder, create a file named `_Layout.cshtml`. (The Visual Studio item template is named **Razor Layout**.)

5. Modify the content of _Layout.cshtml (it is similar to index.cshtml so you can copy and paste the HTML markup from there), as shown in the following markup:

```html
<!doctype html>
<html lang="en">
<head>
  <!-- Required meta tags -->
  <meta charset="utf-8" />
  <meta name="viewport" content=
    "width=device-width, initial-scale=1, shrink-to-fit=no" />
  <!-- Bootstrap CSS -->
  <link href="https://cdn.jsdelivr.net/npm/bootstrap@5.1.3/dist/css/
  bootstrap.min.css" rel="stylesheet" integrity="sha384-1BmE4kWBq78iYhFld
  vKuhfTAU6auU8tT94WrHftjDbrCEXSU1oBoqyl2QvZ6jIW3" crossorigin="anonymous">
  <title>@ViewData["Title"]</title>
</head>
<body>
  <div class="container">
    @RenderBody()
    <hr />
    <footer>
      <p>Copyright &copy; 2022 - @ViewData["Title"]</p>
    </footer>
  </div>
  <!-- JavaScript to enable features like carousel -->
  <script src="https://cdn.jsdelivr.net/npm/bootstrap@5.1.3/dist/js/
  bootstrap.bundle.min.js" integrity="sha384-ka7Sk0Gln4gmtz2MlQnikT1wXgYs
  Og+OMhuP+IlRH9sENBO0LRn5q+8nbTov4+1p" crossorigin="anonymous"></script>
  @RenderSection("Scripts", required: false)
</body>
</html>
```

While reviewing the preceding markup, note the following:

- `<title>` is set dynamically using server-side code from a dictionary named `ViewData`. This is a simple way to pass data between different parts of an ASP.NET Core website. In this case, the data will be set in a Razor Page class file and then output in the shared layout.

- `@RenderBody()` marks the insertion point for the view being requested.

- A horizontal rule and footer will appear at the bottom of each page.

- At the bottom of the layout is a script to implement some cool features of Bootstrap that we can use later, such as a carousel of images.

- After the `<script>` element for Bootstrap, we have defined a section named `Scripts` so that a Razor Page can optionally inject additional scripts that it needs.

6. Modify `index.cshtml` to remove all HTML markup except `<div class="jumbotron">` and its contents, and leave the C# code in the `@functions` block that you added earlier.

7. Add a statement to the `OnGet` method to store a page title in the `ViewData` dictionary, and modify the button to navigate to a suppliers page (which we will create in the next section), as shown highlighted in the following markup:

```
@page
@functions
{
    public string? DayName { get; set; }

    public void OnGet()
    {
        ViewData["Title"] = "Northwind B2B";
        Model.DayName = DateTime.Now.ToString("dddd");
    }
}

<div class="jumbotron">
    <h1 class="display-3">Welcome to Northwind B2B</h1>
    <p class="lead">We supply products to our customers.</p>
    <hr />
    <p>It's @Model.DayName! Our customers include restaurants, hotels,
    and cruise lines.</p>
    <p>
      <a class="btn btn-primary" href="suppliers">
        Learn more about our suppliers</a>
    </p>
</div>
```

8. Start the website, visit it with Chrome, and note that it has similar behavior to before, although clicking the button for suppliers will give a `404 Not Found` error because we have not created that page yet.

Using code-behind files with Razor Pages

Sometimes, it is better to separate the HTML markup from the data and executable code because it is more organized that way. Razor Pages allows you to do this by putting the C# code in **code-behind** class files. They have the same name as the `.cshtml` file but end with `.cshtml.cs`.

You will now create a Razor Page that shows a list of suppliers. In this example, we are focusing on learning about code-behind files. In the next topic, we will load the list of suppliers from a database, but for now, we will simulate that with a hardcoded array of `string` values:

1. In the `Pages` folder, add a new file named `Suppliers.cshtml`:

   • If you are using Visual Studio 2022, then the project item template is named **Razor Page - Empty** and it creates both a markup file and a code-behind file named `Suppliers.cshtml` and `Suppliers.cshtml.cs` respectively.

- If you are using Visual Studio Code, then you will need to create two new files named `Suppliers.cshtml` and `Suppliers.cshtml.cs` manually.

2. In `Suppliers.cshtml.cs`, add statements to define a property to store a list of supplier company names and populate it when an HTTP GET request for this page is made, as shown in the following code:

```
using Microsoft.AspNetCore.Mvc.RazorPages; // PageModel

namespace Northwind.Web.Pages;

public class SuppliersModel : PageModel
{
  public IEnumerable<string>? Suppliers { get; set; }

  public void OnGet()
  {
    ViewData["Title"] = "Northwind B2B - Suppliers";

    Suppliers = new[]
    {
      "Alpha Co", "Beta Limited", "Gamma Corp"
    };
  }
}
```

While reviewing the preceding markup, note the following:

- `SuppliersModel` inherits from `PageModel`, so it has members such as the `ViewData` dictionary for sharing data. You can right-click on `PageModel` and select **Go To Definition** to see that it has lots more useful features, such as the entire `HttpContext` of the current request.
- `SuppliersModel` defines a property for storing a collection of `string` values named `Suppliers`.
- When an HTTP GET request is made for this Razor Page, the `Suppliers` property is populated with some example supplier names from an array of `string` values. Later, we will populate this from the Northwind database.

3. In `Suppliers.cshtml`, modify the markup to render a heading and an HTML table containing the supplier company names, as shown in the following markup:

```
@page
@model Northwind.Web.Pages.SuppliersModel
<div class="row">
  <h1 class="display-2">Suppliers</h1>
  <table class="table">
    <thead class="thead-inverse">
      <tr><th>Company Name</th></tr>
```

```
      </thead>
      <tbody>
      @if (Model.Suppliers is not null)
      {
        @foreach(string name in Model.Suppliers)
        {
          <tr><td>@name</td></tr>
        }
      }
      </tbody>
    </table>
  </div>
```

While reviewing the preceding markup, note the following:

- The model type for this Razor Page is set to SuppliersModel.
- The page outputs an HTML table with Bootstrap styles.
- The data rows in the table are generated by looping through the Suppliers property of Model if it is not null.

4. Start the website and visit it using Chrome.

5. Click on the button to learn more about suppliers, and note the table of suppliers, as shown in *Figure 13.6*:

Figure 13.6: The table of suppliers loaded from an array of strings

Using Entity Framework Core with ASP.NET Core

Entity Framework Core is a natural way to get real data into a website. In *Chapter 12, Introducing Web Development Using ASP.NET Core*, you created two pairs of class libraries: one for the entity models and one for the Northwind database context, for SQLite and/or SQL Server. You will now use them in your website project.

Configuring Entity Framework Core as a service

Functionality, such as Entity Framework Core database contexts, that are needed by ASP.NET Core should be registered as a dependency service during website startup. The code in the GitHub repository solution and below uses SQLite, but you can easily use SQL Server if you prefer.

Let's see how:

1. In the `Northwind.Web` project, add a project reference to the `Northwind.Common.DataContext` project for either SQLite or SQL Server, as shown in the following markup:

   ```
   <!-- change Sqlite to SqlServer if you prefer -->
   <ItemGroup>
     <ProjectReference Include="..\Northwind.Common.DataContext.Sqlite\
     Northwind.Common.DataContext.Sqlite.csproj" />
   </ItemGroup>
   ```

    Warning! The project reference must go all on one line with no line break.

2. Build the `Northwind.Web` project.

3. In `Program.cs`, import the namespace to work with your entity model types, as shown in the following code:

   ```
   using Packt.Shared; // AddNorthwindContext extension method
   ```

4. In `Program.cs`, before the statement that builds the `app`, add a statement to register the `Northwind` database context class, as shown in the following code:

   ```
   builder.Services.AddNorthwindContext();
   ```

5. In the `Northwind.Web` project, in the `Pages` folder, open `Suppliers.cshtml.cs` and import the namespace for our database context, as shown in the following code:

   ```
   using Packt.Shared; // NorthwindContext
   ```

6. In the `SuppliersModel` class, add a private field to store the `Northwind` database context and a constructor to set it, as shown in the following code:

   ```
   private NorthwindContext db;

   public SuppliersModel(NorthwindContext injectedContext)
   {
     db = injectedContext;
   }
   ```

7.   Change the `Suppliers` property to contain `Supplier` objects instead of `string` values, as shown highlighted in the following code:

```
public IEnumerable<Supplier>? Suppliers { get; set; }
```

8.   In the `OnGet` method, modify the statements to set the `Suppliers` property from the `Suppliers` property of the database context, sorted by country and then company name, as shown highlighted in the following code:

```
public void OnGet()
{
  ViewData["Title"] = "Northwind B2B - Suppliers";

  Suppliers = db.Suppliers.OrderBy(c => c.Country).ThenBy(c =>
  c.CompanyName);
}
```

9.   Modify the contents of `Suppliers.cshtml` to import the `Packt.Shared` namespace and render multiple columns for each supplier, as shown highlighted in the following markup:

```
@page
@using Packt.Shared
@model Northwind.Web.Pages.SuppliersModel
<div class="row">
  <h1 class="display-2">Suppliers</h1>
  <table class="table">
    <thead class="thead-inverse">
      <tr>
        <th>Company Name</th>
        <th>Country</th>
        <th>Phone</th>
      </tr>
    </thead>
    <tbody>
    @if (Model.Suppliers is not null)
    {
      @foreach(Supplier s in Model.Suppliers)
      {
        <tr>
          <td>@s.CompanyName</td>
          <td>@s.Country</td>
          <td>@s.Phone</td>
        </tr>
      }
    }
    </tbody>
  </table>
</div>
```

10. Start the website.

11. In **Chrome**, if you started the website project at the command line or terminal, or you have disabled the automatic launch of the browser with the URL already entered, then enter `https://localhost:5001/`.

12. Click **Learn more about our suppliers** and note that the supplier table now loads from the database and the data is sorted first by country and then by company name, as shown in *Figure 13.7*:

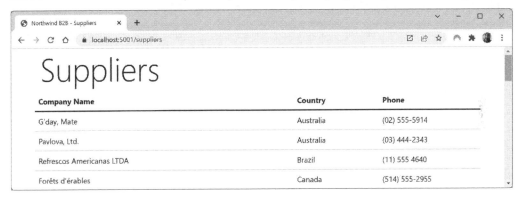

Figure 13.7: The suppliers table loaded from the Northwind database

Manipulating data using Razor Pages

You will now add functionality to insert a new supplier.

Enabling a model to insert entities

First, you will modify the supplier model so that it responds to HTTP POST requests when a visitor submits a form to insert a new supplier:

1. In the `Northwind.Web` project, in the `Pages` folder, open `Suppliers.cshtml.cs` and import the following namespace:

```
using Microsoft.AspNetCore.Mvc; // [BindProperty], IActionResult
```

2. In the `SuppliersModel` class, add a property to store a single supplier and a method named `OnPost` that adds the supplier to the `Suppliers` table in the Northwind database if its model is valid, as shown in the following code:

```
[BindProperty]
public Supplier? Supplier { get; set; }

public IActionResult OnPost()
{
  if ((Supplier is not null) && ModelState.IsValid)
  {
    db.Suppliers.Add(Supplier);
    db.SaveChanges();
    return RedirectToPage("/suppliers");
```

```
    }
    else
    {
      return Page(); // return to original page
    }
  }
```

While reviewing the preceding code, note the following:

- We added a property named `Supplier` that is decorated with the `[BindProperty]` attribute so that we can easily connect HTML elements on the web page to properties in the `Supplier` class.

- We added a method that responds to HTTP `POST` requests. It checks that all property values conform to validation rules on the `Supplier` class entity model (such as `[Required]` and `[StringLength]`) and then adds the supplier to the existing table and saves changes to the database context. This will generate a SQL statement to perform the insert into the database. Then, it redirects to the `Suppliers` page so that the visitor sees the newly added supplier.

Defining a form to insert a new supplier

Next, you will modify the Razor Page to define a form that a visitor can fill in and submit to insert a new supplier:

1. In `Suppliers.cshtml`, after the `@model` declaration, add Microsoft common tag helpers so that we can use the tag helper `asp-for` on this Razor Page, as shown in the following markup:

   ```
   @addTagHelper *, Microsoft.AspNetCore.Mvc.TagHelpers
   ```

2. At the bottom of the file, add a form to insert a new supplier, and use the `asp-for` tag helper to bind the `CompanyName`, `Country`, and `Phone` properties of the `Supplier` class to the input box, as shown in the following markup:

   ```
   <div class="row">
     <p>Enter details for a new supplier:</p>
     <form method="POST">
       <div><input asp-for="Supplier.CompanyName"
                   placeholder="Company Name" /></div>
       <div><input asp-for="Supplier.Country"
                   placeholder="Country" /></div>
       <div><input asp-for="Supplier.Phone"
                   placeholder="Phone" /></div>
       <input type="submit" />
     </form>
   </div>
   ```

While reviewing the preceding markup, note the following:

- The `<form>` element with a `POST` method is normal HTML, so an `<input type="submit" />` element inside it will make an HTTP `POST` request back to the current page with values of any other elements inside that form.

- An `<input>` element with a tag helper named `asp-for` enables data binding to the model behind the Razor Page.

3. Start the website and Chrome.

4. Click **Learn more about our suppliers,** scroll down to the bottom of the page, enter `Bob's Burgers, USA`, and `(603) 555-4567`, and then click **Submit**.

5. Note that you see a refreshed suppliers table with the new supplier added near the bottom because it is sorted with the USA suppliers.

6. Close Chrome and shut down the web server.

Injecting a dependency service into a Razor Page

If you have a `.cshtml` Razor Page that does not have a code-behind file, then you can inject a dependency service using the `@inject` directive instead of constructor parameter injection, and then directly reference the injected database context using Razor syntax in the middle of the markup.

Let's create a simple example:

1. In the `Pages` folder, add a new file named `Orders.cshtml`. (The Visual Studio item template is named **Razor Page - Empty** and it creates two files. Delete the `.cshtml.cs` file.)

2. In `Orders.cshtml`, write code and markup to output the number of orders in the Northwind database, as shown in the following markup:

```
@page
@using Packt.Shared
@inject NorthwindContext db
@{
    string title = "Orders";
    ViewData["Title"] = $"Northwind B2B - {title}";
}
<div class="row">
    <h1 class="display-2">@title</h1>
    <p>
        There are @db.Orders.Count() orders in the Northwind database.
    </p>
</div>
```

3. Start the website.

4. In the browser address bar, navigate to `/orders` and note that you see that there are 830 orders in the Northwind database.

5. Close Chrome and shut down the web server.

Using Razor class libraries

Everything related to a Razor Page can be compiled into a class library for easier reuse in multiple projects. With ASP.NET Core 3.0 and later, this can include static files such as HTML, CSS, JavaScript libraries, and media assets such as image files. A website can either use the Razor Page's view as defined in the class library or override it.

Disabling compact folders for Visual Studio Code

Before we implement our Razor class library, I want to explain a Visual Studio Code feature that confused some readers of a previous edition because the feature was added after publishing.

The compact folders feature means that nested folders such as /Areas/MyFeature/Pages/ are shown in a compact form if the intermediate folders in the hierarchy do not contain files, as shown in *Figure 13.8*:

Figure 13.8: Compact folders enabled or disabled

If you would like to disable the Visual Studio Code compact folders feature, complete the following steps:

1. On Windows, navigate to **File** | **Preferences** | **Settings**. On macOS, navigate to **Code** | **Preferences** | **Settings**.

2. In the **Search** settings box, enter compact.

3. Clear the **Explorer: Compact Folders** checkbox, as shown in *Figure 13.9*:

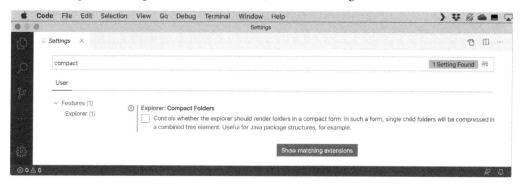

Figure 13.9: Disabling compact folders for Visual Studio Code

4. Close the **Settings** tab.

Creating a Razor class library

Let's create a new Razor class library:

1. Use your preferred code editor to open the PracticalApps solution/workspace and then add a new project, as defined in the following list:

    - Project template: **Razor Class Library**/razorclasslib
    - Project file and folder: Northwind.Razor.Employees
    - Checkbox/switch: **Support pages and views**/-s
    - Workspace/solution file and folder: PracticalApps

 -s is short for the --support-pages-and-views switch, which enables the class library to use Razor Pages and .cshtml file views.

2. In the Northwind.Razor.Employees project, add a project reference to the Northwind.Common.DataContext project for either SQLite or SQL Server and note the SDK is Microsoft.NET.Sdk.Razor, as shown highlighted in the following markup:

```
<Project Sdk="Microsoft.NET.Sdk.Razor">

  <PropertyGroup>
    <TargetFramework>net7.0</TargetFramework>
    <Nullable>enable</Nullable>
    <ImplicitUsings>enable</ImplicitUsings>
    <AddRazorSupportForMvc>true</AddRazorSupportForMvc>
  </PropertyGroup>

  <ItemGroup>
    <FrameworkReference Include="Microsoft.AspNetCore.App" />
  </ItemGroup>

  <!-- change Sqlite to SqlServer if you prefer -->
  <ItemGroup>
    <ProjectReference Include="..\Northwind.Common.DataContext.Sqlite
    \Northwind.Common.DataContext.Sqlite.csproj" />
  </ItemGroup>

</Project>
```

 Warning! The project reference must go all on one line with no line break. Also, do not mix our SQLite and SQL Server projects or you will see compiler errors. If you used SQL Server in the Northwind.Web project, then you must use SQL Server in the Northwind.Razor.Employees project as well.

3. Build the Northwind.Razor.Employees project.

4. Expand the `Areas` folder, right-click the `MyFeature` folder, select **Rename**, enter the new name `PacktFeatures`, and press *Enter*.

5. In the `PacktFeatures` folder, in the `Pages` subfolder, add a new file named `_ViewStart.cshtml`. (The Visual Studio item template is named **Razor View Start**. Or just copy it from the `Northwind. Web` project.)

6. If you are using Visual Studio Code, modify its content to inform this class library that any Razor Pages should look for a layout with the same name as used in the `Northwind.Web` project, as shown in the following markup:

    ```
    @{
        Layout = "_Layout";
    }
    ```

     We do not need to create the `_Layout.cshtml` file in this project. It will use the one in its host project, for example, the one in the `Northwind.Web` project.

7. In the `Pages` subfolder, rename `Page1.cshtml` to `Employees.cshtml`, and, if the code-behind file is not automatically renamed, then manually rename `Page1.cshtml.cs` to `Employees. cshtml.cs`.

8. In `Employees.cshtml.cs`, define a page model with an array of `Employee` entity instances loaded from the Northwind database, as shown in the following code:

    ```
    using Microsoft.AspNetCore.Mvc.RazorPages; // PageModel
    using Packt.Shared; // Employee, NorthwindContext

    namespace PacktFeatures.Pages;

    public class EmployeesPageModel : PageModel
    {
        private NorthwindContext db;

        public EmployeesPageModel(NorthwindContext injectedContext)
        {
            db = injectedContext;
        }

        public Employee[] Employees { get; set; } = null!;

        public void OnGet()
        {
            ViewData["Title"] = "Northwind B2B - Employees";

            Employees = db.Employees.OrderBy(e => e.LastName)
    ```

```
        .ThenBy(e => e.FirstName).ToArray();
    }
}
```

9. In `Employees.cshtml`, add markup to render all of the employees in the page model using a partial view named _Employee, as shown in the following markup:

```
@page
@using Packt.Shared
@addTagHelper *, Microsoft.AspNetCore.Mvc.TagHelpers
@model PacktFeatures.Pages.EmployeesPageModel

<div class="row">
  <h1 class="display-2">Employees</h1>
</div>
<div class="row">
@foreach(Employee employee in Model.Employees)
{
  <div class="col-sm-3">
    <partial name="_Employee" model="employee" />
  </div>
}
</div>
```

While reviewing the preceding markup, note the following:

- We import the `Packt.Shared` namespace so that we can use classes in it such as `Employee`.
- We add support for tag helpers so that we can use the `<partial>` element.
- We declare the `@model` type for this Razor Page to use the page model class that you just defined.
- We enumerate through the `Employees` in the model, outputting each one using a partial view.

Implementing a partial view to show a single employee

The `<partial>` tag helper was introduced in ASP.NET Core 2.1. A partial view is like a piece of a Razor Page. You will create one in the next few steps to render a single employee:

1. In the `Northwind.Razor.Employees` project, in the `Pages` folder, create a `Shared` folder.

2. In the `Shared` folder, create a file named `_Employee.cshtml`. (The Visual Studio item template is named **Razor View - Empty**.)

3. In `_Employee.cshtml`, add markup to output an employee using a Bootstrap card, as shown in the following markup:

```
@model Packt.Shared.Employee

<div class="card border-dark mb-3" style="max-width: 18rem;">
  <div class="card-header">@Model?.LastName, @Model?.FirstName</div>
  <div class="card-body text-dark">
    <h5 class="card-title">@Model?.Country</h5>
```

```
        <p class="card-text">@Model?.Notes</p>
    </div>
</div>
```

While reviewing the preceding markup, note the following:

- By convention, the names of partial views start with an underscore.
- If you put a partial view in the Shared folder, then it can be found automatically.
- The model type for this partial view is a single Employee entity.
- We use Bootstrap card styles to output information about each employee.

Using and testing a Razor class library

You will now reference and use the Razor class library in the website project:

1. In the Northwind.Web project, add a project reference to the Northwind.Razor.Employees project, as shown in the following markup:

```
<ProjectReference Include=
    "..\Northwind.Razor.Employees\Northwind.Razor.Employees.csproj" />
```

2. In Pages\index.cshtml, add a paragraph with a link to the Packt feature employees page after the link to the suppliers page, as shown in the following markup:

```
<p>
    <a class="btn btn-primary" href="packtfeatures/employees">
        Contact our employees
    </a>
</p>
```

3. Start the website, visit the website using Chrome, and click the **Contact our employees** button to see the cards of employees, as shown in *Figure 13.10*:

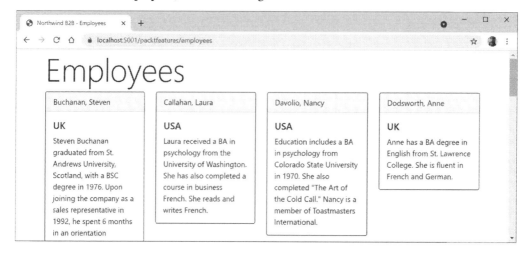

Figure 13.10: A list of employees from a Razor class library feature

Configuring services and the HTTP request pipeline

Now that we have built a website, we can return to the Startup configuration and review how services and the HTTP request pipeline work in more detail.

Understanding endpoint routing

In earlier versions of ASP.NET Core, the routing system and the extendable middleware system did not always work easily together, for example, if you wanted to implement a policy such as CORS in both middleware and MVC. Microsoft has invested in improving routing with a system named **endpoint routing** introduced with ASP.NET Core 2.2.

 Good Practice: Endpoint routing replaces the IRouter-based routing used in ASP.NET Core 2.1 and earlier. Microsoft recommends that every older ASP.NET Core project migrates to endpoint routing if possible.

Endpoint routing is designed to enable better interoperability between frameworks that need routing, such as Razor Pages, MVC, or Web APIs, and middleware that needs to understand how routing affects them, such as localization, authorization, CORS, and so on.

Endpoint routing gets its name because it represents the route table as a compiled tree of endpoints that can be walked efficiently by the routing system. One of the biggest improvements is the performance of routing and action method selection.

It is on by default with ASP.NET Core 2.2 or later if compatibility is set to 2.2 or later. Traditional routes registered using the MapRoute method or with attributes are mapped to the new system.

The new routing system includes a link generation service registered as a dependency service that does not need an HttpContext.

Configuring endpoint routing

Endpoint routing requires a pair of calls to the UseRouting and UseEndpoints methods:

- UseRouting marks the pipeline position where a routing decision is made.
- UseEndpoints marks the pipeline position where the selected endpoint is executed.

Middleware such as localization that runs in between these methods can see the selected endpoint and switch to a different endpoint if necessary.

Endpoint routing uses the same route template syntax that has been used in ASP.NET MVC since 2010 and the [Route] attribute introduced with ASP.NET MVC 5 in 2013. Migration from ASP.NET MVC to ASP.NET Core MVC often only requires changes to the Startup configuration.

MVC controllers, Razor Pages, and frameworks such as SignalR used to be enabled by a call to UseMvc or similar methods, but they are now added inside the UseEndpoints method call because they are all integrated into the same routing system along with middleware.

Reviewing the endpoint routing configuration in our project

Review the statements in `Program.cs`, as shown in the following code:

```
using Packt.Shared; // AddNorthwindContext extension method

// configure services

var builder = WebApplication.CreateBuilder(args);
builder.Services.AddRazorPages();
builder.Services.AddNorthwindContext();
var app = builder.Build();

// configure the HTTP pipeline

if (!app.Environment.IsDevelopment())
{
  app.UseHsts();
}

app.UseHttpsRedirection();

app.UseDefaultFiles(); // index.html, default.html, and so on
app.UseStaticFiles();

app.MapRazorPages();
app.MapGet("/hello", () => "Hello World!");

// start the web server

app.Run();

WriteLine("This executes after the web server has stopped!");
```

The web application `builder` registers services that can then be retrieved when the functionality they provide is needed using dependency injection. The naming convention for a method that registers a service is `AddNameOfService`. Our code registers two services: Razor Pages and an EF Core database context.

Common methods that register dependency services, including services that combine other method calls that register services, are shown in the following table:

Method	Services that it registers
AddMvcCore	Minimum set of services necessary to route requests and invoke controllers. Most websites will need more configuration than this.
AddAuthorization	Authentication and authorization services.
AddDataAnnotations	MVC data annotations service.

`AddCacheTagHelper`	MVC cache tag helper service.

`AddRazorPages`	Razor Pages service including the Razor view engine. Commonly used in simple website projects. It calls the following additional methods:
	`AddMvcCore`
	`AddAuthorization`
	`AddDataAnnotations`
	`AddCacheTagHelper`

`AddApiExplorer`	Web API explorer service.
`AddCors`	CORS support for enhanced security.
`AddFormatterMappings`	Mappings between a URL format and its corresponding media type.

`AddControllers`	Controller services but not services for views or pages. Commonly used in ASP.NET Core Web API projects. It calls the following additional methods:
	`AddMvcCore`
	`AddAuthorization`
	`AddDataAnnotations`
	`AddCacheTagHelper`
	`AddApiExplorer`
	`AddCors`
	`AddFormatterMappings`

`AddViews`	Support for `.cshtml` views including default conventions.
`AddRazorViewEngine`	Support for Razor view engine including processing the @ symbol.

`AddControllersWithViews`	Controller, views, and pages services. Commonly used in ASP.NET Core MVC website projects. It calls the following additional methods:
	`AddMvcCore`
	`AddAuthorization`
	`AddDataAnnotations`
	`AddCacheTagHelper`
	`AddApiExplorer`
	`AddCors`
	`AddFormatterMappings`
	`AddViews`
	`AddRazorViewEngine`

`AddMvc`	Similar to `AddControllersWithViews`, but you should only use it for backward compatibility.
`AddDbContext<T>`	Your `DbContext` type and its optional `DbContextOptions<TContext>`.
`AddNorthwindContext`	A custom extension method we created to make it easier to register the `NorthwindContext` class for either SQLite or SQL Server based on the project referenced.

You will see more examples of using these extension methods for registering services in the next few chapters when working with MVC and Web API services.

Setting up the HTTP pipeline

After building the web application and its services, the next statements configure the HTTP pipeline, through which HTTP requests and responses flow in and out. The pipeline is made up of a connected sequence of delegates that can perform processing and then decide to either return a response themselves or pass processing on to the next delegate in the pipeline. Responses that come back can also be manipulated.

Remember that delegates define a method signature that a delegate implementation can plug into. You might want to refer back to *Chapter 6, Implementing Interfaces and Inheriting Classes*, to refresh your understanding of delegates.

The delegate for the HTTP request pipeline is simple, as shown in the following code:

```
public delegate Task RequestDelegate(HttpContext context);
```

You can see that the input parameter is an `HttpContext`. This provides access to everything you might need to process the incoming HTTP request, including the URL path, query string parameters, cookies, and user agent.

These delegates are often called **middleware** because they sit in between the browser client and the website or web service.

Middleware delegates are configured using one of the following methods or a custom method that calls them itself:

- `Run`: Adds a middleware delegate that terminates the pipeline by immediately returning a response instead of calling the next middleware delegate.

- `Map`: Adds a middleware delegate that creates a branch in the pipeline when there is a matching request usually based on a URL path like `/hello`.

- `Use`: Adds a middleware delegate that forms part of the pipeline so it can decide if it wants to pass the request to the next delegate in the pipeline. It can modify the request and response before and after the next delegate.

For convenience, there are many extension methods that make it easier to build the pipeline, for example, UseMiddleware<T>, where T is a class that has:

- A constructor with a RequestDelegate parameter that will be passed to the next pipeline component.
- An Invoke method with a HttpContext parameter and returns a Task.

Summarizing key middleware extension methods

Key middleware extension methods used in our code include the following:

- UseHsts: Adds middleware for using HSTS, which adds the Strict-Transport-Security header.
- UseHttpsRedirection: Adds middleware for redirecting HTTP requests to HTTPS, so in our code a request for http://localhost:5000 would respond with a 307 status code telling the browser to make a request for https://localhost:5001.
- UseDefaultFiles: Adds middleware that enables default file mapping on the current path, so in our code it would identify files such as index.html.
- UseStaticFiles: Adds middleware that looks in wwwroot for static files to return in the HTTP response.
- MapRazorPages: Adds middleware that will map URL paths such as /suppliers to a Razor Page file in the /Pages folder named suppliers.cshtml and return the results as the HTTP response.
- MapGet: Adds middleware that will map URL paths such as /hello to an inline delegate that writes plain text directly to the HTTP response.

If we had chosen a different project template, for example, for an ASP.NET Core MVC website, then we would have seen other common middleware extension methods that include the following:

- UseDeveloperExceptionPage: Captures synchronous and asynchronous System.Exception instances from the pipeline and generates HTML error responses.
- UseRouting: Adds middleware that defines a point in the pipeline where routing decisions are made, and must be combined with a call to UseEndpoints where the processing is then executed.
- UseEndpoints: Adds middleware to execute to generate responses from decisions made earlier in the pipeline.

Visualizing the HTTP pipeline

The HTTP request and response pipeline can be visualized as a sequence of request delegates, called one after the other, as shown in the simplified diagram shown in *Figure 13.11*, which excludes some middleware delegates, such as UseHsts and MapGet:

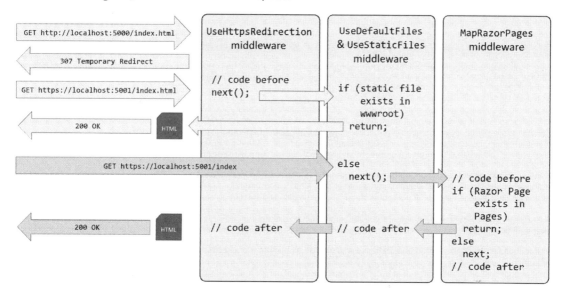

Figure 13.11: The HTTP request and response pipeline

The diagram shows two HTTP requests, as described in the following list:

- First, in yellow, an HTTP request is made for the static file index.html. The first middleware to process this request is HTTPS redirection, which detects that the request is not for HTTPS and responds with a 307 status code and the URL for the secure version of the resource. The browser then makes another request using HTTPS, which gets past the HTTPS redirection middleware and is passed on to the UseDefaultFiles and UseStaticFiles middleware. This finds a matching static file in the wwwroot folder and returns it.

- Second, in blue, an HTTPS request is made for the relative path index. The request uses HTTPS, so the HTTPS redirection middleware passes it through to the next middleware component. No matching static file is found in the wwwroot folder, so the static files middleware passes the request through to the next middleware in the pipeline. A match is found in the Pages folder for the Razor Page file index.cshtml. The Razor Page is executed to generate an HTML page that is returned as the HTTP response. Any code in the middleware that is part of the pipeline could make changes to this HTTP response as it flows back through them if needed, although in this scenario none of them do.

Implementing an anonymous inline delegate as middleware

A delegate can be specified as an inline anonymous method. We will register one that plugs into the pipeline after routing decisions for endpoints have been made.

It will output which endpoint was chosen, as well as handling one specific route: /bonjour. If that route is matched, it will respond with plain text, without calling any further into the pipeline to find a match:

1. In the `Northwind.Web` project, in `Program.cs`, add statements before the call to `UseHttpsRedirection` to use an anonymous method as a middleware delegate, as shown in the following code:

```
app.Use(async (HttpContext context, Func<Task> next) =>
{
  RouteEndpoint? rep = context.GetEndpoint() as RouteEndpoint;

  if (rep is not null)
  {
    WriteLine($"Endpoint name: {rep.DisplayName}");
    WriteLine($"Endpoint route pattern: {rep.RoutePattern.RawText}");
  }

  if (context.Request.Path == "/bonjour")
  {
    // in the case of a match on URL path, this becomes a terminating
    // delegate that returns so does not call the next delegate
    await context.Response.WriteAsync("Bonjour Monde!");
    return;
  }

  // we could modify the request before calling the next delegate
  await next();

  // we could modify the response after calling the next delegate
});
```

2. Start the website.

3. In Chrome, navigate to `https://localhost:5001/`, look at the console output and note that there was a match on an endpoint route /; it was processed as /index, and the `Index.cshtml` Razor Page was executed to return the response, as shown in the following output:

```
Endpoint name: /index
Endpoint route pattern:
```

4. Navigate to `https://localhost:5001/suppliers` and note that you can see that there was a match on an endpoint route /Suppliers, and the `Suppliers.cshtml` Razor Page was executed to return the response, as shown in the following output:

```
Endpoint name: /Suppliers
Endpoint route pattern: Suppliers
```

5. Navigate to `https://localhost:5001/index` and note that there was a match on an endpoint route `/index`, and the `Index.cshtml` Razor Page was executed to return the response, as shown in the following output:

    ```
    Endpoint name: /index
    Endpoint route pattern: index
    ```

6. Navigate to `https://localhost:5001/index.html` and note that there is no output written to the console because there was no match on an endpoint route, but there was a match for a static file, so it was returned as the response.

7. Navigate to `https://localhost:5001/bonjour` and note that there is no output written to the console because there was no match on an endpoint route. Instead, our delegate matched on `/bonjour`, wrote directly to the response stream, and returned with no further processing.

8. Close Chrome and shut down the web server.

Enabling request decompression support

To make HTTP requests and responses more efficient, the HTTP body content can be compressed using standard algorithms like gzip, Brotli, and Deflate, and an HTTP header is added to indicate which was used.

In the past, the developer had to implement decompression before processing the body if a browser sent a compressed request. With ASP.NET Core 7 or later, middleware to do this for you is built in and just needs to be added to the pipeline.

Unfortunately, this is tricky to try out because browsers cannot initiate a compressed request. This is because the browser cannot know if the server can handle it. Compression is normally enabled by the browser sending an uncompressed request with a header informing the server what algorithms the browser understands, as shown in the following request:

```
Accept-Encoding: gzip, deflate, br, compress
```

The server can then decide to compress its response and it sets a similar header in its response if it does, as shown in the following response:

```
Content-Encoding: gzip
```

We will just see how to enable the server side to receive HTTP requests with compressed body content in those rare scenarios where the browser or another client makes one:

1. In the `Northwind.Web` project, in `Program.cs`, add statements after the call to `AddNorthwindContext` to add the request compression middleware, as shown in the following code:

    ```
    builder.Services.AddRequestDecompression();
    ```

2. In `Program.cs`, add statements after the call to use HTTPS redirection to use request decompression, as shown in the following code:

    ```
    app.UseRequestDecompression();
    ```

Enabling HTTP/3 support

HTTP/3 uses the same request methods, like GET and POST, the same status codes, like 200 and 404, and the same headers, but encodes them and maintains session state differently because it runs over QUIC rather than the older and less efficient **Transmission Control Protocol (TCP)**.

At the time of writing, HTTP/3 is supported by about 75% of actively used web browsers, including Chromium-based browsers like Chrome, Edge, and Opera. It is also supported by Firefox and Safari on macOS and iOS (although it is disabled by default).

HTTP/3 brings benefits to all internet-connected apps, but especially mobile, because it supports connection migration using UDP with TLS built in, so the device does not need to reconnect when moving between WiFi and cellular networks. Each frame of data is encrypted separately so it no longer has the head-of-line blocking problem in HTTP/2 that happens if a TCP packet is lost and therefore all the streams are blocked until the data can be recovered.

.NET 6 supported HTTP/3 as a preview feature for both clients and servers. .NET 7 delivers final full support for the following operating systems:

- Windows 11 and Windows Server 2022.
- Linux; you can install QUIC support using sudo apt install libmsquic.

If you have one of the supported operating systems listed above, let's enable HTTP/3 support in the Northwind.Web project; otherwise, skip ahead to the next section:

1. In Program.cs, import the namespace for working with HTTP protocols, as shown in the following code:

    ```
    using Microsoft.AspNetCore.Server.Kestrel.Core; // HttpProtocols
    ```

2. In Program.cs, add statements before the call to Build to enable all three versions of HTTP, as shown in the following code:

    ```
    builder.WebHost.ConfigureKestrel((context, options) =>
    {
      options.ListenAnyIP(5001, listenOptions =>
      {
        listenOptions.Protocols = HttpProtocols.Http1AndHttp2AndHttp3;
        listenOptions.UseHttps(); // HTTP/3 requires secure connections
      });
    });
    ```

 Good Practice: You should not just enable HTTP/3 since about 25% of browsers still do not support it or even HTTP/2.

3. In `appSettings.json`, add an entry to show hosting diagnostics, as shown highlighted in the following configuration:

```json
{
    "Logging": {
        "LogLevel": {
            "Default": "Information",
            "Microsoft.AspNetCore": "Warning",
            "Microsoft.AspNetCore.Hosting.Diagnostics": "Information"
        }
    }
```

4. Start the website.

5. In Chrome, view **Developer tools** and select the **Network** tab.

6. Navigate to `https://localhost:5001/`, and note the **Response Headers** include an entry for **alt-svc** with a value of **h3** indicating HTTP/3 support, as shown in *Figure 13.12*:

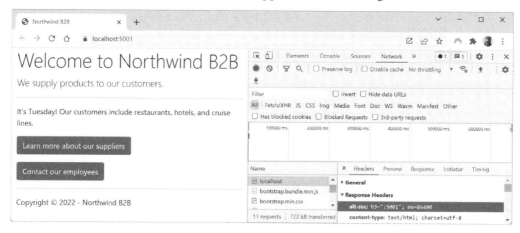

Figure 13.12: Chrome showing support for HTTP/3

7. In the console or terminal output, note the hosting diagnostics logs, as shown in the following output:

```
info: Microsoft.AspNetCore.Hosting.Diagnostics[1]
      Request starting HTTP/3 GET https://localhost:5001/ - -
info: Microsoft.AspNetCore.Hosting.Diagnostics[2]
      Request finished HTTP/3 GET https://localhost:5001/ - - - 200 -
text/html;+charset=utf-8 142.0365ms
warn: Microsoft.AspNetCore.Server.Kestrel[41]
      One or more of the following response headers have been removed
because they are invalid for HTTP/2 and HTTP/3 responses: 'Connection',
'Transfer-Encoding', 'Keep-Alive', 'Upgrade' and 'Proxy-Connection'.
```

8. Close Chrome and shut down the web server.

You can learn more about .NET support for HTTP/3 at the following links:

- HTTP/3 support in .NET: `https://devblogs.microsoft.com/dotnet/http-3-support-in-dotnet-6/`.

- .NET Networking Improvements – HTTP/3 and QUIC: `https://devblogs.microsoft.com/dotnet/dotnet-6-networking-improvements/#http-3-and-quic`.

- Use HTTP/3 with the ASP.NET Core Kestrel web server: `https://docs.microsoft.com/en-us/aspnet/core/fundamentals/servers/kestrel/http3`.

Practicing and exploring

Test your knowledge and understanding by answering some questions, getting some hands-on practice, and exploring this chapter's topics with deeper research.

Exercise 13.1 – Test your knowledge

Answer the following questions:

1. List six method names that can be specified in an HTTP request.
2. List six status codes and their descriptions that can be returned in an HTTP response.
3. In ASP.NET Core, what is the `Program` class used for?
4. What does the acronym HSTS stand for and what does it do?
5. How do you enable static HTML pages for a website?
6. How do you mix C# code into the middle of HTML to create a dynamic page?
7. How can you define shared layouts for Razor Pages?
8. How can you separate the markup from the code-behind in a Razor Page?
9. How do you configure an Entity Framework Core data context for use with an ASP.NET Core website?
10. How can you reuse Razor Pages with ASP.NET Core 2.2 or later?

Exercise 13.2 – Practice building a data-driven web page

Add a Razor Page to the `Northwind.Web` website that enables the user to see a list of customers grouped by country. When the user clicks on a customer record, they should then see a page showing the full contact details of that customer and a list of their orders.

Exercise 13.3 – Practice building web pages for console apps

Reimplement some of the console apps from earlier chapters as Razor Pages; for example, from *Chapter 4, Writing, Debugging, and Testing Functions*, provide a web user interface to output times tables, calculate tax, and generate factorials and the Fibonacci sequence.

Exercise 13.4 – Explore topics

Use the links on the following page to learn more about the topics covered in this chapter:

```
https://github.com/markjprice/cs11dotnet7/blob/main/book-links.md#chapter-13---
building-websites-using-aspnet-core-razor-pages
```

Summary

In this chapter, you learned:

- About the foundations of web development using HTTP.
- How to build a simple website that returns static files.
- How to use ASP.NET Core Razor Pages with Entity Framework Core to create web pages that are dynamically generated from information in a database.
- How to configure the HTTP request and response pipeline, what the helper extension methods do, and how you can add your own middleware that affects processing.

In the next chapter, you will learn how to build more complex websites using ASP.NET Core MVC, which separates the technical concerns of building a website into models, views, and controllers to make them easier to manage.

14

Building Websites Using the Model-View-Controller Pattern

This chapter is about building websites with a modern HTTP architecture on the server side using Microsoft ASP.NET Core MVC, including the configuration, authentication, authorization, routes, request and response pipeline, models, views, and controllers that make up an ASP.NET Core MVC project.

This chapter will cover the following topics:

- Setting up an ASP.NET Core MVC website
- Exploring an ASP.NET Core MVC website
- Customizing an ASP.NET Core MVC website
- Querying a database and using display templates
- Improving scalability using asynchronous tasks

Setting up an ASP.NET Core MVC website

ASP.NET Core Razor Pages are great for simple websites. For more complex websites, it would be better to have a more formal structure to manage that complexity.

This is where the **Model-View-Controller (MVC)** design pattern is useful. It uses technologies like Razor Pages, but allows a cleaner separation between technical concerns, as shown in the following list:

- **Models:** Classes that represent the data entities and view models used on the website.
- **Views:** Razor files, that is, .cshtml files, that render data in view models into HTML web pages. Blazor uses the .razor file extension, but do not confuse them with Razor files!
- **Controllers:** Classes that execute code when an HTTP request arrives at the web server. The controller methods usually create a view model that may contain entity models and passes it to a view to generate an HTTP response to send back to the web browser or other client.

The best way to understand using the MVC design pattern for web development is to see a working example.

Creating an ASP.NET Core MVC website

You will use a project template to create an ASP.NET Core MVC website project that has a database for authenticating and authorizing users. Visual Studio 2022 defaults to using SQL Server LocalDB for the accounts database. Visual Studio Code (or more accurately the dotnet CLI tool) uses SQLite by default and you can specify a switch to use SQL Server LocalDB instead.

Let's see it in action:

1. Use your preferred code editor to open the PracticalApps solution/workspace and then add an MVC website project with authentication accounts stored in a database, as defined in the following list:

   - Project template: **ASP.NET Core Web App (Model-View-Controller) [C#]**/mvc
   - Project file and folder: Northwind.Mvc
   - Workspace/solution file and folder: PracticalApps
   - **Additional information - Authentication type: Individual Accounts**/--auth Individual
   - For Visual Studio 2022, leave all other options as their defaults, for example, HTTPS is enabled, and Docker is disabled

   In Visual Studio Code, select Northwind.Mvc as the active OmniSharp project.

2. Build the Northwind.Mvc project.

3. At the command line or terminal, use the help switch to see other options for this project template, as shown in the following command:

   ```
   dotnet new mvc --help
   ```

4. Note the results, as shown in the following partial output:

   ```
   ASP.NET Core Web App (Model-View-Controller) (C#)
   Author: Microsoft
   Description: A project template for creating an ASP.NET Core application
   with example ASP.NET Core MVC Views and Controllers. This template can
   also be used for RESTful HTTP services.
   This template contains technologies from parties other than Microsoft,
   see https://aka.ms/aspnetcore/7.0-third-party-notices for details.
   ```

There are many options, especially related to authentication, as shown in the following table:

Switches	Description
`-au` or `--auth`	The type of authentication to use: • **None** (default): This choice also allows you to disable HTTPS. • `Individual`: Individual authentication that stores registered users and their passwords in a database (SQLite by default). We will use this in the project we create for this chapter. • `IndividualB2C`: Individual authentication with Azure AD B2C. • `SingleOrg`: Organizational authentication for a single tenant. • `MultiOrg`: Organizational authentication for multiple tenants. • `Windows`: Windows authentication. Mostly useful for intranets.
`-uld` or `--use-local-db`	Whether to use SQL Server LocalDB instead of SQLite. This option only applies if `--auth Individual` or `--auth IndividualB2C` is specified. The value is an optional bool with a default of `false`.
`-rrc` or `--razor-runtime-compilation`	Determines if the project is configured to use Razor runtime compilation in Debug builds. This can improve the performance of startup during debugging because it can defer the compilation of Razor views. The value is an optional bool with a default of `false`.
`-f` or `--framework`	The target framework for the project. Values can be `net7.0` (default), `net6.0`, or `netcoreapp3.1`.

Creating the authentication database for SQL Server LocalDB

If you created the MVC project using Visual Studio 2022, or you used `dotnet new mvc` with the `-uld` or `--use-local-db` switch, then the database for authentication and authorization will be stored in SQL Server LocalDB. But the database does not yet exist.

If you created the MVC project using `dotnet new`, then the database for authentication and authorization will be stored in SQLite and the file has already been created, named `app.db`.

The connection string for the authentication database is named `DefaultConnection` and it is stored in the `appsettings.json` file in the root folder for the MVC website project.

For SQLite, see the following setting:

```
{
  "ConnectionStrings": {
    "DefaultConnection": "DataSource=app.db;Cache=Shared"
  },
```

If you created the MVC project using Visual Studio 2022, then let's create its authentication database now:

1. In the `Northwind.Mvc` project, in `appsettings.json,` note the database connection string named `DefaultConnection,` as shown highlighted in the following configuration:

    ```
    {
      "ConnectionStrings": {
        "DefaultConnection": "Server=(localdb)\\mssqllocaldb;Database=aspnet-
        Northwind.Mvc-440bc3c1-f7e7-4463-99d5-896b6a6500e0;Trusted_
        Connection=True;MultipleActiveResultSets=true"
      },
      "Logging": {
        "LogLevel": {
          "Default": "Information",
          "Microsoft.AspNetCore": "Warning"
        }
      },
      "AllowedHosts": "*"
    }
    ```

     Your database name will use the pattern `aspnet-[ProjectName]-[GUID]` and have a different GUID value from the example above.

2. At a command prompt or terminal, in the `Northwind.Mvc` folder, enter the command to run database migrations so that the database used to store credentials for authentication is created, as shown in the following command:

    ```
    dotnet ef database update
    ```

3. Note the database is created with tables like `AspNetRoles`, as shown in the following partial output:

    ```
    PS C:\cs11dotnet7\PracticalApps\Northwind.Mvc> dotnet ef database update
    Build started...
    Build succeeded.
    info: Microsoft.EntityFrameworkCore.Infrastructure[10403]
          Entity Framework Core 7.0.0 initialized 'ApplicationDbContext'
    using provider 'Microsoft.EntityFrameworkCore.SqlServer:7.0.0' with
    options: None
    info: Microsoft.EntityFrameworkCore.Database.Command[20101]
          Executed DbCommand (129ms) [Parameters=[], CommandType='Text',
    CommandTimeout='60']
          CREATE DATABASE [aspnet-Northwind.Mvc2-440bc3c1-f7e7-4463-99d5-
    896b6a6500e0];
    ...
    ```

```
info: Microsoft.EntityFrameworkCore.Database.Command[20101]
      Executed DbCommand (3ms) [Parameters=[], CommandType='Text',
CommandTimeout='30']
      CREATE TABLE [AspNetRoles] (
          [Id] nvarchar(450) NOT NULL,
          [Name] nvarchar(256) NULL,
          [NormalizedName] nvarchar(256) NULL,
          [ConcurrencyStamp] nvarchar(max) NULL,
          CONSTRAINT [PK_AspNetRoles] PRIMARY KEY ([Id])
      );
...
info: Microsoft.EntityFrameworkCore.Database.Command[20101]
      Executed DbCommand (8ms) [Parameters=[], CommandType='Text',
CommandTimeout='30']
      INSERT INTO [__EFMigrationsHistory] ([MigrationId],
[ProductVersion])
      VALUES (N'00000000000000_CreateIdentitySchema', N'7.0.0');
```

Exploring the default ASP.NET Core MVC website

Let's review the behavior of the default ASP.NET Core MVC website project template:

1. In the Northwind.Mvc project, expand the Properties folder, open the launchSettings.json file, and note the random port numbers (yours will be different) configured for the project for the https and http profiles, as shown in the following settings:

```
{
  "iisSettings": {
    "windowsAuthentication": false,
    "anonymousAuthentication": true,
    "iisExpress": {
      "applicationUrl": "http://localhost:36439",
      "sslPort": 44344
    }
  },
  "profiles": {
    "http": {
      "commandName": "Project",
      "dotnetRunMessages": true,
      "launchBrowser": true,
      "applicationUrl": "http://localhost:5074",
      "environmentVariables": {
        "ASPNETCORE_ENVIRONMENT": "Development"
      }
    },
    "https": {
      "commandName": "Project",
      "dotnetRunMessages": true,
```

```json
      "launchBrowser": true,
      "applicationUrl": "https://localhost:7029;http://localhost:5074",
      "environmentVariables": {
        "ASPNETCORE_ENVIRONMENT": "Development"
      }
    },
    "IIS Express": {
      "commandName": "IISExpress",
      "launchBrowser": true,
      "environmentVariables": {
        "ASPNETCORE_ENVIRONMENT": "Development"
      }
    }
  }
}
```

2. For the http profile, change the port number to 5000, as shown in the following setting:

    ```json
    "applicationUrl": "http://localhost:5000",
    ```

3. For the https profile, change the port numbers to 5001 for HTTPS and 5000 for HTTP, as shown in the following setting:

    ```json
    "applicationUrl": "https://localhost:5001;http://localhost:5000",
    ```

4. Save the changes to the launchSettings.json file.

Starting the MVC website project

1. Start the website:

    *   If you are using Visual Studio 2022, then in the toolbar, select the **https** profile, select **Google Chrome** as the **Web Browser**, and then start the project without debugging.

    *   If you are using Visual Studio Code, then enter the command to start the project with the https profile, as shown in the following command: dotnet run --launch-profile https, and then start Chrome.

2. At the command line or terminal, note the ports that the Northwind.Mvc website project is listening on, as shown in the following output:

```
info: Microsoft.Hosting.Lifetime[14]
      Now listening on: https://localhost:5001
info: Microsoft.Hosting.Lifetime[14]
      Now listening on: http://localhost:5000
info: Microsoft.Hosting.Lifetime[0]
      Application started. Press Ctrl+C to shut down.
info: Microsoft.Hosting.Lifetime[0]
      Hosting environment: Development
info: Microsoft.Hosting.Lifetime[0]
      Content root path: C:\cs11dotnet7\PracticalApps\Northwind.Mvc
```

3. In Chrome, open **Developer Tools**.

4. Navigate to http://localhost:5000/ and note the following, as shown in *Figure 14.1*:

   • Requests for HTTP are automatically redirected to HTTPS on port 5001.

   • The top navigation menu with links to **Home**, **Privacy**, **Register**, and **Login**. If the viewport width is 575 pixels or less, then the navigation collapses into a hamburger menu.

   • The title of the website, **Northwind.Mvc**, shown in the header and footer:

Figure 14.1: The ASP.NET Core MVC project template website home page

Exploring visitor registration

By default, passwords must have at least one non-alphanumeric character, at least one digit (0-9), and at least one uppercase letter (A-Z). I use Pa$$w0rd in scenarios like this when I am just exploring.

The MVC project template follows best practice for **double-opt-in** (**DOI**), meaning that after filling in an email and password to register, an email is sent to the email address, and the visitor must click a link in that email to confirm that they want to register.

We have not yet configured an email provider to send that email, so we must simulate that step:

1. Close the **Developer Tools** pane.

2. In the top navigation menu, click **Register**.

3. Enter an email and password, and then click the **Register** button. (I used test@example.com and Pa$$w0rd.)

4. On the **Register confirmation** page, click the link with the text **Click here to confirm your account** and note that you are redirected to a **Confirm email** web page that you could customize. By default, the **Confirm email** page just says **Thank you for confirming your email**.

5. In the top navigation menu, click **Login**, enter your email and password (note that there is an optional checkbox to remember you, and there are links if the visitor has forgotten their password or wants to register as a new visitor), and then click the **Log in** button.

6. Click your email address in the top navigation menu. This will navigate to an account management page. Note that you can set a phone number, change your email address, change your password, enable two-factor authentication (if you add an authenticator app), and download and delete your personal data. This last feature is good for compliance with legal regulations like the European GDPR.

7. Close Chrome and shut down the web server.

Reviewing an MVC website project structure

In your code editor, in Visual Studio **Solution Explorer** (toggle on **Show All Files**) or in Visual Studio Code **EXPLORER**, review the structure of an MVC website project, as shown in *Figure 14.2*:

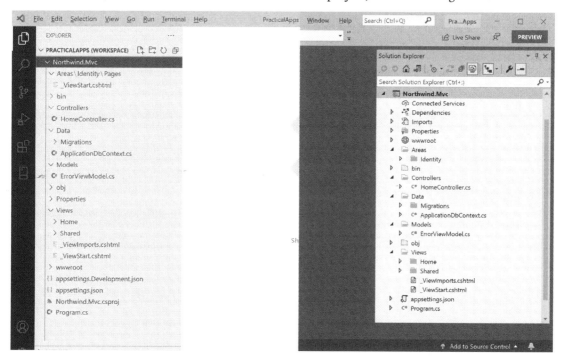

Figure 14.2: The default folder structure of an ASP.NET Core MVC project

We will look in more detail at some of these parts later, but for now, note the following:

*   `Areas`: This folder contains nested folders and a file needed to integrate your website project with **ASP.NET Core Identity**, which is used for authentication.

*   `bin`, `obj`: These folders contain temporary files needed during the build process and the compiled assemblies for the project.

*   `Controllers`: This folder contains C# classes that have methods (known as actions) that fetch a model and pass it to a view, for example, `HomeController.cs`.

*   `Data`: This folder contains Entity Framework Core migration classes used by the ASP.NET Core Identity system to provide data storage for authentication and authorization, for example, `ApplicationDbContext.cs`.

- **Models**: This folder contains C# classes that represent all of the data gathered together by a controller and passed to a view, for example, `ErrorViewModel.cs`.

- **Properties**: This folder contains a configuration file for IIS or IIS Express on Windows and for launching the website during development named `launchSettings.json`. This file is only used on the local development machine and is not deployed to your production website.

- **Views**: This folder contains the `.cshtml` Razor files that combine HTML and C# code to dynamically generate HTML responses. The `_ViewStart` file sets the default layout and `_ViewImports` imports common namespaces used in all views like Tag Helpers:

  - **Home**: This subfolder contains Razor files for the home and privacy pages.

  - **Shared**: This subfolder contains Razor files for the shared layout, an error page, and two partial views for logging in and validation scripts.

- **wwwroot**: This folder contains static content used by the website, such as CSS for styling, libraries of JavaScript, JavaScript for this website project, and a `favicon.ico` file. You also put images and other static file resources like PDF documents in here. The project template includes Bootstrap and jQuery libraries.

- **app.db**: This is the SQLite database that stores registered visitors. (If you used SQL Server LocalDB, then it will not be needed.)

- **appsettings.json** and **appsettings.Development.json**: These files contain settings that your website can load at runtime, for example, the database connection string for the ASP.NET Core Identity system and logging levels.

- **Northwind.Mvc.csproj**: This file contains project settings like the use of the Web .NET SDK, an entry for SQLite to ensure that the `app.db` file is copied to the website's output folder, and a list of NuGet packages that your project requires, including:

  - `Microsoft.AspNetCore.Diagnostics.EntityFrameworkCore`
  - `Microsoft.AspNetCore.Identity.EntityFrameworkCore`
  - `Microsoft.AspNetCore.Identity.UI`
  - `Microsoft.EntityFrameworkCore.Sqlite` or `Microsoft.EntityFrameworkCore.SqlServer`
  - `Microsoft.EntityFrameworkCore.Tools`

- **Northwind.Mvc.csproj.user**: This file contains Visual Studio 2022 session settings for remembering options. For example, which launch profile was selected, like `https`. Visual Studio 2022 hides this file, and it should not normally be included in source code control because it is specific to an individual developer.

- **Program.cs**: This file defines a hidden `Program` class that contains the `<Main>$` entry point. It builds a pipeline for processing incoming HTTP requests and hosts the website using default options like configuring the Kestrel web server and loading `appsettings`. It adds and configures services that your website needs, for example, ASP.NET Core Identity for authentication, SQLite or SQL Server for identity data storage, and so on, and routes for your application.

Reviewing the ASP.NET Core Identity database

Open `appsettings.json` to find the connection string used for the ASP.NET Core Identity database, as shown highlighted for SQL Server LocalDB in the following markup:

```
{
  "ConnectionStrings": {
    "DefaultConnection": "Server=(localdb)\\mssqllocaldb;Database=aspnet-
    Northwind.Mvc-2F6A1E12-F9CF-480C-987D-FEFB4827DE22;Trusted_
    Connection=True;MultipleActiveResultSets=true"
  },
  "Logging": {
    "LogLevel": {
      "Default": "Information",
      "Microsoft.AspNetCore": "Warning"
    }
  },
  "AllowedHosts": "*"
}
```

If you used SQL Server LocalDB for the identity data store, then you can use **Server Explorer** to connect to the database. You can copy and paste the connection string from the `appsettings.json` file, but remove the second backslash between (`localdb`) and `mssqllocaldb`.

If you installed a SQLite tool such as SQLiteStudio, then you can open the SQLite `app.db` database file.

You can then see the tables that the ASP.NET Core Identity system uses to register users and roles, including the `AspNetUsers` table used to store the registered visitor.

Exploring an ASP.NET Core MVC website

Let's walk through the parts that make up a modern ASP.NET Core MVC website.

ASP.NET Core MVC initialization

Appropriately enough, we will start by exploring the MVC website's default initialization and configuration:

1. Open the `Program.cs` file and note that it uses the top-level program feature (so there is a hidden `Program` class with a `<Main>$` method). This file can be considered to be divided into four important sections from top to bottom. As you review the sections, you might want to add comments to remind yourself of what each section is used for.

     .NET 5 and earlier ASP.NET Core project templates used a `Startup` class to separate these parts into separate methods, but with .NET 6 and later, Microsoft encourages putting everything in a single `Program.cs` file.

2. The first section imports some namespaces, as shown in the following code:

```
// Section 1 - import namespaces
using Microsoft.AspNetCore.Identity; // IdentityUser
using Microsoft.EntityFrameworkCore; // UseSqlServer, UseSqlite
using Northwind.Mvc.Data; // ApplicationDbContext
```

> Remember that, by default, many other namespaces are imported using the implicit usings feature of .NET 6 and later. Build the project and then the globally imported namespaces can be found in the following file: obj\Debug\net7.0\Northwind.Mvc.GlobalUsings.g.cs.

3. The second section creates and configures a web host builder that does the following:

   - Registers an application database context using SQL Server or SQLite. The database connection string is loaded from the appsettings.json file.

   - Adds ASP.NET Core Identity for authentication and configures it to use the application database.

   - Adds support for MVC controllers with views, as shown in the following code:

```
// Section 2 - configure the host web server including services
var builder = WebApplication.CreateBuilder(args);

// Add services to the container.
var connectionString = builder.Configuration
  .GetConnectionString("DefaultConnection");
builder.Services.AddDbContext<ApplicationDbContext>(options =>
  options.UseSqlServer(connectionString)); // or UseSqlite
builder.Services.AddDatabaseDeveloperPageExceptionFilter();

builder.Services.AddDefaultIdentity<IdentityUser>(options =>
  options.SignIn.RequireConfirmedAccount = true)
  .AddEntityFrameworkStores<ApplicationDbContext>();
builder.Services.AddControllersWithViews();

var app = builder.Build();
```

The builder object has two commonly used objects, Configuration and Services:

   - Configuration contains merged values from all the places you could set configuration: appsettings.json, environment variables, command-line arguments, and so on.

   - Services is a collection of registered dependency services.

The call to AddDbContext is an example of registering a dependency service. ASP.NET Core implements the **dependency injection (DI)** design pattern so that other components like controllers can request needed services through their constructors. Developers register those services in this section of Program.cs (or if using a Startup class then in its ConfigureServices method.)

4. The third section configures the HTTP pipeline through which requests and responses flow in and out. It configures a relative URL path to run database migrations if the website runs in development, or a friendlier error page and HSTS for production. HTTPS redirection, static files, routing, and ASP.NET Identity are enabled, and an MVC default route and Razor Pages are configured, as shown in the following code:

```
// Section 3 -
// Configure the HTTP request pipeline.
if (app.Environment.IsDevelopment())
{
  app.UseMigrationsEndPoint();
}
else
{
  app.UseExceptionHandler("/Home/Error");
  // The default HSTS value is 30 days. You may want to change this for
  production scenarios, see https://aka.ms/aspnetcore-hsts.
  app.UseHsts();
}

app.UseHttpsRedirection();
app.UseStaticFiles();

app.UseRouting();

app.UseAuthentication();
app.UseAuthorization();

app.MapControllerRoute(
  name: "default",
  pattern: "{controller=Home}/{action=Index}/{id?}");
app.MapRazorPages();
```

We learned about most of these methods and features in *Chapter 13, Building Websites Using ASP.NET Core Razor Pages.*

Good Practice: What does the extension method `UseMigrationsEndPoint` do? You could read the official documentation, but it does not help much. For example, it does not tell us what relative URL path it defines by default: `https://docs.microsoft.com/en-us/dotnet/api/microsoft.aspnetcore.builder.migrationsendpointextensions.usemigrationsendpoint`. Luckily, ASP.NET Core is open-source, so we can read the source code and discover what it does, at the following link: `https://github.com/dotnet/aspnetcore/blob/main/src/Middleware/Diagnostics.EntityFrameworkCore/src/MigrationsEndPointOptions.cs#L18`. Get into the habit of exploring the source code for ASP.NET Core to understand how it works.

Apart from the UseAuthentication and UseAuthorization methods, the most important new method in this section of Program.cs is MapControllerRoute, which maps a default route for use by MVC. This route is very flexible because it will map to almost any incoming URL, as you will see in the next topic.

Although we will not create any Razor Pages in this chapter, we need to leave the method call that maps Razor Page support because our MVC website uses ASP.NET Core Identity for authentication and authorization, and it uses a Razor Class Library for its user interface components, like visitor registration and login.

5.   The fourth and final section has a thread-blocking method call that runs the website and waits for incoming HTTP requests to respond to, as shown in the following code:

```
// Section 4 - start the host web server listening for HTTP requests
app.Run(); // blocking call
```

The default MVC route

The responsibility of a route is to discover the name of a controller class to instantiate and an action method to execute, with an optional id parameter to pass into the method that will generate an HTTP response.

A default route is configured for MVC, as shown in the following code:

```
endpoints.MapControllerRoute(
  name: "default",
  pattern: "{controller=Home}/{action=Index}/{id?}");
```

The route pattern has parts in curly brackets {} called **segments,** and they are like named parameters of a method. The value of these segments can be any string. Segments in URLs are not case-sensitive.

The route pattern looks at any URL path requested by the browser and matches it to extract the name of a controller, the name of an action, and an optional id value (the ? symbol makes it optional).

If the user hasn't entered these names, it uses defaults of Home for the controller and Index for the action (the = assignment sets a default for a named segment).

The following table contains example URLs and how the default route would work out the names of a controller and action:

URL	Controller	Action	ID
/	Home	Index	
/Muppet	Muppet	Index	
/Muppet/Kermit	Muppet	Kermit	
/Muppet/Kermit/Green	Muppet	Kermit	Green
/Products	Products	Index	
/Products/Detail	Products	Detail	
/Products/Detail/3	Products	Detail	3

Controllers and actions

In MVC, the C stands for *controller*. From the route and an incoming URL, ASP.NET Core knows the name of the controller, so it will then look for a class that is decorated with the [Controller] attribute or derives from a class decorated with that attribute, for example, the Microsoft-provided class named ControllerBase, as shown in the following code:

```
namespace Microsoft.AspNetCore.Mvc
{
  //
  // Summary:
  // A base class for an MVC controller without view support.
  [Controller]
  public abstract class ControllerBase
  {
...
```

The ControllerBase class

As you can see in the XML comment, ControllerBase does not support views. It is used for creating web services, as you will see in *Chapter 15, Building and Consuming Web Services*.

ControllerBase has many useful properties for working with the current HTTP context, as shown in the following table:

Property	Description
Request	Just the HTTP request. For example, headers, query string parameters, the body of the request as a stream that you can read from, the content type and length, and cookies.
Response	Just the HTTP response. For example, headers, the body of the response as a stream that you can write to, the content type and length, status code, and cookies. There are also delegates like OnStarting and OnCompleted that you can hook a method up to.
HttpContext	Everything about the current HTTP context including the request and response, information about the connection, a collection of features that have been enabled on the server with middleware, and a User object for authentication and authorization.

The Controller class

Microsoft provides another class named Controller that your classes can inherit from if they do need view support, as shown in the following code:

```
namespace Microsoft.AspNetCore.Mvc
{
  //
  // Summary:
```

```
// A base class for an MVC controller with view support.
public abstract class Controller : ControllerBase,
   IActionFilter, IFilterMetadata, IAsyncActionFilter, IDisposable
{
...
```

`Controller` has many useful properties for working with views, as shown in the following table:

Property	Description
ViewData	A dictionary that the controller can store key/value pairs in that is accessible in a view. The dictionary's lifetime is only for the current request/response.
ViewBag	A dynamic object that wraps the ViewData to provide a friendlier syntax for setting and getting dictionary values.
TempData	A dictionary that the controller can store key/value pairs in that is accessible in a view. The dictionary's lifetime is for the current request/response and the next request/response for the same visitor session. This is useful for storing a value during an initial request, responding with a redirect, and then reading the stored value in the subsequent request.

`Controller` has many useful methods for working with views, as shown in the following table:

Method	Description
View	Returns a ViewResult after executing a view that renders a full response, for example, a dynamically generated web page. The view can be selected using a convention or be specified with a string name. A model can be passed to the view.
PartialView	Returns a PartialViewResult after executing a view that is part of a full response, for example, a dynamically generated chunk of HTML. The view can be selected using a convention or be specified with a string name. A model can be passed to the view.
ViewComponent	Returns a ViewComponentResult after executing a component that dynamically generates HTML. The component must be selected by specifying its type or its name. An object can be passed as an argument.
Json	Returns a JsonResult containing a JSON-serialized object. This can be useful for implementing a simple Web API as part of an MVC controller that primarily returns HTML for a human to view.

The responsibilities of a controller

The responsibilities of a controller are as follows:

- Identify the services that the controller needs to be in a valid state and to function properly in their class constructor(s).
- Use the action name to identify a method to execute.
- Extract parameters from the HTTP request.

- Use the parameters to fetch any additional data needed to construct a view model and pass it to the appropriate view for the client. For example, if the client is a web browser, then a view that renders HTML would be most appropriate. Other clients might prefer alternative renderings, like document formats such as a PDF file or an Excel file, or data formats, like JSON or XML.

- Return the results from the view to the client as an HTTP response with an appropriate status code.

 Good Practice: Controllers should be *thin*, meaning they only perform the above-listed activities but do not implement any business logic. All business logic should be implemented in services that the controller calls when needed.

Let's review the controller used to generate the home, privacy, and error pages:

1. Expand the `Controllers` folder.

2. Open the file named `HomeController.cs`.

3. Note, as shown in the following code, that:

   - Extra namespaces are imported, which I have added comments for to show which types they are needed for.

   - A private read-only field is declared to store a reference to a logger for the `HomeController` that is set in a constructor.

   - All three action methods call a method named `View` and return the results as an `IActionResult` interface to the client.

   - The `Error` action method passes a view model into its view with a request ID used for tracing. The error response will not be cached:

```csharp
using Microsoft.AspNetCore.Mvc; // Controller, IActionResult
using Northwind.Mvc.Models; // ErrorViewModel
using System.Diagnostics; // Activity

namespace Northwind.Mvc.Controllers;

public class HomeController : Controller
{
  private readonly ILogger<HomeController> _logger;

  public HomeController(ILogger<HomeController> logger)
  {
    _logger = logger;
  }
```

```
public IActionResult Index()
{
  return View();
}

public IActionResult Privacy()
{
  return View();
}

[ResponseCache(Duration = 0,
  Location = ResponseCacheLocation.None, NoStore = true)]
public IActionResult Error()
{
  return View(new ErrorViewModel { RequestId =
    Activity.Current?.Id ?? HttpContext.TraceIdentifier });
}
}
```

If the visitor navigates to a path of / or /Home, then it is the equivalent of /Home/Index because those were the default names for the controller and action in the default route.

The view search path convention

The Index and Privacy methods are identical in implementation, yet they return different web pages. This is because of **conventions**. The call to the View method looks in different paths for the Razor file to generate the web page.

Let's deliberately break one of the page names so that we can see the paths searched by default:

1. In the Northwind.Mvc project, expand the Views folder and then the Home folder.
2. Rename the Privacy.cshtml file to Privacy2.cshtml.
3. Start the website.

4. Start Chrome, navigate to `https://localhost:5001/`, click **Privacy**, and note the paths that are searched for a view to render the web page (including in `Shared` folders for MVC views and Razor Pages), as shown in *Figure 14.3*:

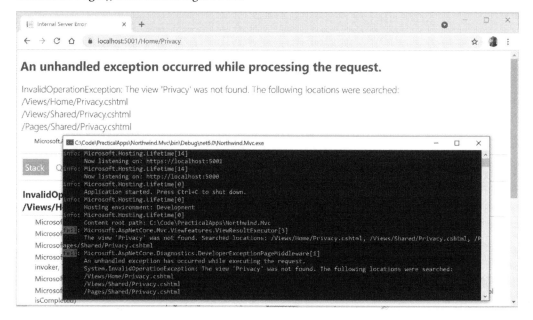

Figure 14.3: An exception showing the default search path for views

5. Close Chrome and shut down the web server.

6. Rename the `Privacy2.cshtml` file back to `Privacy.cshtml`.

You have now seen the view search path convention, as shown in the following list:

- Specific Razor view: `/Views/{controller}/{action}.cshtml`
- Shared Razor view: `/Views/Shared/{action}.cshtml`
- Shared Razor Page: `/Pages/Shared/{action}.cshtml`

Logging using the dependency service

You have just seen that some errors are caught and written to the console. You can write messages to the console in the same way by using the logger.

1. In the `Controllers` folder, in `HomeController.cs`, in the `Index` method, add statements before the `return` statement to use the logger to write some messages of various levels to the console, as shown highlighted in the following code:

```
public IActionResult Index()
{
    _logger.LogError("This is a serious error (not really!)");
    _logger.LogWarning("This is your first warning!");
    _logger.LogWarning("Second warning!");
```

```
_logger.LogInformation("I am in the Index method of the HomeController.");

    return View();
}
```

2. Start the `Northwind.Mvc` website project.

3. Start Chrome and navigate to the home page of the website.

4. At the command prompt or terminal, note the messages, as shown in the following output:

```
fail: Northwind.Mvc.Controllers.HomeController[0]
      This is a serious error (not really!)
warn: Northwind.Mvc.Controllers.HomeController[0]
      This is your first warning!
warn: Northwind.Mvc.Controllers.HomeController[0]
      Second warning!
info: Northwind.Mvc.Controllers.HomeController[0]
      I am in the Index method of the HomeController.
```

5. Close Chrome and shut down the web server.

Entity and view models

In MVC, the M stands for *model*. Models represent the data required to respond to a request. There are two types of models commonly used: entity models and view models.

Entity models represent entities in a database like SQL Server or SQLite. Based on the request, one or more entities might need to be retrieved from data storage. Entity models are defined using classes, since they might need to change and then be used to update the underlying data store.

All the data that we want to show in response to a request is the **MVC model**, sometimes called a **view model**, because it is a model that is passed into a view for rendering into a response format like HTML or JSON. View models should be immutable, so they are commonly defined using records.

For example, the following HTTP GET request might mean that the browser is asking for the product details page for product number 3: `http://www.example.com/products/details/3`.

The controller would need to use the ID route value 3 to retrieve the entity for that product and pass it to a view that can then turn the model into HTML for display in a browser.

Imagine that when a user comes to our website, we want to show them a carousel of categories, a list of products, and a count of the number of visitors we have had this month.

We will reference the Entity Framework Core entity data model for the Northwind database that you created in *Chapter 12, Introducing Web Development Using ASP.NET Core*:

1. In the `Northwind.Mvc` project, add a project reference to `Northwind.Common.DataContext` for either SQLite or SQL Server, as shown in the following markup:

```
<ItemGroup>
  <!-- change Sqlite to SqlServer if you prefer -->
```

```
<ProjectReference Include="..\Northwind.Common.DataContext.Sqlite\
Northwind.Common.DataContext.Sqlite.csproj"/>
</ItemGroup>
```

2. Build the `Northwind.Mvc` project to compile its dependencies.

3. If you are using SQL Server, or might want to switch between SQL Server and SQLite, then in `appsettings.json`, add a connection string for the Northwind database using SQL Server, as shown highlighted in the following markup:

```
{
  "ConnectionStrings": {
    "DefaultConnection": "Server=(localdb)\\mssqllocaldb;Database=aspnet-
    Northwind.Mvc-DC9C4FAF-DD84-4FC9-B925-69A61240EDA7;Trusted_
    Connection=True;MultipleActiveResultSets=true",
    "NorthwindConnection": "Server=.;Database=Northwind;Trusted_
    Connection=True;MultipleActiveResultSets=true"
  },
```

4. In `Program.cs`, import the namespace to work with your entity model types, as shown in the following code:

```
using Packt.Shared; // AddNorthwindContext extension method
```

5. Before the `builder.Build` method call, add statements to load the appropriate connection string and then to register the `Northwind` database context, as shown in the following code:

```
// if you are using SQL Server
string? sqlServerConnection = builder.Configuration
  .GetConnectionString("NorthwindConnection");

if (sqlServerConnection is null)
{
  Console.WriteLine("SQL Server database connection string is missing!");
}
else
{
  builder.Services.AddNorthwindContext(sqlServerConnection);
}

// if you are using SQLite, default is ..\Northwind.db
builder.Services.AddNorthwindContext();
```

6. Add a class file to the `Models` folder and name it `HomeIndexViewModel.cs`.

 Good Practice: Although the `ErrorViewModel` class created by the MVC project template does not follow this convention, I recommend that you use the naming convention `{Controller}{Action}ViewModel` for your view model classes.

7. In `HomeIndexViewModel.cs`, add statements to define a record that has three properties for a count of the number of visitors, and lists of categories and products, as shown in the following code:

```
using Packt.Shared; // Category, Product

namespace Northwind.Mvc.Models;

public record HomeIndexViewModel
(
  int VisitorCount,
  IList<Category> Categories,
  IList<Product> Products
);
```

8. In `HomeController.cs`, import the `Packt.Shared` namespace, as shown in the following code:

```
using Packt.Shared; // NorthwindContext
```

9. Add a field to store a reference to a `Northwind` instance, and initialize it in the constructor, as shown highlighted in the following code:

```
public class HomeController : Controller
{
  private readonly ILogger<HomeController> _logger;
  private readonly NorthwindContext db;

  public HomeController(ILogger<HomeController> logger,
    NorthwindContext injectedContext)
  {
    _logger = logger;
    db = injectedContext;
  }
}
```

 ASP.NET Core will use constructor parameter injection to pass an instance of the `NorthwindContext` database context using the connection string you specified in `Program.cs`.

10. In the `Index` action method, create an instance of the view model for this method, simulating a visitor count using the `Random` class to generate a number between 1 and 1,000, and using the `Northwind` database to get lists of categories and products, and then pass the model to the view, as shown in the following code:

```
HomeIndexViewModel model = new
(
  VisitorCount: Random.Shared.Next(1, 1001),
  Categories: db.Categories.ToList(),
```

```
        Products: db.Products.ToList()
    );

    return View(model); // pass model to view
}
```

Remember the view search convention: when the View method is called in a controller's action method, ASP.NET Core MVC looks in the Views folder for a subfolder with the same name as the current controller, that is, Home. It then looks for a file with the same name as the current action, that is, Index. cshtml. It will also search for views that match the action method name in the Shared folder and for Razor Pages in the Pages folder.

Views

In MVC, the V stands for *view*. The responsibility of a view is to transform a model into HTML or other formats.

There are multiple **view engines** that could be used to do this. The default view engine is called **Razor**, and it uses the @ symbol to indicate server-side code execution. The Razor Pages feature introduced with ASP.NET Core 2.0 uses the same view engine and so can use the same Razor syntax.

Let's modify the home page view to render the lists of categories and products:

1. Expand the Views folder, and then expand the Home folder.
2. Open the Index.cshtml file and note the block of C# code wrapped in @{ }. This will execute first and can be used to store data that needs to be passed into a shared layout file, like the title of the web page, as shown in the following code:

    ```
    @{
        ViewData["Title"] = "Home Page";
    }
    ```

3. Note the static HTML content in the <div> element that uses Bootstrap for styling.

 Good Practice: As well as defining your own styles, base your styles on a common library, such as Bootstrap, that implements responsive design.

Just as with Razor Pages, there is a file named _ViewStart.cshtml that gets executed by the View method. It is used to set defaults that apply to all views.

For example, it sets the Layout property of all views to a shared layout file, as shown in the following markup:

```
@{
    Layout = "_Layout";
}
```

4. In the Views folder, open the `_ViewImports.cshtml` file and note that it imports some namespaces and then adds the ASP.NET Core Tag Helpers, as shown in the following code:

```
@using Northwind.Mvc
@using Northwind.Mvc.Models
@addTagHelper *, Microsoft.AspNetCore.Mvc.TagHelpers
```

5. In the Shared folder, open the `_Layout.cshtml` file.

6. Note that the title is being read from the `ViewData` dictionary that was set earlier in the `Index.cshtml` view, as shown in the following markup:

```
<title>@ViewData["Title"] - Northwind.Mvc</title>
```

7. Note the rendering of links to support Bootstrap and a site stylesheet, where ~ means the `wwwroot` folder, as shown in the following markup:

```
<link rel="stylesheet"
  href="~/lib/bootstrap/dist/css/bootstrap.css" />
<link rel="stylesheet" href="~/css/site.css" />
```

8. Note the rendering of a navigation bar in the header, as shown in the following markup:

```
<body>
  <header>
    <nav class="navbar ...">
```

9. Note the rendering of a collapsible `<div>` containing a partial view for logging in, and hyperlinks to allow users to navigate between pages using ASP.NET Core Tag Helpers with attributes like `asp-controller` and `asp-action`, as shown in the following markup:

```
<div class=
  "navbar-collapse collapse d-sm-inline-flex justify-content-between">
  <ul class="navbar-nav flex-grow-1">
    <li class="nav-item">
      <a class="nav-link text-dark" asp-area=""
        asp-controller="Home" asp-action="Index">Home</a>
    </li>
    <li class="nav-item">
      <a class="nav-link text-dark"
        asp-area="" asp-controller="Home"
        asp-action="Privacy">Privacy</a>
    </li>
  </ul>
  <partial name="_LoginPartial" />
</div>
```

The `<a>` elements use Tag Helper attributes named `asp-controller` and `asp-action` to specify the controller name and action name that will execute when the link is clicked on. If you want to navigate to a feature in a Razor Class Library, like the employees component that you created in the previous chapter, then you use `asp-area` to specify the feature name.

10. Note the rendering of the body inside the `<main>` element, as shown in the following markup:

```
<div class="container">
  <main role="main" class="pb-3">
    @RenderBody()
  </main>
</div>
```

The `RenderBody` method injects the contents of a specific Razor view for a page like the `Index.cshtml` file at that point in the shared layout.

11. Note the rendering of `<script>` elements at the bottom of the page so that it does not slow down the display of the page, and that you can add your own script blocks into an optional defined section named `scripts`, as shown in the following markup:

```
<script src="~/lib/jquery/dist/jquery.min.js"></script>
<script src="~/lib/bootstrap/dist/js/bootstrap.bundle.min.js">
</script>
<script src="~/js/site.js" asp-append-version="true"></script>
@await RenderSectionAsync("Scripts", required: false)
```

Understanding how cache busting with Tag Helpers works

When `asp-append-version` is specified with a true value in a `<link>`, `<img>`, or `<script>` element, the Tag Helper for that tag type is invoked.

They work by automatically appending a query string value named v that is generated from a SHA256 hash of the referenced source file, as shown in the following example generated output:

```
<script src="~/js/site.js?v=Kl_dqr9NVtnMdsM2MUg4qthUnWZm5T1fCEimBPWDNgM">
</script>
```

> You can see this for yourself in the current project because the `_Layout.cshtml` file has the `<script src="~/js/site.js" asp-append-version="true"></script>` element.

If even a single byte within the `site.js` file changes, then its hash value will be different, and therefore if a browser or CDN is caching the script file, then it will bust the cached copy and replace it with the new version.

The `src` attribute must be set to a static file stored on the local web server, usually in the `wwwroot` folder but you can configure additional locations. Remote references are not supported.

Customizing an ASP.NET Core MVC website

Now that you've reviewed the structure of a basic MVC website, you will customize and extend it. You have already registered an EF Core model for the `Northwind` database, so the next task is to output some of that data on the home page.

Defining a custom style

The home page will show a list of the 77 products in the Northwind database. To make efficient use of space, we want to show the list in three columns. To do this, we need to customize the stylesheet for the website:

1. In the wwwroot\css folder, open the site.css file.
2. At the bottom of the file, add a new style that will apply to an element with the product-columns ID, as shown in the following code:

```css
#product-columns
{
  column-count: 3;
}
```

Setting up the category images

The Northwind database includes a table of eight categories, but they do not have images, and websites look better with some colorful pictures:

1. In the wwwroot folder, create a folder named images.
2. In the images folder, add eight image files named category1.jpeg, category2.jpeg, and so on, up to category8.jpeg.

You can download images from the GitHub repository for this book at the following link: https://github.com/markjprice/cs11dotnet7/tree/main/images/Categories.

Razor syntax and expressions

Before we customize the home page view, let's review an example Razor file. The file has an initial Razor code block that instantiates an order with price and quantity, and then outputs information about the order on the web page, as shown in the following markup:

```
@{
  Order order = new()
  {
    OrderId = 123,
    Product = "Sushi",
    Price = 8.49M,
    Quantity = 3
  };
}

<div>Your order for @order.Quantity of @order.Product has a total cost of $@order.Price * @order.Quantity</div>
```

The preceding Razor file would result in the following incorrect output:

```
Your order for 3 of Sushi has a total cost of $8.49 * 3
```

Although Razor markup can include the value of any single property using the `@object.property` syntax, you should wrap expressions in parentheses, as shown in the following markup:

```
<div>Your order for @order.Quantity of @order.Product has a total cost of $@
(order.Price * order.Quantity)</div>
```

The preceding Razor expression results in the following correct output:

```
Your order for 3 of Sushi has a total cost of $25.47
```

Defining a typed view

To improve IntelliSense when writing a view, you can define what type the view can expect using an `@model` directive at the top:

1. In the `Views\Home` folder, open `Index.cshtml`.

2. At the top of the file, add a statement to set the model type to use the `HomeIndexViewModel`, as shown in the following code:

    ```
    @model HomeIndexViewModel
    ```

    Now, whenever we type `Model` in this view, your code editor will know the correct type for the model and will provide IntelliSense for it.

    While entering code in a view, remember the following:

    *   Declare the type for the model using `@model` (with a lowercase m).
    *   Interact with the instance of the model using `@Model` (with an uppercase M).

    Let's continue customizing the view for the home page.

3. In the initial Razor code block, add a statement to declare a `string` variable for the current item. Under the existing `<div>` element, add new markup to output categories in a carousel and products as an unordered list, as shown in the following markup:

    ```
    @using Packt.Shared
    @model HomeIndexViewModel
    @{
      ViewData["Title"] = "Home Page";
      string currentItem = "";
    }

    <div class="text-center">
      <h1 class="display-4">Welcome</h1>
      <p class="alert alert-primary">@DateTime.Now.ToLongTimeString()</p>
    </div>

    @if (Model is not null)
    {
    <div id="categories" class="carousel slide" data-bs-ride="carousel"
        data-bs-interval="3000" data-keyboard="true">
    ```

```
<ol class="carousel-indicators">
@for (int c = 0; c < Model.Categories.Count; c++)
{
  if (c == 0)
  {
    currentItem = "active";
  }
  else
  {
    currentItem = "";
  }
  <li data-bs-target="#categories" data-slide-to="@c"
      class="@currentItem"></li>
}
</ol>

<div class="carousel-inner">
@for (int c = 0; c < Model.Categories.Count; c++)
{
  if (c == 0)
  {
    currentItem = "active";
  }
  else
  {
    currentItem = "";
  }
  <div class="carousel-item @currentItem">
    <img class="d-block w-100" src=
      "~/images/category@(Model.Categories[c].CategoryId).jpeg"
      alt="@Model.Categories[c].CategoryName" />
    <div class="carousel-caption d-none d-md-block">
      <h2>@Model.Categories[c].CategoryName</h2>
      <h3>@Model.Categories[c].Description</h3>
      <p>
        <a class="btn btn-primary"
          href="/category/@Model.Categories[c].CategoryId">View</a>
      </p>
    </div>
  </div>
}
</div>
<a class="carousel-control-prev" href="#categories"
  role="button" data-bs-slide="prev">
  <span class="carousel-control-prev-icon"
    aria-hidden="true"></span>
```

```
        <span class="sr-only">Previous</span>
    </a>
    <a class="carousel-control-next" href="#categories"
      role="button" data-bs-slide="next">
      <span class="carousel-control-next-icon" aria-hidden="true"></span>
      <span class="sr-only">Next</span>
    </a>
  </div>
}

<div class="row">
  <div class="col-md-12">
    <h1>Northwind</h1>
    <p class="lead">
      We have had @Model?.VisitorCount visitors this month.
    </p>
    @if (Model is not null)
    {
    <h2>Products</h2>
    <div id="product-columns">
      <ul class="list-group">
      @foreach (Product p in @Model.Products)
      {
        <li class="list-group-item d-flex justify-content-between
        align-items-start">
          <a asp-controller="Home" asp-action="ProductDetail"
            asp-route-id="@p.ProductId" class="btn btn-outline-primary">
            <div class="ms-2 me-auto">@p.ProductName</div>
            <span class="badge bg-primary rounded-pill">
              @(p.UnitPrice is null ? "zero" : p.UnitPrice.Value.
              ToString("C"))
            </span>
          </a>
        </li>
      }
      </ul>
    </div>
    }
  </div>
</div>
```

While reviewing the preceding Razor markup, note the following:

- It is easy to mix static HTML elements such as <ul> and <li> with C# code to output the carousel of categories and the list of product names.

- The <div> element with the id attribute of product-columns will use the custom style that we defined earlier, so all the content in that element will display in three columns.

- The `<img>` element for each category uses parentheses around a Razor expression to ensure that the compiler does not include the `.jpeg` as part of the expression, as shown in the following markup: `"~/images/category@(Model.Categories[c].CategoryID).jpeg"`.

- The `<a>` elements for the product links use Tag Helpers to generate URL paths. Clicks on these hyperlinks will be handled by the `HomeController` and its `ProductDetail` action method. This action method does not exist yet, but you will add it later in this chapter. The ID of the product is passed as a route segment named `id`, as shown in the following URL path for Ipoh Coffee: `https://localhost:5001/Home/ProductDetail/43`.

Let's see the result of our customized home page:

1. Start the `Northwind.Mvc` website project.

2. Note the home page has a rotating carousel showing categories, a random number of visitors, and a list of products in three columns, as shown in *Figure 14.4*:

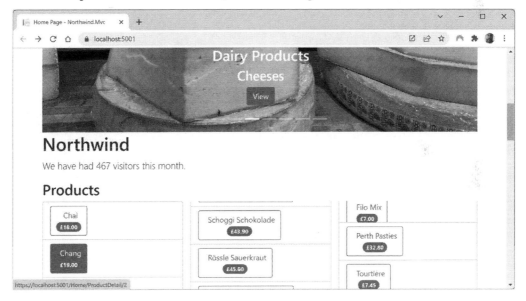

Figure 14.4: The updated Northwind MVC website home page

For now, clicking on any of the categories or product links gives **404 Not Found** errors, so let's see how we can implement pages that use the parameters passed to them to see the details of a product or category.

3. Close Chrome and shut down the web server.

Passing parameters using a route value

One way to pass a simple parameter is to use the `id` segment defined in the default route:

1. In `HomeController.cs`, add an action method named `ProductDetail`, as shown in the following code:

```
public IActionResult ProductDetail(int? id)
{
```

```
if (!id.HasValue)
{
  return BadRequest("You must pass a product ID in the route, for
  example, /Home/ProductDetail/21");
}

Product? model = db.Products.SingleOrDefault(p => p.ProductId == id);

if (model is null)
{
  return NotFound($"ProductId {id} not found.");
}

return View(model); // pass model to view and then return result
}
```

Note the following:

- This method uses a feature of ASP.NET Core called **model binding** to automatically match the id passed in the route to the parameter named id in the method.

- Inside the method, we check to see whether id does not have a value, and if so, we call the BadRequest method to return a 400 status code with a custom message explaining the correct URL path format.

- Otherwise, we can connect to the database and try to retrieve a product using the id value.

- If we find a product, we pass it to a view; otherwise, we call the NotFound method to return a 404 status code and a custom message explaining that a product with that ID was not found in the database.

2. In the Views/Home folder, add a new file named ProductDetail.cshtml. (In Visual Studio, the item template is named **Razor View - Empty**.)

3. Modify the contents, as shown in the following markup:

```
@model Packt.Shared.Product
@{
  ViewData["Title"] = "Product Detail - " + Model.ProductName;
}
<h2>Product Detail</h2>
<hr />
<div>
  <dl class="dl-horizontal">
    <dt>Product Id</dt>
    <dd>@Model.ProductId</dd>
    <dt>Product Name</dt>
    <dd>@Model.ProductName</dd>
    <dt>Category Id</dt>
```

```
        <dd>@Model.CategoryId</dd>
        <dt>Unit Price</dt>
        <dd>@Model.UnitPrice.Value.ToString("C")</dd>
        <dt>Units In Stock</dt>
        <dd>@Model.UnitsInStock</dd>
      </dl>
  </div>
```

4. Start the `Northwind.Mvc` project.

5. When the home page appears with the list of products, click on one of them, for example, the second product, **Chang**.

6. Note the URL path in the browser's address bar, the page title shown in the browser tab, and the product details page, as shown in *Figure 14.5*:

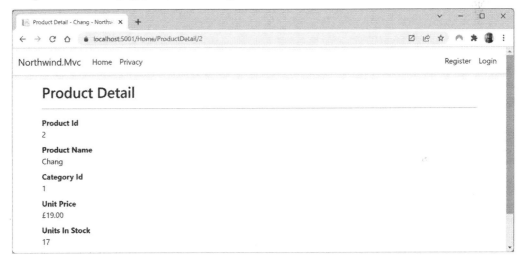

Figure 14.5: The Product Detail page for Chang

7. View **Developer tools**.

8. Edit the URL in the address box of Chrome to request a product ID that does not exist, like 99, and note the `404 Not Found` status code and custom error response.

9. Close Chrome and shut down the web server.

Model binders in more detail

Model binders are a powerful yet easy way to set parameters of action methods based on values passed in an HTTP request, and the default one does a lot for you. After the default route identifies a controller class to instantiate and an action method to call, if that method has parameters, then those parameters need to have values set.

Model binders do this by looking for parameter values passed in the HTTP request as any of the following types of parameters:

- **Route parameter,** like id as we used in the previous section, as shown in the following URL path: /Home/ProductDetail/2
- **Query string parameter,** as shown in the following URL path: /Home/ProductDetail?id=2
- **Form parameter,** as shown in the following markup:

```
<form action="post" action="/Home/ProductDetail">
  <input type="text" name="id" value="2" />
  <input type="submit" />
</form>
```

Model binders can populate almost any type:

- Simple types, like int, string, DateTime, and bool.
- Complex types defined by class, record, or struct.
- Collection types, like arrays and lists.

Let's create a somewhat artificial example to illustrate what can be achieved using the default model binder:

1. In the Models folder, add a new file named Thing.cs.
2. Modify the contents to define a record with two properties for a nullable integer named Id and a string named Color, as shown in the following code:

```
namespace Northwind.Mvc.Models;

public record Thing(int? Id, string? Color);
```

3. In HomeController, add two new action methods, one to show a page with a form and one to display a thing with a parameter using your new model type, as shown in the following code:

```
public IActionResult ModelBinding()
{
  return View(); // the page with a form to submit
}

public IActionResult ModelBinding(Thing thing)
{
  return View(thing); // show the model bound thing
}
```

4. In the Views\Home folder, add a new file named ModelBinding.cshtml.
5. Modify its contents, as shown in the following markup:

```
@model Thing
@{
  ViewData["Title"] = "Model Binding Demo";
}
```

```
<h1>@ViewData["Title"]</h1>
<div>
  Enter values for your thing in the following form:
</div>
<form method="POST" action="/home/modelbinding?id=3">
  <input name="color" value="Red" />
  <input type="submit" />
</form>
@if (Model is not null)
{
<h2>Submitted Thing</h2>
<hr />
<div>
  <dl class="dl-horizontal">
    <dt>Model.Id</dt>
    <dd>@Model.Id</dd>
    <dt>Model.Color</dt>
    <dd>@Model.Color</dd>
  </dl>
</div>
}
```

6. In `Views/Home`, open `Index.cshtml`, and in the first `<div>`, after rendering the current time,
    add a new paragraph with a link to the model binding page, as shown in the following markup:

    ```
    <p><a asp-action="ModelBinding" asp-controller="Home">Binding</a></p>
    ```

7. Start the website.

8. On the home page, click **Binding**.

9. Note the unhandled exception about an ambiguous match, as shown in *Figure 14.6*:

Figure 14.6: An unhandled ambiguous action method mismatch exception

10. Close Chrome and shut down the web server.

Disambiguating action methods

Although the C# compiler can differentiate between the two methods by noting that the signatures are
different, from the routing of an HTTP request's point of view, both methods are potential matches.
We need an HTTP-specific way to disambiguate the action methods.

We could do this by creating different names for the actions or by specifying that one method should be used for a specific HTTP verb, like GET, POST, or DELETE. That is how we will solve the problem:

1. In HomeController, decorate the second ModelBinding action method to indicate that it should be used for processing HTTP POST requests, that is, when a form is submitted, as shown highlighted in the following code:

    ```
    [HttpPost] // use this action method to process POSTs
    public IActionResult ModelBinding(Thing thing)
    ```

> The other ModelBinding action method will implicitly be used for all other types of HTTP request, like GET, PUT, DELETE, and so on.

2. Start the website.
3. On the home page, click **Binding**.
4. Click the **Submit** button and note the value for the Id property is set from the query string parameter and the value for the color property is set from the form parameter, as shown in *Figure 14.7*:

Figure 14.7: The Model Binding Demo page

5. Close Chrome and shut down the web server.

Passing a route parameter

Now we will set the property using a route parameter:

1. Modify the action for the form to pass the value 2 as a route parameter, as shown in the following markup:

    ```
    <form method="POST" action="/home/modelbinding/2?id=3">
    ```

2. Start the website.

3. On the home page, click **Binding**.

4. Click the **Submit** button and note the value for the Id property is set from the route parameter and the value for the Color property is set from the form parameter.

5. Close Chrome and shut down the web server.

Passing a form parameter

Now we will set the property using a form parameter:

1. Modify the action for the form to pass the value 1 as a form parameter, as shown highlighted in the following markup:

```
<form method="POST" action="/home/modelbinding/2?id=3">
  <input name="id" value="1" />
  <input name="color" value="Red" />
  <input type="submit" />
</form>
```

2. Start the website.

3. On the home page, click **Binding**.

4. Click the **Submit** button and note the values for the Id and Color properties are both set from the form parameters.

 Good Practice: If you have multiple parameters with the same name, then remember that form parameters have the highest priority and query string parameters have the lowest priority for automatic model binding.

Validating the model

The process of model binding can cause errors, for example, data type conversions or validation errors if the model has been decorated with validation rules. What data has been bound and any binding or validation errors are stored in ControllerBase.ModelState.

Let's explore what we can do with model state by applying some validation rules to the bound model and then showing invalid data messages in the view:

1. In the Models folder, open Thing.cs.

2. Import the namespace for working with validation attributes, as shown in the following code:

```
using System.ComponentModel.DataAnnotations;
```

3. Decorate the Id property with a validation attribute to limit the range of allowed numbers to 1 to 10, and one to ensure that the visitor supplies a color, and add a new Email property with a regular expression for validation, as shown highlighted in the following code:

```
public record Thing(
  [Range(1, 10)] int? Id,
```

```
[Required] string? Color,
[EmailAddress] string? Email
);
```

4. In the `Models` folder, add a new class file named `HomeModelBindingViewModel.cs`.

5. Modify its contents to define a record with properties to store the bound model, a flag to indicate that there are errors, and a sequence of error messages, as shown in the following code:

```
namespace Northwind.Mvc.Models;

public record HomeModelBindingViewModel(Thing Thing, bool HasErrors,
  IEnumerable<string> ValidationErrors);
```

6. In `HomeController`, in the `ModelBinding` method that handles HTTP POST, delete the previous statement that passed the thing to the view, and instead add statements to create an instance of the view model. Validate the model and store an array of error messages, and then pass the view model to the view, as shown in the following code:

```
HomeModelBindingViewModel model = new(
  Thing: thing, HasErrors: !ModelState.IsValid,
  ValidationErrors: ModelState.Values
    .SelectMany(state => state.Errors)
    .Select(error => error.ErrorMessage)
);
return View(model);
```

7. In `Views\Home`, open `ModelBinding.cshtml`.

8. Modify the model type declaration to use the view model class, as shown in the following markup:

```
@model Northwind.Mvc.Models.HomeModelBindingViewModel
```

9. Add a `<div>` to show any model validation errors, and change the output of the thing's properties because the view model has changed, as shown highlighted in the following markup:

```
<form method="POST" action="/home/modelbinding/2?id=3">
  <input name="id" value="1" />
  <input name="color" value="Red" />
  <input name="email" value="test@example.com" />
  <input type="submit" />
</form>
@if (Model is not null)
{
  <h2>Submitted Thing</h2>
  <hr />
  <div>
    <dl class="dl-horizontal">
      <dt>Model.Thing.Id</dt>
      <dd>@Model.Thing.Id</dd>
```

```
            <dt>Model.Thing.Color</dt>
            <dd>@Model.Thing.Color</dd>
            <dt>Model.Thing.Email</dt>
            <dd>@Model.Thing.Email</dd>
        </dl>
    </div>
    @if (Model.HasErrors)
    {
        <div>
            @foreach(string errorMessage in Model.ValidationErrors)
            {
                <div class="alert alert-danger" role="alert">@errorMessage</div>
            }
        </div>
    }
}
```

10. Start the website.

11. On the home page, click **Binding**.

12. Click the **Submit** button and note that 1, Red, and test@example.com are valid values.

13. Enter an Id of 13, clear the color textbox, delete the @ from the email address, click the **Submit** button, and note the error messages, as shown in *Figure 14.8*:

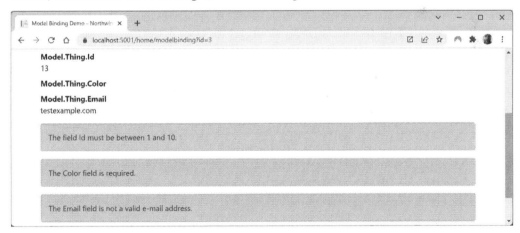

Figure 14.8: The Model Binding Demo page with field validations

14. Close Chrome and shut down the web server.

Good Practice: What regular expression does Microsoft use for the implementation of the EmailAddress validation attribute? Find out at the following link: https://github.com/microsoft/referencesource/blob/5697c29004a34d80acdaf5742d7e699022c64ecd/System.ComponentModel.DataAnnotations/DataAnnotations/EmailAddressAttribute.cs#L54.

Defining views with HTML Helper methods

While creating a view for ASP.NET Core MVC, you can use the `Html` object and its methods to generate markup. When Microsoft first introduced ASP.NET MVC in 2009, these HTML Helper methods were the way to programmatically render HTML. Modern ASP.NET Core retains these HTML Helper methods for backward compatibility and provides Tag Helpers that are usually easier to read and write in most scenarios. But there are notable situations where Tag Helpers cannot be used, like in Razor components.

Some useful methods include the following:

- `ActionLink`: Use this to generate an anchor `<a>` element that contains a URL path to the specified controller and action. For example, `Html.ActionLink(linkText: "Binding", actionName: "ModelBinding", controllerName: "Home")` would generate `<a href="/home/modelbinding">Binding</a>`. You can achieve the same result using the anchor Tag Helper: `<a asp-action="ModelBinding" asp-controller="Home">Binding</a>`.

- `AntiForgeryToken`: Use this inside a `<form>` to insert a `<hidden>` element containing an anti-forgery token that will be validated when the form is submitted.

- `Display` and `DisplayFor`: Use this to generate HTML markup for the expression relative to the current model using a display template. There are built-in display templates for .NET types and custom templates can be created in the `DisplayTemplates` folder. The folder name is case-sensitive on case-sensitive filesystems.

- `DisplayForModel`: Use this to generate HTML markup for an entire model instead of a single expression.

- `Editor` and `EditorFor`: Use this to generate HTML markup for the expression relative to the current model using an editor template. There are built-in editor templates for .NET types that use `<label>` and `<input>` elements, and custom templates can be created in the `EditorTemplates` folder. The folder name is case-sensitive on case-sensitive filesystems.

- `EditorForModel`: Use this to generate HTML markup for an entire model instead of a single expression.

- `Encode`: Use this to safely encode an object or string into HTML. For example, the string value `"<script>"` would be encoded as `"&lt;script&gt;"`. This is not normally necessary since the Razor @ symbol encodes string values by default.

- `Raw`: Use this to render a string value *without* encoding as HTML.

- `PartialAsync` and `RenderPartialAsync`: Use these to generate HTML markup for a partial view. You can optionally pass a model and view data.

Defining views with Tag Helpers

Tag Helpers make it easier to make static HTML elements dynamic. The markup is cleaner and easier to read, edit, and maintain than if you use HTML Helpers.

However, Tag Helpers do not replace HTML Helpers because there are some things that can only be achieved with HTML Helpers, like rendering output that contains multiple nested tags. Tag Helpers also cannot be used in Razor components. So, you must learn about HTML Helpers and treat Tag Helpers as an optional choice that is better in some scenarios.

Tag Helpers are especially useful for **Front End** (**FE**) developers who primarily work with HTML, CSS, and JavaScript because the FE developer does not have to learn C# syntax. Tag Helpers just use what looks like normal HTML attributes on elements. The attribute names and values can also be selected from IntelliSense if your code editor supports that; both Visual Studio 2022 and Visual Studio Code do.

For example, to render a linkable hyperlink to a controller action, you could use an HTML Helper method, as shown in the following markup:

```
@Html.ActionLink("View our privacy policy.", "Privacy", "Index")
```

To make it clearer how it works, you could use named parameters:

```
@Html.ActionLink(linkText: "View our privacy policy.",
   action: "Privacy", controller: "Index")
```

But using a Tag Helper would be even clearer and cleaner for someone who works a lot with HTML:

```
<a asp-action="Privacy" asp-controller="Home">View our privacy policy.</a>
```

All three examples above generate the following rendered HTML element:

```
<a href="/home/privacy">View our privacy policy.</a>
```

Cross-functional filters

When you need to add some functionality to multiple controllers and actions, you can use or define your own filters that are implemented as an attribute class.

Filters can be applied at the following levels:

- At the action level, by decorating an action method with the attribute. This will only affect one action method.
- At the controller level, by decorating the controller class with the attribute. This will affect all methods of the controller.
- At the global level, by adding the attribute type to the Filters collection of the MvcOptions instance that can be used to configure MVC when calling the AddControllersWithViews method, as shown in the following code:

```
builder.Services.AddControllersWithViews(options =>
  {
    options.Filters.Add(typeof(MyCustomFilter));
  });
```

Using a filter to secure an action method

You might want to ensure that one particular action method of a controller class can only be called by members of certain security roles. You do this by decorating the method with the [Authorize] attribute, as described in the following list:

- [Authorize]: Only allow authenticated (non-anonymous, logged-in) visitors to access this action method.

- [Authorize(Roles = "Sales,Marketing")]: Only allow visitors who are members of either of the specified role(s) to access this action method.

Let's see an example:

1. In HomeController.cs, import the Microsoft.AspNetCore.Authorization namespace.

2. Add an attribute to the Privacy method to only allow access to logged-in users who are members of a group/role named Administrators, as shown highlighted in the following code:

```
[Authorize(Roles = "Administrators")]
public IActionResult Privacy()
```

3. Start the website.

4. Click **Privacy** and note that you are redirected to the login page.

5. Enter your email and password.

6. Click **Log in** and note the message, **Access denied - You do not have access to this resource.**

7. Close Chrome and shut down the web server.

Enabling role management and creating a role programmatically

By default, role management is not enabled in an ASP.NET Core MVC project, so we must first enable it before creating roles, and then we will create a controller that will programmatically create an Administrators role (if it does not already exist) and assign our test user to that role:

1. In Program.cs, in the setup of ASP.NET Core Identity and its database, add a call to AddRoles to enable role management, as shown highlighted in the following code:

```
services.AddDefaultIdentity<IdentityUser>(
  options => options.SignIn.RequireConfirmedAccount = true)
  .AddRoles<IdentityRole>() // enable role management
  .AddEntityFrameworkStores<ApplicationDbContext>();
```

2. In Controllers, add an empty controller class named RolesController.cs and modify its contents, as shown in the following code:

```
using Microsoft.AspNetCore.Identity; // RoleManager, UserManager
using Microsoft.AspNetCore.Mvc; // Controller, IActionResult

using static System.Console;

namespace Northwind.Mvc.Controllers;

public class RolesController : Controller
{
  private string AdminRole = "Administrators";
  private string UserEmail = "test@example.com";
  private readonly RoleManager<IdentityRole> roleManager;
  private readonly UserManager<IdentityUser> userManager;
```

```csharp
public RolesController(RoleManager<IdentityRole> roleManager,
  UserManager<IdentityUser> userManager)
{
  this.roleManager = roleManager;
  this.userManager = userManager;
}

public async Task<IActionResult> Index()
{
  if (!(await roleManager.RoleExistsAsync(AdminRole)))
  {
    await roleManager.CreateAsync(new IdentityRole(AdminRole));
  }
  IdentityUser user = await userManager.FindByEmailAsync(UserEmail);

  if (user == null)
  {
    user = new();
    user.UserName = UserEmail;
    user.Email = UserEmail;

    IdentityResult result = await userManager.CreateAsync(
      user, "Pa$$w0rd");

    if (result.Succeeded)
    {
      WriteLine($"User {user.UserName} created successfully.");
    }
    else
    {
      foreach (IdentityError error in result.Errors)
      {
        WriteLine(error.Description);
      }
    }
  }

  if (!user.EmailConfirmed)
  {
    string token = await userManager
      .GenerateEmailConfirmationTokenAsync(user);

    IdentityResult result = await userManager
      .ConfirmEmailAsync(user, token);

    if (result.Succeeded)
    {
```

```
        WriteLine($"User {user.UserName} email confirmed successfully.");
      }
      else
      {
        foreach (IdentityError error in result.Errors)
        {
          WriteLine(error.Description);
        }
      }
    }

    if (!(await userManager.IsInRoleAsync(user, AdminRole)))
    {
      IdentityResult result = await userManager.AddToRoleAsync(user,
      AdminRole);

      if (result.Succeeded)
      {
        WriteLine($"User {user.UserName} added to {AdminRole}
        successfully.");
      }
      else
      {
        foreach (IdentityError error in result.Errors)
        {
          WriteLine(error.Description);
        }
      }
    }
    return Redirect("/");
  }
}
```

Note the following:

- Two fields for the name of the role and email of the user.
- The constructor gets and stores the registered user and role manager dependency services.
- If the Administrators role does not exist, we use the role manager to create it.
- We try to find a test user by its email, create it if it does not exist, and then assign the user to the Administrators role.
- Since the website uses DOI, we must generate an email confirmation token and use it to confirm the new user's email address.
- Success messages and any errors are written out to the console.
- You will be automatically redirected to the home page.

3. Start the website.

4. Click **Privacy** and note that you are redirected to the login page.

5. Enter your email and password. (I used `mark@example.com`.)

6. Click **Log in** and note that you are denied access as before.

7. Click **Home**.

8. In the address bar, manually enter `roles` as a relative URL path, as shown at the following link: `https://localhost:5001/roles`.

9. View the success messages written to the console, as shown in the following output:

```
User test@example.com created successfully.
User test@example.com email confirmed successfully.
User test@example.com added to Administrators successfully.
```

10. Click **Logout**, because you must log out and log back in to load your role memberships when they are created after you have already logged in.

11. Try accessing the **Privacy** page again, enter the email for the new user that was programmatically created, for example, `test@example.com`, and their password, and then click **Log in**, and you should now have access.

12. Close Chrome and shut down the web server.

Using a filter to define a custom route

You might want to define a simplified route for an action method instead of using the default route.

For example, to show the privacy page currently requires the following URL path, which specifies both the controller and action:

`https://localhost:5001/home/privacy`

We could make the route simpler, as shown in the following link:

`https://localhost:5001/private`

Let's see how to do that:

1. In `HomeController.cs`, add an attribute to the `Privacy` method to define a simplified route, as shown highlighted in the following code:

```
[Route("private")]
[Authorize(Roles = "Administrators")]
public IActionResult Privacy()
```

2. Start the website.

3. In the address bar, enter the following URL path:

`https://localhost:5001/private`

4. Enter your email and password, click **Log in**, and note that the simplified path shows the **Privacy** page.

5. Close Chrome and shut down the web server.

Using a filter to cache a response

To improve response times and scalability, you might want to cache the HTTP response that is generated by an action method by decorating the method with the [ResponseCache] attribute.

You control where the response is cached and for how long by setting parameters, as shown in the following list:

- Duration: In seconds. This sets the max-age HTTP response header measured in seconds. Common choices are one hour (3,600 seconds) and one day (86,400 seconds).
- Location: One of the ResponseCacheLocation values, Any, Client, or None. This sets the cache-control HTTP response header.
- NoStore: If true, this ignores Duration and Location and sets the cache-control HTTP response header to no-store.

Let's see an example:

1. In HomeController.cs, add an attribute to the Index method to cache the response for 10 seconds on the browser or any proxies between the server and browser, as shown highlighted in the following code:

   ```
   [ResponseCache(Duration = 10 /* seconds */,
       Location = ResponseCacheLocation.Any)]
   public IActionResult Index()
   ```

2. In Views, in Home, open Index.cshtml, and after the Welcome heading, add a paragraph to output the current time in long format to include seconds, as shown in the following markup:

   ```
   <p class="alert alert-primary">@DateTime.Now.ToLongTimeString()</p>
   ```

3. Start the website.
4. Note the time on the home page.
5. Click **Register** so that you leave the home page.
6. Click **Home** and note the time on the home page is the same because a cached version of the page is used.
7. Click **Register**. Wait at least ten seconds.
8. Click **Home** and note the time has now updated.
9. Click **Log in**, enter your email and password, and then click **Log in**.
10. Note the time on the home page.
11. Click **Privacy**.
12. Click **Home** and note the page is not cached.
13. View the console and note the warning message explaining that your caching has been overridden because the visitor is logged in and, in this scenario, ASP.NET Core uses anti-forgery tokens and they should not be cached, as shown in the following output:

    ```
    warn: Microsoft.AspNetCore.Antiforgery.DefaultAntiforgery[8]
    ```

> The 'Cache-Control' and 'Pragma' headers have been overridden
> and set to 'no-cache, no-store' and 'no-cache' respectively to prevent
> caching of this response. Any response that uses antiforgery should not
> be cached.

14. Close Chrome and shut down the web server.

Using output caching

In some ways, output caching is similar to response caching. Output caching can store dynamically generated responses on the server so that they do not have to be regenerated again for another request. This can improve performance.

Output caching endpoints

Let's see it in action with a really simple example of applying output caching to some endpoints to make sure it is working properly:

1. In the `Northwind.Mvc` project, in `Program.cs`, add statements after the call to `AddNorthwindContext` to add the output cache middleware and override the default expiration timespan to make it only 10 seconds, as shown highlighted in the following code:

    ```
    builder.Services.AddNorthwindContext();

    builder.Services.AddOutputCache(options =>
    {
        options.DefaultExpirationTimeSpan = TimeSpan.FromSeconds(10);
    });
    ```

     Good Practice: The default expiration time span is one minute. Think carefully about what the duration should be.

2. In `Program.cs`, before the call to map controllers, add statements to use the output cache, as shown highlighted in the following code:

    ```
    app.UseOutputCache();

    app.MapControllerRoute(
        name: "default",
        pattern: "{controller=Home}/{action=Index}/{id?}");
    ```

3. In `Program.cs`, add statements after the call to map Razor Pages to create two simple endpoints that respond with plain text, one that is not cached and one that uses the output cache, as shown highlighted in the following code:

    ```
    app.MapRazorPages();
    ```

```
app.MapGet("/notcached", () => DateTime.Now.ToString());
app.MapGet("/cached", () => DateTime.Now.ToString()).CacheOutput();
```

4. In `appsettings.Development.json`, add a log level of `Information` for the output caching middleware, as shown highlighted in the following configuration:

```
{
  "Logging": {
    "LogLevel": {
      "Default": "Information",
      "Microsoft.AspNetCore": "Warning",
      "Microsoft.AspNetCore.OutputCaching": "Information"
    }
  }
}
```

5. Start the `Northwind.Mvc` website project and arrange the browser window and command prompt or terminal window so that you can see both.

6. In the browser, navigate to `https://localhost:5001/notcached`, and note that nothing is written to the command line or terminal.

7. In the browser, click the **Refresh** button several times and note that the time is always updated because it is not served from the output cache.

8. In the browser, navigate to `https://localhost:5001/cached`, and note that messages are written to the console or terminal to tell you that you have made a request for a cached resource but it does not have anything in the output cache so it has now cached the output, as shown in the following output:

```
info: Microsoft.AspNetCore.OutputCaching.OutputCacheMiddleware[7]
      No cached response available for this request.
info: Microsoft.AspNetCore.OutputCaching.OutputCacheMiddleware[9]
      The response has been cached.
```

9. In the browser, click the **Refresh** button several times and note that the time is not updated, and an output caching message tells you that the value was served from the cache, as shown in the following output:

```
info: Microsoft.AspNetCore.OutputCaching.OutputCacheMiddleware[5]
      Serving response from cache.
```

10. Continue refreshing until 10 seconds have passed and note that messages are written to the command line or terminal to tell you that the cached output has been updated.

11. Close the browser and shut down the web server.

Output caching MVC views

Now let's see how we can output cache an MVC view:

1. In the `Views\Home` folder, in `ProductDetail.cshtml`, add a `<div>` to show the current time, as shown in the following markup:

```
<h2>Product Detail</h2>
<p class="alert alert-success">@DateTime.Now.ToLongTimeString()</p>
```

2. Start the `Northwind.Mvc` website project and arrange the browser window and command prompt or terminal window so that you can see both.

3. On the home page, scroll down and then select one of the products.

4. On the product detail page, note the current time, and then refresh the page and note that the time updates every second.

5. Close the browser and shut down the web server.

6. In `Program.cs`, at the end of the call to map controllers, add a call to the `CacheOutput` method, as shown highlighted in the following code:

```
app.MapControllerRoute(
    name: "default",
    pattern: "{controller=Home}/{action=Index}/{id?}")
  .CacheOutput();
```

7. Start the `Northwind.Mvc` website project and arrange the browser window and command prompt or terminal window so that you can see both.

8. On the home page, scroll down, select one of the products, and note that the product detail page is not in the output cache, so SQL commands are executed to get the data, and then once the Razor view generates the page, it is stored in the cache, as shown in the following output:

```
info: Microsoft.AspNetCore.OutputCaching.OutputCacheMiddleware[7]
      No cached response available for this request.
dbug: 20/09/2022 17:23:02.402 RelationalEventId.CommandExecuting[20100]
(Microsoft.EntityFrameworkCore.Database.Command)

      Executing DbCommand [Parameters=[@__id_0='?' (DbType = Int32)],
CommandType='Text', CommandTimeout='30']
      SELECT "p"."ProductId", "p"."CategoryId", "p"."Discontinued",
"p"."ProductName", "p"."QuantityPerUnit", "p"."ReorderLevel",
"p"."SupplierId", "p"."UnitPrice", "p"."UnitsInStock",
"p"."UnitsOnOrder", "c"."CategoryId", "c"."CategoryName",
"c"."Description", "c"."Picture"
      FROM "Products" AS "p"
      LEFT JOIN "Categories" AS "c" ON "p"."CategoryId" =
"c"."CategoryId"
      WHERE "p"."ProductId" = @__id_0
      LIMIT 2
info: Microsoft.EntityFrameworkCore.Database.Command[20101]
      Executed DbCommand (7ms) [Parameters=[@__id_0='?' (DbType =
Int32)], CommandType='Text', CommandTimeout='30']
      SELECT "p"."ProductId", "p"."CategoryId", "p"."Discontinued",
"p"."ProductName", "p"."QuantityPerUnit", "p"."ReorderLevel",
"p"."SupplierId", "p"."UnitPrice", "p"."UnitsInStock",
"p"."UnitsOnOrder", "c"."CategoryId", "c"."CategoryName",
"c"."Description", "c"."Picture"
```

```
        FROM "Products" AS "p"
        LEFT JOIN "Categories" AS "c" ON "p"."CategoryId" =
"c"."CategoryId"
        WHERE "p"."ProductId" = @__id_0
        LIMIT 2
info: Microsoft.AspNetCore.OutputCaching.OutputCacheMiddleware[9]
        The response has been cached.
```

9. On the product detail page, note the current time, and then refresh the page and note that the whole page, including the time and product detail data, is served from the output cache, as shown in the following output:

```
info: Microsoft.AspNetCore.OutputCaching.OutputCacheMiddleware[5]
        Serving response from cache.
```

10. Keep refreshing until 10 seconds have passed and note that the page is then regenerated from the database and the current time is shown.

11. In the browser address bar, change the product ID number to a value between 1 and 77 to request a different product, and note that the time is current, and therefore a new cached version has been created for that product ID, because the ID is part of the relative path.

12. Refresh the browser and note the time is cached (and therefore the whole page is).

13. In the browser address bar, change the product ID number to a value between 1 and 77 to request a different product, and note that the time is current, and therefore a new cached version has been created for that product ID, because the ID is part of the relative path.

14. In the browser address bar, change the product ID number back to the previous ID and note the page is still cached with the time that the previous page was first added to the output cache.

15. Close the browser and shut down the web server.

Varying cached data by query string

If a value is different in the relative path, then output caching automatically treats the request as a different resource and so caches different copies for each, including differences in any query string parameters. Consider the following URLs:

```
https://localhost:5001/Home/ProductDetail/12
```

```
https://localhost:5001/Home/ProductDetail/29
```

```
https://localhost:5001/Home/ProductDetail/12?color=red
```

```
https://localhost:5001/Home/ProductDetail/12?color=blue
```

All four requests will each have their own cached copy of their own page. If the query string parameters have no effect on the generated page, then that is a waste.

Let's see how we can fix this problem. We will start by disabling varying the cache by query string parameter values, and then implement some page functionality that uses a query string parameter:

1. In `Program.cs`, in the call to `AddOutputCache`, increase the default expiration to 20 seconds and add a statement to define a named policy to disable varying by query string parameters, as shown highlighted in the following code:

```
builder.Services.AddOutputCache(options =>
{
  options.DefaultExpirationTimeSpan = TimeSpan.FromSeconds(20);
  options.AddPolicy("views", p => p.VaryByQuery(""));
});
```

2. In `Program.cs`, in the call to `CacheOutput` for MVC, specify the named policy, as shown in the following code:

```
app.MapControllerRoute(
    name: "default",
    pattern: "{controller=Home}/{action=Index}/{id?}")
  .CacheOutput("views");
```

3. In `ProductDetail.cshtml`, modify the `<p>` that outputs the current time to set its alert style based on a value stored in the `ViewData` dictionary, as shown highlighted in the following markup:

```
<p class="alert alert-@ViewData["alertstyle"]">
  @DateTime.Now.ToLongTimeString()</p>
```

4. In the `Controllers` folder, in `HomeController.cs`, in the `ProductDetail` action method, store a query string value in the `ViewData` dictionary, as shown in the following code:

```
public async Task<IActionResult> ProductDetail(int? id,
  string alertstyle = "success")
{
  ViewData["alertstyle"] = alertstyle;
```

5. Start the `Northwind.Mvc` website project and arrange the browser window and command prompt or terminal window so that you can see both.

6. On the home page, scroll down, select one of the products, and note the color of the alert is green because the `alertstyle` defaults to `success`.

7. In the browser address bar, append a query string parameter, `?alertstyle=warning`, and note that it is ignored, because the same cached page is returned.

8. In the browser address bar, change the product ID number to a value between 1 and 77 to request a different product and append a query string parameter, `?alertstyle=warning`, and note that the alert is yellow because it is treated as a new request.

9. In the browser address bar, append a query string parameter, `?alertstyle=info`, and note that it is ignored, because the same cached page is returned.

10. Close the browser and shut down the web server.

11. In `Program.cs`, in the call to `AddOutputCache`, in the call to `AddPolicy`, set `alertstyle` as the only named parameter to vary by for query string parameters, as shown highlighted in the following code:

```
builder.Services.AddOutputCache(options =>
{
  options.DefaultExpirationTimeSpan = TimeSpan.FromSeconds(20);
  options.AddPolicy("views", p => p.VaryByQuery("alertstyle"));
});
```

12. Start the `Northwind.Mvc` website project and repeat the steps above to confirm that requests for different `alertstyle` values do have their own cached copies, but any other query string parameter would be ignored.

There are many other ways to vary the cached results for output caching and the ASP.NET Core team intends to add more capabilities in the future.

Querying a database and using display templates

Let's create a new action method that can have a query string parameter passed to it and use that to query the Northwind database for products that cost more than a specified price.

In previous examples, we defined a view model that contained properties for every value that needed to be rendered in the view. In this example, there will be two values: a list of products and the price the visitor entered. To avoid having to define a class or record for the view model, we will pass the list of products as the model and store the maximum price in the `ViewData` collection.

Let's implement this feature:

1. In `HomeController`, import the `Microsoft.EntityFrameworkCore` namespace. We need this to add the `Include` extension method so that we can include related entities, as you learned in *Chapter 10, Working with Data Using Entity Framework Core*.

2. Add a new action method, as shown in the following code:

```
public IActionResult ProductsThatCostMoreThan(decimal? price)
{
  if (!price.HasValue)
  {
    return BadRequest("You must pass a product price in the query string,
    for example, /Home/ProductsThatCostMoreThan?price=50");
  }

  IEnumerable<Product> model = db.Products
    .Include(p => p.Category)
    .Include(p => p.Supplier)
    .Where(p => p.UnitPrice > price);

  if (!model.Any())
  {
```

```
      return NotFound(
        $"No products cost more than {price:C}.");
    }

    ViewData["MaxPrice"] = price.Value.ToString("C");

    return View(model); // pass model to view
  }
```

3. In the **Views/Home** folder, add a new file named `ProductsThatCostMoreThan.cshtml`.

4. Modify the contents, as shown in the following code:

```
@using Packt.Shared
@model IEnumerable<Product>
@{
  string title =
    "Products That Cost More Than " + ViewData["MaxPrice"];
  ViewData["Title"] = title;
}
<h2>@title</h2>
@if (Model is null)
{
  <div>No products found.</div>
}
else
{
  <table class="table">
    <thead>
      <tr>
        <th>Category Name</th>
        <th>Supplier's Company Name</th>
        <th>Product Name</th>
        <th>Unit Price</th>
        <th>Units In Stock</th>
      </tr>
    </thead>
    <tbody>
    @foreach (Product p in Model)
    {
      <tr>
        <td>
          @Html.DisplayFor(modelItem => p.Category.CategoryName)
        </td>
        <td>
          @Html.DisplayFor(modelItem => p.Supplier.CompanyName)
        </td>
        <td>
```

```
              @Html.DisplayFor(modelItem => p.ProductName)
          </td>
          <td>
              @Html.DisplayFor(modelItem => p.UnitPrice)
          </td>
          <td>
              @Html.DisplayFor(modelItem => p.UnitsInStock)
          </td>
        </tr>
      }
      <tbody>
    </table>
}
```

5. In the Views/Home folder, open Index.cshtml.

6. Add the following form element below the visitor count and above the **Products** heading and its listing of products. This will provide a form for the user to enter a price. The user can then click **Submit** to call the action method that shows only products that cost more than the entered price:

```
<h3>Query products by price</h3>
<form asp-action="ProductsThatCostMoreThan" method="GET">
    <input name="price" placeholder="Enter a product price" />
    <input type="submit" />
</form>
```

7. Start the website.

8. On the home page, enter a price in the form, for example, 50, and then click on **Submit**.

9. Note the table of the products that cost more than the price that you entered, as shown in *Figure 14.9*:

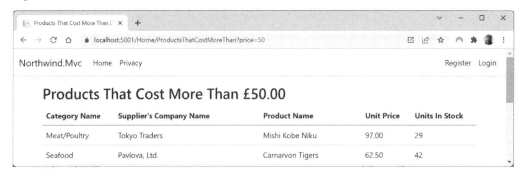

Figure 14.9: A filtered list of products that cost more than £50

10. Close Chrome and shut down the web server.

Improving scalability using asynchronous tasks

When building a desktop or mobile app, multiple tasks (and their underlying threads) can be used to improve responsiveness, because while one thread is busy with the task, another can handle interactions with the user.

Tasks and their threads can be useful on the server side too, especially with websites that work with files, or request data from a store or a web service that could take a while to respond. But they are detrimental to complex calculations that are CPU-bound, so leave these to be processed synchronously as normal.

When an HTTP request arrives at the web server, a thread from its pool is allocated to handle the request. But if that thread must wait for a resource, then it is blocked from handling any more incoming requests. If a website receives more simultaneous requests than it has threads in its pool, then some of those requests will respond with a server timeout error, **503 Service Unavailable**.

The threads that are locked are not doing useful work. They *could* handle one of those other requests, but only if we implement asynchronous code in our websites.

Whenever a thread is waiting for a resource it needs, it can return to the thread pool and handle a different incoming request, improving the scalability of the website, that is, increasing the number of simultaneous requests it can handle.

Why not just have a larger thread pool? In modern operating systems, every thread in the pool has a 1 MB stack. An asynchronous method uses a smaller amount of memory. It also removes the need to create new threads in the pool, which takes time. The rate at which new threads are added to the pool is typically one every two seconds, which is a loooooong time compared to switching between asynchronous threads.

 Good Practice: Make your controller action methods asynchronous.

Making controller action methods asynchronous

It is easy to make an existing action method asynchronous:

1. In `HomeController.cs`, modify the `Index` action method to be asynchronous and await the calls to asynchronous methods to get the categories and products, as shown highlighted in the following code:

    ```
    [ResponseCache(Duration = 10, Location = ResponseCacheLocation.Any)]
    public async Task<IActionResult> Index()
    {
      _logger.LogError("This is a serious error (not really!)");
      _logger.LogWarning("This is your first warning!");
      _logger.LogWarning("Second warning!");
    ```

```
    _logger.LogInformation("I am in the Index method of the
    HomeController.");

    HomeIndexViewModel model = new
    (
      VisitorCount: Random.Shared.Next(1, 1001),
      Categories: await db.Categories.ToListAsync(),
      Products: await db.Products.ToListAsync()
    );

    return View(model); // pass model to view
}
```

2. Modify the `ProductDetail` action method in a similar way, as shown highlighted in the following code:

```
public async Task<IActionResult> ProductDetail(int? id)
```

3. In the `ProductDetail` action method, await the calls to asynchronous methods to get the product, as shown highlighted in the following code:

```
Product? model = await db.Products
    .SingleOrDefaultAsync(p => p.ProductId == id);
```

4. Start the website.

5. Note that the functionality of the website is the same, but trust that it will now scale better.

6. Close Chrome and shut down the web server.

Practicing and exploring

Test your knowledge and understanding by answering some questions, getting some hands-on practice, and exploring this chapter's topics with deeper research.

Exercise 14.1 – Test your knowledge

Answer the following questions:

1. What do the files with the special names _ViewStart and _ViewImports do when created in the Views folder?

2. What are the names of the three segments defined in the default ASP.NET Core MVC route, what do they represent, and which are optional?

3. What does the default model binder do, and what data types can it handle?

4. In a shared layout file like _Layout.cshtml, how do you output the content of the current view?

5. In a shared layout file like _Layout.cshtml, how do you output a section that the current view can supply content for, and how does the view supply the contents for that section?

6. When calling the View method inside a controller's action method, what paths are searched for the view by convention?

7. How can you instruct the visitor's browser to cache the response for 24 hours?

8. Why might you enable Razor Pages even if you are not creating any yourself?

9. How does ASP.NET Core MVC identify classes that can act as controllers?

10. In what ways does ASP.NET Core MVC make it easier to test a website?

Exercise 14.2 – Practice implementing MVC by implementing a category detail page

The `Northwind.Mvc` project has a home page that shows categories, but when the `View` button is clicked, the website returns a `404 Not Found` error, for example, for the following URL:

```
https://localhost:5001/category/1
```

Extend the `Northwind.Mvc` project by adding the ability to show a detail page for a category.

Exercise 14.3 – Practice improving scalability by understanding and implementing async action methods

Almost a decade ago, Stephen Cleary wrote an excellent article for MSDN Magazine explaining the scalability benefits of implementing async action methods for ASP.NET. The same principles apply to ASP.NET Core, but even more so, because unlike the old ASP.NET as described in the article, ASP.NET Core supports asynchronous filters and other components.

Read the article at the following link:

```
https://docs.microsoft.com/en-us/archive/msdn-magazine/2014/october/async-programming-
introduction-to-async-await-on-asp-net
```

Exercise 14.4 – Practice unit testing MVC controllers

Controllers are where the business logic of your website runs, so it is important to test the correctness of that logic using unit tests, as you learned in *Chapter 4, Writing, Debugging, and Testing Functions*.

Write some unit tests for `HomeController`.

 Good Practice: You can read more about how to unit test controllers at the following link: `https://docs.microsoft.com/en-us/aspnet/core/mvc/controllers/testing`

Exercise 14.5 – Explore topics

Use the links on the following page to learn more about the topics covered in this chapter:

```
https://github.com/markjprice/cs11dotnet7/blob/main/book-links.md#chapter-14---
building-websites-using-the-model-view-controller-pattern
```

Summary

In this chapter, you learned how to build large, complex websites in a way that is easy to unit test by registering and injecting dependency services like database contexts and loggers and is easier to manage with teams of programmers using ASP.NET Core MVC. You learned about:

- Configuration
- Authentication
- Routes
- Models
- Views
- Controllers

In the next chapter, you will learn how to build and consume services that use HTTP as the communication layer, aka web services.

15

Building and Consuming Web Services

This chapter is about learning how to build web services (aka HTTP or REST services) using the ASP.NET Core Web API and consuming web services using HTTP clients that could be any other type of .NET app, including a website or a mobile or desktop app.

This chapter requires knowledge and skills that you learned in *Chapter 10, Working with Data Using Entity Framework Core*, and *Chapters 12* to *14*, about building websites using ASP.NET Core.

In this chapter, we will cover the following topics:

- Building web services using the ASP.NET Core Web API
- Documenting and testing web services
- Consuming web services using HTTP clients
- Implementing advanced features for web services (online section)
- Building web services using Minimal APIs

Building web services using the ASP.NET Core Web API

Before we build a modern web service, we need to cover some background to set the context for this chapter.

Understanding web service acronyms

Although HTTP was originally designed to request and respond with HTML and other resources for humans to look at, it is also good for building services.

Roy Fielding stated in his doctoral dissertation, describing the **Representational State Transfer (REST)** architectural style, that the HTTP standard would be good for building services because it defines the following:

- URIs to uniquely identify resources, like `https://localhost:5001/api/products/23`.

- Methods to perform common tasks on those resources, like GET, POST, PUT, and DELETE.
- The ability to negotiate the media type of content exchanged in requests and responses, such as XML and JSON. Content negotiation happens when the client specifies a request header like Accept: application/xml,*/*;q=0.8. The default response format used by the ASP.NET Core Web API is JSON, which means one of the response headers would be Content-Type: application/json; charset=utf-8.

Web services use the HTTP communication standard, so they are sometimes called HTTP or RESTful services. HTTP or RESTful services are what this chapter is about.

Understanding HTTP requests and responses for Web APIs

HTTP defines standard types of requests and standard codes to indicate a type of response. Most of them can be used to implement Web API services.

The most common type of request is GET, to retrieve a resource identified by a unique path, with additional options like what media type is acceptable that are set as request headers, like Accept, as shown in the following example:

```
GET /path/to/resource
Accept: application/json
```

Common responses include success and multiple types of failure, as shown in the following table:

Status code	Description
101 Switching Protocols	The requester has asked the server to switch protocols and the server has agreed to do so. For example, it is common to switch from HTTP to **WS (WebSockets)** for more efficient communication.

103 Early Hints	Used to convey hints that help a client make preparations for processing the final response. For example, the server might send the following response before then sending a normal 200 OK response for a web page that uses a stylesheet and JavaScript file:
	
	`HTTP/1.1 103 Early Hints`
	`Link: </style.css>; rel=preload; as=style`
	`Link: </script.js>; rel=preload; as=script`

200 OK	The path was correctly formed and the resource was successfully found, serialized into an acceptable media type, and then returned in the response body. The response headers specify the Content-Type, Content-Length, and Content-Encoding, for example, GZIP.
301 Moved Permanently	Over time, a web service may change its resource model including the path used to identify an existing resource. The web service can indicate the new path by returning this status code and a response header named Location that has the new path.
302 Found	Similar to 301.

304 Not Modified	If the request included the `If-Modified-Since` header, then the web service can respond with this status code. The response body is empty because the client should use its cached copy of the resource.
400 Bad Request	The request was invalid, for example, it used a path for a product using an integer ID where the ID value is missing.
401 Unauthorized	The request was valid, the resource was found, but the client did not supply credentials or is not authorized to access that resource. Re-authenticating may enable access, for example, by adding or changing the `Authorization` request header.
403 Forbidden	The request was valid, the resource was found, but the client is not authorized to access that resource. Re-authenticating will not fix the issue.
404 Not Found	The request was valid, but the resource was not found. The resource may be found if the request is repeated later. To indicate that a resource will never be found, return `410 Gone`.
406 Not Acceptable	If the request has an `Accept` header that only lists media types that the web service does not support. For example, if the client requests JSON but the web service can only return XML.
451 Unavailable for Legal Reasons	A website hosted in the USA might return this for requests coming from Europe to avoid having to comply with the General Data Protection Regulation (GDPR). The number was chosen as a reference to the novel Fahrenheit 451, in which books are banned and burned.
500 Server Error	The request was valid, but something went wrong on the server side while processing the request. Retrying again later might work.
503 Service Unavailable	The web service is busy and cannot handle the request. Trying again later might work.

Other common types of HTTP requests include POST, PUT, PATCH, and DELETE, which create, modify, or delete resources.

To create a new resource, you might make a POST request with a body that contains the new resource, as shown in the following code:

```
POST /path/to/resource
Content-Length: 123
Content-Type: application/json
```

To create a new resource or update an existing resource, you might make a PUT request with a body that contains a whole new version of the existing resource, and if the resource does not exist, it is created, or if it does exist, it is replaced (sometimes called an **upsert** operation), as shown in the following code:

```
PUT /path/to/resource
Content-Length: 123
Content-Type: application/json
```

To update an existing resource more efficiently, you might make a PATCH request with a body that contains an object with only the properties that need changing, as shown in the following code:

```
PATCH /path/to/resource
Content-Length: 123
Content-Type: application/json
```

To delete an existing resource, you might make a DELETE request, as shown in the following code:

```
DELETE /path/to/resource
```

As well as the responses shown in the table above for a GET request, all the types of requests that create, modify, or delete a resource have additional possible common responses, as shown in the following table:

Status code	Description
201 Created	The new resource was created successfully, the response header named Location contains its path, and the response body contains the newly created resource. Immediately GET-ing the resource should return 200.
202 Accepted	The new resource cannot be created immediately so the request is queued for later processing and immediately GET-ing the resource might return 404. The body can contain a resource that points to some form of status checker or an estimate of when the resource will become available.
204 No Content	Commonly used in response to a DELETE request since returning the resource in the body after deleting it does not usually make sense! Sometimes used in response to POST, PUT, or PATCH requests if the client does not need to confirm that the request was processed correctly.
405 Method Not Allowed	Returned when the request used a method that is not supported. For example, a web service designed to be read-only may explicitly disallow PUT, DELETE, and so on.
415 Unsupported Media Type	Returned when the resource in the request body uses a media type that the web service cannot handle. For example, if the body contains a resource in XML format but the web service can only process JSON.

Creating an ASP.NET Core Web API project

We will build a web service that provides a way to work with data in the Northwind database using ASP.NET Core so that the data can be used by any client application on any platform that can make HTTP requests and receive HTTP responses:

1. Use your preferred code editor to open the PracticalApps solution/workspace and then add a new project, as defined in the following list:

    - Project template: **ASP.NET Core Web API**/webapi
    - Workspace/solution file and folder: PracticalApps
    - Project file and folder: Northwind.WebApi

If you are using Visual Studio 2022, then confirm the following defaults have been chosen. If you are using Visual Studio Code and the dotnet new command, then the following are all the defaults anyway, so no switches are needed:

- **Authentication Type:** None
- **Configure for HTTPS:** Selected
- **Enable Docker:** Cleared
- **Use controllers (uncheck to use minimal APIs):** Selected
- **Enable OpenAPI support:** Selected
- **Do not use top-level statements:** Cleared

- In Visual Studio Code, select `Northwind.WebApi` as the active OmniSharp project.

2. Build the `Northwind.WebApi` project.

3. In the `Controllers` folder, open and review `WeatherForecastController.cs`, as shown in the following code:

```
using Microsoft.AspNetCore.Mvc;

namespace Northwind.WebApi.Controllers;

[ApiController]
[Route("[controller]")]
public class WeatherForecastController : ControllerBase
{
  private static readonly string[] Summaries = new[]
  {
    "Freezing", "Bracing", "Chilly", "Cool", "Mild",
    "Warm", "Balmy", "Hot", "Sweltering", "Scorching"
  };

  private readonly ILogger<WeatherForecastController> _logger;

  public WeatherForecastController(
    ILogger<WeatherForecastController> logger)
  {
    _logger = logger;
  }

  [HttpGet(Name = "GetWeatherForecast")]
  public IEnumerable<WeatherForecast> Get()
  {
    return Enumerable.Range(1, 5).Select(index => new WeatherForecast
      {
        Date = DateTime.Now.AddDays(index),
```

```
        TemperatureC = Random.Shared.Next(-20, 55),
        Summary = Summaries[Random.Shared.Next(Summaries.Length)]
      })
      .ToArray();
  }
}
```

While reviewing the preceding code, note the following:

- The `Controller` class inherits from `ControllerBase`. This is simpler than the `Controller` class used in MVC because it does not have methods like `View` to generate HTML responses by passing a view model to a Razor file.

- The `[Route]` attribute registers the `/weatherforecast` relative URL for clients to use to make HTTP requests that will be handled by this controller. For example, an HTTP request for `https://localhost:5001/weatherforecast/` would be handled by this controller. Some developers like to prefix the controller name with `api/`, which is a convention to differentiate between MVC and Web API in mixed projects. If you use `[controller]` as shown, it uses the characters before `Controller` in the class name, in this case, `WeatherForecast`, or you can simply enter a different name without the square brackets, for example, `[Route("api/forecast")]`.

 Good Practice: Specifying a route using a literal string like this is poor practice. I am only doing so here to keep the example simple. It would be better in practice to define a static class with string constant values and use those instead. Then you have a central place to change routes if needed in the future.

- The `[ApiController]` attribute was introduced with ASP.NET Core 2.1 and it enables REST-specific behavior for controllers, like automatic HTTP `400` responses for invalid models, as you will see later in this chapter.

- The `[HttpGet]` attribute registers the `Get` method in the `Controller` class to respond to HTTP `GET` requests, and its implementation uses the shared `Random` object to return an array of `WeatherForecast` objects with random temperatures and summaries like `Bracing` or `Balmy` for the next five days of weather.

4. In `WeatherForecastController.cs`, add a second `Get` method that allows the call to specify how many days ahead the forecast should be by implementing the following:

   1. Add a comment above the original method to show the action method and URL path that it responds to.

   2. Add a new method with an integer parameter named `days`.

   3. Cut and paste the original `Get` method implementation code statements into the new `Get` method. We are cutting because we need to move the statements from the original method to the new method.

4. Modify the new method to create an `IEnumerable` of integers up to the number of days requested, and modify the original `Get` method to call the new `Get` method and pass the value 5.

Your methods should be as shown in the following code:

```
// GET /weatherforecast
[HttpGet(Name = "GetWeatherForecastFiveDays")]
public IEnumerable<WeatherForecast> Get() // original method
{
  return Get(days: 5); // five day forecast
}

// GET /weatherforecast/7
[HttpGet(template: "{days:int}", Name = "GetWeatherForecast")]
public IEnumerable<WeatherForecast> Get(int days) // new method
{
  return Enumerable.Range(1, days).Select(index => new WeatherForecast
    {
      Date = DateTime.Now.AddDays(index),
      TemperatureC = Random.Shared.Next(-20, 55),
      Summary = Summaries[Random.Shared.Next(Summaries.Length)]
    })
    .ToArray();
}
```

In the `[HttpGet]` attribute, note the route template pattern `{days:int}` constrains the `days` parameter to `int` values.

Reviewing the web service's functionality

Now, we will test the web service's functionality:

1. In **Properties**, open the `launchSettings.json` file, and note that by default, if you are using Visual Studio 2022, it will launch the browser and navigate to the `/swagger` relative URL path, as shown highlighted in the following markup:

```
"profiles": {
  "http": {
    "commandName": "Project",
    "dotnetRunMessages": true,
    "launchBrowser": true,
    "launchUrl": "swagger",
    "applicationUrl": "http://localhost:5000",
    "environmentVariables": {
```

```
        "ASPNETCORE_ENVIRONMENT": "Development"
      }
    },
    "https": {
      "commandName": "Project",
      "dotnetRunMessages": true,
      "launchBrowser": true,
      "launchUrl": "swagger",
      "applicationUrl": "https://localhost:5001;http://localhost:5000",
      "environmentVariables": {
        "ASPNETCORE_ENVIRONMENT": "Development"
      }
    },
```

2. Modify the profiles named http and https to set launchBrowser to false.

3. For the profiles named http and https for the applicationUrl, change the random port number for HTTPS to 5001 and for HTTP to 5000.

 The solution on GitHub is configured to use port 5002 because we will change its configuration later in the book.

4. Start the web service project.

5. Start Chrome.

6. Navigate to https://localhost:5001/ and note you will get a 404 status code response because we have not enabled static files and there is not an index.html, nor is there an MVC controller with a route configured. Remember that this project is not designed for a human to view and interact with, so this is expected behavior for a web service.

7. In Chrome, show **Developer tools**.

8. Navigate to https://localhost:5001/weatherforecast and note the Web API service should return a JSON document with five random weather forecast objects in an array, as shown in *Figure 15.1*:

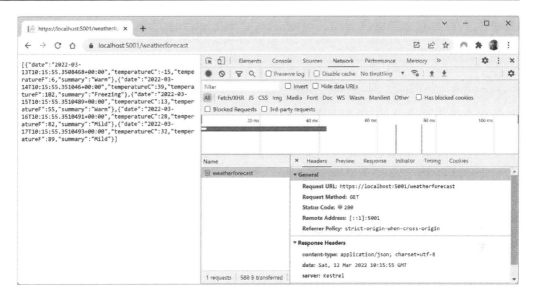

Figure 15.1: A request and response from a weather forecast web service

9. Close **Developer tools**.

10. Navigate to `https://localhost:5001/weatherforecast/14` and note that the response when requesting a two-week weather forecast contains 14 forecasts.

11. Close Chrome and shut down the web server.

Creating a web service for the Northwind database

Unlike MVC controllers, Web API controllers do not call Razor views to return HTML responses for website visitors to see in browsers. Instead, they use **content negotiation** with the client application that made the HTTP request to return data in formats such as XML, JSON, or X-WWW-FORM-URLEN-CODED in their HTTP response.

The client application must then deserialize the data from the negotiated format. The most used format for modern web services is **JavaScript Object Notation** (**JSON**) because it is compact and works natively with JavaScript in a browser when building **Single-Page Applications** (**SPAs**) with client-side technologies like Angular, React, and Vue.

We will reference the Entity Framework Core entity data model for the Northwind database that you created in *Chapter 12, Introducing Web Development Using ASP.NET Core*:

1. In the `Northwind.WebApi` project, add a project reference to `Northwind.Common.DataContext` for either SQLite or SQL Server, as shown in the following markup:

```
<ItemGroup>
  <!-- change Sqlite to SqlServer if you prefer -->
  <ProjectReference Include="..\Northwind.Common.DataContext.Sqlite\
  Northwind.Common.DataContext.Sqlite.csproj" />
</ItemGroup>
```

2. In the `Northwind.WebApi` project, globally and statically import the `System.Console` class.

3. Build the `Northwind.WebApi` project and fix any compile errors in your code.

4. In `Program.cs`, import namespaces for working with web media formatters and the shared Packt classes, as shown in the following code:

```
// IOutputFormatter, OutputFormatter
using Microsoft.AspNetCore.Mvc.Formatters;
using Packt.Shared; // AddNorthwindContext extension method
```

5. In `Program.cs`, add a statement before the call to `AddControllers` to register the `Northwind` database context class (it will use either SQLite or SQL Server depending on which database provider you referenced in the project file), as shown in the following code:

```
builder.Services.AddNorthwindContext();
```

6. In the call to `AddControllers`, add a lambda block with statements to write the names and supported media types of the default output formatters to the console, and then add XML serializer formatters, as shown in the following code:

```
builder.Services.AddControllers(options =>
{
  WriteLine("Default output formatters:");
  foreach (IOutputFormatter formatter in options.OutputFormatters)
  {
    OutputFormatter? mediaFormatter = formatter as OutputFormatter;
    if (mediaFormatter is null)
    {
      WriteLine($"  {formatter.GetType().Name}");
    }
    else // OutputFormatter class has SupportedMediaTypes
    {
      WriteLine("  {0}, Media types: {1}",
        arg0: mediaFormatter.GetType().Name,
        arg1: string.Join(", ", mediaFormatter.SupportedMediaTypes));
    }
```

```
    }
 })
 .AddXmlDataContractSerializerFormatters()
 .AddXmlSerializerFormatters();
```

7. Start the web service.

8. In a command prompt or terminal, note that there are four default output formatters, including ones that convert `null` values into `204` `No` `Content` and ones to support responses that are plain text, byte streams, and JSON, as shown in the following output:

```
Default output formatters:
   HttpNoContentOutputFormatter
   StringOutputFormatter, Media types: text/plain
   StreamOutputFormatter
   SystemTextJsonOutputFormatter, Media types: application/json, text/
json, application/*+json
```

9. Shut down the web server.

Creating data repositories for entities

Defining and implementing a data repository to provide CRUD operations is good practice. The CRUD acronym includes the following operations:

- C for **Create**
- R for **Retrieve** (or **Read**)
- U for **Update**
- D for **Delete**

We will create a data repository for the `Customers` table in Northwind. There are only 91 customers in this table, so we will store a copy of the whole table in memory to improve scalability and performance when reading customer records.

 Good Practice: In a real web service, you should use a distributed cache like Redis, an open-source data structure store that can be used as a high-performance, high-availability database, cache, or message broker.

We will follow a modern good practice and make the repository API asynchronous. It will be instantiated by a `Controller` class using constructor parameter injection, so a new instance is created to handle every HTTP request:

1. In the `Northwind.WebApi` project, create a folder named `Repositories`.

2. Add a new interface file and a class file to the `Repositories` folder named `ICustomerRepository.cs` and `CustomerRepository.cs`.

3. In `ICustomerRepository.cs`, define an interface with five CRUD methods, as shown in the following code:

```
using Packt.Shared; // Customer

namespace Northwind.WebApi.Repositories;

public interface ICustomerRepository
{
  Task<Customer?> CreateAsync(Customer c);
  Task<IEnumerable<Customer>> RetrieveAllAsync();
  Task<Customer?> RetrieveAsync(string id);
  Task<Customer?> UpdateAsync(string id, Customer c);
  Task<bool?> DeleteAsync(string id);
}
```

4. In `CustomerRepository.cs`, define a class with five implemented methods, remembering that methods that use await inside them must be marked as async, as shown in the following code:

```
using Microsoft.EntityFrameworkCore.ChangeTracking; // EntityEntry<T>
using Packt.Shared; // Customer
using System.Collections.Concurrent; // ConcurrentDictionary

namespace Northwind.WebApi.Repositories;

public class CustomerRepository : ICustomerRepository
{
  // Use a static thread-safe dictionary field to cache the customers.
  private static ConcurrentDictionary<string, Customer>? customersCache;

  // Use an instance data context field because it should not be
  // cached due to the data context having internal caching.
  private NorthwindContext db;

  public CustomerRepository(NorthwindContext injectedContext)
  {
    db = injectedContext;

    // Pre-load customers from database as a normal
    // Dictionary with CustomerId as the key,
    // then convert to a thread-safe ConcurrentDictionary.
    if (customersCache is null)
    {
      customersCache = new ConcurrentDictionary<string, Customer>(
        db.Customers.ToDictionary(c => c.CustomerId));
    }
  }
}
```

```
public async Task<Customer?> CreateAsync(Customer c)
{
  // Normalize CustomerId into uppercase.
  c.CustomerId = c.CustomerId.ToUpper();
  // Add to database using EF Core.
  EntityEntry<Customer> added = await db.Customers.AddAsync(c);
  int affected = await db.SaveChangesAsync();
  if (affected == 1)
  {
    if (customersCache is null) return c;
    // If the customer is new, add it to cache, else
    // call UpdateCache method.
    return customersCache.AddOrUpdate(c.CustomerId, c, UpdateCache);
  }
  else
  {
    return null;
  }
}

public Task<IEnumerable<Customer>> RetrieveAllAsync()
{
  // For performance, get from cache.
  return Task.FromResult(customersCache is null
      ? Enumerable.Empty<Customer>() : customersCache.Values);
}

public Task<Customer?> RetrieveAsync(string id)
{
  // For performance, get from cache.
  id = id.ToUpper();
  if (customersCache is null) return null!;
  customersCache.TryGetValue(id, out Customer? c);
  return Task.FromResult(c);
}

private Customer UpdateCache(string id, Customer c)
{
  Customer? old;
  if (customersCache is not null)
  {
    if (customersCache.TryGetValue(id, out old))
    {
      if (customersCache.TryUpdate(id, c, old))
      {
        return c;
```

```
        }
      }
    }
    return null!;
  }

  public async Task<Customer?> UpdateAsync(string id, Customer c)
  {
    // Normalize customer Id.
    id = id.ToUpper();
    c.CustomerId = c.CustomerId.ToUpper();
    // Update in database.
    db.Customers.Update(c);
    int affected = await db.SaveChangesAsync();
    if (affected == 1)
    {
      // update in cache
      return UpdateCache(id, c);
    }
    return null;
  }

  public async Task<bool?> DeleteAsync(string id)
  {
    id = id.ToUpper();
    // Remove from database.
    Customer? c = db.Customers.Find(id);
    if (c is null) return null;
    db.Customers.Remove(c);
    int affected = await db.SaveChangesAsync();
    if (affected == 1)
    {
      if (customersCache is null) return null;
      // Remove from cache.
      return customersCache.TryRemove(id, out c);
    }
    else
    {
      return null;
    }
  }
}
```

Implementing a Web API controller

There are some useful attributes and methods for implementing a controller that returns data instead of HTML.

With MVC controllers, a route like /home/index tells us the controller class name and the action method name, for example, the HomeController class and the Index action method.

With Web API controllers, a route like /weatherforecast only tells us the controller class name, for example, WeatherForecastController. To determine the action method name to execute, we must map HTTP methods like GET and POST to methods in the controller class.

You should decorate controller methods with the following attributes to indicate the HTTP method that they will respond to:

- [HttpGet], [HttpHead]: These action methods respond to GET or HEAD requests to retrieve a resource and return either the resource and its response headers or just the response headers.
- [HttpPost]: This action method responds to POST requests to create a new resource or perform some other action defined by the service.
- [HttpPut], [HttpPatch]: These action methods respond to PUT or PATCH requests to update an existing resource either by replacing it or updating a subset of its properties.
- [HttpDelete]: This action method responds to DELETE requests to remove a resource.
- [HttpOptions]: This action method responds to OPTIONS requests.

Understanding action method return types

An action method can return .NET types like a single string value; complex objects defined by a class, record, or struct; or collections of complex objects. The ASP.NET Core Web API will serialize them into the requested data format set in the HTTP request Accept header, for example, JSON, if a suitable serializer has been registered.

For more control over the response, there are helper methods that return an ActionResult wrapper around the .NET type.

Declare the action method's return type to be IActionResult if it could return different return types based on inputs or other variables. Declare the action method's return type to be ActionResult<T> if it will only return a single type but with different status codes.

Good Practice: Decorate action methods with the [ProducesResponseType] attribute to indicate all the known types and HTTP status codes that the client should expect in a response. This information can then be publicly exposed to document how a client should interact with your web service. Think of it as part of your formal documentation. Later in this chapter, you will learn how you can install a code analyzer to give you warnings when you do not decorate your action methods like this.

For example, an action method that gets a product based on an id parameter would be decorated with three attributes—one to indicate that it responds to GET requests and has an id parameter, and two to indicate what happens when it succeeds and when the client has supplied an invalid product ID, as shown in the following code:

```
[HttpGet("{id}")]
[ProducesResponseType(200, Type = typeof(Product))]
```

```
[ProducesResponseType(404)]
public IActionResult Get(string id)
```

The `ControllerBase` class has methods to make it easy to return different responses, as shown in the following table:

Method	Description
Ok	Returns a 200 status code and a resource converted to the client's preferred format, like JSON or XML. Commonly used in response to a GET request.
CreatedAtRoute	Returns a 201 status code and the path to the new resource. Commonly used in response to a POST request to create a resource that can be performed quickly.
Accepted	Returns a 202 status code to indicate the request is being processed but has not completed. Commonly used in response to a POST, PUT, PATCH, or DELETE request that triggers a background process that takes a long time to complete.
NoContentResult	Returns a 204 status code and an empty response body. Commonly used in response to a PUT, PATCH, or DELETE request when the response does not need to contain the affected resource.
BadRequest	Returns a 400 status code and an optional message string with more details.
NotFound	Returns an e status code and an automatically populated `ProblemDetails` body (requires a compatibility version of 2.2 or later).

Configuring the customer repository and Web API controller

Now you will configure the repository so that it can be called from within a Web API controller.

You will register a scoped dependency service implementation for the repository when the web service starts up, and then use constructor parameter injection to get it in a new Web API controller for working with customers.

To show an example of differentiating between MVC and Web API controllers using routes, we will use the common /api URL prefix convention for the customers controller:

1. In `Program.cs`, import the namespace for working with our customers repository, as shown in the following code:

   ```
   using Northwind.WebApi.Repositories; // ICustomerRepository,
   CustomerRepository
   ```

2. In `Program.cs`, add a statement before the call to the `Build` method, which will register the `CustomerRepository` for use at runtime as a scoped dependency, as shown in the following code:

   ```
   builder.Services.AddScoped<ICustomerRepository, CustomerRepository>();
   ```

Good Practice: Our repository uses a database context that is registered as a scoped dependency. You can only use scoped dependencies inside other scoped dependencies, so we cannot register the repository as a singleton. You can read more about this at the following link: `https://docs.microsoft.com/en-us/dotnet/core/extensions/dependency-injection#scoped`.

3. In the `Controllers` folder, add a new class named `CustomersController.cs`. If you are using Visual Studio 2022, then you can choose the **MVC Controller - Empty** project item template.

4. In `CustomersController.cs`, add statements to define a Web API controller class to work with customers, as shown in the following code:

```csharp
using Microsoft.AspNetCore.Mvc; // [Route], [ApiController], ControllerBase
using Packt.Shared; // Customer
using Northwind.WebApi.Repositories; // ICustomerRepository

namespace Northwind.WebApi.Controllers;

// base address: api/customers
[Route("api/[controller]")]
[ApiController]
public class CustomersController : ControllerBase
{
  private readonly ICustomerRepository repo;

  // constructor injects repository registered in Startup
  public CustomersController(ICustomerRepository repo)
  {
    this.repo = repo;
  }

  // GET: api/customers
  // GET: api/customers/?country=[country]
  // this will always return a list of customers (but it might be empty)
  [HttpGet]
  [ProducesResponseType(200, Type = typeof(IEnumerable<Customer>))]
  public async Task<IEnumerable<Customer>> GetCustomers(string? country)
  {
    if (string.IsNullOrWhiteSpace(country))
    {
      return await repo.RetrieveAllAsync();
    }
    else
    {
      return (await repo.RetrieveAllAsync())
```

```csharp
      .Where(customer => customer.Country == country);
  }
}

// GET: api/customers/[id]
[HttpGet("{id}", Name = nameof(GetCustomer))] // named route
[ProducesResponseType(200, Type = typeof(Customer))]
[ProducesResponseType(404)]
public async Task<IActionResult> GetCustomer(string id)
{
  Customer? c = await repo.RetrieveAsync(id);
  if (c == null)
  {
    return NotFound(); // 404 Resource not found
  }
  return Ok(c); // 200 OK with customer in body
}

// POST: api/customers
// BODY: Customer (JSON, XML)
[HttpPost]
[ProducesResponseType(201, Type = typeof(Customer))]
[ProducesResponseType(400)]
public async Task<IActionResult> Create([FromBody] Customer c)
{
  if (c == null)
  {
    return BadRequest(); // 400 Bad request
  }
  Customer? addedCustomer = await repo.CreateAsync(c);
  if (addedCustomer == null)
  {
    return BadRequest("Repository failed to create customer.");
  }
  else
  {
    return CreatedAtRoute( // 201 Created
      routeName: nameof(GetCustomer),
      routeValues: new { id = addedCustomer.CustomerId.ToLower() },
      value: addedCustomer);
  }
}

// PUT: api/customers/[id]
// BODY: Customer (JSON, XML)
[HttpPut("{id}")]
```

```csharp
[ProducesResponseType(204)]
[ProducesResponseType(400)]
[ProducesResponseType(404)]
public async Task<IActionResult> Update(
  string id, [FromBody] Customer c)
{
  id = id.ToUpper();
  c.CustomerId = c.CustomerId.ToUpper();
  if (c == null || c.CustomerId != id)
  {
    return BadRequest(); // 400 Bad request
  }
  Customer? existing = await repo.RetrieveAsync(id);
  if (existing == null)
  {
    return NotFound(); // 404 Resource not found
  }
  await repo.UpdateAsync(id, c);
  return new NoContentResult(); // 204 No content
}

// DELETE: api/customers/[id]
[HttpDelete("{id}")]
[ProducesResponseType(204)]
[ProducesResponseType(400)]
[ProducesResponseType(404)]
public async Task<IActionResult> Delete(string id)
{
  Customer? existing = await repo.RetrieveAsync(id);
  if (existing == null)
  {
    return NotFound(); // 404 Resource not found
  }
  bool? deleted = await repo.DeleteAsync(id);
  if (deleted.HasValue && deleted.Value) // short circuit AND
  {
    return new NoContentResult(); // 204 No content
  }
  else
  {
    return BadRequest( // 400 Bad request
      $"Customer {id} was found but failed to delete.");
  }
}
}
```

While reviewing this Web API controller class, note the following:

- The `Controller` class registers a route that starts with `api/` and includes the name of the controller, that is, `api/customers`.

- The constructor uses dependency injection to get the registered repository for working with customers.

- There are five action methods to perform CRUD operations on customers—two `GET` methods (for all customers or one customer), `POST` (create), `PUT` (update), and `DELETE`.

- The `GetCustomers` method can have a `string` parameter passed with a country name. If it is missing, all customers are returned. If it is present, it is used to filter customers by country.

- The `GetCustomer` method has a route explicitly named `GetCustomer` so that it can be used to generate a URL after inserting a new customer.

- The `Create` and `Update` methods both decorate the `customer` parameter with `[FromBody]` to tell the model binder to populate it with values from the body of the `POST` request.

- The `Create` method returns a response that uses the `GetCustomer` route so that the client knows how to get the newly created resource in the future. We are matching up two methods to create and then get a customer.

- In the past, the `Create` and `Update` methods would need to check the model state of the customer passed in the body of the HTTP request. If it is invalid, they should return a `400 Bad Request` containing details of the model validation errors. This happens automatically now because the controller is decorated with `[ApiController]`.

When an HTTP request is received by the service, then it will create an instance of the `Controller` class, call the appropriate action method, return the response in the format preferred by the client, and release the resources used by the controller, including the repository and its data context.

Specifying problem details

A feature added in ASP.NET Core 2.1 and later is an implementation of a web standard for specifying problem details.

In Web API controllers decorated with [ApiController] in a project where compatibility with ASP. NET Core 2.2 or later is enabled, action methods that return IActionResult and return a client error status code, that is, 4xx, will automatically include a serialized instance of the `ProblemDetails` class in the response body.

If you want to take control, then you can create a `ProblemDetails` instance yourself and include additional information.

Let's simulate a bad request that needs custom data returned to the client:

1. At the top of the implementation of the `Delete` action method, add statements to check if the id matches the literal string value `"bad"`, and if so, then return a custom problem details object, as shown in the following code:

    ```
    // take control of problem details
    if (id == "bad")
    ```

```
{
  ProblemDetails problemDetails = new()
  {
    Status = StatusCodes.Status400BadRequest,
    Type = "https://localhost:5001/customers/failed-to-delete",
    Title = $"Customer ID {id} found but failed to delete.",
    Detail = "More details like Company Name, Country and so on.",
    Instance = HttpContext.Request.Path
  };
  return BadRequest(problemDetails); // 400 Bad Request
}
```

2. You will test this functionality later.

Controlling XML serialization

In `Program.cs`, we added the `XmlSerializer` so that our Web API service can return XML as well as JSON if the client requests that.

However, the `XmlSerializer` cannot serialize interfaces, and our entity classes use `ICollection<T>` to define related child entities. This causes a warning at runtime, for example, for the `Customer` class and its `Orders` property, as shown in the following output:

```
warn: Microsoft.AspNetCore.Mvc.Formatters.XmlSerializerOutputFormatter[1]
An error occurred while trying to create an XmlSerializer for the type 'Packt.
Shared.Customer'.
System.InvalidOperationException: There was an error reflecting type 'Packt.
Shared.Customer'.
---> System.InvalidOperationException: Cannot serialize member 'Packt.
Shared.Customer.Orders' of type 'System.Collections.Generic.
ICollection'1[[Packt. Shared.Order, Northwind.Common.EntityModels,
Version=1.0.0.0, Culture=neutral, PublicKeyToken=null]]', see inner exception
for more details.
```

We can prevent this warning by excluding the `Orders` property when serializing a `Customer` to XML:

1. In the `Northwind.Common.EntityModels.Sqlite` and `Northwind.Common.EntityModels.SqlServer` projects, open `Customer.cs`.

2. Import the namespace so that we can use the `[XmlIgnore]` attribute, as shown in the following code:

```
using System.Xml.Serialization; // [XmlIgnore]
```

3. Decorate the `Orders` property with an attribute to ignore it when serializing, as shown highlighted in the following code:

```
[InverseProperty(nameof(Order.Customer))]
[XmlIgnore]
public virtual ICollection<Order> Orders { get; set; }
```

4.   If you are using SQL Server, in the `Northwind.Common.EntityModels.SqlServer` project, in `Customer.cs`, decorate the `CustomerTypes` property with `[XmlIgnore]` too.

Documenting and testing web services

You can easily test a web service by making HTTP `GET` requests using a browser. To test other HTTP methods, we need a more advanced tool.

Testing GET requests using a browser

You will use Chrome to test the three implementations of a `GET` request—for all customers, for customers in a specified country, and for a single customer using their unique customer ID:

1.   Start the `Northwind.WebApi` web service project.

2.   Start Chrome.

3.   Navigate to `https://localhost:5001/api/customers` and note the JSON document returned, containing all 91 customers in the Northwind database (unsorted), as shown in *Figure 15.2*:

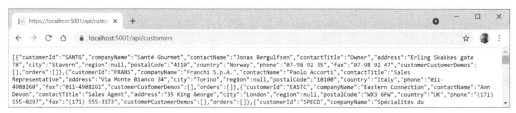

Figure 15.2: Customers from the Northwind database as a JSON document

4.   Navigate to `https://localhost:5001/api/customers?country=Germany` and note the JSON document returned, containing only the customers in Germany.

 If you get an empty array returned, then make sure you have entered the country name using the correct casing, because the database query is case-sensitive. For example, compare the results of uk and **UK**.

5.   Navigate to `https://localhost:5001/api/customers/alfki` and note the JSON document returned containing only the customer named **Alfreds Futterkiste**.

Unlike with country names, we do not need to worry about casing for the customer `id` value because inside the controller class, we normalized the `string` value to uppercase in code.

But how can we test the other HTTP methods, such as `POST`, `PUT`, and `DELETE`? And how can we document our web service so it's easy for anyone to understand how to interact with it?

To solve the first problem, we can install a Visual Studio Code extension named **REST Client**. To solve the second, we can use **Swagger**, the world's most popular technology for documenting and testing HTTP APIs. But first, let's see what is possible with the Visual Studio Code extension.

There are many tools for testing Web APIs, for example, **Postman**. Although Postman is popular, I prefer **REST Client** because it does not hide what is happening. I feel Postman is too GUI-y. But I encourage you to explore different tools and find the ones that fit your style. You can learn more about Postman at the following link: `https://www.postman.com/`.

Testing HTTP requests with the REST Client extension

REST Client is an extension that allows you to send any type of HTTP request and view the response in Visual Studio Code. Even if you prefer to use Visual Studio as your code editor, it is useful to install Visual Studio Code to use an extension like REST Client.

Making GET requests using REST Client

We will start by creating a file for testing GET requests:

1. If you have not already installed REST Client by Huachao Mao (`humao.rest-client`), then install it in Visual Studio Code now.

2. In your preferred code editor, open the `PracticalApps` solution/workspace and then start the `Northwind.WebApi` project web service.

3. In Visual Studio Code, in the `PracticalApps` folder, create a `RestClientTests` folder, and then open the folder.

4. In the `RestClientTests` folder, create a file named `get-customers.http`, and modify its contents to contain an HTTP GET request to retrieve all customers, as shown in the following code:

    ```
    GET https://localhost:5001/api/customers/ HTTP/1.1
    ```

5. In Visual Studio Code, navigate to **View** | **Command Palette**, enter `rest client`, select the command **Rest Client: Send Request**, and press *Enter*, as shown in *Figure 15.3*:

Figure 15.3: Sending an HTTP GET request using REST Client

6. Note the **Response** is shown in a new tabbed window pane vertically and that you can rearrange the open tabs to a horizontal layout by dragging and dropping tabs.

7. In `get-customers.http`, add more GET requests, each separated by three hash symbols, to test getting customers in various countries and getting a single customer using their ID, as shown in the following code:

    ```
    ###
    GET https://localhost:5001/api/customers/?country=Germany HTTP/1.1
    ```

```
###
GET https://localhost:5001/api/customers/?country=USA HTTP/1.1
Accept: application/xml
###
GET https://localhost:5001/api/customers/ALFKI HTTP/1.1
###
GET https://localhost:5001/api/customers/abcxy HTTP/1.1
```

8. Click the **Send Request** link above each request to send it; for example, the GET that has a request header to request customers in the USA as XML instead of JSON, as shown in *Figure 15.4*:

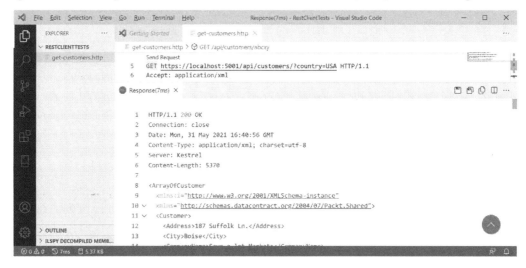

Figure 15.4: Sending a request for XML and getting a response using REST Client

Making other requests using REST Client

Next, we will create a file for testing other requests like POST:

1. In Visual Studio Code, in the RestClientTests folder, create a file named create-customer. http and modify its contents to define a POST request to create a new customer, noting that REST Client will provide IntelliSense while you type common HTTP requests, as shown in the following code:

```
POST https://localhost:5001/api/customers/ HTTP/1.1
Content-Type: application/json
Content-Length: 266

{
  "customerID": "ABCXY",
  "companyName": "ABC Corp",
  "contactName": "John Smith",
  "contactTitle": "Sir",
  "address": "Main Street",
  "city": "New York",
```

```
    "region": "NY",
    "postalCode": "90210",
    "country":  "USA",
    "phone": "(123) 555-1234"
}
```

2. Due to different line endings in different operating systems, the value for the `Content-Length` header will be different on Windows and macOS or Linux. If the value is wrong, then the request will fail. To discover the correct content length, select the body of the request and then look in the status bar for the number of characters, as shown in *Figure 15.5*:

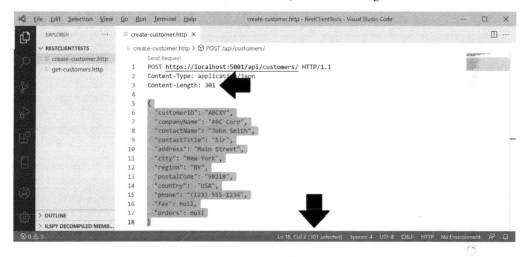

Figure 15.5: Checking the correct Content-Length in the Visual Studio Code status bar

3. Send the request and note the response is `201  Created`. Also note the location (that is, the URL) of the newly created customer is `https://localhost:5001/api/Customers/abcxy`, and includes the newly created customer in the response body, as shown in *Figure 15.6*:

Figure 15.6: Adding a new customer by POSTing to the Web API service

I will leave you an optional challenge to create REST Client files that test updating a customer (using PUT) and deleting a customer (using DELETE). Try them on customers that do exist as well as customers that do not. Solutions are in the GitHub repository for this book.

Now that we've seen a quick and easy way to test our service, which also happens to be a great way to learn HTTP, what about external developers? We want it to be as easy as possible for them to learn and then call our service. For that purpose, we will use Swagger.

Understanding Swagger

The most important part of Swagger is the **OpenAPI Specification**, which defines a REST-style contract for your API, detailing all its resources and operations in a human- and machine-readable format for easy development, discovery, and integration.

Developers can use the OpenAPI Specification for a Web API to automatically generate strongly typed client-side code in their preferred language or library.

For us, another useful feature is **Swagger UI**, because it automatically generates documentation for your API with built-in visual testing capabilities.

Let's review how Swagger is enabled for our web service using the Swashbuckle package:

1. If the web service is running, shut down the web server.

2. In Northwind.WebApi.csproj, note the package reference for Swashbuckle.AspNetCore, as shown in the following markup:

   ```
   <ItemGroup>
     <PackageReference Include="Swashbuckle.AspNetCore" Version="6.2.3" />
   </ItemGroup>
   ```

3. In Program.cs, import Swashbuckle's SwaggerUI namespace, as shown in the following code:

   ```
   using Swashbuckle.AspNetCore.SwaggerUI; // SubmitMethod
   ```

4. In the section that configures the HTTP request pipeline, note the statements to use Swagger and Swagger UI when in development mode, and define an endpoint for the OpenAPI Specification JSON document. Add code to explicitly list the HTTP methods that we want to support in our web service and change the endpoint name, as shown highlighted in the following code:

   ```
   // Configure the HTTP request pipeline.
   if (builder.Environment.IsDevelopment())
   {
     app.UseSwagger();
     app.UseSwaggerUI(c =>
     {
       c.SwaggerEndpoint("/swagger/v1/swagger.json",
         "Northwind Service API Version 1");
       c.SupportedSubmitMethods(new[] {
         SubmitMethod.Get, SubmitMethod.Post,
         SubmitMethod.Put, SubmitMethod.Delete });
   ```

```
    });
}
```

Testing requests with Swagger UI

You are now ready to test an HTTP request using Swagger:

1. Start the Northwind.WebApi web service project.

2. In Chrome, navigate to https://localhost:5001/swagger and note that both the **Customers** and **WeatherForecast** Web API controllers have been discovered and documented, as well as **Schemas** used by the API.

3. Click **GET /api/Customers/{id}** to expand that endpoint and note the required parameter for the **id** of a customer.

4. Click **Try it out**, enter an **id** of ALFKI, and then click the wide blue **Execute** button, as shown in *Figure 15.7*:

Figure 15.7: Inputting a customer ID before clicking the Execute button

5. Scroll down and note the **Request URL**, **Server response** with **Code**, and **Details** including **Response body** and **Response headers**, as shown in *Figure 15.8*:

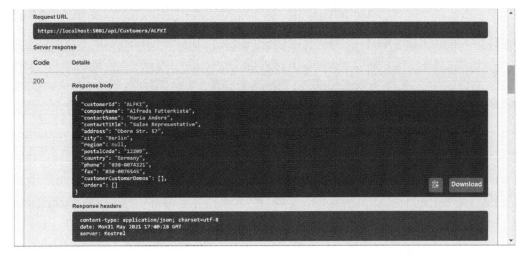

Figure 15.8: Information on ALFKI in a successful Swagger request

6. Scroll back up to the top of the page, click **POST /api/Customers** to expand that section, and then click **Try it out**.

7. Click inside the **Request body** box and modify the JSON to define a new customer, as shown in the following JSON:

```json
{
    "customerID": "SUPER",
    "companyName": "Super Company",
    "contactName": "Rasmus Ibensen",
    "contactTitle": "Sales Leader",
    "address": "Rotterslef 23",
    "city": "Billund",
    "region": null,
    "postalCode": "4371",
    "country": "Denmark",
    "phone": "31 21 43 21",
    "fax": "31 21 43 22"
}
```

8. Click **Execute**, and note the **Request URL**, **Server response** with **Code**, and **Details** including **Response body** and **Response headers**, noting that a response code of 201 means the customer was successfully created, as shown in *Figure 15.9*:

Figure 15.9: Successfully adding a new customer

9. Scroll back up to the top of the page, click **GET /api/Customers**, click **Try it out**, enter Denmark for the country parameter, and click **Execute** to confirm that the new customer was added to the database.

10. Click **DELETE /api/Customers/{id}**, click **Try it out**, enter super for the **id**, click **Execute**, and note that the **Server response Code** is 204, indicating that it was successfully deleted, as shown in *Figure 15.10*:

Figure 15.10: Successfully deleting a customer

11. Click **Execute** again, and note that the **Server response Code** is 404, indicating that the customer does not exist anymore, and the **Response body** contains a problem details JSON document, as shown in *Figure 15.11*:

Figure 15.11: The deleted customer does not exist anymore

12. Enter bad for the **id**, click **Execute** again, and note that the **Server response Code** is 400, indicating that the customer did exist but failed to be deleted (in this case, because the web service is simulating this error), and the **Response body** contains a custom problem details JSON document, as shown in *Figure 15.12*:

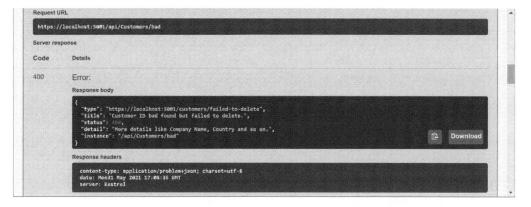

Figure 15.12: The customer did exist but failed to be deleted

 You added the code to implement this in the section titled *Specifying problem details*, where you checked for an id of bad and then returned a bad request with problem details.

13. Use the GET methods to confirm that the new customer has been deleted from the database (there were originally only two customers in Denmark).

 I will leave testing updates to an existing customer by using PUT to the reader.

14. Close Chrome and shut down the web server.

Enabling HTTP logging

HTTP logging is an optional middleware component that logs information about HTTP requests and HTTP responses including the following:

- Information about the HTTP request
- Headers
- Body
- Information about the HTTP response

This is valuable in web services for auditing and debugging scenarios but beware because it can negatively impact performance. You might also log **personally identifiable information (PII),** which can cause compliance issues in some jurisdictions.

Log levels can be set to the following:

- Error: Only Error level logs
- Warning: Error and Warning level logs
- Information: Error, Warning, and Information level logs
- Verbose: All level logs

Log levels can be set for the namespace in which the functionality is defined. Nested namespaces allow us to control which functionality has logging enabled:

- Microsoft: Include all log types in the Microsoft namespace
- Microsoft.AspNetCore: Include all log types in the Microsoft.AspNetCore namespace
- Microsoft.AspNetCore.HttpLogging: Include all log types in the Microsoft.AspNetCore. HttpLogging namespace

Let's see HTTP logging in action:

1. In appsettings.Development.json, add an entry to set the HTTP logging middleware to Information level, as shown highlighted in the following code:

```
{
  "Logging": {
    "LogLevel": {
      "Default": "Information",
```

```
        "Microsoft.AspNetCore": "Warning",
        "Microsoft.AspNetCore.HttpLogging.HttpLoggingMiddleware":
        "Information"
      }
    }
  }
```

 Although the Default log level might be set to Information, more specific configurations take priority. For example, any logging systems in the Microsoft. AspNetCore namespace will use the Warning level. Any logging systems in the Microsoft.AspNetCore. HttpLogging.HttpLoggingMiddleware namespace will now use Information.

2. In Program.cs, import the namespace for working with HTTP logging, as shown in the following code:

```
using Microsoft.AspNetCore.HttpLogging; // HttpLoggingFields
```

3. In the services configuration section, add a statement to configure HTTP logging, as shown in the following code:

```
builder.Services.AddHttpLogging(options =>
{
  options.LoggingFields = HttpLoggingFields.All;
  options.RequestBodyLogLimit = 4096; // default is 32k
  options.ResponseBodyLogLimit = 4096; // default is 32k
});
```

4. In the HTTP pipeline configuration section, add a statement to add HTTP logging before the call to use routing, as shown in the following code:

```
app.UseHttpLogging();
```

5. Start the Northwind.WebApi web service.

6. Start Chrome.

7. Navigate to https://localhost:5001/api/customers.

8. In a command prompt or terminal, note the request and response have been logged, as shown in the following output:

```
info: Microsoft.AspNetCore.HttpLogging.HttpLoggingMiddleware[1]
      Request:
      Protocol: HTTP/1.1
      Method: GET
      Scheme: https
      PathBase:
      Path: /api/customers
      QueryString:
      Connection: keep-alive
```

```
          Accept: */*
          Accept-Encoding: gzip, deflate, br
          Host: localhost:5001

    info: Microsoft.AspNetCore.HttpLogging.HttpLoggingMiddleware[2]
          Response:
          StatusCode: 200
          Content-Type: application/json; charset=utf-8
          ...
          Transfer-Encoding: chunked
```

9. Close Chrome and shut down the web server.

Support for logging additional request headers in W3CLogger

W3CLogger is middleware that writes logs in the W3C standard format. You can:

*   Record details of HTTP requests and responses.
*   Filter which headers and parts of the request and response messages are logged.

 Warning! W3CLogger can reduce the performance of an app.

W3CLogger is similar to HTTP logging so I do not cover details of how to use it in this book. You can learn more about W3CLogger at the following link:

https://learn.microsoft.com/en-us/aspnet/core/fundamentals/w3c-logger/

In ASP.NET Core 7 or later, you can specify to log additional request headers when using the W3CLogger. Call the `AdditionalRequestHeaders` method and pass the name of the header you want to log, as shown in the following code:

```
services.AddW3CLogging(options =>
{
    options.AdditionalRequestHeaders.Add("x-forwarded-for");
    options.AdditionalRequestHeaders.Add("x-client-ssl-protocol");
});
```

You are now ready to build applications that consume your web service.

Consuming web services using HTTP clients

Now that we have built and tested our Northwind service, we will learn how to call it from any .NET app using the `HttpClient` class and its factory.

Understanding HttpClient

The easiest way to consume a web service is to use the `HttpClient` class. However, many people use it wrongly because it implements `IDisposable` and Microsoft's own documentation shows poor usage of it. See the book links in the GitHub repository for articles with more discussion of this.

Usually, when a type implements `IDisposable`, you should create it inside a `using` statement to ensure that it is disposed of as soon as possible. `HttpClient` is different because it is shared, reentrant, and partially thread-safe.

The problem has to do with how the underlying network sockets have to be managed. The bottom line is that you should use a single instance of it for each HTTP endpoint that you consume during the life of your application. This will allow each `HttpClient` instance to have defaults set that are appropriate for the endpoint it works with, while managing the underlying network sockets efficiently.

Configuring HTTP clients using HttpClientFactory

Microsoft is aware of the issue of .NET developers misusing `HttpClient`, and in ASP.NET Core 2.1, they introduced `HttpClientFactory` to encourage best practices; that is the technique we will use.

In the following example, we will use the Northwind MVC website as a client for the Northwind Web API service. Since both need to be hosted on a web server simultaneously, we first need to configure them to use different port numbers, as shown in the following list:

- The Northwind Web API service will listen on port 5002 using HTTPS
- The Northwind MVC website will continue to listen on port 5000 using HTTP and port 5001 using HTTPS

Let's configure those ports:

1. In the `Northwind.WebApi` project, in the `Properties` folder, in `launchSettings.json`, modify the `applicationUrl` setting of the `https` profile to use port 5002, as shown in the following code:

   ```
   "applicationUrl": "https://localhost:5002",
   ```

2. In the `Northwind.Mvc` project, in `Program.cs`, import the namespace for setting a media type header value, as shown in the following code:

   ```
   using System.Net.Http.Headers; // MediaTypeWithQualityHeaderValue
   ```

3. In `Program.cs`, before calling the `Build` method, add a statement to enable `HttpClientFactory` with a named client to make calls to the Northwind Web API service using HTTPS on port 5002 and request JSON as the default response format, as shown in the following code:

   ```
   builder.Services.AddHttpClient(name: "Northwind.WebApi",
     configureClient: options =>
     {
       options.BaseAddress = new Uri("https://localhost:5002/");
       options.DefaultRequestHeaders.Accept.Add(
         new MediaTypeWithQualityHeaderValue(
   ```

```
        mediaType: "application/json", quality: 1.0));
    });
```

Getting customers as JSON in the controller

We can now create an MVC controller action method that:

- Uses the factory to create an HTTP client.

- Makes a GET request for customers.

- Deserializes the JSON response using convenience extension methods introduced with .NET 5 in the System.Net.Http.Json assembly and namespace.

Let's go:

1. In Controllers/HomeController.cs, declare a field to store the HTTP client factory, as shown in the following code:

    ```
    private readonly IHttpClientFactory clientFactory;
    ```

2. Set the field in the constructor, as shown highlighted in the following code:

    ```
    public HomeController(
      ILogger<HomeController> logger,
      NorthwindContext injectedContext,
      IHttpClientFactory httpClientFactory)
    {
      _logger = logger;
      db = injectedContext;
      clientFactory = httpClientFactory;
    }
    ```

3. Create a new action method for calling the Northwind Web API service, fetching all customers, and passing them to a view, as shown in the following code:

    ```
    public async Task<IActionResult> Customers(string country)
    {
      string uri;

      if (string.IsNullOrEmpty(country))
      {
        ViewData["Title"] = "All Customers Worldwide";
        uri = "api/customers";
      }
      else
      {
        ViewData["Title"] = $"Customers in {country}";
        uri = $"api/customers/?country={country}";
      }
    ```

```
HttpClient client = clientFactory.CreateClient(
  name: "Northwind.WebApi");

HttpRequestMessage request = new(
  method: HttpMethod.Get, requestUri: uri);

HttpResponseMessage response = await client.SendAsync(request);

IEnumerable<Customer>? model = await response.Content
  .ReadFromJsonAsync<IEnumerable<Customer>>();

return View(model);
}
```

4. In the `Views/Home` folder, create a Razor file named `Customers.cshtml`.

5. Modify the Razor file to render the customers, as shown in the following markup:

```
@using Packt.Shared
@model IEnumerable<Customer>

<h2>@ViewData["Title"]</h2>
<table class="table">
  <thead>
    <tr>
      <th>Company Name</th>
      <th>Contact Name</th>
      <th>Address</th>
      <th>Phone</th>
    </tr>
  </thead>
  <tbody>
    @if (Model is not null)
    {
      @foreach (Customer c in Model)
      {
        <tr>
          <td>
            @Html.DisplayFor(modelItem => c.CompanyName)
          </td>
          <td>
            @Html.DisplayFor(modelItem => c.ContactName)
          </td>
          <td>
            @Html.DisplayFor(modelItem => c.Address)
            @Html.DisplayFor(modelItem => c.City)
            @Html.DisplayFor(modelItem => c.Region)
            @Html.DisplayFor(modelItem => c.Country)
```

```
        @Html.DisplayFor(modelItem => c.PostalCode)
      </td>
      <td>
        @Html.DisplayFor(modelItem => c.Phone)
      </td>
    </tr>
  }
  }
  </tbody>
</table>
```

6. In `Views/Home/Index.cshtml`, add a form after rendering the visitor count to allow visitors to enter a country and see the customers, as shown in the following markup:

```
<h3>Query customers from a service</h3>
<form asp-action="Customers" method="get">
  <input name="country" placeholder="Enter a country" />
  <input type="submit" />
</form>
```

Starting multiple projects

Up to this point, we have only started one project at a time. Now we have two projects that need to be started, a web service and an MVC client website. In the step-by-step instructions, I will only tell you to start individual projects one at a time, but you should use whatever technique you prefer to start them.

If you are using Visual Studio 2022

Visual Studio 2022 can start multiple projects manually one by one if the debugger is not attached, as described in the following steps:

1. Set the **Startup Project** for the solution to be the **Current selection**.
2. Select a project in **Solution Explorer** so that its name becomes bold.
3. Navigate to **Debug | Start Without Debugging** or press *Ctrl + F5*.
4. Repeat steps 2 and 3 for as many projects as you need.

If you need to debug the projects, then you must start multiple instances of Visual Studio 2022. Each instance can start a single project with debugging.

You can also configure multiple projects to start up at the same time using the following steps:

1. In **Solution Explorer**, right-click the solution and then select **Set Startup Projects...** or select the solution and navigate to **Project | Set Startup Projects...**.
2. In the **Solution '<name>' Property Pages** dialog box, select **Multiple startup projects**, and for any projects that you want to start, select either **Start** or **Start without debugging**, as shown in *Figure 15.13*:

Figure 15.13: Selecting multiple projects to start up in Visual Studio 2022

3. Click **OK**.

4. Navigate to **Debug | Start Debugging** or **Debug | Start Without Debugging** or click the equivalent buttons in the toolbar to start all the projects that you selected.

 You can learn more about multi-project startup using Visual Studio 2022 at the following link: `https://learn.microsoft.com/en-us/visualstudio/ide/how-to-set-multiple-startup-projects`.

If you are using Visual Studio Code

If you need to start multiple projects at the command line with dotnet, then write a script or batch file to execute multiple dotnet run commands, or open multiple command prompt or terminal windows.

If you need to debug multiple projects using Visual Studio Code, then after you've started a first debug session, you can just launch another session. Once the second session is running, the user interface switches to multi-target mode. For example, in the **CALL STACK**, you will see both named projects with their own threads, and then the debug toolbar shows a drop-down list of sessions with the active one selected. Alternatively, you can define compound launch configurations in the launch.json.

 You can learn more about multi-target debugging using Visual Studio Code at the following link: `https://code.visualstudio.com/Docs/editor/debugging#_multitarget-debugging`.

Starting the web service and MVC client projects

Now we can try out the web service with the MVC client calling it:

1. Start the `Northwind.WebApi` project and confirm that the web service is listening only on port 5002, as shown in the following output:

    ```
    info: Microsoft.Hosting.Lifetime[14]
          Now listening on: https://localhost:5002
    ```

2. Start the `Northwind.Mvc` project and confirm that the website is listening on ports 5000 and 5001, as shown in the following output:

    ```
    info: Microsoft.Hosting.Lifetime[14]
          Now listening on: https://localhost:5001
    info: Microsoft.Hosting.Lifetime[14]
          Now listening on: http://localhost:5000
    ```

3. Start Chrome.

4. On the home page, in the customer form, enter a country like Germany, UK, or USA, click **Submit**, and note the list of customers, as shown in *Figure 15.14* for the UK:

Figure 15.14: Customers in the UK

5. Click the **Back** button in your browser, clear the **Country** textbox, click **Submit**, and note the worldwide list of customers.

6. In a command prompt or terminal, note that the `HttpClient` writes each HTTP request that it makes and each HTTP response that it receives, as shown in the following output:

    ```
    info: System.Net.Http.HttpClient.Northwind.WebApi.ClientHandler[100]
          Sending HTTP request GET https://localhost:5002/api/
    customers/?country=UK
    info: System.Net.Http.HttpClient.Northwind.WebApi.ClientHandler[101]
          Received HTTP response headers after 931.864ms - 200
    ```

7. Close Chrome and shut down the two web servers.

Implementing advanced features for web services

This is a bonus section for the chapter that is available online at https://github.com/markjprice/cs11dotnet7/blob/main/docs/bonus/advanced-features.md

Building web services using Minimal APIs

For .NET 6, Microsoft put a lot of effort into adding new features to the C# 10 language and simplifying the ASP.NET Core libraries to enable the creation of web services using Minimal APIs. Minimal APIs are designed to enable the creation of HTTP APIs with minimum lines of code.

 Minimal APIs are covered in more detail in my companion book, *Apps and Services with .NET 7*, in *Chapter 9, Building and Securing Web Services with Minimal APIs*.

You might remember the weather forecast service that is provided in the Web API project template. It shows the use of a controller class to return a five-day weather forecast using faked data. We will now recreate that weather service using Minimal APIs.

It will listen on port 5003 and only GET requests are allowed:

1. Use your preferred code editor to open the PracticalApps solution/workspace and then add a new project, as defined in the following list:

   - Project template: **ASP.NET Core Web API**/webapi
   - Project file and folder: Minimal.WebApi
   - Workspace/solution file and folder: PracticalApps
   - **Authentication Type:** None
   - **Configure for HTTPS:** Selected
   - **Enable Docker:** Cleared
   - **Use controllers** (uncheck to use Minimal APIs): Cleared / -minimal
   - **Enable OpenAPI support:** Selected
   - **Do not use top-level statements:** Cleared

      Warning! If you are using Visual Studio 2022, make sure to clear the check box named **Use controllers** so that it uses Minimal APIs instead. If you are using Visual Studio Code and the dotnet new command, use the --use-minimal-apis or -minimal switch.

   - In Visual Studio Code, select Minimal.WebApi as the active OmniSharp project.

2. Review `Program.cs`, as shown in the following code:

```csharp
var builder = WebApplication.CreateBuilder(args);

// Add services to the container.
// Learn more about configuring Swagger/OpenAPI at
// https://aka.ms/aspnetcore/swashbuckle
builder.Services.AddEndpointsApiExplorer();
builder.Services.AddSwaggerGen();

var app = builder.Build();

// Configure the HTTP request pipeline.
if (app.Environment.IsDevelopment())
{
  app.UseSwagger();
  app.UseSwaggerUI();
}

app.UseHttpsRedirection();

var summaries = new[]
{
    "Freezing", "Bracing", "Chilly", "Cool", "Mild", "Warm", "Balmy",
    "Hot", "Sweltering", "Scorching"
};

app.MapGet("/weatherforecast", () =>
{
  var forecast = Enumerable.Range(1, 5).Select(index =>
    new WeatherForecast
    (
        DateTime.Now.AddDays(index),
        Random.Shared.Next(-20, 55),
        summaries[Random.Shared.Next(summaries.Length)]
    ))
    .ToArray();
  return forecast;
})
.WithName("GetWeatherForecast");

app.Run();

internal record WeatherForecast(DateTime Date, int TemperatureC, string?
Summary)
```

```
{
  public int TemperatureF => 32 + (int)(TemperatureC / 0.5556);
}
```

Note the following:

- A record named `WeatherForecast` is defined at the bottom of `Program.cs` with three data store properties: `Date`, `TemperatureC`, `Summary`, and one calculated property: `TemperatureF`.

- The call to `MapGet` registers a handler for incoming `GET` requests to the relative path `/weatherforecast`. It returns five `WeatherForecast` instances with random values for the `TemperatureC` and `Summary` properties.

- There is no `Controller` folder and no controller classes.

 Good Practice: For simple web services, avoid creating a controller class, and instead use Minimal APIs to put all the configuration and implementation in one place, `Program.cs`.

3. In the `Properties` folder, in `launchSettings.json`, configure the `https` profile to launch the browser using port `5003` in the URL and the relative API path, as shown highlighted in the following markup:

```
"profiles": {
  "http": {
    "commandName": "Project",
    "dotnetRunMessages": true,
    "launchBrowser": true,
    "launchUrl": "weatherforecast",
    "applicationUrl": "http://localhost:5000",
    "environmentVariables": {
      "ASPNETCORE_ENVIRONMENT": "Development"
    }
  },
  "https": {
    "commandName": "Project",
    "dotnetRunMessages": "true",
    "launchBrowser": true,
    "launchUrl": "weatherforecast",
    "applicationUrl": "https://localhost:5003",
    "environmentVariables": {
      "ASPNETCORE_ENVIRONMENT": "Development"
    }
```

Testing the minimal weather service

Before creating a client for the service, let's test that it returns forecasts as JSON:

1. Start the `Minimal.WebApi` web service project.
2. If you are not using Visual Studio 2022, start Chrome and navigate to `https://localhost:5003/weatherforecast`.
3. Note the Web API service should return a JSON document with five random weather forecast objects in an array.
4. Close Chrome and shut down the web server.

Adding weather forecasts to the Northwind website home page

Finally, let's add an HTTP client to the Northwind website so that it can call the weather service and show forecasts on the home page:

1. In the `Northwind.Mvc` project, in the `Models` folder, add a class file named `WeatherForecast.cs`, as shown in the following code:

    ```
    namespace Northwind.Mvc.Models;

    public record WeatherForecast(DateTime Date, int TemperatureC, string?
    Summary)
    {
      public int TemperatureF => 32 + (int)(TemperatureC / 0.5556);
    }
    ```

2. In `Program.cs`, before the call to `Build`, add a statement to configure an HTTP client to call the minimal service on port `5003`, as shown in the following code:

    ```
    builder.Services.AddHttpClient(name: "Minimal.WebApi",
      configureClient: options =>
      {
        options.BaseAddress = new Uri("https://localhost:5003/");
        options.DefaultRequestHeaders.Accept.Add(
          new MediaTypeWithQualityHeaderValue(
          "application/json", 1.0));
      });
    ```

3. In `HomeController.cs`, in the `Index` action method, before the call to `View`, add statements to get and use an HTTP client to call the weather service to get forecasts and store them in `ViewData`, as shown in the following code:

    ```
    try
    {
      HttpClient client = clientFactory.CreateClient(
        name: "Minimal.WebApi");
    ```

```
  HttpRequestMessage request = new(
    method: HttpMethod.Get, requestUri: "weatherforecast");

  HttpResponseMessage response = await client.SendAsync(request);

  ViewData["weather"] = await response.Content
    .ReadFromJsonAsync<WeatherForecast[]>();
}
catch (Exception ex)
{
  _logger.LogWarning(
    $"The Minimal.WebApi service is not responding. Exception:
    {ex.Message}");

  ViewData["weather"] = Enumerable.Empty<WeatherForecast>().ToArray();
}
```

4. In Views/Home, in Index.cshtml, in the top code block, get the weather forecasts from the ViewData dictionary, as shown highlighted in the following markup:

```
@{
  ViewData["Title"] = "Home Page";
  string currentItem = "";
  WeatherForecast[]? weather = ViewData["weather"] as WeatherForecast[];
}
```

5. In the first <div>, after rendering the current time, add markup to enumerate the weather forecasts unless there aren't any, and render them in a table, as shown in the following markup:

```
<p>
  <h4>Five-Day Weather Forecast</h4>
  @if ((weather is null) || (!weather.Any()))
  {
    <p>No weather forecasts found.</p>
  }
  else
  {
  <table class="table table-info">
    <tr>
      @foreach (WeatherForecast w in weather)
      {
        <td>@w.Date.ToString("ddd d MMM") will be @w.Summary</td>
      }
    </tr>
  </table>
  }
</p>
```

6. Start the `Minimal.WebApi` web service project.

7. Start the `Northwind.Mvc` website project.

8. Navigate to `https://localhost:5001/` and note the weather forecast, as shown in *Figure 15.17*:

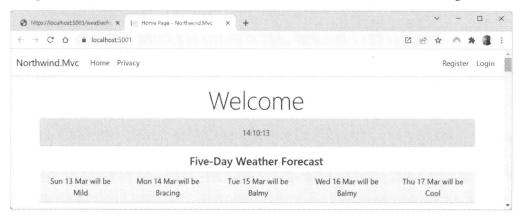

Figure 15.17: A five-day weather forecast on the home page of the Northwind website

9. View the command prompt or terminal for the MVC website and note the info messages that indicate a request was sent to the Minimal API web service `api/weather` endpoint in about 83 ms, as shown in the following output:

```
info: System.Net.Http.HttpClient.Minimal.WebApi.LogicalHandler[100]
      Start processing HTTP request GET https://localhost:5003/
weatherforecast
info: System.Net.Http.HttpClient.Minimal.WebApi.ClientHandler[100]
      Sending HTTP request GET https://localhost:5003/weatherforecast
info: System.Net.Http.HttpClient.Minimal.WebApi.ClientHandler[101]
      Received HTTP response headers after 76.8963ms - 200
info: System.Net.Http.HttpClient.Minimal.WebApi.LogicalHandler[101]
      End processing HTTP request after 82.9515ms - 200
```

10. Stop the `Minimal.WebApi` service, refresh the browser, and note that after a few seconds the MVC website home page appears without weather forecasts because the web service is not responding.

11. Close Chrome and shut down the web server.

Practicing and exploring

Test your knowledge and understanding by answering some questions, getting some hands-on practice, and exploring this chapter's topics with deeper research.

Exercise 15.1 — Test your knowledge

Answer the following questions:

1. Which class should you inherit from to create a controller class for an ASP.NET Core Web API service?

2. When configuring an HTTP client, how do you specify the format of data that you prefer in the response from the web service?

3. What must you do to specify which controller action method will be executed in response to an HTTP request?

4. What must you do to specify what responses should be expected when calling an action method?

5. List three methods that can be called to return responses with different status codes.

6. List four ways that you can test a web service.

7. Why should you not wrap your use of `HttpClient` in a `using` statement to dispose of it when you are finished even though it implements the `IDisposable` interface, and what should you use instead?

8. What are the benefits of HTTP/2 and HTTP/3 compared to HTTP/1.1?

9. How can you enable clients to detect if your web service is healthy with ASP.NET Core 2.2 and later?

10. What benefits does endpoint routing provide?

Exercise 15.2 – Practice creating and deleting customers with HttpClient

Extend the `Northwind.Mvc` website project to have pages where a visitor can fill in a form to create a new customer, or search for a customer and then delete them. The MVC controller should make calls to the Northwind web service to create and delete customers.

Exercise 15.3 – Explore topics

Use the links on the following GitHub repository to learn more detail about the topics covered in this chapter:

```
https://github.com/markjprice/cs11dotnet7/blob/main/book-links.md#chapter-15---
building-and-consuming-web-services
```

Summary

In this chapter, you learned:

- How to build an ASP.NET Core Web API service that can be called by any app on any platform that can make an HTTP request and process an HTTP response.
- How to test and document web service APIs with Swagger.
- How to consume services efficiently.
- How to build a basic HTTP API service using Minimal APIs.

In the next chapter, you will learn how to build user interfaces using Blazor, Microsoft's component technology that enables developers to build client-side SPAs for websites using C# instead of JavaScript, and PWAs or hybrid apps for desktop.

16

Building User Interfaces Using Blazor

This chapter is about using Blazor to build user interfaces. I will describe the different flavors of Blazor and their pros and cons.

You will learn how to build Blazor components that can execute their code on the web server or in the web browser. When hosted with Blazor Server, it uses SignalR to communicate needed updates to the user interface in the browser. When hosted with Blazor WebAssembly, the components execute their code in the client and must make HTTP calls to interact with the server.

In this chapter, we will cover the following topics:

- Understanding Blazor
- Comparing Blazor project templates
- Building components using Blazor Server
- Building components using Blazor WebAssembly
- Improving Blazor WebAssembly apps (online section)

Understanding Blazor

Blazor lets you build shared components and interactive web user interfaces using C# instead of JavaScript. In April 2019, Microsoft announced that Blazor "is no longer experimental and we are committing to ship it as a supported web UI framework, including support for running client side in the browser on WebAssembly." Blazor is supported on all modern browsers.

JavaScript and friends

Traditionally, any code that needs to execute in a web browser is written using the JavaScript programming language or a higher-level technology that **transpiles** (transforms or compiles) into JavaScript. This is because all browsers have supported JavaScript for about two decades, so it has become the lowest common denominator for implementing business logic on the client side.

JavaScript does have some issues, however. Although it has superficial similarities to C-style languages like C# and Java, it is actually very different once you dig beneath the surface. It is a dynamically typed pseudo-functional language that uses prototypes instead of class inheritance for object reuse. It might look human, but you will get a surprise when it's revealed to be a Skrull.

Wouldn't it be great if we could use the same language and libraries in a web browser as we do on the server side?

Even Blazor cannot replace JavaScript completely. For example, some parts of the browser are only accessible to JavaScript. Blazor provides an interop service so that your C# code can call JavaScript code and vice versa. You will see this in the *Interop with JavaScript* section, which is available online.

Silverlight — C# and .NET using a plugin

Microsoft made a previous attempt at achieving this goal with a technology named Silverlight. When Silverlight 2.0 was released in 2008, a C# and .NET developer could use their skills to build libraries and visual components that were executed in the web browser by the Silverlight plugin.

By 2011 and Silverlight 5.0, Apple's success with the iPhone and Steve Jobs' hatred of browser plugins like Flash eventually led to Microsoft abandoning Silverlight since, like Flash, Silverlight is banned from iPhones and iPads.

WebAssembly — a target for Blazor

A recent development in browsers has given Microsoft the opportunity to make another attempt. In 2017, the **WebAssembly Consensus** was completed, and all major browsers now support it: Chromium (Chrome, Edge, Opera, and Brave), Firefox, and WebKit (Safari). Although Blazor Server is supported on Internet Explorer 11, Blazor WebAssembly is not.

WebAssembly (Wasm) is a binary instruction format for a virtual machine that provides a way to run code written in multiple languages on the web at near-native speed. Wasm is designed as a portable target for the compilation of high-level languages like C#.

Blazor hosting models

Blazor is a single programming or app model with multiple hosting models:

- **Blazor Server** runs on the server side, like Razor Pages and ASP.NET Core MVC, so the C# code that you write has full access to all resources that your business logic might need without needing to supply credentials to authenticate. It then uses SignalR to communicate user interface updates to the client side. The server must keep a live SignalR connection to each client and track the current state of every client, so Blazor Server does not scale well if you need to support lots of clients. It first shipped as part of ASP.NET Core 3.0 in September 2019.
- **Blazor WebAssembly** runs on the client side, so the C# code that you write only has access to resources in the browser and it must make HTTP calls (that might require authentication) before it can access resources on the server.

It first shipped as an extension to ASP.NET Core 3.1 in May 2020 and was versioned 3.2 because it was a Current release and therefore not covered by ASP.NET Core 3.1's Long Term Support. The Blazor WebAssembly 3.2 version used the Mono runtime and Mono libraries; .NET 5 and later versions use the Mono runtime and the .NET libraries.

- **.NET MAUI Blazor App,** aka **Blazor Hybrid,** runs in the .NET process, renders its web UI to a web view control using a local interop channel, and is hosted in a .NET MAUI app. It is conceptually like Electron apps that use Node.js.

This multi-host model means that, with careful planning, a developer can write Blazor components once and then run them on the web server side, web client side, or within a desktop app.

Blazor components

It is important to understand that Blazor is used to create **user interface components**. Components define how to render the user interface and react to user events, and can be composed and nested, and compiled into a Razor class library for packaging and distribution.

For example, to provide a user interface for star ratings of products on a commerce site, you might create a component named `Rating.razor`, as shown in the following markup:

```
<div>
@for (int i = 0; i < Maximum; i++)
{
  if (i < Value)
  {
    <span class="oi oi-star-filled" />
  }
  else
  {
    <span class="oi oi-star-empty" />
  }
}
</div>

@code {
  [Parameter]
  public byte Maximum { get; set; }
  [Parameter]
  public byte Value { get; set; }
}
```

You could then use the component on a web page, as shown in the following markup:

```
<h1>Review</h1>
<Rating id="rating" Maximum="5" Value="3" />
<textarea id="comment" />
```

Instead of a single file with both markup and an @code block, the code can be stored in a separate code-behind file named `Rating.razor.cs`. The class in this file must be `partial` and have the same name as the component.

There are many built-in Blazor components, including ones to set elements like `<title>` in the `<head>` section of a web page, and plenty of third parties who will sell you components for common purposes.

In the future, Blazor might not be limited to only creating user interface components using web technologies. Microsoft has an experimental technology known as **Blazor Mobile Bindings** that allows developers to use Blazor to build mobile user interface components. Instead of using HTML and CSS to build a web user interface, it uses XAML and .NET MAUI to build a cross-platform graphical user interface.

What is the difference between Blazor and Razor?

You might wonder why Blazor components use `.razor` as their file extension. Razor is a template markup syntax that allows the mixing of HTML and C#. Older technologies that support Razor syntax use the `.cshtml` file extension to indicate the mix of C# and HTML.

Razor syntax is used for:

- ASP.NET Core MVC **views** and **partial views** that use the `.cshtml` file extension. The business logic is separated into a controller class that treats the view as a template to push the view model to, which then outputs it to a web page.

- **Razor Pages** that use the `.cshtml` file extension. The business logic can be embedded or separated into a file that uses the `.cshtml.cs` file extension. The output is a web page.

- **Blazor components** that use the `.razor` file extension. The output is not a web page, although layouts can be used to wrap a component so it outputs as a web page, and the @page directive can be used to assign a route that defines the URL path to retrieve the component as a page.

Comparing Blazor project templates

One way to understand the choice between the Blazor Server and Blazor WebAssembly hosting models is to review the differences in their default project templates.

> ASP.NET Core 7 introduces some "empty" project templates for Blazor. They are like the project templates that we will review in this chapter except without the demonstration components, **Counter** and **Fetch data** from the weather service, and without Bootstrap. They do still retain a basic home component, so they are not strictly empty. In Visual Studio 2022, the project templates are named **Blazor Server App Empty** and **Blazor WebAssembly App Empty**. At the command-line, they are named `blazorserver-empty` and `blazorwasm-empty`.

Reviewing the Blazor Server project template

Let us look at the default template for a Blazor Server project. Mostly you will see that it is the same as an ASP.NET Core Razor Pages template, with a few key additions:

1. Use your preferred code editor to open the PracticalApps solution/workspace and then add a new project, as defined in the following list:

   - Project template: **Blazor Server App**/blazorserver
   - Workspace/solution file and folder: PracticalApps
   - Project file and folder: Northwind.BlazorServer
   - Other Visual Studio options: **Authentication Type: None; Configure for HTTPS:** Selected; **Enable Docker:** Cleared

- In Visual Studio Code, select Northwind.BlazorServer as the active OmniSharp project.

2. Build the Northwind.BlazorServer project.

3. In Northwind.BlazorServer.csproj, note that it is identical to an ASP.NET Core project that uses the Web SDK and targets .NET 7.0.

4. In Program.cs, note it is almost identical to an ASP.NET Core project. Differences include the section that configures services, with its call to the AddServerSideBlazor method, as shown highlighted in the following code:

```
builder.Services.AddRazorPages();
builder.Services.AddServerSideBlazor();
builder.Services.AddSingleton<WeatherForecastService>();
```

5. Also note the section for configuring the HTTP pipeline, which adds the calls to the MapBlazorHub and MapFallbackToPage methods that configure the ASP.NET Core app to accept incoming SignalR connections for Blazor components, while other requests fall back to a Razor Page named _Host.cshtml, as shown highlighted in the following code:

```
app.UseRouting();

app.MapBlazorHub();
app.MapFallbackToPage("/_Host");

app.Run();
```

6. In the Pages folder, open _Host.cshtml and note that it sets a shared layout named _Layout and renders a Blazor component of type App that is prerendered on the server, as shown in the following markup:

```
@page "/"
@namespace Northwind.BlazorServer.Pages
@addTagHelper *, Microsoft.AspNetCore.Mvc.TagHelpers
@{
    Layout = "_Layout";
}

<component type="typeof(App)" render-mode="ServerPrerendered" />
```

7. In the Pages folder, open the shared layout file named _Layout.cshtml, as shown in the following markup:

```
@using Microsoft.AspNetCore.Components.Web
@namespace Northwind.BlazorServer.Pages
@addTagHelper *, Microsoft.AspNetCore.Mvc.TagHelpers

<!DOCTYPE html>
<html lang="en">
<head>
  <meta charset="utf-8" />
  <meta name="viewport"
        content="width=device-width, initial-scale=1.0" />
  <base href="~/" />
  <link rel="stylesheet" href="css/bootstrap/bootstrap.min.css" />
  <link href="css/site.css" rel="stylesheet" />
  <link href="Northwind.BlazorServer.styles.css" rel="stylesheet" />
  <component type="typeof(HeadOutlet)" render-mode="ServerPrerendered" />
</head>
<body>
  @RenderBody()

  <div id="blazor-error-ui">
    <environment include="Staging,Production">
      An error has occurred. This application may no longer respond until
      reloaded.
    </environment>
    <environment include="Development">
      An unhandled exception has occurred. See browser dev tools for
      details.
    </environment>
    <a href="" class="reload">Reload</a>
    <a class="dismiss">✕</a>
  </div>

  <script src="_framework/blazor.server.js"></script>
</body>
</html>
```

While reviewing the preceding markup, note the following:

- `<div id="blazor-error-ui">` for showing Blazor errors, which will appear as a yellow bar at the bottom of the web page when they occur.
- The script block for blazor.server.js manages the SignalR connection back to the server.

8. In the `Northwind.BlazorServer` folder, open `App.razor` and note that it defines a `Router` for all components found in the current assembly, as shown in the following code:

```
<Router AppAssembly="@typeof(App).Assembly">
  <Found Context="routeData">
    <RouteView RouteData="@routeData"
               DefaultLayout="@typeof(MainLayout)" />
    <FocusOnNavigate RouteData="@routeData" Selector="h1" />
  </Found>
  <NotFound>
    <PageTitle>Not found</PageTitle>
    <LayoutView Layout="@typeof(MainLayout)">
      <p>Sorry, there's nothing at this address.</p>
    </LayoutView>
  </NotFound>
</Router>
```

While reviewing the preceding markup, note the following:

- If a matching route is found, then `RouteView` is executed, which sets the default layout for the component to `MainLayout` and passes any route data parameters to the component.

- If a matching route is not found, then `LayoutView` is executed, which renders the internal markup (in this case, a simple paragraph element with a message telling the visitor there is nothing at this address) inside `MainLayout`.

9. In the `Shared` folder, open `MainLayout.razor` and note that it defines `<div>` for a sidebar containing a navigation menu that is implemented by the `NavMenu.razor` component file in this project, and HTML5 elements like `<main>` and `<article>` for the content, as shown in the following code:

```
@inherits LayoutComponentBase

<PageTitle>Northwind.BlazorServer</PageTitle>

<div class="page">
  <div class="sidebar">
    <NavMenu />
  </div>
  <main>
    <div class="top-row px-4">
      <a href="https://docs.microsoft.com/aspnet/"
         target="_blank">About</a>
    </div>

    <article class="content px-4">
      @Body
```

```
      </article>
    </main>
  </div>
```

10. In the Shared folder, open `MainLayout.razor.css` and note that it contains isolated CSS styles for the component. Due to the naming convention, styles defined in this file take priority over others defined elsewhere that might affect the component.

11. In the Shared folder, open `NavMenu.razor` and note that it has three menu items for **Home**, **Counter**, and **Fetch data**. These are created by using a Microsoft-provided Blazor component named `NavLink`, as shown in the following markup:

```
<div class="top-row ps-3 navbar navbar-dark">
  <div class="container-fluid">
    <a class="navbar-brand" href="">Northwind.BlazorServer</a>
    <button title="Navigation menu" class="navbar-toggler"
            @onclick="ToggleNavMenu">
      <span class="navbar-toggler-icon"></span>
    </button>
  </div>
</div>

<div class="@NavMenuCssClass" @onclick="ToggleNavMenu">
  <nav class="flex-column">
    <div class="nav-item px-3">
      <NavLink class="nav-link" href="" Match="NavLinkMatch.All">
        <span class="oi oi-home" aria-hidden="true"></span> Home
      </NavLink>
    </div>
    <div class="nav-item px-3">
      <NavLink class="nav-link" href="counter">
        <span class="oi oi-plus" aria-hidden="true"></span> Counter
      </NavLink>
    </div>
    <div class="nav-item px-3">
      <NavLink class="nav-link" href="fetchdata">
        <span class="oi oi-list-rich" aria-hidden="true"></span> Fetch
        data
      </NavLink>
    </div>
  </nav>
</div>

@code {
  private bool collapseNavMenu = true;

  private string? NavMenuCssClass => collapseNavMenu ? "collapse" : null;
```

```
    private void ToggleNavMenu()
    {
      collapseNavMenu = !collapseNavMenu;
    }
  }
```

12. In the Pages folder, open FetchData.razor and note that it defines a component that fetches weather forecasts from an injected dependency weather service and then renders them in a table, as shown in the following code:

```
@page "/fetchdata"

<PageTitle>Weather forecast</PageTitle>

@using Northwind.BlazorServer.Data
@inject WeatherForecastService ForecastService

<h1>Weather forecast</h1>

<p>This component demonstrates fetching data from a service.</p>

@if (forecasts == null)
{
  <p><em>Loading...</em></p>
}
else
{
  <table class="table">
    <thead>
      <tr>
        <th>Date</th>
        <th>Temp. (C)</th>
        <th>Temp. (F)</th>
        <th>Summary</th>
      </tr>
    </thead>
    <tbody>
    @foreach (var forecast in forecasts)
    {
      <tr>
        <td>@forecast.Date.ToShortDateString()</td>
        <td>@forecast.TemperatureC</td>
        <td>@forecast.TemperatureF</td>
        <td>@forecast.Summary</td>
      </tr>
    }
    </tbody>
```

```
      </table>
    }

    @code {
      private WeatherForecast[]? forecasts;

      protected override async Task OnInitializedAsync()
      {
        forecasts = await ForecastService.GetForecastAsync(DateTime.Now);
      }
    }
```

13. In the `Data` folder, open `WeatherForecastService.cs` and note that it is *not* a Web API controller class; it is just an ordinary class that returns random weather data, as shown in the following code:

```
namespace Northwind.BlazorServer.Data
{
  public class WeatherForecastService
  {
    private static readonly string[] Summaries = new[]
    {
      "Freezing", "Bracing", "Chilly", "Cool", "Mild", "Warm",
      "Balmy", "Hot", "Sweltering", "Scorching"
    };

    public Task<WeatherForecast[]> GetForecastAsync(DateTime startDate)
    {
      return Task.FromResult(Enumerable.Range(1, 5)
        .Select(index => new WeatherForecast
          {
            Date = startDate.AddDays(index),
            TemperatureC = Random.Shared.Next(-20, 55),
            Summary = Summaries[Random.Shared.Next(Summaries.Length)]
          }).ToArray());
    }
  }
}
```

CSS and JavaScript isolation

Blazor components often need to provide their own CSS to apply styling or JavaScript for activities that cannot be performed purely in C#, like access to browser APIs. To ensure this does not conflict with site-level CSS and JavaScript, Blazor supports CSS and JavaScript isolation. If you have a component named `Index.razor`, simply create a CSS file named `Index.razor.css`. The styles defined within this file will override any other styles in the project.

Blazor routing to page components

The Router component that we saw in the App.razor file enables routing to components. The markup for creating an instance of a component looks like an HTML tag where the name of the tag is the component type. Components can be embedded on a web page using an element, for example, <Rating Stars="5" />, or they can be routed to, like a Razor Page or MVC controller.

How to define a routable page component

To create a routable page component, add the @page directive to the top of a component's .razor file, as shown in the following markup:

```
@page "customers"
```

The preceding code is the equivalent of an MVC controller decorated with the [Route] attribute, as shown in the following code:

```
[Route("customers")]
public class CustomersController
{
```

The Router component scans the assembly specifically in its AppAssembly parameter for components decorated with the [Route] attribute and registers their URL paths.

Any single-page component can have multiple @page directives to register multiple routes.

At runtime, the page component is merged with any specific layout that you have specified, just like an MVC view or Razor Page would be. By default, the Blazor Server project template defines MainLayout. razor as the layout for page components.

 Good Practice: By convention, put routable page Blazor components in the Pages folder.

How to navigate Blazor routes

Microsoft provides a dependency service named NavigationManager that understands Blazor routing and the NavLink component. The NavigateTo method is used to go to the specified URL.

How to pass route parameters

Blazor routes can include case-insensitive named parameters, and your code can most easily access the passed values by binding the parameter to a property in the code block using the [Parameter] attribute, as shown in the following markup:

```
@page "/customers/{country}"

<div>Country parameter as the value: @Country</div>
```

```
@code {
  [Parameter]
  public string Country { get; set; }
}
```

The recommended way to handle a parameter that should have a default value when it is missing is to suffix the parameter with ? and use the null coalescing operator in the OnParametersSet method, as shown in the following markup:

```
@page "/customers/{country?}"

<div>Country parameter as the value: @Country</div>

@code {
  [Parameter]
  public string Country { get; set; }

  protected override void OnParametersSet()
  {
    // if the automatically set property is null
    // set its value to USA
    Country = Country ?? "USA";
  }
}
```

Understanding base component classes

The OnParametersSet method is defined by the base class that components inherit from by default named ComponentBase, as shown in the following code:

```
using Microsoft.AspNetCore.Components;

public abstract class ComponentBase : IComponent, IHandleAfterRender,
IHandleEvent
{
  // members not shown
}
```

ComponentBase has some useful methods that you can call and override, as shown in the following table:

Method(s)	Description
InvokeAsync	Call this method to execute a function on the associated renderer's synchronization context.
OnAfterRender, OnAfterRenderAsync	Override these methods to invoke code after each time the component has been rendered.
OnInitialized, OnInitializedAsync	Override these methods to invoke code after the component has received its initial parameters from its parent in the render tree.

OnParametersSet, OnParametersSetAsync	Override these methods to invoke code after the component has received parameters and the values have been assigned to properties.
ShouldRender	Override this method to indicate if the component should render.
StateHasChanged	Call this method to cause the component to re-render.

Blazor components can have shared layouts in a similar way to MVC views and Razor Pages. You would create a .razor component file and make it explicitly inherit from LayoutComponentBase, as shown in the following markup:

```
@inherits LayoutComponentBase

<div>
  ...
  @Body
  ...
</div>
```

The base class has a property named Body that you can render in the markup at the correct place within the layout.

You can set a default layout for components in the App.razor file and its Router component. To explicitly set a layout for a component, use the @layout directive, as shown in the following markup:

```
@page "/customers"

@layout AlternativeLayout

<div>
  ...
</div>
```

How to use the navigation link component with routes

In HTML, you use the <a> element to define navigation links, as shown in the following markup:

```
<a href="/customers">Customers</a>
```

In Blazor, use the <NavLink> component, as shown in the following markup:

```
<NavLink href="/customers">Customers</NavLink>
```

The NavLink component is better than an anchor element because it automatically sets its class to active if its href is a match on the current location URL. If your CSS uses a different class name, then you can set the class name in the NavLink.ActiveClass property.

By default, in the matching algorithm, the href is a path *prefix*, so if NavLink has an href of /customers, as shown in the preceding code example, then it would match all the following paths and set them all to have the active class style:

```
/customers
/customers/USA
/customers/Germany/Berlin
```

To ensure that the matching algorithm only performs matches on *all* of the text in the path, in other words, there is only a match when the whole complete text matches but not when just part of the path matches, then set the Match parameter to NavLinkMatch.All, as shown in the following code:

```
<NavLink href="/customers" Match="NavLinkMatch.All">Customers</NavLink>
```

If you set other attributes such as target, they are passed through to the underlying <a> element that is generated.

Running the Blazor Server project template

Now that we have reviewed the project template and the important parts that are specific to Blazor Server, we can start the website and review its behavior:

1. In the Properties folder, in launchSettings.json, modify the applicationUrl to use port 5004 for HTTP and port 5005 for HTTPS, as shown highlighted in the following markup:

    ```
    "profiles": {
      "http": {
        "commandName": "Project",
        "dotnetRunMessages": true,
        "launchBrowser": true,
        "applicationUrl": "http://localhost:5004",
        "environmentVariables": {
          "ASPNETCORE_ENVIRONMENT": "Development"
        }
      },
      "https": {
        "commandName": "Project",
        "dotnetRunMessages": true,
        "launchBrowser": true,
        "applicationUrl": "https://localhost:5005;http://localhost:5004",
        "environmentVariables": {
          "ASPNETCORE_ENVIRONMENT": "Development"
        }
      },
    ```

2. Select the https profile and start the website project.

3. Start Chrome and navigate to https://localhost:5005/.

4. In the left navigation menu, click **Fetch data**, as shown in *Figure 16.1*:

Figure 16.1: Fetching weather data into a Blazor Server app

5. In the browser address bar, change the route to /apples and note the missing message, as shown in *Figure 16.2*:

Figure 16.2: The missing component message

6. Close Chrome and shut down the web server.

Reviewing the Blazor WebAssembly project template

Now we will create a Blazor WebAssembly project. I will not show its code in the book if the code is the same as in a Blazor Server project:

1. Use your preferred code editor to open the PracticalApps solution/workspace and then add a new project, as defined in the following list:

   - Project template: **Blazor WebAssembly App**/blazorwasm
   - Project file and folder: Northwind.BlazorWasm
   - dotnet new switches: --pwa --hosted
   - Workspace/solution file and folder: PracticalApps
   - **Authentication Type: None**
   - **Configure for HTTPS:** Checked
   - **ASP.NET Core hosted:** Checked
   - **Progressive Web Application:** Checked

While reviewing the generated folders and files, note that *three* projects are generated, as described in the following list:

- `Northwind.BlazorWasm.Client` is a Blazor WebAssembly project stored in the `Northwind.BlazorWasm\Client` folder.

- `Northwind.BlazorWasm.Server` is an ASP.NET Core project website stored in the `Northwind.BlazorWasm\Server` folder. It hosts the weather service that has the same implementation for returning random weather forecasts as before, but it is implemented as a proper Web API controller class. The project file has project references to `Shared` and `Client`, and a package reference to support Blazor WebAssembly on the server side.

- `Northwind.BlazorWasm.Shared` is a class library stored in the `Northwind.BlazorWasm\ Shared` folder that contains models for the weather service.

The folder structure is simplified, using only the short names like `Client`, `Server`, and `Shared` rather than the full project names, as shown in *Figure 16.3*:

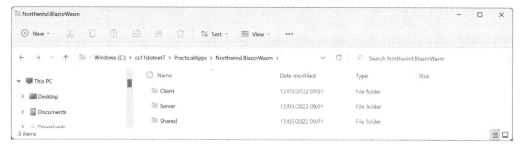

Figure 16.3: The folder structure for the Blazor WebAssembly project template

Deployment choices for Blazor WebAssembly apps

There are two main ways to deploy a Blazor WebAssembly app:

- You could deploy just the `Client` project by placing its published files in any static hosting web server. It could be configured to call the weather service that you created in *Chapter 15, Building and Consuming Web Services*.

- You could deploy the `Server` project, which references the `Client` app and hosts both the weather service and the Blazor WebAssembly app. The Blazor WebAssembly app is placed in the server website `wwwroot` folder along with any other static assets.

 More Information: You can read more about these choices at the following link: `https:// docs.microsoft.com/en-us/aspnet/core/blazor/host-and-deploy/webassembly`.

Differences between Blazor Server and Blazor WebAssembly projects

Now let us review the differences between a Blazor Server and a Blazor WebAssembly project:

1. In the `Client` folder, in `Northwind.BlazorWasm.Client.csproj`, note that it uses the Blazor WebAssembly SDK and references two WebAssembly packages and the `Shared` project, as well as the service worker required for PWA support, as shown in the following markup:

```
<Project Sdk="Microsoft.NET.Sdk.BlazorWebAssembly">

  <PropertyGroup>
    <TargetFramework>net7.0</TargetFramework>
    <Nullable>enable</Nullable>
    <ImplicitUsings>enable</ImplicitUsings>
    <ServiceWorkerAssetsManifest>service-worker-assets.js
      </ServiceWorkerAssetsManifest>
  </PropertyGroup>

  <ItemGroup>
    <PackageReference Include=
      "Microsoft.AspNetCore.Components.WebAssembly"
      Version="7.0.0" />
    <PackageReference Include=
      "Microsoft.AspNetCore.Components.WebAssembly.DevServer"
      Version="7.0.0" PrivateAssets="all" />
  </ItemGroup>

  <ItemGroup>
    <ProjectReference Include=
      "..\Shared\Northwind.BlazorWasm.Shared.csproj" />
  </ItemGroup>

  <ItemGroup>
    <ServiceWorker Include="wwwroot\service-worker.js"
      PublishedContent="wwwroot\service-worker.published.js" />
  </ItemGroup>

</Project>
```

2. In the `Northwind.BlazorWasm.Client` project (in Visual Studio 2022) or the `Client` folder (in Visual Studio Code), in `Program.cs`, note that the host builder is for `WebAssembly` instead of server-side ASP.NET Core and that it registers a dependency service for making HTTP requests, which is an extremely common requirement for Blazor WebAssembly apps, as shown in the following code:

```
using Microsoft.AspNetCore.Components.Web;
using Microsoft.AspNetCore.Components.WebAssembly.Hosting;
using Northwind.BlazorWasm.Client;

var builder = WebAssemblyHostBuilder.CreateDefault(args);
builder.RootComponents.Add<App>("#app");
```

```
builder.RootComponents.Add<HeadOutlet>("head::after");

builder.Services.AddScoped(sp => new HttpClient
  { BaseAddress = new Uri(builder.HostEnvironment.BaseAddress) });

await builder.Build().RunAsync();
```

3. In the `wwwroot` folder, in `index.html`, note the `manifest.json` and `service-worker.js` files supporting offline work, and the `blazor.webassembly.js` script that downloads all the NuGet packages for Blazor WebAssembly, as shown highlighted in the following markup:

```
<!DOCTYPE html>
<html>

<head>
  <meta charset="utf-8" />
  <meta name="viewport" content="width=device-width, initial-scale=1.0,
  maximum-scale=1.0, user-scalable=no" />
  <title>Northwind.BlazorWasm</title>
  <base href="/" />
  <link href="css/bootstrap/bootstrap.min.css" rel="stylesheet" />
  <link href="css/app.css" rel="stylesheet" />
  <link href="Northwind.BlazorWasm.Client.styles.css" rel="stylesheet" />
  <link href="manifest.json" rel="manifest" />
  <link rel="apple-touch-icon" sizes="512x512" href="icon-512.png" />
  <link rel="apple-touch-icon" sizes="192x192" href="icon-192.png" />
</head>

<body>
  <div id="app">Loading...</div>

  <div id="blazor-error-ui">
    An unhandled error has occurred.
    <a href="" class="reload">Reload</a>
    <a class="dismiss">✗</a>
  </div>
  <script src="_framework/blazor.webassembly.js"></script>
  <script>navigator.serviceWorker.register('service-worker.js');</script>
</body>

</html>
```

4. In the `Pages` folder, open `FetchData.razor` and note that the markup is like Blazor Server except for the injected dependency service for making HTTP requests, as shown highlighted in the following partial markup:

```
@page "/fetchdata"
@using Northwind.BlazorWasm.Shared
```

```
@inject HttpClient Http

<PageTitle>Weather forecast</PageTitle>

<h1>Weather forecast</h1>

...

@code {
  private WeatherForecast[]? forecasts;

  protected override async Task OnInitializedAsync()
  {
    forecasts = await
      Http.GetFromJsonAsync<WeatherForecast[]>("WeatherForecast");
  }
}
```

5. In the `Northwind.BlazorWasm.Server` project, in the `Properties` folder, in `launchSettings.json`, modify the `applicationUrl` to use port `5006` for HTTP and port `5007` for HTTPS, as shown highlighted in the following markup:

```
"profiles": {
  "http": {
    "commandName": "Project",
    "dotnetRunMessages": true,
    "launchBrowser": true,
    "applicationUrl": "http://localhost:5006",
    "environmentVariables": {
      "ASPNETCORE_ENVIRONMENT": "Development"
    }
  }
  "https": {
    "commandName": "Project",
    "dotnetRunMessages": true,
    "launchBrowser": true,
    "applicationUrl": "https://localhost:5007;http://localhost:5006",
    "environmentVariables": {
      "ASPNETCORE_ENVIRONMENT": "Development"
    }
  },
```

6. Start the `Northwind.BlazorWasm.Server` project using the `https` profile. Remember that this is an ASP.NET Core website that hosts the Blazor WebAssembly client app project.

7. Note that the app has the same functionality as before. The Blazor WebAssembly component code is executing inside the browser instead of on the server. The weather service is running on the web server. The Blazor WebAssembly app makes HTTP requests each time it wants weather forecasts.

8. Close Chrome and shut down the web server.

Similarities between Blazor Server and Blazor WebAssembly projects

The following `.razor` files are identical to those in a Blazor Server project:

- `App.razor`
- `Shared\MainLayout.razor`
- `Shared\NavMenu.razor`
- `Shared\SurveyPrompt.razor`
- `Pages\Counter.razor`
- `Pages\Index.razor`

Building components using Blazor Server

In this section, we will build a component to list, create, and edit customers in the Northwind database.

We will build it over several steps:

1. Make a Blazor Server component that renders the name of a country set as a parameter.
2. Make it work as a routable page as well as a component.
3. Implement the functionality to perform CRUD operations on customers in a database.
4. Refactor the component to work with both Blazor Server and Blazor WebAssembly.

Defining and testing a simple Blazor Server component

We will add the new component to the existing Blazor Server project:

1. In the `Northwind.BlazorServer` project (*not* the `Northwind.BlazorWasm.Server` project), in the `Pages` folder, add a new file named `Customers.razor`. In Visual Studio, the project item template is named **Razor Component**.

     Good Practice: Component filenames must start with an uppercase letter, or you will have compile errors!

2. Add statements to output a heading for the `Customers` component and define a code block that defines a property to store the name of a country, as shown highlighted in the following markup:

    ```
    <h3>Customers @(string.IsNullOrWhiteSpace(Country)? "Worldwide" : "in " +
    Country)</h3>

    @code {
        [Parameter]
        public string? Country { get; set; }
    }
    ```

3. In the Pages folder, in Index.razor, add statements to the bottom of the file to instantiate the Customers component twice, once setting Germany as the Country parameter, and once without setting the country, as shown in the following markup:

```
<Customers Country="Germany" />
<Customers />
```

4. Start the Northwind.BlazorServer project.

5. Start Chrome, navigate to https://localhost:5005/, and note the Customers components, as shown in *Figure 16.4*:

Figure 16.4: The Customers component with the Country parameter set to Germany, and not set

6. Close Chrome and shut down the web server.

Making the component a routable page component

It is simple to turn this component into a routable page component with a route parameter for the country:

1. In the Pages folder, in the Customers.razor component, add a statement at the top of the file to register /customers as its route with an optional country route parameter, as shown in the following markup:

```
@page "/customers/{country?}"
```

2. In the Shared folder, in NavMenu.razor, at the bottom of the existing list item elements, add two list item elements for our routable page component to show customers worldwide and in Germany that both use an icon of people, as shown in the following markup:

```
<div class="nav-item px-3">
  <NavLink class="nav-link" href="customers" Match="NavLinkMatch.All">
    <span class="oi oi-people" aria-hidden="true"></span>
    Customers Worldwide
  </NavLink>
</div>
<div class="nav-item px-3">
  <NavLink class="nav-link" href="customers/Germany">
    <span class="oi oi-people" aria-hidden="true"></span>
```

```
    Customers in Germany
  </NavLink>
</div>
```

 We used an icon of people for the customers menu item. You can see the other available icons at the following link: https://iconify.design/icon-sets/oi/.

3. Start the Northwind.BlazorServer project.

4. Start Chrome and navigate to https://localhost:5005/.

5. In the left navigation menu, click **Customers in Germany**. Note that the country name is correctly passed to the page component and that the component uses the same shared layout as the other page components, like Index.razor. Also note the URL: https://localhost:5005/customers/Germany.

6. Close Chrome and shut down the web server.

Getting entities into a component

Now that you have seen the minimum implementation of a component, we can add some useful functionality to it. In this case, we will use the Northwind database context to fetch customers from the database:

1. In Northwind.BlazorServer.csproj, add a reference to the Northwind database context project for either SQL Server or SQLite, as shown in the following markup:

    ```
    <ItemGroup>
      <!-- change Sqlite to SqlServer if you prefer -->
      <ProjectReference Include="..\Northwind.Common.DataContext.Sqlite
      \Northwind.Common.DataContext.Sqlite.csproj" />
    </ItemGroup>
    ```

2. Build the Northwind.BlazorServer project.

3. In Program.cs, import the namespace for working with the Northwind database context extension method, as shown in the following code:

    ```
    using Packt.Shared; // AddNorthwindContext extension method
    ```

4. In Program.cs, before the call to Build, add a statement to register the Northwind database context in the dependency services collection, as shown in the following code:

    ```
    builder.Services.AddNorthwindContext();
    ```

5. In the project folder, in _Imports.razor, import the namespace for working with the Northwind entities so that Blazor components that we build do not need to import the namespaces individually, as shown in the following markup:

    ```
    @using Packt.Shared  @* Northwind entities *@
    ```

The `_Imports.razor` file only applies to `.razor` files. If you use code-behind `.cs` files to implement component code, then they must have namespaces imported separately or use global usings to implicitly import the namespaces.

6. In the `Pages` folder, in `Customers.razor`, add statements to inject the Northwind database context and then use it to output a table of all customers, as shown in the following code:

```
@using Microsoft.EntityFrameworkCore  @* ToListAsync extension method *@
@page "/customers/{country?}"
@inject NorthwindContext db

<h3>Customers @(string.IsNullOrWhiteSpace(Country)
    ? "Worldwide" : "in " + Country)</h3>

@if (customers is null)
{
<p><em>Loading...</em></p>
}
else
{
<table class="table">
  <thead>
    <tr>
      <th>Id</th>
      <th>Company Name</th>
      <th>Address</th>
      <th>Phone</th>
      <th></th>
    </tr>
  </thead>
  <tbody>
  @foreach (Customer c in customers)
  {
    <tr>
      <td>@c.CustomerId</td>
      <td>@c.CompanyName</td>
      <td>
        @c.Address<br/>
        @c.City<br/>
        @c.PostalCode<br/>
        @c.Country
      </td>
      <td>@c.Phone</td>
      <td>
        <a class="btn btn-info" href="editcustomer/@c.CustomerId">
```

```
                <i class="oi oi-pencil"></i></a>
           <a class="btn btn-danger" href="deletecustomer/@c.CustomerId">
               <i class="oi oi-trash"></i></a>
        </td>
      </tr>
   }
   </tbody>
</table>
}

@code {
  [Parameter]
  public string? Country { get; set; }

  private IEnumerable<Customer>? customers;

  protected override async Task OnParametersSetAsync()
  {
    if (string.IsNullOrWhiteSpace(Country))
    {
      customers = await db.Customers.ToListAsync();
    }
    else
    {
      customers = await db.Customers.Where(c => c.Country ==
      Country).ToListAsync();
    }
  }
}
```

7. Start the `Northwind.BlazorServer` project.

8. Start Chrome and navigate to `https://localhost:5005/`.

9. In the left navigation menu, click **Customers in Germany**, and note that the table of customers loads from the database and renders in the web page, as shown in *Figure 16.5*:

Figure 16.5: The list of customers in Germany

10. In the browser address bar, change Germany to UK, and note that the table of customers is filtered to only show UK customers.

11. In the left navigation menu, click **Customers Worldwide,** and note that the table of customers is unfiltered by country.

12. In the left navigation menu, click **Home,** and note that the customers component also works correctly when used as an embedded component on a page.

13. Click any of the edit or delete buttons and note that they return a message saying **Sorry, there's nothing at this address** because we have not yet implemented that functionality, and note the link, for example, to edit a customer identified by its five-character Id: https://localhost:5005/editcustomer/ALFKI.

14. Close Chrome and shut down the web server.

Abstracting a service for a Blazor component

Currently, the Blazor component directly calls the Northwind database context to fetch the customers. This works fine in Blazor Server since the component executes on the server. But this component would not work when hosted in Blazor WebAssembly.

We will now create a local dependency service to enable better reuse of the components:

1. In the Northwind.BlazorServer project, in the Data folder, add a new file named INorthwindService.cs. The Visual Studio project item template is named **Interface.**

2. In `INorthwindService.cs`, define a contract for a local service that abstracts CRUD operations, as shown in the following code:

```
namespace Packt.Shared;

public interface INorthwindService
{
  Task<List<Customer>> GetCustomersAsync();
  Task<List<Customer>> GetCustomersAsync(string country);
  Task<Customer?> GetCustomerAsync(string id);
  Task<Customer> CreateCustomerAsync(Customer c);
  Task<Customer> UpdateCustomerAsync(Customer c);
  Task DeleteCustomerAsync(string id);
}
```

3. In the `Data` folder, add a new file named `NorthwindService.cs` and modify its contents to implement the `INorthwindService` interface by using the Northwind database context, as shown in the following code:

```
using Microsoft.EntityFrameworkCore;

namespace Packt.Shared;

public class NorthwindService : INorthwindService
{
  private readonly NorthwindContext db;

  public NorthwindService(NorthwindContext db)
  {
    this.db = db;
  }

  public Task<List<Customer>> GetCustomersAsync()
  {
    return db.Customers.ToListAsync();
  }

  public Task<List<Customer>> GetCustomersAsync(string country)
  {
    return db.Customers.Where(c => c.Country == country).ToListAsync();
  }

  public Task<Customer?> GetCustomerAsync(string id)
  {
    return db.Customers.FirstOrDefaultAsync
      (c => c.CustomerId == id);
  }
```

```
public Task<Customer> CreateCustomerAsync(Customer c)
{
  db.Customers.Add(c);
  db.SaveChangesAsync();
  return Task.FromResult(c);
}

public Task<Customer> UpdateCustomerAsync(Customer c)
{
  db.Entry(c).State = EntityState.Modified;
  db.SaveChangesAsync();
  return Task.FromResult(c);
}

public Task DeleteCustomerAsync(string id)
{
  Customer? customer = db.Customers.FirstOrDefaultAsync
    (c => c.CustomerId == id).Result;

  if (customer == null)
  {
    return Task.CompletedTask;
  }
  else
  {
    db.Customers.Remove(customer);
    return db.SaveChangesAsync();
  }
}
}
}
```

4. In `Program.cs`, before the call to `Build`, add a statement to register `NorthwindService` as a transient service that implements the `INorthwindService` interface, as shown in the following code:

```
builder.Services.AddTransient<INorthwindService, NorthwindService>();
```

 A transient service is one that creates a new instance for each request. You can read more about the different lifetimes for services at the following link: https://docs.microsoft.com/en-us/dotnet/core/extensions/dependency-injection#service-lifetimes.

5. In the `Pages` folder, in `Customers.razor`, replace the directive to inject the Northwind database context with a directive to inject the registered Northwind service, as shown in the following code:

```
@inject INorthwindService service
```

6. In `Customers.razor`, modify the `OnParametersSetAsync` method to call the service instead of the Northwind database context, as shown highlighted in the following code:

```
protected override async Task OnParametersSetAsync()
{
  if (string.IsNullOrWhiteSpace(Country))
  {
    customers = await service.GetCustomersAsync();
  }
  else
  {
    customers = await service.GetCustomersAsync(Country);
  }
}
```

7. Start the `Northwind.BlazorServer` project and confirm that it retains the same functionality as before.

8. Close Chrome and shut down the web server.

So far, the component provides only a read-only table of customers. Now, we will extend it with full CRUD operations.

Defining forms using the EditForm component

Microsoft provides ready-made components for building forms. We will use them to provide create, edit, and delete functionality for customers.

Microsoft provides the `EditForm` component and several form elements such as `InputText` to make it easier to use forms with Blazor.

`EditForm` can have a model set to bind it to an object with properties and event handlers for custom validation, as well as recognize standard Microsoft validation attributes on the model class, as shown in the following code:

```
<EditForm Model="@customer" OnSubmit="ExtraValidation">
  <DataAnnotationsValidator />
  <ValidationSummary />
  <InputText id="name" @bind-Value="customer.CompanyName" />
  <button type="submit">Submit</button>
</EditForm>

@code {
  private Customer customer = new();

  private void ExtraValidation()
  {
    // perform any extra validation
  }
}
```

As an alternative to a `ValidationSummary` component, you can use the `ValidationMessage` component to show a message next to an individual form element.

Building a shared customer detail component

Next, we will create a shared component to show the details of a customer. This will only be a component, never a page:

1. In the `Northwind.BlazorServer` project, in the Shared folder, create a new file named `CustomerDetail.razor`. (The Visual Studio 2022 project item template is named **Razor Component**.)

2. Modify its contents to define a form to edit the properties of a customer, as shown in the following code:

```
<EditForm Model="@Customer" OnValidSubmit="@OnValidSubmit">
  <DataAnnotationsValidator />
  <div class="form-group">
    <div>
      <label>Customer Id</label>
      <div>
        <InputText @bind-Value="@Customer.CustomerId" />
        <ValidationMessage For="@(() => Customer.CustomerId)" />
      </div>
    </div>
  </div>
  <div class="form-group ">
    <div>
      <label>Company Name</label>
      <div>
        <InputText @bind-Value="@Customer.CompanyName" />
        <ValidationMessage For="@(() => Customer.CompanyName)" />
      </div>
    </div>
  </div>
  <div class="form-group ">
    <div>
      <label>Address</label>
      <div>
        <InputText @bind-Value="@Customer.Address" />
        <ValidationMessage For="@(() => Customer.Address)" />
      </div>
    </div>
  </div>
  <div class="form-group ">
    <div>
      <label>Country</label>
      <div>
```

```
            <InputText @bind-Value="@Customer.Country" />
            <ValidationMessage For="@(() => Customer.Country)" />
        </div>
      </div>
    </div>
    <button type="submit" class="btn btn-@ButtonStyle">
      @ButtonText
    </button>
</EditForm>

@code {
    [Parameter]
    public Customer Customer { get; set; } = null!;

    [Parameter]
    public string ButtonText { get; set; } = "Save Changes";

    [Parameter]
    public string ButtonStyle { get; set; } = "info";

    [Parameter]
    public EventCallback OnValidSubmit { get; set; }
}
```

Building customer create, edit, and delete components

Now we can create three routable page components that use the shared component:

1. In the `Northwind.BlazorServer` project, in the Pages folder, create a new file named `CreateCustomer.razor`.

2. In `CreateCustomer.razor`, modify its contents to use the customer detail component to create a new customer, as shown in the following code:

```
@page "/createcustomer"
@inject INorthwindService service
@inject NavigationManager navigation

<h3>Create Customer</h3>

<CustomerDetail ButtonText="Create Customer"
                Customer="@customer"
                OnValidSubmit="@Create" />

@code {
    private Customer customer = new();

    private async Task Create()
```

```
  {
    await service.CreateCustomerAsync(customer);
    navigation.NavigateTo("customers");
  }
}
```

3. In the Pages folder, in Customers.razor, after the <h3> element, add a <div> element with a button to navigate to the create customer page component, as shown in the following markup:

```
<div class="form-group">
  <a class="btn btn-info" href="createcustomer">
  <i class="oi oi-plus"></i> Create New</a>
</div>
```

4. In the Pages folder, create a new file named EditCustomer.razor and modify its contents to use the customer detail component to edit and save changes to an existing customer, as shown in the following code:

```
@page "/editcustomer/{customerid}"
@inject INorthwindService service
@inject NavigationManager navigation

<h3>Edit Customer</h3>

<CustomerDetail ButtonText="Update"
                Customer="@customer"
                OnValidSubmit="@Update" />

@code {
  [Parameter]
  public string CustomerId { get; set; } = null!;

  private Customer? customer = new();

  protected async override Task OnParametersSetAsync()
  {
    customer = await service.GetCustomerAsync(CustomerId);
  }

  private async Task Update()
  {
    if (customer is not null)
    {
      await service.UpdateCustomerAsync(customer);
    }
  }
}
```

5. In the Pages folder, create a new file named `DeleteCustomer.razor` and modify its contents to use the customer detail component to show the customer that is about to be deleted, as shown in the following code:

```razor
@page "/deletecustomer/{customerid}"
@inject INorthwindService service
@inject NavigationManager navigation

<h3>Delete Customer</h3>

<div class="alert alert-danger">Warning! This action cannot be undone!
</div>

<CustomerDetail ButtonText="Delete Customer"
                ButtonStyle="danger"
                Customer="@customer"
                OnValidSubmit="@Delete" />

@code {
  [Parameter]
  public string CustomerId { get; set; } = null!;

  private Customer? customer = new();

  protected async override Task OnParametersSetAsync()
  {
    customer = await service.GetCustomerAsync(CustomerId);
  }

  private async Task Delete()
  {
    if (customer is not null)
    {
      await service.DeleteCustomerAsync(CustomerId);
    }

    navigation.NavigateTo("customers");
  }
}
```

Testing the customer components

Now we can test the customer components and how to use them to create, edit, and delete customers:

1. Start the `Northwind.BlazorServer` project.

2. Start Chrome and navigate to `https://localhost:5005/`.

3. Navigate to **Customers Worldwide** and click the **+ Create New** button.

4. Enter an invalid **Customer Id** like `ABCDEF`, leave the textbox, and note the validation message, as shown in *Figure 16.6*:

Figure 16.6: Creating a new customer and entering an invalid customer ID

5. Change the **Customer Id** to `ABCDE`, enter values for the other textboxes like `Alpha Corp`, `Main Street`, and `USA`, and then click the **Create Customer** button.

6. When the list of customers appears, scroll down to the bottom of the page to see the new customer.

7. On the **ABCDE** customer row, click the **Edit** icon button, change the address to something like `Upper Avenue`, click the **Update** button, and note that the customer record has been updated.

8. On the **ABCDE** customer row, click the **Delete** icon button, note the warning, click the **Delete Customer** button, and note that the customer record has been deleted.

9. Close Chrome and shut down the web server.

Building components using Blazor WebAssembly

Now we will reuse the same functionality in the Blazor WebAssembly project so that you can clearly see the key differences.

Since we abstracted the local dependency service in the `INorthwindService` interface, we will be able to reuse all the components and that interface, as well as the entity model classes. The only part that will need to be rewritten is the implementation of the `NorthwindService` class.

Instead of directly calling the `NorthwindContext` class, it will call a customer Web API controller on the server side, as shown in *Figure 16.7*:

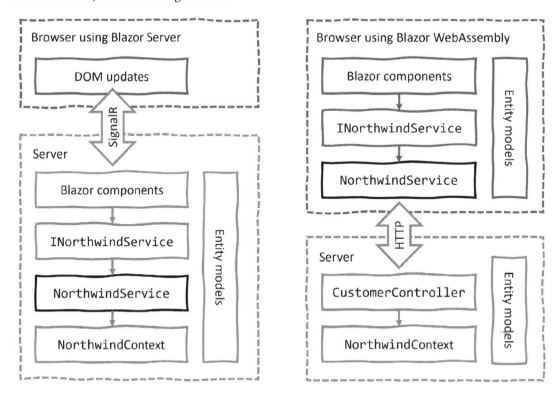

Figure 16.7: Comparing implementations using Blazor Server and Blazor WebAssembly

Configuring the server for Blazor WebAssembly

First, we need a web service that the client app can call to get and manage customers. If you completed *Chapter 15, Building and Consuming Web Services*, then you have a customer service in the `Northwind.WebApi` service project that you could use. However, to keep this chapter more self-contained, let's build a customer Web API controller in the `Northwind.BlazorWasm.Server` project:

 Warning! Unlike previous projects, relative path references for shared projects like the entity models and the database are two levels up, for example, `"..\.."`, because we have an additional layer of folders for `Server`, `Client`, and `Shared`.

1. In the `Server` project/folder, open `Northwind.BlazorWasm.Server.csproj` and add statements to reference the Northwind database context project for either SQL Server or SQLite, as shown in the following markup:

    ```
    <ItemGroup>
      <!-- change Sqlite to SqlServer if you prefer -->
    ```

```
    <ProjectReference Include="..\..\Northwind.Common.DataContext.Sqlite
    \Northwind.Common.DataContext.Sqlite.csproj" />
  </ItemGroup>
```

2. Build the `Northwind.BlazorWasm.Server` project.

3. In the `Server` project/folder, in `Program.cs`, add a statement to import the namespace for working with the Northwind database context extension method, as shown in the following code:

```
using Packt.Shared; // AddNorthwindContext extension method
```

4. In `Program.cs`, before the call to `Build`, add a statement to register the Northwind database context for either SQL Server or SQLite, as shown in the following code:

```
// if using SQL Server
builder.Services.AddNorthwindContext();

// if using SQLite
builder.Services.AddNorthwindContext(relativePath: Path.Combine("..",
".."));
```

5. In the `Server` project, in the `Controllers` folder, create a file named `CustomersController.cs` and add statements to define a Web API controller class with similar CRUD methods as before, as shown in the following code:

```
using Microsoft.AspNetCore.Mvc; // [ApiController], [Route]
using Microsoft.EntityFrameworkCore; // ToListAsync, FirstOrDefaultAsync
using Packt.Shared; // NorthwindContext, Customer

namespace Northwind.BlazorWasm.Server.Controllers;

[ApiController]
[Route("api/[controller]")]
public class CustomersController : ControllerBase
{
  private readonly NorthwindContext db;

  public CustomersController(NorthwindContext db)
  {
    this.db = db;
  }

  [HttpGet]
  public async Task<List<Customer>> GetCustomersAsync()
  {
    return await db.Customers.ToListAsync();
  }

  [HttpGet("in/{country}")] // different path to disambiguate
```

```csharp
public async Task<List<Customer>> GetCustomersAsync(string country)
{
  return await db.Customers
    .Where(c => c.Country == country).ToListAsync();
}

[HttpGet("{id}")]
public async Task<Customer?> GetCustomerAsync(string id)
{
  return await db.Customers
    .FirstOrDefaultAsync(c => c.CustomerId == id);
}

[HttpPost]
public async Task<Customer?> CreateCustomerAsync
  (Customer customerToAdd)
{
  Customer? existing = await db.Customers.FirstOrDefaultAsync
    (c => c.CustomerId == customerToAdd.CustomerId);

  if (existing == null)
  {
    db.Customers.Add(customerToAdd);

    int affected = await db.SaveChangesAsync();

    if (affected == 1)
    {
      return customerToAdd;
    }
  }
  return existing;
}

[HttpPut]
public async Task<Customer?> UpdateCustomerAsync(Customer c)
{
  db.Entry(c).State = EntityState.Modified;

  int affected = await db.SaveChangesAsync();

  if (affected == 1)
  {
    return c;
  }
  return null;
```

```
    }

    [HttpDelete("{id}")]
    public async Task<int> DeleteCustomerAsync(string id)
    {
      Customer? c = await db.Customers.FirstOrDefaultAsync
        (c => c.CustomerId == id);

      if (c != null)
      {
        db.Customers.Remove(c);
        int affected = await db.SaveChangesAsync();
        return affected;
      }
      return 0;
    }
  }
}
```

Configuring the client for Blazor WebAssembly

Now, we can reuse the components from the Blazor Server project. Since the components will be identical, we can copy them and only need to make changes to the local implementation of the abstracted Northwind service:

1. In the Client project, in Northwind.BlazorWasm.Client.csproj, add statements to reference the Northwind entity models library project (not the database context project) for either SQL Server or SQLite, as shown in the following markup:

    ```
    <ItemGroup>
      <!-- change Sqlite to SqlServer if you prefer -->
      <ProjectReference Include="..\..\Northwind.Common.EntityModels.Sqlite\
      Northwind.Common.EntityModels.Sqlite.csproj" />
    </ItemGroup>
    ```

2. Build the Northwind.BlazorWasm.Client project.

3. In the Client project, in _Imports.razor, import the Packt.Shared namespace to make the Northwind entity model types like Customer and Order available in all Blazor components, as shown in the following code:

    ```
    @using Packt.Shared @* Customer, Order, and so on *@
    ```

4. In the Client project, in the Shared folder, in NavMenu.razor, add a NavLink element for customers worldwide and in France, as shown in the following markup:

    ```
    <div class="nav-item px-3">
      <NavLink class="nav-link" href="customers" Match="NavLinkMatch.All">
        <span class="oi oi-people" aria-hidden="true"></span>
        Customers Worldwide
    ```

```
      </NavLink>
    </div>
    <div class="nav-item px-3">
      <NavLink class="nav-link" href="customers/France">
        <span class="oi oi-people" aria-hidden="true"></span>
        Customers in France
      </NavLink>
    </div>
```

5. Copy the `CustomerDetail.razor` component from the `Northwind.BlazorServer` project's Shared folder to the `Northwind.BlazorWasm` Client project's Shared folder.

6. Copy the following routable page components from the `Northwind.BlazorServer` project's Pages folder to the `Northwind.BlazorWasm` Client project's Pages folder:

   - `CreateCustomer.razor`

   - `Customers.razor`

   - `DeleteCustomer.razor`

   - `EditCustomer.razor`

7. In the Client project, create a Data folder.

8. Copy the `INorthwindService.cs` file from the `Northwind.BlazorServer` project's Data folder into the Client project's Data folder.

9. In the Data folder, add a new file named `NorthwindService.cs`, and modify its contents to implement the `INorthwindService` interface by using an `HttpClient` to call the customers Web API service, as shown in the following code:

```csharp
using System.Net.Http.Json; // GetFromJsonAsync, ReadFromJsonAsync
using Packt.Shared; // Customer

namespace Northwind.BlazorWasm.Client.Data;

public class NorthwindService : INorthwindService
{
  private readonly HttpClient http;

  public NorthwindService(HttpClient http)
  {
    this.http = http;
  }

  public Task<List<Customer>> GetCustomersAsync()
  {
    return http.GetFromJsonAsync
      <List<Customer>>("api/customers")!;
  }
```

```
    public Task<List<Customer>> GetCustomersAsync(string country)
    {
      return http.GetFromJsonAsync
        <List<Customer>>($"api/customers/in/{country}")!;
    }

    public Task<Customer?> GetCustomerAsync(string id)
    {
      return http.GetFromJsonAsync
        <Customer>($"api/customers/{id}");
    }

    public async Task<Customer>
      CreateCustomerAsync (Customer c)
    {
      HttpResponseMessage response = await
        http.PostAsJsonAsync("api/customers", c);

      return (await response.Content
        .ReadFromJsonAsync<Customer>())!;
    }

    public async Task<Customer> UpdateCustomerAsync(Customer c)
    {
      HttpResponseMessage response = await
        http.PutAsJsonAsync("api/customers", c);

      return (await response.Content
        .ReadFromJsonAsync<Customer>())!;
    }

    public async Task DeleteCustomerAsync(string id)
    {
      HttpResponseMessage response = await
        http.DeleteAsync($"api/customers/{id}");
    }
}
```

10. In `Program.cs`, import the `Packt.Shared` and `Northwind.BlazorWasm.Client.Data` namespaces.

11. In `Program.cs`, before the call to `Build`, add a statement to register the Northwind dependency service, as shown in the following code:

```
builder.Services.AddTransient<INorthwindService, NorthwindService>();
```

Testing the Blazor WebAssembly components and service

Now we can start the Blazor WebAssembly server hosting project to test if the components work with the abstracted Northwind service that calls the customers Web API service:

1. In the `Server` project/folder, start the `Northwind.BlazorWasm.Server` website project.

2. Start Chrome, show **Developer Tools,** and select the **Network** tab.

3. Navigate to `https://localhost:5007/`.

4. Select the **Console** tab and note that Blazor WebAssembly has loaded .NET assemblies into the browser cache and that they take about 10.65 MB of space, as shown in *Figure 16.8*:

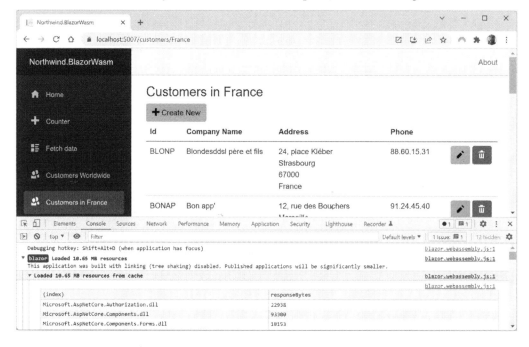

Figure 16.8: Blazor WebAssembly loading .NET assemblies into the browser cache

5. Select the **Network** tab.

6. In the left navigation menu, click **Customers Worldwide** and note the HTTP `GET` request `customers` with the JSON response containing all customers, as shown in *Figure 16.9*:

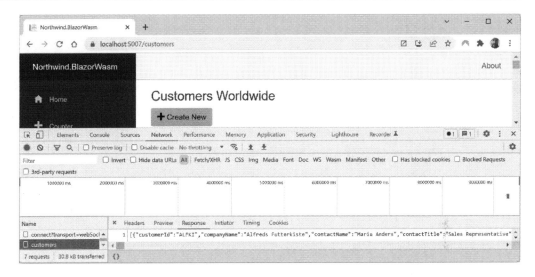

Figure 16.9: The HTTP GET request with the JSON response containing all customers

7. Click the **+ Create New** button, complete the form and click **Add Customer** to add a new customer as before, and note the HTTP POST request made, as shown in *Figure 16.10*:

Figure 16.10: The HTTP POST request for creating a new customer

8. Repeat the steps as before to edit and then delete the newly created customer, and note the requests in the **Network** list.

9. Close Chrome and shut down the web server.

Improving Blazor WebAssembly apps

This is a bonus section for the chapter that is available online at https://github.com/markjprice/
cs11dotnet7/blob/main/docs/bonus/improving-wasm-apps.md

Practicing and exploring

Test your knowledge and understanding by answering some questions, getting some hands-on practice,
and exploring this chapter's topics with deeper research.

Exercise 16.1 – Test your knowledge

Answer the following questions:

1. What are the two primary hosting models for Blazor, and how are they different?
2. In a Blazor Server website project, compared to an ASP.NET Core MVC website project, what extra configuration is required?
3. One of the benefits of Blazor is being able to implement client-side components using C# and .NET instead of JavaScript. Does a Blazor component need any JavaScript?
4. In a Blazor project, what does the App.razor file do?
5. What is the main benefit of using the <NavLink> component?
6. How can you pass a value into a component?
7. What is the main benefit of using the <EditForm> component?
8. How can you execute some statements when parameters are set?
9. How can you execute some statements when a component appears?
10. What are two key differences during initialization between a Blazor Server and Blazor Web-Assembly project?

Exercise 16.2 – Practice by creating a times table component

In the Northwind.BlazorServer project, create a routable page component that renders a times table based on a parameter named Number and then test your component in two ways.

First, by adding an instance of your component to the Index.razor file, as shown in the following markup:

```
<timestable Number="6" />
```

Second, by entering a path in the browser address bar, as shown in the following link:

https://localhost:5005/timestable/6

Exercise 16.3 – Practice by creating a country navigation item

In the Blazor Server project, in the shared NavMenu component, call the customer's web service to get the list of country names and loop through them, creating a menu item for each country.

For example:

1. In the `Northwind.BlazorServer` project, in `INorthwindService.cs`, add the following code:

    ```
    List<string?> GetCountries();
    ```

2. In `NorthwindService.cs`, add the following code:

    ```
    public List<string?> GetCountries()
    {
      return db.Customers.Select(c => c.Country)
        .Distinct().OrderBy(country => country).ToList();
    }
    ```

3. In `NavMenu.razor`, add the following markup:

    ```
    @inject INorthwindService northwind

    ...

    @foreach(string? country in northwind.GetCountries())
    {
        string countryLink = "customers/" + country;

        <div class="nav-item px-3">
            <NavLink class="nav-link" href="@countryLink">
            <span class="oi oi-people" aria-hidden="true"></span>
            Customers in @country
            </NavLink>
        </div>
    }
    ```

 You cannot use `<NavLink class="nav-link" href="customers/@c">` because Blazor does not allow combined text and @ Razor expression in components. That is why the code above creates a local variable to do the combining to make the country URL.

Exercise 16.4 – Explore topics

Use the links on the following page to learn more detail about the topics covered in this chapter:

`https://github.com/markjprice/cs11dotnet7/blob/main/book-links.md#chapter-16---building-user-interfaces-using-blazor`

Summary

In this chapter, you learned:

- How to build Blazor components hosted in Blazor Server.
- How to build Blazor components hosted in Blazor WebAssembly.
- Some of the key differences between the two hosting models, like how data should be managed using dependency services.

In the *Epilogue*, I will make some suggestions for books to take you deeper into C# and .NET.

Join our book's Discord space

Join the book's Discord workspace for *Ask me Anything* sessions with the author.

https://packt.link/csharp11dotnet7

17

Epilogue

I wanted this book to be different from the others on the market. I hope that you found it to be a brisk, fun read, packed with practical hands-on walk-throughs of each subject.

This epilogue contains the following short sections:

- The next steps on your C# and .NET learning journey
- The eighth edition coming November 2023
- Good luck!

The next steps on your C# and .NET learning journey

For subjects that you want to learn more about but I did not have space to include in this book, I hope that the notes, good practice tips, and links in the GitHub repository point you in the right direction:

```
https://github.com/markjprice/cs11dotnet7/blob/main/book-links.md
```

Polishing your skills with design guidelines

Now that you have learned the fundamentals of developing using C# and .NET, you are ready to improve the quality of your code by learning more detailed design guidelines.

Back in the early .NET Framework era, Microsoft published a book that gave good practices in all areas of .NET development. Those recommendations are still very much applicable to modern .NET development.

The following topics are covered:

- Naming Guidelines
- Type Design Guidelines
- Member Design Guidelines
- Designing for Extensibility
- Design Guidelines for Exceptions

- Usage Guidelines
- Common Design Patterns

To make the guidance as easy to follow as possible, the recommendations are simply labeled with the terms **Do, Consider, Avoid,** and **Do not.**

Microsoft has made excerpts of the book available at the following link:

`https://docs.microsoft.com/en-us/dotnet/standard/design-guidelines/`

I strongly recommend that you review all the guidelines and apply them to your code.

A companion book to continue your learning journey

I have created a second book that continues your learning journey, so it acts as a companion to this book.

The first book covers the fundamentals of C#, .NET, and ASP.NET Core for web development. The second book covers more specialized topics such as internationalization, protecting your data and apps, benchmarking and improving performance, and building services with OData, GraphQL, gRPC, SignalR, and Azure Functions. Finally, you will learn how to build graphical user interfaces for websites, desktop, and mobile apps with Blazor and .NET MAUI.

A summary of the two books and their important topics is shown in *Figure 17.1*:

1. **C# language,** including new C# 11 features, object-oriented programming, and debugging and unit testing.
2. **.NET libraries,** including numbers, text, and collections, file I/O, and data with EF Core 7.
3. **Websites and web services** with ASP.NET Core 7 and Blazor.

1. **More .NET libraries** like internationalization, multitasking, and security.
2. **More data** with SQL Server and Azure Cosmos DB.
3. **More services** with Minimal Web API, OData, GraphQL, gRPC, SignalR, and Azure Functions.
4. **More graphical user interfaces** with ASP.NET Core MVC, Razor, Blazor, and .NET MAUI.

Fundamentals   *Practical Applications*

Figure 17.1: A companion book for learning C# and .NET

To see a list of all the books that I have published with Packt, you can use the following link:

`https://subscription.packtpub.com/search?query=mark+j.+price`

Other books to take your learning further

If you are looking for other books from my publisher that cover related subjects, there are many to choose from.

I recommend Harrison Ferrone's *Learning C# by Developing Games with Unity 2021* as a good complement to my book for learning C#. It will likely have an updated edition after my book is published, so keep a watch out for that.

And there are many books that take C# and .NET learning further, as shown in *Figure 17.2*:

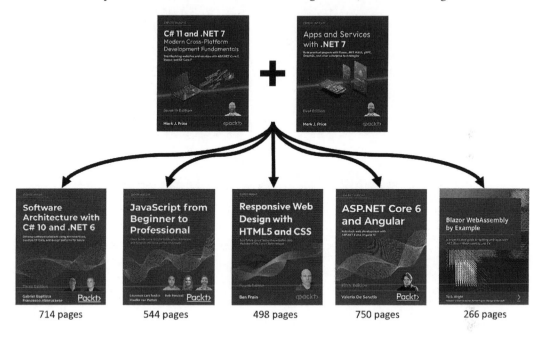

714 pages   544 pages   498 pages   750 pages   266 pages

Figure 17.2: Packt books to take your C# and .NET learning further

You will also find a list of Packt books in the GitHub repository at the following link:

```
https://github.com/markjprice/cs11dotnet7/blob/main/book-links.md#learn-from-other-
packt-books
```

The eighth edition coming November 2023

I have already started working on identifying areas for improvement for the eighth edition, which we plan to publish with the release of .NET 8 in November 2023. While I do not expect major new features at the level of Blazor, I do expect .NET 8 to make worthwhile improvements to all aspects of .NET.

If you have suggestions for topics that you would like to see covered or expanded upon, or you spot mistakes that need fixing in the text or code, then please let me know the details via chat in the Discord channel or the GitHub repository for this book, found at the following link:

```
https://github.com/markjprice/cs11dotnet7
```

Good luck!

I wish you the best of luck with all your C# and .NET projects!

Index

X

Y

Download a free PDF copy of this book

Thanks for purchasing this book!

Do you like to read on the go but are unable to carry your print books everywhere? Is your eBook purchase not compatible with the device of your choice?

Don't worry, now with every Packt book you get a DRM-free PDF version of that book at no cost.

Read anywhere, any place, on any device. Search, copy, and paste code from your favorite technical books directly into your application.

The perks don't stop there, you can get exclusive access to discounts, newsletters, and great free content in your inbox daily

Follow these simple steps to get the benefits:

1. Scan the QR code or visit the link below

https://packt.link/free-ebook/9781803237800

2. Submit your proof of purchase
3. That's it! We'll send your free PDF and other benefits to your email directly

63853297R00448